Communicating

A Social, Career and Cultural Focus

ELEVENTH EDITION

ROY M. BERKO
Notre Dame College (Ohio)
South Euclid, Ohio

ANDREW D. WOLVIN
University of Maryland
College Park, Maryland

DARLYN R. WOLVIN
Prince George's Community College
Largo, Maryland

Allyn & Bacon
Boston   New York   San Francisco
Mexico City   Montreal   Toronto   London   Madrid   Munich   Paris
Hong Kong   Singapore   Tokyo   Cape Town   Sydney

Editor-in-Chief: *Karon Bowers*
Series Editorial Assistant: *Susan Brilling*
Marketing Manager: *Blair Tuckman*
Production Editor: *Patrick Cash-Peterson*
Editorial Production Service: *PD&PS*
Manufacturing Buyer: *JoAnne Sweeney*
Electronic Composition: *PD&PS*
Interior Design: *Denise Hoffman*
Photo Researcher: *Martha Shethar*
Cover Designer: *Joel Gendron*

Printed in the United States of America

10 9 8 7 6 5 4 3 2 1   QW-T   13 12 11 10 09 08

**Allyn & Bacon
is an imprint of**

www.pearsonhighered.com

ISBN-10: 0-205-62489-8
ISBN-13: 978-0-205-62489-8

Ever since the first edition of *Communicating,* Eunice Berko has provided us with editorial assistance and, when things got really rough, plied us with her famous double-double chocolate chip cookies. We dedicate this, the 11th edition, to her!

brief contents

contents

13 Public Speaking: Structuring the Message   352

14 Public Speaking: Presenting the Message   379

15 Informative Public Speaking   398

From its beginning in 1977, *Communicating* has been a forerunner. It was one of the first communication texts to combine the areas of public speaking and intrapersonal and interpersonal communication in a single volume, laying the foundation for what has become known as the "hybrid" communication course.

Even before the academic world was sensitized to cultural awareness, we insisted on using gender-neutral language, photos and illustrations that portrayed many cultures and persons of differences, and an approach that stressed both career and personal aspects of the field.

That's the Past, What's the Present?

We are not resting on our laurels. Long-time users will note changes yet feel comfortable that we have continued to produce a book that is well researched, interesting to read, and pragmatic.

This edition has a new publisher, Allyn & Bacon (Pearson), which has not only shown great faith in our past efforts but has also encouraged us to continue to invent.

Also to be noted is the revised title: *Communicating: A Social, Career and Cultural Focus*. Although the term *cultural* is revised to the title, the concept is not. We have always included references to such factors as gender, race, sexual orientation, age, and nationality. Through the editions, the emphasis on diversity and intercultural communication has been increased. In this edition we decided to give "cultural" an equal place with the social and career aspects and weave them together.

What's New in the Eleventh Edition?

We have fully integrated our "Social, Career and Cultural" themes in this edition by developing a series of boxed features that reinforce key chapter discussions and concepts. Many of these boxes include new, thought-provoking "Reflect on This" questions to encourage the readers to think about the reading or scenario presented, and apply it to their everyday communication situations. Eighty percent of the excerpts and skill-building material in these boxes are new.

- "Socially Communicating" boxes offer guidelines and skills for communicating in relationships and other interpersonal contexts.

- "Communicating in Careers" boxes provide insight into workplace communication with tips on how to communicate more effectively at work and in your career.

- "Culturally Communicating" boxes focus on different cultural communication norms and expectations and how to adapt one's communication in an increasingly diverse world.

Socially Communicating

Capturing Oral Histories

If you've decided to capture some oral histories, it's a good rule of thumb to start with your oldest relatives first. Because most of them won't write down their life stories, they'll need your help. They often lack the writing skills or health, or perhaps even the energy to spend weeks putting their lives on paper or computer. What a blessing it is, then, both for them and for you, to be able to tape- or video-record their life histories. In speaking to family members:

- Start with a question you know they'll love to answer—you want to relax them quickly.
- Stifle the impulse to interrupt—let the narrator tell his or her story and do your best to simply listen.
- Let there be pregnant pauses—you'll often find that the interviewee has something more to say just when you were about to move on to another topic.
- Save questions about details for later—let them answer your broad questions completely before following up with questions about details, clarifications or possible contradictions.
- Do more than just listen—listen for clues to whole new topics that hadn't occurred to you before; if you don't want to interrupt the flow, jot notes to remind you to get back to these new topics later.
- Pursue truth and accurate information—you may occasionally need to ask a question several

different ways or clarify how the interviewer knows something.

- Allow tangents—let them ramble; there can be goldmines in their ramblings and they'll be more natural than if you cut them off.
- Keep your opinions to yourself—this is their interview, not yours.
- Save sensitive matters until late in the interview—if you broach them too early, your interviewee may close up or even end the session.
- Watch for signs that it's time to take a break—look for signs of fatigue and be sensitive to the needs of the interviewee; plan on no more than 2 hours for a session.
- Ask for other family records or a show-and-tell of materials near the end.

Source: "Ancestors: Writing Family History," www.byub.org/ancestors/records/familyhistory/intro.html.

REFLECT ON THIS: Interview a family member in order to get an understanding about your cultures and why your family believes in and carries out traditions and identifies itself. Probe for ethnic, religious, racial identifications as well as the derivation of certain beliefs and attitudes.

Communicating in Careers

Listening in the Global Marketplace

With continued interaction between companies all over the world, the business world is in a global marketplace. Because of this there are some listening guidelines that are appropriate for those involved in international sales and service.

1. Listen for your own cultural/individual values.
2. When you are being introduced to someone from another culture, listen for his or her cultural/individual values.
3. Expand your knowledge of the cultural norms of other peoples.
4. Listen with your eyes and mind open.

REFLECT ON THIS:

1. What kind of education do U.S. businesspeople need in order to fulfill the requirements of listening in the global marketplace?
2. Do you think you are prepared to listen in the global marketplace? Why or why not?
3. Shouldn't those from other nations just accept that the cost of doing business with U.S. companies is the requirement to learn Euro-American language and nonverbal traditions?

Culturally Communicating

Do I Have a Place in This Society?

What does it mean to be Black? . . . My mom worked long hours and she worked so very hard all her life so that she could send me to a private school. I did in fact have some Black friends but not as many as I would have liked. Does this mean I don't consider myself Black? NO! Not at all. I see myself as Black and I love being Black. But I don't know much of Black history. What I know is just the surface, and what I NEED to know is the core. What makes me sad is, I am considered to be the White girl in my family. It saddens me because they don't know my struggle deep inside. Yes, I wish I were strong in being more "ethnic," but I'm not and that scares me. Am I blind? Do I not have a place in this society?
—Lanitra, College Student

Source: Stella Ting-Toomey and Leava C. Chung, *Understanding Intercultural Communication* (Los Angeles, CA: Roxbury Publishing Company, 2005), p. 84.

REFLECT ON THIS:

1. During the 2008 presidential election, Barak Obama faced similar issues as the child of a mixed (white and African) marriage. Do you perceive him as black, African American, white?
2. Golfer Tiger Wood considers himself Cablinasian—Caucasian, black, Indian, and Asian—because of his racially diverse background. Do you agree with his "title" for himself?

Self-Assessment Questionnaires, a valued feature of past editions, have been redesigned so they are easy for the reader to find and assess a variety of skills or issues, from listening ability to communication apprehension.

Numerous pedagogical aids, including chapter objectives and summaries, valuable "Learn by Doing" skill-building activities, boldfaced key terms with a complete end-of-book Glossary, sample speeches and outlines, and extensive examples have been updated and expanded throughout the new edition.

A striking new design for this edition improves the book's appeal and readability, offering a fresh, contemporary look, as well as new photos and custom-drawn cartoons by a former communication student to illustrate key concepts.

A restructuring of the public speaking chapters, including separating the "presentation" material into its own chapter (Chapter 14) more closely mirrors the steps in the public speaking process as outlined in the book, and responds to specific reviewer requests for this revised organization.

We have thoroughly updated and revised this edition by adding, expanding, and revising sources and discussions throughout, including:

- Communication in the emerging "flat" world
- New material and updated references on social networking, blogging, and urban legends
- An added discussion of Knapp's Escalation Model and Termination Model
- Updated information on interpersonal conflict, employment interviewing, and groupthink
- A timely discussion of mediated groups to reflect the increasing popularity of this group format
- New material on virtual conferencing and Web conferencing, as well as off-site employment interviews
- New sources and examples of Internet research for public speaking
- An increased emphasis on intercultural communication, including new discussions of the "Role of Culture" in self-concept, criticism, conflict, apologizing, group process, relationships, public speaking, speech apprehension, and speech preparation and presentation
- A refocused discussion on the Sapir-Whorf Hypothesis
- Revised material on Self-Talk, Self-Esteem, and the role of power in communication

Do You Have Public Speaking Anxiety?

This instrument is composed of six statements concerning feelings about speaking in public.[13] Indicate the degree to which each statement applies to you by marking whether you (1) strongly agree, (2) agree, (3) are undecided, (4) disagree, or (5) strongly disagree. Work quickly. Record your first impression.

_____ a. I have no fear of giving a speech.
_____ b. Certain parts of my body feel very tense and rigid while I am giving a speech.
_____ c. I feel relaxed while giving a speech.
_____ d. My thoughts become confused and jumbled when I am giving a speech.
_____ e. I face the prospect of giving a speech with confidence.
_____ f. While giving a speech, I get so nervous I forget facts that I really know.

Scoring: Add 18 to your scores from items a, c, and e, and then subtract your score from the total of items b, d, and f. This is your final score.

Interpretation: Scores can range from a low of 6 to a high of 30. If your score is 18 or above, you are like the overwhelming majority of Euro-Americans in that you display public speaking apprehension.

- New findings and a restructured discussion of male/masculine–female/feminine communication
- An updated discussion of electronically mediated communication, including updated material on cyber addiction and cyber bullying

A Message from the Students Who Have Used This Book

What do students say about this book? A student in an unsolicited e-mail wrote:

> "Your textbook is fantastic—very readable, easy to understand, and incredibly interesting reading. Having gone back to school later in life, it makes me want to encourage my children to become Communication majors."[1]

An instructor sent us these student comments:[2]

- "This book is easy to understand and reader friendly."
- "It is well organized and it's very applicable."
- "This book is very useful because it gives us good sources, information, and an awesome definition of each and every bold-print word in the text."

And, the comment that means the most to us, your authors:

- "Sometimes I get the urge to go ahead of the class and begin to read and lose myself in the textbook."

A Message to Students

As you undertake the study of communication, you might be asking yourself, "Why do I need to study this? I've been talking and listening all of my life." Research indicates that although you may have been participating in the act of communication your whole life, if you are fairly typical, your skills may not be extremely good. "Educators and researchers express concern that, as young people develop in contemporary society, they may not be learning the critical language, verbal, and oral skills that they will need."[3]

One of the most important skills you need in your career, in your social life, or in relating to people of various cultures is to be an effective communicator. Research shows:

- "All students, including those at the graduate level, need to learn to communicate orally, interpersonally, in small groups and teams, and in public. Interestingly, students also need to learn to communicate effectively outside the classroom with other students and with teachers."[4]

- Communication competency is indispensable for successful participation in careers. Interested in getting a job? The number-one requirement for job attainment and accomplishment is communication skills.

- The ability to communicate is central to a person's self-development and contribution to society, as well as to one's educational and career success.[5]

- Relationships with friends and family depend on your listening and responding to each other.

- As the world becomes "flatter," where communication takes place globally, the ability to understand not only your own culture but that of others becomes imperative.

The purpose of this text is to give you the opportunities to attain communication competency and not only to gain an understanding of the communication process but also to improve the skills that you will possess for the rest of your life.

A Message to Instructors

This text is developed with three philosophical points in mind—what we call the 3 Cs approach: *Concise, Comprehensive, and Creative.*

Conciseness: Communication is an ever-expanding field. As new editions of basic course texts are published, the trend has been for books to get longer and longer, making it difficult for instructors to cover all the material in the time allotted for a course. With this in mind, we have concentrated on stemming this tide. This edition, although it continues to include up-to-date research and approaches to contemporary and emerging communication issues, reinforces the style of conciseness established in previous editions.

Comprehensiveness: We continue to cover the full range of basic communication principles and relevant theory and research. We have specifically updated numerous discussions and references.

Creativity: Historically, students and faculty alike have praised the writing style of the book. As has been the case with previous editions, we have again given special attention to making this book readable, student centered, and practical. We have provided examples of enlightened and entertaining value and have also included custom-drawn cartoons. The cartoonist, a former communication student, not only is creative but also knows the field of communication.

Ancillary Materials

Support materials available to the adopters of *Communicating* include:

Supplements for the Instructor

Print Resources

- **Instructor's Resource Manual** prepared by Laura Janusik, Rockhurst University. This text-specific ancillary is comprehensive, rigorous, and easy to use. The manual includes a sample syllabus, course outlines, more than 125 chapter-by-chapter class activities, and over 20 oral and written assignments with matched assessment instruments.

- **Test Bank** prepared by Laura Janusik, Rockhurst University. The Test Bank contains multiple-choice, true/ false, and essay questions for each chapter. More than 1,200 questions are referenced by text chapter and page number.

- **A Guide for New Teachers of Introduction to Communication, 4th edition,** by Susanna G. Porter, Kennesaw State University with updates and a NEW chapter on incorporating the multimedia capabilities offered with MyCommunicationLab by Heather Dillon. This instructor's guide is designed to help new teachers effectively teach the introductory communication course. Topics such as choosing a text, structuring your course, effectively using group work, dealing with classroom challenges, and giving feedback are included, as well as a number of sample materials in the appendix.

Electronic Resources

- **MyCommunicationLab** is a place where students learn to communicate with confidence! As an interactive and instructive online solution designed to be used as a supplement to a traditional lecture course or completely administered as an online course, MyCommunicationLab combines multimedia, video, communication activities, research support, tests and quizzes to make teaching and learning more relevant and enjoyable. Students benefit from a wealth of video clips that include student and professional speeches, small group scenarios, and interpersonal interactions—some with running commentary and critical questions—all geared to help students learn to communicate with confidence. MyCommunicationLab for Communicating also contains an online career resource, "Finding a Job," as well as speech preparation tools such as a topic selector, research support, and MyOutline, which includes the "Handy Dandy Speech Planner." Available at www.mycommunicationlab.com (access code required).

- **MyTest Computerized Test Bank.** The printed test questions are also available electronically through our new web-based, computerized testing system MyTest. The user-friendly interface enables instructors to view, edit, and add questions, transfer questions to tests, and print tests from any computer with internet access! Available at www .pearsonmytest.com (access code required).

- **PowerPoint Presentation Package,** prepared by Joan Aiken, Park University. These chapter-specific slides include more than 500 slides, many of which are interactive and challenging. Available for download at www.pearsonhighered.com/irc (access code required).

- **Allyn & Bacon Communication Digital Media Archive, Version 3.0,** available on CD-ROM, offers more than 200 still images, video excerpts, and PowerPoint slides that can be used to enliven classroom presentations.

- **VideoWorkshop for Introduction to Communication, Version 2.0,** by Kathryn Dindia, University of Wisconsin. *VideoWorkshop for Introduction to Communication* enables you to bring video into your course for maximized learning. This total teaching and learning system includes quality video footage on an easy-to-use CD-ROM, plus a Student Learning Guide and an Instructor's Teaching Guide. The result? A program that brings textbook concepts to life with ease to help your students understand, analyze, and apply the objectives of the course.

Video Materials

Textbook adopters may choose appropriate video material from Pearson Allyn & Bacon's Communication Video Libraries (some restrictions apply). Please contact your Pearson Allyn & Bacon representative for details and a complete list of videos and their contents to choose which would be most useful to your class.

- **Pearson A&B Interpersonal Communication Video Library.** Each of these videos features a variety of scenarios that illustrate interpersonal concepts and relationships, including topics such as nonverbal acommunication, perception, conflict, and listening.

- **Pearson A&B Small Group Communication Video Library.** This small group communication video collection presents video case studies of groups working in diverse contexts and highlights key concepts of communication, including group problem solving, leadership roles, diversity, power, conflict, virtual group communication, and more.

- **Pearson A&B Public Speaking Video Library.** Pearson Allyn & Bacon's Public Speaking Video Library contains a range of different types of speeches delivered on a multitude of different topics, allowing you to choose the speeches best suited for your students. Samples frem most of our public speaking videos are available on www.mycoursetoolbox.com.

- **A&B Contemporary Classic Speeches DVD.** This exciting supplement includes over 120 minutes of video footage in an easy-to-use DVD format. Each speech is accompanied by a biographical and historical summary that helps students understand the context and motivation behind each speech.

Student Supplements

Print Resources

- **Study Cards for Introduction to Communication.** Colorful, affordable, and packed with useful information, Pearson's Study Cards make studying easier, more efficient, and more enjoyable. Course information is distilled down to the basics, helping you quickly master the fundamentals, review a subject for understanding, or prepare for an exam. Because they're laminated for durability, you can keep these Study Cards for years to come and pull them out whenever you need a quick review.

- **Speech Preparation Workbook,** by Jennifer Dreyer and Gregory H. Patton, San Diego State University. This workbook takes students through the stages of speech creation—from audience analysis to writing the speech—and includes guidelines, tips, and easy to fill-in pages.

- **Preparing Visual Aids for Presentations, 5th edition,** by Dan Cavanaugh. This brief booklet provides a host of ideas for using today's multimedia tools to improve presentations, including suggestions for how to plan a presentation, guidelines for designing visual aids and storyboarding, and a walkthrough that shows how to prepare a visual display using PowerPoint.

- **Public Speaking in the Multicultural Environment, 2nd edition,** by Devorah Lieberman, Portland State University. This two-chapter essay focuses on speaking and listening to a culturally diverse audience and emphasizes preparation, delivery, and how speeches are perceived.

- **Multicultural Activities Workbook,** by Marlene C. Cohen and Susan L. Richardson, both of Prince George's Community College, Maryland. This workbook is filled with hands-on activities with a multicultural focus, such as checklists, surveys, and writing assignments.

- **The Speech Outline: Outlining to Plan, Organize, and Deliver a Speech: Activities and Exercises,** by Reeze L. Hanson and Sharon Condon, both of Haskell Indian Nations University. This brief workbook includes activities, exercises, and answers to help students develop and master the critical skill of outlining.

Electronic Resources

- **Introduction to Communication Study Site,** accessed at www.abintrocomm.com. This website includes web links to sites with speeches in texts, audio, and video formats, as well as links to other valuable websites. The site also contains flashcards and a fully expanded set of practice tests for all major topics.

- **MyCommunicationLab.** MyCommunicationLab is a place where students learn to communicate with confidence! As an interactive and instructive online solution designed to be used as a supplement to a traditional lecture course or completely administered as an online course, MyCommunicationLab combines multimedia, video, communication activities, research support, tests and quizzes to make teaching and learning more relevant and enjoyable. Students benefit from a wealth of video clips that include student and professional speeches, small group scenarios, and interpersonal interactions—some with running commentary and critical questions—all geared to help students learn to communicate with confidence. MyCommunicationLab for Communicating also contains a online career resource, "Finding a Job," as well as speech preparation tools such as a topic selector, research support, and MyOutline, which includes the "Handy Dandy Speech Planner." Access this site at www.mycommunicationlab .com (access code required).

- **VideoLab CD-ROM.** This interactive study tool for students can be used independently or in class. It provides digital video of student speeches that can be viewed in conjunction with corresponding outlines, manuscripts, notecards, and instructor critiques. A series of drills to help students analyze content and delivery follows each speech.

- **Speech Writer's Workshop CD-ROM, Version 2.0.** This exciting public speaking software includes a *Speech Handbook* with tips for researching and preparing speeches; a *Speech Workshop*, which guides students step-by-step through the speech writing process; a *Topics Dictionary*, which gives students hundreds of ideas for speeches; and the *Documentor* citation database, which helps students format bibliographic entries in either MLA or APA style. This product is available for student purchase, or at no additional cost when value-packed with any Allyn & Bacon text (some restrictions apply).

- **VideoWorkshop for Introduction to Communication, Version 2.0,** by Kathryn Dindia, University of Wisconsin. *VideoWorkshop for Introduction to Communication* enables you to bring video into your course for maximized learning. This total teaching and learning system includes quality video footage on an easy-to-use CD-ROM, plus a Student Learning Guide and an Instructor's Teaching Guide. The result? A program that brings textbook concepts to life with ease that helps your students understand, analyze, and apply the objectives of the course.

Acknowledgments

Without the assistance of Joan Aitken of Park University, producing this edition would have been a much more difficult task.

Tony Zupancic of Notre Dame College added a great deal of insight and information to the public speaking chapters and made himself continuously available as a resource person.

We appreciate the efforts of Laura Janusik of Rockhurst University for her development of the Instructor's Manual and Test Banks.

Thanks to Rowena Kirby-Straker and Katie Princiotto at the University of Maryland for their research assistance.

We are also indebted to those professors who have been loyal users of this book through its first ten editions. We hope that you will continue to use the text and to provide us with insightful and helpful comments for future editions.

Appreciation also goes to our professional colleagues who read and critiqued the manuscript through its development: Melissa Barkley Crawford, *University of Central Arkansas*; Kathleen Czech, *Point Loma Nazarene University*; Dan Flickstein, *Brooklyn College*; David S. Hopcroft, *Quinebaug Valley Community College*; Jennifer Lehtinen, *SUNY Orange*; Deborah K. London, *Merrimack College*; Wallis C. Metts, Jr., *Spring Arbor University*; Nancy Petersen, *Los Medanos College*; Esther Rumsey, *Sul Ross State University*; and Anthony J. Zupancic, *Notre Dame College*.

Kudos to Hilary Jackson, Developmental Editor, for her editorial assistance and advice, and to Karon Bowers of Allyn & Bacon (Pearson), our Editor-in-Chief, for her patience and support.

In Conclusion

COMMUNICATE COMPETENTLY!

R.M.B.
A.D.W.
D.R.W.

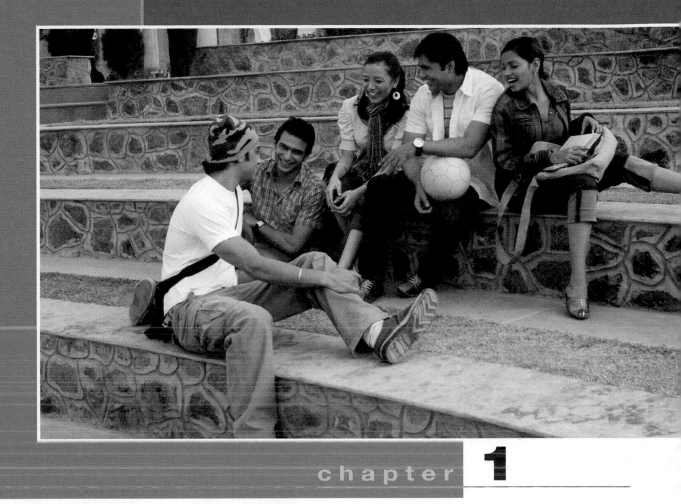

chapter 1

The Human Communication Process

▶ **After reading this chapter, you should be able to**

- List and explain the components of human communication
- Explain the effects of perceptions on the human communication process
- Identify, define, and give examples of the noise factors that affect the human communication process
- Illustrate, define, and give examples of the linear, interactional, and transactional models of communication
- Understand the concept of communication as a system
- Relate to the role of the media as a communicator

- Understand the relationship between communication and culture
- Define and explain ethnocentrism
- Understand the role of First Amendment speech as a rhetorical tool
- Explain the role of the ethical value system in communication
- Understand the basis for ethical career communication

When confronted with the requirement of taking a communication course, students sometimes ask, "Why do I need that? I know how to talk." Communication, though, is more than talking. When you answer a question in class, receive a compliment, challenge another person's ideas, interact with a family member, touch someone, participate in a job interview, take part in a group meeting, listen to a classroom lecture, do a victorious high-five, select clothing to wear, or go through the process of buying a car, you are involved in the act of communicating! Significant friendships, successful family relationships, academic and occupational success, and understandings of others from various cultures depend on communication abilities.

Studying communication and learning how to be an effective communicator are not just academic exercises. "There is emerging consensus among educators, business leaders, and accreditors on what skills are necessary for all students as undergraduates. Those skills include good written and oral communication, a capacity for critical thinking, and the ability to work in teams."[1]

One of the most important skills you must have is to be an effective communicator. "All students, including those at the graduate level, need to learn to communicate orally, interpersonally, in small groups and teams, and in public. Interestingly, students also need to learn to communicate effectively outside the classroom with other students and with teachers."[2]

Communication competency is indispensable for successful participation in careers. Interested in getting a job? The number-one ability for job attainment and accomplishment is communication skills. A survey conducted by the National Association of

Communication competency is indispensable for successful participation in the world of work.

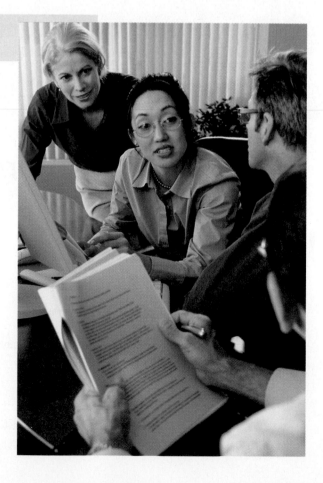

Colleges and Employers (NACE) reveals that communication skills is the most important quality that employers look for in a job candidate.[3] (See Figure 1.1 for the list of the top ten skills sought by employers.) It is interesting to note that employers cited communication as the key ability most *lacking* in new college graduates—specifically, face-to-face communication, interviewing, presentational, telephone, and overall interpersonal skills.[4]

Other findings indicate that the ability to communicate is central to a person's self-development and contribution to society, as well as one's educational and career success.[5] It is interesting to note that listening is considered to be the foundation of effective communication in all settings, yet it is generally recognized that students are lacking abilities in classroom listening.[6]

Communication competency is not limited to the workplace and the classroom. We also need speaking and listening skills to function at the personal level. Relationships with friends and family depend on your listening and responding to each other. The business of life is a communication interaction—whether it is with the supermarket checker, the doctor, the college registrar, the meter reader, the repairperson, your best friend, or the 911 operator.

"As we enter the twenty-first century, direct contact with culturally different people in our neighborhoods, community, schools and workplaces is an inescapable part of life."[7] As the world becomes flatter, where communication takes place internationally, the ability to understand not only your own culture, but that of others, becomes imperative. As the method of communicating with others transfers from one-on-one communication to a *flat world platform* where there is a convergence of the personal computer, with fiber-optic cable, with work flow software (which enables individuals all over the world to collaborate regardless of the distance between them), the knowledge of world cultures and their communication patterns is critical.[8]

There is a growing concern among business leaders about the lack of communication skills among college graduates based on a report by the Business Higher Education Forum, an organization of Fortune 500 executives, which found that "newly hired graduates have impressive academic skills. However, graduates lack communication skills and the ability to work in teams and with people from diverse backgrounds."[9] A Harvard Medical School survey reported "poor communication emerged as the most important factor affecting patients' trust in their doctors and as the most likely reason for dissatisfaction and cause for switching physicians."[10] A review of lawyers indicated that although communication skills are vital between lawyer and client, there is an "imperative need for sustained instruction in the development of communication skills for the lawyer. Especially important are nonverbal communication

1. *Communication skills*

2. *Strong work ethic*

3. *Teamwork skills*

4. *Initiative*

5. *Interpersonal skills*

6. *Problem-solving skills*

7. *Analytical skills*

8. *Flexibility/adaptability*

9. *Computer skills*

10. *Technical skills*

Figure 1.1
Top Ten Qualities Sought by Employers

Source: National Association of Colleges and Employers 2008 Job Outlook Survey.

Communicating in Careers

What Would You Do?

Consider what you might do in the following situations:

- A boss asks you to work on a project you find morally wrong.

- A co-worker spends more time planning a social event than working on a proposal, leaving important tasks undone.

- Customers are being sold merchandise that your company knows is defective.

Do you ignore your conscience, do your work and say nothing? Or do you speak up and run the risk of alienating colleagues and hurting your career?

Source: Kristin Downey Grimsley, *Washington Post* (September 8, 1997): 12.

skills in reading the client during interviews."[11] The apprehension level of those who fear speaking in public is estimated at 50 to 70 percent.[12] To add to our woes is something that many think is a positive aspect of communication: the information explosion, which results in information overload. We are bombarded daily with messages not only directly from other people but also from a number of technological sources. Cell phones, e-mail, pagers, televisions, text messages, and fax machines enable us to receive information quickly and incessantly.

The challenge is how to manage the information so that it doesn't become overwhelming. A 2008 workplace productivity survey commissioned by LexisNexis showed that a majority of professionals feel overwhelmed by the amount of information they encounter daily. According to the survey, 62 percent of the 650 white-collar workers surveyed reported spending a lot of time sorting through irrelevant information to find what they needed, and 40 percent said they would be unable to handle further increases in information flow. Eighty-five percent said that not finding the information they needed at the right time was a major time-waster, and 62 percent wished they could spend less time searching for information and more time using information that came their way.[13]

We started this discussion with an often-asked student question: "Why do I have to take a course in speaking? I've been talking all my life." The answer is: Although you are able to *talk*, if you are typical, you may not be able to *communicate* effectively.

Communication Defined

Communication is a conscious or unconscious, intentional or unintentional process in which feelings and ideas are expressed as verbal and/or nonverbal messages that are sent, received, and comprehended. This process can be *accidental* (having no intent), *expressive* (resulting from the emotional state of the person), or *rhetorical* (resulting from specific goals of the communicator).

Being able to communicate effectively improves your facility to maneuver ideas. Vague impressions gain reality; ideas are examined, set in categories, and eventually added to other ideas.

Human communication occurs on intrapersonal, interpersonal, and public levels. **Intrapersonal communication** is communicating with yourself. It encompasses such activities as thought processing, personal decision making, listening, and determining self-concept. **Interpersonal communication** refers to communication that takes place between two or more persons who establish a communicative relationship. Forms of interpersonal communication include face-to-face or mediated conversations, interviews, and small-group discussions. **Public communication** is characterized by a speaker sending a message to an audience. It may be direct, such as a face-to-face message delivered by a speaker to an audience, or indirect, such as a message relayed over radio or television.

All communication is dynamic, continuous, irreversible, interactive, and contextual.[14]

Communication is *dynamic* because the process is constantly in a state of change. As the attitudes, expectations, feelings, and emotions of persons who are communicating change, the nature of their communication changes as well.

Communication is *continuous* because it never stops. Whether asleep or awake, we are always processing ideas and information through our dreams, thoughts, and expressions. Our brains remain active; we are communicating.

Communication is *irreversible*. Once we send a message, we cannot undo it. Once we make a slip of the tongue, give a meaningful glance, send an angry e-mail, or gen-

Your academic success may well be linked to your ability to communicate.

erate an emotional outburst, we cannot erase it. Our apologies or denials cannot eradicate what has taken place.

Communication is *interactive*. We are constantly in contact with other people and with ourselves. We react to our own speech and actions, and then we react to those reactions, and others react to our speech and actions. Thus, a cycle of action and reaction becomes the basis for our communication.

Communication is *contextual*. The complexity of communication dictates that we develop the awareness and the skills to function effectively as communicators and to adapt to the setting (both where it is taking place and the attitudes of those who are in the environment), the people who are present, and the purpose of the communication. A word-processing advertisement summarized this well: "You don't talk to your mother the same way you talk to your buddies. (Better not, for your sake.) That nice polite talk is perfect for Sunday dinners. Or when you're asking for money. That's why you've got Street talk. Small talk. Back talk. Coffee talk. Baby talk. And—even when you're not saying a word—Body talk, which has absolutely no regard for syntax and grammar. Custom languages made to order."[15]

To be an effective communicator, you need to understand how the communication process operates as a system, how you send and process information, how you reason your way to conclusions and evaluate the ideas that others send, and the relationship between communication and culture. In addition, good communicators know what ethical standards they use in making their decisions.

The Components of Human Communication

As human beings, we are capable of **selective communication.** That is, from the wide repertory available to us, we can choose the symbol we believe best represents the idea or concept we wish to express. We can think in abstractions, plan events in the future, and store and recall information. Selective communication allows us to combine sounds into complicated structures and therefore describe events and objects. This ability to selectively communicate also allows us to decide how to send intentional messages to others.

Figure 1.2
The Components of Communication

Source	Receiver
1. Senses aroused by idea or need to communicate	1. Senses aroused by stimuli or need to communicate
2. Chooses to communicate the message using language symbols (the code)	2. Receives symbols (the code) in distorted form
3. Uses memory and past experiences to find language symbols to communicate the message (encoding)	3. Uses memory and past experiences to attach meaning to symbols (decoding)
	4. Stores information
	5. Sends feedback

Figure 1.2 illustrates how the components of the communication process work. The circles representing the **source** (the originator of the message) and the **receiver** (the recipient of the message) overlap as each person sends **messages** (communication) and **feedback** (response to a message) to the other through a **frame of reference** (a perceptual screen) **noise** (the potential for communication disruption). The overlapping circles suggest that communication is possible only when each communicator understands the other's message. The variables that affect the frame of reference make up the perceptual screen through which verbal and nonverbal messages are communicated.

Communicator Perceptions

Your **perceptions**—the way you view the world—affect your interpretation of a communication stimulus. Many factors make up your perceptual filter. These factors, also listed in Figure 1.2, include your *culture* (the background worldview you hold), *communication skills* (developed from experience and training), *physical and emotional states* (how you feel at this particular time), *experiences* (your cultural background), *attitudes* (negative and positive predispositions to respond to any particular stimulus), *memory* (ability to store and recall information), and *expectations* (what you anticipate will occur). Because of perceptual differences, two people reporting on an incident they have both seen may report their observations differently.

You encode and decode messages through your perceptual filters. These perceptual filters establish expectations for the outcome of the communication, and expectations guide your interpretation of the communicator's message. A person who expects to hear bad news, for instance, probably will interpret what the boss says in a performance review as negative even if the focus of the review highlights many of the positive aspects of the individual's work.

The Communication Process

When we communicate, we **encode** (take ideas and put them into message form), send the ideas through a channel composed of our **primary signal system** (the senses: seeing, hearing, tasting, smelling, and touching) to someone who receives them via her or his primary signal system, and **decode** (translate) the received messages. We express our reactions to what we have sensed by both verbal and nonverbal signs. You might say, "I heard the bell" or "It feels soft." These are examples of verbal communication that are responses to what your senses have received. You also can respond on a nonverbal level. You frown, feel your body tighten up, and wiggle in your chair as you listen to your psychology instructor detail all the homework you have to finish before you can leave for spring vacation. Your frowning, tensing, and wiggling are nonverbal responses of stress that your body is sending to you and to anyone else who is observing you.

In any communication process, the degree to which the communication is effective depends on the communicators' mutual understanding of the signals being used. Suppose you are about to take an examination and suddenly realize you forgot to bring a pencil to class. You ask one of your friends, "May I please borrow a pencil?" She says, "Yes" and gives you a pencil. You have just participated in an effective communication transaction. You (communicator A) *encoded* a message ("May I please borrow a pencil?") and sent it out over a *channel* (vocal tones carried on sound waves) to your friend (communicator B). Your friend *received* the message (by using sensory agents, ears) and *decoded* it (understood that you wanted a pencil). Your friend's *feedback* (the word *yes* and handing the pencil to you) indicated that the message was successfully *received* and *decoded*. (This is illustrated in Figure 1.3.)

Now suppose that the person sitting next to you is from France and speaks no English. The symbol that he uses for pencil is *crayon*. Unless both of you communicate in French, he will be unable to decode your message, so no successful communication takes place. (See Figure 1.4.)

Remember that *the act of speech is not itself communication*. Speech is a biological act: the utterance of sounds, possibly of vocal symbols of language. Communication is vastly more complex. It involves the development of a relationship among people in which there is shared meaning among the participants. That is, the intent of the message received is basically the same as the intent of the message sent.

The Source and the Message

The communication process begins when the source is consciously or unconsciously stimulated by some event, object, or idea. This need to send a message is then followed by a memory search to find the appropriate language (verbal or nonverbal or both) in which to encode the message.

Figure 1.3
Effective Encoding and Decoding without Noise

The Channel

During a communicative act, the encoded message is carried through a **channel** or channels. If the communication occurs face-to-face, these channels may be some or all of the five senses. Typically, we rely on sight and sound as channels in speaking and listening. Instead of communicating face-to-face, however, we may choose an electronic channel that uses sound (e.g., the telephone) or seeing and hearing (e.g., television). In some instances, we may elect to send a message to someone by means of physical contact, such as by tapping the person on the shoulder. In this case, we use the touch channel.

The Receiver and the Message

After receiving verbal and nonverbal signals through the senses, the receiver must decode the message before communication can be accomplished. When gaining verbal and nonverbal signals, the receiver processes them through a memory search so that the signals are translated into the receiver's language system. This decoded message is not identical to the one encoded by the source because each person's symbol system is shaped by a unique set of perceptions. A Euro-American* professor who says, "Assignments should be turned in on time," might be surprised when a student from a culture that has a flexible time system, such as Mexico, attempts to turn in his homework the day after the assignment was due.

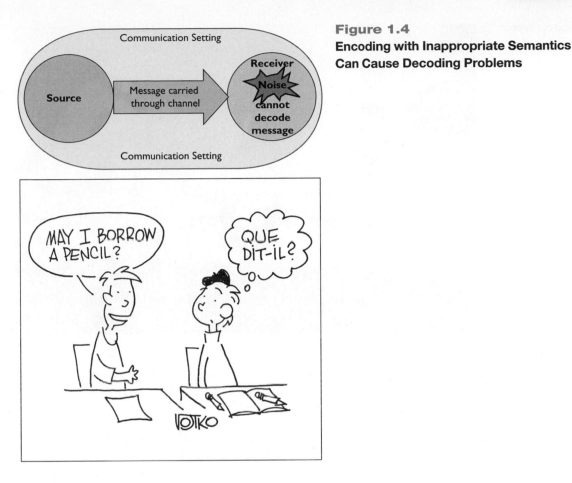

Figure 1.4

Encoding with Inappropriate Semantics Can Cause Decoding Problems

Feedback

Once the receiver assigns meaning to the received message, he is in a position to respond. This response, **feedback,** can be a verbal or a nonverbal reaction to the message, or both. Feedback indicates whether the receiver understands (e.g., by nodding), misunderstands (e.g., by shrugging the shoulders and saying, "I don't understand"), encourages the source to continue (e.g., by leaning forward and saying, "Yes"), or disagrees (e.g., by pulling back and saying, "No way!"). The act of responding, by which the receiver sends feedback to the source, actually shifts the role of the receiver to that of the source.

Noise

Messages are influenced not only by the interpretations of each communicator but also by **noise,** which is any internal or external interference in the communication process.[16] Noise can be caused by environmental obstacles, physiological impairment,

▶ *Note:* Throughout this text the term *Euro-American* or *European American* will be used to designate those people, usually white, who themselves came from or whose relatives came from Europe and live in the United States or identify with living in the United States. The term, like the designations *African American, Chinese American,* and *Jewish American,* is used for those who have a racial, national, or religious identity that they couple with being American.

Others react to our speech and action.

semantic problems, syntactic problems, organizational confusion, cultural influences, and/or psychological problems. The communication breakdown can be caused by one or a combination of the noise factors.

ENVIRONMENTAL NOISE   *Environmental noise* is outside interference that prevents the receiver from gaining the message. This can happen when you are in the kitchen running water and the sound muffles your friend's voice when she asks you a question from the adjoining room.

PHYSIOLOGICAL-IMPAIRMENT NOISE   A physical problem can block the effective sending or receiving of a message, thus creating *physiological-impairment noise*. For

We sometimes find ourselves in situations where stress causes us to send messages ineffectively.

example, people who are deaf or blind do not have the specific sensory capabilities to receive a message in the same way as do people who can hear or see.

SEMANTIC NOISE   Problems may arise regarding the meaning of words—*semantics*—creating *semantic noise*. For example, semantic noise may result when people use language that is common only to one specific group, a particular part of a country, another nation, or a particular field, profession, or organization.

Travelers frequently encounter semantic problems. The U.S. midwesterner who goes into a store in many parts of the country's East Coast and asks for a *soda* will probably get a soft drink (*pop* in the Midwest) rather than a mixture of ice cream, fruit flavoring, and soda water (a *soda* in the Midwest).

Experts—professors, doctors, mechanics—sometimes forget that those who do not have as much knowledge of their field may not be familiar with its vocabulary. For example, clients often complain that lawyers fail to communicate clearly because they use legal jargon, which is confusing to nonlawyers.

Those who instant message or text message frequently forget that not everyone has learned the texting acronyms and abbreviations. Although phrases like "?4U," "LEMENO," and "AFAIK" may make sense to you, as the texter, are you sure the person to whom you are sending the message is aware that those letters mean "I have a question for you," "Let me know," and "As far as I know"?

General Motors discovered the necessity of being sure that the language of the country in which they are selling products is compatible with their product names. When they tried to sell their Nova product line in Mexico, the reaction was very negative and the cars did not sell well. The reason? In Spanish, *nova* means "doesn't go." Obviously that was not a good message to send to prospective car buyers.

SYNTACTICAL NOISE   Each language has a *syntax*, a customary way of putting words together in a grammatical form. *Syntactical noise*, inappropriate grammatical usage, can interfere with clear communication. For example, receivers may become confused if someone changes tenses in the middle of a story ("She *went* down the street and *says* to him . . .").

The usual sequence of a grammatically correct English sentence is noun-verb-object ("I give him the book"). But other languages—Spanish, for example—do not follow this pattern. In Spanish, the same sentence reads *Le doy el libro* ("To him I give the book"). Thus, someone who is learning a new language must master not only its vocabulary but also an entirely different system of grammar. Until this new system becomes natural, the language may be quite difficult both to encode and decode.

ORGANIZATIONAL NOISE   When the source fails to realize that certain ideas are best grasped when presented in a structured order, *organizational noise* may result. A geography instructor presents ideas in a random fashion: first he talks about India, then China, then Greece, then India, and then China. After a while, his students become so confused they have absolutely no idea which country he is discussing.

Using a method of organization can provide a clear structure. In giving directions, a person may set a pattern by starting at the departure point and proceeding in geographical order (e.g., "Go to the first street, turn right, proceed three blocks, and turn left"). If material is presented in a specific pattern, the receiver is likely to grasp the meaning. If the material is not organized, the receiver must not only try to figure out what is said but also sort out the information. However, this pattern of explanation is not universal. When speaking to individuals whose first language is not English, do not assume that their formatting of ideas will follow the usual Euro-American pattern of giving directions. Individuals who come from areas that use an indirect style of communication, such as those from most Asian countries, may hint rather than fill in specifics. Since vagueness, for example, is natural in Japanese communication,[17] a generalized overview, rather than specifics, would be an effective approach to communicating a message.

CULTURAL NOISE   *Cultural noise* results from preconceived, unyielding attitudes derived from a group or society about how members of that culture should act or in what they should or should not believe. Individuals in a culture who believe in a set pattern of rules and regulations might say, "Nice people don't do things like that" and "We do it this way."

An instance of cultural noise is the attitude that any action by a representative of one's own group is always right, whereas the actions by a member of another group are wrong. Thus, a person who has always voted for candidates of one political party may find it difficult to be open-minded when listening to information about the opposing political party's candidates.

Cultural noise may be present when members of two religious or nationality groups interact. Most Jews, Buddhists, and Muslims do not believe in the divinity of Christ as the Messiah. They do not celebrate Christmas, nor do they have Christmas trees or put up Christmas decorations. Although wishing someone "Merry Christmas" may be the tradition among Christians, the phrase may be unnerving to a Jewish, Buddhist, or Muslim acquaintance.

It is a custom among many Russians that when someone in the community dies, money is given to the grieving family to pay for funeral expenses. The common custom among Euro-Americans is to send flowers or make a donation to a charity in the person's name. A Russian, unaware of the Euro-American custom, could offend by giving a mourner money at a funeral.

PSYCHOLOGICAL NOISE   We sometimes find ourselves in situations where *psychological noise*—stress, frustration, or irritation—causes us to send or receive messages ineffectively. Think of what happens when you are so angry that you "can't think straight." For example, as you sit in class, upset over the argument you had with your suitemate before leaving for class, you may be so distracted that you can't concentrate on the professor's lecture.

Some people have severe psychological problems that cause them to communicate in unusual ways. People with schizophrenia (a disintegration of personality) may have great difficulty communicating. They may talk in riddles and rhymes, make up words, switch personalities, or not speak at all.

THE EFFECT OF NOISE   Noise factors can interfere with effective communication in varying stages of the linear, interactional, or transactional models. For example, semantic noise may stop the sender from encoding a message if she does not have the vocabulary to create the message. The message may not get into the channel if there is physiological-impairment noise because the sender has laryngitis. The receiver may not be able to receive the message if she is deaf and can't hear the intended message. The message may not get clearly out of the channel if there is environmental noise that creates static on the telephone line carrying the signal. (See Figure 1.5.) The receiver may be experiencing psychological noise: Although he receives the message, he may be so disoriented that he doesn't really grasp the intent of the information. Or, due to semantic and syntactic noise, he may not be able to decode the message because he doesn't speak the same language as the sender.

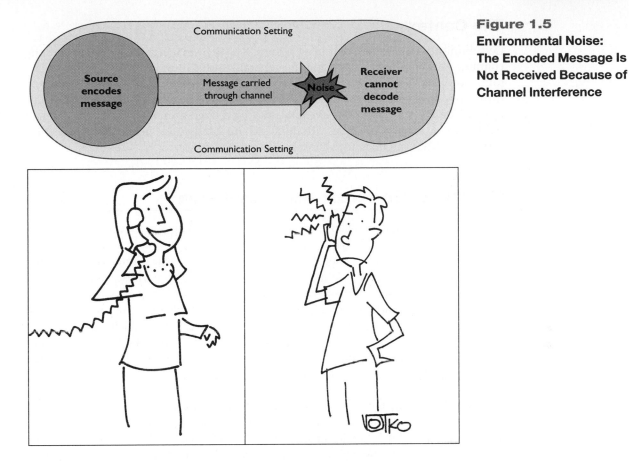

Figure 1.5
Environmental Noise:
The Encoded Message Is
Not Received Because of
Channel Interference

DEALING WITH NOISE   Noise interferes with communication, but because it is commonly present, we must learn to adapt to and compensate for it. For example, a source should offer opportunities for feedback to make sure that a message has been received and understood. Rather than assuming that someone in another room has heard your message, you might word the statement so that it requires an answer: "The phone is for you; are you going to answer it?" Another way to compensate for noise is to define terms that might be misunderstood or may not be part of the receiver's vocabulary. Rather than repeating exactly the same words in a message that has been misunderstood, you can change the terms or the sentence structure to aid the receiver in decoding the message. In the same way, a receiver should ask questions or repeat the message's general ideas to be sure that distractions have not interfered with comprehension.

The way a person does or does not respond may give you some clues as to how to compensate for a noise problem. For instance, consider what happens if you request a sheet of paper, and the other person does not do anything. Environmental noise may have stopped the message from being received, or the person may not have been paying attention because of psychological or cultural noise, or the person may say, "I have difficulty hearing. Could you repeat what you said, and speak up a little?" In this case, you must increase the volume level when you repeat the message. A response of "No comprende!" to the question "Where is the Grande Hotel?" likely indicates that the person of whom you asked the question does not speak English. You may then want to switch to Spanish, if you know the language, or show the person a brochure from the hotel. As a sender, you must keep your eyes and ears open to anticipate a problem and, if one exists, to adjust your communication.

The Context

Communication does not occur in a vacuum. It always relates to the *context:* where the communication is taking place, and the general attitude of those assembled. Such factors as the size of the room, the color of the walls, and the type and placement of the furniture can all affect how we feel, the way we communicate, and the type of communicating we engage in. For example, placing a large number of people in a small work area, as is often the case with direct-phone salespeople, may bring about emotional stress that can be reflected by erratic communication.

Communication as a System

Think of your daily sending and receiving of messages. There is a *system,* a pattern, to the way you communicate with others. The pattern centers on who speaks, what the speaker says or is allowed to say, the way in which the message is sent, and where the speaker and receiver are. The participants, the setting, the purpose, and how they interact form the basis of the *communication system.*

The flow of communication in a consistent pattern allows communication to be regular and predictable, not random, and gives everyone who participates a sense of assurance and security. Identify a communication system with which you are familiar (e.g., your family or work unit). You can probably anticipate what is going to happen and how your actions will affect others before you actually act. Your awareness of how well your ideas will be accepted or of how much encouragement or discouragement you will receive may well dictate what you do and do not say.

The type of communication system used affects who speaks. In a strongly parent-dominated home, for example, a parent may place restrictions on the type of language children may use and the topics they can discuss. Any attempt by the children to challenge the system may be met with strongly negative reactions and may result in verbal or even physical punishment.

A communication system can be shaped by the communicators' age, status, gender, attraction for each other, and cultural heritage. For example, in a family system, the rules for male members may be different from those for female members, regulations may alter as the children get older, and favored children may be allowed more freedom than the others. Certain families may be influenced by a historical ethnic pattern that dictates how much public display of emotion is allowable and whether family members may express opinions. In many households, when children reach adolescence, their attempts to change the rules and not to be treated as children are often at the core of many family conflicts.

A particular setting may encourage or discourage communication. In some settings, people may feel free to disagree, whereas in others they may feel restricted. Some instructors, for example, encourage differences of opinion in their classrooms; others demand adherence to their philosophy and discourage interpretations. Students quickly learn the rules in classrooms and conform accordingly; if they do not, they may be faced with lowered grades or verbal reprimands.

The purpose of the communicative act also may result in limits to the system. Trying to tell someone what you believe is a different task and experience from attempting to persuade that person to take some action you desire. An employee may not like a particular regulation, for instance, but if it has been made clear that the supervisor is not interested in input regarding company policies, and that she has the power to fire an employee, it is probably unwise for an employee who wants to retain his job to present his thoughts about perceived changes.

In some instances, the role of gender may dictate how communication is accepted. In Orthodox Judaism, for example, where men are considered to have more power than women, a woman may want to get a divorce, but she cannot get a *get*, a document of religious divorce, unless her husband agrees.

An artistic mobile is a good analogy for visualizing a system. It swings around until, by addition, subtraction, and other alterations, it attains balance. It remains that way until something disturbs the balance. In human communication, once a system is set up and operating, any attempt to alter that system and its pattern of rules can impair the system or cause it to stop functioning. This does not mean that all systems that are working are good ones. It merely suggests that when a system is functioning, regardless of whether the participants are happy with the pattern, at least there is a basis for understanding how the communication of the people within that system will take place. For instance, if you are aware that your supervisor is not going to accept anyone else's ideas, you learn to live with the system or find another job. A relationship in which there is abuse may function well because of a clear pattern of action–reaction. The abuser says, "You do what I say or I will punish you." The recipient of the abuse accepts and operates under those rules. Thus, a functional system is established. This does not mean the system is healthy, but it is functional.

Interestingly, positive results can emerge from a system that is not working well because awareness of a problem may halt a negative system. For example, if a family unit has been operating under a reign of physical and verbal abuse, something that happens to stop the abuse could result in a much-needed change or could bring the system to an end.

Once the rules become nonexistent or fuzzy, chaos may result. The basis of good communication patterns between any two or more people is the ability to alter the system with little chaos in the process. When a new supervisor comes into a workplace, there may be a disintegration of the previously developed system, as the newcomer may have a different communication style. She may be less open to input from the employees, while the former supervisor encouraged input.

A physical problem can block the effective sending or receiving of a message, thus creating physiological-impairment noise.

In the complex process of human communication, it is not enough simply to be able to identify the component parts and realize that communication is systematized. We must also understand how these components fit together. A useful way of doing this is to look at models of the process of communication that illustrate how the various elements relate to each other.

Models of Human Communication

Any model is a simplification that may leave out steps or omit details. Despite this limitation, communication models can help us see the components of the system from a perspective that will be useful in analyzing and understanding the process.

Although there are many models that can be used to illustrate the act of communication, three are used here to illustrate the process: the linear, the interactional, and the transactional.

Linear Model of Communication

Early theoretical work concerning verbal communication evolved from ancient Greek and Roman rhetoricians who were concerned with the proper training of orators. For this reason, early theories of communication stressed the role of the orator, the public speaker. The theories reflected what might be called a one-directional view of communication, in which a person performs specific actions in a specific sequence during a speech and elicits specific desired responses from listeners. This view is called the linear model of communication. (See Figure 1.6.)

In the **linear model of communication,** a source encodes a message and sends it to a receiver through one or more sensory channels. The receiver then receives and decodes the message. For example, after you buy a computer, you view and listen to the message on a CD provided by the manufacturer. The CD explains how to download the operating system. When you follow the directions and the computer boots up and operates, the communication has been successful.

When using one-directional communication, unless there is careful analysis by the speaker of the intended audience, the setting, and the purpose, noise factors may be present. To illustrate this, let us consider an example. José (the speaker/source) says, "Please put the book on the table when you are done with it." He then turns and walks from the room. Brooke (the listener/receiver) has a stack of books in front of her; she is not certain which one to place on the table. In this example, José is assuming that this sending of a message is all there is to communicating.

Does this mean that a sender should not use the linear model? No. Sometimes senders have no choice about whether they should use the linear model. Advertisers, public speakers appearing on television, people leaving messages on answering machines, and producers of documentaries have no choice but to use the linear model. Therefore, they must give careful consideration to figuring out the most appropriate language, clarifying examples, and what structure should be used to assist in avoiding listener or viewer communication noise.

Interactional Model of Communication

The linear model of communication does not take into account all of the variables in the communication process. For this reason, some early behavioral scientists, influenced by research in psychology, expanded the notion of the process to encompass

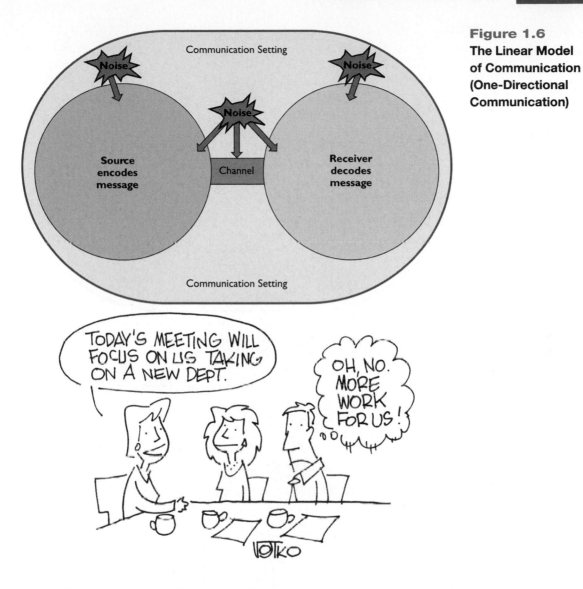

Figure 1.6
The Linear Model of Communication (One-Directional Communication)

greater interaction and to demonstrate the dynamic, ongoing nature of communication. Communication scholars point to David Berlo's *The Process of Communication*[18] as the influential work that introduced this perspective. The interactional model of communication is displayed in Figure 1.7.

In the **interactional model of communication,** a source encodes and sends a message to a receiver (through one or more of the sensory channels). The receiver receives and decodes the message, as in linear communication, but then encodes *feedback* and sends it back to the source, thus making the process two-directional. The source then decodes the feedback message. Based on the original message sent and the feedback received, the source encodes a new message that adjusts to the feedback *(adaptation).* For example, José says to Brooke, "Please hand me the book." Brooke looks at the pile of books in front of her and says, "Which one?" (feedback). José responds, "The red one on the top of the pile" (adaptation).

This view of communication accounts for the influence of the receiver's responses. It suggests a process that is somewhat circular: sending and receiving, receiving and sending, and so on.

Figure 1.7
The Interactional Model of Communication (Two-Directional Communication)

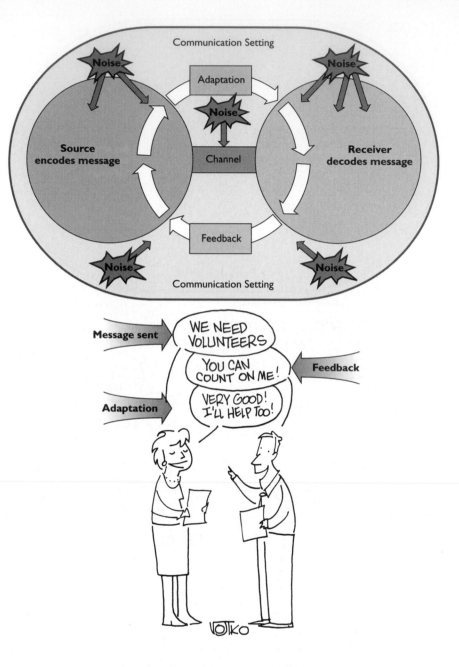

Whenever possible, communicators should attempt to interact so that they can find out how effective their communication actually is. For example, José's analysis of the number of books available might have led him to the conclusion that he needed to be more specific, and he therefore could have said, "Please hand me the red book on the top of the pile." Or he might have wanted to ask, "Do you know which book I want?," after saying "Hand me the book." Or he might have waited to see which volume Brooke put on the table to see whether she understood him. If she did not, he could have corrected his error by being more specific in his directions.

Managers in organizations, parents, and professors should make use of this communication model in order to ensure that their employees, customers, children, and students have received and can react appropriately to their messages.

Transactional Model of Communication

Theorists have suggested that communication may not be as simple a process of stimulus and response as the linear and interactional models suggest. This view supports the idea that communication is a transaction in which source and receiver play interchangeable roles throughout the act of communication. Because of the complexity of this process, a clear-cut model of the process is not easy to construct. Figure 1.8 is designed to illustrate the **transactional model of communication.** In this model, the communicators simultaneously process messages. Communicator A encodes a

Figure 1.8
The Transactional Model of Communication (Multidirectional Communication)

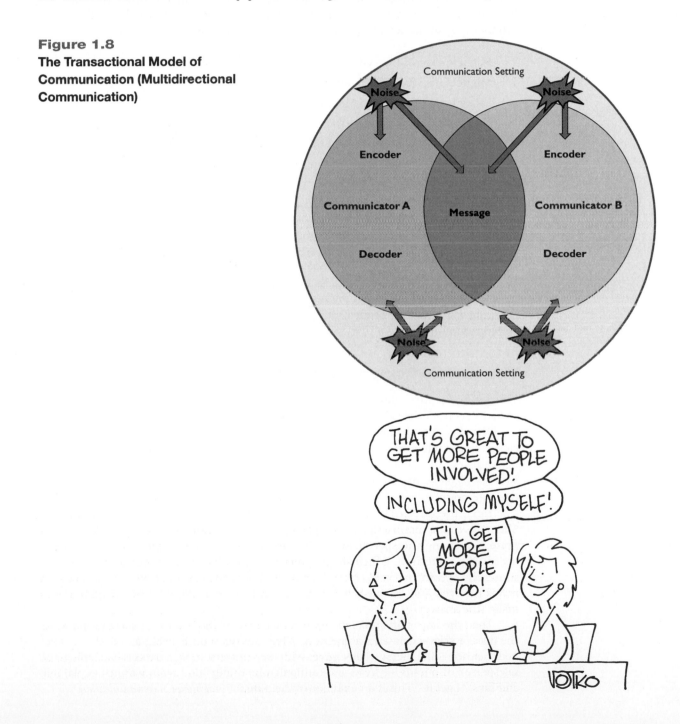

message and sends it. Communicator B then encodes feedback and sends it to A, who decodes it. But these steps are not mutually exclusive; encoding and decoding may occur simultaneously. Speakers may send a verbal message and at the same time receive and decode a nonverbal feedback message from listeners. Because messages can be sent and received at the same time, this model is multidirectional and the message overlaps. Think of the instances when you were speaking to someone and he simultaneously nodded as you were speaking, said, "Yes," and then, "and?," which gave you his message while you were simultaneously giving yours.

Notice that one person is not labeled the source and the other the receiver. Instead, both communicators assume the roles of encoder and decoder in the transaction, thus simultaneously communicating—for example:

Miguele says, "I love you," *while*

Miguele sees Latica walk away as he is speaking, *while*

Latica walks away from Miguele, *while*

Latica says, "I love you," *while*

Miguele stops, turns, frowns, and says, "I'm not sure you mean that," *while*

Latica sees Miguele nod his head and walk toward her as she speaks, *while*

Miguele hears her words, *while*

Miguele smiles and nods his head and walks toward Latica as she speaks.

Throughout the encounter, both Miguele and Latica are simultaneously sending and receiving (encoding and decoding) verbal and nonverbal messages.

Although use of the transactional model may result in the most effective communication, applying this model will be successful only if the communicators are continually aware of adapting the communication by being alert to feedback, anticipating potential noise factors, and considering the participants, setting, and purpose of the communication act.

The Models Compared

Comparing the three models in an example may enhance your understanding of how each differs from the others.

The director of public relations of a major corporation presents a speech over closed-circuit television from the headquarters' media studio to the marketing personnel at district offices located throughout the country. This is an example of the *linear model of communication* (one-directional, no chance for feedback, no opportunity to evaluate noise).

Next, the director gives the same presentation in the corporation's boardroom. She sticks to the manuscript she prepared, making no effort to seek feedback or detect noise. Following the speech, she asks if there are any questions. A member of the board asks a question, which she answers. The question-and-answer session demonstrates the *interactional model of communication:* The sender encoded and sent a message, it was received and decoded, feedback was given (the question), and adaptation was made (the answer).

Then the sales staff enters the room. The public relations director starts to speak. As she does, a salesperson asks a question. While the question is being asked, the speaker nods her head. She then verbally agrees with the salesperson. While this is happening, the salesperson also nods his head, indicating that he understood what was just explained, and says, "I get it." This is an example of the *transactional model of communication.*

Besides understanding what the communication process is, it also is important to understand how we are affected not only by communication that is face-to-face but also by communication that is media derived.

The Media as Communicators

We are influenced by **media**—radio, television, the Internet, magazines, newspapers, and film. Radio and television play a role in the communication lives of many people. "There is a long history (or tradition) of sociological theories of mass communication and critical studies of culture that attempt to understand these many effects."[19]

When you consider that the typical American spends more than half of his or her leisure time watching television, you can appreciate the potential influence the media can have.[20] Add to this that in 2007, 70.2 percent of the people in the United States were using the Internet,[21] it is easy to understand why media is considered by many to be the major communication tool in the twenty-first century. Some lives are shaped by the media. People develop role models based on seeing sports and entertainment celebrities on television, listening to them being interviewed on radio, or reading what is being said about them on the Internet. The images that the media project tell us how to dress, how to spend our time, and how to be a consumer. As political, business, and social attitudes are relayed, we form our beliefs on war, what stocks to buy or sell, or whom to vote for in an upcoming election. MTV and compact discs not only influence our music tastes but they also send political, religious, and social messages.

The result of this media exposure can be positive. Children learn the alphabet and numbers through *Sesame Street*. They learn values from *Barney*. *National Geographic* specials and print sources provide information about people, animals, and places. We attend symphonies and dance performances without leaving our homes. Oprah introduces us to cultural perspectives, and Dr. Phil (McGraw) informs us about how to cope with trauma.

But there can be a downside to media exposure. As people spend time in front of television sets, listening to the radio, attending movies, going online, and texting, they have less time to engage in direct conversations with others and participate in other activities. Critics point to television, for example, as a key to the declining reading and academic scores of students and in the rising incidence of violence in the United States. The perception of the influence of media violence on the perpetrators of the 1999 shootings at Columbine High School in Littleton, Colorado, led then-President Clinton to order the Federal Trade Commission to undertake a study. The goal was to determine if television and film companies use violent language and imagery to lure young, impressionable consumers and whether the amount of violence on television and in the movies has desensitized people to death and destruction.

There is also the question of whether exposing people to information about violence can result in further violence. The number of copycat crimes after the Columbine shootings was perceived to have resulted from exposure to the coverage of the murders on television. For example, in March 2005, a sixteen-year-old Red Lake (Minnesota) High School student killed a security guard, teacher, and five fellow students and then shot himself. The crime had direct echoes of the Columbine massacre: the killer's adoration of Hitler, his social isolation, his frightening Web postings, his Goth clothing and trench coat, and his being a loner with no friends.[22]

Radio and television have profound effects on our everyday lives. The products you buy, the attitudes you hold, and the political candidates you choose to vote for or against may well be influenced by the media you listen to and watch. History, too, has been influenced by media events. For example, it is perceived that major radio and television presentations have been influential in changing history. Dr. Martin Luther King's "I Have a Dream" speech (August 28, 1963) is credited as being a pivotal force in advancing the civil rights movement.[23] President Franklin Delano Roosevelt's Fireside Chats (which started on March 12, 1933), in which he presented casual conversations about problems that faced the nation at the height of the 1930s economic depression, is credited with calming down an anxious populace.[24] The Nixon–Kennedy television debate (September 26, 1960), which is considered to be the pivotal factor in John F. Kennedy's election, illustrated the necessity of being aware of the visual effects of television. Richard Nixon, the Republican candidate, was recovering from the flu and did not look very well. Kennedy, on the other hand, appeared tan and relaxed. Although not normally considered to be an effective speaker, George W. Bush used "his former cheerleader skills" to inspire when someone put a bullhorn in his hand as he inspected the rubble of the World Trade Center three days after 9/11 (September 14, 2001) and set a course for his presidency.[25] Barack Obama catapulted himself onto the national scene when he gave his "The Audacity of Hope" speech at the Democratic National Convention on July 27, 2004.

Like television, the Internet has become a major mediated communication channel. It is estimated that more than 400 million people throughout the world use the Internet.[26] Facebook, a social networking website, has over 55 million users,[27] and "reportedly signs up 100,000 new users every day."[28] As more and more people spend time at their computers getting information, e-mailing friends and family, participating in online educational opportunities, and in social networking, the impact of this medium has been profound. The rapid advances of the system now enable us to watch films, listen to the radio, place phone calls, do banking, be in constant contact with friends, watch each other, and shop online with our computers, I-phones, and Blackberries.[29] Some critics fear that this will turn us into social isolates who interact less with each other and more with our computer screens. Others point out, however, that the Internet brings friends and families together in meaningful ways as people maintain ongoing e-conversations and connections as well as allowing them to conduct personal and professional business without leaving their homes or businesses.

A media critic maintains that we have to be trained to "read" television and other media in order to use them positively. He argues, "Only when we recover a critical distance from the technology which seduces us with its amusing appeal, can we recover the appropriate balance of mediums that will make us an intelligent culture."[30] An intelligent culture is one in which the inhabitants are competent communicators. Understanding how culture affects communication is another important concept to investigate in order to understand the world of communication.

Communication and Culture

What phrases or terms immediately come to mind when you are asked, "What is your culture?" How do your cultural affiliations affect you? How do they affect your communication?

Intercultural and Intracultural Communication

Usually when one speaks of culture, nationality comes to mind. In reality, *nationality* refers to the nation in which one was born, now resides, or has lived or studied for enough time to become familiar with the customs of the area. Some nationality

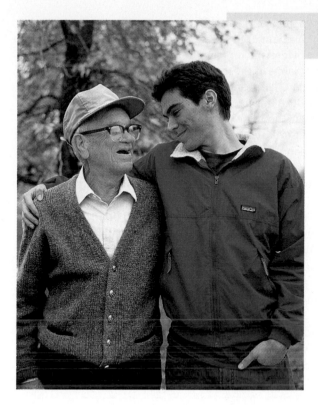

Culture is a communication phenomenon because it is passed from generation to generation through interactions.

identifiers are Irish and Korean. Nationality is only one factor of culture, however. Other cultural group identifiers are the region of a country (e.g., the southern part of the United States), religious affiliation or orientation (e.g., Muslim), political orientation (e.g., Democrat), socioeconomic status (e.g., upper middle class), gender (e.g., female), sexual orientation (e.g., gay male), age or generation (e.g., senior citizen), vocation (e.g., executive), avocation (e.g., stamp collector), family background (e.g., Italian Catholic from a large family), marital status (e.g., married), and parental status (e.g., single father).

We are each culture-filled, a combination of many cultures. You may not have thought about it, but you are the sum total of your environmental influences—the influences of your family, your community, your religious or lack of religious upbringing, your education, and the media with which you have come in contact. Because you have so many cultural influences, you are a multicultural being.

It is culture that gives us our language, ethics, morals, and social and political ideals. It is culture that gives us our art forms, our way of relating to others, and our value system. In other words, in many ways, it is culture that makes us human. The words you utter and think, the actions you take, and your ability to interact with others have all been laid out for you by your cultural influences. You are human because you have the ability to selectively use language to think about what has happened, use those experiences to perceive in the present tense, and project into the future. You can convey ideas, perceptions, and beliefs because of the language your culture has taught you. You are your culture, and your culture is you.

Communication and culture have a direct link. A *culture* consists of all those individuals who have a shared system of interpretation. Culture is a communication phenomenon because it is passed among its adherents by communication: written and oral, verbal and nonverbal. You might think of it this way: Culture is the software that allows the hardware (the person) to operate. Your parents, the schools you have attended, and the media were all influential in aiding you to develop your belief system through communication. You were spoken to and listened to, and you saw and read about the rules, customs, and habits of those with whom you lived in your home, region of the country, and nation. This is an ongoing process; it was and is done through communication. Your culture has been passed on to you through proverbs, family stories, fairytales, songs, poetry, and literature.

A great deal of your daily communication centers on your cultural identifications. As a student, for example, how many times do you refer to student-oriented topics, including the institution you attend and how your education will help you in the future? You probably compare and contrast your "studentness" with qualities of other students and nonstudents.

When you interact with those with whom you have a cultural bond, you are participating in **intracultural communication.** For example, a baseball fan speaking to another baseball fan has a cultural bond. When you speak to those with whom you have little or no cultural bond, you are engaging in **intercultural communication.** A Japanese citizen with little knowledge of New Zealand and a New Zealander with little knowledge of Japan or its customs who are speaking with each other are involved on an intercultural level.

Have you ever wondered how comfortable you are in speaking to people from cultures other than your own? If so, fill out the Personal Report of Intercultural Communication Apprehension questionnaire on page 25.

Multiculturalism

When people from various cultures live in the same place, unique multicultural situations can emerge. The term *multiculture* refers to a society consisting of varied cultural groups. The United States is a multicultural country. It is ethnically composed of African Americans, Hispanic Americans, Irish Americans, and many other cultures. It is also multicultural as it relates to the broader definition of culture because it is made up of such differences as women and men, homosexuals and heterosexuals, and religious believers and atheists.

The multicultural view is one of *pluralism.*[31] Individuals can maintain their individual identities and still be part of the larger group. For example, using the analogist term *salad bowl* to describe the United States describes that each person is uniquely different and does not have to become the same. Each item in a salad is identifiable: tomato, lettuce, cucumber, and so on. Historically, the term *melting pot* was used to describe the United States. In other words, everyone was supposed to be the same, lose their individuality, lose their individual cultural components, and become part of the blend, rather than remain individual and identifiable.

Much attention has been given to *multiculturalism,* a political and attitudinal movement to ensure cultural freedom. The movement evolved because "a lot of people are ignorant about people of color, gays and lesbians, or whatever [e.g., Hispanics, Spanish Americans, Asians]. These groups often feel like they are marginalized."[32]

"The United States as a whole is moving in the direction of its two most populous states, California and Texas, where members of racial and ethnic minorities account for more than half the population, according to the Census Bureau."[33] "Non-Hispanic whites now make up two-thirds of the total U.S. population, the bureau said, but that proportion will dip to one-half by 2050, according to the agency's latest projections."[34]

Personal Report of Intercultural Communication Apprehension (PRICA)[35]

This measure was developed to address communication apprehension in the intercultural context.

Directions: The 14 statements below are comments frequently made by people with regard to communication with people from other cultures. Please indicate how much you agree with these statements by marking a number representing your response to each statement using the following choices: Strongly Disagree = 1; Disagree = 2; Neutral = 3; Agree = 4; Strongly Agree = 5

_____ 1. Generally, I am comfortable interacting with a group of people from different cultures.

_____ 2. I am tense and nervous while interacting with people from different cultures.

_____ 3. I like to get involved in group discussion with others who are from different cultures.

_____ 4. Engaging in a group discussion with people from different cultures makes me nervous.

_____ 5. I am calm and relaxed when interacting with a group of people who are from different cultures.

_____ 6. While participating in a conversation with a person from a different culture, I get nervous.

_____ 7. I have no fear of speaking up in a conversation with a person from a different culture.

_____ 8. Ordinarily I am very tense and nervous in a conversation with person from a different culture.

_____ 9. Ordinarily I am very calm and relaxed in conversations with a person from a different culture.

_____ 10. While conversing with a person from a different culture, I feel very relaxed.

_____ 11. I am afraid to speak up in conversations with a person from a different culture.

_____ 12. I face the prospect of interacting with people from different cultures with confidence.

_____ 13. My thoughts become confused and jumbled when interacting with people from different cultures.

_____ 14. Communicating with people from different cultures makes me feel uncomfortable.

Scoring: To compute the PRICA score, complete the following steps:

Step 1. Add the scores for the following items: 1, 3, 5, 7, 9, 10, and 12

Step 2. Add the scores for the following items: 2, 4, 6, 8, 11, 13, and 14

Step 3. Complete the following formula:
PRICA score = 42 – Total from Step 1 + Total from Step 2.

Scores can range from 14 to 70. Scores below 32 indicate low intercultural communication apprehension (CA). Scores above 52 indicate high intercultural CA. Scores ranging between 32 and 52 indicate a moderate level of intercultural CA.

Many people who are long-time residents of the United States have verbal and nonverbal patterns quite different from those of European Americans because of their cultural background—in this case, their ethnic or racial group.

People from ethnic and racial minority groups face a different and sometimes hostile and alien culture, value system, and communication system when entering school systems and corporate, social service, and governmental environments. As a result, some minority students might perform poorly in school classes because they lack competence in the majority culture's language and rules of communication.

The ethnic majority often doesn't understand or has biases against those who are in the minority, and the culturally different may not understand the motives and patterns of the mainstream.

Accepting that you are a cultural being, understanding the process you use to discuss cultural affiliations as well as other aspects of yourself, is an important part of learning to be a competent communicator. Ask yourself, "What is my cultural composite?" "What is my gender, ethnicity, race and sexual orientation?" How do these factors affect your communication?

Culturally Communicating

You Are a Citizen of a Very Diverse World

If we shrank the earth's population to a "global village" of only 100 people and kept all the existing human ratios, there'd be:

61	from Asia
21	from China
17	from India
13	from Africa
12	from Europe
5	from the U.S.
1	from Australia and New Zealand
22	who speak a Chinese dialect,
18	of whom speak Mandarin
9	who speak English
8	who speak Hindi
50	females
50	males
32	Christians
68	non-Christians,
15	of whom are nonreligious
19	Muslims
6	Buddhists
1	Jew
30	who have enough to eat
88	old enough to read,
17	of whom cannot read at all
1	teacher

and you are one person traveling that world.

Source: worldcitizensguide.org.

Ethnocentrism

Jon, a Christian European American male, is introduced to Aaron and thinks it is ridiculous that he wears a skullcap (a *yarmulke*) all the time. He is invited to Sanjav's home and is repulsed when he is told that the meat being served at dinner is snake. He is amazed when he hears that in many Arabic countries women have to cover their entire bodies when they are in public. His reactions reflect ethnocentrism.

"*Ethnocentrism* means that we consider the views and standards of our own in-group as much more important than any out-groups."[36] The founder of sociology in the United States explained the concept of ethnocentrism as the result of people's perceptions that they belong to an *in-group*, defined as a collectivity with which an individual identifies. An *out-group* is a collectivity with which an individual does not identify. The in-group's beliefs are perceived to be right, the out-group's wrong. As a result of ethnocentrism, out-groups are often at a disadvantage because we constantly make judgments about them based on our standards and values and reject the other group's standards and values. When Jon encountered Aaron, Sanjav, and the notion of an Arabic woman enclosed in a *burka*, he put into effect his concept system of what he is used to, what his culture's rules are, what he believes to be the "right" way.

Generally, we view life in terms of our own group being the center of everything, and all others being scaled and rated with reference to it. Think of the clothing worn on your campus by the majority of students. That's the "in" clothing. On many campuses in the early 2000s, that consisted of jeans or shorts, T-shirts, and jogging shoes, flip-flops, or sandals. A student showing up for class in an African *dashiki* or an Indian *sari* may be met with strange looks. That's ethnocentrism in action. The in-group's style is considered the only right one.

Ethnocentrism pervades every aspect of a culture's existence. Examples range from the insignificant to the significant. Students in the United States, if asked to identify the great books of the world, would likely produce a list of books mainly by Western, white, male authors. You probably have been taught in your literature classes that these are the classics. With few exceptions, books written by women or by non-Westerners may be noteworthy, but they don't normally reach the high levels of being "classics."

National conflicts often center on the perception that what is in our national interest is right. What is in the national interest of another country is not acceptable. In reality, no one can claim that only certain groups have a cultural perspective or identity that is superior to another's perspective or identity. Although we might like to think so, the "American way" is not superior to the "Chinese way" or the "Egyptian way." Some Polish people eat duck blood soup and pierogies; many people from Thailand eat kaeng

The United States is a multicultural country as it relates to ethnic derivation.

hang, larb, som tam, and kai; Americans eat hamburgers and French fries. Which of these foods is best? None, per se. What a person eats is based on cultural patterns, availability, and sometimes necessity.

Ethnocentrism is not a new concept. It was expressed, and reinforced in many ways, by the European colonizers. White-skinned colonists considered themselves more advanced than the natives, who were people of color. They subjugated the native peoples of Southern and Latin America, Africa, and Asia, whom they considered inferior. Strong attempts were made to convert the natives to the religion and views of the invaders. Often, if they would not convert to these cultural values, the natives were killed or enslaved. Entire cultures were wiped out or nearly destroyed because of ethnocentrism. The definition of what it means to be an "American" is under constant redefinition. Nationality diversity is part of the present national perspective. Among some in the Euro-American community this means that "our" country is no longer ours. It is this fear of losing control of their country that motivates some to attack any immigration into the United States. Indeed, some individuals and organizations have taken strong stands against the move toward immigration. For example, one organization bannered the phrase, "Illegal Immigration must be stopped and reversed!"[37] The issue evolved as one of the most important issues of the 2008 presidential and congressional elections. Immigration placed second in concerns of Republican voters in exit polls conducted during the Super Tuesday 2008 voting to select presidential candidates,[38] ahead of such issues as the Iraq war and health care.

Realistically, we also must recognize that the tendency to see things from our own cultural viewpoint is very natural. However, we must additionally realize that ethnocentrism can have many negative impacts, including shutting out others. In its highest forms, extreme ethnocentrism leads to a rejection of the richness and knowledge of other cultures. It impedes communication and blocks the exchange of ideas and skills among peoples. Because it excludes other points of view, an ethnocentric orientation is restrictive and limiting. It can lead and has led to racism, sexism, and even war.

Can ethnocentrism be decreased or eliminated? Two major actions might help change the perspective: direct, personal (one-on-one) contact with an unlike other and intercultural communication training that is experiential. These actions can be implemented by increasing contact between unlike individuals. In this way, through

Culturally Communicating

Cross-Cultural Communication

If you work with people whose native language is not your own, follow these tips to communicate instructions clearly:

- Avoid complicated and lengthy explanations. Keep instructions short.

- Make it clear that you welcome questions when something is unclear.

- Ask them to repeat your instructions in their own words. *Reason:* if they repeat the instructions in your words, they may have memorized the words but not the message.

Source: Sondra Thiederman, PhD, president of Cross-Cultural Communications, cited in *Leadership for the Front Lines*, 24 Rope Ferry Road, Waterford, CT 60386.

travel and interactions, people can become aware of others' patterns and learn to accept them as being as valid as their own patterns. And through training, individuals can understand the nature of their ethnocentric beliefs and increase their empathy by experiencing the unalike culture. An example is a two-week training course in India that was designed to decrease the sexism of male government employees. This Women's Awareness Training puts male trainees in the daily role of an Indian woman. The trainees carry water from a distant well, wash their clothes and dishes, cook, and clean their living quarters. The male trainees are not allowed to go outside of their residences without permission of a female trainer. Nor are the trainees permitted to drive a vehicle. Thus, the Indian men are taught to empathize with the subservient role of traditional Indian women. Individuals who have completed this training say that it has had a powerful effect on their sexist attitudes and has decreased their ethnocentrism.

Some communication experts feel that ethnocentrism must be replaced by *cultural relativism* through a concentrated effort to educate students about the dangers of being self-absorbed. "*Cultural relativism* is a worldview and standpoint that no culture as such is superior to any other one, and that any culture deserves to be described, understood, and judged on its own premises."[39]

They further contend that to counter ethnocentrism, students must be taught and given the opportunity to recognize individual differences and the uniqueness of each person and culture. The Semester at Sea program is an academic attempt to help students gain such experience. Students travel to ten to fifteen countries during a single academic semester. Before visiting each country, students are instructed about the unique features of each nation, including its language, treatment of the sexes, nonverbal patterns, and religions. A student in the program who took an Intercultural Communication class expressed the point in a letter to one of your authors who was his instructor: "When people ask me about the voyage and what it taught me about cultures, I often respond with the statement, 'It's not good. It's not bad. It's just different.' Those words of yours brought home a new-found awareness that I can use every day as I continue to encounter people and cultures different from my own. I truly learned the meaning of differences."[40]

First Amendment Speech

In the United States, one of our cultural cornerstones is freedom of speech. As a competent communicator, you should know your privileges and responsibilities concerning your constitutional rights. Your communication liberties are soundly influenced by the First Amendment to the U.S. Constitution, which bans Congress from passing laws "abridging the freedom of speech." Therefore, when we are confronted with the question of the meaning of **freedom of speech,** the answer tends to be that it is the protected right to speak without restrictions—to be free to say what we want. In reality, however, the simple language of the First Amendment leaves much to interpretation. Because of this, courts have been called on to establish standards and guidelines to resolve free-speech disputes An examination of cases shows the complexity of the issue of freedom of speech:

- A group of student organizations, known collectively as the Free Speech Coalition of West Virginia University, sued the university in June 2002 over the school's free-speech zone policy. In *Free Speech Coalition of West Virginia University v. Hardesty,* the student groups allege that the policy, which now allows for seven campus free-speech zones, violates the students' First Amendment rights.[41] In February 2002, students and a few faculty members began protesting the policy. In response, the university expanded its number of free-speech zones from two to seven. But that was not enough to satisfy the student groups.

- Officials at New Mexico State University adopted a new free-speech policy in the 1980s. This policy said members of the university community were free to speak on any topic so long as they did so in three designated areas. In September 2000, a student activist was arrested for distributing leaflets criticizing the university's policy on freedom of speech. The American Civil Liberties Union intervened and filed a lawsuit contending that NMSU has designated unusable areas in which to distribute literature to other students.[42]

- In April 2003, two students sued Shippensburg University in Pennsylvania, arguing that several part of the school's conduct code and diversity polices intimidated them into keeping silent about their conservative politics and beliefs. The lawsuit is part of the FIRE (Foundation for Individual Rights in Education) campaign to abolish campus speech codes.[43]

Is there justification for limitations placed on freedom of speech, or are such restrictions unacceptable?

One of the justifications offered for limitations on freedom of speech is that *words are deeds.* It contends that some symbolic behavior may be so harmful that we are justified in restraining it. A presidential assassin might plead that he or she acted for the purpose of sending a political message to the public. To regard such a claim as legitimate may blur the line that must be maintained between speech and action.[44]

A further contention against limitations on freedom of speech proposes that "more often than not, *the free-speech issue becomes a weapon to fight some other cause . . . flag burning, blocking access to abortion clinics, pornography.*"[45] This assertion suggests that it is not freedom of speech or the First Amendment that is being dealt with in these cases, but rather the causes themselves.

Also questioned is: If one speaker is banned, must every speaker be banned?

A leading civil libertarian wonders where the founding fathers, those who wrote the Constitution of the United States, would draw the line. He concludes "that we ought not to censor the speech of even the most violent religious leaders."[46] Echoing Jefferson, he adds that any censorship would not prevent either violence or incitement.[47]

In her U.S. Supreme Court nomination hearings, Ruth Bader Ginsburg stated, "We are a society that has given, beyond any other, maximum protection for the speech that we hate, and on the other hand, are concerned for the quality and dignity of individuals. Those two principles collide in this area [hate speech]."[48]

Following the September 11, 2001, terrorist attacks on New York and Washington, DC, much controversy arose concerning how many and what kind of restrictions

Socially Communicating

Conundrum: University Speech Policies

A civil liberties group has filed suit against Shippensburg University, saying the state school's policy on speech is among the most unconstitutionally restrictive in the nation.

The complaint cites what it alleges is unconstitutionally vague or overly broad language in the school's racism and cultural diversity policy, which cautions among other things against "unconscious attitudes toward individuals which surface through the use of discriminatory semantics."

"Too many colleges and universities attempt to outlaw free speech and expression that does not conform to a specific orthodoxy."

Source: Based on JoAnn Loviglio, "Group Sues Pennsylvania University Over 'Speech Codes,'" April 23, 2003. Fire-Foundation for Individual Rights in Education, www.thefire.org.

REFLECT ON THIS:

1. Does your school have a policy on speech?

2. Does your school have a policy on racism and cultural diversity?

3. Do you think colleges should outlaw speech that does not conform to a specific orthodoxy?

could or should be placed on an individual's rights. "Free speech versus public safety is familiar territory for the court [Supreme Court,] which has tended to side with those favoring less restriction on expression."[49] However, six weeks after the terrorist attacks, Congress, over vigorous objections from civil liberties organizations, approved the Uniting and Strengthening America by Providing Appropriate Tools Required to Intercept and Obstruct Terrorism Act, better known as the USA PATRIOT Act.[50] The act has allowed surveillance of U.S. citizens even when there was no probable cause and minimal judicial involvement, roving wiretaps, eavesdropping on inmates' attorney–client conversations, and the questioning of 5,000 people, who appear to have been selected according to their ethnicity or religion.[51]

How might this conflict affect you on a personal level? Should your communication instructor limit what topics you may speak about in a speech? Should Internet providers be allowed to censor what you send or receive? Should your collegiate organization be allowed to bring a speaker to campus who attacks others' religious or ethnic heritage? Should an instructor lower your grade because you speak out in class in opposition to her view?

Not only is what you are allowed to and not allowed to communicate an issue, but also important is knowing what your ethical standards are as you act as a speaker and as a listener.

Ethics

Ethics is the systematic study of what should be the grounds and principles for acceptable and unacceptable behavior.[52] Ethics are not just something that individuals practice; instead, they are the perceived values shared by a society. The importance of conducting our human affairs in ethical, responsible ways has recently been highlighted by corporate financial scandals, political campaigns that used lies and innuendoes to coerce voters and perhaps even to take this country to war in Iraq, the role of pharmaceutical and health-care companies in influencing government decisions regarding their industries, and the role of advertising in persuading people to buy products and services that are often unnecessary and sometimes dangerous. These situations have prompted a renewed emphasis on ethics.

Your *personal ethical value system* is the basis for your decision making and your understanding of why you will or will not take a particular stand or action. It is the basis for your communication ethics.

Communication Ethics

Over the decades, speech communication instructors and theorists have stressed that competent speakers should, by definition, be ethical speakers. "Potential ethical issues are inherent in any instance of communication between humans to the degree that the communication can be judged on a right–wrong dimension, involves possible significant influence on other humans, and to the degree that the communicator consciously chooses specific ends sought and communicative means to achieve those ends."[53] Therefore, it is contended that speakers should give the audience assistance

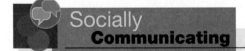

Socially
Communicating

Feel Your Way to Be Ethical

Thinking FEEL when you face an ethical dilemma can keep you on the right path, says James Melton, a consultant in Palm Springs, Calif.:

- **Feeling** Do you feel comfortable about the situation, or does something about it worry your conscience?

- **Equity** Will what you've decided to do be fair to everyone involved?

- **Emotion** Have you let emotion overrule reason in your decision-making process?

- **Legality** Will what you plan to do violate any laws?

Source: Management Review, March 1998, American Management Association, 1601 Broadway, New York, NY 10019. © Communications Briefings, www.briefings.com, 1101 King St., Alexandria, VA 22314. Used with permission.

in making wise decisions and that speakers' decisions about what to say should be based on moral principles. Following this concept, in the 2004 national election, Democratic challenger John Kerry sought to counter Republican attacks on his Vietnam war record by accusing the Bush campaign of using "tactics of fear and smear" to evade discussion of the administration's record on jobs, health care, and U.S. alliances frayed as a result of the war in Iraq. He stated, "They have decided that some people will believe anything, no matter how fictional or how far-fetched, if they just repeat it often enough. That's how they've run their administration, that's how they're running their campaign."[54]

Ethical Communicators

Ethical communicators are those who "respect the integrity of ideas and concerns from the listeners."[55] They are generally defined as those who conform to the moral standards a society establishes for its communicators. Although this definition seems plausible, it contains a major flaw: The words ring hollow because it is impossible either to list or to gain acceptance for *universal* moral standards. Although some people claim they have the true answer, in reality there is no universal agreement on what exactly it means to be moral.

The National Communication Association, the major voice of communication educators, has approved a Code of Ethic for Speakers. (See Figure 1.9.) It isolates specific traits that define an ethical speaker in the European American culture. It also may have some implications for global communication as the organization has international members.

Because most readers of this book live in a society that stresses Western philosophy, the discussion of what it means to be an ethical communicator centers on this viewpoint. Nevertheless, this perspective may not be appropriate or acceptable to you, based on your ethnic, racial, and other cultural influences. As a student of communication, the credo stresses that you should realize you:

- Should not knowingly expose an audience to lies
- Should not alter the truth

In public communication, an implied assumption is that words can be trusted and people will be truthful, but this does not mean you should accept everything that is said.

Figure 1.9
NCA Credo for Ethical Communication

Source: Approved by the NCA Legislative Council in 1999 (National Communication Association, Washington, DC, www.natcom.org/policies /External/EthicalComm.htm.)

Questions of right and wrong arise whenever people communicate. Ethical communication is fundamental to responsible thinking, decision making, and the development of relationships and communities within and across contexts, cultures, channels, and media. Moreover, ethical communication enhances human worth and dignity by fostering truthfulness, fairness, responsibility, personal integrity, and respect for self and others. We believe that unethical communication threatens the quality of all communication and consequently the well-being of individuals and the society in which we live. Therefore we, the members of the National Communication Association, endorse and are committed to practicing the following principles of ethical communication:

- We advocate truthfulness, accuracy, honesty, and reason as essential to the integrity of communication.
- We endorse freedom of expression, diversity of perspective, and tolerance of dissent to achieve the informed and responsible decision making fundamental to a civil society.
- We strive to understand and respect other communicators before evaluating and responding to their messages.
- We promote access to communication resources and opportunities as necessary to fulfill human potential and contribute to the well-being of families, communities, and society.
- We promote communication climates of caring and mutual understanding that respect the unique needs and characteristics of individual communicators.
- We condemn communication that degrades individuals and humanity through distortion, intimidation, coercion, and violence, and through the expression of intolerance and hatred.
- We are committed to the courageous expression of personal convictions in pursuit of fairness and justice.
- We advocate sharing information, opinions, and feelings when facing significant choices while also respecting privacy and confidentiality.
- We accept responsibility for the short- and long-term consequences for our own communication and expect the same of others.

- Should tell the truth as you understand it
- Should supply the necessary facts, definitions, descriptions, and substantiating information to lead the speaker to a reasonable conclusion
- Should not invent or fabricate statistics or other information intended to serve as a basis for proof of a contention or belief
- Should give credit to the source of information

Be aware that speakers who are unethical can lose their credibility. A 2007 report indicated that then "US President George W. Bush and his top officials ran roughshod over the truth in the run-up to the Iraq war lying a total of 935 times."[56] A parallel study indicated that as the information concerning the questionable information was given to the public by Bush and his staff, the president's popularity dropped considerably. A compilation of major polling sources indicates that when taking office for his first term, Bush's approval rating was 55 percent. After his positively perceived speech on terrorism on January 20, his rating was 90 percent. By September 20, 2007, when the information about the number of so-called untruths was documented, his approval rating was 30 percent.[57]

Not only speakers but also listeners need to operate within an ethical framework. From the standpoint of the receiver, in most public and private communication, a fundamental implied and unspoken assumption is that words can be trusted and people will be truthful. This does not mean that you should accept everything that is said; doing so would be naive. To be an ethical receiver, you should listen carefully to the information presented and ask yourself whether the conclusions reached are reasonable and expected.

Be aware that there are urban legends, myths consisting of stories thought to be factual by those circulating them. They are not necessarily untrue, but they are often distorted, exaggerated, or sensationalized. These stories are often spread on the Internet. Before accepting accounts that may seem questionable, check them on www.snopes.com, which is a site that specializes in tracking down the facts concerning urban legends.

Ethical Career Communicators

What is the responsibility of organizations to be ethical communicators? One expert in business communication states, "It is incumbent upon managers in business, education, and industry today, to be very sensitive and forthright in their communications, and in response to privacy requests regarding communications from their employees. To be less than totally forthright can result in some very unsavory results from disenfranchised employees."[58] These results may include legal action against the perpetrator of the unethical act and the organization.

To attempt to ensure ethical communication in organizations, the International Association of Business Communicators has established a code of ethics that indicates that the activities of business communicators must practice "honest, candid and timely communication and [foster] the free flow of essential information in accord with the public interest."[59] The IABC code indicates that its members must:

- Engage in communication that is not only legal but also ethical and sensitive to cultural values and beliefs
- Engage in truthful, accurate and fair communication that facilitates respect and mutual understanding.[60]

In Conclusion

Communication is a conscious or unconscious, intentional or unintentional process in which feelings and ideas are expressed as verbal and/or nonverbal messages sent, received, and comprehended. It can take the form of intrapersonal, interpersonal, or public messages. Three factors are present in any communicative event: the communicators, the purpose, and the setting. We communicate through our senses. The process of communication can be understood by investigating the linear, the interactional, and the transactional communication models and the components that make up the process. As a system, communication is directly influenced by culture. Media is an important source of communication. In the United States, multiculturalism is an important aspect of communication, as are freedom of speech and an understanding of what is meant by ethical communication.

Learn by Doing

1. Design a model of communication that differs from any of the three presented in this chapter, and explain it to the class.

2. Identify an experience in which your attempt to communicate was a failure. Use the classification of sources of noise given in the text to label the type of interference you encountered. Why

did this happen? What, if anything, could you have done to correct the interference problem?

3. Describe a context in which you find it difficult to communicate. Describe a context in which you find it easy to communicate. Why did you select each one? What implications for communication are involved in your choices?

4. Describe the system of communication by which your family operates (or operated) by investigating the patterns of communication and the rules of operation. What were the advantages and disadvantages of that system?

5. Write one phrase or expression that is unique to your family or group of friends. It should be an expression that has meaning only for that group, not one commonly used in society as a whole. It may be an ethnic expression, an in-group reference, or some other special phrase. The other students will read the expression and try to figure out what it means. Draw inferences about semantic noise from this activity.

6. Individually, each student decides what he or she would do in each of the following situations. You will then be divided into small groups to discuss your answers and report back to the class as a whole on the choices made by each group.

   a. You are taking a public speaking course. The instructor requires three quoted references in the speech that you are to present in about five minutes. You had a week to get ready but did not have time to do the necessary research. Would you make up three references, not give the speech and get a failing grade, give the speech without the references and hope for the best, or take some other action? If you would take another action, what would it be?

   b. You have just finished eating in a restaurant. You check the bill and realize that the waiter has made a $10 error in your favor. The waiter sees your reaction and asks if anything is wrong. How do you respond?

   c. You look up during a test and see that your best friend, who needs a passing grade in this class to get off academic probation, is using cheat notes. You think the instructor also saw the action. As you hand in your paper, the instructor says to you, "Remember, this class operates on the honor system. Is there anything you want to say to me?" How do you respond?

7. Your class will discuss or debate the following resolution: "Resolved: A higher educational institution must be a platform for the debate of social issues. Therefore, it is resolved that [name of your college/university] allow, encourage, and invite *all* speakers to present their views in public forums on this campus."

8. Your class will discuss: Is it realistically possible to be an ethical communicator?

9. Write a list of words or phrases that answer the question, "What factors or identities constitute my culture?" Your answers will be used by your instructor as the basis for a discussion of "What is culture?" communication.

10. Answer this question. A class discussion will follow in which you need to state and defend your answer. A colleague and friend knocks on the door of your home one evening. "I've got great news," he says. "I'm buying the house of my dreams." Now, you know that your friend will lose his job in the next few weeks as your company reorganizes. But your company has sworn you to secrecy until the announcement is made. What do you do?

Key Terms

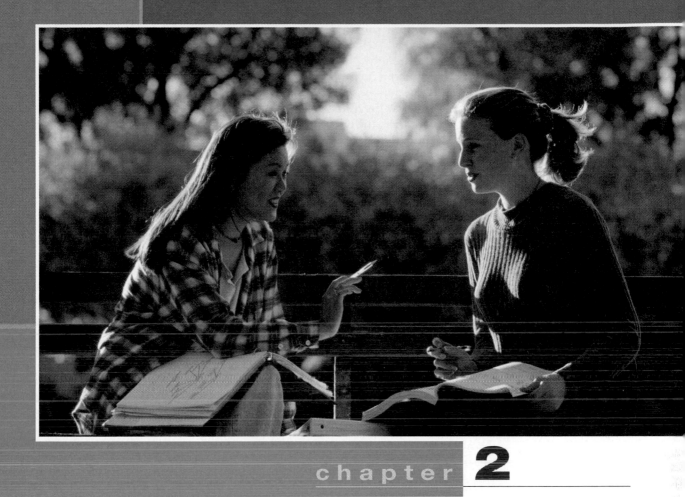

chapter 2

Foundations of Verbal Language

▶ **After reading this chapter, you should be able to**

- Name and describe several theories of the origins of human language
- Understand how thought is shaped by language
- Explain and illustrate how people select, process, use, and learn symbols
- Identify the features common to all languages
- Define and illustrate the emotive, phatic, cognitive, rhetorical, and identifying functions of language
- Explain the roles of ambiguity, vagueness, inference, and message adjustment in relation to language distortion

- Define and contrast standard versus nonstandard dialects, and relate the effects of speaking a nonstandard dialect
- Analyze slang as it relates to standard dialects
- Compare and contrast Standard American English, Ebonics/Black English, Spanglish, Asian American dialect, and Native American languages
- Relate the effects of speaking a dialect or nonstandard language
- Be aware of the effects of using verbal language

Each culture conveys a value system to its children. These assumptions are reflected and reinforced in language, and language thus creates or recreates the culture's social reality. There is a connection between the language we use, our self-perception, and our behavior. Language reflects our attitudes. Words can create categories and expectations so deep-seated that only such devices as affirmative action and anti-hate laws can force individuals to act differently than their language seems to allow. For example, the Supreme Court's decision in 1954 regarding *Brown v. Board of Education* caused widespread concerns in southern states and brought up not only changes in attitudes but also changes in the language used to describe white–black relations. Another vivid example took place during the lead-up to the 2008 presidential election. Democratic candidate Barack Obama "denounced his former pastor [Rev. Wright] for divisive and destructive remarks on race, seeking to divorce himself from the incendiary speaker."[1] Obama, speaking about the power of words, stated, "I am outraged by the comments that were made and saddened over the spectacle."[2] Wright had "criticized the U.S. government as imperialist and stood by his suggestion that the United States invented the HIV virus as a means of genocide against minorities."[3]

What is **language?** It is a system of arbitrary signals, such as sounds, gestures, or symbols, used by a nation, people, or distinct community to communicate thoughts and feelings. The system includes rules for combining its components, which is referred to as *grammar*.[4]

The *study of language* involves the study of meaning. The meaning is based on words, the way the words are placed together, and the backgrounds and experiences of the communicators. The channels by which the words are conveyed help create their meaning. When they appear on a printed page, words are linear, one-dimensional; their meaning is based on what the reader thinks the words mean, with no other clues for interpretation. But the words pick up additional dimensions when they are spoken because the rate, pitch, pause, and volume of the spoken words help us figure out the meaning of the words and the intent of the sender. Even more dimensions are available when the receiver can see the speaker and note facial expressions, gesture patterns, and body positions.

Origins of Human Language

The origin of language remains one of human evolution's enduring puzzles. Some anthropologists believe that two critical mutations in our human ancestors 200,000 years ago provided for a degree of control over mouth and throat muscles. They maintain that this control gave our ancestors the ability to create sounds that served as the foundation of language.[5]

Another researcher has proposed that language has its roots in gestures, not vocalics. He suggests that speech evolved from grunts and vocal cries that were voluntary, emotional responses to human movements of the hands and face, gestures that people used to communicate with each other.[6]

Others maintain that language evolved from primate grooming behavior.[7] A computer neuroscientist believes that speech is based on mental reflexes.[8]

However it started, "once speech caught on, it gave Homo sapiens a decisive advantage over less verbal rivals, including Homo erectus and the Neanderthals, whose lines eventually died out."[9] As one researcher puts it, "We talked them out of existence."[10]

Once verbal language was developed, an additional way to convey messages was needed, which resulted in the creation of written codes.

Language does not remain static; it is constantly changing. Changes in technology, lifestyles, and social attitudes lead to new words and phrases. For example, in the English language, each year, Merriam-Webster adds about 100 words to its dictionary.[11] Words recently added include *himbo* (an attractive but vacuous man), *empty suit* (an ineffective executive), *drama queen* (a person given to often excessively emotional performances or reactions), *sandwich generation* (a generation of people who are caring for their aging parents while supporting their own children), and *supersize* (to increase considerably the size, amount, or extent of).[12] The same publication crowned *truthiness,* meaning "truth that comes from the gut, not books," which was coined by television satirist Stephen Colbert as the Word of the Year (2005) and *crackberry,* meaning "a constant-flow-of-communication quality," as the 2006 winner.[13]

Sometimes when words are added due to usage, there is a protest regarding the word. When *ain't* was included for the first time, there were protests from semanticists that the word was not an acceptable word to be in common usage. Recently, McDonald's Corporation started a campaign to "ditch the dictionary definition of *McJob.*"[14] It had been defined in *The Oxford English Dictionary* as "an unstimulating, low-paid job with few prospects."[15] McDonald's contends that "the definition is demeaning to its workers."[16] Both *The Oxford English Dictionary* and *Merriam-Webster Dictionary* declined to remove or change their definition, declaring that the definition was "accurate and appropriate."[17]

Not only are new words added to individual languages, but some languages disappear entirely. "While there are an estimated 7,000 languages spoken around the world today, one of them dies out about every two weeks."[18] "Roughly a third of those are spoken in Africa and about 200 have fewer than 500 speakers."[19] You might be surprised to know that several of the disappearing languages are spoken by people in the United States. Included are Siletz Dee-ni, the last of twenty-seven languages once spoken on the Siletz reservation in Oregon and Yuchi, a language once spoken by the Yuchi tribe. As of 2005, there were only five fluent speakers alive.[20] "Experts estimate that half the world's people now use just eight languages. These are Chinese, English, Hindi, Spanish, Russian, Arabic, Portuguese, and French.[21]

Selecting and Processing Symbols

How are we able to select the symbols we want to use at the split second when the need arises to use them? Our senses bombard us with signals that beg to be interpreted and stored in our information bank. In response, the cortex, an area of the human brain that stores, computes, and eventually processes some of these incoming signals, puts forth the necessary information. This operation, the **cybernetic process,** functions much like a computer. It is schematized in Figure 2.1. The process can be clarified with an example. If I hold up a cylindrical piece of graphite about one-eighth of an inch in diameter, covered with wood, painted it yellowish gold, put an eraser on one end and a sharpened point on the other, and ask you what the object is, if you speak English, you will probably respond, "A pencil."

Culturally Communicating

Language Mirrors Life

Within each speech community, the language spoken mirrors human life—the personalities of the speakers, their attitudes and beliefs, their styles of thought and expression, their interactions with one another. Language so interpenetrates the experience of being human that neither language nor behavior can be understood without knowledge of both.

Source: Peter Farb, *Word Play: What Happens When People Talk* (New York: Knopf, 1974), pp. 366–367.

REFLECT ON THIS:

1. Your family and friends influence your language. Name several phrases or words you use that are unique to your family or friends.

2. Name several attitudes you hold, which you express verbally or nonverbally, that display who you are.

Figure 2.1
The Cybernetic Process

By investigating the process you used to identify the pencil, you can gain an understanding of the operation of the *cybernetic process* (Figure 2.1). You have been taught the word *pencil (input)*, and it has been placed *(stored)* in your cortex along with the image of a pencil. Thus, when you see an object made of graphite, wood, and an eraser, the sight of the object *(stimulus)* activates your storage system to sort through its stored visual signals *(search)*, find the symbol that represents the image *(recall)*, and allows you to identify the combination of the stored term and the object, and you say, "Pencil" *(output)*. You have just experienced the cybernetic process in action.

A mathematician/logician who played an important role in the development of high-speed computers coined the term *cybernetics*.[22] It comes from the Greek word for "steersman." The term is significant in that the means for internal control and communication in an animal—its nervous system—are similar to those of self-regulating machines, such as furnaces with thermostats. In each one, a measuring device feeds back information about performance. In human beings, the input comes in the form of a sense image *(taste, smell, sight, sound, touch)* that is tested against stored material *(symbols, images)*; the output *(feedback)* represents the symbol or image. Because humans can't be flawlessly programmed, there is always the possibility of human communication being less than perfect. This error factor accounts for some of our language problems, such as why you sometimes can't remember the information when you take a test, even though you studied. Sometimes the stored information is incorrect. Sometimes not enough information has been stored. Sometimes an overload occurs. Just as machines trip circuit breakers because the demand placed on their circuitry is too great, so too can you trip psychological breakers from too much pressure. It is possible to get so upset that you block messages from coming forth. But when the emotional pressure is removed, the normal flow returns. That is why experts advise people taking a test or under other stress to "turn off" every so often—look out the window, put their head down, walk around, sing a song to themselves to break the tension—and then return to their work.

Cybernetic processing starts to develop in humans at about the third month after birth. It does not become fully operative, however, until a child is capable of processing the image–symbol relationship, selecting symbols, and articulating the symbols.

Look at your surroundings, focus on an object, and identify it. Did you respond quickly with a word for the object? Now think back to the experience. Did you (as you did with *pencil*) think of all the parts that describe the object you just named? Probably not. Instead, you looked at the object, recognized it, assigned the symbol to it if you could, and then spoke or thought the relevant word. All of this happened below your level of awareness.

Try another experiment. Picture these objects: a pen, an apple, and a glass of milk. You probably had little trouble "seeing" these objects. This means that you have been exposed to the objects and can identify their symbols. Try the experiment again and picture these objects: a finger, a book, and a jerboa. The first two words in the series were probably familiar, but what about the third? *Jerboa?* A jerboa is a mouse-like rodent found in North Africa and Asia that has long hind legs for jumping and looks a little like a miniature kangaroo with the head of a mouse. You had no trouble with the words *finger* and *book* because you have already come in contact with these objects and have been told what to call them. But few Americans—with the exception of those who have traveled or lived in Asia or Africa or who have stumbled on a book or a television show that included information about this type of rodent—have had any exposure to the word *jerboa.*

Consider your symbol selection in this way. As you acquire language, you do so by hooking ideas together. When you pictured the "pencil," you saw the form of what you have been taught was identified with the word *pencil.* You saw the image and searched for the word identification you have been taught, *the symbol.* It is easy to do this with those items in our vocabulary that we can visualize. It is more difficult with abstract words. For example, what is your image of *nice* or *good* or *bad?* These conceptual words cause us problems because they have no exact definition, no image. In these cases, we probably imagine a definition and hook the word that describes it to the concept. That explains why we can often get a universal agreement in English on what a pencil is but not on what a *good* person is.

Learning Symbols

There are varying views of how we acquire our unique language along with our beliefs, values, and attitudes. Included are the Language-Explosion Theory and the Significant-Other Theory.

LANGUAGE-EXPLOSION THEORY The **Language-Explosion Theory** proposes that we build communication skills from the core of language we develop early in life. If you were asked to name the one person who had the most influence on your ability to communicate, you probably would name an immediate family member. The most common

The Language-Explosion Theory proposes that we build communication skills from the core of language we develop early in life.

Socially Communicating

One Word at a Time

Babies understand more than they can say at first, so don't be discouraged if your child's first words take time. Speak to your child constantly. During the second year, a toddler discovers that everything has a name, and vocabulary explodes:

Age	Average Number of Words
12 months	3
18 months	22
2 years	272
3 years	896

Age	Sounds Mastered
4–7 months	First language-like sounds: "eee-eee," "ooo-ooo"
7–9 months	First well-formed syllables: "ma-ma," "da-da"
9–12 months	Melodic babbling
Around 12 months	First words
18–20 months	First word combinations
Around 2 years	First sentences

Source: Jennifer Lach, "Cultivating the Mind," *Newsweek,* www.newsweek.com/id/95368.

response is "my mother." In some instances the mother–infant *dyad* (pair) is replaced by a father–infant, sibling–infant, or grandparent–infant dyad. And in still other situations, the day care center or other caregiver may replace the family member. It all depends on who spoke to the child the most. Adults with a weak language base often were not spoken to or read to on a regular basis as youngsters.

Whatever the child's primary influence, his or her circles of influence quickly expand to include the communication patterns of many other people. The child's neighborhood, the area of the country in which he or she lives, and the schools attended all influence overall ability to communicate, as do religious institutions and exposure to the media.

SIGNIFICANT-OTHER THEORY When we are young, all of the sources around us influence us. But at a certain stage in our lives, we start selecting specific people or groups whose language, ideals, and beliefs we allow to influence us. These people become the significant others in our lives, and their effect is great. Indeed, social psychologists contend that we have no identity whatsoever except in relationship to others. This view is called the **Significant-Other Theory**[23] (see Figure 2.2), which centers on the principle that our understanding of self is built by those who react to and comment on our language, actions, ideas,

Figure 2.2

Significant-Other Theory: Circles of Friends

A baby's first friends are usually the child's parents. Interaction with them prepares the child for future relationships in larger social circles. As a child grows, he/she comes in contact with others and is also exposed to media. These influencers are called the *significant others.*

Source: Reprinted by permission from *Newsweek,* "Your Child," *Newsweek* Special Edition, Spring/Summer 1997 (April 23, 1997). Copyright © 1997 by *Newsweek.*

Age in Years

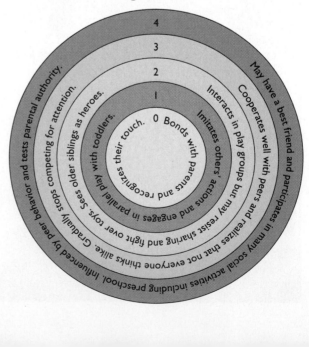

beliefs, and mannerisms. Thus, if we respect someone, we are likely to adjust our behavior and our messages to derive the most encouraging evaluation from that person. We may be influenced by such people's messages because of the position they hold, as is the case with politicians, sports heroes, or movie stars, or the control they have over us, as is true of a supervisor, teacher, religious leader, or parent.

We constantly come into contact with people who have the potential to be significant others in our lives. If you think about who you are today and compare your current language, beliefs, values, and attitudes with those you held five years ago, you probably will find some noticeable differences. These very likely were brought about by your acceptance of someone else's influence. No one can change you except you, but the significant others in your life can alert you to new concepts and help lay the foundation for the changes that come if you accept them.

The Concept of Meaning

Understanding what language is, and how we acquire and access it, gives us an important basis for understanding how meaning results. The study of the sounds, structure, and rules of human language is **linguistics.** It tells us that certain features are common to all languages. Among these are:

- *Languages are based on a set of symbols, both verbal and nonverbal.* In English, we use the letters *s-c-i-s-s-o-r-s*, for example, to represent an instrument that is used for cutting. Or in the Euro-American culture, forming a circle with the thumb and index finger and extending the other three fingers signifies that everything is "okay."

- *Languages that are alphabetically based recognize the differences between vowels and consonants.* In English, the vowel sounds are represented by the letters *a, e, i, o,* and *u,* singly or in combination. The consonants are such letters as *b, c, r,* and *m.* Not all languages use an alphabet. Some languages—for example, Chinese—are pictographical. A symbol represents a single word and is not made up of letters, as is the case with such languages as Turkish, Russian, and Portuguese.

- *Languages have ordered structural categories, such as verbs, nouns, and objects.* English is symbolic; we use words to represent objects and ideas. The sentence *The car is beautiful* designates the object *(car)* and expresses an idea about the car *(is beautiful).*

- *Words in and of themselves are not inherently meaningful.* The meaning derived from our language stems from how we interpret the symbols used in that language. Because words carry no meaning as such, we derive our meaning for the symbols through our own backgrounds, experiences, and perceptions. Two generations can be divided by the same language. Examine this conversation between a father and son who are shopping for clothing for the youth.

> *Father:* (picks up a shirt) Do you like this?
>
> *Boy:* That's bad.
>
> The father puts down the shirt and starts to walk away.
>
> *Boy:* Where are you going? I want that shirt.
>
> *Father:* You said you didn't like it; it was bad.
>
> *Boy:* No, not bad bad, bad good.

The *Sapir-Whorf hypothesis,* also known as the *linguistic relativity hypothesis,* theorizes that a person's understanding of the world and how the person behaves in it are based on the language a person speaks.[24] The theory, which is controversial due to the lack of definitive research, indicates that different language patterns yield differing patterns of thought. For example, various cultures have differing viewpoints regarding color perception. As Figure 2.3 illustrates, those speaking English tend to perceive a rainbow as "seeing" six bands of color. The Shona Indians describe the rainbow with four bands, whereas the Bassa perceive two bands.[25] These descriptions create our "color reality" of the world. Doubt this? What's your visual and linguistic image/description of the colors amaranth, fuchsia, and puce? Don't have an image/description? Those who believe in the concept of linguistic relativity would say that since you don't have those words in your vocabulary, you are incapable of having an image/description. Curious about amaranth, fuchsia, and puce? In English, they are all words that represent varying shades of pink. This could account for why, when listening, since we have different *frames of reference,* our interpretation may vary from the sender's intent.

We assign words **denotative meanings**—direct, explicit meanings—when we want to categorize them. For instance, the denotative word *dog* carries the denotative meaning of a "four-legged, furry animal; a canine." This denotation enables anyone to classify the animal and understand the literal characteristics of the term. In contrast, *connotative words* have an implied or suggested meaning. Words such as *good, pretty,* and *nice* have **connotative meanings.** It is difficult for people to agree on exactly what these words mean.

To make matters even more confusing, all meanings for symbols are not easily definable. Our language is filled with connotative meanings that derive from denotative words. Thus, the denotative word *dog* may carry pleasant connotations, such as *lovable, friendly,* and *warm,* if we have had pleasant associations with these animals. A child once attacked by a dog, however, may find that the word has negative connotations; to them, *dog* may carry the connotative meaning of *a mean, snarling, biting animal.*

Along with making us aware of connotative problems, people who study **semantics**—the relationship of language and meaning—warn us to avoid a rigid orientation that sees everything as falling into a *two-valued orientation* that only allows for the options of good or bad, or right or wrong. This type of narrow reasoning leaves no room for "neither right nor wrong" or "could be right or could be wrong."

Have you, as a student, ever taken a true-or-false test and found that when the instructor gave back the exam, the "correct" answers differed from yours? If a question

| ENGLISH | red | orange | yellow | green | blue | purple |

| SHONA | cipsuka | cicena | citema | cipsuka |

| BASSA | ziza | hui |

Figure 2.3   Colors of a Rainbow

When you look at a rainbow, how many colors do you see? Each language encourages its speakers to tell certain things and to ignore others. All human eyes see the same colors because colors have their own reality in the physical world. But when speakers in most European [and U.S.] communities look at a rainbow, they imagine they see six sharp bands of colors. People elsewhere in the world, who speak languages unrelated to European ones, have their own ways of partitioning the color spectrum.

Source: From *Word Play:* "What Happens When People Talk" by Peter Farb, p. 197. Copyright © 1973 by Peter Farb. Used by permission of Alfred A. Knopf, a division of Random House, Inc.

asked for a specific definition, date, or name of a person, there was no issue—your answer was clearly right or wrong. However, if a question contained connotative words that could be interpreted in various ways, then you and the instructor may have been at odds. To compensate for this either–or situation, some instructors tell students, "Read the question. If you can't clearly identify a true or false answer, pick the answer that you think is correct and explain your choice, or indicate that the answer could be either true or false and tell why."

Also, how irritated do you get when your literature instructor says, "This is what the poem means." This manner of thinking—in which something that is not provable is put into a two-valued format ("my way or wrong")—reflects irrational thinking. There may be numerous ways of interpreting the poem. On the other hand, if a chemistry exam question asks whether "combining two parts of hydrogen and one part of oxygen under ideal testing conditions results in water," the answer is "yes." This is a clearly provable, nondebatable two-valued question.

Social issues are sometimes forced into a right or wrong/good or bad structure. For example, consider these questions: Should the United States have become involved in the war in Iraq? Is the death penalty justified? Should gay marriage be legalized? There may be political, cultural, or religious perceptions of the "correct" answers to them, but that doesn't make the conclusions two-valued. If these questions had clear "yes" or "no" answers, there would be no controversies. However, controversy is based on differences of perceptions and no clear way to prove whatever conclusion is reached. Therefore, these questions are not candidates for two-valued/either-or answers.

Are you interested in finding out if you use two-valued reasoning? If so, fill out the Two-Valued Reasoning Questionnaire below.

A sender should attempt to use language as precisely as possible to reduce misunderstanding and thus avoid semantic noise. The use of definitions, examples, synonyms, and explanations can serve to clarify terminology. Consider an example: A dentist says to an assistant, "Hand me the instrument." The assistant looks at a tray of fifteen different instruments and responds, "Which one?" Obviously, the word *instrument* was so imprecise in this situation that the assistant was unable to determine the intended meaning.

Remember that not just the source has a responsibility in the transaction; the receiver is also an active participant and must filter for potential noise factors. Following the format of the interactional model of communication (page 18)—giving feedback, such as asking questions and repeating the message—can aid in clarifying the meaning

▶ Two-Valued Reasoning Questionnaire

Directions: This activity is designed to ascertain your value orientation. Read each statement and indicate if it is *T* (true, proved accurate by information provided in the story); *F* (false, proved inaccurate by the information provided in the story); or *I* (inconclusive or cannot be proved accurate or inaccurate because the story does not indicate whether the information is true or false). (Your instructor will find the correct answers in the instructor's manual that accompanies this book.)

Dale went to a travel agency to arrange some plane reservations. When Dale arrived in St. Louis, it was only two days before the wedding. After the wedding, the bride and groom took a trip to Hawaii.

a. Dale arrived in St. Louis two days before the wedding.

b. Dale got married in St. Louis.

c. She went to a travel agency.

d. The plane reservation to get to the wedding in St. Louis was made by a travel agent.

e. Dale went to Hawaii on her honeymoon.

in a communication transaction. Further feedback may be beneficial. For example, asking the person to structure ideas in a different way can eliminate organizational noise, and stating that the words of the message need defining can eliminate semantic noise.

The Functions of Language

The way in which a person uses language is affected not only by the vocabulary available but also by the functions of language.[26] These functions are generally classified into five categories: emotive, phatic, cognitive, rhetorical, and identifying.

1. **Emotive language** employs emotional connotative words to express the feelings, attitudes, and emotions of the speaker. In discussing a movie, for example, a person who says that a film is *riveting* and *gripping* is using emotive language.

2. **Phatic language** is one whose only function is to perform a social task, as opposed to conveying information.[27] For example, the question, "How are you?," usually is not said to elicit information, but is an automatic component of a social encounter. In fact, if a person actually starts to tell about his physical health, the reaction may be one of surprise. Language functions such as greetings, farewells, and small-talk exchanges are phatic aspects of language.

3. The function of **cognitive language** is to convey information. Cognitive language tends to be denotative. This section on the functions of language is an example of cognitive language.

4. The purpose of **rhetorical language** is to influence thoughts and behaviors. The speaker employs connotative terms to be persuasive by using emotionally vivid pictures and drawing implications while developing logical appeals. Advertisements to sell products or a speech supporting organ donations that uses examples of people who died because organs weren't available are examples of the rhetorical function of language.

5. The role of **identifying language** centers on naming persons or things specifically, thus being able to clarify exactly what we are speaking about—for example, *Ming went to Midway Mall.* Using the name *Ming,* rather than *she* or *someone,* is identifying language that clarifies who (Ming) and where she went (Midway Mall). Compare that sentence to, *She went to the mall.* Which is clearer?

Identification also carries implications beyond just hanging a name on something. There are cultural inferences for many people, places, and things. In Sanskrit, for example, the word for *name* is derived from *gna,* meaning "to know."[28] Naming defines

Communicating in Careers

Send Messages That Grab the Guts

Which warning sign is more effective: "Private beach; no swimming" or "Please don't feed the sharks"?

Before you distribute your next "basic" message to employees, make sure you're telling them something that not only provides information they need but also grabs their attention.

Source: Adapted from *The Joy of Thinking Big,* by Ernie J. Zelinski, Ten Speed Press, P.O. Box 7123, Berkeley, CA 94707.

REFLECT ON THIS:

1. Can you think of phrases that illustrate this example?

2. This is from the book *The Joy of Thinking Big.* Why is using language like that illustrated in the example "thinking big"?

people and influences communication responses. In the Bible, the book of Genesis reports that Adam's dominion over animals was demonstrated by his being given the *power* to name them. And the North American Indian "regards his [her] name as a distinct part of his [her] personality, just as much as his [her] eyes or teeth."[29]

To be unnamed is to be unknown, to have no identity, such as the Unknown Soldier. Names can be positive, elevating the in-group with positive terms, or negative, stigmatizing the out-group. The out-group is generally dehumanized, and this justifies oppression or even extermination. Hitler used the technique of dehumanization before and during World War II to attack Jews by labeling them *enemies of the country* and taking away their name identities and branding them with numbers, making them no more than cattle. Thus, it was "okay" to slaughter them. Native Americans were debased when they were given the names *savages* and *primitives*, implying they were less than civilized, less than human. For years, male terms for females included demeaning names such as *chick* (dumb fowl) and *doll* (a toy to be played with). To avoid the results of negative labels, some groups have changed their names. For example, in the 1960s, civil rights leaders rejected the terms *Negro* and *colored* as historical terms that identified a weak and controlled people, and labeled themselves *black* as a clear identifier of their individuality, their skin color. Later came the belief that a name should connect the people to their country of origin, so the name was changed to *African American*.[30] Much of what is called hate speech falls within the realm of identification. People use those images to construct their social reality, and the group being oppressed then starts to be a group at risk. The labels become the identification that demoralizes the recipient, and a tool to be used as the reason for psychological or physical destruction. From this perspective, it becomes acceptable to bash a *faggot*, burn down the store of a *rag head*, or sexually abuse a *bitch*.

Language Distortion

Words stand for different meanings. People intentionally or unintentionally distort information as they process it, and people intentionally or unintentionally use language that is unclear. These factors lead to **language distortion,** which is caused by ambiguity, vagueness, inferences, or message adjustment.[31]

Ambiguity can be present when a word has more than one interpretation. For example, does the word *hog* mean "a fat pig," "someone who eats too much," "a person who controls others' attention," "a large car," or "a motorcycle"? All of these definitions are appropriate depending on the context. Fortunately, ambiguity can often be overcome if the listener refers to the word's context to determine whether it describes an overindulging dinner guest or the purchase of a Harley motorcycle, or if the sender defines the term when used.

Vagueness results when words or sentences lack clarity. Use of words such as *they, he,* and *things like that* are vague unless we specifically know to whom or to what the speaker is referring.

Many connotative words, because they have no specific definition, are vague. A form of vagueness that is deceptive, evasive, or confusing is **doublespeak.**[32] It is the intended or accidental purpose of doublespeak to mislead, distort reality, make the bad seem good, create a false verbal map of the world, or create incongruity between reality and what is said or not said. Examples of doublespeak abound.

In his run for the 2008 presidential nomination, Mitt Romney stated that he had not raised taxes while he was the governor of Massachusetts.[33] When it was pointed out that his "efforts raised tax bills on business by $300 million," Romney used doublespeak when he explained that he "merely closed loopholes in the tax code."[34] He went on to say, "That's called tax enforcement."[35]

In another instance of doublespeak, President George W. Bush appeared to use a language of his own, which became known as *Bushism*, "peculiar words, phrases, pronunciations, malapropisms and semantic or linguistic errors and gaffes that appeared in his speeches."[36] He stated, for example, "We're going to—we'll be sending a person on the ground there pretty soon to help implement the malaria initiative, and that initiative will mean spreading nets and insecticides throughout the country so that we can see a reduction in the death of young children that—a death that we can cure."[37] In another speech he stated, "You know, when you give a man more money in his pocket—in this case, a woman more money in her pocket to expand a business, it—they build new buildings. And when somebody builds a new building somebody has to come and build the building. And when the building expanded it prevented additional opportunities for people to work."[38]

Doublespeak is a conscious use of language as a weapon or tool by those in power to achieve their ends at the expense of others, or it can be making statements that make little sense, but that the speaker perceives to be clear. Some doublespeak is funny, but much of it is frightening. It can be a weapon of power, exploitation, manipulation, and oppression.[39]

Inferences result when we interpret beyond available information or jump to conclusions without using all of the information available. Because communicating is a creative process, inferences are an inevitable part of processing information. If we do not have enough material, we complete an idea with what seems logical to us, what we have experienced in the past, or what we hope or fear will be the potential outcome. Read the following sentence quickly:

The cow jump over
over thee noon.

Language does not remain static; it is constantly changing. These alterations reflect changes in technology, lifestyles, and social attitudes.

Did you see *jump,* or did you read the word as *jumped?* What about the first and the second *over,* or *thee* and *noon?* Many people see the first couple of words and, based on their experience, instinctively infer the nursery rhyme statement, "The cow jumped over the moon."

The Languages We Use

Language, like chemical compounds, has a structure. There is a limited set of elements—vowels and consonants—and these are combined to produce words, which in turn can be compounded into sentences.[40] It is the work of the **linguist**—a social scientist who studies the structures of various languages—to provide concepts that describe languages.

"Systematic and rule-governed differences exist between languages,"[41] reported one linguist. "Each language is a collection of similar dialects [a social or regional variation of a language]. Dialects, like languages, differ from each other in terms of pronunciation, vocabulary, grammar, and *prosody* [accent or tone]."[42] A **dialect** is a social or regional variation of a language. Over long periods of time, dialects may develop into separate languages. For instance, French, Italian, and Spanish were originally dialects of Latin.[43] Each speaker of a language speaks some dialect of it or a combination of dialects.

There are significant variations in languages within the United States based on region, social class, religious and ethnic group, gender, and age. The same item may carry different word identifiers according to the region of the country. Philadelphia's *hoagie* is a *bomber* in upstate New York, a *hero* in New York City, a *grinder* or *sub* in Boston, a *Cuban sandwich* in Miami, and an *Italian* in Kansas City.

In reality, the dialects of the English language have more similarities than differences. For this reason, speakers of different English dialects can communicate with relative ease, although sometimes, an **accent**—the pronunciation and intonation used by a person—may cause some difficulty in understanding. Southerners, for example, may be difficult for some northerners to understand, and the "New York–New Jersey" sound is clearly identifiable yet not easily understood by those outside that area.

A common mistake is to view one dialect as best. No single dialect of a language is *the* language. But in every language, there is a continuum of prestige dialects from the lowest to the highest. High-prestige dialects are called **standard dialects,** and low-prestige dialects are called **nonstandard dialects.** The dialects of those who are in power, have influence, and are educated become the standard dialects of a language; and the literature, science, and official records are written using the vocabulary and grammar that approximate the standard dialects.[44] Historically, groups in power have used the lack of out-group standard language ability as a way to keep the out-groups from gaining power. Some of the push for making Standard American English the legal language of the United States is to ensure the supremacy of those who speak that defined dialect, excluding those who do not use it. In some instances, there is a conscious effort for some people to rid themselves or others of regional dialects. For example, across the fast-growing South, accents are under assault. As one linguist indicates, "Notions of Southern upward mobility require dropping the drawl, and stereotypes that 'ya'alls' and 'suhs' signal low status or lack of intelligence."[45]

Not only do dialects and accents create some difficulties, but the choice of which to use also can create controversy.

Standard American English

It may surprise you, but the United States does not have a legally declared language. By tradition, English has been the standard language used for most speaking, public school instruction, and commerce. However, to date, nothing within the Constitution declares English as the country's legal language.

The English-only movement, based on the concept that the glue that holds a society together is the ability of the citizens to interact with each other, is attempting to make English the country's official language through a constitutional amendment. English has been declared the official language of some states. The movement is not without controversy. In February 2007, the mayor of Nashville vetoed a measure to make English the city's official language. He did so because he thought it was both unconstitutional and unnecessary. Others don't agree, as communities such as Taneytown, Maryland, Cherokee County, Georgia, and Farmers Branch, Texas, have passed English-only laws.[46]

Some linguists contend that so long as no single pattern of language has been legally declared, there can be no such thing as a standard by which American English can be judged. In spite of this contention, there are generally accepted patterns of pronunciation, semantics, and syntax.

Standard American English is the language generally recognized by linguists as representative of the general population of the United States.[47] It is the oral form usually spoken by national news personalities and generally characterized by the oral sounds of the residents of the Midwest and West. The pronunciation is identified by articulating the final r (*father* versus *fa'da*) and the r before consonants in words (as in *park* versus *pahk*). In these and other respects, Standard American English differs from the dialects spoken in the other principal regional-pronunciation areas: the Midland, New England, and the South. (See Figure 2.4.) In New England and the Midland, the a in such words as *fast* is generally pronounced like the a in *father,* and the r is not pronounced when it is a final consonant or precedes a final consonant. In the South, the r is not pronounced after vowels (*for* becomes *fo*), and simple stressed vowels are diphthonged (*him* becomes *he-im*). Out-of-the-mainstream pronunciation often is used as a source of humor. Entertainers Rosie O'Donnell and Fran Drescher, for example, have made their accents one of the focal points of their careers.

Although there may not be one "best" way of pronunciation, if some pronunciations are used, they become problematic. The words *pitcher* and *picture* do not have the same meaning and are not pronounced the same way. Such words as "hunderd" *(hundred),* "liberry" *(library),* "secatary" *(secretary),* and "alls" *(all)* linguistically do not

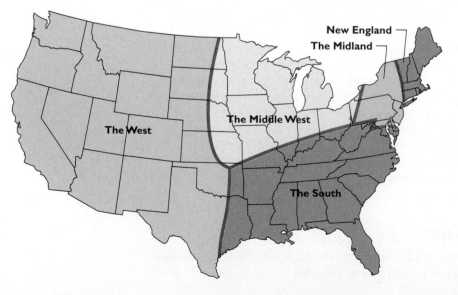

Figure 2.4
Principal Regional Pronunciation Areas

Source: From Wilbur Zelinsky, *The Cultural Geography of the United States,* Revised Edition, © 1992, p. 118. Adapted by permission of Prentice-Hall, Englewood Cliffs, New Jersey.

New England
The Midland
The West
The Middle West
The South

Figure 2.5
The Average American's Vocabulary

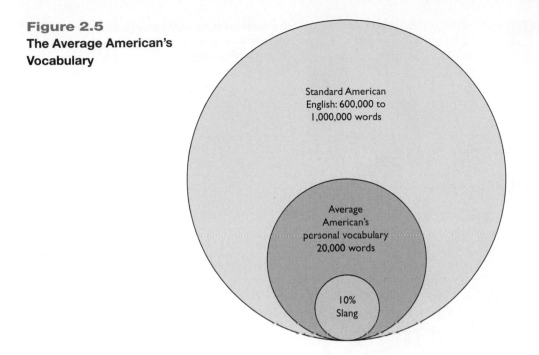

Standard American
English: 600,000 to
1,000,000 words

Average
American's
personal vocabulary
20,000 words

10%
Slang

exist. Words ending with -ing, such as *going* and *coming,* when pronounced as "goin" and "comin" can result in negative listener reaction regarding the speaker's sophistication. Saying "jeet yit?" is not a substitute for *Did you eat yet? Many* isn't "minnie," and *didn't* is not "dint," and there is no such word as "nu-uh" (often used as a negative response to "uh-huh").

The Standard American English words and grammatical forms are those of nationally published magazines (such as *Time* and *Newsweek*) and newspapers (*USA Today* and the *New York Times*). These words tend to represent the vocabulary of the West, the Midwest, the Midland, and the southern section of New England.

In addition to dialects and accents, slang plays a role in language.

Slang

The English language contains somewhere between 600,000 and 1 million words. (See Figure 2.5.) But the average American's vocabulary consists of only about 20,000 words, 2,000 of which may be slang.[48]

Slang denotes words that are related to a specific activity or incident and are immediately understood by members of a particular group. Sometimes slang terms such as *cool* start out as an in-group term and become a generally used term. *Cool,* which, early on, was used commonly to describe a smooth sound of jazz, has continued to change in meaning. Interestingly, the word *cool* remains the gold standard of slang in the twenty-first century, surviving like few expressions in our constantly evolving language."[49]

Slang comes into being because a group needs words to describe their ideas and "things." The slang forms a bond among the people of the group who use their unique terms.

TYPES OF SLANG Slang may come from anywhere. All it requires is a group of people who use and understand it. Computer users have developed *techno-babble,* which is computer language used for personal communications. Techno-babblers *interface with each other* and *debug their relationships.*[50] Because of the prevalence of computers in our

Computer users have developed *techno-babble*, which is a computer language that has been adapted for use in other meanings.

society, techno-babble is becoming a permanent part of Standard American English, so it is losing its status as slang. Once slang becomes mainstream language, it is no longer slang and is included in dictionaries, the chronicles of language.

Regional slang is prevalent. In New England, a *flatlander* is anybody who does not live in that geographical area. People in the Midwest may refer to a brown paper bag as a *sack*, whereas in some parts of the South, the same item is referred to as a *poke*. A linguist, in evaluating slang usage in the United States declared that, because of excessive slang usage, the "worst English" was spoken in Philadelphia, New York City, Honolulu, and Pittsburgh.[51]

Inarticulates

Inarticulates are uttered sounds, words, or phrases that have no meaning or do not help the listener gain a clear understanding of the message, such as the phrase *stuff like that*. They constitute what is considered to be "powerless language," language usage that diminishes rather than enhances the communication effect you wish to achieve. Studies of the negative perceptions of powerless language extend to tag questions ("Put away your toys, *okay?*"), hedges ("It's *like* difficult to concentrate"), hesitations (*"um," "you know"*), and intensifiers ("It's *so awesome* of you to come"). Such inarticulates become conversational mannerisms that can distract from the substance of the message and from the speaker's credibility.[52]

Some recent thinking regarding inarticulates perceive "um" and "er" to be part of the cycle of thinking and speaking, not a display of lack of knowledge.[53] This is based on studies that indicate "the causes are the discrepancies between the planning and executing functions of the brain—between planning what we are going to say and saying it."[54] They further indicate that, in spite of the idea that people can multitask, "the old warning is true: We can't think and talk at the same time."[55] Lesson to be learned: When speaking, stop and let your thoughts form rather than speaking without time to let ideas develop.

Nonstandard English Dialects

Many people in the United States speak languages or dialects that differ from Standard American English. Some of these speakers use a recognizable alternative language form, such as Spanish, French, Chinese, or one of the Native American tongues. In some cases, speakers present their ideas in identifiable dialects of Standard American English, such as Spanglish. Still others speak a separate but definite rule-based communication system called Ebonics, which fulfills the definition of language because it has a distinct grammatical and symbolic system; but because it has so many similarities to Standard American English, it is considered by some to be a dialect or "bad English."

One of the major problems confronting U.S. public schools is how to handle nonstandard American English speakers. Most schools have adopted the attitude that "we accept the language the students bring from home, but we teach them that Standard English is a tool they must have. They may not use it all the time, but when you need it, you need it."[56]

A classic concept of dialect recognizes that "there are many dialects and some get a lot of respect and some don't get any. In some cases, the respect given to the dialect is in the same amount that is given to the people who speak it."[57] A brief examination of Black English, Spanglish, Asian American English, and Native American languages can lead to some understanding of their nature, their history, the speakers who use them, and the perceived effects of speaking an alternative language or dialect.

EBONICS/BLACK ENGLISH   A "Vernacular Black English [Ebonics] is the most common dialect [language] used by African Americans. This is not street talk, it is not broken English, and it is not slang."[58] It is "a private vocabulary of many Black people which serves the users as a powerful medium."[59] Moreover, Black English is not a regional dialect. It reflects the common national culture of the African American community.

"**Ebonics** is characterized by a systematic grammar, for example, the frequent use of the habitual tense [e.g., "I be sick."—"I have been and still am sick."]"[60] This is not present in Standard American English, but is part of the syntactic system of both French and Spanish. In addition, there are "particular sound patterns [e.g., "wif" rather than "with"], and in some cases, words that deviate in their meanings from standard English [e.g., "the man"]. These elements are thought to have some linguistic basis in West African languages, particularly those belonging to the Niger-Congo language family."[61]

Culturally Communicating

Vocal Behavior of African Americans and European Americans

African American children speak to each other less than do European American children. European Americans tend to talk to males for longer periods, while African Americans spend more time talking to females. Both African Americans and European Americans pause longer in response to racially oriented questions.

Source: From Michael Hecht, Ronald Jackson, and Sidney Ribeau, *African American Communication*, 2nd edition (Lawrence Erlbaum Associates, Publishers, 2003). Reprinted with permission of the author.

REFLECT ON THIS:

1. Why do you think this is so?

2. Have you ever been involved in a scenario in which this principle was enacted? If so, what was the situation?

3. Do you think these differences of communication style have an effect on why there is sometimes difficulty in the communication between African Americans and European Americans?

"Ebonics, a term introduced by Black linguists in the mid-1970s, refers not only to a particular grammar and syntax, but also to paralinguistic (i.e., noises such as laughing and crying) and gestural (movement) features of African American communication."[62] A Black linguist contended that "African American modes of communication and expression are grounded in African World View—a view which she claimed emphasizes rhythm, analogy, metaphor, and intuition."[63] Other Black linguists have maintained that "Ebonics is based on an African perspective which, they say, differs radically from Euro-Western views of nature and reality.[64] This contention reinforces the Sapir-Whorf hypothesis that the language we use creates our worldview.

The distinctiveness of African American speech style has been problematic for group members with Standard American speakers and in the world of work. In order for African Americans to be able to better participate in the general U.S. community, they have often been encouraged to learn Standard American English, and learn to be *code switchers* who selectively use Black English and mainstream American English depending on the situation.

SPANGLISH   A significant number of Americans speak Spanish, the language of not only Spain but also Mexico, Central America, and much of South America and the Caribbean. Many also speak a dialect referred to as **Spanglish**.[65] It is common linguistic currency wherever concentrations of Hispanics are found. Spanglish takes a variety of forms, ranging from *hasta la bye-bye* and *lonche* (a quick lunch rather than a leisurely one), the description of a group of *los teenagers*, and the almost universally used *no problema*. Spanglish sentences are mostly Spanish, with a quick detour for a few English words and some fractured syntax.[66]

A professor of linguistics who speaks Spanglish with relatives and neighbors said, "Among Latinos, Spanglish conversations often flow easily from Spanish into several sentences of English and back again. It's unconscious. I couldn't even tell you minutes later if I said something in Spanglish, Spanish, or English."[67]

ASIAN AMERICAN DIALECT   The last several decades have seen a large immigration of Asian Pacific language speakers into the United States. People have come from such countries as Vietnam, China, Korea, Taiwan, Japan, and Cambodia. They bring with them languages that differ from English and often from each other.

As with Spanish speakers, when Asian Pacific speakers develop **Asian American dialects** by adapting their language to English, both vocabulary and pronunciation can be major stumbling blocks.

Aside from the vocabulary and pronunciation, Asian Pacifics confronted by English often have difficulty in developing arguments. English is a language whose relative preciseness encourages not just argumentation and debate, but detailed analysis, Western logic, and thorough explanations. This is not true of such languages as Chinese and Japanese. In these languages, ordinary speech is necessarily vague and depends heavily on the cooperative imagination and sympathy of the listener. Fewer words are required in Asian-language arguments because the concepts are shared in the experiences of the communicators, therefore, details are unnecessary.[68]

NATIVE AMERICAN LANGUAGES Controversy surrounds any attempt to discuss **Native American/American Indian dialects.** This centers on what constitutes "Indianness" and therefore their language(s). Indian identity is not the same as tribal identity because tribes have differing languages and customs.[69]

Research in Native American language and customs has resulted in the identification of eight prominent modes of communication behavior: "(a) reticence with regard to interaction with strangers, (b) the acceptance of obligations, (c) razzing, (d) attaining harmony in face-to-face interactions, (e) modesty and doing one's part, (f) taking on familial relations, (g) permissible and required silence, and (h) a unique style of public speaking."[70] Since permissible and required silence is encouraged, many Native Americans are misperceived by Euro-Americans as being communicatively apprehensive.

The idea of harmony pervades the Native American belief system of what things are and what they ought to be. "Rhetoric in such a universe has as its primary function not in discovery but in use, and its uses are carefully prescribed, sanctioned by ancestral tradition, and functional in maintaining the world as it ought to be."[71] The basic concepts are that talking it over is a way to straighten things out, talking is the most important means of persuasion, and speaking and thinking are ways to energize and secure knowledge. Decisions must be discussed with all who happen to be around, which accounts for the importance of family councils.[72]

Indian identity is not the same as tribal identity, as many tribes have differing languages and customs.

The use of razzing is a communication format unique to Native Americans. "*Razzing* is a collective form of storytelling in which participants take some episode, humorous or not, from a present or past experience and relate it humorously to the others in attendance. The story, which is often lengthy, is then characteristically embellished and altered by others who are present."[73] Razzing serves as a method to "determine cultural competency, identify in-group and out-group members, and as a form of instruction."[74]

A difficulty some Native Americans encounter in conversing with Standard American English speakers centers on the use of narration. Traditionally, Native Americans have relied on razzing and telling historical or experiential stories to clarify their points. Often the tales only allude to the general point being made rather than directly relating to the specific issue. It is called the *spiral structure of argument*. This is similar to the narrative communication patterns of many Hispanics and Arabs. The format strikes many Standard American English speakers as abstract and imprecise since it does not set up a clear purpose and use evidence to clarify and prove.

EFFECTS OF SPEAKING A DIALECT OR NONSTANDARD ENGLISH   Recent studies have reinforced the concept that for those living in the United States, speaking a non-standard dialect rather than Standard American English can be detrimental to a person's educational and economic health. The message seems clear: "You need to speak right to go to college, to get a good job."[75]

Children entering schools with weak Standard American English skills are at a definite disadvantage.[76] Since they may not know the alphabet or have the vocabulary, learning to read and understanding class discussions become extremely difficult. They often quickly turn off and eventually drop out. Research shows that "while 75 percent of white students graduated from high school, only 50 percent of all Black students, 51 percent of Native American students, and 53 percent of all Hispanic students got a high school diploma. The study also found that the drop-out problem was even worse for Black, Native American, and Hispanic young men at 43 percent, 47 percent and 48 percent, respectively."[77]

In economic terms, nonstandard speakers are given shorter interviews and fewer job offers than Standard American English speakers. When job offers are presented, nonstandard speakers are offered positions paying as much as 35 percent less than those offered Standard American English speakers.[78]

In social terms, speakers of nonstandard dialects often are confronted with mistaken, negative assumptions concerning their intelligence, dependability, and creativity. Many different languages and accents make the United States a rich tapestry; however, people speaking dialects should be aware that in some instances, education and speech therapy can make alterations in their vocabulary and speaking patterns if they desire change. That desire is usually based on a person's awareness that her or his career and social goals include particular language requirements that the person does not possess.

Using Verbal Language

Because language is symbolic, it is necessary to be as clear and precise as possible when using words. You need to consider the other person's frame of reference and whether he or she will share your interpretation of the language used. If not, it is important to adjust your vocabulary level and word choice to fit that of the listener. For example, you must be careful not to use technical terms that are beyond your listener's experience. Have you ever found yourself confused in a classroom because the instructor was using terms you didn't understand? The problem may well have centered on the fact that as an expert in the field, the instructor was using words with which she was familiar, but you, as a neophyte to the subject area, weren't familiar with them. You can increase your clarity by defining your terms, offering synonyms, or providing examples of terms you are using. Remember that slang expressions, words unique to a culture or a region, and euphemisms work against clarity and precision.

In addition to striving to be clear, it also is necessary to consider ways to make your language memorable. To be attention getting, words and phrases should be colorful, rhythmical, and compelling. After listening to a speech, a listener often will remember only one phrase. In fact, some speeches are identified by a single phrase. Martin Luther King Jr.'s stirring civil rights speech is identified as his "I Have a Dream" speech, based on a phrase he used over and over to make his point.

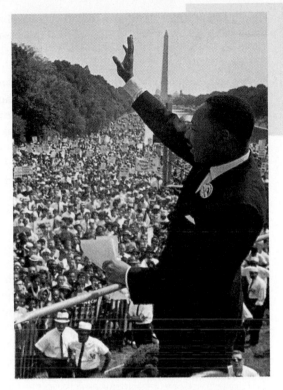

Martin Luther King Jr.'s stirring civil rights speech is identified as his "I Have a Dream" speech based on the phrase he used over and over to make his point.

Words have an impact. "There are words whose effects are subtle and unperceived; there are words that comfort ["I'm very sorry for your loss"] and words that pain ["You are so dumb!"]; words that support ["I believe you are doing the right thing"] and that undermine ("That's a bad decision"); words that inform ["Thank you for being such a good friend"] and that mislead ["Call me soon" (when you don't want him to call)]; that foster rationality ["Think before you speak"] and that impede it ["You'll never do it right"]; words that unite ["All for one and one for all"] and words that divide ["You are either with us or against us"]."[79]

Research shows that the adage "Sticks and stones will break my bones, but words will never hurt me" is not true. Words can, according to the findings, "cause physical harm."[80] Investigations of emotionally abused women discovered that they suffered from illnesses strikingly similar "to those affecting physically abused women."[81] As a result of these findings, health-care providers are being encouraged to regularly screen women for psychological abuse as well as for physical and sexual violence.[82]

Communicating in Careers

"Affect" and "Effect"

Many people confuse "affect" and "effect." As verbs, "affect" means "to influence" or "stir the emotions of" and "effect" means "to bring about" or "to accomplish." *Examples:* "His dismissal affected me." "The boss effected a compromise."

As a noun, "effect" has a number of meanings and is more commonly used than "affect." One *example:* "The pay raise has a positive effect on him."

"Affect" on the other hand, is used only as a specialized psychological term.

Source: The Glossary of Misused Words and Phrases, Briefing Publishing Group, 1101 King Street, Suite 110, Alexandria, VA.

REFLECT ON THIS:

1. Write an example in which *affect* is used only as a specialized psychological term.

2. Illustrate that you understand the concept explained by writing an example like that stated in the first paragraph.

A high school student who had slandered another student was asked to write an essay about the effect of his words. His essay was entitled "The Impact of Our Words."[83]

It can build cities and destroy empires. It could move people to the brink of tears or inspire hate. It can be beautiful or disgusting. It can create love or destroy it. It can help people find common ground or destroy reputations. Using it carelessly has started wars. Such is the power of speech and the words that accompany. According to many, speech is the most dangerous and oft-used weapon in man's arsenal.

Speech is the definition of a man, whether he is refined or crude, vulgar or complicated, appropriate or not. There is a good saying for this, "Better to remain silent and be thought a fool, than to open one's mouth and remove all doubt."

Words can hurt, too. Just think of insults and how they sting, especially from people whose opinion matters to you. Also, arguments can increase tensions between people until they snap, causing a fight. Psychological scars also take longer to heal than physical scars.

Speech can destroy reputations through slander: the vilest form of speech by far. Millions of people each year fall victim to this most heinous form of killing, for it not only destroys their reputations; it makes them wish they were dead, or at the very least someplace else.

Words and speech can be good, too. Many important cities and projects would not exist if the builders had not had the force of will to continue, motivated by words. Words can also give encouragement, comfort, help, and sooth tempers, but used wrongly they can and will destroy anything.

Unfortunately, in the modern world, many people prefer slander, insults, and diminishing one's fellow man to make themselves feel big and important.

Also speech and words can entertain. Think of the happiness and release caused by a good joke. Comedy is the universal communicator. Where language can fail, humor can cross the gaps between cultures.

Speech and words can be used for good or evil. It all depends on the user.

In Conclusion

In this chapter, the foundations of verbal language were discussed. Although there is no one accepted theory of the origins of human language, the operation of the human brain in acquiring, retaining, and allowing for language usage can be explained by the cybernetic process. We acquire our language, beliefs, values, and attitudes from people and influences surrounding us. Languages are based on a set of symbols, both verbal and nonverbal. Successful communication takes place when the sender adapts the message to the background and knowledge of the particular person or audience being addressed. A dialect is used by people from the same geographical region, occupational group, or social or educational class.

Standard American English is the language usually recognized by linguists as being representative of the general society of the United States. Aspects of language are slang, inarticulates, and dialects.

Learn by Doing

1. A major controversy was ignited when the Oakland, California, school district recognized Ebonics as a language. Research the topic, and have a class discussion or debate that agrees or disagrees with this statement: "Resolved: Accepting Black English as a language is a sellout to street slang and puts the users in a position of being second-class citizens."

2. Find an example of doublespeak in a speech, a letter to the editor, or a newspaper or magazine article. Bring the material to class. Discuss what you think the speaker was trying to hide or manipulate by using doublespeak.

3. Write down one phrase or expression that has meaning only for a select group. It may be an ethnic expression or an in-group reference. You will read the expression to other students, who will try to figure out what it means.

4. Make a list of five people who have had a significant effect on your own language use. Identify which of these people was the most influential and why.

5. List five words that have different meanings depending on the people who use them or the place in which they are used. See how many different definitions you can develop for each word.

Key Terms

chapter 3

Nonverbal Communication

▶ ## After reading this chapter, you should be able to

- Explain the importance of nonverbal communication as a message-sending system

- Categorize and discuss the origins of nonverbal messages

- State and explain the relationship between verbal and nonverbal communication

- List and illustrate the categories of nonverbal communication

- Analyze the role of culture in the development and use of nonverbal communication

D o you believe that when you communicate with another person, your *words* carry the majority of the meaning of the message? If you answered "yes," you are mistaken. There has long been an awareness that it is possible to communicate a great deal without using verbal language (spoken words). "Nonverbal communication is a major force in our lives."[1] Nonverbal behaviors such as smiling, crying, pointing, caressing, and staring appear to be used and understood the world over.[2]

Nonverbal communication is composed of "all those messages that people exchange beyond the words themselves."[3] Historically, people have interpreted body talk, perhaps without knowing they were doing so, but only in recent years have attempts been made to analyze and explain nonverbal communication in a scientific manner.

Are you interested in finding out how much you know about nonverbal communication? If so, fill out the research-based questionnaire below.

Research has established that nonverbal language is an important means of expression. Experts in the field have identified patterns of body language usage through the study of films and videotapes and through direct observation. Nonverbal acts, like all communication acts, are sensitive to the relationship between the sender and receiver. They have meaning based on their setting (the place of the communication and the attitude of the communicators) and on the purpose of the communication.

Because the formal study of nonverbal communication is more recent than the study of verbal communication, we do not yet have a dictionary of its terms or a thorough understanding of the process involved.

Traditionally, experts tend to agree that nonverbal communication itself carries the impact of a message. "The figure most cited to support this claim is the estimate that 93 percent of all meaning in a social situation comes from nonverbal information, while only 7 percent comes from verbal information."[4] The figure is deceiving, however.[5] It is based on two 1976 studies that compared vocal cues with facial cues.[6] It appears that the "percentage of our total communication [that] is nonverbal ranges from 60 percent to 93 percent. But the percent of emotional communication that is nonverbal exceeds 99 percent. When it comes to emotions, instead of verbalizing how we feel, our bodies do the talking."[7]

In the effort to read nonverbal communication, we must remember that no one signal carries much meaning. Instead, such factors as gestures, posture, eye contact, clothing styles, and movement must all be regarded together. This grouping of factors is called a *cluster*.

▶ Nonverbal Communication Pretest[8]

Directions: Answer *true* or *false*, then check your answers.

1. Females are more sensitive than males to nonverbal cues—especially facial cues—and they transmit more accurate nonverbal cues to others.

2. When contradictory messages are sent through both verbal and nonverbal channels, most adults see the nonverbal message as more accurate.

3. People with low self-esteem use more eye contact when receiving negative messages than when receiving positive ones, whereas while those with high self-esteem do just the opposite in each case.

4. When people are conjuring up a lie, their pupils tend to become smaller. However, when they tell the lie, their pupils tend to dilate.

5. The three nonverbal cues an interviewer remembers most about a job applicant are gestures, posture, and handshake.

Answers: 1. true, 2. true, 3. true, 4. true, 5. false—interviewers remember eye contact, appearance, and facial expressions.

Few of us realize how much we depend on nonverbal communication to encourage and discourage conversations and transactions.

We also must remember that, just as in verbal communication, nonverbal signs can have many different meanings. For example, crossing the arms over the chest may suggest that a person is cold. But crossed arms accompanied by erect posture, tightened body muscles, setting of the jaw, and narrowing of the eyes could indicate anger.

A person's background and past patterns of behavior also must be considered when we analyze nonverbal communication. The relationship between current and past patterns of behavior, as well as the harmony between verbal and nonverbal communication, is termed *congruency*. When you say to a friend, "You don't look well today," you are basing your statement on an evaluation of the person's appearance today compared with her appearance in the past. In other words, something has changed, and you have become aware of a difference. If you did not have experience to draw on, you would not have noticed the change.

Few of us realize how much we depend on nonverbal communication to encourage and discourage conversations and transactions. For instance, we consciously wave at waiters and raise our hands to get a teacher's attention. Much of our opening and closing of channels, however, occurs without our consciously realizing it.

As you observe people conversing, you might notice that they may indicate they are listening by moving their heads. If they agree with what is said, they may nod affirmatively. They may also smile to show pleasure or agreement. If, however, they glance several times at their watch, look away from the speaker, cross and uncross their legs, and stand up, they are probably signaling that they have closed the channel and wish to end the transaction. Be aware that these patterns are not the same in all parts of the world. There are some cultures in which people move their heads from left to right to signal agreement. Or, in China, the head nod often simply means, "I'm listening."

Sources of Nonverbal Signs

We learn to read words through a step-by-step process in which we are taught to use our written, oral and reading forms of communication. But how do we acquire nonverbal signs? There are two basic sources: innate neurological programs and behaviors common to a culture or a family.

Neurological Programs

Innate neurological programs are those automatic nonverbal reactions to stimuli with which we are born. These nonverbal "automatic reactions" are *reflexive* because of neurological drives. These reflexive drives seem to be tied to our need drives. For example, we blink our eyes automatically when we hear a loud noise (survival need drive) or when a pebble hits the windshield of the car we are driving (survival and territorial need drives). Our stomach muscles tighten and our hands sweat when we feel insecure (security need drive).

That we are born with some of our nonverbal tendencies is illustrated by the fact that "when the facial expressions of these [blind]children were compared with normal-sighted, normal-hearing children, nearly identical facial expressions were produced for sadness, crying, smiling, laughing, pouting, fear and anger."[9] This "seems to confirm that our expressive faces are part of human nature rather than collective learning."[10] A study of eye-accessing cues indicates "every movement is an important source of body language."[11] Most people, according to neuro-linguistic programming (NLP) research, will look up for visual accessing, down for linguistic accessing, to the left for past experiences, to the right for future perceptions, and straight ahead for present-tense thinking.[12] (See Figure 3.1.) "Some NLP experts consider eye movements to be an aid to accessing inner speech since the eye movements stimulate different parts of the brain."[13] If this is true, then following the advice that one should maintain good eye contact when speaking to someone would render "a person unable to make the accessing movements"[14] and could "interfere with and slow down the [person's] normal thinking style."[15] In academia, teachers often make the mistake of misinterpreting students' actions. For example, a professor asks a question, and you struggle to visualize the answer, your eyes moving up or down and to the left or right (depending on whether you are looking for past learned ideas or inventing new material). The professor states, "Well, you won't find the answer on the ceiling." The teacher is wrong. The answer may be found by glancing up and to the left if your normal eye-glance pattern for past tense and picturing concepts is up.[16] A recent study backed up this concept when it showed that "children who avert their gaze when considering their response to a question are more likely to come up with the right answer."[17]

A student who knows his or her eye-shift pattern may be able to access past-tense learning by moving his or her eyes in the direction of his or her past-tense triggering and looking up or down, depending on whether he or she is trying to access images or words.

Cultural and Intercultural Behavior

Some nonverbal behavior is learned in the same way as spoken language. When we display these culturally taught nonverbal behaviors, they are said to be *reflective*—reflective of the culture from which they were learned.

As children, we observe and imitate people around us; thus, we learn not only to speak but also to behave as they do. Every culture has its own body language, and the young learn the culture's nonverbal patterns along with those of spoken language. As a research anthropologist indicated, "The important thing to remember is that culture is very persistent. In this country, we've noted the existence of culture patterns that determine physical distance between people in the third and fourth generations of some families, despite their prolonged contact with people of very different cultural heritages."[18] These cultural patterns are readily identifiable. Italians, for example, are generally noted for using their hands when they speak. In contrast, the British generally are noted for controlling their use of gestures.

Figure 3.1
Eye-Accessing Cues

Source: "People Who Read People." *Psychology Today,* July 1979. Reprinted with permission from *Psychology Today* magazine, copyright © 2008 Sussex Publishers, LLC. For further information see *The Pegsasus Mind-Body Newsletter,* Issue 9, January 4, 2002, and research on neuro-linguistic programming.

The proponents of NLP (Neurolingistic Programming) believe that eye movements are linked to the sensory processing that goes on in a person's mind when he or she is thinking. The eye movement may be a flicker or it may be held for several seconds. This movement happens when a person is organizing incoming sensations, recalling past experiences, or imagining never previously experienced phenomena.

Eyes up and to the left: Recalling something seen before—a visual memory.

Eyes up and to the right: Visualizing something that has not been seen before.

Eyes centered, looking up: present tense visual memory; eyes centered, looking down: present tense verbal memory; eyes centered, staring (no matter whether eyes are up or down): daydreaming or not engaged in decoding any information being sent.

Culturally Communicating

Nonverbal Messages Styles

My Son's Silent Language. An aboriginal mother wrote to her son's new teachers asking them to examine their own biases and expectations:

He doesn't speak standard English, but he is in no way *linguistically handicapped.* If you take the time and courtesy to listen and observe carefully, you will see that he and the other Aboriginal children communicate very well, both among themselves and with other Aboriginees. They speak *functional English,* very effectively augmented by their fluency in the silent language, the subtle unspoken communication of facial expressions, gestures, body movement, and the use of personal space.

You will be well advised to remember that our children are skillful interpreters of the silent language. They will know your feelings and attitudes with unerring precision no matter how carefully you

arrange your smile or modulate your voice. They will learn in your classroom because children learn involuntarily. What they learn will depend on you.

Source: Jock Smith, "Inclusiveness in Learning Media," 27 January 1997, unpublished document. Originally from the Northian Newsletter, submitted by Jock Smith, Surrey School trustee and educational counselor for the Department of Indian Affairs to *Focus on Equality,* March 17, 1991.

REFLECT ON THIS:

1. What are the implications for a classroom teacher of knowing this information?

2. What are the implications for you about knowing this information if you become acquainted with an Aborigine?

3. Based on this exposition, what advantages do you think Aborigines have over most Euro-Americans when communicating with others?

"Gestures are a powerful language in any culture."[19] A person who speaks more than one verbal language gestures according to the language he or she is speaking. Fiorello La Guardia, New York City's mayor in the 1930s and early 1940s, carried on his political campaigns in English, Italian, and Yiddish—the languages of the major voting blocs in the city. He was observed using one set of gestures for speaking English, another for Italian, and still another for Yiddish. If you fluently speak more than one language, do you notice that your gestures, your facial expressions, and sometimes your volume reflect which language your are using?

Nonverbal gestures and behaviors convey different messages throughout the world. An Arabic male, for example, commonly strokes his chin to show appreciation for a woman, whereas a Portuguese man does it by pulling his ear. But in Italy a similar kind of ear tugging may be considered a deliberate insult.[20]

In communicating nonverbally, people also operate on different action chains. An *action chain* is a behavioral sequence with two or more participating organisms, in which there are standard steps for reaching a goal. If an individual leaves out a step, the chain gets broken, and the person has to start all over again. Different cultures operate under different action chains. For example, to an American, being on time normally means making contact within five minutes or so of a designated hour. To a Mexican, however, being on time often means within a reasonable time. A European American businessperson, having been kept waiting for twenty minutes in a Mexico City client's office, may decide to leave the office, feeling that she is being ignored and that the client's lateness is a sign of lack of interest in the business deal. But the Mexican client may not consider himself at all tardy and may be totally confused by the person's quick exit.

European Americans engaged in business dealings with Arabs, for example, should understand and adhere to their customs of hospitality to be successful. The initial meeting with an Arab businessperson is typically devoted to fact finding. No commitments are implied or made, but the initial session is usually lengthy and thorough. Based on their pattern of working quickly so as not to waste time, European Americans often feel that the process is tedious. The next meeting is taken up with additional rituals. It is not unusual for a business deal to take as long as thirty days to complete.

Gesture patterns, which have verbal meanings, also vary. For instance, the thumb-and-forefinger-in-a-circle gesture means "okay" in the United States. In France or Belgium, however, it means the recipient is worth zero. The same gesture in Greece and Turkey may be construed as a sexual invitation. Similarly, an index finger tapping to the temple with the other fingers curled against the palm usually means "you're smart" in the United States, whereas it communicates "you're stupid" in most of Europe.

The use of space also varies widely around the world. Arabs, South Americans, and Eastern Europeans generally favor close conversational encounters, which may make some European Americans feel somewhat uncomfortable and many Germans and Scandinavians totally uncomfortable.

Culturally Communicating

Waving Hello and Good-Bye

In most European countries, the accepted way to wave hello and good-bye is palm out, hand and arm stationary, fingers wagging up and down. The traditional U.S. waving of hello or goodbye, holding the arms upward, fingers extended, wiggling the wrist from right to left, means "no" in many countries. In Greece it is an insult.

Source: worldcitizensguide.org.

REFLECT ON THIS: This is just one example of a gesture that is different according to the country you are visiting or living in. In this chapter others are listed. Your task is to go online or check in a resource book and

1. Identify an emblem (a gesture that has nonverbal meanings) that has different interpretations in varying cultures.

2. Identify an emblem that has one meaning in the Euro-American culture and a different meaning in another culture.

3. Identify an emblem or color that has a positive meaning in the Euro-American culture, but a negative meaning in another culture.

We tend to read nonverbal signs on the basis of our own personal background and experiences, and we assume that others share the same interpretations—an assumption that can be misleading, even dangerous. We must remember that in all forms of communication, an understanding of the receiver is necessary. And, as if matters were not complicated enough, we also must be aware that although cultural patterns are reported to be persistent, not all the people within a given culture share identical patterns.*

Emotional Influences on Nonverbal Communication

Emotions have a direct effect on the size of people's personal territory and their resulting nonverbal responses. When people are insecure, they tend to avoid closeness. People who are emotionally upset may even become violent if someone invades their territory. Again, these are representative of basic human needs and what happens when needs are not being satisfied.

When people are upset, their bodies may become rigid. For example, many people who are nervous about public speaking report that their throats tighten and their stomach muscles contract when they must present a speech. Under great tension, the pitch of the voice also rises because vocal cords tighten.

Those who attempt to mask their emotional upsets may become physically ill. The body must release its pent-up feelings. Suppressed emotions must get out somehow, and the result may be a headache or an upset stomach.

People under stress also find that others loom larger and closer than they actually are. To a frightened child, an adult can seem like a giant. Because of this, adults who are dealing with crying or hysterical children should kneel to talk with them. By the same token, police interrogators and trial lawyers know that moving in close to an interviewee may cause him or her to get upset and say something that would be controlled under normal conditions. This invasion of territory may result in the breaking down of defenses.

Sometimes nonverbal patterns change because of outside influences. For instance, a vast difference exists between normal nonverbal communication and deviant communication, such as that caused by drugs, alcohol, or shock. Patterns change as people lose control of their ability to make decisions and value judgments. A person under the influence of alcohol or drugs does not walk, talk, or have the same bodily controls as he or she would when sober. This has resulted in the development of drunk-driver-walking-a-straight-line and touching-the-nose tests, with the assumption being that a sober person can perform these acts but a drunk person can't.

Verbal and Nonverbal Relationships

Obviously, a link exists between verbal and nonverbal communication. Because they are so tightly interwoven, it is necessary to identify, analyze, and understand their various relationships. The main relationships of nonverbal to verbal communication can be described as substituting, complementing, conflicting, and accenting. (See Figure 3.2.)

▶ *Note:* Throughout this text generalizations are presented regarding trends of various cultural groups. These are based, whenever possible, on research findings and expert observations. They are in no way intended to lead to the conclusion that all members of the noted cultural group conform to the generalized patterns.

Substituting relationship Nonverbal message replaces the verbal message	**Complementing relationship** Nonverbal message accompanies the verbal message
Verbal message: (none)	**Verbal message:** "Yes"
Nonverbal message: Nod head vertically to indicate yes	**Nonverbal message:** Nod head vertically to indicate yes
Conflicting relationship Verbal and nonverbal message are in contrast to one another	**Accenting relationship** Nonverbal message stresses the verbal message
Verbal message: "Yes"	**Verbal message:** "Yes"
Nonverbal message: Body language indicates *no*	**Nonverbal message:** Body language indicates yes

Figure 3.2
Verbal and Nonverbal Relationships

Substituting Relationship

Suppose someone asks you a question. Instead of answering verbally, you nod your head up and down. In doing so, you have used the *substituting relationship*. In the Euro-American tradition, you have replaced the word meaning "yes" for the action *yes*.

Complementing Relationship

Body language can complement a verbal message. For example, shaking your head horizontally from side to side while saying "no" reinforces the negative verbalization. The simultaneous saying and doing creates a nonverbal *complementing relationship* in which a nonverbal message accompanies a verbal message and adds dimension to communication.

Conflicting Relationship

A person's physical movements sometimes can conflict with his or her verbal message. For example, suppose a professor is confronted by a student after a class session. The student asks, "May I speak with you?" The professor says, "Sure, I have lots of time." While making this reply, however, the professor is packing books, glancing at the clock, and taking several steps away. A conflict exists between the verbal and nonverbal messages.

When actions conflict with verbal messages, forming a *conflicting relationship* between the verbal and nonverbal, the receiver probably should rely more on the nonverbal aspect of communication. Nonverbal clues often are more difficult to fake than verbal ones. When you were young, you might have been surprised to find that your parents knew when you were not telling the truth. There you stood, looking at the floor, twisting your hands, with a flushed face, as you insisted, "I didn't do it." The father of the modern psychology movement is reported to have said, "He that has eyes to see and ears to hear may convince himself that no mortal can keep a secret. If his lips are silent he chatters with his fingertips; betrayal oozes out of him at every pore."[21]

A leading expert in nonverbal communication developed the Expectancy Violations Theory.[22] "*Expectancy Violation Theory* sees communication as the exchange of information that is high in relational content and that can be used to violate the expectations of another, which will be perceived either positively or negatively

Body shifts can encourage or discourage conversation.

depending on how much the two people like each other.[23] The theory assumes that there are norms for all communication activities and if these norms are violated, there will be specific, predictable outcomes. For example, if you feel comfortable with about three feet between you and the person with whom you are communicating, and the person stays outside of that distance, you are comfortable. But, if the other person gets closer to you than your comfortable distance, you will feel violated and will display that by backing away from the person, breaking eye contact, and/or requesting space.

Polygraphs, or lie detectors, read the body's nonverbal reactions by measuring changes in blood pressure, respiration, and skin response—in other words, by attempting to detect a conflicting relationship between the verbal and the nonverbal. This is accomplished by hooking up a meter to the fingers, measuring perspiration, or checking heart rate on an electrocardiograph machine. "Most psychologists agree that there is little evidence that polygraph tests can accurately detect lies."[24] (The estimate of accuracy is about 61 percent.) Because of the question of validity, questions have arisen as to whether federal agencies should rely on lie detectors to screen workers and job applicants. The conclusion reached by the National Research Council was that "the machines are simply too inaccurate."[25] The report also contends that "almost a century of research in scientific psychology and physiology provides little basis for the expectation that a polygraph test could have extremely high accuracy."[26]

Because of the lack of dependability, television programs such as *The Moment Of Truth* have come under attack. On that show, real people, whose lives could be affected by the consequences, are accused of various indiscretions by their accusers. The accused is then evaluated by a "lie detector expert" with the assumed attitude that the lie detector and the interpreter are wholly accurate—this, in spite of research that demonstrates the conclusion is problematic. Since research shows that the present process of detecting deception is so questionable, the question arises as to whether nonverbal techniques should be relied on. Part of the answer may be to go beyond historical methods. A new technique, functional magnetic resonance imaging (fMRI), "scans the brain and could well morph into a forensic tool far more potent than the flawed polygraph test."[27] "Forensics experts are hopeful because fMRIs measure complex mental processes, whereas polygraph tests pick up skin and blood pressure changes that can be misleading."[28] Another method, MERMER, a system of brain fingerprinting that records messages emitted by the brain before the body physically reacts, has been developed.[29] Although some scientists argue that the technology isn't ready for widespread use in the criminal court system, an Iowa judge ruled brain fingerprinting admissible in court after it was tested and peer reviewed.[30]

Accenting Relationship

Nonverbal behavior may accent parts of a verbal message, much as underlining or italicizing emphasizes written language. In the *accenting relationship*, the nonverbal message stresses the verbal one. Jabbing someone's shoulder with a finger as you turn the person to look at you while commanding, "When I speak to you, look at me!" emphatically accents the verbal message with nonverbal signs.

Categories of Nonverbal Communication

Nonverbal channels can be divided into many categories. Our discussion of these categories centers on kinesics, proxemics, paravocalics, chronemics, olfactics, aesthetics, and gustorics.[31] (See Figure 3.3.)

Figure 3.3
Categories of Nonverbal Communication

Kinesics: Body Communication

Kinesics is the study of communication through the body and its movements. We communicate through the gestures we use, the way we walk and stand, the expressions on our faces and in our eyes, the manner in which we combine these variables to open or close channels, and what we look like. Specific areas studied in the area of kinesics are facsics; ocalics; gestics; haptics; posture, walk, and stance; artifactics; and physical characteristics.

FACSICS   **Facsics** is the study of how the face communicates. Facial expressions range from communicating our internal states such as anger or fear, to carrying messages to others of whether we want to interrupt what they are saying or are interested and want them to continue to speak. The face sends information about our personality, interests, responsiveness, and emotional states. How we perceive another person is often based on that person's facial expressions as we observe or interact with her or him.

Research about the face and its messages has been conducted through the Facial Action Coding System (FACS).[32] Through this process, we have more data about the face than about any other area of nonverbal communication. What has been determined is that facial expressions, movements of brief duration, are so subtle that they can just pass us by as observers. An upturn of the corners of the mouth, nasal cavity expansions, an eyebrow arching, a dropping jaw, or open mouth are often overlooked and the message is not conveyed.

OCALICS   The eye, unlike other organs of the body, is an extension of the brain. Because of this, it is almost impossible for an individual to disguise eye meaning from someone who is a member of the same culture. **Ocalics** is the study of the eyes. Your eyes are the primary way to receive body language. They are the primary way you send body language as well. Eye contact, eye avoidance, and eye blinks all carry messages.

A person's eye blinks have an effect on how he or she is perceived by others. For example, the slowness or rapidity of eye blinks can indicate nervousness. The normal blink rate for someone speaking is 31 to 50 blinks per minute. During the presidential debate in 1996 between President Bill Clinton and his Republican opponent, Senator Bob Dole, polls indicated that Dole was considered to be very nervous. A review of the videotape of the debate revealed why people had come to that conclusion. Dole averaged 147 eye blinks per minute, almost three times the normal rate.[33]

Experts on nonverbal signs created by the eyes, mouth, and hands offered a guide to viewers of how to nonverbally read President George W. Bush's mannerisms during his 2006 State of the Union address.[34] This is illustrated in Figure 3.4.

A theory known as *pupilometrics* indicates that pupils dilate when the eyes are focused on a pleasurable object and contract when focused on an unpleasurable one.[35] Enlarged pupils signify interest, and contracted pupils reflect boredom. Thus, knowledgeable teachers often watch the pupils of their students' eyes to ascertain their interest in a particular lesson. The idea of wide-eyed wonder and interest is not new. Members of different social classes, generations, ethnic groups, and cultures use their eyes differently to express messages. European Americans often complain that they feel some foreigners stare at them too intensely or hold a glance too long. This is because a gaze of longer than ten seconds is likely to induce discomfort in a European American. But lengthy eye contact may be comfortable as long as the communicating people have sufficient distance between them.

Figure 3.4
Nonverbal Clues That Help to Interpret a Message

Source: CLEVELAND PLAIN DEALER by Staff Writer. Copyright 2006 by Plain Dealer Publishing Company (Cleveland OH). Reproduced with permission of Plain Dealer Publishing Company (Cleveland OH) in the format Textbook via Copyright Clearance Center.

- **Eyes:** Rapid side-to-side eye movement connotes stress. Steady movement suggests command. When comfortable, Bush shares his narrow gaze with individuals all around the room; when less so, he shares it mainly with supporters. To suggest gravity, disdain or the significance of his words, he often narrows his eyes.

- **Mouth:** Bush pushes his lip to the side and bites it when frustrated. Experts disagree on the grin. Some say his smiles at inappropriate moments mean "I don't get it." To others, these read, "Why don't you get it?" He bares his teeth, enunciates slowly, to "educate" on a point he considers key.

- **Hands:** Uses an abrupt hand chop to frame short, simple points. Too much jerkiness suggests agitation. Aggressive or frequent pointing says "I'm being defensive; back off." Firm handshakes, upper arm clasps and slaps on the back: jocular confidence.

Photo source: Baltimore Sun

When individuals in the European American culture are intent on hiding an inner feeling, they may try to avoid eye contact. Thus, the child who has eaten forbidden candy will likely not look at a questioning parent during the interrogation. (European American children are often told, "Look me in the eye and say that.")

GESTICS   **Gestics** is the study of the movements of the body, such as gestures, which can give clues about a person's status, mood, cultural affiliations, and self-perception. Why do people gesture when they talk? Linguists have theorized that speech and gesturing function together and may help us think and form words.[36] In addition, gesturing helps people retrieve words from memory. "When asked to keep their hands still by holding onto a bar, people had a more difficult time recalling words than those whose hands were free."[37] Nods of the head and body shifts can encourage or discourage conversation. Other movements may show internal feelings. For example, those who are bored may tap their fingers on a table or bounce a crossed leg.

As people attempt to communicate, they use gestures. These gestures may be classified as speech independent or speech related. *Speech-independent gestures* are not tied to speech. These gestures are referred to as emblems. *Speech-related gestures* are directly tied to, or accompany, speech. These gestures are illustrators, affect displays, regulators, and adaptors.

Emblems are nonverbal acts that have a direct verbal translation or dictionary definition consisting of one or two words.[38] The sign language of the deaf, gestures used by off-camera television personnel, and signals between two underwater swimmers are all examples of the use of emblems. It is important to realize that not all emblems are universal. In fact, they tend to be *culture specific;* in other words, an emblem's meaning in one culture may not be the same as that same emblem's meaning in another. For example, The fig—a clenched fist with the thumb coming through between the knuckle of the index and middle fingers means "good luck" in Brazil, but in Greece and Turkey it is considered an insulting gesture, and in Tunisia and Holland it has strong sexual connotations."[39] "In everyday life, Americans regularly use more than 100 emblems."[40]

Illustrators are "kinesic acts accompanying speech that are used to aid in the description of what is being said or trace the direction of speech."[41] They are used to sketch a path, point to an object, or show spatial relationships. Saying, "*Josh, please stand up* (point at Josh and bring your hand upward), *go out the door* (point at the door), *turn to the left* (point to the left), and *walk straight ahead* (point straight ahead)" is an example of a cluster of illustrators.

Affect displays are facial gestures that show emotions and feelings, such as sadness or happiness. Pouting, winking, and raising or lowering the eyelids and eyebrows are examples of affect displays. Different people and cultures tend to use facial expressions in different ways. For example, many European American males mask and internalize their facial expressions because they have been taught that to show emotion is not manly; Italian males, however, tend to express their emotions outwardly.

Regulators are nonverbal acts that maintain and control the back-and-forth nature of speaking and listening between two or more people. Nods of the head, eye movements, and body shifts are all regulators used to encourage or discourage conversation. Imagine, for example, a conversation between a department manager and an employee who has asked for a raise. The manager glances at her watch, her fingers fidget with the telephone, and she glances through some materials on the desk. The manager's regulator signs indicate that she views the transaction as completed.

Adaptors are movements that accompany boredom, show internal feelings, or regulate a situation. People who are waiting for someone who is late, for example, often stand with their arms crossed, fingers tapping on upper arms, foot tapping the pavement, and checking the time every few seconds.

Culturally Communicating

A Hands-On Approach

Lingering handshakes, hand-holding, embraces, and sometimes kisses between heterosexual men are the norm in much of the Muslim world. In Senegal, men walk with arms draped around each other's shoulders. In Saudi Arabia, greetings between men are almost always extended with kisses on the cheek. In Afghanistan, men write love poems to friends, and Taliban fighters give one another flowers.

Source: "A Hands-On Approach: Muslim Men Are Affectionate in Ways That Would Make an American Male Blush," *Psychology Today* (November/December 2007): 24.

REFLECT ON THIS:

1. The title of the article from which this activity derived is "A Hands-On Approach: Muslim Men Are Affectionate in Ways That Would Make an American Male Blush." Why would American men blush?

2. Why do you think there is such a difference in views regarding male–male displays of affection in the Arabic world and the United States?

HAPTICS **Haptics** is the study of the use of touch as communication. *Touch* is defined as the physical placing of a part of one person's body on another's body, such as putting your hand on another person's shoulder. This may be done with or without permission. Your skin is a receiver of communication: pats, pinches, strokes, slaps, punches, shakes, and kisses all convey meaning. A doctor touches your body to ascertain sensitivity and possible illness. You shake hands to satisfy social and business welcoming needs. You intimately touch through kisses and use sexually arousing touch in the act of lovemaking. The messages that touch communicates depend on how, where, and by whom you are touched.

The importance of touch is well documented. Many people find that when they are upset, they rub their hands together or stroke a part of their body, such as the arm. We reassure others by touching them on the shoulder or patting them on the hand. "Throughout life, touch is your deepest and most intimate connection to the ones you love."[42] "Researchers have found that tactile deprivation is terrible for a child and can actually be life-threatening."[43] Most people (except those who have been abused, raped, or brought up in a low- or no-touch family or society) associate appropriate touching with positive messages. Those whose bodies have been invaded without permission, however, as in the case of sexual abuse, often pull back or feel uncomfortable when touched. In fact, touch avoidance is one of the signs counselors sometimes use to aid in the identification of clients who have been physically or sexually abused.

If you have ever wondered why you felt comfortable, or uncomfortable, when you were touched, it could well have to do with your upbringing. Different cultures regard touch in different ways. Some avoid touch, but others encourage it. The same is true within families. For example, in the United States, a moderate-touch society, it is not unusual for a person to touch another with either hand, but, "to touch an Arab Muslin with the left hand, which is reserved for toilet use, is considered a social insult."[44] In the United States, a handshake is appropriate as a business greeting, a bow fulfills the same purpose in Japan, and kissing on both cheeks is an acceptable French custom.

Touch is not only culture specific but also gender specific. Women in the European American culture tend to engage in more intimate same-sex touch than do men. Female pairs are more likely than male pairs to exchange hugs, kisses, and touches on the arm or back, and to do so for longer duration. Heterosexual men touch one another using only narrowly circumscribed behaviors, such as handshaking or, in instances of extreme emotion (e.g., athletic accomplishments), hugging, butt slapping, or kissing. The acceptability of showing physical affection by women may be one of the reasons lesbians may be less discriminated against than gay men.[45]

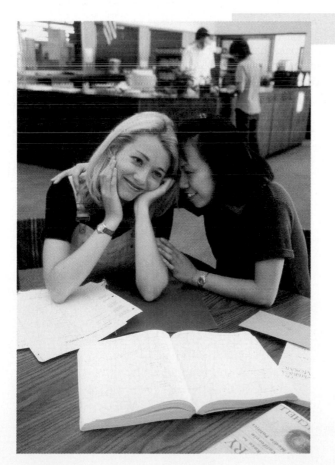

Touch is not only culture specific but gender specific.

European Americans tend to react less to physical displays between women than between men. This is not true in other countries. "Public displays of affection between men have deep historical roots in Muslim culture."[46] Lingering handshakes, handholding, embraces, and sometimes kisses between heterosexual men are the norm in much of the Muslim world. In Senegal, men walk with arms draped around each other's shoulders. In Saudi Arabia, greetings between men are almost always extended with kisses on the check. In Egypt and much of the Arab world, it is acceptable for men to hold hands or kiss. In the United States, when men touch, kiss, or hug each other, attention is drawn to the activity, and since it is not generally part of the cultural norm, except in the homosexual culture, it is perceived by some in a negative way.[47]

Permission to touch tends to follow an action chain sequence. If you have ever wondered why someone with whom you'd like to be intimate pulls away or gets rigid when one of you is touched, it may well be that you have jumped forward in the sequence too quickly. For a person brought up in a moderate- to low-touch society, there is an appropriate time not to touch, then to touch, then to kiss, and then to fondle. If one person feels he or she is at the no-touch stage, and the partner acts at the fondle stage, strong negative verbal and physical reactions may follow.

Individuals differ dramatically in the degree to which they like or dislike touch. The degree to which an individual dislikes being touched is identified as *touch avoidance*.[48]

If you would like to measure your touch/touch avoidance, fill out the Touch Avoidance Scale[49] on the next page. Remember in evaluating your scores that your cultural background, including your nationality, sexual orientation, and gender, has a great deal to do with your score, your desire to touch, and with whom you feel comfortable touching you.

POSTURE, WALK, AND STANCE: BODY SYNCHRONY   Research in **body synchrony,** the study of posture and the way a person walks and stands, indicates that these nonverbal indicators do say something about a person.[50] A person's walk can give us clues about status, mood, ethnic and cultural affiliation, and self-perception.

Nonverbal communication is composed of all those messages that people exchange beyond the words themselves.

The Touch Avoidance Scale

Directions: This instrument is composed of 18 statements concerning feelings about touching other people and being touched. Please indicate the degree to which each statement applies to you by circling whether you (1) Strongly Disagree, (2) Disagree, (3) Are Undecided, (4) Agree, or (5) Strongly Agree with each statement. While some of these statements may seem repetitious, take your time and try to be as honest as possible.

1. A hug from a same-sex friend is a true sign of friendship.   1 2 3 4 5
2. Opposite-sex friends enjoy it when I touch them.   1 2 3 4 5
3. I often put my arm around friends of the same sex.   1 2 3 4 5
4. When I see two people of the same sex hugging, it revolts me.   1 2 3 4 5
5. I like it when members of the opposite sex touch me.   1 2 3 4 5
6. People shouldn't be so uptight about touching persons of the same sex.   1 2 3 4 5
7. I think it is vulgar when members of the opposite sex touch me.   1 2 3 4 5
8. When a member of the opposite sex touches me, I find it unpleasant.   1 2 3 4 5
9. I wish I were free to show emotions by touching members of the same sex.   1 2 3 4 5
10. I'd enjoy giving a massage to an opposite-sex friend.   1 2 3 4 5
11. I enjoy kissing persons of the same sex.   1 2 3 4 5
12. I like to touch friends that are the same sex as I am.   1 2 3 4 5
13. Touching a friend of the same sex does not make me uncomfortable.   1 2 3 4 5
14. I find it enjoyable when a close opposite-sex friend and I embrace.   1 2 3 4 5
15. I enjoy getting a back rub from a member of the opposite sex.   1 2 3 4 5
16. I dislike kissing relatives of the same sex.   1 2 3 4 5
17. Intimate touching with members of the opposite sex is pleasurable.   1 2 3 4 5
18. I find it difficult to be touched by a member of my own sex.   1 2 3 4 5

Directions for scoring:

A. Add up the circled numbers for items 1, 2, 3, 5, 6, 9, 10, 11, 12, 13, 14, 15, and 17: _____

B. Score items 4, 7, 8, 16, and 18 in reverse so a circled 1 is scored as 5, 2 as 4, 3 as 3, 4 as 2, and 5 as 1, and add them up: _____

C. Add up items (A) and (B) above to get your score: _____

A score of 70 or higher indicates a very strong motivation to touch. Less than 14% (about one-seventh) of the population scores this high. If your score is right around 60, your motivation is about average, but still generally positive, since the midpoint between positive and negative on the scale is 54. A score of 50 or lower would place you approximately in the lower 14% in terms of motivation for touch.

Note: Item 14 from the original scale (Andersen & Leibowitz, 1978) has been altered from "when my date and I embrace" to "when a close opposite-sex friend and I embrace." Also, the scoring has been reversed from the original so that a higher score indicates a more positive attitude toward touch.

Even walking follows cultural patterns: Europeans, European Americans, and Asians have different walks. Some Europeans coming to the United States often ask why people are in such a hurry, an impression that comes from the quick pace at which European Americans typically walk.

In general, the way you walk and stand tells more about you than you probably realize. When someone enters a room, you instantly form conclusions about that person. Some people walk with confidence and stand with head high, shoulders back, and jaw set. Others walk slowly with a stance of sloping shoulders, eyes down, withdrawing within their bodies. This posture may indicate a lack of confidence as interpreted in the Euro-American culture. Detectives and airline security personnel are trained to pick out suspicious people by the way they walk.

ARTIFACTICS   **Artifactics** centers on the study of those things that adorn the body and send messages to others about us as well as say something about us and our selection of these items. A person's clothing, makeup, eyeglasses, and jewelry carry distinct messages.

Clothing is probably the most obvious of the artifact communicators. It is almost like a substitute body, telling an observer something about who you are. Because you have made a choice about what to wear, it follows that this is the image you want to portray, this is the attitude you want to present about the type of person you are, and this is the way you want others to perceive you. Wearing something out of the mainstream can influence others' reactions to you. Black trench coats were banned in many high schools after two students who went on a shooting rampage at Columbine High School in Littleton, Colorado, were known to have worn such coats. In addition, some pressure has been put on academic administrators to limit clothing choices because wearing certain clothing indicates gang affiliation.[51]

For those interested in climbing the business ladder, the corporate uniform is still the norm for interviews. It is known, for example, that the clothing you wear to a job interview may be a deciding factor on whether you get hired. For women, a dark blue suit and a cream-colored shirt are recommended. Hems on skirts should be at the knees, and stay away from pants. For men, a dark blue suit, a white shirt, and a red or blue tie are generally the way to go.

In spite of the emphasis on corporate clothing for interviews, casual attire on the job, sometimes referred to as *business casual*, became popular during the last decade of the twentieth century and peaked toward the turn of the century.[52] Business casual attire was meant to create a more relaxed working environment while still appearing professional, but some workers went overboard trading slacks for jeans and shirts for T-shirts.[53] In a 2006 poll of over 2,000 job seekers and active employees and over 900 job recruiters, 25 percent of employees and nearly 45 percent of recruiters said that their employers instituted casual Fridays.[54] However, another study indicated a decline in the number of employers who allow casual Fridays.[55] A corporate executive states, "I see a return to more traditional business wear, people dress up more in times of financial uncertainty and intense competition. It helps their sense of stability."[56]

Be aware, however, that even though some U.S. companies are allowing casualness, this trend is not universal. Companies dealing in foreign markets know that the business suit, which originally rose in nineteenth-century Europe as a costume to make managerial workers stand out from production workers, is still very much the business garb. In countries such as Japan, England, and Germany, casual is definitely not the "in" style.

Legal professionals also are aware of the effect of clothing worn by themselves and their clients. Lawyers advise clients to dress conservatively and to reinforce their credibility with a professional appearance.

PHYSICAL CHARACTERISTICS   A person's **physical characteristics**—for instance, height, weight, and skin color—communicate something about him or her to others. We find some people appealing and others unappealing by how they appear physically.

Attractiveness   We often are drawn to or repulsed by people according to how they appear physically. The prejudice against unattractive people is deeply ingrained in European American society. This attitude may, in part, be the result of the emphasis projected by the advertising industry on attractiveness in their magazine, newspaper, and television ads.

The attitude toward the way people look carries over into the way people are evaluated. Attractive people are often given credit—known as the *halo effect*—for other qualities such as high intelligence and better job performance. Meanwhile, unattractive people may be cast by the *devil effect*—a negative evaluation because of the way they look, regardless of their intelligence or job performance.[57]

Attractiveness is in the eye of the beholder. What it means to be attractive differs from culture to culture. For example, judges at international beauty contests have difficulty determining the winner because of the vast physical differences among the contestants and the lack of a universal definition of *beauty*. And, although thinness for women might be the "in" beauty criterion in white European American culture, that is not necessarily true in African American culture. In a study of teenage girls, white girls painted attractiveness as 5'7", between 100 and 110 pounds, with blue eyes and long flowing hair. However, the black girls in the study named full hips and large thighs as the signs of attractiveness.[58]

It is generally assumed that females are more vain, more concerned about their physical appearance, and more dissatisfied with their bodies than are males. It is known, for example, that more females than males have eating disorders such as bulimia and anorexia. However, it's not just women who are dissatisfied with their bodies; men seem to be, too. Men's dissatisfaction stems primarily from believing themselves to be less muscular than they really are. Body image is linked to depression, eating pathology, low self-esteem, and using performance-enhancing substances."[59]

A jury's decision can be affected by both the plaintiff's and the defendant's physical appearances. In one study, participants in an automobile-negligence trial heard tape-recorded testimony. The first set of jurors was shown photographs of an attractive male plaintiff and an unattractive male defendant; the second set of jurors saw

Communicating in Careers

How Do Australians and Americans Display Similar and Different Nonverbal Clues?

According to Doug Ash, general sales manager for the Hutton Group, a meeting and event management company based in Pittsburgh, Pennsylvania:

The Australian culture is very similar to [that of] the United States, and because of that it's extremely easy to assimilate American business practices into the Australian culture and vice versa. One difference is that the Australians aren't big on business formalities. They don't want to do business over lunch; they want to get to know you personally. And outside Sydney's financial area—called the suit area because it is about the only place people wear suits—dress is more casual. If you go to a pub for lunch, dress will be slacks and a shirt. When we travel to Australia, the suits and ties come off, and it's a much more relaxed atmosphere.

Attractiveness is in the eye of the beholder.

the reverse. A third panel saw no pictures but heard the testimony. The results: The attractive plaintiff received a 49 percent positive vote from the first jury, the unattractive plaintiff got only a 17 percent positive vote from the second jury, and 41 percent of the third group, which did not see any pictures, ruled for the plaintiff.[60]

Height   It should not be surprising that height can be a communicator. People often are judged purely by their physical presence. Size can affect a man's life. "Short men are discriminated against with respect to job offers and salaries."[61] Men under 5′ 6″ are considered short. People regard them as having less power. Short men may be perceived as *submissive* and *weak;* tall men garner such descriptions as *mature* and *respected.*

A comparison of the starting pay of business-school graduates indicates that tall males received $600 per inch of height more in yearly salary[62] or "1.8 percent increase per additional inch of height."[63] What are the implications? Shorter men may need to be better prepared, be aware that they must exceed in grades and talent, and sell themselves during job interviews. However, success for short men is not impossible. For example, two-term U.S. President James Madison was 5′ 4″; Attila the Hun, 5′; and, of course, there was Napoleon.

Although European American society seems to show a preference for taller men, tall women often are labeled "ungainly"; short businesswomen, in fact, may have an advantage in not acquiring whatever threatening overtones may attend to increasing height. But very short women may be perceived differently than taller women. A well-qualified 5′ 1″, size 2, master-degreed audiologist reports that her patients often call and ask for "the little girl doctor." Overweight women also find themselves "prejudiced against."[64]

We communicate through the gestures we use, the way we walk and stand, and the expressions on our faces and in our eyes.

Proxemics: Spatial Communication

A basic difference among people can be seen in how they operate within the space around them—how they use their territory. The study of how people use and perceive their social and personal space is called **proxemics**.

Every person is surrounded by a psychological bubble of space. This bubble contracts and expands depending on the person's cultural background, emotional state, and the activity in which he or she is participating. Northern Europeans—English, Scandinavians, and Germans—tend to have a need for a larger zone of personal space and often avoid touching and close contact. They require more room around them and structure their lifestyles to meet the need for this space. Thus, the English are stereotyped as being distant and impersonal, not showing great emotion through hugging, kissing, and touching. This stereotype derives from the respect they exhibit for each other's territory. In contrast, many Italians, Russians, Spaniards, Latin Americans, Middle Easterners, and the French prefer close personal contact.

Culture has an effect on how people perceive themselves in space and how they use space.

CULTURE AND SPACE When people from different cultural backgrounds come into contact, they may assume they have the same concept of space. This, of course, is not true. In fact, "cultures can be distinguished by the distances at which members interact and how frequently members touch."[65] It has been proposed that there are

Most European-Americans feel most comfortable keeping eighteen inches to four feet space around them. Invasion of this personal territory will cause discomfort.

contact cultures—those characterized by tactile modes of communication (e.g., Latin Americans, Mediterraneans, French, Arabs)—and *noncontact cultures* (Germans, Japanese, English, North Americans).[66] Although heterosexual men in the United States and England rarely touch other men, except in times of great emotion (such as athletic game victories) or shaking hands when welcoming or meeting someone, arm linking between two men is common in Turkey, Morocco, and many Latin American countries.[67]

Even within our own culture, the space bubble varies according to our emotional state and the activity. Although European Americans usually keep well beyond the three-foot personal circle of space, this can change very quickly. If you are on a crowded bus and someone presses against you, you may tolerate it. If, however, you are standing at a bus stop and someone presses against you, you will probably object. This situation brings into play your idea of public distance.

Your emotional state also can change your idea of space. For instance, when some people are angry, they may grab someone by the front of the shirt, step in close, get "nose to nose," and shout.

Space Distances   An examination of space distances allows for an understanding of space as it relates to culture. Everyone has spatial needs. Studies of space distances as they relate to white middle-class Americans indicate that there are four classifications that explain their spatial needs: intimate, personal, social, and public. (See Figure 3.5.)[68]

Intimate distance covers a space varying from direct physical contact with another person to a distance of eighteen inches. It is used for our most private activities: caressing, making love, and sharing intimate ideas and emotions. We can often get clues about a relationship by noticing whether the other person allows us to use his or her intimate space. For example, if you have been on a hand-holding/physically touching basis with someone, and suddenly he or she will not let you near or pulls away when you get very close, a change in the relationship may have occurred. If a nontoucher suddenly encourages close body proximity, this also may indicate a change in attitude.

Personal distance, eighteen inches to four feet, is sometimes called the *comfort bubble*. Generally, European Americans feel most comfortable maintaining this distance when talking with others, and invasion of this personal territory will cause us to back away. If we are backed into a corner, sitting in a chair, or somehow trapped, we will lean away, pull in, and tense up. To avoid invasion of our territory, we might place a leg on the rung of a chair or on a stair. Some of us even arrange furniture so that no one can invade our territory. For example, businesspeople may place their desks so that

| 18 in. | 18 in. to 4 ft | 4 ft to 12 ft | 12 ft to 25 ft |

Intimate distance   **Personal distance**   **Social distance**   **Public distance**

Figure 3.5   Space Distances

employees must sit on one side and the boss on the other. In contrast, interviewers have reported a completely different atmosphere when talking to job applicants if the two chairs are placed facing each other about three to four feet apart instead of on opposite sides of the desk.

Social distance covers a four- to twelve-foot zone that is used during business transactions and casual social exchanges. Also part of social distance is the *standing–seated interaction*, in which the person in control stands and the other person sits. Standing–seated positions occur, among others, in teacher–pupil and police officer–arrestee transactions.

Public distance may dictate a separation of as little as twelve feet, but it is usually more than twenty-five feet. It is used by professors in lecture rooms and speakers at public gatherings as well as by public figures who wish to place a barrier between themselves and their audiences.

An important aspect of proxemics is the arrangement of seating and how people are spaced at meetings and in homes.

Small-Group Ecology   The physical placement of members of small groups in relation to one another has an effect on their behavior. This *small-group ecology,* which includes the placement of chairs, the placement of the person conducting a meeting, and the setting for a small-group encounter, clearly influences the group's operation. If, for example, people are seated in a tight circle, they will probably feel more comfortable and interact more than they if they were sitting in straight rows. They will be able to see each other's nonverbal reactions, and, because there is no inhibiting physical distance, they will lose their self-consciousness as they become members of the group.

Business organizations make considerable use of such nonverbal strategies in small-scale conferences. One technique is to seat key members of the group in prominent positions to stimulate discussion or even direct it.

Paravocalics: Vocal Communication

The vocal effects that accompany words, such as tone of voice—but not the words themselves—are paralanguage or **paravocalics**.[69] Vocal quality communicates nonverbally to the listening ear. The rate (speed), volume (power), pitch (such as soprano or bass), pause (stopping), and stress (intensity) of sounds all have particular meanings. These paravocal tools are often referred to as *vocal cues.* "People spontaneously use a system of communicating when they speak that either reinforces their message or provides additional information not conveyed by the words alone."[70] The vocal changes "happen with little intention on the part of the speaker, although it is possible to use this expression explicitly to dramatize an utterance."[71] For example, "someone will raise his voice slightly at the end of the sentence when saying 'the stock market is going up' or lower it when saying 'the stock market is going down.'"[72]

Vocal cues offer clues to determine the sex, age, and status of a speaker. We also can make

Socially Communicating

Voices Weigh In

People can estimate a speaker's height, weight and age from his voice as accurately as they can after viewing his photo.

Source: "Voice Messages, The Science of Your Sound," *Psychology Today,* (November/December 2006): 15.

REFLECT ON THIS:

1. Did you ever meet someone who you "knew" only by phone or when listening to him or her on the radio? If so, did the person "look" like what you expected? What clues did you use to come to your first impression?

2. While talking to someone on the phone, does your image of what that person looks like influence how you speak to him or her?

Formal time is the way in which a culture defines its time and the role it plays in regulating our lives.

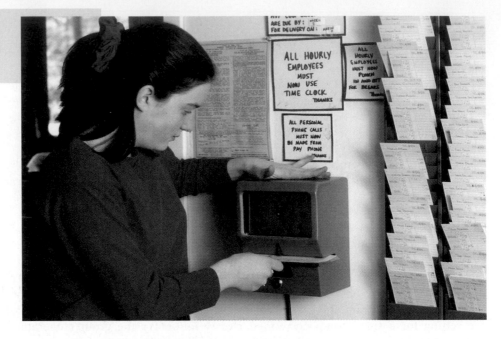

some pretty accurate judgments about the emotions and feelings of the people with whom we communicate by their paralinguistic presentation. If you are very angry, the pitch of your voice may go up. And when you are very, very angry, you sometimes say words slowly and distinctly, pausing after each word for special effect.

The voice also may be important in some aspects of persuasion.[73] A faster rate of speech, more intonation, greater volume, and a less halting manner seem to be related to successful attempts at persuasion. If a person sounds assured, the receiver credits him or her with a higher degree of credibility. Network television anchors, for example, work to cultivate an assured broadcast voice.

Vocal cues can provide much information about a speaker, and our overall reaction to another person is colored at least somewhat by our reactions to these cues. Perceptions of vocal cues, combined with other verbal and nonverbal stimuli, mold the conceptions we use as bases for communicating.

Chronemics: Time as Communication

You communicate to yourself and others by the way you use time. The way people handle and structure their time is known as **chronemics.** Time, as a communication tool, is sometimes greatly misunderstood. Only within certain societies, for example, is precise time of great significance. Some cultures, such as Native Americans and some eastern societies,[74] relate to time as a *circular phenomenon* in which there is no pressure or anxiety about the future. Existence follows the cycle of the seasons of planting and harvesting, the daily rising and setting of the sun, birth and death. In *circular time,* there is no pressing need to achieve or create newness, or to produce more than is needed to survive. Nor is there fear of death. Such societies have successfully integrated the past and future into a peaceful sense of the present.[75] Some societies operate on *linear time,* centered primarily on the future. These societies focus on the factual and technical information needed to fulfill impending demands. In most of Western Europe, North America, and Japan, punctuality is considered good manners.

Another way of viewing time is to understand its technical, formal, and informal uses. *Technical time* is precise time, as in the way some scientists look at how things happen in milliseconds. Few of us come in direct contact with this usage. *Formal time* is the way in which a culture defines its time, and it plays a daily role in most of our lives. It refers to centuries, years, months, weeks, days, hours, and minutes. As a student, you may think in formal-time terms of semesters or terms. *Informal time* refers to a rather flexible use of time, such as "soon" or "right away." These terms often cause communicative difficulty because they are arbitrary and mean different things to different people. For example, how long is "pretty soon"?

Time has become a critical factor in the U.S. workplace. Throughout a person's career, punctuality is often used as a measure of effectiveness. A person who arrives late for a job interview probably will have difficulty overcoming such a negative first impression, and employees who arrive late or leave early may be reprimanded and even dismissed.

Time is culture based. European Americans, Euro-Canadians, and Western Europeans, in general, are clock bound; African, Latin American, and some Asian Pacific cultures are not clock bound. European Americans traveling abroad often are irritated by the seeming lack of concern for time commitments among residents of some countries. In Mexico and Central America, tours may be late; guides may fail to indicate exact arrival and departure times. Yet in other places, such as Switzerland, travelers can set their watch by the promptness of the trains. Businesspeople may get confused over what "on time" means as they meet those from other cultures. In Latin America, one is expected to arrive late to an appointment. This same tardiness for Germans or European Americans would be perceived as rudeness.[76]

The differences in the use of time have been noted when college students arrive for classes and turn in assignments. For instance, one of your authors found that some of his Arabic and South American students showed few signs of concern for lateness, arriving as much as an hour late for a two-hour class, but also feeling comfortable about asking questions long after the class had officially ended. As one of them explained it, "Things just don't start on time, at least U.S. time, where we come from."[77] Some people from some cultures, such as gays, Hispanics, and African Americans, are amused by their use of time and even have names that refer to habitual lateness such as *gay-late, mañana time*.[78] (*Note:* Remember, as in all generalizations, not everyone in a particular culture follows the same patterns.)

In cultures that value promptness, one of the questions raised about time centers on the person who is constantly late. What does habitual tardiness reveal about the person? Chronic lateness, in a formal-time culture, may be deeply rooted in a person's psyche. Compulsive tardiness is rewarding on some level. A key emotional conflict for the chronically late person involves his or her need to feel special. Such a person may not gain enough recognition in other ways; people must be special in some way, so the person is special by being late. Other reasons include needs for punishment or power or as an expression of hostility.[79] Tardiness can also be a sign that a person wants to avoid something or that the activity or person to be met is not important enough to warrant the effort to be on time. Procrastinators are often not valued in a linear time-focused culture.[80]

Olfactics: Smell as Communication

Olfactics is the study of smell. We communicate through our smells. The sense of smell is extraordinarily precise. "Scents can have positive effects on mood, stress reduction, sleep enhancement, self-confidence, and physical and cognitive performance."[81] "It has been demonstrated that odor remains in our memory much longer than things we see or hear."[82] Our sense of smell is very selective and helps us reach

Socially Communicating

Using Smell to Improve Your Test Taking

An odor has no personal significance until it becomes connected to something that has meaning. On a practical level, that means that you may be able to use your sense of smell to prompt your memory when taking a test. Research suggests that your ability to recall information may be improved by inhaling an odor you breathed while absorbing information—so fire up a stick of incense while studying, then bring a vial of that aroma's essential oil to a big test.

REFLECT ON THIS: Some students have used this technique to improve their grades. See if it works for you. The next time you study for an exam, expose yourself to a particular odor. For example, put your favorite cologne, after-shave, vanilla extract, or some other positive smell on a handkerchief. Smell it occasionally as you study. The day of the test, saturate the handkerchief and bring it to class with you. Smell it during an exam and see if you have any intrapersonal flashback memory that helps you remember answers.

conclusions. Some people find certain body odors offensive. This is especially true in a country such as the United States, where we have been taught by advertisers and medical people to wash off natural odors and replace them with neutral, fragrance-free, or substitute smells. This is not the case in other cultures such as India and many Arabic countries.

We often make decisions without realizing that these choices are based on odors. Several phenomena provide insight into how smell serves as a nonverbal communication tool: smell blindness, smell adaptation, smell memory, smell overload, and smell discrimination.[83]

Each person has a unique ability to identify and distinguish smells. *Smell blindness* occurs when a person is unable to detect smells. It parallels color blindness or deafness because it is a physiological blockage. It accounts for the fact that some people do not smell differences in the odors of various foods. Because smell and taste are so closely aligned, this can explain why people who are smell-blind may also have taste-identification difficulties.

Smell adaptation occurs when we gradually lose the distinctiveness of a particular smell through repeated contact with it. When you walk into a bakery, you may be aware of the wonderful odors. The clerks who work there, however, may have become so used to the odors that they are not aware of them.

The ability to recall previous situations when encountering a particular smell associated with them is *smell memory*. Smelling a crayon may trigger flashbacks to experiences you had in kindergarten or passing a perfume counter with samples of a cologne a former lover wore may trigger intrapersonal smell memories. Smell memory may even have an affect on your academic career, since your sense of smell may be able to "prompt memory when taking a test."[84] Research suggests that "your ability to recall information may be improved by inhaling an odor you breathed while absorbing information."[85] The implications might be to bring a vial of whatever aroma was present when you were studying to your next exam.[86]

Smell overload takes place when an exceptionally large number of odors or one extremely strong odor overpowers you. Walking down a detergent aisle in a store can trigger smell overload for some people; it can also occur when on an elevator with someone who is saturated with perfume.

The ability to identify people, places, and things on the basis of their smells is *smell discrimination*. Smell discrimination allows us to tell the difference between cinnamon and garlic, bananas and oranges, and one person and another.

Aesthetics: Mood and Beauty as Communication

The study of communication of a message or mood through color or music is **aesthetics.** When you are driving a car, the type of music on the radio affects your driving, alertness, and concentration. And the music in an elevator is almost never loud and pulsating because such strong sounds would be too emotionally stressful for people in a small, contained area.

As you stroll through the supermarket, you may not even be aware of how music affects you. During a nine-week test, the music in one supermarket was randomly played at a slow 60 beats a minute on some days and at 108 beats a minute on others. On slow-tempo days the store's gross receipts were 38.2 percent higher as people walked at a leisurely pace and purchased more.[87]

Music does many things for the human body, including masking unpleasant sounds and feelings; slowing down and equalizing brain waves; affecting respiration; affecting heartbeat, pulse rate, and blood pressure; reducing muscle tension and improving body movement and coordination; affecting body temperature; regulating stress-related hormones; boosting the immune function; changing our perception of space and time; strengthening our memory and learning; boosting productivity; enhancing romance and sexuality; stimulating digestion; fostering endurance; enhancing unconscious receptivity to symbolism; and generating a sense of safety and well-being. The next few paragraphs will provide an understanding of how something like music can affect our bodies in such a large way.[88]

A study on the impact of rock music tested more than 20,000 records for their effect on muscle strength: "Listening to rock music frequently causes all the muscles in the body to go weak."[89] This relationship may account for the drugged and dreamlike feelings of some people who attend rock concerts. It is theorized that some rock music has a stopped quality that is not present in other types of music—that is, the beat is stopped at the end of each bar or measure. Because the music stops and then must start again, the listener subconsciously comes to a halt at the end of each measure; this may tire the listener.

Music has been credited with easing pain, and a type of music therapy is being used in hospices in working with dying patients. A recent study found signs that harp music might help regulate a patient's irregular heartbeat.[90] Other researchers believe music can alleviate some of the mental and physical symptoms of disease, including normalizing sick newborns' heart rates and after surgery to reduce patients' anxiety.[91]

Colors also affect people, and many institutions are putting into practice this awareness. For example, hospitals are experimenting with using various colors for their rooms in hopes that the colors may motivate sick people to get well or ease pain. Hospitals also are painting large pieces of equipment, such as x-ray machines, the same color as the background walls so they do not appear as frightening to patients.

Other studies regarding the power of colors to communicate reveal that when otherwise equally matched with their opponent in fitness and skill, athletes wearing red are more likely to win.[92] The reason, according to scientists, is that red correlates to male dominance and testosterone levels. Anger is associated with reddening of the skin due to increased blood flow.[93] However, the wearing of or sitting next to someone who is wearing red when you take a test could negatively affect your performance.[94] The conclusion reached is, "care must be taken in how red is used in achievement contexts."[95]

Gustorics: Taste as Communication

Every time we place a substance in our mouths, our sense of taste communicates. Like our other senses, the sense of taste acts as a medium that carries messages of pleasure, displeasure, and warning to our brains.[96] **Gustorics** is the study of how taste communicates. It encompasses the communication aspects of such factors as the classifications of taste, the role of culture on taste, the role of food deprivation, food preferences, taste expectations, and color and textures as an encourager or discourager of eating and drinking.

Taste qualities have been classified as bitter, salty, sweet, and sour. We receive these signals much the same as we do smells. We come in physical contact with the object that brings about the sense reaction within us. These sense reactions are located not on our tongue but in various regions of our mouth and throat. The taste buds of the mouth are the most common tasters.

It is interesting to note that just as some people have smell blindness, and others can't smell all or some odors, some people have *taste blindness*—the inability to taste. This can either be a defect in their senses at birth or the destruction of the tasters through an accident or illness. This condition can be long or short term. Expectant mothers, for example, temporarily suffer taste loss during the first three months of pregnancy. Some people have extremely sensitive tasting abilities. They react very strongly to the slightest taste, they may find slightly spicy foods to be very offensive, and the taste of certain foods may stimulate allergic reactions.

Another phenomenon associated with gustorics is taste adaptation. *Taste adaptation* takes place when a person becomes used to a taste to the degree that he or she can eat a substance and not taste it. People who eat a lot of very spicy foods may eventually develop an insensitivity to the tang.

Socially Communicating

Nonverbals' Role in Persuasion

Perhaps you believe visuals won't help you persuade. If so, consider a Columbia University study that shows the percentages each sense usually plays in interpreting messages.

Touch	65%
Taste	1.5%
Smell	6%
Hearing	11%
Sight	80%

Source: Creative Negotiating Proven Techniques for Getting What You Want From Any Negotiation, by Stephen Kozicki, Adams Media Corp., 260 Center St. Holbrook, MA 02343.

REFLECT ON THIS: Select a real situation in which you are trying to persuade someone. Using the information in this study, indicate what specific appeals you could use in carrying out the action you desire them to take.

Using Nonverbal Communication

Nonverbal communication has become a weapon in the war on terrorism. Law-enforcement officers are being exposed to *behavior pattern recognition*, which is training in detecting signs that could indicate a terrorist plot. The officers are taught to look for something outside the normal range of behavior—such as people exhibiting odd or suspicious nonverbal behavior, including wearing heavy or large baggy clothes on a hot day, loitering without luggage, or going through checkpoints and glancing around excessively or looking nervous—and to listen for verbal stammering when a person is answering questions. The technique is not new to the government. Customs agents use similar techniques to look for smugglers at border crossings.[97]

A question arises as to why, if nonverbal communication is such an important aspect of communication, most people aren't aware of it or don't pay much overt attention to its powers. One reason is that most people have not been taught that actions communicate as clearly as words communicate, so they don't look for nonverbal components. Schools don't generally teach courses in the subject, and what we do learn tends to be through subtle cultural communication. You may have been told that if you didn't look someone in the eye as you speak, that person might not believe you, or that you should stand up straight and walk with pride, or that you are judged by what you wear. These messages actually say, "Pay attention to the nonverbals," but most of us don't tie that to the fact that nonverbal communication is carrying messages.

Being aware that nonverbal communication exists, being aware that you need to listen to others with your eyes as well as your ears, and monitoring what you do as a nonverbal communicator will help you to become a more competent communicator.

In Conclusion

Nonverbal communication is composed of all those messages that people exchange beyond the words themselves. Nonverbal communication is a major force in our lives. There are two basic sources of nonverbals: innate neurological programs and behavior common to a culture. Research shows a relationship between nonverbal and verbal communication. In attempting to read nonverbal communication, we must remember that no one signal carries much meaning. Nonverbal communication includes the categories of kinesics, physical characteristics, proxemics, paravocalics, chronemics, olfactics, aesthetics, and gustorics. Through all of these channels, humans are always sending messages, even when no words are used.

Learn by Doing

1. Research one of these topics or people and be prepared to give a two-minute speech on what you have learned regarding the topic of nonverbal communication: neuro-linguistic programming, Ray Birdwhistell, Albert Mehrabian, Edward Hall, pupilometrics, biorhythms, Muzak

2. Give examples of your own recent use of substituting, complementing, conflicting, and accenting.

3. Carefully observe members of your family or think of the nonverbal patterns they display. Can you find any similarities between their patterns and your own?

4. Identify a cultural-specific nonverbal trait and describe it to the class.

5. Make a list of five emblems used by you, by members of your family, or within your culture. Be prepared to demonstrate them. Compare your explanations of what they mean with those of your classmates.

6. Carry on a conversation with a person outside your classroom. As you speak, slowly move closer to him or her. Continue to move in on the person gradually. Observe his or her reaction. Did the person back up? Cross his or her arms? Report to the class on the results of the experiment.

Key Terms

nonverbal communication 59

kinesics 68

facsics 68

ocalics 68

gestics 69

emblems 69

haptics 70

body synchrony 72

artifactics 74

physical characteristics 74

proxemics 77

paravocalics 79

chronemics 80

olfactics 81

aesthetics 83

gustorics 84

chapter 4

Listening

▶ **After reading this chapter, you should be able to**

- Explain the importance of listening in daily communication
- Contrast hearing and listening
- Define and identify the roles of reception, perception, attention, the assignment of meaning, and response as they relate to the listening process
- List and explain some of the listening influencers

- Describe discriminative, comprehension, therapeutic, critical, and appreciative listening
- Understand how to listen to the media
- Identify and explain some of the techniques available for improving personal listening
- Discuss the causes of listening apprehension and approaches to dealing with it

If you are fairly typical, you have had little, if any, training as a listener. Most elementary schools operate on the assumption that you don't know how to read or write when you come to school, so they teach you how to perform those skills. They also assume that since you can talk and hear, you can communicate and listen. This assumption is incorrect. Talking and hearing are biological functions. Listening and communicating, like reading and writing, are learned skills. Listening is a complex combination of skills and emotions. As Figure 4.1, the symbol for listening in Chinese, indicates, listening involves a combination of the ears, eyes, undivided attention and the heart.

How effective a listener do you think you are? Are you interested in finding out? If so, try the self-assessment on pages 88 and 89.

How much of your time do you spend listening? Research shows that the average working person spends 40 percent of his or her time listening. This is in contrast to 9 percent writing, 16 percent reading, and 35 percent talking.[1] "That's right. You listen more than you use any other form of communication. In fact, you spend more time listening than you do reading and writing combined!"[2]

The Importance of Listening

Your academic success, employment achievement, and personal happiness may well depend on your ability to listen efficiently.

Listening is an important means for learning at all academic levels. Students listen to the equivalent of a book a day, talk the equivalent of a book a week, read the equivalent of a book a month, and write the equivalent of a book a year.[3] A recent study showed that students spend 8 percent their time writing, 6 percent reading, 20 percent speaking, and 50 percent in listening-related activities.[4]

Frequently, listening is considered to be a passive process. But this image is an illusion. A good listener has to be patient, suspend judgment, and analyze what is said. It is an active, rather than a passive, process.

Several years ago, the former Sperry Computer Corporation launched a major advertising campaign to point out how important it is to listen effectively in both our personal lives and our careers. Like many other U.S. organizations such as Pfizer, International Paper, the World Bank, and the Central Intelligence Agency, Sperry instituted training programs to prepare its executives, managers, and employees to be better listeners. The

Eyes

Ear

Undivided
Attention

Heart

Figure 4.1

Chinese Symbol for "Listening"

The Chinese characters that make up the verb *to listen* explain the significance and complexity of the learned skill.

cost of poor listening can be catastrophic. Federal investigators, for example, observe that poor listening is as much at fault as mechanical problems in airline crashes.[5]

You learn about your culture by listening as your family, clergy, government officials, and the media explain your gender, ethnic, and racial roles. It is also through listening that you gain your language.

As an educated person, you have an obligation to strive to be an effective listener. And to be a responsible listener, you must know what the process is about, what it takes to be an effective listener, how to evaluate your own listening, and how to work toward improving your weaknesses while retaining your strengths.

Janusik/Wolvin Student Listening Inventory

Directions: The process of listening includes the five steps of Reception, Attention, Perception, Assignment of Meaning, and Response. As a process, listening can break down at any of the five steps. This inventory will help you identify your strengths and weaknesses in terms of the steps within the context of the classroom. After reading each of the following statements, code the item with the most appropriate response within the context of the college classroom. Remember, "speaker" can mean the instructor or fellow students, so you may have to average your responses.

(1) almost never, (2) not often, (3) sometimes, (4) more often than not, (5) almost always

_____ 1. I block out external and internal distractions, such as other conversations or what happened yesterday, when someone is speaking.

_____ 2. I feel comfortable asking questions when I don't understand something the speaker said.

_____ 3. When a speaker uses words that I'm not familiar with, I jot them down and look them up later.

_____ 4. I identify the speaker's credibility while listening.

_____ 5. I paraphrase the speaker's main ideas in my head as he or she speaks.

_____ 6. I concentrate on the main ideas instead of the specific details.

_____ 7. I am able to understand those who are direct as easily as I can understand those who are indirect.

_____ 8. Before making a decision, I confirm my understanding of the other person's message with her or him.

_____ 9. I concentrate on the speaker's message even when what she or he is saying is complex.

_____ 10. I really want to understand what the other person has to say, so I focus solely on his or her message.

_____ 11. When I listen to someone from another culture, I understand that the speaker may use time and space differently, and I factor that into my understanding.

_____ 12. I make certain to watch a speaker's facial expressions and body language for further clues to what he or she means.

_____ 13. I encourage the speaker through my facial expressions and verbal utterances.

_____ 14. When others are speaking to me, I make sure to establish eye contact and quit doing other tasks.

_____ 15. When I hear something with which I disagree, I tune out the speaker.

_____ 16. When an emotional trigger is activated, I recognize it for what it is, set aside my feelings, and continue to concentrate on the speaker's message.

_____ 17. I try to be sure that my nonverbal response matches my verbal response.

_____ 18. When someone begins speaking, I focus my attention on her or his message.

_____ 19. I understand that my past experiences play a role in how I interpret a message, so I try to be aware of their influence when listening.

_____ 20. I attempt to eliminate outside interruptions and distractions.

_____ 21. I look the speaker in the eye to focus on her or his message.

_____ 22. I tune out messages that are too complicated to understand.

_____ 23. I try to understand the other person's point of view and why she or he feels that way even when it is different from what I believe.

_____ 24. I am nonjudgmental and noncritical when I listen.

_____ 25. As appropriate, I self-disclose a similar amount of personal information as the other person shares with me.

Janusik/Wolvin Student Listening Inventory

Scoring Directions: Write your responses in the appropriate positions. For example, if you gave yourself a "3" for the first statement, transfer the 3 to the first slot under Reception. When you have transferred all of your scores, add up all five scores for each step. The step with the highest score is your strength. The step with the lowest score is the step that can use the most improvement.

Reception	Attention	Perception	Assignment of Meaning	Response
1. ____	5. ____	3. ____	4. ____	2. ____
9. ____	10. ____	6. ____	7. ____	8. ____
12. ____	14. ____	15. ____	11. ____	13. ____
18. ____	20. ____	16. ____	19. ____	17. ____
21. ____	22. ____	23. ____	24. ____	25. ____
Total ____	____	____	____	____

Now add up your scores for all five steps, and use the following as a general guideline:

125–112 You perceive yourself to be an outstanding listener in the classroom.

111–87 You perceive yourself to be a good listener in the classroom, but there are some steps that could use improvement.

86–63 You perceive yourself to be an adequate listener in the classroom, but attention to some steps could really improve your listening effectiveness.

62–0 You perceive yourself to be a poor listener in the classroom, and attention to all of the steps could really improve your listening effectiveness.

Consider:

a. In which step or steps did you excel? What do you consciously do?

b. Which step or steps indicated the most need for improvement? What two specific actions could you take for each step to improve your listening effectiveness?

c. Did you find yourself averaging scores because you were considering both the instructor and peers? What does that say about your perception of both?

Communicating in Careers

Listening in the Global Marketplace

With continued interaction between companies all over the world, the business world is in a global marketplace. Because of this there are some listening guidelines that are appropriate for those involved in international sales and service.

1. Listen for your own cultural/individual values.

2. When you are being introduced to someone from another culture, listen for his or her cultural/individual values.

3. Expand your knowledge of the cultural norms of other peoples.

4. Listen with your eyes and mind open.

REFLECT ON THIS:

1. What kind of education do U.S. businesspeople need in order to fulfill the requirements of listening in the global marketplace?

2. Do you think you are prepared to listen in the global marketplace? Why or why not?

3. Shouldn't those from other nations just accept that the cost of doing business with U.S. companies is the requirement to learn Euro-American language and nonverbal traditions?

The Listening Process

Many people wrongly assume that hearing and listening are the same. **Hearing** is a biological activity that involves reception of a message through sensory channels. Hearing is only one part of **listening,** a process that involves reception, attention, perception, the assignment of meaning, and the listener's response to the message presented. (See Figure 4.2.)

Reception

The initial step in the listening process is the *reception* of a stimulus or message—both the auditory message and the visual message. The hearing process is based on a complex set of physical interactions between the ear and the brain. Proper care of the ear is important because auditory acuity enhances the ability to listen efficiently. It is estimated that about 15 percent of American adults report some level of hearing loss.[6] Also estimated is that 10 percent of Americans between 20 and 69 years have sustained permanent damage to their hearing as a result of exposure to loud sounds and noises on the job or during leisure activities.[7] To keep these statistics from rising, people who work near loud machinery are often required to wear ear protectors. But the workplace is not the only source of potential danger. For example, individuals who expose themselves to excessive amounts of loud music or listen to music through earphones should be aware that they can damage their hearing mechanism. In fact, the use of earphones to listen to music is considered to be a major source of hearing damage.[8] An audiologist warns, "As you enjoy the blaring music in your car, home, or your headsets, or at a concert, be aware that you can be permanently damaging one of your most important biological tools . . . your hearing mechanism."[9]

In addition to using the hearing mechanism, people listen visually. As you engage in conversations, or as a receiver of public speeches, you should observe facial expression, posture, movement, and appearance, which provide important cues that may not be obvious by listening only to the verbal part of the message.

Figure 4.2
The Listening Process

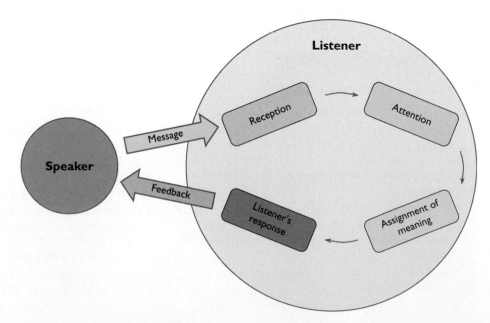

Figure 4.3
Dale's Cone of Learning

Source: Reprinted by permission from Lilly Walters, *Secrets of Successful Speakers.* Copyright © 1993 by the McGraw-Hill Companies.

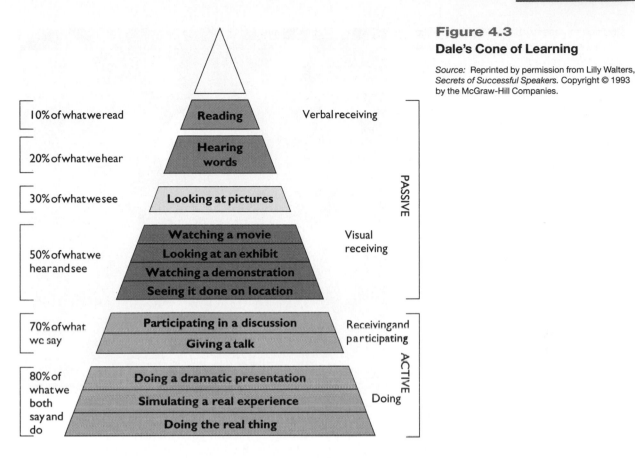

You also should be aware that the way in which information is presented will have an affect on how you perceive the message. As the Dale's Cone of Learning indicates (Figure 4.3), the most effective method of presenting material so that it is remembered involves directed, purposeful learning experiences such as hands-on or field experiences.[10]

Both speakers and listeners must realize that listeners can recall only about 26 percent of what they hear.[11] Thus, speakers must attempt to stimulate listeners by doing "the real thing," simulating a real experience, or doing something dramatic. Unfortunately, many speakers don't know this, so you, as a listener, must concentrate when hearing information. Try to get involved in the process and ask questions using the concepts of the interactional model of communication so that you can ensure active listing and comprehending.

Receiving the message through the visual and the auditory channels is but one component of the listening process. The listener also must attend to the message.

Attention

Once the stimulus—the word or visual symbol, or both—is received, it reaches the attention stage of the human processing system.

ROLE OF ATTENTION In listening, *attention* represents the focus on a specific stimulus selected from all the stimuli received at any given moment. In this phase, the other stimuli recede so that we can concentrate on a specific word or visual symbol. Normally your attention is divided between what you are attempting to listen to, what is

Attention represents the focus on a specific stimulus selected from all the stimuli received at any given moment.

currently happening in the rest of the environment, and what else is going on in your mind. Consider, for example, what happens if you go to a movie. Perhaps the person in front of you is constantly whispering to the person next to him, there is a buzz in the sound system, and you are worried because you left your car in a no-parking zone. Your attention is being pulled in several directions. But if the film is interesting enough, you will focus on it, and the other factors will be relegated to the back of your consciousness.

Culturally Communicating

The Haka Race of Taipei, Taiwan's View of Listening

When you listen, you use your ears, eyes and heart to determine *the* meaning. The eyes are actually more important than the ears. You have to learn to listen to the content, but you have to know what people mean.

Source: Pamela Cooper, Carolyn Calloway-Thomas, and Cheri Simonds, *Intercultural Communication: A Text with Readings* (Boston: Pearson, 2007), p. 158.

REFLECT ON THIS:

1. What do you think the authors mean by "listen with your heart" as it relates to the meaning of messages you receive?

2. What do you think is meant by "but you have to know what people mean"?

The listener's ability to focus attention is limited. Estimates are that the range of attention span of an adult (the amount of time a person can concentrate on a single activity) is from seven[12] to twenty minutes.[13] To informally check this out, during your next classroom lecture, look around after twenty minutes and see how many people are doing other things, such as doodling, looking out the window, daydreaming, playing with their cells, or dozing. The implication is that in giving a speech, for example, ensure that, at a maximum, the first twenty minutes include any material that you want your audience to remember.[14] To "prolong attention span, periodically give your audience a rest by telling a story, giving a demo, or doing something else that gives the brain a break."[15]

Cognitive psychologists have come to understand this as a dual-task process of what they call the working memory. A person's *working memory* capacity is made up of both the memory and the attention functions, and listeners shift in and out of the long-term memory to retrieve and to store stimuli while, at the same time, attempting to pay attention to the speaker's message.[16] Your working memory may be impacted by your television viewing. Individuals who have been raised watching television have come to expect a seven- to ten-minute viewing format followed by a commercial break and that may be the guideline for the patterning of their working memory.

ROLE OF MOTIVATION/CONCENTRATION   Undoubtedly one of the most difficult tasks we have to perform as listeners is concentration, put in action by your motivation. For example, if you really want to listen to a speaker, this desire will put you in a more positive frame of mind than will anticipating that the speaker will be boring, thus encouraging concentration on the speaker and subject matter. Realistically, some messages may be boring, but if you need to get the information, careful concentration is imperative. For example, you may not find the chemistry professor's ideas fascinating, but if you do not listen effectively, you probably will fail the next test. You also may find the information so difficult that you tune out. Again, if it is imperative for you to understand the ideas, then you have to force yourself to figure out what you do not understand and find a way of grasping the meaning.

The average American rate of speech is 130 to 200 words per minute.[17] In conversations, the average rate is 125 words per minute; whereas a speaker before an audience slows down to about 100 words per minute.[18] How fast do listeners listen? Or, to put the question in a better form, how many words a minute do people normally *think* as they listen? Listeners probably average 400 to 500 words per minute as they listen.[19]

Because we can receive messages much more quickly than the other person can talk, we tend to tune in and tune out throughout a message. The mind can absorb only so much material. Indeed, the brain operates much like a computer: It turns off, recycles itself, and turns back on to avoid information overload. It is no wonder, then, that our attention fluctuates even when we are actively involved as listeners. Think back to any class you have attended. Do you recall a slight gap in your listening at times? This is a natural part of the listening process. When you tune out, the major danger is that you may daydream rather than quickly turn back to the message. But by taking notes or forcing yourself to paraphrase, you can avoid this difficulty.

Research with compressed speech illustrates the human capacity for efficient listening. In this technique, taped material is speeded up mechanically to more than 300 words per minute. Incredibly, there is no loss of comprehension at this faster rate. Tests even reveal increased comprehension, much as the tests given to people who have been taught to speed-read show an increase in their retention of information. Because of the rapid speeds, the test participants anticipated retention problems and thus forced themselves to listen more attentively and concentrate more fully than they would otherwise have done.[20]

Concentration also requires the listener to control for distractions. As a listener, you probably have a whole list of things that you have to attend to in addition to the speaker's message. Rather than attempting to dismiss them, control your concentration by mentally setting these other issues aside for the moment to give the speaker your full attention. It takes mental and physical energy to do this, but concentration is the key to successful listening.

ROLE OF PARAPHRASING   Paraphrasing—making a summary of the ideas you have just received—will provide you with a concise restatement of what has been presented. It also will allow you to determine whether you understand the material. If you cannot repeat or write down a summary of what was said, then you probably did not get the whole message or did not understand it. Keep this in mind when you are listening to an instructor and taking notes. Try to paraphrase the material, putting it into your own words, instead of writing down direct quotations. If you cannot paraphrase, you should ask for clarification or make a note to look up that particular material later on.

Try verbally paraphrasing the next time you are engaged in a demanding conversation, such as when you are receiving directions. Repeat back to the speaker what you think she or he just said in order to check whether you both received and understood the same things. One of the benefits of paraphrasing is that it eliminates the common complaint that you weren't listening. Giving people back the ideas they have just presented makes it impossible for them to support the claim that you were not paying attention.

Perception

As the message is received and attended to, the listener's perceptions play an important role. Perceiving is an active process. During the act of **perception,** a person takes the material received and attempts to analyze what has been input. Perception is a screening process. The *perceptual filter* strains the stimuli you receive to separate what makes sense from what doesn't so that you can organize and interpret the message.

The act of perception might be compared to the actions of a chef who strains ingredients in order to filter what he wants from what he is not interested in using— for example, separating pasta from water by passing it through a colander. The strainer can be compared to your perceptual filter. As you listen to a message, your perceptual filter (the colander) strains the information to which you are listening. This filter is your frame of reference through which you screen messages. It is made up of your life experiences, including your background, culture, roles you play (e.g., child, student, parent), mental and physical states, beliefs, attitudes, and values.

As listeners, we use our *selective perception* to narrow our attention to specific bits or pieces of information. The uniqueness of an idea, or whether the idea triggers a need in you, forms the basis on which you will decide to pay attention or not pay attention to a particular message. The more relevant, or the more novel the stimuli, the more likely it will be perceived by the listener.

The perceptual screen through which you receive and interpret messages is, essentially, your sensorium. This *sensorium* frames your perceptual filter so that all of your senses are brought to bear as you logically and emotionally respond to information. Through this sensorium, listeners perceptually select those messages that will be received, attended to, and interpreted. The perceptual screen is a constant process of tuning in and tuning out stimuli.

Perception plays a major role in how you function as a listener. Essentially, the principle is that "you hear what you want to see and hear." As a result, a patient returning to a physician to get the results of medical tests may have a perceptual mindset that he is very ill. Therefore, he may not hear the physician say, "Your test results are fine," and instead will come out of the doctor's office convinced that he's going to die or that the doctor was not telling him the truth.

Likewise, listeners' perceptual filters frame interpretations so that no two people ever share the exact meaning of a message. Because everyone experiences life differently, every person's perceptual filter is basically different. Thus, we come to understand information in subtly different or even extremely different ways. For example, have you ever heard a speech and then, after discussing it with a friend with whom you had attended the event, realized that you each had come to a very different conclusion about what the speaker had said?

Assignment of Meaning

Once you have paid attention to the material presented, the next stage in the listening process is to categorize the message so as to assign meanings to its verbal and nonverbal stimuli.

ROLE OF ASSIGNING MEANING The *assignment of meaning*—the process of putting the stimulus into some predetermined category—develops as we acquire our language system. We develop mental categories for interpreting the messages we receive. For instance, our categorizing system for the word *cheese* may include such factors as food, dairy products, taste, and nourishment, all of which help us relate the word *cheese* to the context in which it is used.

The categorical assignment of meaning creates *schema*—scripts for processing information. The mental representations that we carry in our brains—*schemata*—are shaped by the language categories and the way our brains process information. Our individual culture, background, family, education, and experience all serve as the framework for creating the schema that enable us to deal with incoming information. The cognitive process draws on all of a person's schemata for the purpose of interpretation, and these schemata provide the mental links for understanding and creating meaning from the verbal and the nonverbal stimuli we receive.[21] Understanding a discussion of some of the customs and traditions on a college campus, for example, may be difficult for first-year students because they do not have the cognitive schema to relate to the information.

ROLE OF GLOBAL/LINEAR THINKING/LISTENING Each of us is unique in the way we listen and learn. Some of the differences among us are based on the way our brains work. The human brain is divided into hemispheres, and research shows that some people are prone to use one hemisphere more than the other. This *brain dominance* accounts for learning and listening in patterned ways.[22] The Linear Global Dominance activity on page 96 can help you identify your brain dominance pattern.

The left hemisphere of the brain is most responsible for rational, logical, sequential, linear, and abstract thinking. People who are left-hemisphere dominant listen and learn best when materials are presented in structured ways. They tend to prefer specifics and logic-based arguments. Because they tend to take information at face value, abstractions and generalizations don't add much to their learning. Because they are so straight-line in their learning preferences, they are **linear learners/listeners.**

The right hemisphere of the brain is responsible for intuitive, spatial, visual, and concrete matters. It is from the right hemisphere of the brain that we are able to visualize. Those with this listening and learning dominance prefer examples rather than technical explanations. They prefer knowing that the information can be useful and applied. The right-brain–dominant

Socially Communicating

Linear and Global Listeners in Relationships

Linear listeners prefer what might be termed deliberate listening. This is a process of sorting out the acceptable and unacceptable elements of the messages. This doesn't meet the needs of the global listener who needs to be empathized with and contributes to chronic frustration with the linear partner and eventually dissatisfaction with the relationship itself.

Source: Rebecca Cutter, *When Opposites Attract: Right Brain/Left Brain Relationships and How to Make Them Work* (New York: Dutton Books, 1994), p. 65.

REFLECT ON THIS:

You are in a relationship with a person whose listening style is not parallel to yours (e.g., he is linear, you are global; she is global, you are linear).

1. What specific things can you do to ensure that you receive the other person's message as effectively as possible?

2. What can you suggest that the other person do to receive your message as effectively as possible?

Linear/Global Dominance[23]

Answer all of the questions quickly; do not stop to analyze them. When you have no clear preference, choose the one that most closely represents your normal attitudes or behaviors.

1. When I buy a new product, I
   ____ a. usually read the directions and carefully follow them.
   ____ b. refer to the directions, but really try to figure out how the thing operates or is put together on my own.

2. Which of these words best describes the way I perceive myself in dealing with others?
   ____ a. Structured/rigid
   ____ b. Flexible/open-minded

3. Concerning hunches:
   ____ a. I generally would not rely on hunches to help me make decisions.
   ____ b. I have hunches and follow many of them.

4. I make decisions mainly based on
   ____ a. what experts say will work.
   ____ b. a willingness to try things that I think might work.

5. In traveling or going to a destination, I prefer
   ____ a. to read and follow a map.
   ____ b. get directions and map things out "my" way.

6. In school, I preferred
   ____ a. geometry.
   ____ b. algebra.

7. When I read a play or novel, I
   ____ a. see the play or novel in my head as if it were a movie or TV drama.
   ____ b. read the words to obtain information.

8. When I want to remember directions, a name, or a news item, I
   ____ a. visualize the information or write notes that help me create a picture and maybe even draw the directions.
   ____ b. write structured and detailed notes.

9. I prefer to be in the class of a teacher who
   ____ a. has the class do activities and encourages class participation and discussions.
   ____ b. primarily lectures.

10. In writing, speaking, and problem solving, I am
   ____ a. usually creative, preferring to try new things.
   ____ b. seldom creative, preferring traditional solutions.

Scoring and Interpretation: Give yourself one point for each question you answered *b* on items 1 to 5 and *a* on 6 to 10. This total is your score. To assess your degree of linear or global preference, locate your final score on this continuum:

1 2 3 4 5 6 7 8 9 10

The lower the score, the more linear tendency you have. People with a score of 1 or 2 are considered highly linear. Scores of 3 and possibly 4 show a linear tendency.

The higher the score, the more global tendency you have. People with scores of 9 or 10 are considered highly global. Scores of 7 and possibly 6 indicate a global tendency.

If you scored between 4 and 7, you have indicated you probably do not tend to favor either tendency and are probably flexible in your learning and listening style.

Bear in mind that neither tendency is superior to the other. If you are extremely linear or global, it is possible to develop some of the traits associated with the other hemisphere, or you may already have them.

person tends to be creative and rely on intuitive thinking, can follow visual and pictographic rather than written instructions, likes to explore information without necessarily coming to a conclusion, and enjoys interaction rather than lecturing. Because of their preference for a generalized rather than specific description, right-brain–dominant persons are often labeled as **global listeners/learners.** Global learners may find much of the traditional lecture method of teaching in U.S. schools and universities, a linear methodology, to be dull and frustrating.

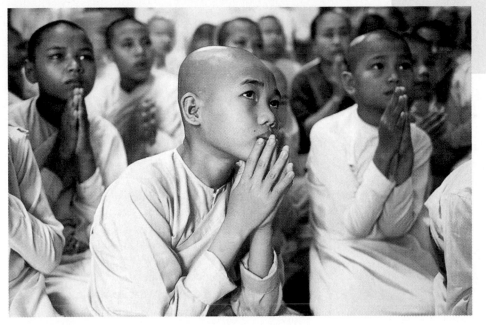

Some cultures stress being mindful, giving complete and full attention, in order to be a good listener.

Many people are a combination of global and linear learners and listeners. If you fall into this classification, you tend to be more flexible in how you listen and learn than those with extreme style preferences.

It is helpful for you to recognize your listening and learning-processing styles because this understanding can make a difference in the way you approach listening and learning environments. If you know that you need examples and the speaker is not giving them, you should ask for them. If the speaker is not drawing specific conclusions and not speaking in a structured format, and these are necessary for your understanding, then you must probe for information that will allow you to organize the ideas. Don't assume that the speaker knows how you need to receive information; the person doesn't. Most classroom instructors teach based on his or her own listening and learning style, forgetting that all students don't learn that way. If you are a global listener and learner, this may explain why you had trouble with some math or science classes. On the other hand, if you are a linear listener and learner, literature and poetry classes may have been difficult for you.

For a comparison between linear and global characteristics, see Figure 4.4.

ROLE OF CULTURE IN LISTENING   Like brain dominance, a person's culture influences listening and learning abilities. Some cultures, such as many in Asia, stress good listening by being a silent communicator in order to receive messages. People in Japan, for example, are likely to spend less time talking on the job than do European Americans, stressing instead the listening aspect of communication. In addition, some cultures stress concentration, which results in longer attention spans. Buddhism adheres to a principle called "being mindful." This means giving whatever you are doing your complete and full attention. Training to have long attention spans starts in childhood. To those raised in a typical European American environment, these listening-enhancing concepts may not be part of their background.[24]

Edward Hall's Theory of High and Low Context Cultures[25] postulates that in *low-context cultures*, such as the United States and Canada, communicators expect to give and receive a great deal of information, since these cultures perceive that most message information is contained in words. In *high-context cultures*, such as Japan and Saudi

Research shows that the following are the tendencies of people with left-brain or right-brain characteristics. The characteristics listed are for those who have extreme right- or left-brain tendencies. Of course, some people have been taught to adjust to their patterns and may not presently act exactly as described.

Linear-Brain Characteristics

- Prefers maps to oral directions.
- When trying something new, he or she likes to think about it before doing it.
- Likes to do things one at a time.
- Has a serious attitude about things.
- Is time conscious, likes for meetings to start and end on time.
- Likes agendas, program booklets, outlines, lists, written contracts, and agreements.
- Likes neatness in self and others.
- Fairly long attention span, able to concentrate on one subject for a long period of time.
- Is not a risk taker; careful, does not like to make mistakes.
- Likes to follow written directions that are numbered.
- Will ask many questions before making a decision.
- Is sometimes stubborn and very cautious when placed in a problem-solving situation.
- Likes multiple-choice and true-or-false tests rather than essay exams.

Global-Brain Characteristics

- Prefers directions that are explained or demonstrated; doesn't like maps.
- Likes to try things that he or she has not tried before.
- Likes to do several things at once.
- Likes essay tests for which he or she writes out the answer rather than multiple-choice or true-or-false tests.
- Is good at thinking up funny things to say or creative solutions to problems.
- Can tell whether or not someone is happy without the person's telling him or her (good at reading nonverbal signs).
- Often has own concept of time.
- Dislikes structured situations, details, and agendas.
- High tolerance for clutter, disorganization.
- Is a risk taker, does not always fear failure.
- Has a short attention span; daydreamer, mind wanders easily.
- Likes to picture the answers to a problem in his or her head.
- Likes to guess at the answer or use intuition in a problem-solving situation.
- When reading a book, sees the images as if he or she were watching a TV show or movie.

Figure 4.4   A Comparsion of Linear-Mode and Global-Mode Characteristics

Source: Based on concepts developed by Dr. Paul Torrance and Dr. Bernice McCarthy, Excell, Inc., P. O. Box 6, Fox River Grove, IL.

Arabia, more of the information is situated in the communicators themselves and in the communication setting, so fewer words are necessary. In high-context cultures, it is the responsibility of the listener to understand; in low-context cultures, it is the speaker who is responsible for making sure the listener comprehends all. This concept translates into communication patterns for certain people. For example, in some cultures, such as the Navajo culture, listening is the most valued communication skill.[26]

ROLE OF EVALUATION   One of the greatest barriers to effective listening is the tendency to evaluate the stimuli we receive, regardless of whether the stimuli are relevant to the message. In fact, this tendency has long been thought to be the most persistent barrier to communication that we have to overcome.[27] Although assigning meaning to stimuli often requires a quick evaluation, listeners should attempt to avoid instant judgments based primarily on superficial factors. Sometimes if you feel you don't have enough information, or you need to study the information, it may be better for you not to come to a conclusion yet.

A strategy useful to listeners in assigning meaning to messages is to differentiate *factual statements* (those based on observable phenomena or common acceptance) from *opinions* (inferences or judgments made by the speaker).

It also is helpful for the listener to sift through verbal obscurities and work for clarification of meanings. Unclear terms and phrases, euphemisms, and evasive language make interpretation difficult. The effective listener asks questions and seeks clarification from speakers and the contextual cues in their messages.

Listeners also benefit from recognizing what their emotional biases are and how those biases affect interpretations of messages. One way to discover such biases is to draw up a list of terms and phrases that serve as *red flags* (negative reactions) or *green flags* (positive stimulators) that trigger emotional responses. Recognition of such emotional triggers is a good first step toward compensating for the knee-jerk reactions that effectively tune out the speaker or cause you to daydream. Some people have red flag reactions, for example, to such words and concepts as *gay rights, taxes, abortion,* and, yes, *grades.* Some have green flag reactions to such ideas as *vacation, new car,* or *the name of a favorite sports team.*

The assignment of meaning is a complex process involving categorizing, evaluating, filtering through verbal obscurity, and recognizing emotional biases.

Culturally Communicating

Listening: Collective versus Individual Cultures

Collectivist cultures (e.g., Japan, Korea, and China) place a higher value on listening than do individualistic cultures (the U.S. and Canada). Native Americans tend to be more collectivist and are similar to people from Asia in their views of storytelling as a means of preserving and maintaining the traditions of the culture.

Source: Pamela Cooper, Carolyn Calloway-Thomas, and Cheri Simonds, *Intercultural Communication: A Text with Readings* (Boston: Pearson, 2007), p. 157.

REFLECT ON THIS:

1. What are the implications of individualism versus collectivism for a U.S. American or a Canadian communicator when interacting with someone from Japan, Korea, or China, or a Native American?

2. Why do you think that cultures have different attitudes toward the role of listening?

Response

Once we have assigned meaning to a message, we continue the information processing with an internal and/or external response—an intellectual or emotional reaction—to

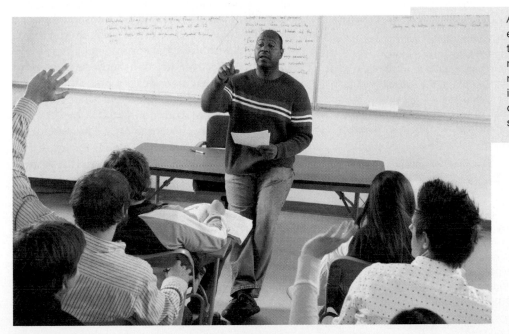

Asking questions enables the listener to ensure that the message he or she has received and interpreted is consistent with the original intent of the speaker.

the message. It is hypothesized that every stimulus we receive is stored internally some-where in our brain. In addition, over time the information may be moved from our short-term memory to our long-term memory. Externally, we react to the stimulus by providing feedback to the speaker in order to further the communication.

ROLE OF MEMORY TECHNIQUES   Throughout the process of listening, the working memory plays an important role. The listener must be willing (and able) to hold the message received in short-term memory long enough to attend to it while, at the same time, accessing the long-term memory to find the category "match" to assign meaning. This activity requires sufficient auditory and visual memory to maintain focus long enough to process the message.

Many people find remembering names a problem. In some cases, it may be that you don't remember because you don't listen when the name is spoken, or you don't immediately repeat the name to entrench it in your memory. But there are techniques that you can learn to improve your memory, including name recall. For example, when you are introduced to someone, you must first decide that you want to remember this person's name and then get ready to remember it. If you tend to remember things by pictures, picture the person in a particular setting—perhaps the location where you are meeting him or what she is wearing. You can remember the person either by picturing him with a sign across his chest, emblazoned with his name, or you can tie the person's name to some other mental picture. (This is a good technique for global learners who tend to remember pictures, not words.) If you tend to remember words better than pic-tures, concentrate on the name and repeat it several times to yourself, or select a famil-iar word with which the name rhymes (a good technique for linear learners since words, rather than pictures, are generally their way of remembering). Finally, repeat the name several times as you speak to the person. If you carry through on this process, the odds of your remembering the name increase greatly.

Culturally Communicating

Asian Students and Listening

When some Asian students interact with others, whether it is in a class or in an interpersonal communication event, they expect to understand what is being said, and if they do not, they usually will not express their lack of understanding because in their own cultures, it is their duty to understand without asking questions or making their lack of knowledge or understanding known to others.

Source: Pamela Cooper, Carolyn Calloway-Thomas, and Cheri Simonds, *Intercultural Communication: A Text with Readings* (Boston: Pearson, 2007), p. 157.

REFLECT ON THIS: One of your authors taught at a university with a very large Asian population. He encouraged class discussion and question-asking during classes. He found that almost none of the Asian students would participate in the discussions or ask questions. What strategies could he have used to get the Asian students to participate?

ROLE OF QUESTIONS   One area of response that can assist listeners in storing information in long-term memory and, at the same time, provide meaningful feedback to speakers, is asking ques-tions. This enables listeners to ensure that the message they have received and interpreted is consistent with the speaker's original intent.

To be effective, questions must be relevant to the message that the speaker presented. When asking questions, try to figure out what you don't understand. Most commonly, difficulties in per-ceiving information center on a lack of under-standing of vocabulary, a need for clarifying examples, or a need for the material to be pre-sented in a different format or order.

For example, you are taking notes in class and can't paraphrase the instructor's ideas so that you can write them down. One of the mistakes students often make is not to say anything. If it is important for you to gain the information, you must probe for meaning. If an opportunity is available, such as when a teacher indicates that questions are welcome, use that invitation to your advantage. When asking for information, just don't say, "I don't understand." The instructor won't be able to clarify; you haven't provided the clues needed to be of help. It is common in certain academic subjects for the vocabulary to be new and unusual. If you don't understand the terms being used, ask, "Would you please define [fill in the term]?" Or if you vaguely understand but need something more, you could ask, "Would you please give several examples to illustrate [insert the specific topic]?" (This is often what people who are global learners need to have in order to grasp the idea, because they require examples they can picture rather than memorizing words.) If you don't understand the concept, you could ask, "Could you restate the concept of [fill in the topic] in a step-by-step process?" (This is a technique for linear learners, who need the structure to understand what may be confusing because it was not put in a patterned manner.) In each case, you are specifically centering on what needs to be done to help you gain information. The same techniques work on the job and in other situations in which getting and using information is important.

ROLE OF FEEDBACK   Good listeners are conscious of the role of *feedback cues;* they recognize the importance of giving the speaker an understanding of whether they received the message. Asking questions, nodding or shaking your head, smiling or frowning, and verbalization such as "uh-huh" or "um?" are all forms of listener feedback. Feedback responses can be verbal or nonverbal, and they should function to enhance or reinforce the communication.

Rather than enter into the listening process passively, assume an active role as a listening communicator, sending feedback that will help both you and the speaker accomplish the goal of meaningful communication.

Listening Influencers

It should be clear that the process of listening, through which the listener receives, attends to, perceives, assigns meaning to, and responds to messages, is complex. To be effective, the listener must be actively involved throughout this process and work to overcome barriers that may arise. Certain key influencers can facilitate or hinder the process.

ROLE OF THE SPEAKER   The speaker's credibility—that is, the listener's perception of the speaker's trustworthiness, competence, and dynamism—can lead the listener to

Noise (interference in the communication process) can diminish the effectiveness of the speaker–listener interaction.

accept or reject a message. Unfortunately, some listeners are so in awe of a particular speaker that they may lose all objectivity in analyzing the person's message. For example, if the speaker is a Hollywood celebrity or an athletic superstar, the listener may overlook that he is not an expert in the specific subject in question. If the listener accepts the speaker's message simply because he is a celebrity, the receiver may be overlooking the logical weaknesses of the presentation. To be a discerning listener, it is important to listen to the message, not just to the status of the speaker.

The speaker's physical presentation—animation, appearance, clothing—can have an instantaneous effect on listener attention. A speaker who is dynamic and humorous may be able to get past the critical listening abilities of certain listeners. During the 2008 presidential nomination process both Barack Obama and Mike Huckabee were noted as being charismatic speakers and, as a result, gained many followers, even those whose political viewpoints were different from those of the candidates.

ROLE OF THE MESSAGE   Another major influencer is the message itself. If the presentation is not clearly organized—if the arguments are not well ordered—the listener may have difficulty concentrating on and staying tuned in to the message.

The tone and the treatment of the message can also affect a person's listening abilities. Some religious speakers, for example, are known for their ability to put fear into the minds of their listeners when they prophesy eternal damnation. Listeners must ascertain whether the message is appropriate for them and whether they believe in the prophecies presented.

ROLE OF THE CHANNEL   The communication channel can influence listening ability. Some people are more auditory, while some are more visual in orientation. The public speaker, for example, who couples the message with clear visual aids may assist listeners in comprehending the material. Electronic channels versus face-to-face presence also can have an effect. For instance, television has changed the nature of political campaigning. Historically, candidates had to appear in person before an audience, where listeners could have some physical contact with them. Now, sound bites, thirty-second spots, videotaped messages, and debates in which listeners can't actively participate in the experience have made for drastic differences. Likewise, candidates are making increased use of voice mail and the Internet, including blogs and social networks, to reach potential voters.

Students have reacted both positively and negatively to varying channels of communication. For example, the concept of distance learning, in which television sets and computer screens replace a live instructor, has met with mixed reactions. Some like that the instructor cannot call on the listener, that the message can be viewed whenever the receiver wants to listen or watch, and that they can replay the material for reinforcement. On the other hand, some students think that using the linear model of communication in which there is a separation between the listener and speaker causes a sterile environment and eliminates the possibility for feedback and adaptation.

ROLE OF EXTERNAL AND INTERNAL VARIABLES   Noise (any sort of interference) in the communication channel can diminish the effectiveness of the listener. Static on the telephone or distortions on the television screen can interrupt good listening. Noise from the environment also affects listeners. If the lighting is poor or the room temperature is too cold or too hot, the listener may have greater difficulty concentrating on the speaker's message. Control of or adjustment for the distraction may be necessary—for example, moving to a different spot so that you can see or hear the speaker more readily, adjusting the auditory or visual channel in some way, or negotiating with the speaker to move to a better environment.

Listeners are influenced not only by a vast array of external factors but also by internal ones. Receivers are affected by their physical state (general or psychological health), experiences (background, life history, training), attitudes (predispositions), memory, and expectations. The listener's culture also can be influential. People from different cultures have different ways of attending to each other, as indicated by the amount of eye contact, distance between each other, and the degree of patience. For example, in some South American cultures, it is perceived as bad manners to look directly into the eyes of a speaker, especially if the presenter is an authority figure. Some Arabic and Asian cultures stress standing very close to people while conversing, often holding hands, which causes many European Americans to be uncomfortable, thus making concentration difficult.

The positive or negative attitude the listener carries into a listening situation (in conjunction with expectations for the experience) is important. For example, a listener who goes to a training session convinced beforehand that it will be a waste of time will probably carry that negative attitude into the session and refuse to suspend judgment and listen comprehensively.

The listener's positive or negative attitude extends to himself or herself as a listener. Just as speakers have self-concepts, so too do listeners. Most people have had very little praise or external rewards for good listening but have probably heard lots of negative messages such as, "Keep quiet and listen" and "Why don't you ever listen to me?" These negative messages, which are often received from a very early age, can create a negative attitude in people about their listening abilities.

ROLE OF TIME   The listener has to have the time, and be willing to take the time, to listen with discrimination and comprehension. Well-intentioned listeners find it useful to recognize that they are busy and distracted. You must be willing, however, to mentally set aside or "bracket" the other internal factors competing for your attention ("Yes, I do have to finish that memo") and focus on the speaker and his or her message at the moment (". . . but first I need to listen to . . .").

> ### Socially Communicating
>
> **Listening by Quieting Your Inner and Outer Voice**
>
> The first thing to notice about our intrapersonal communication, is how it can interfere with the process of listening effectively to others. We need to quiet our inner voice, as well as our outer voice, if we are to fully comprehend what others have to tell us. We cannot fill a full cup. If we are to truly listen to friends and colleagues we must first empty our own cup (our mind) of thoughts so we have room for the ideas of the speaker. The process of quieting the mind takes personal effort and discipline.
>
> *Source:* Deborah Borisoff and Michael Purdy, *Listening in Everyday Life: A Personal and Professional Approach* (Lanham, MD: University Press of America, 1991), p. 25.
>
> **REFLECT ON THIS:** The author encourages you to "quiet [your] inner voice." That is easy to say, but hard to do. What specifically can you, as a listener, do to quiet your inner voice so that it doesn't interfere with receipt of the message?

Purposes of Listening

We listen on a number of levels, for a variety of purposes: to distinguish among sounds, gain ideas, discriminate among ideas, aid others, and appreciate sounds or symbols. Awareness of the purposes of listening sometimes helps a listener select the listening techniques that best fit the desired outcome.[28]

Discriminative Listening

In **discriminative listening,** we attempt to distinguish auditory and visual stimuli. Through discrimination, we can come to understand differences in verbal sounds (dialects, pronunciation) and nonverbal behavior (gestures, facial reactions). By understanding such differences, we gain sensitivity to the sights and sounds of our world. We can then determine, for example, whether a person is being sarcastic,

Communicating in Careers

Business Listening: Don't Multitask

Don't multitask if you are supposed to be listening. For example, if you are on a conference call, don't try to read your emails at the same time. You wind up listening to only part of what someone says, or pretending to listen while you think about or do something else. You also sacrifice important nonverbal cues and information about their intent, their confidence level, and their commitment level. Even if you think that you can get enough of what people say while multitasking to serve your immediate purpose, you should assume as a general rule that people notice when you don't listen to them attentively.

Source: "How to Listen (Attentive Listening Skills)," businesslistening.com.

REFLECT ON THIS: Have you ever tried to multitask while listening? For example, have you ever driven your car and listened to a friend, or carried on business on a cell? Or have you ever carried on a face-to-face conversation while texting someone? What was the result?

cautious, negative, or uncooperative because we realize that the same set of words can be taken in a variety of ways.

Discriminative listening also is important when we come in contact with some of the non-human features of our everyday lives. We may listen, for instance, to household appliances to determine whether they are functioning properly. People in professions such as music, medicine, and technology often find discrimination to be their most important listening skill.

It is interesting to check your own level of listening discrimination. Read the directions for the rest of this paragraph. *Directions:* Stop reading. Close your eyes for about one minute. Listen to the sounds around you, then open your eyes and answer these questions: What sounds did you recognize? What sounds were unfamiliar to you? What effect did these sounds have on you as you processed them?

Is it important for you to be a discriminative listener? Daily you encounter sounds to the point that you just screen out most of them. However, if your vehicle's engine is making an unusual whining noise, you should know that you need to get it to a service technician right away. Or listen to your own voice as you are involved in a conflict. When the pitch and volume increase, these changes may indicate that you are getting stressed and could become verbally or physically abusive. Discriminative listening is an important but overlooked type of listening.

Comprehension Listening

In **comprehension listening,** the objective is to recognize and retain the information in a message. This need for understanding has led to the development of the Theory of Listening Fidelity, which postulates that how much listeners understand a speaker's message is consistent with the speaker's understanding of the message received.[29]

To comprehend a message consistent with the speaker's intent, the listener must first discriminate the message to recognize its auditory and visual components. But listening for comprehension goes beyond the objective of discriminating a message. At this point in the process, heightened concentration is needed. In the academic world, comprehension is imperative. The very purpose of education is often to carefully listen, understand, and remember concepts, facts and ideas.

Some techniques have been found to enhance listening comprehension to achieve listening fidelity. In the academic setting, knowing how to take notes effectively is a vital skill. "Students spend roughly 80 percent of their weekly in-class activity listening to lectures."[30] This situation is problematic for comprehensive listening since "notes provide students with an external storage mechanism for information."[31] They allow students to encode information into memory because in order to take notes, they must pay attention to, organize, and interpret lecture information. The problem with most students' note taking is that "in lecture situations, some students seem to want to record everything said by the lecturer."[32] What students need to know is how to select, organize, and interpret lecture information.[33]

There are various strategies to aid in the selection and organization of material and to concentrate on getting the main points of a message rather than all of the supporting details. That is, listen to an instructor by focusing on the main points rather than on the elaboration and details, sorting the main points and the supporting details. This can be done, for example, by drawing a vertical line down the middle of the paper, putting the main points in the left-hand column, and noting the supporting ideas in the right-hand column. Using abbreviations of commonly used words saves time in writing, which allows for more listening time. For instance, if the early part of this chapter ("The Listening Process") was given as a lecture, effectively taken notes might look like those in Figure 4.5.

The student whose notes are shown in Figure 4.5 obviously felt there were sufficient cues for understanding the material so that examples were not essential. Nevertheless, many note takers like to provide examples to help clarify material. Each note taker has to determine how much detail and how much reinforcement are necessary.

Some communication experts[34] recommend a technique called *clarifying and confirming* to improve concentration. This strategy calls for the listener to ask for additional information or explanation. This system works well when added to a technique known as *bridging:* relating one part of the message to another. Good radio and television talk-show hosts use this system when interviewing guests. National Public Radio's award-winning interviewer Terri Gross is excellent at using paraphrasing (repeating ideas), verbal feedback ("uh-huh" and "that's an interesting idea"), internal summaries (summarizing one topic before going on to the next), and bridging (indicating what topic or idea she'd like to talk about next by referring to a quotation in a book or one just made by the speaker). The abilities of clarifying, confirming, and bridging are important tools for individuals going

| Lstn
Lstn Process | Hearing—biological process
Ltng—active processing of info heard
Reception—get message
Attention
　focus on ideas
　anticipate next point
　paraphrase—restate in own words
　get ready to lstn
Perception—screen info
Assignment of meaning—categorize symbols
　global—linear thinking
　role of culture
　role of evaluation
Response—info storage
　choose to remember
　visualize what is to be remembered
　associate info
　practice material
Lstng influences
　speaker |
| Purposes of Lstng | 　message
　channel
　noise
　internal variables
　attitude
　memory
　time |

Figure 4.5
Note-Taking Format

into listening professions such as counseling, social work, police work, newscasting, and reporting.

Remembering the main points at a later time also may require the development of a number of memory techniques. Some research indicates that a person can lose as much as half of any given information after the first day without taking notes and reviewing them. Because it is so easy to lose information in memory storage, good listeners work to gain the information presented. Some students have found, for example, that they retain ideas best if they review the information immediately after it is presented and then go over it daily rather than waiting until the night before an examination to cram.

Using comprehension and discriminative listening as the foundation, people listen for special purposes: to provide a therapeutic setting for a person to talk through a problem, critically evaluating a persuasive message, or appreciating aspects of a particular message.

Therapeutic Listening

Listening at the therapeutic level is important for those in such fields as mental health, social work, speech therapy, and counseling. **Therapeutic listening** requires a listener to learn when to ask questions, when to stimulate further discussion, and when, if ever, to give advice.

Therapeutic listening is not restricted to professional counselors. In daily life, people often need a listener when dealing with a problem. The listener can help the speaker talk through the situation. To be effective in this role, therapeutic listeners must have empathy for the other person—the ability to understand that person's problem from her own perspective by momentarily putting themselves into her shoes and attempting to see the world as she sees it. This is difficult for many people to do, as there is a tendency to want to solve the other person's problem and help rid her of the pain.

How can you learn to be an effective therapeutic listener? The training given to hot-line volunteers includes teaching them to resist the temptation to jump in with statements such as "The same thing happened to me" or "If I were you, I would . . ." Don't diminish the person's feeling pain. Saying, "That's no big problem" doesn't help diminish the hurt. In addition, remember that there is nothing wrong with silence. Listen patiently. The person in pain may need time to feel the ache and get in touch with her thoughts and feelings. Inserting any sound may interfere with that inner speech process.

A direct device that can be helpful is for the listener to help the speaker generate a list of possible alternatives from which that person may choose. Allowing the person to choose, rather than you giving him your solution, will allow the person to develop a commitment to carrying out the action.

Skill in therapeutic listening is important, not only for mental and medical health professionals but also for managers, parents, teachers, colleagues, and friends to provide for emotional support. Having someone to listen to stories, experiences, and fears is a way many cope with tragedy and frightening situations such as the terrorist attacks that occurred on September 11, 2001, school and drive-by shootings and violence, and the deaths and traumas of family members and friends.

Critical Listening

Critical listening centers on the listener's comprehending and evaluating the message that has been received. A critical listener assesses the arguments and the appeals in a message and then decides whether to accept or reject them.

An understanding of the tools of persuasion and the process of logic and reasoning enables critical listeners to make judgments about the merits of the messages they receive. Judgments should take into account such factors as:

- *The personal appeal of the speaker.* The speaker's credibility stems from the position held (e.g., sports celebrity), expertise, trustworthiness, and dynamism. The critical listener needs to recognize how much this credibility is influencing how the message is being understood and analyzed.

- *The speaker's arguments and evidence.* Does the speaker present a logical argument supported by substantive and relevant data?

- *The speaker's motivational appeals.* How is the speaker attempting to get the listener involved in the message? What appeals to the listener's needs are used to get the listener to respond to a persuasive message?

- *Assumptions on the part of the speaker.* Does the speaker assume that something is a fact before it has been established as such? Just because someone says, "It is readily apparent that . . ." doesn't make it so.

- *What is not said.* In some cases, the speaker implies rather than states ideas, so the listener is forced to read between the lines to supply the message. "You know what I mean" is a remark to which the listener should be alert. What do you really know from what was said?

Critical listeners should be aware of these factors and assess the merits of a particular message. Sales pitches, advertising messages, campaign speeches, and persuasive briefings all require critical analysis.

As a communication student, you probably will be called on to critique the speeches of fellow students. In this mode of critical listening, your role is to provide information to help speakers improve their work. Offer comments on what the speaker does effectively as well as what the speaker needs to improve. Deal with content (topic choice, structure, supporting materials, clarity, and interest) and delivery (animation, vocal dynamics, and eye contact).

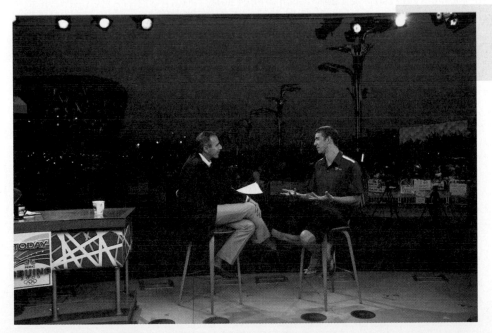

A media interviewer uses paraphrasing, verbal feedback, internal summaries, and bridging.

Appreciative Listening

Appreciative listening takes place when a person engages in enjoyment of or sensory stimulation to a message, such as listening to humorous speakers, comedians, or music videos. Appreciation is a highly individual matter. Some people believe that the more knowledge they have about a particular subject or artistic form, the more they can appreciate it. Others feel that the more they know about something, the more they lose their ability to appreciate all but the best.

Listening Apprehension

Not only are some people apprehensive when they speak, but they may also be apprehensive when they must or are given the opportunity to listen. **Listener apprehension,** "the fear of misinterpreting, inadequately processing, and/or not being able to adjust psychologically to messages sent by others,"[35] is a concern for many people. It may be a short-term fear, such as the anxiety associated with knowing you are going to receive a negative evaluation, or the fear of the person who is going to talk to you or what he might say. For example, in the context of physician–patient interaction, the difference in power roles between you as a patient and the doctor as the expert may interfere with your ability to listen to your physician calmly and accurately. You also might be afraid of what the doctor might say, so you dread listening.

Listener apprehension also may be a long-term disability. There are individuals who have lived their entire lives being told they are poor listeners and have come to believe it. There are others who have a hearing or vision disability and fear that they will miss the core of the message in listening situations.

Listening anxiety may make it difficult to understand, process, and remember a message. It may make a person less able to interact effectively, less willing to communicate, and less confident about communication abilities. Further, if a listener is emotional about the content of the message, that emotional response may take so much attention energy that it can increase apprehension.

If you experience listening apprehension, here are some suggestions that might help:

- Realize that worrying isn't going to make you a better listener, so if you can't avoid the situation, then you must force yourself to participate and accept that you will do the best job you can.

- If appropriate, have a writing instrument and paper to take notes. Taking notes forces you to listen and, if you paraphrase the message, it allows you to know if you understand. If not, ask questions to clarify what has been said.

- Repeat back the ideas of the speaker as you listen so that you can assure yourself that you are receiving the message and that you are letting the other person know that you are listening and understanding.

- Prepare questions and formulate ideas in advance if you know you are going to be evaluated or will need to defend yourself or your ideas.

- If there has been an agenda, memo, or outline of what will be discussed, such as for a meeting or a class, go over the material ahead of time and get ready to listen.

- Get ready for the session. If you are at work, have the ideas researched. For the classroom situation, read and prepare the assignment.

- Prepare notes to use during the discussion. That way you won't have to worry about not having anything of value to say.

Improving Your Listening

Effective listening is a complex, involved, and involving process requiring a great deal of commitment on the part of the listener. Despite its complexities, you can do a great deal to improve your skill as a listener.

Improvement of listening skills requires breaking old habits, putting new strategies in their place, and practicing these new skills until they feel comfortable and are part of your listening repertoire.

Here are some suggestions to help listeners develop greater skills:

1   *Recognize that both the sender and receiver share responsibility for effective communication.* If you are sending a message, you should define terms, structure your message clearly, and give your receiver the necessary background to respond effectively. As a receiver, you should ask questions and provide feedback if you cannot understand the speaker's point. If possible, repeat the major ideas so that the speaker can check to be sure you have grasped the meaning.

2   *Suspend judgment.* One of the greatest barriers to human communication is the tendency to form instant judgments about information we encounter. As listeners, we are prone to assess speakers prematurely, before we have even comprehended the entire message. Unstated thoughts such as "I don't like his voice" and "This is a boring lecture" set up barriers to effective listening. Good listening requires setting aside these judgments and listening for the message.

3   *Be a patient listener.* Avoid interrupting or tuning out until the entire message has been communicated. We often find ourselves beginning to act before we have totally understood what is being said. This is especially true of global listeners, who often act intuitively on perceived information.

Think about how difficult it is to assemble a new product until you thoroughly comprehend the instructions. Or remember the times you filled out a form, only to realize later that you put down your first name when the directions

Socially Communicating

Listening: Send "Tell-Me-More" Signals

Good listeners use these techniques to get all the information they need before they act on what they've heard:

- **Examples.** "Please give me an example so I'll have a better idea of what you mean."

- **Illustrations.** "Could you illustrate that point to show me how it works?"

- **Statistics.** "What's the date on that information?" "Can you get more data on that?"

- **Authorities.** "Who said that?" "Do the experts you cite agree on this?" "Do these experts have other positions on this subject?"

- **Analogies.** "Can you compare that to the situation we faced last week?" "How does this model compare to the other one?"

- **Explanations.** "What are some of the specific problems you're having?" "Can you give me more details?" "Please explain how it works."

- **Restatements.** "Would you repeat that? I want to make sure I've got it right."

Source: The New Time Manager, by Angela V. Woodhull, Gower Publishing, Ltd., Gower House, Croft Road, Hampshire GU11 3HR, UK.

REFLECT ON THIS: In order for you to get all the information given by a speaker, which of these questions is generally most important for you to ask? Why? Which is the next most important? Why?

said your last name should come first. Patience in listening will help you avoid having to go back over messages you missed the first time or did not understand because you did not let the whole message come through.

4 *Avoid egospeak.* **Egospeak** is the "art of boosting our own ego by speaking only about what we want to talk about, and not giving a hoot in hell about what the [other] person is speaking about."[36] When you jump into a conversation and speak your piece without noticing what the other person is trying to communicate or listen only to the beginning of another's sentence before saying, "Yes, but . . . ," you are engaging in egospeak. As a result, you do not receive the whole message because you are so busy thinking of what you want to say or saying it. Although egospeak is a very natural temptation, it can easily become a real barrier to communication.

Several techniques can be used to control egospeaking. First, monitor your body. Individuals who are about to interrupt have a tendency to lean forward as if to jump into the conversation and poise an arm and hand so that they can thrust them forward to cut in. If you feel your body taking these actions, be aware that you are about to egospeak—and don't.

Another way to deter yourself from egospeaking is to repeat the ideas of the speaker before you give your point of view. Be aware that if you can't summarize, you may not have listened long enough to gain the message. In future conversations, see if you can repeat the message of the speaker to yourself before you jump in.

5 *Be careful with emotional responses to words.* Inciting words, red and green flags, are those words or phrases that trigger strong feelings, either positive or negative, within us. How do you react to the words *recession, rapist,* and *spring vacation?* Words like these often send us off on tangents. In an everyday situation, you may tighten up and block out the rest of the message when your friend mentions the name of a person with whom you have just had an argument. Or you might start daydreaming about the beach when your instructor uses the word *sunshine.* Speakers should be aware that listeners can be sent off on tangents by certain words, resulting in interference with the effort to communicate. As receivers, we should be aware that we can be led astray and lose our concentration through our emotional responses.

There is no quick way to prevent yourself from reacting to inciting words. By monitoring your body, however, you might catch yourself physically pulling in, feel yourself flushing as you become upset, or catch yourself daydreaming. These responses are typical of the emotional triggers that set us off while listening.

6 *Be aware that your posture affects your listening.* When you listen to an exciting lecture, how do you sit? Usually you lean slightly forward, with your feet on the floor, and look directly at the presenter. If you slump down and stare out the window, it's unlikely that you're actively participating in the communication act taking place.

Have you ever left a classroom and felt totally exhausted? You may have been concentrating so hard that you became physically tired. After all, good listening is hard work. An effective listener learns when it is necessary to listen in a totally active way and when it is possible to relax. An analogy can explain the concept. When you're driving a car with an automatic transmission, the car shifts gears when it needs more or less power. Unfortunately, people don't come equipped with automatic transmissions; we have to shift gears for ourselves.

When you need to concentrate, shift into your active listening position: feet on the floor, posture erect, and looking directly at the speaker to pick up any necessary nonverbal clues. Once you feel that you understand the point being made (a test is the ability to paraphrase what has been said), you may want to shift your posture to a more comfortable position. When a new subject arises or when you hear transitional words or phrases such as *therefore* or *in summary,* then you shift back into your active listening position.

7   *Control distractions.* All of us are surrounded by environmental noise—the sound of machinery, people talking, music playing—that can interfere with efficient listening. If the message is important to you, try to adjust the interference or control it. If possible, turn off the machinery, or move away from it. Tell someone who is speaking to you while you are talking on the telephone that you cannot listen to both people at the same time. Turn off the radio or raise your voice so that others can hear you over the sound. Remember that there is little point in continuing the attempted communication if you cannot hear the other person or that person cannot hear you.

8   *Tune in to the speaker's cues.* An effective speaker provides the listener with verbal and nonverbal cues. You should recognize transitions (words indicating a change of idea or topic: *therefore* or *finally*), forecasts of ideas (statements that show a series of ideas: "There are three ideas that . . . ," or "The next point is . . ."), and internal summaries (restatements of ideas that have just been explained: "and so I've illustrated that . . ."). These are all vehicles for furthering your grasp of the major points the speaker is presenting.

The rate, volume, pitch, and pauses that the speaker uses also can help you understand the points being developed. By stressing words, pausing before an idea, or increasing the volume of a phrase, the speaker is telling you that something is important or significant.

The speaker's physical movements can carry a meaning that may reinforce or contradict a verbal message. For example, a speaker who uses a forceful gesture or enumerates points with the fingers can assist listeners in following the main points. We often have to listen with our eyes as well as our ears to pick up all the cues to help us understand the real message.

9   *Paraphrase.* Paraphrasing can be one of the most effective ways to sharpen concentration, because it requires careful focus and storage in short-term memory. By repeating the ideas in your answer, you let the speaker know what you have received. If your paraphrase is not correct, the speaker can clarify to help you understand what was really intended. The use of active feedback allows both of you to be sure that the message sent was the message received.

10   *Visualize.* To engage in successful communication, a good technique, especially for the global learner and listener, is to visualize the speaker's points or what he is doing when certain concepts are presented. Visual associations are a useful way to improve storage and retrieval in long-term memory. For example, a student relayed to a former instructor that even today when she hears certain topics discussed, she visualizes where the instructor stood in class and can remember what he said.

Not all the listening you do is one-on-one. People spend a great deal of time receiving media messages, including listening to iPods, cell phones, televisions, and radios. You need to understand how these messages influence the way meaning are framed and shared by society. One media specialist recommends these strategies for listeners to increase their media literacy:[37]

- Think about how realistic or how fantasized the images are.

- Compare media approaches to how a particular message is treated.

- Think about what is communicated in the presentation. Is it reasonable? Is it biased? Is it trying to manipulate you by appealing to your weaknesses?

- If you tend to believe the appeal, ask yourself why you are opening yourself to that belief.

- Be aware of when someone is trying to change your point of view. Apply this awareness by challenging the contentions before you go along with the idea.

- Recognize that much of what is on the media seeks to manipulate you to buy products or services. Recognize that commercials and factual news are not the same.

- Recognize that situation comedies, dramas, and other fictionalized stories are not reality. Real life doesn't always have happy endings, cures are not always found for diseases, and life doesn't go from beginning to end in thirty or sixty minutes.

In Conclusion

Listening is a central part of the communication process. It is a process of receiving, attending to, perceiving, assigning meaning to, and responding to messages. We listen to discriminate among auditory and visual stimuli, comprehend information, provide therapeutic support to other communicators, critically evaluate messages, and appreciate messages.

Various strategies can be undertaken to improve a person's listening skills, including shared responsibility for effective communication with the speaker, suspending judgment and being a patient listener, avoiding egospeaking, being careful with emotional responses to words, being aware that your posture affects your listening, making a conscious effort to listen, controlling distractions, tuning in to the speaker's cues, learning how to use paraphrasing, and using visualization.

People spend a great deal of time processing television, radio, and Internet messages; therefore, they need to understand how words, images, and sounds influence the way meanings are created and shared.

Learn by Doing

1. Contrast hearing and listening. Develop a verbal analogy between listening and reading.

2. Analyze your own listening. Name one listening behavior you have that does not match the characteristics of a good listener as described in this chapter. Consider how you can change this listening behavior to be more effective.

3. Now that you are aware of some of the principles of effective listening, put them into practice. At the next speech or lecture you attend, sit up, concentrate on what the speaker is saying, and focus all your attention and energy on comprehending the material. Make internal summaries and paraphrase to assist yourself. After the session is over, analyze your listening behavior and determine what you can still do to improve your comprehension.

4. Critically analyze an editorial on television. Listen for the arguments and appeals, and determine

how those persuasive elements were arranged to get a positive response from you, the listener.

5. Make a list of your "red flags" and "green flags." Go back and review these terms. Why do you think they incite you? If class time is available, your instructor will divide the class into groups of four to six students. Discuss your "red flags" and what implications they have for your communication.

6. To learn how to paraphrase, do this three-step activity:

   a. Indicate whether you thoroughly agree (TA), agree (A), disagree (D), or thoroughly disagree (TD) with each of these statements:

      (1) Prayer should be allowed in the public schools.

      (2) Stem cell research should be sanctioned and financially supported by the federal government.

      (3) Homosexual marriages should be legally sanctioned.

      (4) College students should not have required courses outside of their major area of concentration.

      (5) Gun ownership and possession should be outlawed in the United States for everyone except those entrusted with the defense of citizens (e.g., police, armed forces personnel, security guards).

   b. Your class is divided into groups of four to six students. Your task is to get everyone in the group to accept one of the attitudes (TA, A, D, or TD) for each of the preceding statements. You must paraphrase during the entire discussion. You may not give your opinion until you have summarized the statement of the person who preceded you. One member of the group acts as referee and says, "Foul" if anyone speaks without summarizing. (If time does not allow for a discussion of all five questions, your instructor will select one for discussion.)

   c. Now make a list of the positive aspects of paraphrasing as a listening technique; then list the frustrations it causes.

7. The text mentions National Public Radio's Terri Gross as an excellent interviewer and listener. Listen to a radio interview or watch a television interview and critique the listening, feedback, and follow-up skills of the interviewer. Be prepared to discuss the interviewer and specifically tell what she or he did to enhance or distract from the quality of the interview.

8. Your instructor will play a short video of a political candidate or office holder. Each class member is to critically listen to the speech. You may, as the speech proceeds, take notes. At the end of the speech, list the major points the speaker made and his or her "back-up statement" for each of those points. There will be a class discussion that will first list the major points and their back-ups (comprehensive listening), followed by a critical listening evaluation of the back-ups.

Key Terms

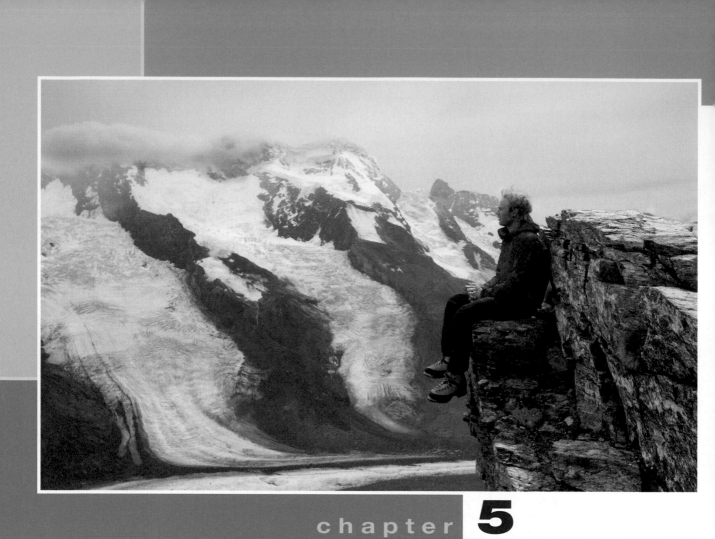

chapter 5

Intrapersonal Communication

▶ **After reading this chapter, you should be able to**

- Define and explain the concept of intrapersonal communication

- State and discuss the theory of basic drive forces as they affect inner communication

- Explain self-concept and its role as a guiding factor in a person's actions

- Define self-talk and explain its relation to our communication accomplishments

- List some options and sources for improving self-concept, self-confidence, and self-esteem (or all of them)

- Define and explain the causes, results, effects, and aids for communication apprehension

- Understand that culture has an effect on intrapersonal communication and the development of self-concept

When you lie in bed at night before you fall asleep, perhaps you review the events of the day. When you take a test, you might carry on a conversation with yourself to arrive at the answers. In both cases, you are participating in the act of **intrapersonal communication,** internally communicating with yourself.

The basis for communication with others is the ability to communicate with oneself. Those people who tend to know who they are, what they believe in, and what their attitudes are, and have a clear understanding of their beliefs, values, and expectations are much more likely to be able to communicate these ideas to others. People who can internally process ideas and decide how to present them can communicate that information to others.[1]

There is disagreement about where to draw the line as to what constitutes intrapersonal communication. For our purposes, assume that at times we talk to ourselves, such as when we debate during a test which of the multiple-choice answers is correct. Our bodies can "speak" to us nonverbally, as when muscles in the back of the neck tighten when we get emotionally upset or when our stomachs churn just before giving a speech. Also, intrapersonal communication may occur below our level of awareness, such as when we dream or daydream.

One way of understanding your intrapersonal communication and, if necessary, improving your communication skills is by understanding your self-talk.

There is a saying that it is okay to talk to yourself, but when you start answering back, it is time to worry! That tongue-in-cheek contention is basically incorrect. Indelible links exist between what we say to ourselves and what we accomplish.

Self-Talk

The starting point of any communication is **self-talk**—intrapersonally communicating within yourself. We all engage in this inner dialogue. Sometimes you are conscious of your vocalizing aloud within your head, but self-talk is often silent thinking, an internal whisper of which you are scarcely aware, or our automatic nonverbal reactions.

Culturally Communicating

Do I Have a Place in This Society?

What does it mean to be Black? . . . My mom worked long hours and she worked so very hard all her life so that she could send me to a private school. I did in fact have some Black friends but not as many as I would have liked. Does this mean I don't consider myself Black? NO! Not at all. I see myself as Black and I love being Black. But I don't know much of Black history. What I know is just the surface, and what I NEED to know is the core. What makes me sad is, I am considered to be the White girl in my family. It saddens me because they don't know my struggle deep inside. Yes, I wish I were strong in being more "ethnic," but I'm not and that scares me. Am I blind? Do I not have a place in this society?
—Lanitra, *College Student*

Source: Stella Ting-Toomey and Leava C. Chung, *Understanding Intercultural Communication* (Los Angeles, CA: Roxbury Publishing Company, 2005), p. 84.

REFLECT ON THIS:

1. During the 2008 presidential election, Barak Obama faced similar issues as the child of a mixed (white and African) marriage. Do you perceive him as black, African American, white?

2. Golfer Tiger Wood considers himself Cablinasian— Caucasian, black, Indian, and Asian—because of his racially diverse background. Do you agree with his "title" for himself?

Even though it may be quiet, its impact can be enormous. "Your behavior, your feelings, your self-esteem, and even your level of stress are influenced by your inner speech."[2] Everything that you do begins as self-talk. Self-talk shapes our inner attitudes, our attitudes shape our behavior, and of course our behavior—what we do—shapes the results we get.[3] The self-talk often triggers confidences and inquiries you have about yourself, which then affect your interpersonal communication decisions.

Think of the inner struggles you often have concerning whether you will believe something, will take a particular action, or will make a certain decision. Awake or asleep, you are constantly in touch with yourself. You mumble, daydream, dream, fantasize, and feel tension. These are all forms of inner speech.

There is controversy over whether inner speech and symbolic thought are the same thing. The major theorist in thinking and speaking postulated that "inner speech was solely thinking silently to oneself, while symbolic thought is used to make associations between or among words or concepts, thus creating word meanings."[4] For our purposes, "the term *inner speech* refers to subvocalized or silent intrapersonal spoken language used to generate symbolic and conceptual thought while in the process of creating word meanings (italics added)."[5] This inner speech allows us to silently produce words that remind us of things we need to do, things that have happened, or things we want to do. We tend to think, self-talk, continually. The voice rarely stops.[6]

In order to understand how inner speech works, it is important to be aware of how people acquire and develop language. Children go through a series of stages that enable them to develop linguistic skills. These skills enhance the ability to develop concepts and is the basis for inner speech. Given a stable environment, normally functioning senses, and a functioning cortex, all children, no matter what their nationality, learn language in a series of sequential steps.[7] (See Figure 5.1.) There is seems to be no significant difference in the speech development of boys versus girls.[8] If a child is denied normal interaction with other humans, the child will not naturally develop proficient language abilities, no matter his or her gender. When a child is born, he or she is neurologically wired to learn language and develop the ability to think in abstractions.[9] "The human brain has been tuned for social learning. We have a general-purpose device for acquiring culture, technology and language."[10] The first point of linguistic development is the involuntary cries of a child, expressing the feeling of being frightened, lonesome, hungry, wet, or in pain. At this point the child is not selecting the sound, although cries of babies can be differentiated. A baby, for

**Figure 5.1
Sequential Steps
of Linguistic
Development**

Rhetorical strategies	**Rhetorical stage**
Concept formulation	**Conceptual stage**
Sentence building	**Linguistic stage**
Selective ability	
Echoing	**Prelinguistic and**
Babbling	**preconceptual**
Reflexive vocalization	**stage**

example, who is hungry will cry with a sucking sound. The child, at this point, has no inner speech. Beginning around the sixth to the ninth month, a child starts to make sounds beyond crying. By the ninth to twelfth month, there is an echoing of the words that surround the infant. Sometime between the twelfth and fifteenth month, the child starts to select words to represent ideas, such as *coat* or *milk*. The word selected—for example, *milk*—generally represents whole ideas, such as "I want some milk."

As they grow older, children continue to develop language. A two-year-old child may have a vocabulary of 300 to 400 words, but he or she still externalizes them instead of processing information intrapersonally. A child of age four has learned the grammar of her language, but she still does not have internal speech. That is why if you watch four-year-olds playing, you will notice that they often talk out the activities they are performing to think things through. Younger children tell themselves to go, run, or hurry. The same thing happens when a child goes to bed and talks himself to sleep. Their external speech parallels an adult's self-talk, except that kids speak the ideas aloud. Children often need to talk out loud to solve problems or make decisions. Teachers who insist on a silent classroom in the first and second grades may be closing off any means their students have of adding numbers, planning activities, or understanding what they are reading. Teachers and parents who tell children to "keep quiet" teach them to internalize, often before they are ready to do so. This forced silence can lead to emotional trauma and may restrict their ability to learn. You may have experienced this when your early grade teacher didn't let you count aloud during arithmetic class or didn't let you talk as you tried to write a story. You may have become frustrated and given up, unable to carry out the task.

Children normally don't develop internalized speech until some time around age nine, when they can conceptualize—think in abstraction. Interestingly, some adults find that they need to use external processing, including reading aloud and talking to themselves while writing or taking tests, in order to comprehend. This is especially true with creative, globally-oriented speakers and listeners.

Once individuals have a usable vocabulary and the ability to think in abstractions, they begin to learn strategies to manipulate ideas and enter into the rhetorical stage. In this stage, they can adjust their speech according to the person(s) to whom they are speaking, to the purpose of the communication, and to the place where the communication is taking place. This usually occurs at age twelve or thirteen. It is at this stage that the person also has full functioning inner speech.

Self-Concept

Self-concept, your idea or picture of yourself, "is the accumulation of knowledge about the self, such as beliefs regarding personality traits, physical characteristics, abilities, values, goals and roles."[11] Your concept of your self-esteem begins in infancy and is acquired as you interact with cultural forces such as your family, religious influences and influencers, media, friends, teachers, and the others with whom you come in contact. Although you may think of your self-esteem as being a single unit, those who study self-esteem have been able to identify four areas of esteem: physical, moral-ethical, family, and social. The *physical* refers to how your perceive your body. Do you evaluate highly such aspects as your height, weight, or attractiveness? *Moral-ethical* relates to your evaluation of your belief system, your moral behavior. The *family* aspects of your self-esteem relate to your views of your family relationships, the functional system of your family, how you were treated by your parents or whoever was responsible for your upbringing. And the *social* aspects of your self-esteem are your evaluations of yourself as you regard yourself in social situations—your pleasing others and your treatment of others. The sum total of these add up to your total concept of your self-esteem.

The more positively you perceive yourself, the more likely it is that you will have self-confidence—that is, a sense of competence and effectiveness.

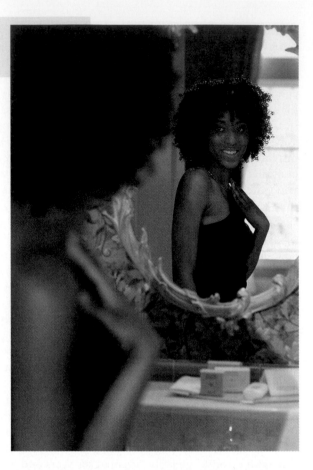

Communicating in Careers

A Business Professional Shares Her Views on Self-Concept

Profile: Linda Eaton, senior consultant, Franklin Quest Company, Salt Lake City, consultant to many of the Fortune 1000 companies.

How does a person develop a strong self-concept?
A great self-concept is acquirable. Martin Seligman's *Learned Optimism* is a great guide for businesspersons to use to assist them in the development. It basically stresses that positive people (a) take credit for their actions, (b) take responsibility, and (c) identify negative experiences as learning opportunities, not things that happen to them (a "victim") but rather things they had a hand in shaping.

Is there a correlation between positive self-confidence and leadership?
Leaders have positive self-concepts, a vision, and the confidence to develop and share that vision. Leadership builds on the belief in the self and a positive self-concept.

How does a person's self-concept affect business-people in the changing work environment, especially as it relates to downsizing and mergers?
As George Bernard Shaw once said, "Luck is the marriage of opportunity and preparation." A downsizing, a merger, or an acquisition is not necessarily a good or a bad thing. Those with strong self-concepts view their jobs as a vehicle for self-development, and therefore are less negatively emotionally impacted by change.

Source: Roy Berko, Andrew Wolvin, and Rebecca Ray, *Business Communication in a Changing World* (New York: St. Martin's Press, 1997), p. 145.

REFLECT ON THIS:

1. In this era of corporate downsizing, mergers, and layoffs, how do you think a person who has a positive self-concept will react versus a person with a negative self-concept?

2. Think of a person your know who has a positive self-concept. How do you think he or she developed that attitude?

Analyzing My Specific Self-Esteem[12]

Directions: Indicate the degree to which each item is true or false for you.

If it is completely false, mark the item 1.

If it is mostly false, mark the item 2.

If it is partly false and partly true, 3.

If it is mostly true, 4.

If it is completely true, 5.

_____ 1. I am satisfied with my weight.

_____ 2. I am satisfied with my looks.

_____ 3. I am satisfied with my height.

_____ 4. I am satisfied with my moral behavior.

_____ 5. I am satisfied with the extent to which I am religious.

_____ 6. I am satisfied with my relationship with a Supreme Being.

_____ 7. I am satisfied with my family relationships.

_____ 8. I am satisfied with how well I understand my family.

_____ 9. I am satisfied with how I treat (treated) my parents.

_____ 10. I am satisfied with how sociable I am.

_____ 11. I am satisfied with the extent to which I try to please others.

_____ 12. I am satisfied with the way I treat other people.

Scoring:

Add items 1, 2, and 3:_____. This is your _physical self-esteem score._

Add items 4, 5, and 6:_____. This is your _moral-ethical self-esteem score._

Add items 7, 8, and 9:_____. This is your _family self-esteem score._

Add items 10, 11 and 12:___. This is your _social self-esteem score._

Scores in any category between 12 and 15 indicate high self-esteem; scores between 3 and 6 indicate low self-esteem; and scores from 7 through 11 indicate moderate self-esteem.

Are you interested in probing into your self-esteem? If so, try the Analyzing My Specific Self-Esteem activity above.

Your concept of self is important because how you act and communicate with others is connected closely with your self perception.[13] Your self-esteem rises and falls, acting as an internal barometer of how well you perceive you are doing in your personal, social, and career environments. The degree to which you are comfortable with yourself has been found to affect many areas of your psychological functioning.[14] Self-esteem is perceived to relate to overall adjustment. Those with high levels tend to be less anxious in social situations than those with lower self-perceived esteem. They also tend to be less likely to be depressed, irritable, or aggressive.[15]

From the communication perspective, your self-concept often determines what you will say and to whom you will say it. For example, if you perceive yourself to be a good communicator, then you are likely to feel confident in your communication. But if you label yourself as shy or apprehensive, then you may find it difficult to express yourself. At the heart of this dynamic process is the premise that if you do not accept yourself, probably no one else will, either. A lack of confidence is easily detected by those with whom you interact.

Research shows that there seven signs that are common among those with a weak sense of self. Most people have some of these, but the person with a negative self-belief system displays many of these signs.[16]

- _Sensitivity to criticism._ This is displayed by a person not liking it when people point out any shortcomings.

- _Inappropriate response to flattery._ Most people accept flattery—in fact, they are honored by it. Those with negative self-esteem, however, tend to refuse to believe anything positive about themselves because it is inconsistent with their own perceptions. Do not mix up modest with negative reactions.

- *Hypercritical attitude.* People who do not feel good about themselves often have trouble feeling good about anyone else.
- *Tendency toward blaming.* Some people project their perceived weaknesses onto others in order to lessen the pain of thinking of themselves as inferior.
- *Feelings of persecution.* People with low self-esteem tend to believe the world is against them and constantly picking on them.
- *Negative feelings about competition.* Many of us like to win, but in order to avoid the feeling of loss, those with weak self-perceptions avoid competition because they believe they cannot win, and not winning will reinforce their negative self-views.
- *Tendency toward seclusion and timidity.* People who think they are inferior believe that they may not be as intelligent or talented or attractive or sociable as others, so they tend to avoid social situations. Or, if they do participate, they avoid speaking up so as not to embarrass themselves or reinforce their negative self-perceptions.

Some people worry about appearing too self-confident and being considered a braggart. Accepting yourself as a worthy person does not necessarily mean that you are boasting. Sometimes you have to "blow your own horn" because no one else knows how to play the tune. You know yourself better than others and know more about yourself and your skills and talents than others do. There is a difference, however, between tooting your own horn and playing a symphony (e.g., the distinction between sharing your accomplishments with others and going on and on about them or exaggerating). In this vein, consider this advice:

Your self-concept can work for or against you. "We have a choice each time we think, to think positively or negatively. Many of us don't believe it, but that absolutely is our choice. Once we understand that our private thoughts are ours alone to determine, we can select to program ourselves with empowering, confidence-building thoughts."[17] It's up to you. If you tell yourself that you're clumsy or that you aren't comfortable in social situations, that is what you probably will be, how you will act. If you create a positive scenario, positive actions will probably result.

ATTACKING NEGATIVE SELF-THOUGHTS AND BELIEFS Consider for a moment the vulture, an unattractive bird with sharp claws and a pointy beak whose favorite activity is picking on the weak, the helpless, and, preferably, the dead. It dives into the flesh and picks away at it. The *psychological vulture* does much the same thing. It attacks a person's perceived weaknesses and eats at the person's self-worth.

Are you interested in finding out about your vultures? If so, try the Identifying Your Vultures activity on the next page.

What do you call yourself when you lock your keys in the car? What do you call yourself when you trip over the edge of the carpet? Every self–put-down—"Idiot!" "Klutz!"—summons the vultures!

Put-downs may be either obvious or subtle. The obvious ones have a clear physical referent, like the keys dangling in the ignition of the locked car, or the frayed edge of the carpet on which you tripped, or the words you called yourself because of your actions or perceived actions. The subtle put-downs impose limitations on you that, though not obvious, are equally as destructive. Sample vultures include:

"I could never write a paper longer than five pages."

"I could never stick to a diet for more than a week."

"I just can't stop smoking."

Identifying Your Vultures

Directions: List as many negative statements about yourself as you can for each statement. (Don't be concerned if you can't fill in all the blanks, but try to be honest!)

My *intelligence* (e.g., "I'm dumb," "I'm no good in math.")

_____

My *creativity* (e.g., "I'm not imaginative," "I can't sing.")

_____

My *family* (e.g., "I'm the odd-ball in the family," "My brother is the favorite.")

_____

My *physicality* ("I'm too fat.")

_____

My *sexuality* ("I'm not sexy.")

_____

Me and my *relationships* ("I can't make friends," "Nobody likes me.")

_____

Psychological vultures tend to nest in six areas: *intelligence* vultures ("I'm dumb," "I'm no good in math," "I'm no good at foreign languages"); *creativity* vultures ("I'm not imaginative," "I can't draw as well as Zander," "I can't sing like Eric"); *family* vultures ("I'm the odd-ball in the family," "My brother is the favorite child"); *relationship* vultures ("I'm no good at meeting people," "I can't make friends," "I'm shy"); *physical* vultures ("I'm too short/tall/fat/thin," "My nose is too big," "My teeth are crooked"); and *sexual* vultures ("I'm not sexy," "Only a person who was desperate would want to have a relationship with me").

The results of self–put-downs are obvious: A person avoids the areas where the vultures lurk. Depending on the perceived vultures, he or she avoids such things as math classes, drawing, dates, singing, and going to social events. He or she wears large clothing to cover up their body or makes excuses for not participating in parties.

Communicating in Careers

How to Keep Your Composure

Your boss or coworker says something that irritates you—and you want to lash back. But you don't want to lose your cool at work. How can you keep your composure without experiencing a lot of stress? Some suggestions:

■ Step away and do what's called "a perception check." Ask yourself what you're really upset about. Does the situation revive something that happened to you as a child?

■ Try to understand why the person behaved that way. You might realize that the intent was not vindictive.

■ Let your feelings out on paper. Don't edit or censor a thing. Then look over what you've written and destroy the piece of paper. You'll feel better.

■ Talk with coworkers you can trust. You'll release some emotions—and you might also get an objective assessment in the situation.

■ Try to determine if you're overreacting. Ask yourself: "If this happened to my best friend, would I think that she or he was no good?" Your answer should help keep things in perspective.

■ Before you decide to confront the offender, ask yourself these questions:

"What will I gain by taking this action?"

"Will I achieve my goals with this particular person?"

Source: Nancy Monson, writing in *New Woman*, 215 Lexington Ave., New York, NY 10016.

REFLECT ON THIS: Have you ever been in a work or school situation where knowing these principles would have been of value? If so, describe the situation. Which of these principles would have been of value? Why?

Your self-talk can work for or against you. It's up to you. Tell yourself you're clumsy, or you aren't comfortable in social situations, and that is what you probably will be. "We have a choice each time we think, to think positively or negatively. Once we understand that our private thoughts are ours alone to determine, we can select to program our brains with empowering, confidence-building thoughts."[18]

How do you use self-talk to kill off your vultures? A theory regarding changing your self-defeating self-talk encourages:[19]

- Pat yourself on the back by saying something good and true about yourself. You can surely think of something for which to compliment yourself.

- Pat someone else on the back by saying something good and true about her or him. Not only will you feel good about yourself for complimenting another person, but you'll also find that compliments beget compliments.

- Recognize your self–put-downs. To make sure you catch them, you may want to ask a friend for help. Be sure to identify both the obvious and the subtle ones (and don't argue when your friend points them out). This step is crucial: You can't cure what you don't recognize! Once you start focusing on the positives, the negatives tend to go away. Negative self-talk can't survive if you don't feed it.[20]

The replacement method has been used with athletes to overcome negatives. In one study, basketball players were divided into three groups for foul-shot practice. The first group used imagery (internally picturing that they were shooting and making their shots) and negative-message elimination but did not practice shooting. The second group practiced shooting, and the third group did both corrective imaging and practicing. Although all three groups improved, the first and third groups improved by the same amount, and the second group improved less. "Positive self-talk really can turn your life around and make any life more successful."[21]

Self-Love

Self-love means accepting yourself as a worthy person because you choose to do so. Self-love has nothing to do with the sort of behavior characterized by telling everyone how wonderful you are. It means to love yourself; it doesn't demand the love of others. Self-love is the basis for accepting who and what you are and for realizing that if others can't accept you as you are, that is their problem and not yours. This is not to say that you can't listen to the input of others and attempt to make changes in yourself, but the bottom line is exercising your ability to accept yourself as a viable human being. This does not, of course, allow you to physically, sexually, or psychologically be aggressive toward others.

In addition to self-talk, self-concept, and self-love, another important aspect of intrapersonal communication is how we process the information we receive.

Cognitive Processing

Your culture, background, family, education, and experiences all serve as the framework for shaping how you deal with incoming information and affect the way you decide on what actions to take or avoid. The act of *cognitive processing* is the comprehending, organizing, and storing of ideas. An aspect of intrapersonal communication, it is how we process information in relationship to our values, attitudes, and beliefs.

Each of us carries with us *values* (what we perceive to be of positive or negative worth), *attitudes* (our predispositions), and *beliefs* (our convictions). Most people try to keep their actions parallel to their values, beliefs, and attitudes. If things are in balance, we feel fairly good about ourselves and the world around us. If they are not, we may intrapersonally become confused and frustrated, which may cause us to act negatively toward ourselves or others, maybe even blaming them for what's wrong. This imbalance happens, for example, when you know that a certain action you are about to take is wrong based on your value system. Your "internal voice" cries out, "Be careful! Don't do that!" Before the event, you may have a sleepless night as you toss and turn with the internal voice speaking messages, or you may dream about the negative things that are going to happen as a result of your taking the action.

The *imbalance* between your values, attitudes, and beliefs is called *cognitive dissonance.*[22] Cognitive dissonance often leads to a *guilty conscience:* the real or perceived fear that we are going to get caught, get punished, or otherwise be "found out." For example, an individual who believes cheating is wrong yet cheats on a test may feel cognitive dissonance following the act, no matter what grade she receives.

If you become aware of cognitive dissonance before you act and decide not to do the deed, you could chalk it up to your conscience warning you and saving you from a perceived disaster. If you take the negative action and then brood about the action afterward, then you may need to accept that you took the action, there is nothing you can do about it now, and go on from there, with the internal pledge to not do it again. Our internal voice, through its self-talk technique, often continues to shout at us until we can put the imbalance to rest. Sometimes apologizing to a person is in order if the action hurt him or her.

The Self

How a human being views himself or herself will determine most of that individual's actions and choices in life. Essentially a person is going to choose what he or she feels he or she is worth.[23] Thus, the more positively you perceive yourself, the more likely it is that you will have *self-confidence*—that is, a sense of competence and effectiveness.

Each of us possesses a real self, an ideal self, and a public self. (See Figure 5.2.) The *real self* is what you think of yourself when you are being most honest about your interests, thoughts, emotions, and needs. For many people, the real self is dynamic and changing. This accounts for why you may feel as if you are in constant turmoil, searching for who and what you are, questioning your motives for doing and not doing certain things.

The *ideal self* is who you would like to be or think you should be. This is the "perfect you," perceived as being "perfect" by yourself or others (or both of you). It's often the you the significant others in your life (relatives, employers, the media, advertising) have told you that you should be, or who they want you to be.

The *public self* is the one you let others know. It is the person that you have decided to let others see. It is based on the concept that "if others believe the right things about me, I can get them to like me; I can persuade them and generally get my way." It acknowledges that "if others

Figure 5.2
Your Many Selves

Communicating in Careers

Managing Self-Communication

I left the manager's office in a daze. I had an armful . . . the proposal, quarterly reports, profiles, a stack of recent press clippings from the public relations department, and a legal pad full of notes from the two-hour planning session. I had been assigned to lead a project team for the first time. I had to figure out how to manage the boss's perceptions, influence peers, and manage multiple deadlines. How could I do it? Every failure of my life flashed before my eyes. By the time I got back to my office I was filled with self-doubt. I was sure I was going to fail. I wish I had more self-confidence. I wish I thought of myself as a winner instead of a loser.

Source: Roy Berko, Andrew Wolvin, and Rebecca Ray, *Business Communication in a Changing World* (New York: St. Martin's Press, 1997), p. 131.

REFLECT ON THIS:

1. Specifically, what could this person have done to help her feel more confident and gain her composure?

2. Have you ever been in such a situation? If so, what did you do or how could you have better handled yourself?

believe the wrong things about me, I can be rejected and blocked from my goals. Not only actors and politicians shape their public selves, we all do."[24]

Recognition of the importance of self-esteem and self-concept has a long tradition in the Euro-American culture. Psychologists and educators have been interested in the study of the self for many years and have developed different theories about it. Communication theorists have examined the self and self-esteem based on observing and studying what we intrapersonally communicate to ourselves about ourselves and what we interpersonally communicate to others.

The classic theory about the self is that it is composed of four aspects: the *spiritual,* what we are thinking and feeling; the *material,* represented by our possessions and physical surroundings; the *social,* represented by our interactions with others; and the *physical,* our physical being.[25] Much of our self-talk centers on how we perceive the four aspects.

Another theory stresses that the self evolves from the interactions we have with other people and how we intrapersonally integrate these interactions into our self-thought. This evolution takes place in stages. For example, a child aims for a sense of self as a separate person while developing gender identity; the adolescent tries to establish a stable sense of identity; the middle-aged person emphasizes independence while adjusting to changes in body competence; and the elderly person seeks to come to terms with aging.[26] As we go through these changes, our self-communication reflects the alterations that are taking place, and for this reason we experience over our lifetime multiple concepts, rather than a single one, of who we are. Thus, at any one time in our lives, we may perceive ourselves to be a different person than we were at another time. You are probably not the same person today that you were five years ago, and you are not the same person today that you perceive yourself to be five years from now.

Self-concept also seems to be situational. Who you are with one person or in one place may not be the same as who you are with someone else or in a different place. In one relationship, you may take on the role of student, and in another the role of friend. At work you may be the leader, and at home the follower. Many of these role-plays are based on our intrapersonal perception of who we should or who we need to be with these people in this environment.

It is important that you understand yourself and your perceptions of yourself. This is the basis of self-awareness, which is the basis for much of your self-talk.

Socially Communicating

Your Self-Esteem Helps You Navigate Social Waters

According to Mark Leary, director of social psychology at Duke University, our way of thinking about self-esteem has been backward for decades. Instead of regarding low self-esteem as an anathema—and trying desperately to pump up self-esteem to stratospheric levels so that everyone feels super about themselves all the time—we should instead recognize that self-esteem provides a gauge of how we're doing in our social interactions. "Self-esteem rises and falls, acting as an internal barometer of how well you're faring, telling you to fix this problem here, and helping you understand that you don't have to worry about it there," says Leary.

Source: Erika Casriel, "My Friend Joe Raffetto, A Desert Guide," *Psychology Today* (March/April, 2007): 73.

REFLECT ON THIS:

1. Do you agree with the author? Why or why not?
2. How does or could Leary's theory apply to you?

Understanding Yourself

Most people have only a general idea of who they are and what they really believe in. This explains why many of us don't understand why we think the thoughts we do and are intrapersonally motivated to act in particular ways.

It is often of great personal value to attempt to discover the you who is within you—the you who carries on your self-talk, cognitively processes, and acts on your self-concept.

It has been said that you are what you are based on your verb *to be*.[27] Are you interested in finding out your verb "to be?" If so, try the Perceiving My Verb "To Be" activity on page 126.

A good part of our lives is devoted to communicating our pleasure or lack of pleasure as we exploit our conquests, stress our influences, and reinforce our accomplishments.

Perceiving My Verb "To Be"

Directions: Complete these statements:

I am _____.

I would like to be _____.

I like to _____.

I believe that _____.

I have been _____.

I wouldn't want to _____.

The quality I possess that I am most proud of is

_____.

My biggest flaw is _____.

Something that I would prefer others not know about me is _____.

When you are finished responding to these items, write a two-sentence description of yourself based on the answers to the statements you completed.

_____

_____

_____

If you completed this activity, your two-sentence summary is your view of your perceived "to be." You have used your intrapersonally stored data to examine your past experiences (*I have been/done*), current attitudes and actions (*I am*), and future expectations or hopes (*I would like to be/do*). If you were honest and revealed what you really think and feel, you have just gained a glimpse of your perceived self.

Another way of looking at yourself is through the model known as the **Johari window,**[28] which allows you to ascertain your willingness to disclose who you are and allows others to disclose to you. From an intrapersonal perspective, the Johari window helps you understand a great deal about yourself and some cultural underpinnings of your self-thinking.

If you are interested in finding out your Johari Window, try the "Johari Window" activity below.[29]

Based on your answers to the questionnaire, use Figure 5.3 to plot your scores. Compare your pattern with those in Figure 5.4 to ascertain your self-disclosure/receive-feedback style. What is revealed are the four common styles people use in receiving and giving personal information and feedback.

Johari Window Questionnaire

Directions:

Before each item in Part I, place a number from 1 to 6 to indicate how much you are *willing to reveal.* A 1 indicates that you are willing to self-disclose nothing or almost nothing, and a 6 indicates that you are willing to reveal everything or almost everything. Use the values 2, 3, 4, and 5 to represent the points between these extremes.

Before each item in Part II, place a number from 1 to 6 to indicate how *willing you are to receive feedback* about what you self-disclose. A 1 indicates that you refuse or resist feedback, and a 6 indicates that you consistently encourage feedback. Use the values 2, 3, 4, and 5 to represent the points between these extremes.

PART I: Extent to which I am willing to self-disclose my

____ 1. goals

____ 2. strengths

____ 3. weaknesses

____ 4. positive feelings

____ 5. negative feelings

____ 6. values

____ 7. ideas

____ 8. beliefs

____ 9. fears and insecurities

____ 10. mistakes

____ Total

PART II: Extent to which I am willing to receive feedback about my

____ 1. goals

____ 2. strengths

____ 3. weaknesses

____ 4. positive feelings

____ 5. negative feelings

____ 6. values

____ 7. ideas

____ 8. beliefs

____ 9. fears and insecurities

____ 10. mistakes

____ Total

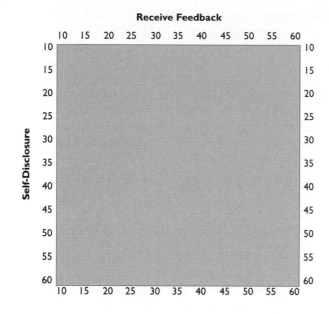

Receive Feedback

Self-Disclosure

Figure 5.3
Plotting Your Johari Window

Circle the number on the top line of the square, designated "Receive Feedback," that corresponds to your score on Part II of the activity. Circle the same number on the bottom line of the square. Connect the two circles with a straight line. Then circle the number on the left side line of the square, designated "Self-Disclosure," that corresponds to your score on Part I of the activity. Circle the same number on the right side line of the square. Connect the two circles with a straight line.

Figure 5.4
Johari Style Indicator

Source: Reprinted by permission from Ronald B. Adler, Lawrence B. Rosenfeld, and Neil Towne, *Interplay: The Process of Personal Communication*, 5/e. Copyright © 1992 by Oxford University Press Inc.

- *Style I* people spend little time disclosing or giving feedback. They tend to be perceived as good listeners and fairly shy or quiet; sometimes they are labeled as introverts.

- *Style II* people spend a great deal of time listening and not much time sending out personal information. After you have been with a Style II type of person for a while, he or she tends to know a great deal about you, but you don't know much about him or her. This is the style that generally describes introverts.

- *Style III* people give a great deal of personal information but don't like to receive very much. They tell you about themselves and are often perceived as great talkers but not very good listeners. You tend to know a great deal about them, but they don't know much about you.

- *Style IV* people like to give and get information. People who are very open and easily share themselves with others normally have

a large, free area and smaller blind, hidden, and unknown areas. Because these people share, they are known to themselves and to others. They are often referred to as extroverts; they are outgoing and interactive.

If your four-sided figures are approximately the same size, you do not have a predominant self-disclosure/receive-feedback style.

What you should gain from the Johari window exercise is an understanding of not only your perception of yourself and how it affects your intrapersonal communication but also how others may perceive you based on your willingness or unwillingness to disclose and receive information.

In application terms, Style II people and Style III people would appear to make excellent partners in relationships as one likes to disclose and the other to receive but not disclose. The problem with this combination may be that after a while the Style III person realizes that he doesn't know much about the Style II person, and the Style II person realizes that while she knows a lot about her partner, the partner knows practically nothing about her. The relationship is sometimes perceived as not being balanced.

Style IV people often scare those who are Style I individuals. A Style IV person dominates the conversation by telling about himself and probing to find out about the other person, who really doesn't necessarily want to learn about the other person nor reveal anything about herself. This can be unnerving to Style I individuals.

Need Drives Affecting Communication

We are each born with certain biological tools that allow us to communicate: a brain, sound-producing organs (mouth, tongue, larynx), and a receiving apparatus (ears, eyes). We also, according to *ethnographers*—researchers who study cultures—are born with need drives that must be satisfied. Some communication theorists think that these intrapersonal drives are the basis for our communication: what we think, what we express, what inspires us to act the way we do, and how we react to the way others express and use their drives. This concept explains why we communicate in ways that go beyond our usual understanding of communication.[30]

The basic forces that determine human behavior are survival of the species, pleasure seeking, security, and territoriality.[31] These drives are not manifested equally in every person. One person may have a pleasure need that is stronger than any of the other forces, whereas another may have strong needs for security and territoriality. This view offers a contrast to the earlier proposed hierarchy of needs theory, which suggests that each need must be satisfied before a person can move on to the next one.

We choose to communicate in those situations in which we perceive we will get pleasure.

Survival

A person who is threatened screams out for help; when a pebble flies against the windshield of your moving car, you duck. These are examples of attempts to ensure *survival*. These actions are reflexive—inborn reactions that we instinctively use to communicate our fear of a possible ending of our existence.

Our ability to communicate selectively gives us a distinct survival advantage. For example, we can call for help, plead, explain our needs, or try to convince attackers that their action is unwise. In addition, we are aware of our own evolution, an awareness that is probably not found in other animals. Because of this, we can communicate about how we reproduce, what causes us to die, and how we can attempt to alter conditions to prolong our lives and those of our descendants. We have been able to communicate these ideas from person to person and thus build on the experience of the past in developing intrapersonal understanding.

Pleasure Seeking

We are basically *pleasure-seeking* beings. A good part of our lives is devoted to communicating our pleasure or lack of pleasure as we exploit our conquests, stress our influences, and reinforce our accomplishments. We talk about our awards, citations, and good grades to communicate to others that we have succeeded, thus satisfying our pleasure need.

People find different events pleasurable, and each of us may find both pleasure and pain in a single event. Moreover, we may find pleasure in satisfying not only our own needs but also the needs of others, or in fulfilling our long-term goals as well as our immediate desires. What pleases one person may well torture another. One person happily gives a speech before a large audience; another is petrified by any speaking situation.

If given the opportunity, we choose to communicate in those situations in which we perceive we will get pleasure. You raise your hand to answer a question in class if you think you know the right answer. Unless forced to do so, individuals who fear public speaking avoid putting themselves in a position of giving a speech. But a speaker who has received positive reactions from an audience is much more likely to try the experience again. We are constantly sending ourselves intrapersonal messages relating to whether some experience was or was not pleasurable, or whether a perceived activity will render pleasure.

Security

You enter a classroom for the first meeting of a class. You see a place that is unfamiliar, people you do not know, a professor who is an unknown entity. You feel insecure. Your desire to participate and your comfort in this situation can be affected directly by the messages you send yourself.

The need for *security* causes us to seek equilibrium, a balance. When security is absent, when we feel a lack of control, most of us are uneasy, overly cautious, and uncertain.

Our concept of ourselves in situations of security or insecurity motivates our verbal and nonverbal communication. Fear causes the vocal pitch to rise, the body to shake, and the stomach to churn. We find ourselves afraid to speak, or speaking incessantly, or stammering. But as we become more comfortable in a situation and learn the rules of the game, we find ourselves acting quite differently because we send ourselves positive messages. The first day of class, for instance, you may not say a word. But as you acclimate yourself to the situation, you may feel secure enough to participate.

Hearing intrapersonal messages of fear of the unknown explains why some people will not wander down the unmapped paths of life. The messages they send themselves center on the warning "Beware of the unknown, the uncomfortable."

Territoriality

We intrapersonally define a particular *territory*, whether physical or perceptual, and then feel secure within that territory. We defend it from invasion and use it for protection. We mark off land by defining it precisely with a deed indicating length, width, and location. We mark our territory with fences, signs, and numbers that specifically say "This belongs to me." We tend to feel most secure when we are in our own territory, and we often identify ourselves by our hometown, our school, and our social groups, all of which are territorial markers.

We act differently in different territories. When friends come to visit you, conditions are not the same as when you go to visit them. The friend you invite over for dinner does not act the same at your house as when you go to his house for dinner. In the same way, there is a definite difference between playing an athletic game at home and playing it on the road. The home team is estimated to have an advantage of about one touchdown in football and ten points in basketball.

In addition to physical territory, we have ideas and areas of expertise that we identify as ours. Inventors obtain patents to protect their inventions; writers copyright their books. Both are attempts to establish a territory and to communicate the boundaries to others.

The more insecure a person is within a territory, the greater is that person's intrapersonal fear of losing the territory. Once people have defined something as theirs, they will tend to defend it. Thus, an invasion of someone else's territory is likely to invite a counterattack.

We mark off territory by marking it with objects, fences, signs, and numbers.

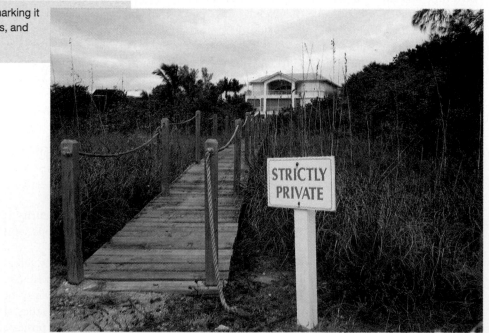

Clearly, one's basic drives have a significant influence on intrapersonal communication.

The field of communication relies on research in psychology, sociology, and anthropology as well as communication to develop many of its concepts. One area related to intrapersonal communication is exclusively the property of the communication field: communication apprehension.

Anxiety: Communication Apprehension

Anxiety—the perception of a real or perceived threat or danger[32]—may affect your perceptions and intrapersonal or interpersonal performance. Anxiety is based on negative intrapersonal messages as they specifically relate to pleasure and security needs. Much anxiety comes from perceiving that something is wrong or could happen and our body's reaction to those perceptions.

Anxiety is normal.[33] It is your body's way of protecting you. It is the "in-wired reaction to high arousal."[34] The ingredients in anxiety are a combination of *biological reaction* (a sensitivity to protect yourself from danger), *personality type* (highly perfectionistic individuals and those who have a strong desire to please others tend to have high anxiety levels), and the *normal stresses of life* that center on a fear of failure (being tested in school, giving a public speech, competing in sports).[35]

Think of times when you have felt anxious. You probably displayed one or more of these symptoms of stress:[36]

- *Physical signs:* nausea, headaches, difficulty in breathing, talking fast, heart racing, palms sweating, and dry mouth
- *Cognitive signs:* worry, self-messages of "I should do . . . ," catastrophizing (self-prediction that horrible things are going to happen), and disorganized thoughts

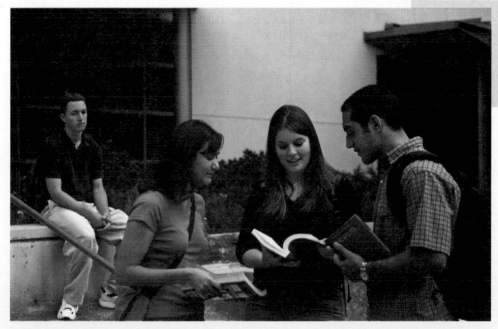

The communicatively anxious person is aware of the anxiety because intrapersonal messages clearly warn of the fear.

■ *Behavioral signs:* visual images of negative things that might happen, avoidance of tasks and situations for fear of the negative event happening, restlessness, and agitation

Most people realize that because stress is natural, they need to confront it, so they ask themselves, "What is the worst thing that can happen?" In most instances the consequences aren't that great, and those in charge of themselves will confront an issue or simply let the situation pass, with the perceived anxiety also passing. Those who understand the workings of anxiety also realize that "most of the things people worry about never happen."[37] Another coping mechanism is realizing that "what you think others are thinking of you is what you are really thinking of yourself."[38] In other words, if you can think positively about yourself, you can counter the perceptions of the negative things that you fear people might be thinking about you.

Realistically, however, anxiety can overcome some people. "One in four people will develop an anxiety disorder."[39] The good news is that learning what anxiety is and some techniques for overcoming it (such as what you are doing in this class) can help considerably. Much of the problem can be relieved through counseling, or a combination of counseling and drug therapy,[40] and/or using self-induced coping techniques such as the following:

■ *Relaxation skills*

practice yoga

learn and practice self-hypnosis

■ *Stress management*

setting up a regular exercise routine

learning how to do square breathing (breath in to a count of four, hold the breath to a count of four, breath out to a count of four)

■ *Dietary controls*

avoiding foods containing high concentrations of caffeine, artificial flavors, and sugar

■ *Cognitive habits*

learning to block stressing messages by using a directive such as "Cool it," "Relax," or "Forget it; it's not that important"

using affirmations (saying something that inspires positive beliefs and actions), applying social skills, or choosing not to be anxious

An *affirmation* consists of an "I" statement presented in present tense with an action verb that is positive—for example, "I will use the blocking message 'Relax' when I feel stress." This technique may sound very theoretical and not practical, but research shows that affirmations do work because "if you say something that is true and believe it, it becomes your reality."[41]

Communication Anxiety Defined

In the field of communication, the term used for speech anxiety is **communication apprehension.** It is also identified as *shyness, social anxiety disorder,* and *social phobia.*[42] The communicatively anxious person is aware of the anxiety because intrapersonal messages clearly warn of the fear. The messages warn of unfavorable outcomes, and the person experiences a sense of impending doom.

Although many think of communication anxiety only in regard to public speaking, it is actually much broader.[43] Worries, concerns, and fears interfere with efficient listening, communicating in groups, talking in class and on the telephone, and verbalizing during interviews. Anxiety can make us so preoccupied that we do not get the message being communicated, or we become incapable of sending a message.

Individuals who are considered to have high communication anxiety often think and feel that one or more of their basic needs is being attacked. They may feel so endangered that they perceive their very existence is endangered (survival need). Because they do not think that the experience of communicating is or will be positive, they do not perceive it as positive (pleasure need). They often are uncomfortable thinking about communicating in conversations, or giving speeches, that they are off-balance, up-tight (security need). Going into a setting (territorial need) where communication will take place (e.g., a classroom where a report is due or a job where a speech must be given) may be unnerving.

"Shy people have inaccurate self-concepts."[44] They often believe that they are inadequate when they are not. "They tend to blame themselves for failure and credit others for success. They tend to erase themselves: They avoid eye contact, speak softly or less than others, and rarely take a strong position on a topic."[45] People who experience speech anxiety think poorly of themselves, feel fearful, and often perform in an inadequate fashion.[46]

Is there a difference between men and women regarding communication apprehension? Research shows that "more women than men are thought to suffer anxiety, but because shyness and demureness are smiled upon in females and less acceptable in males, more men turn to professionals for help."[47]

Almost 95 percent of the population reports having apprehension about communicating with some person or group in their lives.[48] Referring to the 1980s, researchers reported, "A decade ago, 40 percent of people said they were shy."[49] Two decades later, but in today's "nation of strangers"—in which computers, texting, and ATMs make face-to-face relations less and less common—that number is nearing 50 percent.[50] Of those, 30 percent classify themselves as extremely shy, so introverted that they chose careers or just naturally evolve into jobs and lifestyles that center on avoiding communication situations.[51] It is reasoned that the increase is due to people being able to avoid interacting directly with others. Thus, they avoid practicing the very skills that they need to hone. "Social phobia is the third most common mental disorder in the United States, behind depression and alcoholism."[52] Not all shyness is the same, however. There are degrees of communication apprehension. (See Figure 5.5.)

Communication apprehension may be situation specific or general. For example, some people only feel fear when confronted with giving a speech. A survey indicates that 40.6 percent of respondents identified their major fear to be speaking before groups,

Socially Communicating

Comedian Will Ferrell Reveals His Shyness

Comedic superstar Will Ferrell, who once considered himself painfully shy, forced himself to do crazy things in public. "In college, I would push an overhead projector across campus with my pants just low enough to show my butt," Ferrell told *People*. "Then my friend would incite the crowd to be like, 'Look at that idiot!' That's how I got over being shy."

Source: Erika Casriel, "My Friend Joe Raffetto, A Desert Guide," *Psychology Today* (March/April, 2007): 73.

REFLECT ON THIS:

1. How did Ferrell's actions help him to overcome his shyness?

2. If you consider yourself to be shy, what one or two specific actions could you take to help you overcome your shyness?

NORMAL SHYNESS	EXTREME SHYNESS	SOCIAL ANXIETY	SEVERE SOCIAL ANXIETY
■ You are jittery beginning a public speech, but afterward you are glad you did it.	■ You clam up and your heart races when you know people are looking at you.	■ You will do anything, even skip work, to avoid being introduced to new people.	■ You are free of nervousness only when alone and you can barely leave the house.
■ Your mind goes blank on a first date, but eventually you relax and find things to talk about.	■ You tremble when speaking up at a meeting, even if it is only to say your name.	■ You have trouble swallowing in public, making it hard to dine out or go to parties.	■ You constantly worry about being embarrassed or humiliated by others.
■ Your palms sweat in a job interview, but you ask and answer thoughtful questions.	■ You avoid starting conversations for fear of saying something awkward.	■ You feel you never make a good impression and that you are a social failure.	

Figure 5.5   A Spectrum of Shyness

Source: U.S. News & World Report, June 21, 1999, pp. 52–53.

exceeding fear of heights, death, and loneliness.[53] On the other hand, some people report perceived discomfort only in one-on-one conversations or in groups. Others indicate experiencing anxiety in any speaking situation.

Are you interested in finding out whether you considered yourself communicative apprehensive and, if so, in what situations? If so, take the Personal Report of Communication Apprehension (PRCA-24) activity on the next page.

The Effects of Communication Anxiety

Most people with communication anxiety believe that they suffer negative consequences, that they have given up control of themselves to someone else or to an unknown force, or that they are puppets whose strings are being pulled by their master, *fear*.

There are some demonstrated effects of communication anxiety.[54] In classroom situations, communicatively anxious students rarely volunteer, if at all.[55] They often drop classes that require oral communication or miss class when oral participation is necessary. These behavior patterns can affect both learning and grades.[56] Some anxious college students even fail to graduate when they have only one course to complete—a required course in speech communication.[57]

People with communication anxiety often choose college majors that require few, if any, oral presentations, such as research or technical fields. In the workplace, if they must participate orally—whether one-on-one, in a group, or in a public setting—they fail to do so, thus missing out on promotions and pay increases because they are handicapped by their fear.[58]

In interpersonal situations, people with communication anxiety talk very little about themselves and seem overly concerned that the other person understand and agree with them.[59] They are also nonassertive, tending to yield to the other person and submitting themselves to others' directions. Insofar as perceptions of communicatively anxious people are concerned, after interacting for only a short period of time with strangers, communicatively anxious people are perceived as less socially attractive, trustworthy, and satisfied than people who are not communicatively anxious.[60]

Finally, although they may have as much desire for social relationships as those who are not communicatively anxious, people who are afraid to communicate have fewer steady dates than those who are less anxious.[61]

Personal Report of Communication Apprehension (PRCA-24)[62]

Directions: This instrument is composed of twenty-four statements concerning feelings about communicating with other people. Indicate the degree to which each statement applies to you by marking whether you (1) strongly agree, (2) agree, (3) are undecided, (4) disagree, or (5) strongly disagree. Record your first impression.

_____ 1. I dislike participating in group discussions.

_____ 2. Generally, I am comfortable while participating in a group discussion.

_____ 3. I am tense and nervous while participating in group discussions.

_____ 4. I like to get involved in group discussions.

_____ 5. Engaging in a group discussion with new people makes me tense and nervous.

_____ 6. I am calm and relaxed while participating in group discussions.

_____ 7. Generally, I am nervous when I have to participate in a meeting.

_____ 8. Usually I am calm and relaxed while participating in meetings.

_____ 9. I am very calm and relaxed when I am called upon to express an opinion at a meeting.

_____ 10. I am afraid to express myself at meetings.

_____ 11. Communicating at meetings usually makes me uncomfortable.

_____ 12. I am very relaxed when answering questions at a meeting.

_____ 13. While participating in a conversation with a new acquaintance, I feel very nervous.

_____ 14. I have no fear of speaking up in conversations.

_____ 15. Ordinarily I am very tense and nervous in conversations.

_____ 16. Ordinarily I am very calm and relaxed in conversations.

_____ 17. While conversing with a new acquaintance, I feel very relaxed.

_____ 18. I'm afraid to speak up in conversations.

_____ 19. I have no fear of giving a speech.

_____ 20. Certain parts of my body feel very tense and rigid while I am giving a speech.

_____ 21. I feel relaxed while giving a speech.

_____ 22. My thoughts become confused and jumbled when I am giving a speech.

_____ 23. I face the prospect of giving a speech with confidence.

_____ 24. While giving a speech, I get so nervous I forget facts I really know.

Scoring:

18+ scores for items 2, 4, 6; minus the scores for items 1, 3, 5 = Group discussion score

18+ scores for 8, 9, 12; minus the scores for 7, 10, 11 = Meetings score

18+ scores for 14, 16, 17; minus the scores for 13, 15, 18 = Interpersonal conversations score

18+ scores for 19, 21, 23; minus the scores for 20, 22, 24 = Public speaking score

Add your group, meetings, interpersonal, and public speaking scores = Total score

Your score should range between 24 and 120. If your score is below 24 or above 120, you have made a mistake in computing the score. (Your instructor will refer to the _Instructor's Manual_ for this textbook to tell you the meaning of your scores.)

The Causes of Communication Apprehension

Studies in brain biology indicate that communication apprehension can result from heredity. Some people, according to brain scans, have a natural predisposition to be shy and uncomfortable with others.[63] "Scientists using sophisticated scanning tools to monitor brains have detected differences between introverts and extroverts that last from infancy to adulthood."[64] And although shyness can be overcome, or at least managed, researchers say born introverts might be more likely than their gregarious brethren to develop phobias, anxiety disorders and depression.[65]

Approximately 10 to 15 percent of babies reportedly are born apprehensive, as demonstrated by their crying when exposed to unfamiliar things. Tests on children progressing from two weeks of life to seven years indicated that at twenty-one months, they clung to their caretakers in new situations and hesitated before interacting with new persons; at four years they remained quiet in the presence of an unknown adult; at seven years they exhibited a greater degree of reaction to imagined threats than other children did.[66] Biologically shy children react more intensely to the stimuli around them than other children do, as exhibited by racing hearts, widening pupils, and vocal cord tenseness.

Communication apprehension also can spring from social conditioning. Children may imitate or model such behaviors as observed in others. Apprehensive parents often have apprehensive children. Another potential cause includes an individual's having been brought up in environments where perfection was stressed, often causing the person to fear being evaluated, which is a major fear of many communicatively anxious people.[67] In addition, a person's anxiousness may be reinforced by the negative feedback received because of his or her avoidance of communicative activities.[68]

It should be noted that communication apprehension, as it is generally understood, focuses on *speaker* apprehension. Receiver apprehension, however, is also significant as a communication barrier. Listener apprehension has been conceptualized as "the fear of misinterpreting, inadequately processing, and/or not being able to adjust psychologically to messages sent by others."[69] It is possible that a listener can be so anxious about the outcome of a communication (getting a test report from a physician, for example) that he or she approaches listening with a high level of apprehension. Receiver apprehension can stem from inexperience and/or lack of familiarity with the speaker, the situation, or the subject itself.

Help for Communication Apprehension

Communication apprehension is not a mental disorder.[70] Except for those born with the anxiety, communication apprehension is an attribute a person applies to himself or herself, and it can be removed. The easiest way to do this, of course, is for the person to declare that he or she doesn't want or need the title. Sound silly and oversimplistic that you can declare yourself no longer a communication apprehensive? It's not. A change of self-perception can result in a change of action. Just as some people declare, "I will no longer smoke" and they never light up again, people have successfully overcome shyness by declaring that their self perceived social phobia is over.[71] Doing this is very difficult for many to do, however, so be reassured that aid is available to those who want to rid themselves of the title. Such actions as skill training, systematic desensitization, cognitive modification, a willingness to communicate, and drug therapy are forms of help.

SKILL TRAINING   One of the factors that is perceived to be a problem among communicatively anxious people is their lack of oral communication skills. Not knowing how to structure or organize a speech, how to start and continue a conversation, or how to participate in a group can manifest itself by triggering the negative aspect of two basic human needs—security and pleasure.

"Socially confident people deliberately learn specific skills, like displaying friendly body language, understanding the predictable format for conversation with new people, and focusing on the topic rather than on how they are perceived."[72]

Those who have learned the skills needed to be an effective communicator feel secure and anticipate pleasure. Many of the theories and skills stressed in this book—and taught in other communication classes—can teach a person the necessary skills.

Socially Communicating

What Is Your Life Script?

How fixed beliefs define our roles:
Our fixed beliefs define the roles we play in life. The scripts that are running follow a play's script of lines, actions and attitude. We follow life scripts according to what our fixed beliefs tell us. Are you telling yourself that you are a tragic character or heroic character? Are you playing the loving mother, abusive husband, frustrated artist or successful businessman?

Why scripts are dangerous:
Whatever your fixed beliefs are, you have practiced your script for so long that you believe what it says about your potential. This is why life scripts are dangerous. We begin to perceive them as being set in stone. We even allow them to shape the way we expect things to turn out. Fixed beliefs also influence the casting, location and wardrobe of our script. Who is "right" for the part in our script and who isn't? What type of living arrangement and attire are the character we are playing, etc.?

When life scripts become limiting:
Because our scripts are based on fixed beliefs, we tend to resist any challenges or changes to them. If we are happy and fulfilled, but our script says that we should feel sad and hopeless, we tend to panic because we script." It just doesn't feel right and besides, the happy role belongs to someone else, doesn't it? This is an example of why most fixed beliefs are also limiting beliefs. They limit our scripts by dictating what we can't do, don't deserve and aren't qualified for.

Source: Dr. Phil McGraw, www.dr.phil.com.

REFLECT ON THIS:
1. Name two entries in your life script.
2. What are two of your fixed beliefs?
3. At this point in your life, how set is your life script?
4. Are you willing to change any or all of your life script?
5. What would get you to change any or all of your life script?

SYSTEMATIC DESENSITIZATION   People's fear of humiliation and embarrassment when they are around unfamiliar people or of being evaluated negatively by others are major apprehension inducers.[73] Through systematic desensitization, people are taught first to recognize tension in their bodies and then how to relax.[74] As many as 80 or 90 percent of the people treated professionally by this system report the complete elimination of their apprehension.[75] Nevertheless, such a program works only if the person wants to change and has the skills to modify his or her behavior. If the individual does not have the necessary abilities, then skill training must precede systematic desensitization.

COGNITIVE MODIFICATION   The basic concept behind cognitive modification is that people have learned to think negatively and must be taught to think positively. The first step in this process is for people to learn how to recognize when they are thinking negatively and to identify their own negative statements about their communication. Then they learn to replace negative statements with positive ones. Rather than saying, for example, "I really say stupid things," they may change their response to "I can present clear ideas; it isn't that hard." The last stage of the training is to practice substituting positive statements for negative ones. This may sound very theoretical, but in reality, it works. The success achieved by using this technique is quite high.[76]

WILLINGNESS TO COMMUNICATE   Your personal communication must stem from a willingness to communicate. People who are willing to communicate are willing to take risks, to analyze their communication, and to make adjustments as needed.

To be a willing communicator, you must realize that

- There is no such thing as a perfect communicator. We all make mistakes.
- You need to interact with others, no matter what you perceive to be the negatives of that communication, such as being embarrassed.

- Most often, the perceived fear of what will go wrong never happens (deaths caused by speaking in public just don't happen, for example).

- Accomplishing your communicative task is more important than your perceived fear of "what others might think."

- You must assume that if someone doesn't like what you say, or how you say it, that it is their problem, not yours. Maintaining this attitude allows you to be immune to the personal negative self-doubts that are often present in those who are communicative apprehensive.

"Willingness to communicate is the one, overwhelming communication personality construct which permeates every facet of an individual's life and contributes significantly to the social, educational, and organizational achievements of the individual."[77]

DRUG THERAPY "Pasted on bus shelters nationwide, a poster asks passersby to imagine being allergic to people."[78] The purpose of the billboards is to alert individuals with social anxiety disorder that, in extreme cases, there may be some help for dealing with the problem by using drug therapy as a support for psychological and speech communication assistance. Several prescription drugs have been found to assist those who are communicative apprehensive in managing their problems. These are available only through medical professionals, such as psychiatrists, and should be prescribed only after carefully medical and psychological evaluation.[79]

The Role of Culture in Intrapersonal Communication

The basis for your identity is anchored in your *social orientation*, which includes all aspects of your culture: your nationality, race, gender, sexual orientation and religion.[80] How your culture deals with and teaches about boastfulness, orientations toward life, spirituality, relationship to nature, attitudes toward others, and what it means to be a successful communicator affects your development of self-concept.

In this discussion of cultural tendencies, please be aware that the statements are assertions based on research findings. This means that any individual member of a culture may not follow the patterns described. Testing looks for norm patterns—patterns of the general members of the group. If you are a member of the culture being discussed, for example, you may fall outside of the statistical sample description being described.

Aspects of Culture That Affect the Self

Varying cultural concepts affect a person's concept of self. These include self-credentialing and self-humbling; relationship to the spirit world, nature, and other living things; doing or being orientation to life; attitudes toward others; and, high and low context communication.

SELF-CREDENTIALING/SELF-HUMBLING VERBAL SOCIETIES

In cultures that stress a *self-credentialing verbal mode*, emphasis is placed on drawing attention to or boasting about one's accomplishments. For example, "In the Swiss and U.S. cultures, individuals are encouraged to sell themselves and boast about their achievements."[81] The same pattern is found in Arab and African cultures.[82]

In *self-humbling verbal mode societies*, we see the importance of lowering oneself via modest talk, verbal restraints and the use of self-deprecation. Native Americans and those from some areas of West Africa, may have difficulty understanding and applying the concept of self-credentialing because of their linguistic patterns of underplaying, rather than overplaying, their sense of self.[83]

Your self-concept is obviously based on different criteria, depending on if you are from a self-credentialing or a self-humbling verbal society.

RELATIONSHIP TO THE SPIRIT WORLD, NATURE, AND OTHER LIVING THINGS Cultural patterns may tell people how to locate themselves in relation to the spiritual world, nature, and other living things. If they are not from a fundamentalist religious background, European Americans generally view humans as separate and distinct from nature. "The general belief is to regard nature as something to be manipulated and controlled in order to make human life better."[84]

"In an African and African American world view, however, human beings live in an interactive state with the natural and spirit world."[85] There is a personal closeness to God. Native Americans view "humans as living in harmony with Nature."[86]

Socially Communicating

The Stolen Generation: Positive Self-Concept Denied

"For the indignity and degradation thus inflicted on a proud people and a proud culture, we say sorry."

Australian Prime Minister Kevin Rudd, apologizing to members of the "Stolen Generation" of Aborigines, an estimated 100,000 children who until the 1970s were forcibly taken from indigenous parents under now discredited assimilation policies.

Source: "Perspective," Newsweek (February 25, 2008): 25.

REFLECT ON THIS: Do you think the President of the United States should make an apology to:

1. Japanese Americans who were imprisoned by the U.S. government during World War II?

2. African Americans for being enslaved?

3. Gays and lesbians for the discrimination against them caused by laws restricting their rights and the lack of protection for their rights?

Believing that God, or some other source, creates you and you are beholden to that creator can encourage individuals to develop a self-image in a different way from those who act independently of that perception.

DOING OR BEING ORIENTATION TO LIFE Middle-class African Americans, Asian Americans, Latino Americans, and European Americans focus on a *doing oriented approach to life*.[87] They tend to be achievement oriented. Much of the self-image of a person who believes in the doing orientation is based on his or her financial gains and/or obtaining the respect of others through accomplishments. Their concept of self is often based on what others think or say about their deeds.

On the other hand, Africans, Native Americans, Hindus, and Buddhists are more in tune with the *being oriented approach to life*.[88] In this orientation, a person may strive for life goals, but this is not something to use as an evaluation of a person's self-worth or self-value. They often do not talk about their accomplishments, and therefore the idea of self-worth is a nonissue.

ATTITUDES TOWARD OTHERS Some societies have respect for all. Societies, for example, where Buddhism is practiced are likely to avoid evaluating the life style and beliefs of others. This is in opposition to those societies where there are strong religious traditions by Muslims, Orthodox Jews, fundamentalist Christians, and traditional Catholics. These religions teach that there are good versus bad behaviors, desirable and undesirable practices. This creates an atmosphere where those who are pointed out as being deviant or different have challenges in developing positive self-images.

Gay men and women, for example, in the United States, because of years of exclusion by the general society and its laws, and some religious teaching, have found it necessary to hide who they are. Thus, a gay person's self-concept may have been negatively influenced.[89]

HIGH-CONTEXT, LOW-CONTEXT COMMUNICATION   In *low-context communication societies,* the emphasis is on the expression of ideas through explicit verbal messages.[90] In *high-context communication societies,* the emphasis is on how the verbal message can best be conveyed through indirect language and the nonverbal channels of silence and subtle tone of voice.

The British, Germans, Danes, Swedes, Euro-Americans, Canadians, and Australians tend to be low-context communicators, using the low-context mode.[91] The speaker is expected to construct a persuasive message that the listener can easily decode.

"The Arabic and Spanish language systems tend toward a more status-based, high context verbal model." Other high context nationalities are Japan, China, South Korea, Vietnam, Nigeria, Mexico, Kuwait, and Saudi Arabia.[92]

In comparing the two contexts, "The Japanese disclose less because they highly value harmony, group interest, formal relationships, private selves and nonverbal forms of disclosure, while U.S. Americans emphasize informal relationships, personal interests, greater social spontaneity, public selves and direct expressions."[93]

These communication styles influence the formation of self-concepts. For example, praise or criticism are given for acting the way in which a culture dictates, as well as setting up how one should perceive himself or herself as a social being. In the United States, respect is given for extroversion, and introversion is considered a disadvantage. On the other hand, in Japan, where being thoughtful and a good listener is revered, communication apprehension, as defined by Euro-American standards, is a positive way of acting.

In Conclusion

The basis for communication with others is the ability to communicate with oneself. The internal messages that we send to ourselves are called intrapersonal communication. Each person's culture, background, family, education, and experiences serve as the framework for shaping how he or she deals with incoming information and affects the way he or she decides on what actions to take or avoid. How a human being views himself or herself will determine most of his or her actions and choices in life; however, most people have only a general idea of who they are and what they really believe in. Some communication theorists believe that the intrapersonal drives we are born with are the bases for our communication: what we think, what we express, what inspires us to act the way we do, and how we react to the way others express and use their drives. Most people experience and subsequently deal with some form of communication apprehension. Culture has a strong affect on self-concept and self-perception.

Learn by Doing

1. Prepare a list of ten questions an interviewer should ask to get an accurate picture of who you really are. These questions should allow the interviewer to understand your personal history, beliefs, and future plans. Phrase the questions so that they require more than a one- or two-word reply. Your instructor will then match you with another member of the class. You will interview each other using the questions that each of you has prepared. Then introduce each other in a two- to three-minute presentation to the class. After the class presentation, answer the following questions:

   a. What did it feel like to reveal myself to a stranger?

   b. Did I conceal things about myself during the interview? If so, why?

   c. How did I feel and what did I do while my partner was introducing me to the class?

2. Bring to class a painting, poem, or piece of music you like. Share it with the class or a small group, and indicate why you have positive feelings about it. What does your choice indicate about you? Did you find it difficult to share something so personal with strangers?

3. State whether you agree or disagree with these statements: "A person is changeable and can alter behavior patterns if she or he really wants to do so." "No one can change anyone else; only the individual can change himself or herself." Explain the reasons for your answers.

4. Get one of your friends to fill out the Johari Window form (see p. 126) as if she or he were you. Compare that person's answers with yours. What did you learn about yourself from this activity?

5. Make a shield like coat of arms out of a piece of cardboard large enough for the class to see. Draw or cut out and paste at least four pictures, symbols, or words on the coat of arms that represent you: your beliefs, attitudes, bodily image, hobbies, future plans, past successes or failures. The class will be divided into groups. Each person is to explain his or her coat of arms and why he or she selected these things as self-representations.

Key Terms

intrapersonal communication   115

self-talk   115

self-concept   117

self-love   122

Johari window   126

communication apprehension   132

chapter 6

The Concepts of Interpersonal Communication

▶ After reading this chapter, you should be able to

- Illustrate how self-disclosure plays a role in both self-understanding and understanding of another person
- Explain the roles of trust, approval seeking, emotions, and power as they relate to interpersonal communication
- Explain the similarities and differences in the communication of males and females and their effect on interpersonal communication
- Be aware of the role of gender communication in the workplace

- Understand the role of bullying as a verbal and nonverbal communication weapon
- Be aware of the causes of relational conflict
- Define what relationships are and demonstrate how they develop, continue, and end
- Explain the role of, positive and negative aspects of, and how to be a better online interpersonal communicator

The concept of interpersonal communication developed in the early 1950s.[1] As a result of research on the subject, the field of speech expanded from study focused on public speaking into the broader field of communication, encompassing such areas as self-disclosure, approval seeking, relational communication, family communication, small-group communication, nonverbal communication, conversational communication, intercultural communication, organizational communication, and conflict resolution. The term *interpersonal communication* can be defined as "communication that is based on communicators' recognition of each other's uniqueness and the development of messages that reflect that recognition."[2] It also can be described as an interactional process in which two people send and receive messages. Two primary themes underlie this process: Communication necessitates give and take, and communication involves relationships and information.

Because there can be no interpersonal communication unless the communicators give and take information, the basis for interpersonal transactions is the sending and receiving of messages in such a way that they are successfully encoded and decoded. The more experiences the communicators have in common and the more openness they have between them, the more likely it is that their communication will be successful.

Our interpersonal relationships bring together the most important people, roles, contexts, and energies we experience. Interpersonal communication functions to combat loneliness, shape self-concepts, confirm experiences, renew personal and intrapersonal growth, and aid us in understanding who we are and how we relate to others.

Interpersonal skills have been identified by business executives as one of the three most important abilities that employees must have (good listening and effective problem solving are the others).[3] On the personal level, family and relational communication is dependent on your being a competent interpersonal communicator. Interpersonal communication is at the core of collegiate success. Your interpersonal abilities can affect your academic success, roommate rapport, and social connectedness.

Basic Concepts of Interpersonal Communication

As you read about interpersonal communication, keep these basic concepts in mind:

1. *Communication takes place within a system.* As we enter into communicative relationships with others, we set a pattern by which we will interact. For example, in a family, there are flow patterns of message sending and receiving: who speaks to whom, who controls the interactions, who has the power to praise and punish, who can encourage or stop the message flow, and so on. If you examine any relationship you are in, you will recognize patterns by which the communication flows.

   A change in the system results in a change of the communication. If someone in the system changes roles (e.g., a teenager leaves for college) or outside factors change the system (a grandparent becomes ill and moves in), that changes the communicative system.

   There may be resistance to changing the system because this may also shift the power structure. If your supervisor, spouse, lover, or friend likes being in control, and you are proposing a change, problems may arise. At the other extreme, there also may be situations in which the system requires adjustment so that a person is forced to assume responsibility after having been dependent on someone else. The communication system remains unchanged as long as the status quo is maintained.

2. *We teach others how to treat us.* The system in which communication takes place needs to be structured. Each person plays a role when a system is developing. If

both people accept their roles, then those roles become part of the system. If a role is rejected, then it does not become a system rule. Often we wonder why people treat us as they do. In many instances it is because when they treat us in a particular way, we don't object; therefore, it becomes the pattern. For example, habitual physical abusers at one point hit someone who didn't object or feel that they had the power to defend themselves. Consequently, the next time the abuser got angry, he or she repeated the action. The cycle is set unless the abused takes action to teach the aggressor a new way to act or leaves the relationship.

3 *We communicate what and who we are.* Every time we communicate, we tell a great deal about ourselves. Our selection of words, the tone of our voice, and the gestures we use combine to give a picture of our values, likes and dislikes, and self-perceptions. We give clues to our background by our pronunciation patterns and the attitudes we express. As receivers, we form conclusions about senders and react to these conclusions based on our own culture—our background, experiences, and beliefs.

4 *Much of our interpersonal communication centers on our wanting others to act or think or feel as we do; in other words, much of it is an attempt at persuasion.* In our interpersonal relations with parents, children, and friends, we often attempt to alter or reinforce behavior, gain compliance, give advice, or elicit some type of action.

5 *Meaning is in people, not in words.* A word has a meaning only by virtue of the meaning people give to that word. In communicating with others, we must be aware that what a particular symbol means to us is not necessarily what it means to the other person. A homeowner hearing the word *grass* may think of the *lawn*. A drug counselor probably thinks of *marijuana*. Unless some basis for understanding exists, ineffective communication may be the result. Thus, we must define terms and give examples, keeping our audience in mind and adjusting our messages accordingly.

6 *We cannot not communicate.* Communication does not necessarily stop simply because people stop talking or listening. Suppose you do not answer a question your instructor has asked. Or suppose you sit quietly at the dinner table instead of joining in the conversation. In these cases, you are still sending messages, although your lips are silent. Remember that much communicating is done below the verbal level. You may think that if you do not actively participate, you are not sending messages—but you are! In many instances, your body is communicating nonverbally, and the very fact that you are not saying something may be interpreted as if you were telling the other person that you are not interested, don't care, or disagree.

7 *People react to our actions.* We constantly are demonstrating the *action–reaction principle.* When we smile, others are likely to smile back; when we display anger, others tend to do the same. Try an experiment. The next time you walk down a hallway or a sidewalk, smile as others come toward you. You probably will find that the people you pass smile back, often saying *hello*—action–reaction. Think back to the last time you had an argument. If you raised your voice, what did the other person do? No doubt that person also raised his or her voice—action–reaction.

8 *We do what we do because in the end we expect to achieve happiness.* When we choose to enter into communication, we do so hoping to gain from the experience, but certainly to be in no worse psychological shape than when we entered. Consequently, many people try to avoid any situation in which they feel they may get negative feedback or be unsuccessful in communicating their ideas.

9 *We cannot always have the same understandings and feelings as others.* As we communicate, we must recognize that because of differences in cultures, the only areas we share are those in which we have a common experiential background. To illustrate

Figure 6.1
Commonality of Experiences between Two Persons

this, let us assume that all our knowledge and experience is contained within one circle and that all the knowledge and experience of the person with whom we are communicating is contained within another circle. The only commonality—the only place where our ideas, concepts, beliefs, and vocabulary will overlap—is where we have had similar exposure. Figure 6.1 illustrates this idea. Only in the area where the circles overlap are there any common unities.

If we add a third person to the conversation, the problem becomes even greater, as Figure 6.2 illustrates. Here, there are areas of overlap that exist between persons A and B, between persons A and C, and between persons B and C. But notice the small area of overlap among all three. The difficulty of communicating with large groups of people can easily be demonstrated when this process of drawing representative circles is continued.

 Self-Disclosure

Self-disclosure is "intentionally letting the other person know who you are by communicating self-revealing information."[4] This revealing can be accomplished through verbal or nonverbal messages.

Figure 6.2
Commonality of Experiences among Three Persons

Whether the atmosphere is supportive or defensive is a large factor in determining how much will be revealed and how vulnerable you will allow yourself to become. The amount and type of disclosure will also be based on the relationship between the people involved. The deepest level of self-disclosure occurs when two people open themselves in such a way that each can be hurt by the other's actions. In addition,

Culturally Communicating

Ethnic Self-Disclosure: Euro-Americans and Afro-Americans

In the area of ethnic self-disclosure, European Americans tend to self-disclose more with people they do not know than do African Americans. However, in close friendship situations, African Americans tend to self-disclose more and at a deeper level than do European Americans.

In addition, African Americans repeatedly emphasize the importance of *acceptance, problem-solving,* and *life-time support* in close friendships; in comparison, European Americans emphasize *confiding in each other* and being *free to be myself;* Mexican American interviewees emphasize terms such as *mutual sharing* and *mutual understanding* in explaining close friendships.

Source: Stella Ting-Toomey and Leeva C. Chung, *Understanding Intercultural Communication* (Los Angeles: Roxbury Publishing Company, 2005), p. 299, referencing M. Hecht and S. Ribeau, "Sociocultural Roots of Ethnic Identity," *Journal of Black Studies,* 21 (1984), pp. 501–513; M. J. Collier, "Conflict Competence within African, Mexican and Anglo American Friendships," as printed in S. Ting-Toomey and F. Korzenny (Eds.), *Cross-Cultural Interpersonal Communication* (Newbury Park, CA: Sage), 1991.

REFLECT ON THIS:

1. What do these descriptions tell you about each of the three cultural groups described?

2. Using this information, describe why individuals from different cultures may not get along together or understand each other.

Self-disclosure is "intentionally letting the other person know who you are by communicating self-revealing information."

your attitude toward disclosing is an important factor. Think back to the Johari Window activity that you did in Chapter 5 (see pages 126–127). Are you a discloser or a concealer?

Self-disclosure allows others to understand you, and it allows you to understand yourself. As you talk about yourself, the other person is not the only one exposed to you; you may also learn something about yourself. One of the activities in psychotherapy, for example, is to get clients to talk about themselves in order to talk out what they think and feel, with the intent of having them learn who they really are.

The Self and Others

Your image of yourself makes up your "I."[5] The *self-perceived I* is the image you project, the way you perceive yourself. It is revealed through the words, ideas, actions, clothing, and lifestyle you choose. All of these communicate your "I" to others.

Those with whom you come into contact also build their own images of you for themselves, and they sometimes communicate this image to you. For example, friends comment about what they like and dislike about you; teachers and parents praise and criticize; significant others and supervisors evaluate. These collective judgments by significant others develop into a "Me." The *other-perceived Me* is the person that others perceive you to be. It may be the same as or different from your self-perceived I.

One of the best ways to understand how the I–Me dichotomy affects your communication is to examine the entire process as a mathematical formula. Under ideal conditions, we come as close to I = Me (I equals Me) as we can. Just as in algebra, when the equation balances, there is no basic

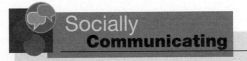

Socially Communicating

First Impression

Try this simple tip to help you project a good first impression: Notice the color of a person's eyes as you shake hands. *Why it works:* You'll gain strong eye contact in a way that shows you care.

Source: Secrets of Power Persuasion by Roger Dawson, Prentice-Hall, Englewood Cliffs, NJ 07632. © Communication Briefings, www.briefings.com, 1101 King Street, Alexandria, VA 22314.

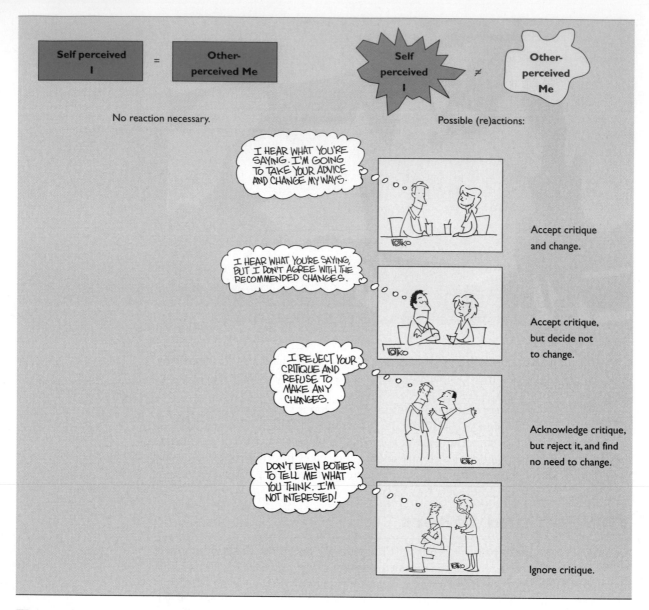

Figure 6.3   I = Me or I ≠ Me

error. If your perception of self (I) and the perception of you that significant others hold (Me) are basically the same—if these perceptions balance—then you maintain your equilibrium and continue to function as before. As a result, you continue to communicate in the same manner as previously. (See Figure 6.3.)

When the I and the Me are not in balance (I ≠ Me), you have four options for how to communicatively react:

1   *You can alter your communication actions.* You attempt to make the specific changes the significant other has indicated. In the play *Our Town*, George, one of the play's young lovers, must decide whether to alter his behavior as a result of a conversation with his girlfriend, Emily. She tells George that he is spending all his time playing

baseball and that he has become stuck-up and conceited. As the conversation continues, George offers to buy Emily an ice cream soda to celebrate not only their recent election as class officers but also his good fortune in having a friend who tells him what he should be told. The scene ends with George's promise to take Emily's advice and change his ways.

You can change on your own, or you can get help from mental health professionals, friends, or relatives. You have probably known someone whose personality changed suddenly, or even over a period of time, because of an alteration of attitudes and ideas as expressed through verbal and nonverbal communication.

2 *You can accept an evaluation by acknowledging that it exists, but you feel the recommended change is not desirable.* Consequently, you accept the evaluation but do not change. For example, a member may take the leadership role after a group makes no progress toward accomplishing its goal. Another member may accuse the newly emerged leader of exerting too much power. Because the group made no previous progress and is now well on its way to fulfilling its goal, the newly emerged leader may decide to accept the evaluation but not make any changes in her behavior pattern.

3 *You completely reject the input.* You consider the information, decide it is not true, and do nothing about making any changes. This happens, for example, when a student in a communication class, rather than accepting comments about his speech presentation, refuses to consider any suggestions. It can take place in a work environment when an employee fails to make the adjustments presented by a manager.

4 *You can ignore any evaluation.* You don't seek out criticism, and if someone attempts to give it, you can refuse even to listen to what is said. Ignorers use statements such as "Don't even bother to tell me what you think—I'm not interested" or "Let me be me." Sometimes you block out all criticism because you find it potentially depresses you or forces you to think about who you really are. Think, for example, of people who adopt the attitude "I am what I am, and I'll be that way no matter what you say!"

Seeking Approval

A great deal of interpersonal communication is spent on trying to get the approval of others. In some instances, people seek approval at the expense of diminishing their self-worth. Some people are so controlled by others and the fear that others (friends, relatives, employers) won't like them that they almost become immobile. Thus, not being able to make decisions for themselves, they turn over their destiny to others.

If you want to eliminate approval-seeking behavior as a major need in your life, keep these guidelines in mind:

- If you think someone else is trying to control you by withholding approval, say so.
- When you are faced with disapproval, ask yourself, "If they agreed with me, would I be better off?"
- Accept that some people will never understand you and that this situation is perfectly acceptable.
- You can refuse to argue or try convincing anyone of the rightness of your stance and still simply believe it.
- Trust yourself.

- Stop verifying your ideas by having them substantiated by others.
- Work at eliminating the apologies you make even when you are not wrong or not sorry for what you have said or done.

The **self-fulfilled person**—the person who confidently chooses what to reveal and to whom—is not intimidated into a negative self-concept and realizes that there will always be problems, frustrations, and failures in life. These people have learned to be happy and are therefore confident of their ability in interpersonal communication.

Gaining Compliance

In our relationships with other people, we often need to get others to do something for us, agree with us, or otherwise engage with us. As a result, it is sometimes necessary to apply the skills of persuasion to our interpersonal communication to *gain compliance*. Physicians, for instance, must work to get patients to comply with their recommended treatment plan. Teachers must be persuasive in getting students to do the work required in a course. Parents rely on persuasive strategies to gain their children's compliance with their wishes.

Research on compliance-gaining strategies reinforces how much securing compliance is a transactional, give-and-take process. Some of the strategies that have been found to work effectively include:[6]

- *Pregiving.* In pregiving, you give the person something he or she may want in order to help convince the person to act as you might want him or her to act. For example, you could give your significant other a gift and then request agreement with your plan to vacation in the mountains.

- *Liking.* In order to assist in the persuasive interpersonal act, you may try to put the other person in a receptive mood by being friendly to him or her. For example, you could offer to help a coworker with a project she is doing so that she has positive feelings toward you and might, therefore, be open to a suggestion that she assist you on your next project.

- *Promise.* In proposing assistance or conformity with your view, you might make a promise. For example, a candidate running for public office, in a face-to-face interaction with you, might promise that in exchange for your vote, he will attempt to get funding for the local YMCA, which is one of your favorite projects.

- *Threat.* You could include in your proposal the intention to use influence or control over the other person if he or she doesn't conform to your request. A teacher does this, for example, when she discusses academic work with a student and warns that the student will fail if he doesn't study and pass the next test.

- *Self-feelings.* You might include a statement of guilt in your proposal. A parent does this when, for instance, he tells his son that he will feel bad, and so should the child, if the child doesn't stop being a bully on the playground.

- *Esteem.* One of our basic needs is pleasure, and people often strive to achieve personal recognition as part of that need. Indicating that there is a reward, recognition, or praise that could result from conforming with your request may sway the person to your side. For example, as a manager at a business, you might indicate to a worker that she could be a candidate for the Employee of the Month Award, which carries a $500 stipend. This incentive might inspire her to work harder.

- *Debt.* You may decide to indicate to a person who is indebted to you for a past favor that he "owes you one" in order to get him to comply with your request.

For example, you could ask a friend to drive you to the airport and include the comment that he owes you a return favor since you gave him your sociology class notes when he had missed class.

Of course, these strategies can backfire if you aren't careful about when and how you use them. As always, you must consider the participants, the setting, and your purpose in evaluating which, if any, of these strategies you will use. It's necessary to assess the situation thoroughly so that you can anticipate how the other person will respond to your appeals. Consider how much is at stake. Realistically, people might consider your using any of these tactics as being manipulative, so be ready for a potential rejection. The bottom line is that you should determine what is the best strategy, make sure that you plan your proposal and compliance-gaining strategy as carefully as you can, and consider what the ramifications of your actions may be before you proceed.

Emotions

A theory that relates to how the brain works suggests that in the process of human development, two brains developed. These are parallel to the right and left lobes of the brain. The first brain to develop was the emotional brain (the right lobe), and therefore it triggers first. Then the second brain, the logical brain, is triggered.[7] The logical brain contains the information we are taught: reasoning patterns, the rules of civilized behavior, and cultural rules. This also parallels the concept that we instinctively act; then we logically reason to conclusions. It has been estimated that 90 percent of our actions are emotional, leaving only 10 percent intellectual.[8]

Any message we communicate is made up of both logic and emotion. Emotional states include fear, anger, disgust, grief, joy, surprise, and yearning. You probably have grown up believing that you can control your emotions—that anger, fear, and hate, as well as love, ecstasy, and joy, are things that happen to you but can be stuffed (held inside). This pattern of conduct is especially true if you are a typical European American male. If you were brought up to believe that it is good to control your emotions, whether love or hate, that nice people do not display their emotions, or that men do not cry, then this statement may startle you: *There is nothing wrong with expressing your feelings; it is normal and natural!*

One of the most feared interpersonal displays of emotion is anger, yet anger is a natural, normal emotion. To react with anger to a situation or set of events is not bad. Anger serves as an emotional defense mechanism to relieve the stress of an overly stressful situation. Suppressed anger leads to ill health, emotional disturbance, and a general feeling of unhappiness.[9] Expressions of anger, however, can be constructive or destructive. Letting out your anger by saying how you feel while not verbally or physically attacking another person can be a positive outlet. But physically or verbally abusing a person is not a positive way of showing emotions. If we use someone as a scapegoat, blaming him or her for our own shortcomings, we are not being fair to ourselves or the other person. Each of us must assume responsibility for our feelings and for our reactions to them.

Power

"**Power** is the ability to control what happens—to create things you want to happen and to block things you don't want to happen."[10] Power is the ability to choose for yourself or to control the choice of others.

Defining *power* as the ability to control what happens and to make choices clarifies several preconceptions. First, the power to choose is not bad, and it is something that is exercised in every human transaction. The view of power as bad may stem from its abuse (often in the form of winning at someone else's expense), from the perception that it contradicts the belief that all humans should be equal, or from its waste (as when there's really no opportunity to gain anything and large amounts of resources are being thrown away in the process, such as when a person spends time and money on a former romantic partner who does not intend to begin a new relationship with him). In fact, power—the ability to make choices—is desirable, not bad.

Every person may be more or less powerful or powerless, depending on the situation and its participants. Thus, you have power, and you are powerful—maybe not with everyone, at all times, and in every circumstance, but certainly with some people, at some times, and in particular settings. For example, a father may be powerful at home when dealing with his four-year-old son but powerless in a work situation in which his boss has made it clear that all decisions must be approved by her.

Interested in finding out how powerful you think you are, how powerful you feel? If so, try the assessment questionnaire below.

People who feel powerless often lack the ability to make choices about their relationships, such as deciding which to maintain and which to terminate. They may feel that they don't have the ability to make choices, and therefore they settle for unsatisfying relationships. Also, people who feel powerless in one situation may take out their hostilities and frustrations in other situations. For example, a parent having

How Powerful Do You Feel? Questionnaire[11]

Think of one of your important relationships and keep it in mind as you respond to the following questionnaire. Each item has two alternatives. Your task is to divide 10 points between the two alternatives according to how well each describes you. You may give all 10 points to one alternative and none to the other; split the points evenly, 5 and 5; or assign any other combination of 10 points that seems appropriate.

1. When the other person says something with which I disagree, I

   ____ a. assume my position is correct.

   ____ b. assume what the other person says is correct.

2. When I get angry at the other person, I

   ____ a. ask the other person to stop the behavior that offends me.

   ____ b. say little, not knowing quite what to do.

3. When something goes wrong in the relationship, I

   ____ a. try to solve the problem.

   ____ b. try to find out who's at fault.

4. When I participate in the relationship, it is important that I

   ____ a. live up to my own expectations.

   ____ b. live up to the expectations of the other person.

5. In general, I try to surround myself with people

   ____ a. whom I respect.

   ____ b. who respect me.

Scoring:

Add all of your *a* responses. *a* = _____

Add all of your *b* responses. *b* = _____

Each of the two totals, *a* and *b*, indicate how powerful you feel in the relationship you chose. The total number of points is 50, so one score could be 50 and the other zero, although that is unlikely.

If your *b* score is greater than your *a* score by 10 or more points, you probably feel somewhat powerless in your relationship because you see the other person's choices as more important than your own.

If your two scores are within 10 points of each other, you are probably unsure of your own power and your potential to influence others.

If your *a* score is greater than your *b* score by 10 or more points, you most likely feel quite powerful and in control of the choices you make in a relationship.

problems with her boss at work—and who feels powerless to do anything about it—may be unusually harsh with her children.

Many European Americans are raised to believe that they have great power over their own lives and even over the lives of others, that they are "masters of their own fate," and that they can "pull themselves up by their bootstraps." Not only do they want power and think that they deserve it; they also do not want other people to have power over them. They may leave home so that their parents will not have power over them. Women and minority groups ask for power so that they can have freedom from internal and external restraints. In short, Euro-Americans are taught not to be powerless. This, of course, is not the case with all cultures. Most of the world's people, in fact, believe that an outside source or fate—be it "God," "the gods," "reincarnation," or "nature"—controls their lives. Muslims use the expression "It is Allah's will," and Hindus believe that their karma is being acted out. In such instances, these people do not feel powerless per se, but instead they believe in a philosophy of "what will be, will be." It is not their mission to seek power, nor in most instances do they rebel against the fact that they do not have power. In most situations, they hold the view that the legitimacy of power is irrelevant.[12]

People telling others about their power is not a universal trait. There are cultures, such as those in parts of Asia, in which people do not talk about themselves. First, too much self-focus is considered a form of bragging or boasting. Individuality is "systematically repressed."[13] Second, cultures that have a nonverbal rather than a verbal tradition believe that people possess intuitive *feelings* about each other and therefore do not have to state what is "known" by both parties. If an individual has power, others will just know it. In these cultures there is a belief that "it is the heart always that sees, before the head can see."[14]

Have you ever considered that there are different types of power and that you may possess all or none of these? The types include expert power, referent power, reward power, coercive power, and legitimate power.

Expert power is your capacity to influence another person because of the knowledge and skills you are presumed to have. Are you knowledgeable about how to operate a computer, throw a knuckle ball in baseball, or bake the world's best chocolate-chip cookies? To build expert power, you need to communicate or demonstrate your expertise to others. You can do this by mentioning your background and training, demonstrating that you are well informed on various topics, and accomplishing tasks competently.

Referent power is probably the most important source of power because it's based on personal loyalty, friendship, affection, and admiration. The key to securing this power base is to demonstrate your friendliness and trustworthiness. For example, emphasize the similarities between yourself and the other person, such as your background, goals, attitudes, and values. It also helps to communicate your support for the other person, give her or him the benefit of the doubt, and create symbols that bind you together, such as in-jokes and a special language.

Reward power requires that you be perceived as the best or only source of desired rewards. To a child, for example, parents may be the ultimate possessors of reward power. Instructors and bosses also have reward power in the form of grades and pay increases.

Coercive power is based on possible negative outcomes that are used as weapons. To exercise coercive power, you need to (1) know what weapons the other person fears most, (2) acquire them, (3) communicate that you have them, and (4) persuade the other person that you're willing to use them. A boss who threatens to fire an employee unless she works overtime without pay is exercising coercive power—power that forces the person to decide between two options, neither of which is desirable. In this case, the employee can either work for free or get fired.

Legitimate power stems from one person's perception that another person has the right to make requests of him or her because of the position that the other person occupies or because of the nature of the relationship. For example, in an academic relationship, students perceive that the professor has the right to make requests of them such as asking them to do homework and take tests. In a committed relationship, companions often feel that their partners have the right to ask favors of them. To increase your legitimate power, you must either move into a new position or role that has more authority (e.g., become the boss), change the nature of the relationship (from acquaintance to friend), or persuade another person that you have more authority by changing the expectations associated with your position.

When we are involved in interpersonal communication, we must recognize that we can lose a great deal by failing to realize the consequences of what we say and to whom. If a person has the power to control us, we must be willing to pay the price for any show of strength we may make. The price of challenging the power can include losing a job, failing a class, or getting a traffic ticket. If, however, we are in a position of power, we can, if we so desire, demand obedience based purely on our ability to manipulate, reward, and control.

Ideally, the use of power is controlled to the extent that it becomes a tool of cooperation rather than a weapon of punishment. A Hindu proverb says, "There is nothing noble in being superior to another man; true nobility is in being superior to your former self." Realistically, however, we must recognize that many people do not hold this attitude, and we should take this into consideration in our dealings with others.

Besides power as a communication factor, gender considerations impact much of our interpersonal communication.

Male/Masculine–Female/Feminine Communication

"Some people become angry at the mere suggestion that women and men are different."[15] For example, "[In 2005] Harvard University president Lawrence Summers suffered condemnation and jeopardized his job for suggesting that the underrepresentation of women in engineering and some scientific fields may be due to in part to inherent differences in the intellectual abilities of the sexes."[16] Those who took Summers's side contended that "among people who do the research, it's not so controversial. Many studies show that men's and women's brains are different." As a female researcher states, "I know it's not politically correct to say this and I've been torn for years between my politics and what science is telling us. But I believe that women actually perceive the world differently than men."[17] According to a neuropsychiatrist, "Advances in neuro-imaging and neuro-endrocrinology have began supplying exciting new insights into how women and men use their brains differently."[18] On the other hand, a prominent psychologist "examined decades of studies that compared the emotional and behavioral lives of men and women and concluded that most differences between the genders were statistically close to zero."[19] One expert states, "Women have 11 percent more neurons in the area of the brain devoted to emotions and memory. Because they have 'mirror neurons' they are also better at observing emotions in others."[20] But another states, "Nurture plays such a huge role in human behavior that focusing on biology is next to meaningless."[21]

This controversy has directly affected the field of communication. In the early 1990s, research in the area seemed to strongly indicate that there were vast differences between the communication styles of males and females. However, more recently, a set of communication scholars has investigated the research background of one of the first books to expose the differences between male and female communication. They concluded that the text "makes quantitative claims based on thin sources, generalizes from small and unrepresentative study samples, and overlooks studies that support other explanations of differences in conversational styles."[22] The investigators contend that "the best evidence on gender and communication suggests that men and women are far more alike than different."[23]

While scholars accept that there are many similarities, there also appears to be enough evidence beyond that of the initial writings in the field that indicates that differences between male and female communication do exist—enough so that the different tendencies deserve to be discussed.[24]

In this discussion of male and female tendencies, please be aware that the statements are assertions based on research findings. This means that any individual male or female may not follow the patterns described. Testing looks for norm patterns, patterns of the general members of the group. You, for example, may fall outside of the statistical sample description for the particular gender or sex being described.

Sex and Gender

"Sex refers to one's biological or physical self [male/female] while gender refers to one's psychological, social, and interactive characteristics [man/woman]."[25]

From the sexual perspective, biological research has "produced a body of findings which paints a remarkably consistent picture of sexual asymmetry. The sexes are different because the brain, the chief administrative and emotional organ of life, is differently constructed in men and in women. It processes information in a different way, which results in different perceptions, priorities and behavior."[26]

These biological underpinnings can have a profound effect on communicating. For example, scientists suggest that the differences in emotional response between men and women can be explained by the differences in the structure and organization of the brain. Because the two halves of a man's brain are connected by a smaller

Communication between men and women is essentially cross-cultural communication.

number of fibers than a woman's, the flow of information between one side of the brain and the other is more restricted. It is proposed, therefore, that a woman can express her emotions better in words because what she feels has been transmitted more effectively to the verbal side of her brain.[27]

Parallel to this view are findings about gender. This research shows that "gender is socially constructed. Because of the lessons we learn about ourselves and our world, people may develop differently. As children and later as adults, females and males often are treated differently, so it hardly is surprising that our ways of knowing and ways of being are distinct.[28] "From infancy on, males generally learn masculine traits—independence, self-absorption, competition, aggression."[29] "Men value power, competency, efficiency, and achievement. They are more interested in objects and things than people and feelings."[30] "Females learn feminine traits—dependence, other-absorption, nurturance, sensitivity."[31] However, recognize that there are some children who learn and use reverse gender roles.

Another factor to keep in mind is that the terms *men's traits* and *women's traits* really refer to "masculine traits" and "feminine traits." In fact, it has been suggested that discussion of male and female communication should refer to "mannish tendencies" and "womanish tendencies."[32]

Remember that gender tendencies are not sexual descriptors. Someone whose gestures, walk, voice pitch, and language better fit the stereotype of what a member of the opposite sex uses does not make the user sexually that gender.

Are you interested in finding out how you perceive yourself on a masculine/feminine scale? If so, try the BEM Sex-Role Inventory questionnaire.

BEM Sex-Role Inventory[33] Questionnaire

Indicate the degree to which each statement is true of you.

Write 1 if the statement is never or almost never true of you.

Write 2 if it is usually not true of you.

Write 3 if it is sometimes but infrequently true of you.

Write 4 if it is occasionally true of you.

Write 5 if it is usually true of you.

Write 6 if it is always or almost always true of you.

_____ 1. I am self-reliant.

_____ 2. I am cheerful.

_____ 3. I am independent.

_____ 4. I am affectionate.

_____ 5. I have a strong personality.

_____ 6. I am sympathetic.

_____ 7. I act as a leader.

_____ 8. I am eager to soothe hurt feelings.

_____ 9. I am analytical.

_____ 10. I am warm.

The odd-numbered items represent a stereotypical "masculine" personality and the even-numbered items represent a stereotypical "feminine" personality. Add your responses to the odd items to obtain your "masculine" score. Then add your responses to the even items to obtain your "feminine" score. Total scores above 22 in either category are considered high and scores below 22 are considered low.

If you scored high on masculine and low on feminine, you would be classified by this instrument as having those personality characteristics that research shows are indicative of a person called "masculine." If you scored low on masculine and high on feminine, you would be classified by this instrument as "feminine." High scores on both lead to classification as "androgynous," a balance of both masculine and feminine personality characteristics, and low scores on both lead to classification as "undifferentiated." These classifications exist apart from your biological-sex categorization. Both males and females fall into all four personality categories.

How Men and Women Communicate Differently

Accepting that males and females generally communicate in somewhat the same patterns, it can also be reasoned that communication between men and women can be cross-cultural communication. It appears sometimes that the dual communication patterns can be as confusion ridden as talk between people from two different countries. Because men and women often approach one another from distinct worlds, the simplest phrase can carry separate, and sometimes conflicting, meanings to members of the opposite sex. Men and women sometimes use language to contrary purposes and effect. "Men use speech to report, to compete, to gain attention, and to maintain their positions in a social hierarchy. Women use speech to gain rapport, maintain relationships, and reflect a sense of community."[34] Women tend to use language to create intimacy and connection, whereas men tend to use language to preserve their independence and negotiate their status.

How do these differences develop? Research shows that girls and boys grow up in different worlds of words. Boys and girls tend to have different ways of talking to their friends. Boys tend to play in large groups that are hierarchically structured; there is a leader and/or a competition for leadership; there are winners and losers in the games they play, as well as complex rules. The emphasis is on skill and who is best. Girls tend to play in small groups or pairs and usually have a best friend; intimacy is the key. Everyone gets a turn, there are usually no winners and losers, and girls are not expected to boast about their successes. Girls don't generally give orders; they express their preferences as suggestions. Boys say, "Gimme that!" and "Get out of here!" Girls say, "Can we do this?" and "How about doing that?" Gender differences in language can be observed in children as young as age three.[35]

Both male and female styles are valid in their own ways. Misunderstandings arise because the styles are different.

There are general patterns of communication that can generally be identifiably male and female. For example, which of these do you think tend to be true, false, or questionable? As stated earlier, please be aware that the "answers" that follow these assertions are based on generalized research findings. This means that any individual male or female may not follow the patterns described.

- Women use more words to make their point.
- Men are more competitive in their speaking.
- Men tend to be more task oriented.
- Women are more supportive conversationalists.
- Men are more direct in their communication.
- Women disclose more personal information to others than men do.
- Women have larger vocabularies for describing emotions and aesthetics.

The myth that *women use many more words per day than men* is questionable. The numbers usually quoted vary from 7,000 a day for women to 2,000 for men; other counts are as high as 24,000 for women and 10,000 for men. Recent research, using an electronically activated recorder (EAR), however, says the "data fails to reveal a reliable sex difference in daily word use. Women and men both use on the average about 16,000 words per day, with very large individual differences around this mean."[36]

Yes, *men are more competitive in their speaking*. They have been socialized to "take charge" and get things done. Typically men engage in *competitive turn taking*, grabbing the floor by interrupting another speaker. Women have been conditioned from childhood to believe that to interrupt is impolite. Indeed, research on male–female communication patterns found that 96 percent of the interruptions and 100 percent of the overlaps in mixed pairs in daily conversations were performed by men.[37]

Yes, *men do tend to be more task oriented; women tend to be more maintenance oriented.* Men tend to want results at any cost. Women are usually more concerned about the process used, about keeping things going smoothly, and about doing business in the least disruptive manner. Women characteristically use tentative phrases such as "I guess" and turn direct statements into indirect ones. For example, a woman may say, "Don't you think it would be better to send that report first?" A man will typically say, "Send the report."[38] Men will say, "What's next on the agenda?" and "What's the bottom line?" Women tend to ask, "You haven't spoken; what do you think?" or "How does everyone feel about this?"

Yes, *women are more supportive conversationalists.* They are much more likely to check the connection of conversations. Women tend to ask more questions and work harder than men do to keep the conversational ball rolling. In fact, women ask questions three times as often as men do. Women often feel that it is their role to make sure that the conversation goes well, and they assume that if it is not proceeding well, they have to remedy the situation.

Yes, *men tend to be more direct.* When men want something, they ask for it directly; women tend to be more indirect.[39] A man may ask a woman, "Will you please go to the store?" He wants something; he feels that he has the status to ask for it and get it. But a woman asking a man may say, "Gee, I really need a few things from the store, but I'm so tired." Often she speaks this way because she feels she is in a low-status position that does not include the right to make a request.[40] A man may well describe the manner in which a woman makes a request as "beating around the bush," and he may ask, "Why, if you want something, don't you just ask for it?" Women also tend to use more **tag questions**—questions added onto the end of statements, such as "That movie was terrific, don't you think?" The intent is to get the partner to enter the conversation. Men sometimes construe the tag question as continuing what has already been discussed.

Yes, findings indicate that *women disclose more personal information than men do.* In their vocabulary selections, females tend to be people oriented and concerned with internal psychological and emotional states, whereas men are self-oriented and concerned with action.

Yes, *women have larger vocabularies for describing emotions and aesthetics.* Women have been taught to express their feelings; many men have been taught to hide or disregard their feelings. Therefore, women tend to have a larger repertoire of words to describe what they are feeling. Women also have broader vocabularies that can finitely separate aesthetics such as colors. Men, for example, will describe the color as red; women describe specific shadings such as ruby, magenta, or rose. Other factors also seem to be present in male–female patterns:

- When a man resists a woman's suggestion, she feels as though he doesn't care and that her needs are not being respected. As a result, she may feel unsupported and stop trusting him.[41] But "when a woman resists a man's solutions, he feels his competence is being questioned. As a result he feels mistrusted, unappreciated, and stops caring. His willingness to listen understandably lessens."[42]

- The most frequently expressed complaint women have about men is that they don't listen. Underlying this is that she wants empathy, yet he thinks she wants a solution; she thinks she's nurturing him, but he feels he's being controlled.[43]

- "Men are more interested in visual stimulation, or physical details. Women are more interested in tactile sensations, emotional overtones, and intimacy."[44]

- Men prefer to talk about actions rather than emotions.[45]

- Men tend to pull away and silently think about what's bothering them; women feel an instinctive need to talk about what's bothering them.[46]

- Men are motivated when they feel needed; women are motivated when they feel cherished.

- Men primarily need a kind of love that is trusting, accepting, and appreciative; women primarily need a kind of love that is caring, understanding, and respectful.[47]

Whose communication patterns are right? Neither gender holds the key to being a competent communicator. For the past decade, some people have believed that men need to change since it is perceived that women are more effective communicators and more sensitive to human needs. In fact, a review of communication books leads to the conclusion that feminine patterns of being supportive, talking through issues, and not interrupting are positive; however, the task orientation, the directness, and the lack of tentativeness of males also gain points. Some communication theorists feel that one approach to a "best" communication pattern centers on a person who acts with *androgyny*—a person who communicates with both masculine and feminine patterns. That individual has the largest repertoire of communication behaviors to call on. For example, this person may behave both emphatically and objectively, and both assertively and cooperatively, which increases the person's adaptability—one of the qualities of the competent communicator.

Gender Communication in the Workplace

Understanding the differences between the way men and women tend to communicate is especially critical in the workplace because it often determines salaries, promotions, and power.[48]

Although the concepts are generalizations, research in gender and organizations indicates that "men go to work as if they're going to battle, whereas women go to work as if they're going to the village square."[49] "Men don't like to ask questions, because they've been brought up and conditioned to think that their job as a man is

What we say and what we'd like to say are not necessarily the same.

to have all the answers. For women, asking questions is a very valid way of getting information that works well for them. But men look at a woman and think, 'She must not know enough to do her job.'"[50] "Men communicate to share what they know; women communicate to establish relationships."[51] All of these findings aid in understanding why, in the workplace environment, when males and females communicate, they are perceived differently.

So what can be done about these differences? "For men, some of the things they need to do is to become more considerate, caring, trusting—basically to become good communicators. Give women enough time to finish their ideas. Avoid interrupting them, finishing their sentences or being sarcastic and condescending."[52]

Another difference is that "women don't want to focus on the solution until they've finished venting, and men don't want to hear all the details."[53] Recognizing these differences and working to accommodate the styles of each gender would facilitate communication.

"A more balanced workplace would include allowing both genders to display emotion and accept that display as healthy. We don't want a passionless workplace."[54]

Sexual Harassment and Bullying

Issues that can affect both males and females are sexual harassment and bullying.

SEXUAL HARASSMENT   **Sexual harassment** may be described as "generalized sexist remarks or behavior; inappropriate and offensive, but essentially sanction-free, sexual advances; solicitation of sexual activity or other sex-linked behavior by promise of rewards; coercion of sexual activity by threat of punishment; and assaults."[55] It also includes "unwanted and unwelcome sexual actions in work and educational contexts."[56]

How much do you know about sexual harassment? Do you want to find out? If so, try the Sexual Harassment Quiz below.

As illustrated in Figure 6.4, sexual harassment is prevalent in the workplace. In spite of the fact that "62% of companies now offer sexual harassment prevention

---

A Sexual Harassment Quiz[57]

How much do you know about sexual harassment? Here are some questions based on court rulings in sexual harassment cases. Answer "true" or "false."

1. A single incident or statement does not normally constitute sexual harassment.

2. If a person participates voluntarily in an unwelcome sexual relationship, sexual harassment is not an issue.

3. The courts recognize that fear of retaliation can prevent a victim from communicating that a harasser's conduct is unwelcome—even though the victim is expected to communicate this fact.

4. For vulgar language or sexual flirtation to be considered as creating a hostile environment,

behavior has to adversely affect the working environment—in the judgment of a reasonable person.

5. If a sexual harassment problem is common knowledge at work, the employer is presumed to know about it.

6. Displaying "girlie" pictures can constitute a hostile work environment—even though some workers think they are harmless.

Answers:

1. True. Usually a sustained pattern is necessary—unless the incident was severe or physical. 2. False. The Supreme Court has ruled that volunteering is not a defense. 3. True. 4. True. 5. True. 6. True.

Figure 6.4
**Sexual Harassment
in the Workplace**

Source: From Louis Harris and
Associates Telephone Poll
of U.S. Workers, Equal
Opportunity Employment
Commission (EEOC) document,
www.sexualharassmentsupport
.org/SHworkplace.html.

- 31% of the female workers reported they had been harassed at work
- 7% of the male workers reported they had been harassed at work
- 62% of targets took no action
- 100% of women reported the harasser was a man
- 59% of men reported the harasser was a woman
- 41% of men reported the harasser was another man

Of the women who had been harassed:

- 43% were harassed by a supervisor
- 27% were harassed by an employee senior to them
- 19% were harassed by a coworker at their level
- 8% were harassed by a junior employee

Note: The Gender Public Policy Coalition stated recently that increasing numbers of men are filing against other men. Seventeen percent of men said they had experienced sexual harassment, vs. 35% of women.

training programs, and 97% have a written sexual harassment policy,"[58] "approximately 15,000 sexual harassment cases are brought to the EEOC (Equal Employment Opportunity Commission) each year."[59] As might be expected, the majority of complaints come from women; however, the number of complaints filed by men is rapidly increasing.[60] Eleven percent of the claims involved men filing against female supervisors.[61]

Communication is the primary medium through which sexual harassment is expressed. It is the means by which those who are harassed respond to harassment.

The causes of sexual harassment at work can be complex, and steeped in socialization, politics, and psychology. Work relationships can be quite intimate and intense. Supervisors and employers can grow accustomed to the power they have over their employees. Such closeness and intensity can blur professional boundaries. "No occupation is immune from sexual harassment; however, reports of harassment of women is higher in fields that have traditionally excluded them, including the blue collar environment such as mining, firefighting [and law enforcement], and white collar environments such as surgery and technology."[62]

Sexual harassment takes place not only in the workplace but also on college campuses. Students at one university reported that as many as 89 percent of women experienced sexual harassment at least once and that many experienced it more than once.[63]

Although "sexual harassment is experienced primarily by women,"[64] this does not mean that men are not also victims. However, in our society, where men may perceive a come-on as positive, women perceive the same advances as negative. Instead of feeling like victims, men may perceive harassment as an ego booster and a cause for bragging.

Men's perceptions of what their behavior communicates are vastly different from women's. The harasser may see himself as intending to exercise his power over women, protect his professional turf, boost his macho self-image, and demonstrate his friendliness and helpfulness. The person who is harassed may want to stop the harassment; deter future incidents; preserve her reputation; avoid retaliation; maintain rapport; and preserve self-respect, physical safety, and psychological well-being.[65]

Sexual harassment has not changed over the years. "What has changed is that people now are more willing to label these behaviors as being sexual harassment, people are more willing to talk about it, and people are more angry about it."[66]

Responding to Sexual Harassment   One of the questions often asked regarding sexual harassment is "What should I do if I am a recipient of unwelcome behavior?" In general, if you question a person's actions as being inappropriate,[67] you should:

- *Trust your instincts.* If you think it is harassment, it may well be harassment.
- *Don't blame yourself.* You are the victim, not the perpetrator. A common ploy by harassers is to intimate that the victim brought the harassment on or encouraged the actions or advances by the type of clothing she or he wore, the way the person looked at the harasser, or the type of language she or he used. In almost all instances, this is a ploy to turn the innocent person into the guilty party. People with weak self-concepts often fall for this ploy.
- *Get emotional support.* Turn to a mental health professional, an expert in harassment, or a support telephone service or hot-line that deals with harassment.
- *Say no clearly and early to the person whose behavior and/or comments make you uncomfortable.* Don't allow him or her to continue with the actions or verbalizations. Call a halt to it immediately by saying emphatically, "I will not allow you to . . . (speak to me like that, *or* put up with that type of talk, *or* allow you to touch me)."
- *Document every incident in detail.* Keep a record. Write down everything that happened, including exactly what was said and done, with dates and times and any other supporting evidence. Share the information with another person to verify that the acts have taken place. If possible, get a witness to attest to the action(s).
- *Find a way to speak out.* Make a statement to someone in the personnel or human resources department of your organization or university. Also alert your supervisor or campus counselor.
- *Seek out supportive individuals.* More and more businesses and institutions are designating safe zones: a person or department responsible for providing resources for persons who perceive that they have been harassed.
- *Seek out institutional and company channels and use them.*
- *File a charge with a local, state, or federal antidiscrimination agency if necessary.* As with any other legal action, it will be your responsibility to prove the harassing actions or verbalizations. Be sure you can document the accusations.

If a friend tells you that he or she has been or is being harassed, you should:

- *Listen without judging.*
- *Validate that sexual harassment is wrong.*
- *Offer to help explore resources and support the recipient's efforts to seek help.*
- *Be prepared for displaced anger because the recipient may not be able to channel it appropriately.* In some instances, a person who is feeling stressed attacks the nearest source, so don't be surprised if the victim turns her or his wrath on you, even if you are trying to be helpful. The person is not really attacking you but is just acting out of frustration.
- *Offer affirmation to the recipient that whatever feelings are being expressed are his or her right to have.* Victims sometimes are confused and don't trust their own judgment. They need affirmation as to their rights and responsibilities.
- *Reassure the recipient that you care and are there to be supportive.* Offer to be of assistance in whatever way you can, but be aware that you are not the person who was harassed.

■ *Do not take matters into your own hands; rather, help the individual find the appropriate channels either inside or outside the company or other institution.* Unless you are a lawyer or a mental health professional, be aware of your limitations.

BULLYING   It is often perceived that **bullying,** verbally or physically attacking someone, takes place in junior and senior high school. However, research now shows that employees are bullied and belittled in many U.S. workplaces.[68] "Managers at about one out of four workplaces reported bullying. And three out of five said uncivil behavior, such as berating employees and 'the silent treatment,' had happened."[69]

"About three out of four workers report these experiences, but most don't complain to higher-ups, so a lot of bosses wouldn't necessarily know what's going on."[70] "In larger corporations the abuse can be buried in corporate layers, and if bosses don't dig deep, they won't find it."[71]

Communicating
in Careers

Workplace Bullying

One in three employees personally experiences bullying at some point in their working lives. At any given time, 1 out of 10 employees is a target of workplace bullying. Nearly half of all American workers (59%) have been affected by workplace bullying, either being a target themselves or having witnessed abusive behavior against a co-worker.

Source: "Workplace Bullying Defined," Waitt Institute for Violence Prevention, www.waittinstitute.org.

REFLECT ON THIS:

1. Based on this statement, what effect do you think workplace bullying has on the U.S. workforce?

2. Have you ever been bullied at work or in school? If so, what did the bullying make you feel like? What did you do about it?

The consequences of the bullying are multileveled. "Verbal abuse at work fosters depression, insomnia, and alcohol and drug abuse. It also lowers productivity, motivation, and job satisfaction."[72] It can have the additional effect of causing conflicts in home environments as employees carry home their frustration and anger.

The actions that someone who is being bullied should take are the same as those one should take to remedy sexual harassment—the person should indicate to the bully that she or he will not accept that type of action, document the incidents in detail, find a way to speak out to those who are responsible for protecting an employee in the workplace (a union, governmental agencies, the organization's human resources office), and file charges.

Relationships

Throughout our lives, we find ourselves in relationships with other people: parents, siblings, friends, and coworkers. This reality makes it extremely important that we understand how relationships develop, how they continue, what constitutes a positive relationship, how to communicate effectively within the structure of a relationship, and how to deal with relational endings.

Interpersonal relationships are social associations, connections, or affiliations between two or more people. They can vary from intimacy and sharing to establishing a common ground, and are usually centered around something shared in common. Relationships may be described with such terms as *romantic, friendship, business partners,* or *family.*

Development of Relationships

Relationships vary so greatly that it is almost impossible to formulate any rules about them. Nevertheless, some general principles explain how they develop.[73] Within the first moments of a relationship, internal (that is, intrapersonal) decisions are being formulated that can determine the functions and goals of the relationship. Whether the relationship will be primarily task oriented, friendship oriented, or intimate oriented more often than not is formulated with the initial interaction.[74]

When two persons meet for the first time, their levels of uncertainty about each other and themselves are fairly high. This uncertainty is generated because people can behave in a number of ways; thus, accurate prediction of behavior and beliefs is difficult. And initial encounters can cause uncertainty in the future as well because predicting behavior is always difficult, and little or no information has been exchanged between the two.

Powerful barriers to establishing intimate connections exist: *fear of exposure* (the decision not to tell certain things because they may be perceived as weaknesses or make you an undesirable partner); *fear of abandonment* (if the relationship begins, what happens if the other person decides to leave it?); *fear of reprisal or attack* (what if something goes wrong, and the other person physically or verbally assaults me?); *fear of loss of control* (especially a male issue, based on not being able to make decisions for and about oneself); *fear of loss of individuality* (the potential loss of *me* as *I* and *you* become a *we*); and *fear of creating a power imbalance* (the potential for relinquishing power to the partner, thus losing your own power).

Think back to your first meeting with a good friend, your spouse or lover, or a coworker. What happened during that first encounter? Why did you decide to pursue

Intimacy depends on clear communication, maintaining a balance of independence and interdependence, and knowledge of the sequential patterns of relational development and maintenance.

the relationship? Did your attitudes change as you got to know the person better? How long did it take you to decide to pursue the relationship? We ask all these questions each time we encounter others and decide how far to allow the interaction to go.

It also is recognized that developing intimacy is difficult. Intimacy depends on accepting one's self as well as others, communicating clearly, maintaining a balance of power, maintaining a balance of independence and interdependence, and knowing the sequential patterns of relational development and maintenance.

Role of Culture in Relationships

In any relationship, culture has an effect. Differences between the participants' religions, nationalities, and race can be a factor in forming and retaining relationships. Since each person enters into a relationship, whether it is friendship or a bonded coupling, they bring with them their backgrounds concerning such factors as language, food preferences, modes of religious beliefs, methods of conflict resolution, sexual patterns, and much more.

Whenever there is a clash between individuals' cultural patterns, there is likely to be conflict. The potential for *intercultural-intimate conflict* centers on "any antagonistic friction or disagreement between two partners due, in part, to cultural or ethnic group membership differences."[75] In Figure 6.5, Alan (who has a strong African American identity) and Sara (with a strong sense of Jewish identity) illustrate the point.

Some of the conflict sources include attitudes toward individualism/collectivism (Is each member of the relationship important, or is the relationship the most important?); value orientations (What is important and what is unimportant concerning relationships with other family members, religious affiliations, and the rules of having or not having a religious system of ethics?); power (Who is responsible for making decisions? Is the system matriarchal or patriarchal?); and certainty/uncertainty (To what degree can each participant stand uncertainty in his or her life regarding rules of relational operation and how decisions are to be made?).

Stages of Relationships

Relationships have a sequential pattern. The **Knapp's Relationship Escalation Model**[76] is a communication-based explanation of how relationships develop and continue. (See Figure 6.6.) Knapp describes the escalation stages as initiation, experimenting, intensifying, integrating, and bonding.

The *initiation stage* tends to be short, sometimes only 15 seconds. Think of the first time you met someone who later became your friend. It is usually keyed by basic information being exchanged such as each other's names. Standard greetings or observing each other's appearance

Figure 6.5
Different Identities Can Affect Relationships

ALAN: How can you know what it means to be discriminated against? You grew up in a comfortable, safe neighborhood. You got to choose whether or not you revealed to others that you were Jewish. My ancestors were brought here as slaves.

SARA: I can't believe you're saying this stuff. You know that I lost great-aunts and great-uncles in the Holocaust. You don't have any monopoly on suffering. What right does the past give you to say how we lead our lives?

Alan and Sara's identity conflict issues—cultural, racial, and religious identities—obviously tapped into very intense, core emotions in their own identity construction. They will need time to really get to know the identity of each other and to find meaningful ways to connect to each other's cultures as well as their own.

Source: Reprinted by permission from Stella Ting-Toomey and Leeva C. Chung, *Understanding Intercultural Communication.* Copyright © 2005 by Oxford University Press Inc.

Figure 6.6
Knapp's Relationship Escalation
Model (KREM)

or mannerisms takes place. Although superficial, this stage is critical in determining whether there is interest on the part of either person to progress to the next relational level—the relational escalation level. Much of the information at this level is at the superficial nonverbal level. Evaluations are made as to physical appearance, clothing, strength of the handshake, or sincerity of the smile. Whether the person gets good or bad "vibes" (feelings about the person) may be the determinant of interest.

The *experimenting stage* centers on asking questions of each other in order to gain more information, which will allow for determining whether there is interest in furthering the relationship. More demographic information may be investigated (e.g., Where do you go to school? Where are you from?). Light probing about belief systems and attitudes may be included.

In the *intensifying stage*, self-disclosure becomes more common. The relationship often becomes less formal, the interactants start regarding each other as individuals, personal nicknames and knowledge below the surface level are known. Information about each other is known and there is growing awareness about attitudes, beliefs, family, and other friendships. There is often common "language" about actions that have been coexperienced.

The *integrating stage* normally includes such terms as *best friends, couple, boyfriend–girlfriend/boyfriend–boyfriend/girlfriend–girlfriend,* or *engaged* associated with the duo. Others perceive the dyad as a pair, as they have developed a shared relational identity.

During the *bonding stage,* a formal, sometimes legal, announcement of the relationship takes place. Terms that describe this phase include getting engaged, going through a marriage or civil union, or forming a business partnership. Other actions that may indicate that the couple is bonded may include living together, or having or adopting a child. Very few relationships reach this level.

Continuing a Relationship

People make judgments about interpersonal contacts by comparing relational rewards and costs—the **Economic Model of Relationships.**[77] As long as rewards are equal to or exceed costs, the relationship will usually become more intimate; however, once costs exceed rewards, the relationship may begin to stagnate and eventually dissolve.

If one person believes that the investment *(relational costs)* of such factors as money, time, and emotion is met with such factors as security and affection *(relational rewards)*, then that person will want to continue the relationship. If one person is doing all the giving and the partner is only taking, then the relationship will probably end.

With this in mind, examine a relationship that you have. You probably have continued to associate with this person because you receive at least as much as you are giving from knowing and being with the person. In contrast, if you have taken the initiative to end an association with someone, you probably believed that you were giving too much and not receiving enough; the relationship was tilted against you, or it was one-sided.

POSITIVE RELATIONSHIPS   A good relationship allows freedom of expression and reflects acceptance of the idea that the feelings of both people are important. We should remember, however, that any alliance experiences times of uncertainty and anxiety. The persons may change as individuals, what appeared to be fulfilling the economic model may no longer do so, and the reason for the relationship may cease to be.

Family and relational communication is dependent on one's being a competent interpersonal communicator.

We also must recognize that we cannot achieve happiness through someone else. If it is to be found, it must be found within ourselves. Unfortunately, this desire to find happiness in someone else causes us to try changing people we supposedly love when in fact we should allow them to be themselves and do what they feel is best for themselves. Love is the ability and willingness to allow those for whom you care to be what they choose for themselves without any insistence that they satisfy you. Unfortunately, this idea is easier to present as a concept than to live as a reality. Most of us spend a great deal of our time trying to alter and change the people we supposedly love.

Communication is the key to creating and maintaining positive relationships. Research shows that couples who are happily married argue no less vigorously for their own positions than do those who are not happily married. But happily married couples come to agreement fairly readily through one partner conceding to the other without resentment or compromise. Unhappily married people tend to get caught in a situation that seems like cross-complaining. Neither partner is willing to come halfway to resolve a dispute; each must continue to have his or her own way.[78]

One approach to successful relational communication centers on five guidelines for making a relationship flourish:

1. *When you are speaking, get into the habit of using "I" messages instead of "you" messages.* Indicate what you are feeling or how you are reacting to the situation rather than accusing the other person. Say "I feel . . ." or "I think . . ." rather than "You did . . ." or "You make me . . . ." Report facts to back up your contentions. Rather than saying, "You are always late," try "I get angry when you tell me you will be here at 2:00 and you arrive at 2:45."

2. *Respond to what the other person has said.* When you go off on a tangent without first having replied to the original statement, you are catching the other person unaware.

3. *Give the other person freedom of speech.* If you want to have the opportunity to state your view, you must also be willing to hear out the other person.

Communication is the key to creating and maintaining positive relationships.

4. *Set aside frequent talking time for just the two of you.* We often get so busy that we forget to talk to each other. Don't assume the other person knows what you are thinking.

5. *Do not put labels on either yourself or the other person.* Name calling doesn't solve issues; stating the issue and discussing it can possibly solve it or at least get it out into the open. Moreover, when people get angry, labeling can become the source of attack and conflict. Saying, "You're stupid," is an invitation to a battle.

Also, watch out for some specific communication patterns that cause conflict in intimate relationships. Included among these are blaming, putting someone down, and teasing. In the case of teasing, what can start out as fun usually has an underlying message behind it that is not humor.

Game playing can result in relational trouble. Such activities as trying to make a person measure up to preset expectations, making an individual prove how much he or she loves you, and forcing someone with whom you have a relationship to follow your wishes can result in conflicts that are irreconcilable.

Another problem is *relational fusion,* which takes place when one partner defines, or attempts to define, reality for the other. In other words, the controller dictates what is good, right, and acceptable for the partner. If the partner allows that to happen, the pattern for the future can be set. Then, when the defined partner wants to break the pattern, abuse may result.

People who are unhappy in their relationships tend to talk at each other, past each other, or through each other, but rarely with or to each other. Just because you're talking doesn't mean you are communicating. Although couples may spend time talking to each other, many lack the skills to get their messages across effectively, express their feelings, or resolve conflicts without hurting each other or provoking anger.

COMMUNICATION IN RELATIONSHIPS All relationships have a structure, and each person has a role. As long as no one changes the system, and each member of the relationship maintains the assigned role, the structure is working. But if someone wants alterations, wants to do things that are not normally done, then the system can become a *dysfunctional system.* A system that is operating to the general satisfaction of the participants is a *functional system.* Assume, for example, that you are dating someone. You and that person look forward to your times together. When conflicts do arise, you are capable of working out the problems without destroying the relationship or building up bad feelings. In contrast, a dysfunctional system is one in which its members are confused about the roles they are to play. For example, if a woman who has been a stay-at-home mother decides to go to college, there will have to be a redistribution of her former chores in the family, and the family's old system of operation will be thrown out of kilter. Some members in the system may not want to change roles. The husband may not want to do the cooking or child care, or the children may resent not having their mother around. Before the system can become normal again, a new balance has to be established. This does not mean that the system has to return to the past mode of operation, but a mode of operation in which a pattern of cooperation exists must be instituted.

This does not mean to suggest that dysfunctional systems are not operational. The individuals in the relationship may continue to function quite effectively as they make changes. The usual result of the dysfunction, however, is confusion because each person lacks clarity about what role to play and what rules to follow. For example, questions and protests may arise as to who is responsible for the tasks formerly done by the mother and wife who is now going to college. Common complaints may include "Why should I have to make the meals now?" or "I've never cooked before, and it's not fair for that job to be shoved on me."

The need to reestablish a system is not necessarily disastrous. In fact, most relationships go through adjustments on a regular basis. As a system is being *recalibrated*—restructured—growth can take place. People learn to assume new roles, develop new respect for each other, or make a new team effort. On the other hand, chaos may result as people fight for new role identities, defend their emotional territories, or feel compelled to make changes not to their liking.

In a positive relationship, the participants attempt to adjust to alterations in the normal patterns so that the dysfunctional period is kept to a minimum. This usually takes place because the partners in the *dyad* (a relationship of two people) have developed effective communication skills and a positive method for solving problems.

RELATIONAL CONFLICT[79]   One of the concerns of individuals who are in any type of relationship—be it friendship, family, bonded, or work—is whether there will be *relational conflict*. Conflict in any relationship is normal. However, when conflict is unresolved, it can be difficult for people to continue their relationship.

Typically, relational conflict has four recognizable stages: tension development, false ignoring, resentment, and unforgiveness. Recognizing these stages can assist individuals in attempting to save the relationship.

During the first stage, *tension develops*. Causes might include disagreements regarding finances, division of labor, intimacy, respect, or behavioral quirks. For instance, one partner may be irritated because he or she cleans up after the other person. These disagreements are normal, but are not always discussed, so one partner holds in his or her thoughts while the other is clueless about the problem until there is an explosion.

The second stage of conflict is *false ignoring,* the decision to stop talking about the topic of disagreement or to pretend nothing is wrong. This occurs when attempts to discuss the topic have proven to be fruitless. That is, either no behavioral change has been forthcoming, or any discussion of the issue has quickly ended in anger and/or hurt feelings.

Resentment, the third stage, is the end result of repeated disappointment. The person who is resentful distances himself or herself emotionally and shares little information regarding his or her thinking. Sometimes both partners feel resentful at the same time, which only intensifies the strain. If this situation continues long enough, often one partner will without warning demand to terminate the relationship (e.g., divorce, firing of an employee, moving out on a roommate, or violence in the form of battering or murder).

As the relational conflict develops, some couples maintain an uneasy truce with each other, telling themselves, "If we are not raising our voices at each other, things are going relatively well." Ordinarily, most people cannot maintain an uneasy truce indefinitely.

The fourth stage, *unforgiveness,* can, and often does, occur. In this stage, one partner has crossed over (in the other partner's mind) from being a misguided person to being "bad." If one or both partners do something that the other considers unforgivable (e.g., committing infidelity or physical abuse), trust and respect are not possible. Forgiveness, although possible at this stage, is often not considered an option.

Heading into the downward spiral of relational conflict can be avoided through honest and open communication. Some people can recognize the decline, resolve to talk about the relationship problem, and work it out on their own. Others have difficulty helping themselves due to a lack of conflict-resolution skills because they have not had good parental modeling or have not taken a communication course such as the one you are taking, which teaches the necessary skills. In some cases, professional assistance by a relational therapist may be required.

Figure 6.7
**Knapp's Relationship
Termination Model (KRTM)**

Differentiating
↓
Circumscribing
↓
Stagnating
↓
Avoiding
↓
Terminating

STAGES OF TERMINATING RELATIONSHIPS[80]   **Knapp's Relationship Termination Model** (Figure 6.7) describes how, at any stage of the model, participants may work toward ending the relationship. The ending stages are differentiating, circumscribing, stagnating, avoiding, and terminating.

The *differentiating stage* is highlighted by one or both of the partners being aware that he or she needs to assert independence. This may result in one or both persons realizing that "we" is no longer as important as "me." In terms of the Economic Theory of Costs and Rewards, the costs of being in the relationship are exceeding the rewards being received. This could be a warning sign that the relationship needs to be recalibrated or that it is beyond help.

Circumscribing stage is illustrated by the diminishment of volume and quality of the intercouple communication. Again, this awareness can be used as a sign that the relationship needs to be discussed and may be recalibrated.

During the *stagnating stage*, the individuals may start to avoid discussing the relationship because one or both think they know what the other will say and are afraid of the consequences. The relationship may take on the air of suspended animation, with little or no mutual feelings or actions taking place. If there has been a sexual component to the relationship, those actions may cease or become automatic rather than meaningful. Often, words of endearment start to disappear during this stage.

The *avoiding stage* is noted for the partners physically separating. Little or no discussion takes place, as it is often thought that the relationship is on a strong downhill slope and is basically over.

The *terminating stage*, the final stage, may come naturally, such as at the end of the semester when roommates move out, or arbitrarily, through divorce or legal separation.

A breakup of a relationship can be hurtful. And this hurt usually comes with the realization that there has been heavy emotional and sometimes physical investment.

At such times, we feel loss, question who we are, feel alone, search for the reason for the break, and sometimes experience guilt. These emotional difficulties are compounded when one party wants to terminate the relationship and the other does not.

Relationship endings can take many forms. In some cases, the people decide on a mutual split, go their separate ways, and feel little regret. In other cases, as, for instance, when your best friend moved, you tried to keep in touch for a while, and then your interests and need for each other faltered, and eventually memories faded away.

Sometimes, it is possible to leave a relationship, if not on a positive note, at least with a feeling of not being rejected or with some positive gain from the experience. This sort of ending is most likely to occur in a face-to-face meeting in which the participants take time to discuss their own observations and inferences about the relationship and each other in a productive fashion. Although this is seldom done, it can be an insightful experience.

Some intimate relationships end with the individuals agreeing to "still be friends." This is very difficult. Being friends is not the same as being in an intimate relationship. Much time and effort often have gone into the relationship, and reverting to a shallow version of the former relationship is almost impossible. Unfortunately, the endings of many relationships tend to be charged with tension and hostility and feelings of loss, failure, or rejection.

The role of computer-mediated communication as a means of interacting with others, including the development of relationships, is an important interpersonal communication issue.[81]

Electronically Mediated Communication

Electronically mediated communication (EMC) includes all forms of communication using electronic devices. Cell phones, electronic mail, instant messages, blogs, social networks (e.g., texting, Facebook, MySpace, Twitter, YouTube), and computer conferencing have become substitutes, in many instances, for faxes, voicemail, letters, and even face-to-face interactions.

Although EMC is made possible through an electronic vehicle, in reality it is about intrapersonal and interpersonal communication,[82] not just about computers and cells. The technology doesn't communicate. You communicate as you use the technology.

Celluar Phones

Cellular phones are an important part of interpersonal communication in modern life. In addition to serving as telephones, cells are cameras, wireless e-mail devices, address and calendar books, Internet servers, and audio systems.[83]

As a result of the popularity of cell phones, interpersonal communication has changed dramatically. Rather than connect in face-to-face conversation, many people rely on cell phones and text messaging. Cell phones offer the advantage of a quick, easy, and instant means of communicating, so you truly can stay connected.

In spite of the positives, cells can be distracting. A cell phone can interrupt face-to-face conversations and meetings. Driving and using a cell simultaneously can be dangerous. It has been discovered that even though conversing involves different parts of the brain than those used for driving, the ability to drive is impaired by cell phone conversation.[84]

The cell phone requires a unique style of communication. Mediated interpersonal communication specialists offer some useful advice for communicating via cell phone:[85]

- Don't interrupt a face-to-face conversation to answer your cell phone.

- Go to a private area to engage in a cell phone conversation so people around you won't have to be engaged in the conversation too.

- Put the volume level of your cell phone on low and speak softly when talking into the instrument; don't engage in "cell yell!"

- If you are expecting an important call, let those in your conversation know that you may have to excuse yourself.

- Avoid discussing personal matters if you are in a public space (i.e., retail store, sidewalk) where others might overhear you.

The Internet

The use of the computer as an interpersonal communication tool is growing at an astronomical rate. Nearly half (47 percent) of all adult Americans now have a high-speed Internet connection at home.[86] It is estimated that internationally, over one billion people use the Internet.[87] It is fast becoming the basic feature for communication in the personal and organizational global civilization.[88]

POSITIVE ASPECTS OF INTERNET USE Some people use the Internet to improve themselves by taking courses. Others use the Internet to look for employment and to conduct business *(e-commerce).*

Through the Internet, people who would never come together under traditional face-to-face circumstances have the opportunity to connect online. This interaction with strangers can offer unique opportunities for growth and confrontation of prejudices.

Socially Communicating

"A Little Mouse Killed Me"

I committed suicide a year ago. Well, Internet suicide. As suicides go, it was very quick. I told no one. I left no signs. Chat buddies only found out via instant messages in chat rooms I used to visit. Their condolences were the type of dialogue you commonly find in chat rooms. For example, "He was a good man" was never used to pay homage. Instead, offerings were more along the lines of "Man, he was so hot" or "He will be missed, I heard he was a top."

I remember holding the weapon in my hand, thinking, do I really want to terminate this alter ego that has been a self-indulgent validation tool for so many years? I struggle with the thought. I even recall the last words that go through my head: "Are you sure you want to delete this screen name?" Then, with one simple tap of my finger, I'm dead. A little mouse killed me.

Source: Thom, "Sex and the Internet," gay.com (online partner.com), September 13, 2002.

REFLECT ON THIS:

1. This entry appeared on a gay online source. Besides the source note, what wording was your clue to this being a gay-oriented commentary?

2. Have you ever thought you wanted to delete any of your personal internet accounts? If so, why didn't you?

3. What would you lose by eliminating a personal Internet or MySpace or Facebook account?

4. What would be the gain in eliminating a personal Internet or MySpace or Facebook account?

Chat rooms are group interactions that allow simultaneous communicating between people on the Internet who select to participate according to their interests.

The Internet offers enormous flexibility. The noninvasive nature of e-mail allows each individual to handle communications in her or his own time and own way. A person can take a break from working at his or her desk, and still talk to someone via e-mail. They can go online with their cell, I-phone, or Blackberry when desired.

E-mail is fast. Most people can keyboard a message faster than they can place and carry on a phone call. It also can be time saving because e-mail messages tend to be brief and to the point with little or no side conversations, such as happens during phone calls.

Today, in most business situations, work is being conducted through computers. Even what was once a tradition of face-to-face decision making has become a subject for collaborating by electronic mail through such programs as *Gotomeeting,* a web conferencing tool that enables coworkers, customers, and prospects to view any application running on your PC in real time.[89]

In the collegiate environment, not only can the net be used for research and making contacts with other students to find assignments and share class notes, but students can also contact instructors who otherwise might not be available face-to-face, and faculty members can send individual or group mailings to students.

The Internet can open avenues of academic communication. Sometimes out of fear of negative face-to-face reactions, or cultural patterns that restrict a student from speaking directly to an authority figure, or out of shyness, students may not approach professors. For example, some Asian students have been brought up not to lose face by admitting they don't know information, or cause others to lose face, such as asking questions of authority figures who may not know the answers. These students feel more comfortable asking for information online.

Some schools have created virtual classrooms that bring together distance education students, allowing them to work online without ever stepping onto a conventional campus. Some people have turned to chat rooms to supplement their psychological needs. People in remote areas can find others who can be of assistance. For example, an isolated gay youth or a woman with breast cancer can find interactive voices on the net.

NEGATIVE ASPECTS OF INTERNET USE   In spite of all the positive features of the Internet, it still has its negative aspects. Most people will use the Internet with discretion and will experience few, if any, problems. However, there are some individuals who become so involved in Internet usage that they use it to the point of neglecting personal and work responsibilities, and become socially isolated. For example, a survey indicated that 13 percent of college students thought that their computer use interfered with personal functioning.[90]

Negative aspects of Internet use include cyber addiction, negative social impact, flaming, cyber bullying, cyber stalking, and diminishment of writing skills.

Cyber Addiction   **Cyber addiction** is considered the major negative aspect of net usage.[91] It is classified as an addiction because it fits into the addiction cycle,[92] which is *need* that leads to *use* that leads to *trouble* that leads to *repeating the action* to satisfy the *need*. (See Figure 6.8.) The problem has caught the attention of the American Psychological Association, which is considering whether to include it in its newest official manual of psychological disorders.[93] The problem on college campuses has reached the level that institutions are now offering support for Internet addiction. For example, at The University of Maryland at College Park the assistant director of the counseling center said the reported addiction rose from 2 to 3 percent in the late 1990s to about 13 percent in 2005 and 2006 surveys.[94]

Symptoms of cyber addiction include lying about or hiding your level of Internet usage, being preoccupied with using the Internet, and neglecting almost everything else in your life.[95] Are you interested in finding out if you are a cyber addict? If so, do this assessment questionnaire.

Figure 6.8
Addiction Cycle

Explanation: In the case of the cyber addict, there is a *need* to escape from the real world due to angst, boredom, or depression. The *use* is to create the world "I" want, which provides the needed escape. The *trouble* that results centers on the time spent on the Internet, which causes missed work or classes and the person's being constantly tired. The trouble leads to deeper *need*, so the cycle is repeated.

Source: Patrick Carnes, "The Criteria of Problematic Online Sexual Behavior," stated in a workshop presented at the Free Clinic of Cleveland, February 27, 2004.

Are You a Possible Cyber Addict? Questionnaire[96]

Directions: How many of the following statements describe your tendencies regarding the use of the Internet?

1. Given a choice, I would generally choose to go on the Internet than go to a social event.

2. I often stay on the Internet for longer periods of time than I originally intended.

3. I have made repeated, unsuccessful efforts to control, cut back on, or stop engaging in my use of the Internet.

4. I am restless or irritable when attempting to limit or stop engaging in my use of the Internet.

5. Using the Internet is a way for me to escape from problems or relieve feelings of helplessness, guilt, anxiety, or depression.

6. I return to the Internet day after day in search of a more intense or higher-risk experience.

7. I lie to friends, family members, therapists, or others to conceal my involvement on the Internet.

8. I commit illegal or unethical acts online (e.g., downloading pornography, gambling, creating a computer virus, or exchanging test or homework answers).

9. I have jeopardized or lost a significant relationship, a job, or an educational or career opportunity because of online behavior.

10. I have incurred significant financial consequences as a result of engaging in online behavior.

Scoring Guide: Answering *yes* to three or more of these indicates problematic online addictive behavior.

Even if you are not cyber addicted, ask, "Is my online time disrupting my face-to-face relationships, allowing me to hide from directly interacting with real people? Also, are other aspects of my life suffering because of my using the computer or my cell to get onto the Internet?"

Those who are obsessive in their use of the Internet may experience such consequences as lost jobs, academic problems, marital strife, mounting debts, broken trust, and being caught in lies and cover-ups.[97]

The psychological "causes" of excessive usage may be long or short term. For example, in the short term, a college freshman who feels isolated after leaving the security of home may turn to the Internet to counteract her social isolation until she gains school friends and feels secure in her new environment. Long-term causes center on a person's having an addictive personality, being compulsively shy, or being obsessive-compulsive. In these cases, the users find the computer a safe haven for satisfying their needs.

If you think that you are overdoing the computer connectedness, ask yourself, "What could I do instead of spending all my time online?" If your answers indicate that your time would be better spent in other pursuits, but you simply can't motivate yourself to cease your overuse, realize that you can choose to act differently and that there are ways to make changes. You might want to consider learning how to control the computer so that it doesn't control you. Set specific start and stop times when you can use the computer. If you can't control the time on your own, place a locking device on the machine and give the key to a family member or friend to monitor your time. Or have a friend enter a new password and turn on the device for you. You may also connect your computer to a timer that turns off the machine at a designated time. If you can't do this on your own, you may want to get involved in some face-to-face therapy or search out a support group for cyber addicts.[98]

Flaming   People online can become the victims of flaming. **Flaming,** which is a form of e-mail aggression, occurs when individuals exchange hostile or insulting remarks.

Because there is no direct personal contact online, some people feel they can get away with verbally abusing others. There are few consequences for the abuser.

The Net can offer power without responsibility.[99] Although many people would not argue with their boss or disagree with their partner in person, on the Internet, especially when dealing with strangers, the meek can become bold. They feel they have nothing to lose. The person on the other end often can't punish, fire, or divorce the writer.

Even when there are repercussions for certain actions, they may not be severe. If a moderator banishes an individual from an e-mail discussion group, for example, the person can simply join another group or use a new e-mail address to resubscribe to the group. The risks are often low compared with those associated with face-to-face communication.

Interestingly, the person who has been victimized in face-to-face communication sometimes may become a flamer.[100] He or she may feel power in being able to get away with what he or she wouldn't do in face-to-face interactions.

Cyber Bullying and Cyber Stalking   "Cyber bullying—also known as digital bullying or Internet bullying—is harassment that takes place using an electronic medium."[101] In some cases, cyber bullying is even more cruel than the in-person kind "because the cyber bullies can often hide their true identities."[102]

Although commonly thought to be a tool of teens and preteens, the phenomenon has been found on college campuses as well as in the rest of the adult world.

Cyber bullying has become so pervasive that municipalities have passed measures to make online harassment a crime.[103] Such laws were stimulated by a case in Missouri, where a 13-year-old-teenage girl committed suicide after receiving "cruel messages on the Internet."[104] The girl, who thought she had met and developed a relationship with a 16-year-old boy on MySpace, began receiving nasty messages, including one that said "she was a bad person and the world would be better without her."[105] The "boy," in fact, had been created by the mother of a neighbor girl who had had a falling out with the girl. An FBI investigation followed. The community became outraged when the emailing mother received no legal penalty because there were no laws forbidding cyber harassment. This pressured the legislature to pass such regulation with stiff penalties.[106]

Another negative aspect of the Internet is that people may use it for **cyber stalking**—following and harassing others. Given the enormous amount of personal information available through the Internet, a cyber stalker can easily locate private information about a potential victim with a few mouse clicks or key strokes.[107]

In order to protect yourself from cyber stalking, you might want to follow these suggestions:

1. Create a gender-neutral name, not one that reveals your interests or your gender.

2. Remove all gender and personal information from your user profile.

3. Make your e-mail signature dull, businesslike, and gender neutral.

4. Check your e-mail headers, which may be sending information without your knowledge.

5. If you find yourself being victimized online, ignore the stalker. Erase the message and block the person's identification. Even responding to say "Leave me alone" just encourages him or her. "Your best bet is to hope that your cyber stalker will get bored by your lack of response."[108]

Diminishment of Writing Skills   A person's writing skills may deteriorate if she or he uses e-mail to correspond. Devotees may exhibit bad writing habits that include:

- Dashing off notes without stopping to think about what they're writing or to whom they're writing, resulting in misspellings, little audience analysis, and poor grammatical constructions

- Using *e-lingo* and *e-bbreviations*—computer shorthand and Internet nonverbal indicators—such as LOL, BRB, JK, :(, and :)—without concern for whether or not the receiver understands the argots (translations) for e-lingo illiterates: LOL (laughing out loud), BRB (be right back), JK (just kidding), :((sadness) and :) (happiness).

Blogging

"A **blog** is a website with dated entries, usually by a single author, often accompanied by links to other blogs. Think of a blog as one person's public diary or suggestion list."[109]

Personal uses for blogging include knowledge sharing, self-expression, learning, gaining self-awareness, self-marketing, campaigning for social reform, community building and storytelling.[110] Blogging has even found its way into the corporate world. When a work team uses blogging, the team can exchange information and provide information to other people in and outside the company. Blogging in business can increase accountability because the project is organized, documented, and visible to others.[111]

BLOGGING DANGERS   One of the major problems with blogging is that separating truth from fiction can be difficult. Some people blindly accept anything they read as being true, even though many blogs are opinion pieces that have not been researched or fact checked.

An example of how rumors can be spread centers on Marcia Cross, a member of the cast of the television show *Desperate Housewives*. "The news broke [on a blog] that Marcia Cross was a lesbian."[112] "The press latched onto this story and ran with it."[113] Things got so out of control that she had to deny on national television that she was gay. Two aspects of the story are cause for concern: Legitimate news sources were picking up on an anonymous Web posting and running it as news without checking the source, and an anonymous posting was being used to sway public opinion without the media substantiating the source of the story.[114] The moral is that blogs are sometimes nothing more than people spouting their opinions without thinking about the need to substantiate their views; therefore, information on blogs should be viewed with suspicion.

EFFECTIVE BLOGGING   As with any interpersonal means of communication, there are certain tips that can help you be competent. In blogging, these include:

- Once you have sent a blog into cyberspace, you cannot retrieve it. Do not write anything that you don't want the entire global population to know.

- Normally, do not include your address or phone number. Harassment, stalking, and death have resulted from the wrong information getting into the wrong hands.

- Remember that the laws related to defamation of character and slander are in effect on the Internet.

- It is usually wise to protect the privacy of others by using fictitious names of people, places, schools, and businesses.

- Writing something in haste, especially when you have strong feelings about a subject, can result in your saying things that you might not want in public view.

- Blogs are generally forever. Do you want this information to still be "out there" in five, ten, or twenty years? People have been compromised and blackmailed by things they have said in the past that they now regret having said.[115]

There are several sites that may be particularly useful to those who are bloggers or who wish to join the blogging ranks. For example, blogger.com, which is a free service, has a three-step format that takes less than thirty seconds to follow. Other blog sites include Kinja.com, Bloglines.com, and Feedster.com.[116]

Ways to Be a Better Interpersonal Online Communicator

How can you be a competent interpersonal cyber communicator?

- Know that you may not always get a response to your e-mail messages. Many people receive a large volume of e-mail, may delete days' worth of mail, may select the "No Mail" option, or may be selective about responding when busy. You might have to repeat your message or alter your channel of communication—using a telephone or fax—to make sure that the message has arrived.

- Some e-mail users become irritated with comments that continue back and forth needlessly. Watch for cues that indicate that a correspondence has reached its climax. Such statements as "That about does it for this topic," "We seem to have concluded this," or "I'll get back to you when I have something more to say," are forecasters of conversational closings.

- Be aware that there is no such thing as a private e-mail conversation. In many businesses, a device that allows managers to monitor e-mail has been integrated into the organization's computer system. If you don't want others to know the sites you are visiting or the content of your personal messages, don't use your business computer or a home computer to which others have access.

■ Your computer provides "cookies" to most Internet sites so that companies, law enforcement, and stalkers can track back to you and/or your computer. The illusions of Internet safety and anonymity are just that—illusions.

■ Be aware that if you are using a university or company computer, the organization owns your e-mails, and your e-mail messages are encoded by their computers and are kept on the organization's Internet provider. A rule of good sense is "Don't say anything on the Internet that you would be ashamed to have your family, boss, or best friend read."

■ Harassment charges can be lodged regarding e-mail. For example, if you send a private e-mail to a friend that contains gender-centered jokes, or if you send racist humor to another person, you can be charged with harassment.

■ Remember that you can't recall e-mail. Once it is sent, it is sent. If you are angry or upset, don't pound your feelings out on the keyboard, or if you do, consider whether you want to wait awhile and then delete the message once you have vented your frustrations. Is today's message really what you will want to say tomorrow?

■ Before you flame, you might want to consider extinguishing the message. You are libel for any abusive, aggressive, or deliberately antisocial e-mail you send.

■ Remember that "there is no intonation, affect, facial expression, as e-mail offers only bare words."[117] To make your e-mail more expressive, pretend you are writing a novel. Include in your message any necessary descriptive information so your receiver can picture what you are talking about and know the feelings you are expressing.

■ If you use e-bbreviations, make sure the person receiving the message will understand their meaning. If not, don't use them.

Social Networking

If you are a typical college student, you spend much time **social networking,** talking online in such communities as Facebook.com, MySpace.com and Twitter.com. These sites allow you to interact with other students from down the hall, across the campus, or around the world.

FACEBOOK   Facebook has become so well known among students that a common comment on some college campuses is "Facebook me," much like previous generations said, "Give me a buzz [phone me]" or even "e-mail me." In fact, the verb, *facebooking*, meaning to facebook someone, has reached the status of being entered into standard dictionaries.[118]

Facebook is a hot-button issue. It has been praised and damned. Specifically, positive aspects of Facebook include:

■ Offers people who aren't socially outgoing the opportunity to meet others and for everyone to potentially create a positive self-image.

■ Allows students to create social networks and stay connected with past and present friends.

■ Removes the requirement of being able to meet someone only face-to-face. Instead of a handshake, students are *poking* each other, nudging each other to interact by attracting the other person's attention.

■ Allows campus surveys and event listings to be accomplished easily.

On other hand, negative aspects of Facebook include:

- Because students' personal information is available to anyone, stalking or harassing someone can be done with little effort. For example, in an attempt to rattle him, the week before the 2007 Ohio state high school football championship game, fans of one of the schools began a poke campaign against the opposing team's quarterback, which resulted in hundreds of entries on his Facebook site.[119]

- *Facebook addiction,* chronic obsession with using the site, can take place. Some people's lives literally revolve around Facebook.[120]

- Identification with certain interest groups may lead to negative evaluations by prospective employers or campus authorities.

- Potential future employers can find out information about an interviewee that may exclude the person from employment or force the person to explain his/her actions.

- Students can get in trouble with university administrators for incriminating and inappropriate information or pictures that are violations of school policy or the code of conduct. For example, several residence advisors at a southern university lost their jobs when photos of them drinking in a residence hall were discovered,[121] a student was punished for hate speech against homosexuals on his blog,[122] and students were expelled because of racist images posted on their Facebook accounts.[123]

- Listings can be used for attempted blackmail and humiliation. In an effort to embarrass Rudy Giuliani, who was attempting to win the Republican Presidential nomination, a rival revealed that Giuliani had joined a Facebook group supporting Barack Obama (Democratic candidate for the presidential nomination).[124]

Protecting Yourself on Facebook   Since there can be negative results from being a Facebook participant, you can avoid some of the problems by protecting yourself by realizing that the Web is not secure. Do not put anything on your page that you would not want everyone to know.

Do not post private information such as your land or cell phone number, address, class schedule, date of birth, social security number, or social plans. In spite of warnings not to list sensitive information, a recent investigation of Facebook accounts found that "41% of users divulge personal information."[125]

Be careful about even listing yourself on Facebook if you do not want to be contacted or traced by others. As of October 2007, anyone who searches the Internet can gain access to members' names and photos.[126]

Recognize that employers use sites like Facebook, MySpace, LiveJournal, and Friendster to check on potential hires. How would you feel about your potential employer seeing what you have posted? What about your parents or grandparents?

Google yourself to see how your name or identity is used. Subscribe to www.pubsub.com to keep track of your name and identity on the Web.[127]

Don't assume that if you remove a blog or site it is gone. For example, one of your authors went to www.alexa.com and entered the name of a website that had been "erased" several years ago. The materials were still "active."

Before going to a job interview, check over your Facebook account. Be prepared to answer questions about your listing during job interviews.

Text Messaging

Text messaging, the sending of short messages (160 characters or fewer, using the Short Message Service from mobile phones) has evolved into a major part of everyday communication for many people, particularly high school and college students. Ninety-five percent of 16- to 24-year-olds use text messaging regularly, each sending an average of 100 texts per month.[128]

Texting is a quick and easy way to keep in touch. Since it can be used anywhere, it allows people who are not near computers to send a quick message. Since it is silent and discreet, you can text without anyone knowing it and not disturb anyone.

Besides personal use, this technology has all the makings of something that could become a highly effective means of communication between various segments of society. Organizations are starting to understand the value of texting. An analysis of the poor communication at Virginia Tech during the 2007 massacre, in which 32 students were killed, has brought about communication patterns on many college campuses that alert students via texting of potential or real dangers on campus.

TEXTING PROBLEMS   In spite of its positive effects, texting can cause difficulties that include poor academic achievement, physical danger, physical impairment, academic cheating, financial hardship, texting addiction, and diminishment of writing skills.

Academically, students may lose their ability to correctly spell words, use appropriate grammar, and develop complete thoughts with a back-up of ideas. Teachers have found that some students have actually started to turn in assignments in texting format and language.[129] Another effect is the sheer corruption of the language that it brings about. Texting can cause problems with writing skills. "Instant-messaging shorthand is creeping into the essays of high school and college students."[130] A professor at Syracuse University cites an example of a student who left him this note: "hi prof how are u culd u tell me my sm grade—tim[.]"[131]

Physical danger can result from texting. For example, deaths have been recorded of people texting while driving.[132] An 18-year-old who was text messaging while driving was killed and killed the driver of another car when her auto drifted into oncoming traffic.[133]

There may be a temptation to use texting for cheating in academic settings. Since students can text an outside-of-class accomplice to look up materials while taking exams, many academic institutions forbid students from bringing or activating phones during classes.

Texting can be addictive.[134] There are students who are so obsessed with their text messages that they must check their phones constantly, thus not listening attentively in class, not eating properly because of the need to be available for quickly answering messages, and losing sleep because of the need to be present so that they don't miss a message.[135] In Germany, where texting has been in vogue for many years, it is reported that there are about 380,000 texting addicts.[136]

In Conclusion

This chapter dealt with interpersonal communication, especially self-disclosure and relationships. Interpersonal communication is an interactional process in which meaning is stimulated through the sending and receiving of messages between two people. Our interpersonal communication is made up of both logic and emotion. The role of power is important in any relationship. There is a sequential pattern for developing and exiting a relationship. People make judgments about interpersonal relationships based on comparisons of rewards and costs. In a functional system, members are clear about the roles they are to play. Males and females may not communicate in the same way. Electronic mediated communication (EMC) is an integral part of our daily communication on campus, at home, and in the workplace. Senders and receivers of EMC should be responsible communicators, and be aware of the potential pitfalls of relying on electronic communication, including its effect on interpersonal communication.

Learn by Doing

1. Think of an interpersonal problem you have had. Then, on a 3″ × 5″ card, describe your role and the role taken by the other person. The class will be divided into groups of three. Read your card to the other two people in your group, and find out how each of them would have handled the situation. After the discussion, tell them what you did and what the outcome was.

2. Relate to the class a recent personal experience that illustrates the action–reaction principle.

3. Think back to a relationship you had that has ended. Examine it from the standpoint of the costs and rewards theory discussed in the chapter.

4. What do you consider the most difficult part of developing a relationship? Give examples to back up your contention.

5. Relate an experience you had in which power was an important element in a relationship. Was the power used to aid or destroy the relationship? If the power structure had been eliminated, would the relationship have been the same? Why or why not?

6. Relate a personal experience in which your emotions totally dominated your logic, and you said or did something for which you were sorry later.

7. Discuss this statement: "Sometimes you have to blow your own horn because no one else knows how to play the tune."

8. Be prepared to take a stand on these topics:
   a. Men are being verbally bashed by women as women attempt to get what they call *equal rights*.
   b. Stereotyping males and females by their communication patterns is a disservice because it teaches people how others act and sets those patterns for others to follow.
   c. The pop-psychology treatment of male and female communication has trivialized the valid research on the subject.

9. Select one of the following topics, and relate a personal experience or an incident a friend or relative has had: developing personal relationships online, cyber addiction, people changing demographics online, flaming, e-lingo, e-bbreviations, Facebook problems.

10. Use EMC to connect creatively with your friends and family.
   a. Send an online greeting card for silly holidays (e.g., for a friend's nonbirthday, passing a math test, or a twelfth-day anniversary for wearing the same sweatshirt). Yahoo.com, among others, offers a free greeting card service.
   b. Use e-commerce to order a gift to be delivered to an acquaintance's pet.
   c. Create and send an ASC art picture to a friend.
   d. Set up an "add on to this" type of chain letter for a group of friends. Doing this will save the time of writing individual messages to each person on the list.

Be prepared to report on what the reactions were to your efforts.

Key Terms

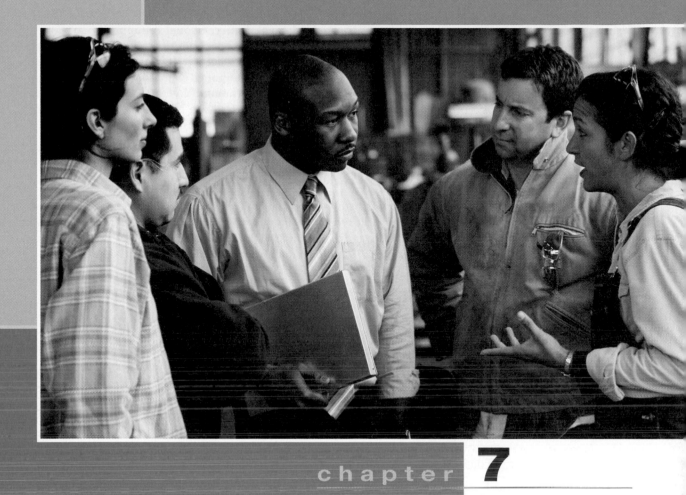

chapter 7

Interpersonal Skills

▶ **After reading this chapter, you should be able to**

- Explain the presentational, listening, and nonverbal concepts of conversation
- State the rules for giving details, organizing ideas, and using appropriate terms in giving directions
- Discuss the process of ascertaining information, asking for change, and questioning
- Discuss the process of apologizing
- Define conflict and interpersonal conflict
- Define anger and explain it as a negative and positive emotion

- Explain negotiation, avoidance, accommodation/smoothing over, compromise, competition, integration, and fighting fair as ways to deal with conflict
- Differentiate the win–lose, lose–lose, and win–win styles of negotiation
- Demonstrate the simple, empathic, and follow-up assertions, and DESC scripting
- Explain techniques for handling rejection and criticism
- Understand the role of culture as it relates to conflict resolution, apologizing, and criticism

E very day you participate in the act of interpersonal communication. You converse with friends, negotiate with members of your family, become involved in conflicts, and send messages to and receive messages from your instructors. To participate successfully in all of these interactions, you need to master certain interpersonal skills, including how to participate in conversations, give directions, make requests, ask questions, resolve conflicts, accomplish goals, and handle rejection and criticism. You should also be aware of the cultural influences that affect these concepts.

Participating in Conversations

A **conversation** is an interaction with at least one other person. Almost all of us possess basic conversational skills. Nevertheless, some people try to avoid conversations. Others have difficulty starting and maintaining social interactions even if they are not communicatively apprehensive. Still others need improvement in their conversational skills.

Conversational Presentation Skills

Conversations usually start with small talk and then move to more in-depth sharing. **Small talk** is an exchange of information with someone on a surface level. It takes place at informal gatherings, parties, and meetings. The information exchange centers on *biographics* (e.g., name, occupation or college major, hometown, college attended or attending) or slightly more personal information (e.g., hobbies, interests, future plans, acquaintances). Small talk usually lasts for about fifteen minutes, and then in-depth conversation starts. The ground level of communication has been passed when people start talking about personal matters, such as attitudes, beliefs, goals, and specific ways of behaving, or express the desire for a social or business interaction, such as a date or a business lunch.

You will find that people usually like to talk about themselves and their experiences. For example, you can ask about where a person lives, what it is like to live there, and what his or her job is. You can ask whether a person likes her or his job and how she or he chose it. The key to good conversation is to hit on a common interest between you and the other person.

Other approaches can help you become a good conversationalist. Keep track of current events, watch nonverbal clues, show interest. If you disagree and want to state your opinion but do not want to offend, try to be tactful. You can say, for instance, "I see your point. Have you considered . . . ?" Another approach is to make a comment about an aspect of the situation you are both in or an observation about the person you are talking with. Say something positive about the person's appearance, request advice, or ask a question.

A vital part of being a good conversationalist is to understand that a person's name is usually important to him or her. As you are introduced or the person reveals his name, repeat it immediately. Then, as the conversation proceeds, use the person's name several times. For example, "That's really interesting, Ian." Several interchanges later, add, "I never thought of it from that perspective, Ian." This reinforces the person's name in your memory and also lets the person know that you are interested in him.

Questions are powerful devices for building conversations. In using questions, remember:

- *Questions encourage people to open up by drawing them out* (e.g., What university do you go to? What's your major? I've been considering switching my major to communication; do you think that's a good idea?).

- *Questions aid you in discovering the other's attitudes* (e.g., Why did you decide to be a communication major?).

- *Questions keep the conversation to the topic at hand.* Whenever a response is irrelevant, ask a follow-up question that probes for more information about the topic (e.g., What do you feel the future job market is for communication majors?).

- *Questions can be used to direct the conversation.* A question can change the topic, probe for more information, or keep the conversation going.

- *Questions help you gain information and clarify meanings.* If what the person says is not clear, ask for definitions or examples or for the source or basis of information.

- *Ask questions that require the person to give more than a yes or no response.* For example, ask "What's your favorite movie?" rather than "Do you like movies?" This gets the person to talk and opens up the possibility of *follow-up questions*, where you probe for additional information. For example, you might respond, "Gee, Ian, that's my favorite movie as well," and then elaborate on why and probe why it is his favorite movie.

One of the biggest problems for people who are nervous about conversations is staying calm and not giving themselves negative intrapersonal messages like "I'm really messing this up." Periods of silence are all right. If the other person does not want to talk to you, that is his or her issue, not yours. If you convince yourself that you cannot carry on a conversation and that the other person is superior to you, then you become your own worst enemy.

Specific suggestions for conversational improvement include:

- Turn the spotlight on the other person. Discover the person's interests. People are usually flattered by your interest in them.

- Listen closely for a nugget to explore that will interest you both. Follow these up with such comments as "What did you mean by that?," "Oh, that must have been exciting," or "It sounds as if that was tough on you."

- Keep it light. Stay away from controversial subjects on your first meeting. If you need to voice your opinion, indicate it with a soft phrase such as "I can see we look at that differently" or "That's an interesting opinion."[1]

Remember that some people are difficult to get to know and that there are some people you may not want to get to know any better. The small talk at the start of a conversation often gives you and a new acquaintance an opportunity to determine whether a closer relationship merits exploring.

The Effect of Culture on Conversations

Be aware that not all people converse in the same way. In the United States, people are constantly coming into contact with individuals from other cultures. In general, white European American males engage in focused conversations; they get right to the point. Behind this is the assumption that a speaker ought to know explicitly the idea or information he or she wishes to convey. European Americans often speak in thought patterns emphasizing *analytical thinking,* which dissects events and concepts into pieces that can be linked into chains of statements backed up by facts and/or examples. Analytical thinking is not typical for all cultures, however. *Holistic thinking,* which doesn't dissect events or concepts, is more typical in some South American and Asian cultures and for people descended from those cultures.[2] Storytelling and the use of parables are common. Although the stories may be interesting, they sometimes

Culturally Communicating

Intercultural Conversation: Misinterpretation of Common U.S. Phrases

American Phrase	Foreign Interpretation
"See ya later."	To schedule a definite future contact.
"Y'all come for another visit."	Bring more people next time. "Y'all" interpreted to mean "more."
"You're on a roll."	I look like a hot dog or hamburger?
"Let's use a shotgun approach."	Shoot our competition?
"Let's organize this like a Chinese menu."	Very offensive to Chinese counterparts.
"Send me your response ASAP."	Have no idea what you're talking about.
"I have to find a bathroom."	You're going to take a bath now?
"It'll take me the better part of the day to finish this report."	Which is the better part? Morning, midday, or evening?
"We need to cover all the bases."	Do we need a blanket?

Source: Reprinted by permission from James W. Neuliep, *Intercultural Communication: A Contextual Approach.* Copyright © 2003 by Houghton Mifflin.

confuse European Americans, since stories don't prove the original contention or answer posed questions, and often don't come to conclusions, but leave it up to the listener to ascertain the point(s) being made.

In addition, European Americans generally are open to approaching strangers, often start conversations with strangers, and are responsive to strangers who approach them. Those from other cultures may not be as open to invasion of personal space. Asians and Native Americans are generally more "stand-offish" toward strangers, more reluctant to approach them, and respond less favorably to conversations initiated by people they do not know.[3]

Conversational Listening Skills

Listening is a very important part of conversations. People who can converse well with strangers are invariably good listeners. To be a good conversationalist, maintain eye contact. You might want to force yourself to discover the color of your conversational partner's eyes. This ensures that you are making eye contact. Learn how to paraphrase the speaker's ideas, but be sure to allow the speaker to finish a point before you repeat your understanding of what was just said or respond to it. Interruptions can be very annoying, especially to those from mannerly cultures such as Japan.

Listening in conversations requires some strategies:

- *Listen to the concerns of others.* Conversations should be two-sided, with both people having the opportunity to participate. Often, people ask questions only so that they can give their own answers. You already know what you think. If you are interested in a conversation, not in giving a personal speech, find out what others think and address their ideas. An "I-I" conversation can be very unsatisfying.

- *Don't assume.* Too often we assume one thing and later find we were mistaken. Because physical and oral first impressions are not always accurate, give the other person a chance to prove he or she is worthy of your conversation or repugnant enough to cast aside.

- *Before speaking, ask yourself what message is needed.* Some people do not like to participate in small talk because it appears to offer no opportunity for in-depth discussion or because finding out little tidbits about people in whom they are not interested seems a waste of time. These contentions may be true, but you cannot get to know a person to the degree necessary to have an in-depth conversation until you get to know him or her on a basic level and build rapport. People who start right off by stating strong viewpoints and getting too personal often are rebuffed.

Conversational Nonverbal Skills

Nonverbal communication plays an important role in conversation. For example, quick glances away may indicate that the person is anxious to leave, and the same may be implied when that person glances repeatedly at a watch, looks around the room, or shifts from one foot to the other. If, however, the person leans forward, is intently looking at you, or is directly facing you, then the interaction is probably positive. Consider whether to continue or end the interaction based on the other person's comments as well as both of your nonverbal cues.

CONVERSATIONAL SALONS　An interesting application of conversation skills is the development of *salon conversation clubs*, formed by people who enjoy the opportunity to participate in interactions about various topics, such as books, politics, religion, or the arts.[4] The purpose is to get a group of people together not only to discuss a topic but also to retrieve the lost art of conversation, which some think may have diminished in this age of the computer, text messaging, and excessive television watching.[5]

Salons have been held on college campuses in dorm rooms or student center lounges, and by the general public in private homes and in recreation centers. Members are attracted through online advertisements, newspaper and radio announcements, and one-on-one recruiting. College professors have formed conversational salons with their students to encourage discussions of topics beyond the classroom and, since the setting is informal, the professor can become part of the group rather than its leader.

Giving Directions

We often find ourselves giving other people **directions**—for example, instructions for accomplishing a task, achieving an effect, or getting somewhere. In giving directions, include all the necessary details, organize the ideas in a specific order, and use clearly understood terms.

Giving Details

How many times have you asked someone for directions and been given only a very general description? Others assume that because they know what they are talking about, you do also. "Go down the street to the corner and make a right" may be very clear if you know what street and which corner the person means. Unfortunately, such is not always the case. On the other hand, too many details can be confusing.

Have you ever been frustrated by your attempt to assemble an electronic device that was accompanied by vague directions? Directions are commonly written by the experts who designed the item. They often assume that because they know what to do, you too can figure out how to do the assembling.

We often find ourselves giving other people directions.

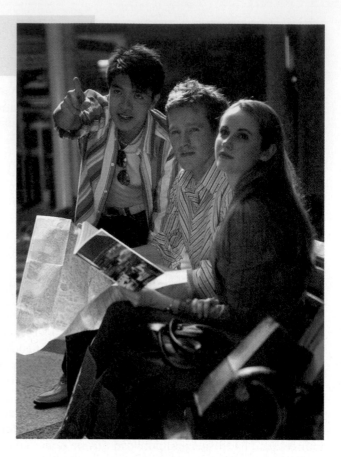

When providing directions, try to be as specific and clear as possible. Include such information as names, references (north, south; left, right), descriptions (the size of the item, a sketch of what it looks like), and warnings about where confusion may set in. The procedure should be the same whether you are giving travel directions, assembly information, or a recipe.

Communicating
in Careers

Ways to Give Instructions

Here are some ways to help you communicate better when assigning tasks:

- Explain the purpose of the assignment. Employees are more likely to give their best when they feel they're being brought into the big picture.

- Give employees the real deadline. Even if an employee has a reputation for being chronically late, you'll earn more respect with your honesty than by lying about an early deadline.

- Tell them who else is involved in the task. Your explanation may forestall deadline problems. Explain, too, whom the employee can ask for help if you're not available.

- Explain why you chose them. This will make employees want to do a good job for you, because you've singled them out for positive attention.

- Don't allow sloppy work to sneak by you. And don't make a habit of "redoing" the drafts sent to you. If you do, the employees will start saying to themselves, "Oh well, if there is anything wrong, the boss will catch it."

- Summarize what you told them. Then, instead of asking if they have any questions, ask them a question or two.

Source: The Personnel News, 4701 Patrick Henry Drive, Suite 1301, Santa Clara, CA 95054.

Organizing Ideas

Directions are easiest to follow when they are given in a chronological or a spatial order. In a chronological order, you indicate the step-by-step procedure by telling what is to be done first, second, third, and so on. This is a good method to use when explaining how something should be assembled.

Spatial orders involve providing descriptions according to geographic directions. A travel plan from the auto club indicating the exact place where you start and the place-by-place order of the cities you will go through is an example of directions that are in spatial order. Automobile navigation devices follow this procedure.

Knowing if someone is a linear or global thinker (see Chapter 4, pp. 95–96, for details and a test to determine your style) can aid you in deciding how to package the directions. Linear thinkers prefer maps and written-out directions. Global thinkers prefer pictures and oral directions with specific landmarks (e.g., the identification of indicators such as restaurants and gas stations by name).

Requesting

Requesting is the process of expressing a desire for something. It centers on asking, expressing a desire or soliciting for something wanted or desired.[6] Requests usually fall into one of two categories: requesting information or asking questions.

Requesting Information

When you request information, specify the exact nature of the information you want and make the request in language that includes a suggestion as to how the request is to be carried out. If you ask the research librarian, for example, to tell you about Lucerne, Switzerland, she or he can give you volumes of information. But what specifically do you want to know? Maybe you are interested in finding out the most recent population statistics. Try to be as specific as possible.

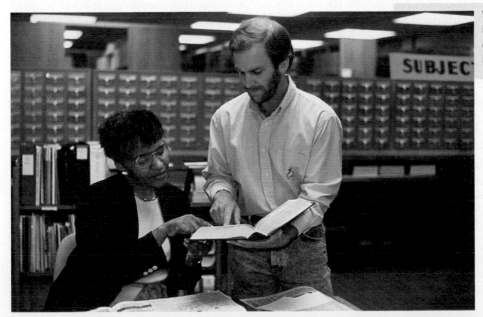

When you request information, specify the exact nature of the information you want.

If you are not presenting the request in person, indicate how you wish to receive the reply: by telephone, e-mail, fax, letter, text messaging, or in person. If the information must be received by a deadline, be sure to specify this as well.

Make sure that both you and the other person understand exactly what is wanted and how the request is to be processed.

Asking Questions

People often do not ask questions because they are afraid to do so, do not know how to ask them, or do not know what to ask. The reluctance to ask questions has become a major communication problem in academic, personal, and professional environments.[7] Students may sit in class not understanding the concepts being presented. However, when the instructor asks if there are any questions, they fail to take advantage of the opportunity for clarity. Employees, when given instructions for accomplishing a task, may not ask for clarification, even though they don't understand them. Personal relationships may be endangered because participants don't understand what another person is saying but won't state their lack of knowledge. Gaining the skills involved in **asking**—seeking out information by inquiring—will help you to eliminate misunderstandings, aid you in ensuring receipt of your intended message, reassure you that you gained the proper information, and convince the sender that you really do understand.

Asking is important. If, for example, a person receives directions to institute a new procedure at work, he or she may need to ask questions of the supervisor or trainer who is providing the instructions. A worker who is reluctant to ask for clarification for fear of appearing uninformed is probably just creating more problems for himself. Later, when called on to perform the new procedure, he may be unable to do so. Remember that if something is important to understand, it is important enough to ask questions about if you don't comprehend the concept.

When you ask questions that probe for information, word the queries in a way so that the listener will know exactly what you need. To do this, determine what it is that you do not understand. Ask a specific question that will clarify your dilemma. If you cannot identify what you do not understand, recognize that confusion usually centers on the need for restatement, definition, or clarification.

ASKING FOR RESTATEMENT Sometimes in explaining, people state their ideas in such a way that the concepts are unclear. This confusion may be caused by the order in which the ideas were presented. For example, an explanation of an accounting procedure that does not tell the first step, the second step, and so on, will probably lead to confusion. In this case, ask for the ideas to be presented in a step-by-step sequence. This is especially true if you are a linear listener and learner. Linear listeners generally need a clear step-by-step structure to organize the ideas, thus leading to clarity.

ASKING FOR DEFINITIONS Unclear vocabulary is a major problem in understanding information. Asking someone to define terms often clears up the misunderstanding. Many professionals forget that the average person does not have much expertise in the subject and therefore does not have access to technical terminology. This is usually the problem, for example, with physicians who use medical terms to explain a patient's illness. An explanation appropriate to the layperson's vocabulary is necessary.

Each time you are introduced to a new subject area, you must learn its vocabulary. Chemistry, psychology, and communication, for example, all have specialized vocabularies. Students who do poorly in these subjects often do so because they are weak in the subject's vocabulary. In asking for a definition, be specific. Ask, "What does [fill in the word] mean?"

ASKING FOR CLARIFICATION   Sometimes the basic information in a message is simply not enough. In this case, clarification can be achieved through the use of examples, illustrations, and analogies. For example, while listening to a lecture, you will find that the first few sentences dealing with each new concept tell the idea, and the rest of the statements enlarge the idea. Sometimes, however, senders forget to give examples, illustrations, or analogies. If the illustrations used are not clear, ask for new or additional ones. This is especially true if you are a global listener and learner. Global listeners generally need examples to clarify and make abstract ideas concrete.

As you sit in class, participate in a medical examination, or are being trained to operate a piece of equipment, try to paraphrase what the speaker is saying. If you cannot do so, you probably do not understand the message. In that case, ask questions—specific questions!

Dealing with Interpersonal Conflict

When you hear the word *conflict,* what do you think? If you are fairly typical, your list includes such terms as a *fight, dissension, friction, strife, and confrontation.* These terms tend to be negative, and many of us have been taught to think of conflict as a totally negative experience—something to be avoided. In truth, conflict in and of itself is a natural process that can be negative or positive, depending on how it is used. The Chinese word for *conflict* or *crisis* is made up of two components. (See Figure 7.1.) The top figure stands for "danger" and the bottom section stands for "opportunity." Most people recognize the danger part in a crisis or conflict, but few recognize the opportunity. Conflict can promote relational changes, bring people together, precipitate personal growth, or aid in gaining personal and relational insights.

Figure 7.1

In Chinese, the words *danger* (top) and *opportunity* (bottom) are components of the word *crisis.*

危
機

Conflict Defined

"A **conflict** is any situation in which you perceive that another person, with whom you're interdependent, is frustrating or might frustrate the satisfaction of some concern, need, want, or desire of yours."[8] "The source of conflict or crisis could be your perception of a limited resource (such as money) or an individual difference between you and the other person (such as differences in how you and the other person define your relationship)."[9] Conflict is part of everyone's life.

The process of conflict begins when one person perceives that another person has caused him or her to experience some type of frustration, thus they experience interference from each other in accomplishing their goals.[10] This frustration, if put into words, would sound like this: "I *want* [your personal concern, need, want], *but* [the person perceived as frustrating you] *wants* [his or her concern, need, want]." From these statements comes a conflict or crisis situation in which incompatible thoughts are present. These thoughts prevent, block, or interfere with each other or in some way irritate the participants. "Any situation in which one person perceives that another person, with whom he or she is interdependent, is interfering with his or her goal achievement may be defined as a conflict situation. . . . If it is not expressed in some way, but kept bottled up inside, it is an intrapersonal conflict."[11]

Some people try to avoid conflict at any cost. Indeed, one study indicated that "students try to avoid about 56 percent of their conflicts. They become skilled at turning away from conflict."[12] This sort of behavior may not desirable. If handled constructively, conflict can be healthy because it allows for the communication of differing points of view, which can lead to important awareness and changes.

Just as conflict can serve a useful function, so too can it be detrimental. Conflict is detrimental when it stops you from doing your work; threatens the integrity of a relationship; endangers the continuation of a relationship or your ability to function within it; causes physical, mental, or sexual abuse; or leads a person to give up and become inactive in a relationship or life in general.

Since most of the readers of this book will be dealing with conflict in the predominantly Euro-American society, an investigation of that society's conflict patterns will be undertaken. However, even if you are European American, remember that because the United States and Canada are nations of immigrants, a great number of the people with whom you come in contact have strong other-cultural ties and may follow the patterns of their native cultures. In addition, not all people within a culture act exactly the same. The patterns described are based on research but probably don't describe the actions of everyone in a specific culture.

Causes of Conflict

Think back to instances when you were involved in a conflict. What preceded the conflict? What were the causes of the conflict that ensued? Four major issues have been identified as the root causes of conflicts.[13] These issues center on goals, allocation of resources, decision making, and behaviors.

- *Goals to be pursued.* Communication often centers on someone's desire that you do what he or she wants you to do while you are interested in doing what you want to do. A friend asks you to do her a favor that you don't want to do. A parent tells a high school senior what college to attend or what major to pursue. A boss insists that the only right way to perform the employee's job is the boss's way. These are examples of goals one person is trying to set for someone else.

- *Allocation of resources.* We only have so much time. We only have so much money. When someone asks us to expend our resources, we may get stressed. This stress can lead to conflict. You have a term paper due in two days. A friend asks you to go to a party with her. You indicate that you are on a short calendar. She insists that you have lots of time and that the party will be fun. Or remember the time

Sometimes in conversation, a person gets caught between two opposing points of view.

when you asked your parents for new designer jeans, a car, or a computer? They tried to explain that money was short, but that meant little, as your needs were the most important issue. A battle followed. Often the acting out of these conflicts escalated with your saying something like, "You're stingy" or "Everyone else's parents get them what they need."

- *Decisions to be made.* Decisions that are appropriate for one person may not be appropriate for another. This situation becomes a source of conflict when Mia attempts to force Sheiva to go along with Mia's decision. Another source of conflict centers on how decisions are made. People generally don't want to go along with decisions that concern them but that don't include their input. Employers who impose working hours on employees without obtaining the employees' input may find themselves at the center of a storm. Teenagers may rebel over what they consider to be imposed solutions to their problems. Conflicts may erupt concerning what person she can date, and even what she can wear out of the house.

- *Behaviors that are considered inappropriate.* Each of us has certain parameters by which we live our lives, and we often expect others to follow our lead. If a person deviates from that course, we may consider the person's behavior inappropriate. A person displaying a lack of manners in a restaurant, wearing inappropriate clothing, or drawing unnecessary attention to himself or herself may be the cause of conflict. "You embarrass me when you act like that" may be the statement that stimulates conflict.

Levels of Conflict

As with all other ascending levels of emotions, conflict develops sequentially and can be understood by examining the levels it travels through. These steps seem present in every type of conflict, ranging from neighborly spats to family disagreements, marital problems, labor negotiations, and international incidents. (See Figure 7.2.)[14]

Level 1. No conflict. The individuals face no key differences in goals.

Level 2: Latent conflict. One person senses a problem and believes that goal differences exist. Yet the other gives no sign of noticing such differences or tries to deny that differences exist.

Level 3: Problems to solve. The people express concerns that focus on interests. They choose to confront the problem and have the courage to face the risks associated with that confrontation. The goals do not include personal attacks that move the conflict toward a destructive orientation.

Level 4: Dispute. There is a problem to solve that carries with it a needs-centered conflict. The individuals fight about an issue but insert frequent personal attacks that move the conflict toward a destructive orientation.

Level 5: Help. When people can no longer manage their dispute because it has gotten out of control, they often seek help. The help can be from friends, relatives, or a professional such as a mental health worker, conciliator, mediator, arbitrator, or adjudicator. It is best if the third party is neutral and invited to participate rather than one who intrudes. The assistance can be directive or nondirective, but unless required to do so by law, the third party should manage the procedure, not solve the conflict. Individuals forced into a solution, such as in court-decreed divorces and child custody cases and arbitrated labor–management conflicts, almost always hold resentments.

Figure 7.2
Levels of Conflict

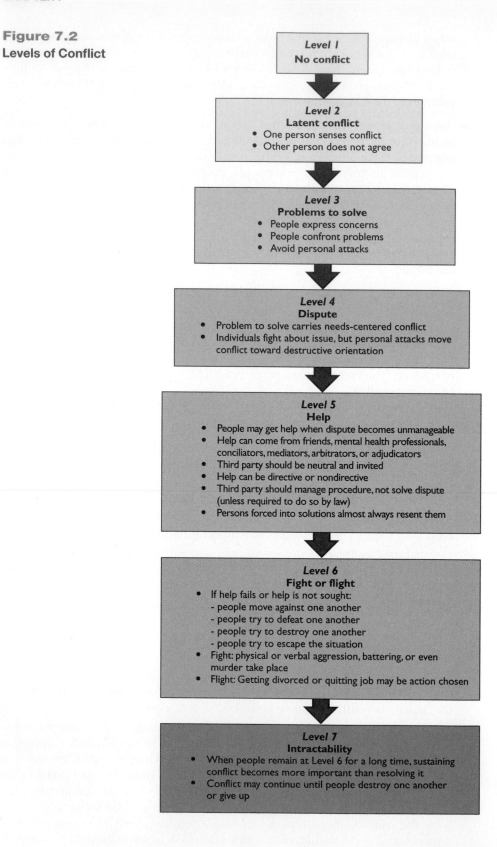

Level 6: Fight or flight. If the help fails or the parties become so angry that they don't think of asking for help, they either move against and try to defeat or destroy one another (such as in declaring war) or they try to escape from the situation, such as when a teenager runs away from home. It is at the fight stage that physical and verbal aggression, battering, or even murder may take place. At the flight level, getting divorced or quitting a job may be the chosen action.

Level 7: Intractability. When people remain at the fight-or-flight level for a long period of time, sustaining the conflict becomes more important than resolving it. That is, the conflict gains a life of its own. People abandon hope for a constructive solution. The conflict may continue until the parties destroy one another or lose the will to continue to fight.

Role of Personal Anger in Conflict

Explaining reactions to conflict, a person may say, "He made me mad" or "I was so angry I couldn't control myself." These are statements expressing the emotion of anger.

Anger is the feeling of being upset with yourself or others (or both). "Anger is a signal, and one worth listening to. Our anger may be a message that we are being hurt, that our rights are being violated, that our needs or wants are not being adequately met, or simply that something is not right."[15] With the possible exception of anger caused by illness, most angry episodes are social events. The participants are you and yourself, or you and someone or some group of others. You can be angry at yourself because you allowed yourself to be taken advantage of, for not standing up for your rights, or for doing something that you now know was not the right way to act. Or your anger may be aimed at another or others for what you perceive he, she, or they did to you, or said to you or about you, or didn't say or do.

Anger is not a condition with a single cause; it is a process, a transaction, a way of communicating. You communicate to yourself first that something is wrong, and then, in some cases, you communicate that knowledge to others. Sometimes your anger is below your level of awareness; you know something is wrong, but you don't know what it is. Anger assumes meaning only when you are aware of it or express it to yourself or others. Anger is emotional, not logical. You get angry emotionally, and you often express that emotion by attacking yourself or someone else. Anger isn't a problem, but the way you express that anger can make it into a problem.

When you get angry, there are various forms that the expression may take (see Figure 7.3). Your actions may follow an internal or outward form that has negative implications, or you could take a positive action by asserting yourself in a clear, direct, and expressive way. The negative implications tend to follow a pattern—first, internal and/or external actions, then passive resistance, acting out, and, finally, violence. The expression of anger may stop at any step of the process.

Anger can be *implosive.* You can beat yourself up in various ways: negative self-talk; overuse of drugs, alcohol, or food; self-mutilation; or suicide. Or anger can be *explosive:* You attack others through physical or verbal abuse, cut off verbal or social contact, remove love, restrict financial support, or disown them.

Once you are aware of the feeling of anger, you can identify what it is and its cause by putting your thoughts into words. Think back to the last time you were feeling angry. Using that information, fill in the blanks in this statement: *I want/wanted* _____, *but* [name the person(s)] _____ *wants/wanted* or *didn't want/doesn't want to* _____. For example, "I wanted to leave to go to dinner, but James kept wasting time." Being able to verbalize what is bothering you often makes it possible for you to understand what is happening and decide what to do about it.

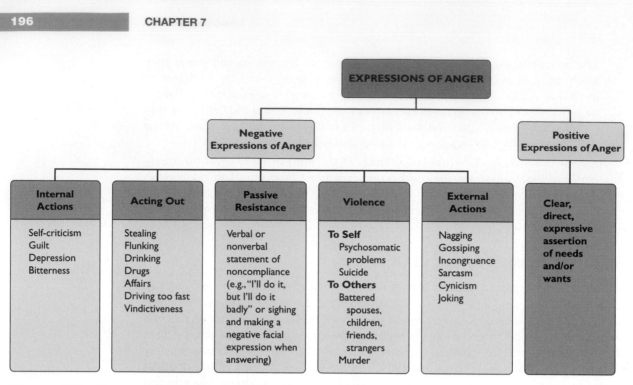

Figure 7.3   Forms of Expression for Anger

Source: Diagram by Judith K. Beebe, LPC, Lorain, OH, and Sandra J. Nowkowski, PhD, Las Vegas, NV. Reprinted by permission.

Normally we perceive anger to be a negative feeling. You get mad at yourself for not taking action or because you did the wrong thing, and you deal with it negatively by getting depressed, reacting with defensive behavior, allowing it to affect you physically, or starting to doubt yourself. We know that internalized anger can result in headaches, tension, and depression. It can also result in legal and psychological effects if you attack someone verbally or physically. On the other hand, it can be positive if you use the anger to alert yourself to what's wrong, figure out how to deal with it constructively, and act in a responsible way.

There are some techniques that can affect your interpersonal expression of anger so that it can be a constructive rather than a destructive action. Consider, for example:[16]

- *Do not react immediately when you are angered.* The count-to-ten technique is often effective. It stops you from acting on only your emotions and allows you to think through the ramifications of your actions.

- *If possible, don't make important decisions in the heat of an angry moment.* A moment of emotional stress is not the time to fire anybody or tell your spouse or lover that your relationship is over.

- *Use the extra energy generated by anger to act constructively.* When you experience anger (or its first cousin, fear), your body activates its *fight-or-flight mechanism* (stay and battle it out or run away). This results in an increased flow of adrenaline that makes you temporarily stronger than usual. But instead of beating up someone, go for a fast-paced walk.

- *Apologize if necessary.* If you really behave badly during a fit of anger, an apology to those who have been affected is in order. A simple "I'm sorry; I was angry" will probably do. Sometimes you need to go further and make an "I" statement of what motivated your outburst (e.g., "I really get upset when I feel my ideas are being totally ignored. I'm sorry I left the meeting. I'd appreciate it if next time you'd let me finish my entire presentation before telling me that it is not a good idea").

Dealing with Another Person's Anger in Conflict

To deal with someone else's anger, one expert advises, "Don't let them dump on you; it only encourages their craziness."[17] Instead, you must determine what is the best behavior for you and then carry it out. If you give in to another's emotional blackmail (e.g., threats that he will leave you or stop being your friend), you have set a pattern by which that person can control you in the future. And the more you give in, the more the person will use the same ploy again.[18] We teach people how to treat us. Once the pattern is set, the other person will likely assume that you will let him or her aggress against you in the future, and that's how you will be treated.

Remember that in a conflict situation, the other person often is attacking you when you may not be the cause of the problem or cannot solve the problem. It may be simply that you are the first person who wandered on the scene after an incident happened. The best approach is to allow the person to vent her frustrations while you remember that the attack is not really against you and try not to react personally. If the person continually uses you as her scapegoat, recount factually what the pattern has been and that you will not allow yourself to be a scapegoat. State the facts and how you want to be treated. It's hard to argue with facts! You could say, "Yesterday you yelled at me when Maria didn't get her report in on time and when LeBron didn't reach his sales quota. I wasn't responsible for either of those things. I know you were angry, but I'd appreciate it in the future if you discussed other people's problems with them, not take your anger out on me."

Disagreements actually can end up being constructive if you follow the basic principles of fighting fair.[19]

Fair Fighting

In **fair fighting,** participants work toward an amicable solution to the problem and keep in mind that although the issue is important, the relationship is also important, such as with marital or other relational partners, children and parents, and friends. Some fair-fighting strategies include the following:

- *Get as much information as you can, and attempt to adjust to the problem based on this information.* Fact, rather than hearsay, may show that the supposed cause of the conflict is not the actual cause.

- *Keep arguments in the present tense.* Do not argue about what happened in the past; that can't be changed.

- *Do not try to make the other person change things that cannot be altered.* We cannot trade in our relatives, extensively alter our physical appearance, or become a totally different person.

- *Do not start a fight when it cannot be finished.* It is not appropriate to start a stressful discussion when a person is walking out the door on the way to work or on a tight schedule or when one or both parties are extremely tired.

- *The setting can affect a conflict.* Disagreeing in public or in front of individuals who are not part of the conflict is not a good strategy. It can bring about embarrassment not only to the participants but also to the observers.

- *A fight can take place only if both parties participate.* If the conflict is getting out of hand or has gone on too long, then one party should simply stop participating.

In fair fighting, participants work toward an amicable solution to the problem and keep in mind that although the issue is important, the relationship is also important.

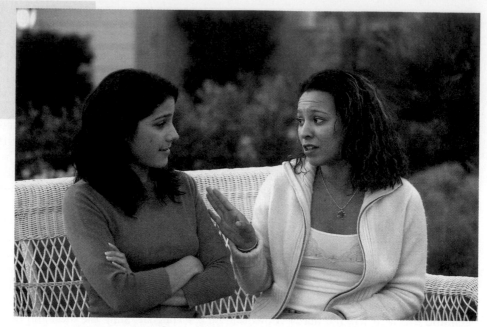

The length of a constructive argument is normally about twenty minutes; people get tired, and their reasonable intentions break down after that. When the participants start repeating the same arguments, they have run out of concepts regarding the issue, and it is not uncommon, at that point, for one of the participants to start attacking the other person rather than dealing with the issue.[20]

- *Listen to your body.* If you are aware of your voice getting louder or your body tightening up, or you are making fighting fists, you should either physically leave or limit your role to that of a passive listener for a while.

- *Identify realistically what you need to get out of the transaction.* Often we enter into a conflict situation without having identified our goals, which means we have no clarity of purpose and don't even know if the conflict is over.[21]

Individual Approaches to Dealing with Conflict

People react differently in dealing with conflict. Some people pull back, some attack, and others take responsibility for themselves and their needs. Most of us use a primary style for confronting conflict. Are you interested in determining your usual conflict management style? If so, do the Conflict Questionnaire on pages 199–200.

Knowing your style and its ramifications can be helpful in determining whether you are pleased with your interpersonal communication conflict management style. If you are not, you may need to acquire the skills to make a change in your habitual pattern. The styles of conflict management are avoidance, accommodation/smoothing over, compromise, competition/aggression, and integration. (See Figure 7.4 on page 201.)

AVOIDANCE   Some people choose to engage in **conflict avoidance**—not confronting the conflict. They sidestep, postpone, or ignore the issue.[22] They simply put up with the status quo, no matter how unpleasant. Although seemingly unproductive, avoidance may actually be a good style if the situation is a short-term one or of minor importance. If, however, the problem is really bothering you or is persistent, then it should be dealt with. Avoiding the issue often uses up a great deal of energy without

Conflict Questionnaire

We each have a general pattern by which we deal with conflict. To learn your approach to dealing with conflict, circle T (true) or F (false) to indicate how you would respond in each of the situations. Although you may not agree with either choice, you must select either T or F. Read quickly, and react quickly.

Directions: Circle T (true) or F (false) to indicate which of the following statements best describes how you would respond in each of these situations. Although you may not agree with either choice, you must select either true (T) or false (F). Your first instinct will be your best response.

	1	2	3	4	5
1. When there is a difference of opinion, wants, or needs, I would rather explore our differences than try to convince the other person that I am right and he or she is wrong.	F				T
2. When there is a difference of opinion, wants, or needs, I would rather disagree openly and explore our differences than agree with the other point of view simply to have someone agree with my point of view.				F	T
3. When asked to perform an unpleasant task, I would rather postpone the task indefinitely than follow orders without discussion.		F	T		
4. When there is a difference of opinion, wants, or needs, I would rather try to win the other person over than withdraw from the conversation.	T		F		
5. Sometimes it's easier to agree and appear to go along with something without discussion than to avoid making any comment on a controversial subject.		T	F		
6. During a disagreement, I would rather admit that I may be half wrong than try to convince the other person that I am 100 percent right.	F		T		
7. When there is a difference of opinion, wants, or needs, I would rather give in totally than try to change the other person's mind or opinion.	F		T		
8. I would rather postpone a potential disagreement than explore our different points of view.			T		F
9. During a disagreement, I would rather meet the person halfway than give in totally.		F		T	
10. Sometimes it's easier to agree without discussion than to try to convince the other person I'm right.	F	T			
11. During a disagreement, I would rather admit that I am half wrong than not say anything and withdraw from the conversation.			F	T	
12. When asked to perform a task I don't want to do, I would rather postpone it indefinitely than make someone else do the task.	F		T		
13. During a disagreement, I would rather try to win the other person over than to split our differences.	T			F	
14. When there is a difference of opinion, wants, or needs, I would rather explore our differences and reach a mutually satisfactory solution than withdraw from the conversation or conflict.	F		T		
15. When asked to perform a task I don't want to do, I would rather postpone the task indefinitely than discuss my feelings and attempt to find a solution we can both agree on.			T		F
16. During a difference of opinion, wants, or needs, I would rather try to convince the other person that I am right than explore our differences.	T				F
17. During a disagreement, I would rather admit that I am half wrong than explore our differences.				T	F

(continued)

Conflict Questionnaire (continued)

18. Sometimes it is easier just to agree without discussion than to give up half of what I believe to reach an agreement.		T		F	
19. When there is a difference of opinion, wants, or needs, I would rather explore our differences than give in without a discussion.			F		T
20. During a difference of opinion, wants, or needs, I would rather try to win the discussion than sacrifice my point of view by not discussing it.	T		F		
21. During a disagreement, I would rather try to find a solution that satisfies both of us than to let the other person find a solution without my input.			F		T
22. During a disagreement, I would rather try to win the other person over than give in totally.	T		F		
23. When asked to perform a task I don't want to do, I would rather agree to perform just half the task than to find a solution that is mutually satisfactory.				T	F

Scoring Instructions:

1. Count the number of items circled in each of the five columns. Record your totals in the boxes below. Multiply each score by 10.

	1	2	3	4	5
× 10 =					

2. Chart your score on the graph below. Place an X next to your score for each of the five strategies. Draw a straight line connecting the Xs from one column to the next. This will give you your conflict management strategy pattern.

	1 Competition/ Aggression	2 Accommodation/ Smoothing Over	3 Avoidance	4 Compromise	5 Integration
120					
110					
100					
90					
80					
70					
60					
50					
40					
30					
20					
10					
0					

Let's assume that I want to go to the movies and you want to go to a rock concert. This is a chart about the choices I make when you and I want different things.

Figure 7.4
Personal Styles of Conflict Management

Source: National Conference for Community and Justice, Northern Ohio Region, adaptation of "Activity 1," handout developed by Mary Adams Trujillo and Laurie Miller and distributed at the workshop "Responding to Conflict Around Issues of Difference," February 19, 1999, Cleveland, Ohio.

COMPETITION/ AGGRESSION
I go to the movie. (I want to go to the movie so I do what I want, when I want to do it. Your wants are not important to me.)

INTEGRATION
I go to the movie, you go to the concert and we meet afterwards at our favorite restaurant for a midnight snack. (We are both happy with this plan.)

I want to go to the movie. I like the freedom to see what I want, when I want.

COMPROMISE
We agree to go to the movies tonight and a rock concert next week. (We are both happy with this plan.)

AVOIDANCE
I don't say anything and go to the concert with you. (I don't want to make problems.)

ACCOMMODATION/ SMOOTHING OVER
I tell you that our friendship is more important than the movie so I'll go to the concert with you. (I may not go where I want; but, I'm "kind of" okay with that.)

resolving the aggravating situation. Very seldom do avoiders feel that they have been in a win-win situation. Avoiders usually lose a chunk of their self-respect since they so clearly downplay their own concerns in favor of the other person's. Avoiders frequently were brought up in environments in which they were told to be nice and not to argue, and eventually bad things would go away. Or they were brought up in homes where verbal or physical abuse were present, and to avoid these types of reactions, they hide from conflict.

ACCOMMODATION/SMOOTHING OVER People who attempt to manage conflict through **conflict accommodation** put the needs of others ahead of their own, thereby giving in. Accommodators meet the needs of others and don't assert their own.[23] In this situation, the accommodator often feels like the "good person" for having given the other person his or her own way. This is perfectly acceptable if the other person's needs really are more important. But unfortunately, accommodators tend to follow the pattern no matter what the situation. Thus, they often are taken advantage of, and they seldom get their needs met. Accommodators commonly come from backgrounds where they were exposed to a martyr who gave and gave and got little, but put on a happy face. They also tend to be people who have little self-respect and try to earn praise by being nice to everyone.

A form of accommodation known as **conflict smoothing over** seeks above all else to preserve the image that everything is okay. Through smoothing over, people sometimes get what they want, but just as often they do not. Usually they feel they have more to say and have not totally satisfied themselves.

As with avoidance and accommodation, smoothing over occasionally can be useful. If, for example, the relationship between two people is more important than the subject they happen to be disagreeing about, then smoothing over may be the best approach. Keep in mind, however, that smoothing over does not solve the conflict; it just pushes it aside. It may very well recur in the future.

Those who use this technique as their normal means of confronting conflict often come from backgrounds in which being nice was considered the best way to be liked and popular. And being liked and popular was more important than satisfying their needs.

COMPROMISE   **Conflict compromise** brings concerns out into the open in an attempt to satisfy the needs of both parties. It usually means "trading some of what you want for some of what I want. It's meeting each other half way."[24] The definition of the word *compromise*, however, indicates the potential weakness of this approach, for it means that both individuals give in to some degree, to give something up, to reach a solution. As a result, neither usually completely achieves what she or he wants. This is not to say that compromise is an inherently poor method of conflict management, but it can lead to frustration unless both participants are willing to continue to work until both of their needs are being met. Those who are effective compromisers normally have had experience with negotiations and know that they have to give to get, but they don't have to give until it hurts. Those who tend to be weak in working toward a fair and equitable compromise believe that getting something is better than getting nothing at all. Therefore, they are willing to settle for anything, no matter how little.

COMPETITION/AGGRESSION   The main element in **conflict competition** is power. Its purpose is to "get another person to comply with or accept your point of view, or to do something that person may not want to do."[25] Someone has to win, and someone has to lose. This forcing mode, unfortunately, has been the European American way of operation in many situations—in athletic events, business deals, and interpersonal relations. Indeed, many people do not seem to be happy unless they are clear winners. Realize that if someone wins, someone else must lose. The overaggressive driver must force the other car off the road.

The value of winning at all costs is debatable. Sometimes, even though we win, we lose in the long run. The hatred of a child for a parent caused by continuous losing, or the negative work environment resulting from a supervisor who must always be on top, may be much worse than the occasional loss of a battle. In dealing with persons from other cultures, European Americans sometimes are perceived as being pushy and aggressive. Many sales, friendships, and relationships have been lost based on the win-at-all-costs philosophy. Many of the aggressive behaviors in the personal lives of professional athletes are directly credited to their not being able to leave their win-at-all-costs attitude on the athletic field.

INTEGRATION   Communicators who handle their conflicts through **conflict integration** are concerned about their own needs as well as those of the other person. But unlike compromisers, they will not settle for only a partially satisfying solution.

Integrators keep in mind that both parties can participate in a win-win resolution and are willing to collaborate. Thus, the most important aspect of integration is the realization that the relationship, the value of self-worth, and the issue are equally important. For this reason, integrative solutions often take a good deal of time and energy.

People who are competitive, who are communication apprehensive, or who are nonassertive find it nearly impossible to use an integrative style of negotiation. They think that they must win, or that they cannot stand up for their rights, or that they have no right to negotiate. In contrast, people who tend to have assertiveness skills and value the nature of relationships usually attempt to work toward integration.

Avoidance, accommodation, and smoothing over are all nonassertive acts; the person's needs are not met. Competition is an aggressive act in that the person gets his or her needs met at the expense of others. Integration is assertive, since the objective is to get one's needs met without taking away the rights of someone else. Compromise, depending on how it is acted out, can be either nonassertive or assertive.

Communication Approaches to Managing Conflict

The communicative approaches to managing conflict are assertive communication, negotiation, arbitration, litigation, and mediation.

Assertive Communication

Have you ever found yourself saying, "I didn't want to come here, but she made me," or "I ordered this steak well done, and it's rare. Oh well, I guess I'll eat it anyway"? If so, the communication skill you probably were missing was the ability to be assertive.

Socially Communicating

Here's How You Can Say "No"

The more you take on, the greater the chance that you'll lose effectiveness. And although it's sometimes hard to say "no," you can make it easier if you use these strategies:

- Set clear goals and focus your energy on things that will move you toward them. Being purposeful about how you manage your time will make it easier to say "no" to new activities that seem less important. Don't be rigid and inflexible if a new assignment or opportunity comes along, but let your goals become your reality check.

- State clearly the consequences of doing one more thing. *Examples:* "If I do this, I won't be able to get to do the other things that I've committed to" or "With what I've got going on right now, I feel certain that I won't do as good a job as I'd like and we'll both be disappointed."

- Suggest someone else who you feel could perform the task better or who may be available sooner. *Note:* If the request comes from your manager, suggest a project or priority that you're doing that you could drop, delay or give to someone else. Or ask the manager to do the same.

Source: Ken Blanchard. *The Blanchard Management Report*, 125 State Place. Escondido, CA 92029.

REFLECT ON THIS: Have you ever found yourself overwhelmed because you had too much to do and someone asked you to do something else? How did you feel? Did you assert yourself and say no? Of what value is knowing this?

ASSERTIVE BEHAVIOR DEFINED   **Assertive communication** takes place when a person stands up for and tries to achieve personal right without damaging others. It begins by acknowledging that you have a right to choose and control your life. A person who is assertive takes action instead of just thinking about it. Rather than saying, "Why didn't I tell her?" or "If the waiter was here now, I'd say . . . ," the assertive person takes action at the appropriate time. "Assertive people say "no" when they don't want to do something, express their feelings without hurting others and initiate and terminate conversations."[26]

The root of many communication problems is the lack of assertion. You know you are being taken advantage of and are upset because others are getting their needs met and you aren't. You may know how you feel but are afraid to state your needs because you're afraid somebody won't like you, you'll get in trouble, or you don't know exactly how to go about making your needs clear.

ASSERTION, NONASSERTION, AND AGGRESSION   As illustrated in Figure 7.5, the goal of assertive behavior is to communicate your needs through honest and direct communication.[27] **Assertiveness** does not mean taking advantage of others; it means taking charge of yourself and your world.

In contrast, the goal of **nonassertive behavior** is to avoid conflict. Nonassertive statements include "Think of others first," "Be modest," and "Let's keep the peace."

	Nonassertive	Assertive	Aggressive
Characteristics of the behavior	Does not express wants, ideas, and feelings, or expresses them in self-deprecating way Intent: to please	Expresses wants, ideas, and feelings in direct and appropriate ways Intent: to communicate	Expresses wants, ideas, and feelings at the expense of others Intent: to dominate or humiliate
Your feelings when you act this way	Anxious: Disappointed with yourself. Often angry and resentful later	Confident: You feel good about yourself at the time and later.	Self-righteous: Superior, sometimes embarrassed later
Other people's feelings about themselves when you act this way	Guilty or superior	Respected, valued	Humiliated, hurt
Other people's feelings about you when you act this way	Irritation, pity, disgust	Usually respect	Anger, vengefulness
Outcome	Don't get what you want; anger builds up.	Often get what you want	Often get what you want at the expense of others. Others feel justified in "getting even."
Payoff	Avoids unpleasant situation, conflict, tension, and confrontation	Feels good; respected by others. Improved self-confidence. Relationships are improved.	Vents anger; feels superior.

Figure 7.5   A Comparison of Nonassertive, Assertive, and Aggressive Behavior

Source: Created by Phyllis DeMark. Used with permission.

The consequence of nonassertive behavior is that you do not get what you want. Because of this, anger may build, and you may be alienated from yourself and others.

The goal of **aggressive behavior** is to dominate, to get your own way. If you are aggressive, you are likely to make such statements as "Win at all costs," "Give them what they gave you," and "They only understand if they're yelled at." Aggressive behavior may well get you what you want, but it can also lead to alienation, thereby putting emotional distance between you and others that can lead to loneliness and frustration. *Direct aggression* is the outward expression of dominating or humiliating communication—for example: "That's the way it's going to be, and if you don't like it, that's tough. I'm bigger, and I'm stronger. You lose!" *Passive aggression* attacks or embarrasses in a manipulative way. This can be done by pretending that there is nothing wrong but, at the same time, derailing any attempt to solve a problem that isn't to your liking in a way that doesn't appear to be aggressive. Devices for passive aggression include using sarcasm that sounds like teasing, withholding something from the other person (some service, compliance with a request), or being sweet and polite but in fact controlling what is being done. Passive aggression is a common cultural pattern in places where direct aggression is considered bad manners, such as England, China, and Japan. In the United States, the direct aggressive sign would read, "No Dogs Allowed. This Means You and Your Mutt!" In Britain, the sign would say, "We Regret That in the Interest of Hygiene, Dogs Are Not Allowed on These Premises."

PRINCIPLES OF ASSERTIVENESS To learn to use assertive communication, you might keep these basic principles in mind:

- *People are not mind readers.* You must ask for what you want. You must share your feelings if you are hurt, have been taken advantage of, or need assistance.

- *Habit is no reason for doing anything.* "That's the way it always has been," and "Our family tradition is . . ." are patterned statements. But the presence of a past pattern does not mean that change cannot occur.

- *You cannot make others happy.* Others make themselves happy, just as you make yourself happy. Much of our guilt has come from parents and friends who make us believe that if we do not act as they want us to, then we are causing them unhappiness.

- *Remind yourself that parents, spouses, friends, bosses, children, and others will often disapprove of your behavior and that their disapproval has nothing to do with who or what you are.* In almost any relationship, you will incur some disapproval.

- *Whenever you find yourself avoiding taking some action, ask yourself, "What's the worst thing that could happen to me?"* Before you let fear act on you, determine what the consequences of the action, the communication, may be. If you would prefer to avoid these consequences, then by all means avoid the situation. But in most instances you will probably realize that the potential consequences aren't that bad.

- *Do not be victimized.* A *victimizer* is a person or establishment that interferes with another person's right to decide how to live his or her own life, and a *victim* is a person who is denied that right. Recent cases of sexual harassment illustrate that women and men have been made victims because they would not stand up to a victimizer. Victimization may be enacted by others, but it also can take the form of *self-victimization*, in which a person prevents himself or herself from deciding how to live. Self-victimizers often go through life thinking of themselves as failures or losers with no capability to achieve anything worthy.

When people are functioning as assertive human beings, they use available resources to get out of victimizing situations and victimizing relationships. They report a sexual abuser or leave situations in which they are being victimized. These are communicative actions that say, "I am too valuable a person to be taken advantage of."

- *Worrying about something will not change it; only action will.* Worrying will not alter the past, the present, or the future. Instead, you must take some action to relieve yourself of anxiety.

- *Adopt the attitude that you will do the best you can, and if someone else does not like it, that is her or his problem, not yours.* You are responsible to only one person: you. If others cannot and will not accept that idea, that is their problem, not yours. This does not mean that you should not seek out information and advice from those whose opinions you respect; instead, it means that you do not need to seek reassurance for everything you do, think, and feel.

- *When you decide to be assertive, be aware of the consequences.* Actions have consequences. If you threaten to quit your job if you do not get a raise, you should be ready to start looking for another employer. Don't make a threat unless you are willing to accept the responsibility and take the action.

ASSERTIVENESS SKILLS   If you are not already assertive, you may have decided that you would like to be. Or if you are basically assertive but have not been extremely successful at it, it may be that you lack sufficient techniques to handle a variety of situations. In either case, some strategies can be of assistance to you.

One assertiveness strategy is composed of simple, empathic, and follow-up assertions. The use of this technique follows several stages. (See Figure 7.6.) When you feel the need to be assertive, start with a **simple assertion** in which you state the facts relating to the existence of a problem. This may be enough to solve the problem because people are often unaware that something is bothering you or that they have done something you consider wrong. A simple assertion alerts them to the problem. If they act to eliminate the problem, the solution is at hand.

Sometimes, however, you need to recognize the other person's position but state your own needs. This is an **empathic assertion.** It may follow a simple assertion or be the first step in the assertive process. By recognizing the other person's problems or rights, you may find that she or he understands that you are not on the attack and may then become quite cooperative.

A **follow-up assertion** is used when the simple or empathic assertion is not successful in getting the desired action. It takes the form of a restatement of the simple or empathic assertion and then a statement of your own position, which may include a direct statement of the action you need or want.

Do not assume that by being assertive, you will always get your way. You may not, but you definitely have a better chance than if you are nonassertive. And

Figure 7.6
Three Types of Assertive Responses

Source: Based on a concept of Judith Spencer. Used with permission.

1. *Simple assertion:* State the facts. If someone shoves ahead of you in the supermarket, you say, "I was here first."*

2. *Empathic assertion:* You recognize the other's position but state your own needs. "I know you're probably in a hurry, but I was here first."*

3. *Follow-up assertion:* Repeat a description of the person's behavior, then state your own position. "I was here first. I'd like you to go to the end of the line."*

* Remember that assertions should be made in a nonaccusatory oral manner.

you probably won't get the negative reactions that you might receive if you were aggressive.

DESC SCRIPTING   DESC scripting is a way of dealing with interpersonal conflicts that centers on the process of **D**escribing, **E**xpressing, **S**pecifying, and stating **C**onsequences. This system allows you to "analyze conflicts, determine your needs and rights, propose a resolution to the conflict, and, if necessary, negotiate a contract for change."[28]

The process of DESC scripting also allows you to plan ahead, if desirable, to avoid being unable to think of what to say. Most people, especially those who are communicatively anxious, tend to feel more secure if they know exactly what they are going to say. This system enables them to rehearse and eliminate bad scripts or self-defeating statements. There are four steps of DESC scripting:

1. *Describe.* Describe as specifically and objectively as possible the behavior that is bothersome to you—for example, "I was told these repairs would cost $35, and I've been given a bill for $100."

2. *Express.* Say what you think and feel about this behavior—for example, "This makes me frustrated because I feel I was not told the truth."

3. *Specify.* Ask for a different, specific behavior—for example, "I would like my bill adjusted to the original estimate."

4. *Consequences.* Spell out concretely and simply what the punishment will be for not changing the behavior. The consequence should be something that you are willing to do and are capable of doing. Threats that go beyond reasonableness will be ignored. For example, you may say, "In the state of Ohio, I know you can charge me only $50 over the amount of the estimate. If the change isn't made, I'll contact the state's Consumer Protection Office and lodge an official complaint." (Since this is the law, you can carry through.)

DESC scripting can be used for requesting an adjustment, asking for information or help, clarifying instructions, reconciling with someone, saying *no* to unreasonable demands, protesting annoying habits, and dealing with unjust criticism.

Negotiation

Whether it's with an employer, family member, friend, or salesperson, we all negotiate for things each day. We negotiate for a higher salary; better service; solving a dispute with a coworker, roommate, or spouse; extending a homework assignment due date; or deciding where to go on a date.

Negotiation is the act of bargaining to reach an agreement with at least two people or groups working on a mutual problem.[29] It is a process in which the participants search for an agreement that satisfies all the parties. When negotiating, both parties must be explicit about what they want and why. In order to negotiate, it is important to understand the principles and styles of negotiation.

THE PRINCIPLES OF NEGOTIATION[30]   Every time you deal with someone—be it a friend, a colleague, or a stranger—you have to decide what you owe that person (if anything) in terms of fairness, candor, and the use of pressure tactics. Whatever poster or credo you may hang on the wall of your office or dorm room doesn't mean very much if your actions don't really match those values.[31]

Negotiation is the act of bargaining to reach an agreement with at least two people working on a mutual problem.

You should keep in mind four principles of negotiation during the process:[32]

- If possible, prepare in advance.
- Reframe the questions and the arguments.
- Respond; don't react.
- Identify and alter tactics.

Prepare   Whenever possible, *prepare in advance*. Consider what your needs are and what the other person's needs are. Consider outcomes that would address more of what you both want.

If you are interested in getting the best for both sides, *commit yourself to a win-win approach,* even if the tactics used by the other person seem unfair. Be clear that your task will be to steer the negotiation in a positive direction. Realistically, some people go into the negotiation prepared to battle to the end and will do anything to get their way or their idea accepted. Entering with this attitude almost always ensures that the negotiation will not go smoothly and that the odds of getting to an amicable agreement will be slim.

Reframe   During the proceedings, if you need clarification or want to ensure that the other person understands what you or he or she has proposed, *restate what you heard in your own words or ask a question to reframe,* such as, "I just want to make sure I understand your proposal. Do you believe that if the fraternity eliminates its pledging procedures, it will increase membership?" Or "What I heard you suggest was a 5 percent salary increase." Or "You want me to loan you my car for two weeks in exchange for your paying the rent this month?"

Respond; Don't React   *Try to manage your emotions.* Remember that you want to reach an agreement that is acceptable to both parties. Win-win negotiation is not an "I win; you lose" situation. Attack the problem or the issue, not the other person.

It is often difficult for people to admit that they are wrong or that their ideas have not been accepted. So, if it is appropriate, *make it possible for the other party to back down without feeling humiliated by identifying changed circumstances that could justify a changed position on the issue*—for example: "Since we've been negotiating, we seem to have made some adjustments in our requests. As I understand it, the proposal now is that you are willing to take less in alimony if I am willing to grant partial custody of Mark." This is better than saying, "I told you that you wouldn't get full custody and all the money!"

Maintain the relationship while trying to resolve the issue. A statement such as "Our friendship is more important than solving this issue" may, in fact, help solve the issue as well. Focus on being partners solving the problem rather than opponents by using statements such as "If we really work at this together, I'm sure we can come up with a solution that satisfies both of us."

Invite trading (e.g., "If you will do . . . , then I will do . . . ."). Trading allows both sides to feel that they have participated in the final outcome.

Once a person has proposed a solution, he or she may push for that solution simply because it is "my" idea. To eliminate this possibility, *explore best and worst alternatives to negotiating an acceptable agreement by making a list of the alternatives without discussing their positive or negative implications.* Often, just making the list opens up new possibilities and clarifies the ideas for all parties. It also takes the onus off the discussion of who proposed which solution.

Identify and Alter Tactics　　*If attacks or aggressive methods are present, name the behavior as a tactic.* For example, if someone starts making personal attacks, you can say, "I realize this is getting stressful, but name calling isn't going to get us to an agreeable solution."

Take a break. If things are getting heated, it might be wise to cool things off by saying, "I think it's getting a little intense in here. I think it's time for us to take a break and reorganize our thoughts."

Change locations or seating arrangements. Meeting in a person's home or office makes that person feel that he or she is in charge. Perhaps adjourning to another setting may change the dynamics of the discussion. If you think this might be true, suggest the change. Or change your seat so that you are sitting across from someone whom you want to address directly rather than looking at him or her over a table or desk.

Go into smaller groups. Often, meeting in large groups can lead to chaos. Meeting in smaller groups tends to work better. For example, one of your authors was chairperson of a salary and fringe benefits committee. The two sides each consisted of six people. When no progress was being made, your author suggested that the chairs of the committees meet privately. In a very short time, a negotiated settlement was reached.

Sometimes it is wise to *call for the meeting to end now and resume later,* perhaps "to give an opportunity for reflection."

Select the appropriate negotiation technique. The following are the most common approaches:

- *Spiraling agreements.* Begin by reaching a minimum agreement, even though it is not related to the objectives, and build, bit by bit, on this first agreement.
- *Changing of position.* Formulate the proposals in a different way, without changing the final result.
- *Gathering information.* Ask for information from the other party to clarify its position.
- *Making the cake bigger.* Offer alternatives that may be more agreeable to the other party, without changing the terms.
- *Commitments.* Formalize agreements orally and in writing before ending the negotiation.

Culturally Communicating

U.S. and Japanese Negotiation Styles

Brett and Okumura studied the negotiation styles of U.S. and Japanese managers. They reasoned that because U.S. culture is individualistic and egalitarian and Japanese culture is collectivistic and hierarchical, managers from the two cultures would exercise different styles of negotiation. Their results showed that Japanese negotiators paid significantly more attention to power during negotiations than did U.S. negotiators. Brett and Okumura also found a difference in the two cultures' focus on self-interest during negotiations. The American negotiators were much more focused on self-interest than were the Japanese. The two researchers also found that joint gains in negotiations were significantly higher in intracultural negotiations than in intercultural ones. In other words, when U.S. managers negotiated with other U.S. managers, there were higher gains than when U.S. managers negotiated with Japanese managers. The same result was found among Japanese managers.

Source: J. M. Brett and T. G. Okumura, "Inter- and Intracultural Negotiation: U.S. and Japanese Negotiators," *Academy of Management Journal,* 41 (1998): pp. 495–510 as printed in James W. Neuliep, *Intercultural Communication: A Contextual Approach* (Boston: Houghton Mifflin, 2003,) p. 320.

NEGOTIATING STYLES   Each of us has developed a negotiating style. Children may lay on the floor and kick their feet or cry, or they may ask nicely. Teens may pout or plead, or they may do whatever is asked, knowing that this is the only way to get something they want. As an adult, you might scream or threaten, thinking this tactic will get you your way, or you may offer to do someone a favor in return for getting what you want.

We learn our style by trying out various approaches and figuring out which one works best with which individual in what setting. Since one pattern does not work in all situations, if you are a good negotiator, you recognize that you must fit the approach to the individual. This method goes back to the concept that in any communicative situation, there are always participants, a setting, and a purpose that set the parameters for the communication.

Much of your strategy settles on whether you are interested in a win-lose, lose-lose, or win-win resolution. (See Figure 7.7.)

Win-lose negotiations center on one person's getting what he or she wants while the other comes up short. In **lose-lose negotiations,** neither person is satisfied with the outcome because neither gets what he or she wants. In a **win-win negotiation,** the goal is to find a solution that is satisfying to everyone. Although the latter seems to be the ideal for which most people strive, some may aim for a different option. There are times when people feel they must win at all costs, and if they cannot win, then the other person is not going to win, either.

If you are interested in a win-win resolution, take these concepts into consideration:

- *Set up a conducive climate for negotiating.* If the atmosphere is positive, the negotiation will probably go forward. If the atmosphere is negative, however, there may be no way of avoiding a win-lose or lose-lose situation, both of which are fostered by competition. Are you really interested in amicably settling the issue? If so, make an effort to be cooperative. Try to set up a "we" rather than a "you versus me" atmosphere.

- *Consider the impact of the setting.* Trying to negotiate in front of others often places a strain on the participants that can result in a less than desirable solution. If the participants feel rushed, tired, or under pressure to meet a deadline, this feeling can influence both their thinking and their emotional attitude.

Win-lose negotiation	Lose-lose negotiation	Win-win negotiation
• One person gets what s/he wants • Other comes up short	• Neither person is satisfied with the outcome	• All parties try to find a solution that is satisfying to everyone

Figure 7.7   Options for Negotiation Resolution

- *Keep the discussion focused.* Avoid attacking the other person; rather, deal with the issue itself.

In many instances, no one has to lose in a negotiation. If both people are satisfied with what has been decided, then their needs have been met and a win-win situation results.

Arbitration

Arbitration is an alternative process for deciding disputes.[33] Instead of being decided by a judge or jury, cases are decided by a third party who is an expert in a particular field. The third party hears evidence and then makes a decision on how the conflict will be resolved. In arbitration, both sides have previously agreed that they will abide by the decision. Instead of being decided in a courtroom, as in litigation, cases are dealt with in an office and decisions are final, with no right to appeal.[34] Arbitration advocates think this system is better than litigation due to its speed (litigation can take years), costs (a lawsuit may run into tens of thousands of dollars), and informality (no presence of a judge, jury, or observers).

Arbitration is an accepted pattern in such circumstances as disputes in professional baseball, in which a player who does not agree with the salary and/or contract offered by the team that holds the rights to his playing can apply for arbitration. Some workers and corporations and professors and their institutions will agree to binding arbitration as a means of avoiding a work stoppage or settling a strike.

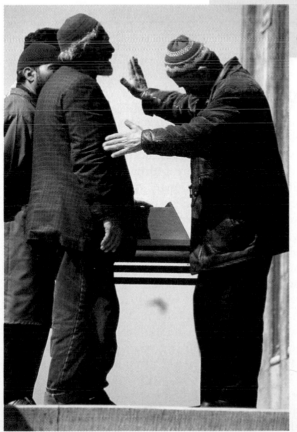

In most of the Middle Eastern and Mediterranean cultures, conflict is accepted as an important part of life, and men especially take great delight in haggling and arguing.

Litigation

Litigation is adversarial communication in which a dispute is settled by presenting evidence to a judge or a jury, who decides who is right. Litigation is usually conducted by lawyers who call witnesses and question them to reveal information while following a prescribed set of rules that have been established by law and interpreted by the person in charge, usually a judge.

Mediation

Mediation is a process in which a neutral person who has no vested interest in the outcome facilitates communication between parties and, without imposing a solution on the parties, enables them to understand and resolve their dispute.[35] Mediation is becoming a communication technique that many courts are mandating instead of litigation in such matters as custody, divorce, and neighbor disputes. It tends to work well in situations in which the parties want to have a win-win outcome and are not interested in litigation.

Mediators are specially trained in specific communication techniques and are often licensed to perform the act of mediation.

The basic principle in mediation is to get those in conflict to communicate with each other so that they can reach a win-win decision, thus ensuring that the dispute will remain settled.[36] It is imperative in mediation that the participants keep the discussion in the present tense and discuss how to solve the issue. Therefore, mediation rules usually indicate that the first session may be used by disputants to blame each other, but then they are not to revert to blaming each other again for the rest of the time but instead should work toward agreement.

Since most people are not trained to deal with each other in a nonconfrontational manner when they are involved in a conflict, a mediator acts as both guide and teacher in getting the disputants through the process.

The Role of Culture in Conflict

A person's attitudes, dispositions, and beliefs, which are developed by his or her various cultural influences, lay the foundation for how that individual approaches conflicts. The conflict styles discussed so far in this chapter basically reflect the research on Euro-Americans and nations such as Australia, Great Britain, and Canada. This research reflects that the rights of individuals are strongly stressed. In most Middle Eastern and Mediterranean cultures, which are considered *conflict-active societies*, conflict is accepted as an important part of life, and men especially take great delight and pleasure in haggling and arguing. Haggling is expected when purchasing goods in many Central and South American and Arabic countries.[37]

In contrast, in nations where the group is stressed over the individual, such as Guatemala, Ecuador, Panama, and Venezuela, care is taken not to directly confront individuals. People from *conflict-avoidance societies* believe that face-to-face confrontations are to be avoided.[38] Asians may find haggling and confrontation distasteful.[39] For example, a Chinese proverb states, "The first person to raise his voice loses the argument." "Asian culture doesn't allow for them to tell you what you're doing wrong. Asians avoid conflict at all cost and will not risk loss of face through telling you directly what is on their minds."[40]

The conflict-avoidance aversion in Japan includes not resolving disputes with lawyers. It is estimated that the Japanese have only one lawyer for every ten thousand people; in the United States, a conflict-active society, there is one lawyer for every fifty people.[41]

Another factor that affects the conflict style is face. *Face* is concerns "socially approved self-image and other-image."[42] It is expressed as *facework,* "the verbal and nonverbal strategies that we use to maintain, defend or upgrade our own social self-image and attack or defend the social images of others."[43] In countries where face is stressed, such as in China, Hong Kong, Japan, Korea, Taiwan, and Mexico, direct confrontations are generally avoided. The use of self-defensive, controlling, dominating and competitive styles in managing conflict is discouraged.[44] Avoidance, accommodating, and compromise styles are more appropriate. Using a competition/aggression style will probably cause embarrassment. Recently, one of your authors was in a Vietnamese restaurant. A patron at another table yelled to the young waiter, "I've been waiting for my check. Get it now!" The young man bowed his head, shuffled away and didn't come back into the dining room. Another server brought the bill.

In some cultures, conflicts are not directly dealt with by the participants in the disagreement. The decision is turned over to others, such as the elders, village leaders, or the tribal chief.

Remember, as in any discussion of culture, variations exist within specific cultures so that not everyone in a cultural group reacts in exactly the same way, but there are patterns based on how research illustrates generalized patterns.

Handling Criticism

Criticism—the act of judging—is typically considered to be a negative act by the receiver. Few of us handle criticism well. In many instances we attempt to deny or dismiss it. Criticism often triggers within us memories of being corrected by our parents, teachers, coaches, or clergy. It may make us feel inadequate and unacceptable.[45]

But like it or not, sometime in your life, you are going to be the recipient of criticism. To handle criticism as constructively as possible, without feeling the need to justify yourself, get angry, withdraw, or counterattack, you can try these strategies:

- *When criticized, seek more information.* If someone accuses you of having done something, ask for specifics. For example, if a friend says that you are selfish and do not respect anyone's feelings, ask for some specific examples or the specific instance that led to the comment.

Communicating in Careers

Feedback: Try This Response to Criticism

Benefit from both positive and negative feedback with STAFF:

- *Say thanks.* Even if the feedback is negative, avoid the urge to defend yourself. If you agree, say so and thank the person. If you don't agree, say nothing except "Thank you."

- *Think about what the person said.* Walk away and take time to honestly answer this question: "Was the feedback accurate?" Don't waste time trying to think of ways to defend yourself or to criticize your criticizer.

- *Ask for more information, if you feel you need it.* Even if you disagree with the feedback, it can help to know the reasons for it. Also, you both need to agree on the problem and how serious it is before moving to the next step.

- *Find out what you need to change.* Ask for specifics. If the other person has none, and if you feel you deserved the criticism, try to think of how you might do better. But also consider this: The lack of specifics could also mean the criticism was unfounded.

- *Follow through on any changes you've agreed to try on your own.*

Source: Dawn Hudson, writing in *Office Hours,* The Economics Press, Inc., 12 Daniel Road, Fairfield, NJ 07004. © Communication Briefings, www.briefings.com, 1101 King Street, Alexandria, VA 22314. Used with permission.

- *Paraphrase the ideas of the person making the criticism to clarify them for both of you.* Repeat the accusation, and ask if that is what the accuser really meant. That way, you will be dealing with exactly what has been said.

- *Ask yourself what consequences will result from your not altering the behavior being criticized.* Will you personally gain from making the changes, or is the criticism based solely on satisfying the needs of the criticizer?

- *Listen to the person; if the criticism is just, accept the opinion.* Use such techniques as agreeing with the truth, agreeing with the odds (if it is a projection into the future, agree with the odds for its occurrence), agreeing in principle (if the criticism comes in the form of an abstract ideal against which you are being unfavorably compared, you can agree with it in principle without agreeing with the comparison), or agreeing with the critic's perception (agreeing with the right of the critic to perceive things the way he or she does). For example, if you are accused of spending too much time studying and not enough socializing, and you feel this is true, why not simply agree rather than arguing that you have a right to spend your time as you wish?[46]

In dealing with criticism, recognize that much of it is well intentioned. Often, family members, friends, and your supervisor are telling you how to change for (what they perceive is) "your own good." This does not mean that they are right or wrong or that you have to take their suggestions. Remember that none of us has a crystal ball allowing us to see into the future. Your desires, needs, and goals are ultimately your responsibility, and you can do as you wish as long as you are also willing to accept the consequences.

The Role of Culture in Criticism

The discussion, so far, regarding criticism, centers on Euro-American attitudes and techniques regarding commenting on the actions of others as well as attempting to guide the other person toward correcting or improving his or her actions or deeds. These concepts are not universal.

The Asian concept of face enters into the act of criticism. "Direct criticism of individuals in the Chinese culture, particularly in front of other needs to be handled delicately."[47] What is considered constructive criticism in many Western societies can

There are times when people feel they must win at all costs and if they cannot win, the other person is not going to win either.

cause deep embarrassment with many Asians. For example, a communication professor teaching Chinese students in Hong Kong found that "whenever anyone did offer some form of criticism it was striking that everyone's head in the class went down." Even if the criticism was couched with praise, the reaction was the same. Both criticism and praise, the teacher found, brought attention to the individual, and that individual attention was not part of the collective concept of being part of a group. Interestingly, the instructor found that by allowing the students to prepare the speech as a group, and having one person selected by and representing the group, allowed for constructive criticism, since the group, not the individual, was being evaluated.[48]

Apologizing

Have you ever angrily said something to another person? Have you ever offended someone by being sarcastic or joking around when your remark was perceived to be serious and not funny? Have you ever acted inappropriately toward someone whom you really like? If the answer to any of these is *yes*, what did you do about it?

We all have said or done something we know has hurt or offended a personal friend, a significant other, or even a stranger. For many people brought up in the European American culture, **apologizing,** saying you are sorry, although it is a key to getting along with others, is a difficult task. How you react to having offended someone has a great deal to do with your background. If you've been brought up to fight for being right, not to give in, or to hold a grudge, you are not likely to consider apologizing. If you've been brought up to believe that the feelings of others supersede your own feelings, then making an apology is probably an automatic reaction.

Questions arise as to when it is appropriate to apologize and how to do it. For many people, it is both hard to know when to apologize and difficult to apologize. You may be ashamed of your negative actions or have too much pride to admit to another that you did something wrong. Sometimes, even though you may want to apologize, you just may not know how. But remember that apologizing often solves the small problems and keeps them from getting bigger.

Traditionally, an apology basically has three stages. First, the person who has done the wrong states what he or she did. For example, the person could say, "I yelled at you after you told me that the idea I had presented at the meeting was wrong." Second, the perpetrator explains why he or she took the action. For example, the person could say, "I spent a lot of time on that solution, and I felt I had to defend myself." Third, a statement of remorse is made. For instance, the person could say, "I was upset, but I shouldn't have yelled. It didn't do anything to help deal with the task on which we were working." The reason the second step is optional is that you may not know why you took the action, or an explanation may incite further anxiety. If either of these situations is the case, it may be wise to skip that part of the process.

Does the process sound too formulaic or unnatural? It may well be, especially if you aren't in the habit of apologizing, but it lays out a pattern for verbalization that can and does work. Once you adopt the style, you may make adjustments to fit your own personality and situations, but at least you now have a format for the apology process.

The person who has been wronged may reject your apology. That is not your problem. If you offer an apology, and the apology is sincerely worded and felt, then whether the other person accepts or rejects the action is not the issue. You have fulfilled your obligation. You have recognized that what you did or said was wrong and have taken an action to let the other person know that you are remorseful. You can only be responsible for one person's actions—your own. You cannot make the other person act as you would like him or her to act. Therefore, acceptance of the apology is out of your hands. Don't go into the process of apologizing to receive forgiveness. Go in accepting that you are doing the right thing.

Here are some additional tips that may make it easier to say you're sorry:[49]

- *Take responsibility.* The starting point of any change of behavior is self-admission. Admit to yourself that you have offended someone. You may know this right away, the other person's reaction may let you know you have done something hurtful, someone else might alert you to the situation, or you may realize it yourself at a later time. However you find out, you must admit that you have done wrong and accept responsibility for your actions or you won't be prone to take action.

- *Explain.* Recognize that your actions caused a problem for the other person. If you can do so, and it is appropriate, explain why you acted as you did. For example, if you were angry and blurted out something, you might say, "I was really having a bad day, and what I said wasn't really aimed at you. I was mad at myself, and I took my anger out on you. I'm sorry."

- *Show your regret.* The other person needs to see that you are aware that what you did was wrong. That is, if you think you were wrong, say that you are sorry or ashamed with a statement such as "I felt bad the minute I told your secret. You trusted me, and I betrayed your trust. I shouldn't have done that." This, of course, is appropriate only if you are regretful. If not, the apology will sound phony and may cause a bigger conflict.

- *Repair the damage.* To be complete, an apology should attempt to correct the injury. If you damaged someone's property, offer to fix it. If the damage is emotional, you might ask, "I'm really sorry. What can I do to make it up to you?" There may be nothing concrete you can do, but the offer is usually enough and shows your sincerity. You might follow up by saying something appropriate, such as "I'll try to be more considerate in the future. In the meantime, how about if I buy you a cup of coffee."

- *Use good timing.* If possible, apologize right away for little things. For example, if you bump into someone, say you're sorry right away. However, if you have done something more serious, like insult a friend out of anger, you may need some time to figure out exactly what to say. A quick apology might not give you time to realize what you've done, why you did it, and what the ramifications might be.

- *Choose an appropriate conduit.* What's the best conduit for an apology? Letters, e-mail, text messaging, voicemail, the phone, and speaking face-to-face are all message channels that are available. The first four are definitely impersonal. Using them may be easier and might save you from facing the person directly, but they are usually not as effective as other channels. Resort to using them only if there is no way to meet face-to-face. If a person lives far away, then there may be no choice. If that's the case, using the phone is probably a better alternative than a written presentation. At least hearing the tone of your voice can be a clue to the honesty of your message. If you do apologize by voicemail, "it is best to plan exactly what you want to say, and keep it to 30 seconds, never more than a minute."[50] Long, rambling messages quickly lose their impact.

A face-to-face apology is often best because you can display your honesty. It can be a humbling experience, as you must see the other person's expressions, show yours, and probably hear a verbal reply. As one expert states, it is worth the anxiety because "you will be respected by the person you are addressing as well as by yourself more if you are able and willing to make your apology in this manner [face to face]. Smiles, laughter, hugs, handshakes, and other displays of appreciation and affection are added benefits for both parties that are all possible when apologizing this way!"[51]

■ *It's not about who "won" or who "lost."* Remember, life is not a war unless you or the other person makes it a war. Stubborn pride often leads to a loss of friends and can result in physical confrontations. "An apology is a tool to affirm the primacy of our connection with others."[52]

The Role of Culture in Apologizing

There is no universal "truth" regarding apology. The concepts just discussed so far are those typical in the Euro-American culture.

Research shows that "the Japanese typically apologize far more frequently than Westerners."[53] Although, in many instances, those from Western countries seem reluctant to admit their own failure, this is not the case in Asian countries, where the concept of "apologizing is considered a virtue."[54] This may come from the individualistic concept in Western cultures where the person is solely responsible for his actions and is often reluctant to acknowledge that responsibility, thus appearing to have done something wrong. In many Asian/Eastern countries, the collective concept of a person as part of a group, and not wanting to insult any member of that group, comes into play. When one apologizes and shows one's remorse, he or she is not blaming others, not embarrassing them so that they lose face. The attitude is expressed in the proverb "The more you feel sorry, the more deeply you bow,"[55] meaning that you are showing respect for the other person. It is also interesting that in English, we have basically one word for apology, whereas the Japanese have at least seven, each indicating a deeper degree of remorse.[56] Not only are there nationality differences but there are also gender differences. For example, in the Euro-American culture, females both offer and receive more apologies then men.[37] Also, males and females often perceived apologies differently. "Men may regard apologies as signals of social distance or as devices to be used only in cases of relatively serious offenses . . . women's motivation for apologies may be related to their perception of what is necessary to maintain the relationship with the person offended."[58] In addition, males were more likely to apologize to strangers than to friends, but females were likely to apologize to friends and to strangers."[59]

In Conclusion

Every day we participate in interpersonal communication. The basic principle of good conversation is to find a common interest between yourself and the other person. Directions include instructions for how to accomplish a task, achieve an effect, or get somewhere. Requesting is the process of seeking out information or change. Conflict is natural, the inevitable result of individual differences, limited resources, and differences in role definitions. Apologizing is saying you are sorry. The communicative approaches to resolve conflict include assertive communication, negotiation, arbitration, litigation, and mediation. Knowing how to handle criticism is an important communication skill. Culture impacts all aspects of interpersonal communication.

Learn by Doing

1. Select a place on your campus, and write directions from your classroom to that place. Your instructor will divide the class into pairs. One partner gives the directions orally to the other partner without revealing the chosen destination. See if by following your directions, your partner can figure out the place you selected. Then reverse roles.

2. Select an object and write a description of it without revealing its identity. Then read your description to your classmates. At the end of the entire description, they will attempt to name the object. When everyone has read his or her description, discuss why the class members could or could not identify certain objects.

3. Do this activity over a period of several days, completing the tasks in the order given. When you are finished, share your experiences with the class, and discuss what you learned about the process of assertiveness. In the discussion, figure out why activities a and b were assertive acts.

   a. Do something you have wanted to do for yourself but for some reason have not (e.g., call a friend you have wanted to talk to for a while). This is an assertive act. Record what you did and how you felt.

   b. Do something you have wanted to do for someone else but for some reason have not (e.g., visit an ill relative). This is an assertive, selfless act. Record what you did and how you felt.

   c. Think of something that someone is doing that bothers you. Using the DESC or the simple/empathic/follow-up assertion format, tell that person how you feel, remembering to be assertive, not aggressive (e.g., tell your roommate you would appreciate her not borrowing your clothes without asking). This is an assertive act. Record what you did and how you felt.

4. Think of a specific situation in which you should have been assertive but were not. Why did you not assert yourself? How could you have asserted yourself? What do you think might have happened if you had asserted yourself? Use your answers as the basis for a discussion on assertiveness.

Key Terms

conversation   184

small talk   184

directions   187

requesting   189

asking   190

conflict   191

anger   195

fair fighting   197

conflict avoidance   198

conflict accommodation   201

conflict smoothing over   202

conflict compromise   202

conflict competition   202

conflict integration   202

assertive communication   204

assertiveness   204

nonassertive behavior   204

aggressive behavior   205

simple assertion   206

empathic assertion   206

follow-up assertion   206

DESC scripting   207

negotiation   207

win-lose negotiation   210

lose-lose negotiation   210

win-win negotiation   210

arbitration   211

litigation   212

mediation   212

criticism   213

apologizing   215

chapter 8

The Interview

▶ ## After reading this chapter, you should be able to

- Define what an interview is and identify the types of interviews

- List and explain the different purposes for interviews and how those purposes affect what happens in the interview

- Demonstrate the organizational structure of an interview

- State the principles of preparing for and functioning as an interviewee and an interviewer

- Identify and illustrate the types of questions used in an interview

An **interview** is a purposeful conversation between two or more persons that follows a basic question-and-answer format. The participants in an interview are the **interviewer,** the person responsible for arranging for and conducting the interview, and the **interviewee,** the person who is the subject of the interview. In some instances, there may be a team of interviewers or a number of interviewees.

Interviewing Roles

The most effective interviews are conducted in a conversational mode, with a structured format. In contrast to traditional conversation, one person, the interviewer, conducts the interaction.

Role of the Interviewer

The interviewer is responsible for the interview's arrangements and takes the lead in conducting the process. This person usually establishes the time, location, and purpose of the meeting. The interviewer usually prepares an **interview agenda,** which outlines the procedures that will be followed to achieve the interaction's purpose.

A good interviewer tries to build a climate of trust and support and is aware of and adapts to the verbal and nonverbal cues of the interviewee. The interviewer also should be a good listener so that she or he can adapt to the needs and concerns expressed by the interviewee.

Interviewers should be aware that it is the purpose of the interview to find out about the interviewee, and therefore the interviewer should not talk too much. Although there are not specific parameters, about two-thirds of the time should be spent with the interviewer speaking. It is also wise to remember as an interviewer that your role is not to dominate by telling your beliefs, unless you are involved in a reprimanding, persuasive, or appraisal interview. Unfortunately, some interviewers forget this and insist that the interviewee parrot the interviewer. If, as the interviewer, you say such things as, "You agree with me, don't you?" or "What I believe is . . . " you may well be leading the interviewee, which is not your role.

SETTING THE INTERVIEW FORMAT   Once the objectives of the interview have been established, the interviewer should prepare the interview agenda. The basic format, regardless of the interview's purpose, is divided into the opening, the body, and the closing.

Opening the Interview   Interviewees generally are nervous at the start of an interview. They are in an unfamiliar environment, are stressed, have little control over the process, and have a strong desire to impress. This places the responsibility on the interviewer to make the interviewee comfortable. With a warm welcome, including smiling, sounding positive, and establishing the goals and procedure for the process, the interviewer can ease some of the stress.

Body of the Interview   In the body of the interview, the interviewer asks a variety of questions in an attempt to accomplish the purpose of the session. Types of interview questions include:

1. *Direct questions* are explicit and require specific replies—for example, "Where did you last work?"
2. *Open questions* are less direct and specify only the topic—for example, "What is your educational background?"

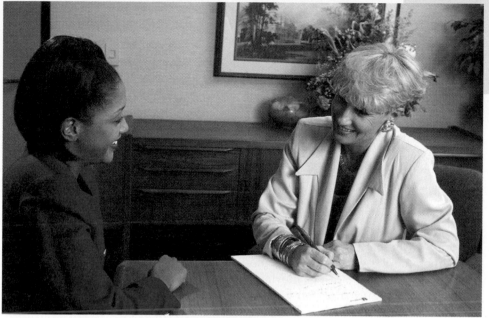

A good interviewer works at establishing a rapport with the interviewee by providing a climate of trust and support.

3. *Closed questions* provide alternatives, narrowing the possibilities for response, and probing for opinions on opposite ends of a continuum—for example, "Do you think knowledge of a product or possessing communication skills is the most important asset of a salesperson?"

4. *Bipolar questions*, a form of closed question, require a yes or no response—for example, "Would you like to work for this company?"

5. *Leading questions* encourage a specific answer—for example, "You wouldn't say you favor gun control legislation, would you?" This is a leading question because it implies how the interviewee shuld answer the question.

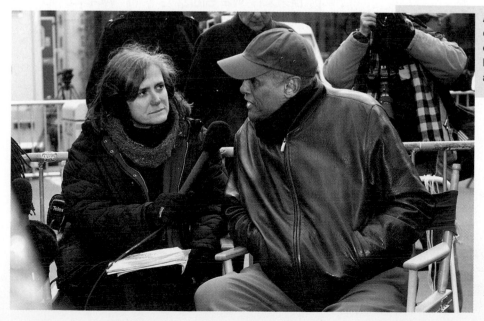

An interviewer has a variety of questions to use: direct, open, closed, bipolar, leading, loaded, yes-response, mirror, and the probe.

6. *Loaded questions,* a type of leading question, are designed to elicit an emotional response. Asking a job applicant who was an officer of the union at a previous job to defend this company's policy of nonunion affiliation would, for example, be a loaded question.

7. *Yes-response questions,* another form of leading question, are stated in such a way that the respondent is encouraged to agree with the interviewer—for example, "You would agree with me, wouldn't you, that this company's policies are fair?"

Leading, loaded, and yes-response questions are used by interviewers who feel that the only way to get responses that reveal the true personality and beliefs of the interviewee is to put him or her on the spot. Consequently, interviewees should be aware that questions can carry implications going far beyond what is actually being asked. The mirror question and the probe are used to follow up on the initial question:

8. *Mirror questions* are intended to get a person to reflect on what he or she has said and expand on it. For example, the interviewer may say, "I've worked for this corporation for years, and I'm getting nowhere." The mirror question might be, "Do you think you're not moving ahead in the corporation as rapidly as you would like?" Such a response may encourage the interviewee to disclose more about her or his feelings.

9. *Probes* are used to elicit a more detailed response—for example, "Why do you feel that way?" This question encourages the interviewee to discuss his or her point with more direction and depth.

Closing the Interview   An interview's conclusion should summarize what has been accomplished. If appropriate, discussion of the next step to be taken after the interview has ended should finish the session. When the interview is nearing its end, the interviewer should give the interviewee an opportunity to make statements or ask questions.

In interviewing, the participants usually have a preset purpose.

The employment interviewer might say, "You are one of three candidates for the position. By next Tuesday we will finish the interviews and will call all three candidates by noon on Wednesday to give each our decision. Before we conclude, are there any questions?"

DEVELOPING AN INTERVIEW AGENDA   To accomplish the purpose of an interview, the interviewer usually develops an agenda. It includes the format for the interview, including a checklist of questions he or she wants to cover. To do this, the interviewer must first determine the type of information that is desired from and about the interviewee. For example, in the following job interview outline, the interviewer may decide there are four categories of information needed: educational background, experience, job-related outside activities, and communication skills. These categories and the questions within them are set up in a format consistent with the communication goal.

The order of questions often takes the form of a *funnel schedule* in which the questions are sequenced to take the interview from more general to more specific information. An interviewer can arrange the questions in each category with a range from those that are easiest to answer to those that are more difficult. He or she might decide to ask those that require factual information first, followed by those that probe attitudes. The interviewer should provide transitions at the end of each category of questions so that the interviewee knows when the questions are changing directions. Specifically, the interviewer could say, "Now that we've covered your educational background, let's turn to your on-the-job experience."

In this agenda, the interviewer is a corporate personnel director seeking to hire a civilian computer programmer to work on a military base. The interviewee is a computer programmer.

I. Open Interview
   A. Specify details of position
      1. Duties
      2. Workdays, hours, benefits, and pay
   (Transition to next topic) "I'd now like to examine your educational background."

II. Education
   A. Why did you choose computer science as your educational major?
   B. Which courses do you feel best prepared you for this position?
   C. Why?
   (Transition to next topic) "Let's now examine how your experiences relate to this position."

III. Experience
   A. Describe one problem for which you devised a solution on your last job.
   B. If you were rushing to meet a deadline, how would you complete the assignment while keeping quality high? Give an example from your last job.
   (Transition to next topic) "Let's move on to discussing your skills as they relate to this position."

IV. Job-Related Activities
   A. In which computer language or languages are you fluent?
   B. Which language do you like the most? Why?
   C. What specific computer-security measures do you feel should be carried out to protect military information?
   (Transition to next topic) "You appear to have good communication skills. Let's now find out how you apply them to a specific task."

V. Test of the Ability to Display Clear Communication Skills
  A. We cannot read the VTOC on any of a string of disk drives. The CE is stumped and strongly suggests that it is a software problem. You are 100 percent sure that it is a hardware, not a software, problem. If I am the CE, convince me that I am wrong and you are right.
  B. If I were to offer you the following two jobs, which would you choose and why?
    1. One with a $65,000 salary and a job description and responsibility level with which you are not very happy.
    2. One with a $50,000 salary and a job description that fits the type of position you really want.
  (Transition to next topic) "I'd like to wrap up the interview by restating some of the major ideas we've discussed, find out if you have any questions, and tell you about what our procedure is for informing potential employees of their status."

VI. Conclude Interview
  A. Summarize briefly.
  B. Ask for any questions.
  C. Tell interviewee when to expect to hear from you regarding the final hiring decision.

Role of the Interviewee

The interviewee, the person who is being interviewed, should prepare for the session by knowing the purpose of the meeting, what her role and responsibilities are, and the information she needs to provide. As an interviewee, anticipate what you will be asked and think about how you can best respond. But don't assume that your only role is to answer questions. It is fairly common during interviews for the interviewee to be given the opportunity to probe for information.

ANSWERING INTERVIEW QUESTIONS   The interviewer carries the burden of determining the sequence of questions. The interviewee's responsibility is to answer with accuracy, clarity, and specificity. The answers should be backed up with supporting material for clarification and evidence. Here are some suggestions for answering interview questions.

■ *If you don't understand the question, ask for clarification.* For example, you might ask, "Would you please restate the question?"

■ *Restate the question in the answer.* If asked, "What are your responsibilities in your present job?" the interviewee might begin with, "In my current job, I . . . ." In this way, the questioner knows you are listening, and you are clarifying exactly what you are answering.

■ *Answer one question at a time.* Too often interviewers group questions together. In general, it is best to answer one question at a time to make sure that the questioner knows specifically which piece of information you are giving. For example, should the interviewer ask, "Would you describe the working conditions and what you like best about your job?" you could divide your answer into two parts, such as "My working conditions are . . ." and "I like the fact that at my job I can . . . ."

■ *Try to turn negative questions into positive answers.* A commonly asked job interview question is "What do you think your greatest weakness is?" This negative can be turned into a positive by stating, for example, "I am aware that I am rather compulsive about my work, so I spend a great deal of time making sure that what I do is done correctly."

Types of Interviews

There are numerous types of interviews. The commonly used formats are employment, information gathering, oral history, problem solving, counseling, persuasive, appraisal, reprimanding, interrogatory, and media. Although not all the varieties may be relevant to you at this point in your academic or employment career, you may well be called on to participate in them in the future. Therefore, it is useful to investigate some considerations of each type.

Employment Interview

The most crucial interview for many people is the **employment interview.** It is both a way of entering the job market *and* a means for changing positions, getting promotions, and achieving salary increases. The job interview format may also be part of the admission processes for universities, internships or assistantships, and graduate and professional programs.

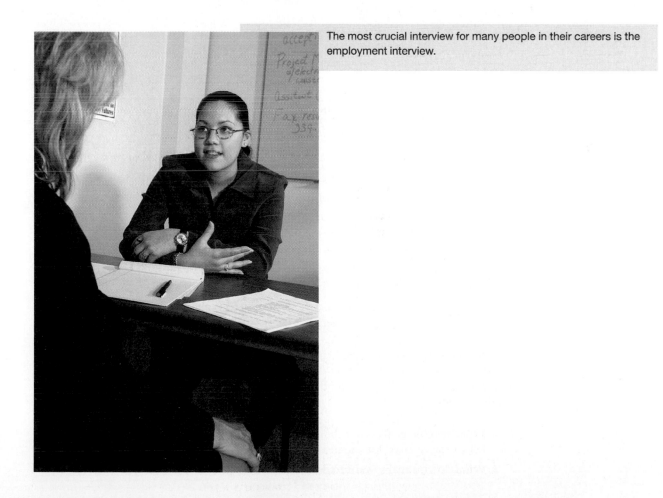

The most crucial interview for many people in their careers is the employment interview.

Culturally Communicating

Job Interviewing in the United Arab Emirates

- In the United Arab Emirates it is widely accepted to be late, but this is not applicable to you! So, arrive at least 10 minutes before the job interview.

- *Prepare yourself*—find out information about the company you want to work for. Remember that it is customary to present a business card, originals and copies of qualifications and certificates, passport photos, passport, written *references,* application forms (where appropriate) and marriage certificate at the initial job interview. An extra CV can be handy too. You will never get a second chance to make a first impression!

- If no one is available to introduce you, shake each person's hand and introduce yourself. Maintain brief eye contact while talking with someone. Use professional titles, or Mr., Mrs., Miss with the last name when addressing someone.

- Do not sit until invited. *Talk effectively* demonstrating your knowledge of the industry and/or the company, do not interrupt the interviewer and criticize former employers.

- Prepare for all kinds of *questions* about yourself, your skills, qualifications, experience and hobbies, and answer them as fully as you can, avoiding yes and no answers.

- When listening to a local person talking in English, it is very important to nod, showing that you are listening and understand the speaker.

- Ask questions about the job, the lines of authority and your future responsibilities, but avoid raising the issue of salary or benefits early in the process.

- *UAE Job Interview Dress Code:* Dress neatly and conservatively. Men should wear jackets and ties. Women should wear dresses or suits.

Source: Jobera.com.

REFLECT ON THIS: What about these suggestions do you perceive to be different from being interviewed for a job in a U.S. company?

There are a number of communication factors that may be important for a candidate's success. These include:

- Listening (the ability to listen, to paraphrase messages, to give appropriate feedback)
- Leadership (the ability to set clear goals and lead others in a constructive manner)
- Language abilities (the use of acceptable standard language regarding grammar and vocabulary)
- Ability to develop a logical argument (provide support for arguments and display a clear pattern of organization to the thoughts presented)
- Social skills (exhibit a positive attitude, being strongly motivated to succeed, and appearing to have a personality that fits into the specific organization's culture)
- Communication style (the use of appropriate verbal and nonverbal communication skills that fit the position and the organization's culture)

It has been recommended that interviewers go beyond the standard interview questions and ask questions that develop more than a superficial level of information and reveal a realistic and in-depth view of the potential employee. These questions might include:[1]

- What specific goals other than those related to your occupation, have you established for yourself for the next ten years?
- What do you really want to do in life?

Culturally Communicating

Job Interviewing in the United Kingdom

- The job *interview* is a time of mutual assessment. You may be confronted by a panel of three or more selectors for the purpose of assessing your technical competencies.

- Punctuality is expected, so arrive at least 10 minutes before the job interview. *Prepare yourself*—find out information about the company you want to work for.

- Remember to bring with you copies of professional and academic qualifications. An extra CV can be handy too. You will never get a second chance to make a first impression!

- The meeting begins with introductions and hand shakes. Shake hands with everyone present when arriving and leaving. Titles are important—particularly Dr., Professor and even those such as Mr., Mrs. and Ms. Normally those present do not exchange business cards at the job interview.

- Remember that it is best to avoid body contact and to keep a wide distance when conversing. One should also avoid emotional responses, loudness, overuse of hand gestures and patting on the back!

- Do not sit until invited. *Talk effectively* demonstrating your knowledge of the industry and/or the company, do not interrupt the interviewer and criticize former

employers. Answer questions respectfully and directly, and avoid arrogance or boasting.

- Prepare for all kinds of *questions* about yourself, your skills, qualifications, experience and hobbies, and answer them as fully as you can, avoiding yes and no answers. Also ask interviewers questions about the internal operations, responsibilities and even benefits.

- UK companies make extensive use of Assessment Centres. The tendency among some companies is to use them even at the beginning of the selection process, before the interviews. During such tests, which can last up to three days, intelligence, social and communication skills and management qualities are tested.

- *United Kingdom Job Interview Dress Code:* It is important to demonstrate at the job interview good appearance as well as good manners. Dress neatly and conservatively. Men usually wear black, blue or gray suits and ties. Women wear dresses or conservative skirt suits, with simple accessories.

Source: Jobera.com.

REFLECT ON THIS: What about these suggestions do you perceive to be different from being interviewed for a job in a U.S. company?

- What are the most important rewards you expect in your career?
- How well do you work with people? Do you prefer working alone or in teams?
- How would you evaluate your ability to deal with conflict?
- Have you ever had difficulty with a supervisor? How did you resolve the conflict?
- How would a good friend describe you?

EMPLOYMENT INTERVIEWER   In an employment interview, the interviewer's purpose is to find out about the job applicant as well as selling the organization or the position.

Legal ramifications may result from the failure to have clear criteria and procedures because of federal, state, and municipal employment laws. Since interviewers vary widely in their selection decisions, and are highly idiosyncratic in their approach to employment interviews, selection interviewers are advised to develop selection criteria, determine how the criteria will be assessed, and establish a criteria-based interview guide.[2]

It is important, as an interviewer, to recognize and adapt to cultural differences as they relate to an interview. Those whose first language is not English, who are not familiar with Euro-American nonverbal customs such as greeting procedures, or whose life experiences do not include the spotlight being shone on them may be uncomfortable in the interview process. Sarcasm, slang, abstract terms, and having to explain ideas in specific rather than general terms may make interviewees unable to respond and react in the expected. Some useful guidelines for managing cultural variations in interviews include:

- Be aware that slight changes in words can alter meanings, that languages have different grammatical patterns, and that words may take on different meanings when processed through the perceptual filter of a non-native English speaker.
- Define technical terms and abbreviations. Being part of a profession gives a person the privilege of knowing the terminology of that vocation. Those outside that profession cannot be expected to know or understand that specific jargon.
- Gain as much knowledge as you can concerning the cultural background of the person you are interviewing.

EMPLOYMENT INTERVIEWEE   The interviewee has the responsibility to provide information about his or her background and experiences and, at the same time, convince the recruiter that he or she is the best applicant for the position. As the job seeker, don't overlook the importance of preparing for an employment interview.

Preparing for the Employment Interview   One of the first steps in preparation is to research and understand the position for which you are interviewing and the nature of the organization.

An excellent source for finding information about most positions is the *Occupational Outlook Handbook*, which can be found online at www.bls.gov/oco. Another source is *Choices Planner*, which can be found online at www.career.fsu.edu/occupations/choices .html. It provides up-to-date information regarding job responsibilities, employment outlook, educational requirements, and starting salaries.

In examining organizations, learn about their function, mission and goal, products and services, size, and local and international locations. For large organizations, a Google search may suffice. If you are called for an interview, ask the contact source to send you information about the organization.

Normally, if you are applying for a job at a new place of employment, you will be asked to provide a résumé and a letter of interest so that the recruiter has background information. A résumé and cover letter ought to be tailored to the specific company and position for which you are applying. (Information on preparing a résumé and a sample résumé are presented in online materials that accompany this text.)

Be aware that many organizations electronically screen application materials. Make sure to include the key words used in the position announcement or job description. Use the exact words. For example, if the announcement says, "Operational knowledge of Word and Excel required," state in your cover letter and in the résumé "I have operating knowledge of Word and Excel," not, "I am computer literate." The electronic scanners will pick up the designated words and ignore the other terms, no matter how close the meanings.

Another important aspect of preparation is to be ready to answer the questions posed. Here is a list of the most-asked interview questions for entry-level positions and some ideas about how you might answer them:[3]

1. *What are your future plans?*
   Connect your response to the goals of the organization with which you're interviewing. For example, since your pre-interview investigation revealed that the company is growth oriented, you might state, "Since I have strong training and

experience in computer graphics, I really want to be part of an organization that is exploring new and innovative ways of entering into the graphics field."

2. *In what school activities have you participated?*

Highlight any activities that demonstrate your leadership abilities and how you are good at time management, assuming responsibility, and multitasking. An appropriate answer would be "I served as President of the Student Government Association and was on the Student Government Council for two years. This activity allowed me to assume leadership responsibilities, balance school work with other responsibilities, and develop skills in working well with others."

3. *How do you spend your spare time?*

Be selective in what you disclose. Focus on those activities that reflect your physical, intellectual, and community service activities that are applicable to the position. Consider including your religious or ethical activities only if you perceive that the organization and interviewer are aligned with your views. Usually, it is wise to avoid making political comments or talking about social activities, especially those that would put you in a bad light. A solid answer might be "I enjoy working out at the gym, going to professional sports games, working with Habitat for Humanity, and volunteering as a Big Brother." If your list is not strong, you might add wishes for the future by stating, "I have been busy getting my degree, but as soon as I have a job, I'm planning on becoming involved in Habitat for Humanity and volunteering as a Big Brother."

4. *In what type of position are you most interested?*

Try to tailor your response to this company and this position. If you are interviewing for an entry-level position, it would be appropriate to state, "As a recent college graduate, I am interested in your opening because it will give me the necessary basis for understanding the field of accounting." If the interviewer asks, "Is that your career goal?" you could respond by saying, "Realistically, I need to know more information about the field, which I can acquire in this position, before I can make decisions about the future." This response doesn't close doors on your ambition and indicates that the job is at your appropriate level. Avoid saying, "I'm willing to do anything." It makes you sound desperate and unfocused.

5. *Why do you think you may like to work for our company?*

In answering this question, refer to your pre-interview research about the company and reflect on those features of the firm that are attractive to you and that the organization also stresses. For example, you could say, "I'm very excited that your company has on-the-grounds recreation facilities, encourages its employees to participate in community service projects, and recently was recognized as one of the area's most family-friendly places to work."

6. *What jobs have you held?*

Include those positions that are relevant to the job for which you are interviewing. Even if you have only had part-time jobs, you can successfully weave those into your answer. If you are interviewing for a customer-service position at a bank, try stating something like "While at Home Depot's customer-service department, I learned to understand why people become frustrated with organizations and their rules. I think this background will be helpful in this job."

7. *What courses did you like best? What courses did you like least?*

Be sure in answering these questions that your response doesn't contradict what your transcript reveals. If you got a D in Introduction to Physics, you might have to substantiate why you received that grade. If you are interviewing for your first teaching position, you could say, "I've always wanted to be a history teacher, so I was really pleased with the fact that my university had a top-notch history department and a strong education program. As for what courses I liked the least, science isn't my favorite subject. Given a choice, I would always take a history class over a science course."

8. *Why did you choose your particular field of work?*
   Demonstrate that you have passion for the field, not that you just fell into it for lack of anything else to study or do. An acceptable answer might be "When I was in junior high, I came home and asked my father what career someone goes into if everyone is always asking his for advice and when he gives it, they take it. My dad said, 'Sounds like a psychologist to me.' So I set my goals right then to become a psychologist, and here I am today interviewing for a position on your psych staff."

9. *What are your strengths? Your weaknesses?*
   Interviewers know that in communication and job preparation courses, students are prepped to answer interview questions. The general rule is that when answering these questions, try not to sound conceited but let the interviewer know of your strengths as they relate to the potential job. And try to turn your weaknesses into strengths. Consider saying something like "I've been told over and over that my strength as a person is my ability to analyze what's going on around me and to assume a role in dealing with the circumstances. I work creatively and efficiently. My creativity sometimes gets me into trouble because I think of solutions that others haven't considered. If they are fairly traditional, they might think my ideas are off the wall. In the long run, however, my solutions do give people some options to think about."

10. *What is your ideal work environment?*
    Ideally, you should reflect about your ideas for what comprises a good work routine, your preferred supervisory style, and the role you like to play in creating a good working setting. You might say, "I tend to work best when I'm given clear directions and then am trusted to carry out the tasks" or "As a former athlete, I've learned to be a team player. I work well with others and feel comfortable to play the role of either the follower or the leader."

If you are interested in an in-depth examination of employment interviewing and practicing for an interview, you might want to go to JobBankUSA.com. In addition, an interviewing coach suggests that you "list all the questions you think the interviewer might ask, particularly the questions you are most afraid you will get, and prepare a short answer to each."[4] Another technique is to "find an interview buddy and practice, practice, practice. Buy a deck of three-by-five cards, put each question on a card and have your friend drill you just like you're learning the multiplication tables with flash cards. You might also practice a few short stories about your accomplishments to back up claims about your skills."[5]

Dressing for the Employment Interview   Appearance is an important factor for success in employment interviews. A consultant who advises businesspersons on what to wear states, "Walk though a door into an office, and instantly people draw a dozen conclusions about you, from how much money you make (or should make) to how trustworthy you are."[6] "An initial salary of 8 to 20 percent higher is a result of upgrading a mediocre business appearance to one that is crisp and effective."[7]

Although some organizations have turned to a more relaxed look, this doesn't normally apply to clothing choices for employment interviews. If you want to succeed, you must package yourself to turn off the least number of people and turn on the greatest number of opportunities. This generally translates into the conservative, trustworthy look.

For men, that means solid color suits (navy or dark grey), color-coordinated long-sleeved shirts, tie, dark socks, and conservative leather shoes.[8] In other words, leave the Nike running shoes and Mickey Mouse tie at home.

For women, navy, black, or dark grey suits are recommended with a color-coordinated blouse and a skirt long enough to allow for comfortable sitting. Shoes should be conservative with neutral-colored hosiery.[9]

For both men and women, a portfolio or briefcase is recommended, neat and professional hairstyle, neatly manicured nails, and limited jewelry (no earrings for men).[10] Items that should be left at home include body-piercing jewelry and iPods. Don't forget to turn off your cell phone.[11] A list of top twenty interview fashion faux pas includes unnatural hair colors, sunglasses on top of your head, headphones, and backpacks. The fashion faux pas list also suggests that women avoid skirts that are too short, more than one set of earrings, long fingernails with bright polish, heavy makeup, patterned hosiery, and bare legs. Men should avoid earrings and short-sleeved shirts.[12]

Actions During the Employment Interview   What should you do during the interview? In general, it is wise to keep in mind the following advice:[13]

- If asked, be prepared to tell the employer your specific job preferences. This gives you a chance to explain your training and strengths, and it displays knowledge about the organization and what positions are available.

- Stress your qualifications without exaggeration. Be specific as to what you actually did. Rather than saying, "I did office work," say, "I entered data using both Word and Excel, did Internet searches to be used in product development, and edited letters and advertising copy before they were sent out."

- When you discuss your previous jobs, avoid criticizing former employers and fellow workers. If you complain, you may well be perceived as a malcontent.

- Few people can fake a role or lie well. Even if you can, employers will hire you for what they see and hear, and if you are not the person you have pretended to be or cannot perform at that level, you'll be terminated.

- Ask questions—for example, ask about what your initial duties will be and what kind of training you will receive.

- Take notes during the interview that you can use to remind yourself of questions you want to ask or refer to later. Be careful of interrupting as ideas pop into your mind. Wait for an appropriate time. For example, most interviewers will say, "Are there any questions?" It is wise to ask appropriate questions so that the interviewer knows you have been listening and inquisitive.

- If the employer does not definitely offer you the job or indicate when you will hear about it, ask when you may call to learn of the decision.

Dealing with Legal Restrictions During the Employment Interview   An important consideration for both the interviewer and the interviewee are the legal issues that relate to the selection process.[14] Both the interviewer and the interviewee should know the federal guidelines as to what questions can and cannot be asked in employment interviews. Unfortunately, the laws are constantly being changed, so a review of the current standards must be made. At the time this book was published, these were some of the regulations:

An interviewer *may* ask:

> How many years' experience do you have?
>
> What are your career goals?
>
> Who were your prior employers?
>
> Why did you leave your previous job?
>
> Are you a veteran? Did the military provide you with job-related experience?
>
> What languages do you speak?
>
> Do you have any objection if we check with your former employer for a reference?

An interviewer may *not* ask:

> What is your age?
>
> What is your date of birth?
>
> What is your race?
>
> What church do you attend?
>
> Are you married, divorced, separated, widowed, or single?
>
> Have you ever been arrested?
>
> What organizations or clubs do you belong to?
>
> What does your spouse do?
>
> Have your wages ever been attached or garnished?
>
> What was your maiden name?

Unfortunately, in spite of these guidelines, job applicants still report that they are subjected to inappropriate questions.

What should you do if an illegal question is asked? You might say, "I'm not trying to be difficult, but I was told in one of the classes I took that asking that question is illegal. I'm afraid if I answer it we could both get into trouble, so, if it's all right with you, I'll not respond." Another approach is to compliment the questioner but refuse to answer the question—for example, "That's an interesting question. Normally I'd love to answer it, but in my business class, the professor told us that we aren't legally allowed to answer that." On the other hand, if you think the answer will not be negatively perceived, you might decide to answer the question and hope for the best.

If you feel that you have been discriminated against because of gender, age, or any of the other classifications approved by your state or legislative district, you have the right to take action. If you plan to take action, be certain that you can document the questions that were asked or the procedure that was followed.

Second Employment Interview   Many organizations use the initial employment interview as a recruitment tool to gain a pool of applicants for a particular position. The candidates whom the company wishes to consider seriously are invited to a second interview.

Second employment interviews provide more detailed information about the position and, at the same time, further determine the candidate's fit to the organization and the job. This is the appropriate time to ask questions about salary, benefits, retirement plans, and projected plans or profits of the company.

Behavioral Interview As part of the initial or second employment interview, a prospective employee may be asked to participate in a **behavioral interview,** which is designed to allow employers to know what skills you, the applicant, may have and how these skills would translate into performance on the job. In applying for a teaching position, an applicant should be prepared to teach a class. In business organizations, the interviewer may stress questions that ask you to talk in detail about your skills or demonstrate job-related skills. For instance, you might be asked about a time that you assumed leadership, such as, "How did you do this?" or "How did you perform?" You also might be asked to perform a specific function, perhaps to edit a document if you are applying for an executive assistant position.

If you know you are going to participate in a behavioral interview, you might want to review the types of skills needed for the position and what skills might be tested, and then prepare for the test by rehearsing your abilities.

Employment Stress Interview The **employment stress interview** is designed to determine how you might function under pressure. Because many employment positions operate in a crisis management mode, an employee's ability to handle stress can be a necessary criterion for employment. You may face two or more interviewers who are firing questions at you, or the interviewers may act in ways that induce stress, such as standing very close to you while interviewing or asking you personal questions that are intended to embarrass you. They may ask rapid-fire questions, interrupt before you are finished with an idea, or belittle your answers. These are all meant to see how you react.

The key to handling this type of interview is to stay as calm as you can, realizing that this is a type of game intended to rattle you. Assume the attitude that you personally are not under attack. You win the game when you don't allow the harassment to bother you.

The stress interview may be of value to you as a potential employee. It may be an indication that this is not the right job for you. If you can't handle the stress, you may not be happy with this position.

OFF-SITE INTERVIEWS Some organizations conduct off-site interviews. Procedures for these include telephone interviews, online interviews, and virtual interviews.

The key to handling a stress interview is to stay calm and realize that this is a type of game with the purpose of rattling you.

Telephone Job Interview   At many organizations the *telephone job interview* has replaced the first personal interview that an applicant used to have with a company.[15] This is done in an attempt to save time and money. Weeding out undesirable candidates; cutting down on airplane, hotel, and meal costs; and eliminating the interruption of the normal organizational routine are regarded as offsetting the lack of face-to-face interaction. Some feel that this is a positive step because it eliminates the interviewer's possible prejudice toward certain people regarding their race, physical appearance, or disabilities.

As a result of this trend, the principles of employment interviewing must be adapted to how best to use the telephone as a conduit for the message. Here are some suggestions for being a participant in a telephone interview:

- Confirm the time of the interview and be sure your telephone is going to be available.

- Select a quiet setting, one in which you will not be interrupted. If other people use the phone, tell them not to place a call between *x* time and *y* time. Make your setting secure by informing others not to enter your space and, if possible, put up a sign asking for privacy and quiet.

- Prepare your desk or working space with items you may need. These might include a pencil, a pad for taking notes, your résumé, and any materials to which you might want to refer, such as the organization's financial report or research notes you've made about the company.

- Use a corded phone so that you don't run the risk that the signal will fade or a battery will expire during the interview.

- Try to maintain a positive attitude and high energy throughout the interview. Smile as you answer the phone. Sit erect in the chair, feet on the floor, to ensure an active listening posture. Don't play with anything on the desk. Concentrate on the phone and the caller. Don't get distracted by objects in the room.

- Hold the phone in one hand and leave the other free to gesture or take notes. Animated speakers are vocally more expressive.

- Listen carefully. Write down the name(s) of the interviewer(s) during the introductions. Refer to the interviewer(s) by name when addressing them. Directing questions and answers to specific people is imperative if there is a team of interviewers.

- Ask questions. You may prepare these questions in advance, or you can generate them during the interview. Because the interviewer can't see you, you can write down the questions as they occur to you so that you don't have to interrupt the interviewer's flow of questions. If the interviewer clarifies something you have been curious about, remove that question from your list.

Online Interview   Another cost-saving technique is to conduct *online interviews,* using cyberspace for recruiters to meet with candidates. The interview may take place on instant messaging, with or without the use of web cameras.

From the standpoint of the interviewee, unless you lack technical skills (e.g., poor keyboarding abilities), the online interview should be no greater problem than the face-to-face interview. The same type of questions will normally be asked and your strategies to sell yourself as effectively as possible will be essential.

Virtual Interview   *Virtual interviewing* is another approach to screening job candidates.[16] Some companies have established websites where recruiters and job seekers can create computer-generated images of themselves *(avatars)* and use their computer keyboards to navigate through the interview site. When it is the interviewee's turn, he or she enters the "virtual world called Second Life, and meets the interviewees by either typing questions and answers or talking."[17] Much like an online video game,

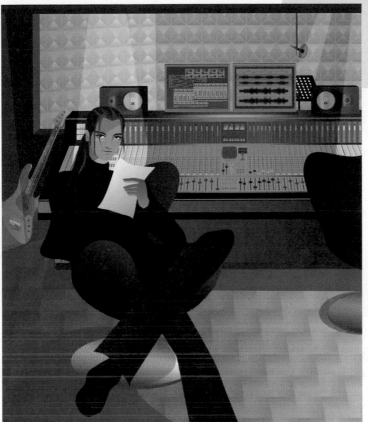

In virtual conferencing, each participant inter-acts with others through the use of an avatar, which is a computer user's three-dimensional model or picture which represents himself/ herself.

virtual interviewing requires the technical expertise to create your avatar and to be comfortable moving and conversing in this futuristic format. According to a human resource person who has used the process, the advantage over online interviewing is, "You get to know a candidate better. You see what they chose to wear, you see what they laugh at or what they interact with."[18]

Managing a virtual interview takes practice with the browser so that you don't simulate sitting down on the desk instead of the chair. Despite glitches that you would expect in any computerized format, some technology employers like it because it offers a measure of one's level of computer expertise and adaptive style.[19]

Information-Gathering Interview

In an **information-gathering interview,** the interviewer sets out to obtain information from a respondent. This type of interview is important to journalists, law-enforcement authorities, health-care workers, students, businesspeople, and mental health profes-sionals. As a student, for example, you may want to conduct an information-gathering interview to collect data to use in a speech or a term paper. Reporters and news people depend on information-gathering interviews to obtain information.

CONDUCTING AN INFORMATION-GATHERING INTERVIEW Information-gathering interviews may be transacted in person, by telephone, or through e-mail. Some guide-lines for information-gathering interviews include:

1. Make an appointment to interview the potential interviewee if you are appearing in person or conducting a telephone interview.
2. Preplan the questions you want to ask.

In an information-gathering interview, the interviewer sets out to obtain information from a respondent.

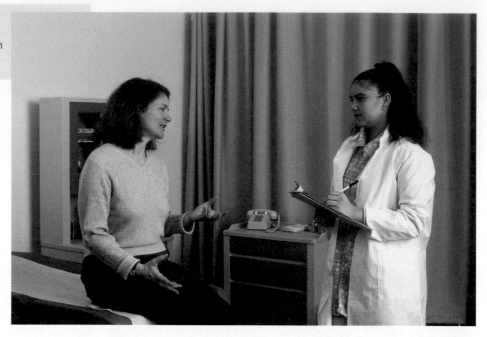

3. If possible, send your list of queries to the interviewee in advance of the session. However, avoid sending the questions if you wish to catch the interviewee off guard and get a spontaneous response.

4. Consider using the *five-Ws-and-an-H approach* developed by journalists for getting facts: who, what, when, where, why, and how? *Who* has to do with the person or persons involved in an event. *What* asks for a description or explanation of the event. *Where* indicates the place the incident happened. *When* provides such information as the date and time of the occurrence. *Why* is an explanation of the reason the event took place. And *how* centers on the exact details of what occurred.

5. Actively listen during the interview. Ask follow-up questions. Make sure that you understand and get all the information you need; you may not be able to do a follow-up session.

6. Take careful notes. If you are going to use quoted material, repeat back what the person has said to be certain you have the information correctly recorded. Or to ensure that you have the exact information, use a tape recorder. Be sure to ask permission when you make your original appointment as to whether recording equipment can be used.

7. Remember that you are taking up valuable time. Ask your questions and leave.

8. Be aware that certain people can be highly evasive, hard to pin down. You just have to persevere and keep after them: "I understand what you're saying, but you haven't answered my question." If this person has something to hide or if the information could be used in a legal action, then it well may be impossible to find out exactly what you want.

BEING THE SUBJECT OF AN INFORMATION-GATHERING INTERVIEW   You may find yourself in the role of the interviewee, giving information. If so, be sure that you understand the questions being asked and that you don't feel pressured into answering against your will.

If you are a witness, say, to a traffic accident, you may be asked to provide information as to what happened. If you are unable to give facts, make sure the interviewer is aware that you are communicating your opinion. There is a vast difference between saying, "The driver turned left on the red light" and "I couldn't see the light clearly, but I think it was red when the driver turned left." It is advisable, if you know you could possibly be called as a witness, to write down or tape-record everything you can remember as soon as you can, following the incident. Time often alters memory.

You need to make a decision about what and how much you are willing to share. Do not allow yourself to be pressured into an answer you may regret later. Remember that even in a court of law, you always have the Fifth Amendment right not to reveal information that may be used against you.

As the interviewee, you legitimately may be concerned about how your responses will be used. You may want to stipulate that the information may not be used until you are given a copy of the article or speech in which the ideas are to be used.

The information interview can be used for an entrance into careers. Students may use this format to interview someone in a position that they may be interested in attaining after completing their studies or to obtain an internship.

Oral History Interview

A valuable application of informative interviewing is the **oral history interview.** It is a way for families to preserve their history by interviewing members of the family who

Socially Communicating

Capturing Oral Histories

If you've decided to capture some oral histories, it's a good rule of thumb to start with your oldest relatives first. Because most of them won't write down their life stories, they'll need your help. They often lack the writing skills or health, or perhaps even the energy to spend weeks putting their lives on paper or computer. What a blessing it is, then, both for them and for you, to be able to tape- or video-record their life histories.

In speaking to family members:

- Start with a question you know they'll love to answer—you want to relax them quickly.

- Stifle the impulse to interrupt—let the narrator tell his or her story and do your best to simply listen.

- Let there be pregnant pauses—you'll often find that the interviewee has something more to say just when you were about to move on to another topic.

- Save questions about details for later—let them answer your broad questions completely before following up with questions about details, clarifications or possible contradictions.

- Do more than just listen—listen for clues to whole new topics that hadn't occurred to you before; if you don't want to interrupt the flow, jot notes to remind you to get back to these new topics later.

- Pursue truth and accurate information—you might occasionally need to ask a question several

different ways or clarify how the interviewer knows something.

- Allow tangents—let them ramble; there can be goldmines in their ramblings and they'll be more natural than if you cut them off.

- Keep your opinions to yourself—this is their interview, not yours.

- Save sensitive matters until late in the interview—if you broach them too early, your interviewee may close up or even end the session.

- Watch for signs that it's time to take a break—look for signs of fatigue and be sensitive to the needs of the interviewee; plan on no more than 2 hours for a session.

- Ask for other family records or a show-and-tell of materials near the end.

Source: "Ancestors: Writing Family History," www.byub.org/ancestors/records/familyhistory/intro.html.

REFLECT ON THIS: Interview a family member in order to get an understanding about your cultures and why your family believes in and carries out traditions and identifies itself. Probe for ethnic, religious, racial identifications as well as the derivation of certain beliefs and attitudes.

have stories and customs they can share on audiotape or videotape. Organizations are also using the oral history interview to establish and maintain an archive of people and their stories. Knowledge of historical events is also stored this way, as in the series of interviews done with Jewish survivors of the Holocaust. The recordings can be kept in family archives or by organizations.

An oral history is best conducted in an informal atmosphere so that the interviewee feels free to tell his or her story. It's usually important to make a recording of the session in order to preserve the authenticity of the events in the words of the participant. People may experience a sense of discomfort when they know they are being videotaped or audiotaped, but most people forget about the mechanical devices once the interview is underway. If, in spite of assurances, the interviewee is still stressed by the presence of the recorder, turn it off, take notes, and try for a recorded session at another time.

The interviewer should normally start by putting the interviewee at ease by asking for the person's name, age, and any other relevant background information such as place of birth. Establishing a chronological order, starting as far back as the person can remember, often helps the speaker organize his or her thoughts. If a pattern is not followed, there is a danger that random ideas may be presented, much history left out, and details omitted. Use prompts such as "What happened next?" If the person objects to this method or can't remember things chronologically, you might try a topical arrangement, such as discussing individuals in the person's life or referring to specific stories you've been told and asking for clarification or amplification.

As the interviewer, you must learn to be comfortable with silence. Sometimes people need time to think or to make a decision as to whether they want to share certain information. You should also be prepared to participate in the interview. You might want to model an answer by stating, "I remember a story about how you and your sisters finally got Grandma's Russian tea biscuit recipe written down. I'd love to hear that story again. What happened?" You might be able to fill in any gaps of information by asking questions about things that you've discovered in family documents and genealogy records. Some interviewers find that a subject who is agitated often will reveal details that a calmer person would omit, and thus they intentionally will attempt to arouse the anxiety of an interviewee. A determination was made to try this tactic during some of the interviews with Holocaust survivors who had resisted being interviewed because of the trauma of their experiences. Since it had been deemed psychologically therapeutic for the individuals to "let loose," interviewers were sometimes encouraged to push the people. In general, doing this is not a good idea unless the consequences have been clearly considered, and the decision has been made that this would be the most appropriate approach.

As you proceed with the interview, be aware that an older person might tire easily. If that's the case, divide the session into segments with breaks. Each time you reenter the interview, remind the person what was discussed at the last session. In order to stimulate memory, you might say, "You were saying something about your grandfather Kwan. I'm curious about when he was born and where he grew up."

The conclusion of the oral history interview should include a comment of appreciation and a discussion of what will be done with the information. If it is appropriate, present the interviewee with a final copy of the report or video.

Problem-Solving Interview

In a **problem-solving interview,** the interviewer and interviewee meet to solve a dilemma. The end goal is to develop a solution that can solve the problem, won't cause bigger problems, and can be put into effect.

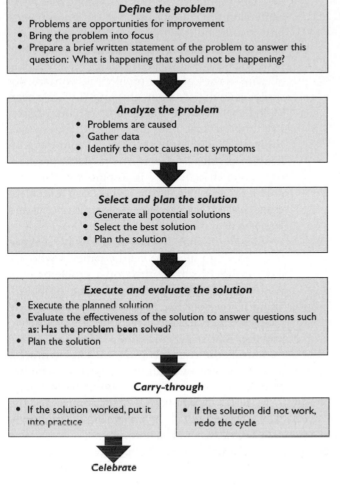

Figure 8.1

A Problem-Solving Cycle

Source: "Tool Kit for Quality," by Joann Horal, Association Management, November 1993, p. 65, copyright 1993, American Society Executives, Washington, DC. Reprinted with permission.

In working toward the solution, the interviewer usually proposes a series of steps to assist in addressing and solving a problem. There are many formats for this to take place. For example, as illustrated in Figure 8.1, "a problem-solving cycle" could be the format employed.

An effective problem-solving format commonly relies on a give-and-take in which the interviewer and interviewee shift roles, following the transactional model of communication. Questions are used to seek information, probe thoughts, and discover points of view.

Counseling Interview

We all have problems; some require we have assistance in working through them. The **counseling interview** is designed to provide guidance and support to the interviewee. It is used by mental health professionals, friends, and family members, among others.

In some organizations, managers have been urged to develop basic counseling skills to improve communication with their employees. In this way, counseling can provide a service to both the organization and to individuals within it who have particular problems. A manager or a colleague might be helpful to someone who has a problem that is interfering with his or her work. Remember, however, that serious psychological issues warrant interventions by professional therapists and counselors.

Socially Communicating

Helping Others Solve Problems

Would you like to encourage others to work on problems that are bothering them? The key is to get them to open up and express themselves. Here are two approaches:

- Ask open-ended questions—such as those that begin with "what," "which," "why," "how," etc. Also use open-ended comments—such as "Tell me more." Examples:
  - —"How do you feel about . . .?"
  - —"What do you think of . . .?"
  - —"Give me a complete picture of how you see things."

- Mirror others' feelings by reflecting what they say or imply. Examples:
  - —"I sense that you're . . ."
  - —"When you talk that way, it seems to me . . ."

Source: Adapted from *Why Didn't I Say That?! What to Say and How to Say It in Tough Situations on the Job,* by Donald H. Weiss, AMACOM. American Management Association, 135 W. 50th St., New York, NY 10020.

REFLECT ON THIS: Which of these approaches do you think is best? Why?

One approach to the counseling interview centers on the concept that it should not include any evaluation by the interviewer. Using this approach, in talking to a friend who is doing poorly in school, instead of saying, "You're failing all your classes and the problem is, you are not studying enough," you might say, "You have been saying that you are failing most of your classes. I've noticed that you don't spend much time studying. Could that be the cause of your class difficulties problem?" Such *nondirective techniques*—not taking an active role in a solution—can work only if the troubled person accepts that a problem exists, has the skills to identify what is wrong, and wants to deal with it.

Some mental health professionals believe that allowing unlimited talk by patients who are not capable of solving their own problems only wastes time and leads to even more problems. These counselors use a *directive intervention*: The counselor takes a stand that there should be active probing, that specific activities should be carried on outside the counseling session (e.g., writing a letter to or directly confronting a person who has abused the client), that there should be role playing and activities during counseling (e.g., releasing emotions by envisioning that the victimizer is sitting in a chair nearby so the client can tell the imagined person exactly how he or she feels), and that therapeutic hypnosis could be used.[20]

Therapeutic interviews go through a series of stages: The objectives of the counseling are spelled out; the interviewee elaborates on his or her emotional and logical perceptions of the problem; the problem is explored and the interviewee's perceptions are examined to establish their validity; further probing is done to continue to clarify the problem and the interviewee's perceptions concerning the problem; the interviewee's options are discussed; the options are examined; and a plan of action is put into effect as to what the interviewee will do if necessary. If all the steps have not been accomplished in a single session, further sessions are planned.

Persuasive Interview

The purpose of a **persuasive interview** is to change or reinforce a person's beliefs or behavior. The selection and organization of persuasive points depends on the initial position of the interviewer. If she or he agrees with the beliefs or purpose of the interviewee, then the interviewee's task is to reinforce the agreement. For instance, if a person comes to a volunteer agency already convinced that she wants to volunteer, then the volunteer coordinator does not have to persuade her to give her time to the cause. Instead, the coordinator can concentrate on explaining the opportunities available.

If, however, the interviewee disagrees with the interviewer's beliefs or purpose, then the interviewer should find some points of agreement and try to build on these before leading the interviewee into areas of controversy. For example, a management consultant may have to begin with praise and recognition for some aspect of a company's management program before attempting to persuade its executives that their organization needs to develop better internal communication.

The uncertain or neutral interviewee may require more background information before persuasive appeals can be introduced. If, for example, a voter does not know anything about your preferred candidate for mayor, you will have to provide that person with some background information on the candidate before giving any reasons to vote for her or him.

Compliance-gaining strategies can be used to influence people to do what you want them to do. Among the more familiar techniques are asking for a favor, calling in a debt, and appealing to guilt. Health professionals recognize the value of these strategies to assure that patients will take the full course of a medication, for instance, by reinforcing how much the patients have at stake in the outcome of the treatment.

SALES INTERVIEW   The sales process is a persuasive interview. The sales interview process is generally culture specific. The techniques are different according to the cultural group (e.g., nationality, gender, and race). Different cultures may approach the process differently. In many Middle Eastern cultures, for example, an exchange of personal information and the establishment of a friendship are imperative for a successful sale. In Turkey, for example, where one of your authors purchased several carpets, the sales process included having tea, talking about families, and then being shown the products. Haggling or negotiation is part of the customs of some cultures, such as those in many parts of Mexico and South America, where the buyer and seller are expected to negotiate the final price.

On the other hand, in the United States, Canada, Japan, and most European countries, the procedure is quite different. The **sales interview** usually begins with the salesperson establishing rapport, arousing interest, and getting the customer involved. The salesperson then explores the customer's needs through probing, careful listening, and observing so that the product and the presentation can be linked to these needs. The next step is to present the product or service and illustrate how it will meet the customer's needs. This is followed by an acknowledgment of the potential buyer's objections, in which the salesperson probes and answers them. Finally, on

The sales interview usually begins with the salesperson establishing a rapport, arousing interest, and getting the customer involved.

closing the sale, the salesperson reiterates the reasons to decide favorably, asks for a commitment, and paves the way for future business.

If a sales pitch is legitimate, and the product or proposal is going to meet your needs, then your acceptance of it may be in order. But remember that many salespersons are trained to close a sale in order to make a commission or reach a quota; thus, they have strong motivations to do whatever they can to disarm and manipulate you during the negotiation. Don't be intimidated by appeal to guilt (e.g., "I've spent a lot of time with you when I could have been helping other customers, so . . . ") or pressure (e.g., "This deal is only good for today").

As a salesperson who is seeking to counter the often negative perception of sales personnel, keep in mind that trust can be built by showing knowledge of the product and concern for the needs of the customer, using sales techniques that are not manipulative, being sincere without being condescending, and showing concern for the finances and welfare of the customer.

Appraisal Interview

In an **appraisal interview,** sometimes referred to as a *performance review,* the interviewer helps the interviewee realize the strengths and weaknesses of his or her performance. An appraisal interview takes place when you meet with an instructor to review your English theme or in-class speech; however, this type of interview is usually more associated with career settings.

Employees are often rated on their performance. Many governmental units, organizations, nonprofit agencies, and educational institutions have formal systems of personnel assessment. Performance appraisal interviews are useful in improving individual performance by (1) clarifying job requirements and standards, (2) providing feedback on an employee's progress in meeting the requirements, and (3) guiding future performance on the job.[21]

Unfortunately, appraisal interviews may be misunderstood, abused, and too frequently used only for negative criticism instead of positive reinforcement. But when handled well, an appraisal interview can present methods for change while reinforcing the positive aspects of a person's performance.

Certain techniques in performance appraisal have been found to yield better results than others. When these procedures are followed, employees are more likely to view the appraisal process as accurate and fair.[22]

- *Discussion encouragement.* Employees are likely to feel more satisfied with their appraisal results if they have the chance to talk freely and discuss their performances.

- *Constructive intention.* It is very important that employees recognize that negative appraisal feedback is provided with a constructive intention (i.e., to help them overcome present difficulties and to improve their future performance).

- *Performance goals.* Goal setting is an important element in employee motivation. Goals can stimulate employee effort, focus attention, increase persistence, and encourage employees to find new and better ways to work.

- *Appraiser credibility.* It is important that the appraiser (usually the employee's supervisor) be well informed and credible. Appraisers should feel comfortable with the techniques of appraisal, and should be knowledgeable about the employee's job and performance.

As in many phases of organizations, electronic methods have been incorporated into appraisals. One such device, *Halogen eAppraisal,* is intended to enhance the appraisal process and save you time and money, while aligning employee goals and developing a high-performing workforce.[23]

Just as it requires skill to present constructive criticism in a performance appraisal, so too does it take ability to receive criticism. Unfortunately, criticism can engender a great deal of defensiveness. People are ego centered; most of them have a need to be right. Even when we recognize we are wrong, we want to defend our actions. Performance appraisals, from the viewpoint of the receiver, will be most productive when the interviewee

- Listens carefully to the criticism.

- Paraphrases the criticism.

- Asks for specifics.

- Monitors nonverbal behavior and is aware of the physical signs that indicate possible upset: hand twisting, teeth grinding, face flushing, wiggling in the chair or shifting from foot to foot if standing, or feeling sudden tightness in the back of the neck or the temples.

- Responds by agreeing to take the steps necessary to change the situation, or, if he or she feels the criticism is not legitimate or beneficial, refusing to take the recommended actions and indicating why.

Remember that if you refuse to accept the recommendations or input, you may be punished for that action: fired, denied a promotion, put on warning for insubordination, fail a course. Therefore, if you choose to take such an action, be sure you are willing to accept the consequences.

The goal of performance appraisal in any field is to improve performance, but improvement can result only if a specific plan is established during the interview. For this reason, the performance appraisal interview should conclude with a concrete plan in which both parties jointly explore several possible actions; concentrate on one or two specific actions; specify to whom those actions will happen and what will happen; provide for follow-up on the work; and set out in writing the plan to be followed.

Communicating in Careers

If You Must Criticize Someone

Here are some suggestions for giving criticism in a way that motivates others to do a better job:

- See yourself as a teacher or coach—as being helpful. Keep in mind that you're trying to help someone improve.

- Show you care. Express your sincere concern about sharing ways the other person can boost his or her success.

- Pick the right moment to offer criticism. Make sure the person hasn't just been shaken by some incident.

- Avoid telling people they "*should* do such and such" or "*should* have done such and such." "Shoulds" make you appear rigid and pedantic.

- Avoid giving the impression that you're more concerned with seeing your recommendations put into practice than in helping the other person improve.

- Show how the person will benefit from taking the actions you suggest.

- Give specific suggestions. Being vague might only make the situation worse by creating anxiety and doubt.

Tip: Be sure you can take criticism yourself. If not, you may not be perceived as a credible source.

Source: How to Love the Job You Hate, by Jane Boucher, Thomas Nelson Publishers, P.O. Box 141000, Nashville, TN 37214.

REFLECT ON THIS:

1. What is the hardest part of giving criticism? Why?

2. What is the hardest part of receiving criticism? Why?

Reprimanding Interview

In a **reprimanding interview,** the interviewer helps the interviewee analyze problems caused by the latter so that corrections can be made. A reprimand is usually scheduled after an appraisal interview so that an employee has had an opportunity to correct problematic behavior. Unlike most of the other types of interviews, the *inverted funnel schedule* is usually most appropriate for the reprimand. In this format, the interview starts out with a specific statement of the problematic performance so that there is no question as to what the difficulty is. After revealing the problem(s), the discussion should move to what barriers are interfering with an acceptable level of functioning.

In reprimanding interviews, communicators should attempt to avoid accusatory statements and stick to factual statements. They should ask questions that permit each person to express feelings or explain behaviors, stay away from verbalizing conclusions during the body of the interview, and try to conclude the interview on a neutral note. Because the interviewer can be held legally liable for any type of punishment that is given, she or he must use factual evidence as a basis for any final decision. The evidence should be documented and available for any legal action that may follow.

Interrogatory Interview

An **interrogation interview** is designed to secure information from an interviewee through extensive use of probing techniques. Lawyers, credit officers, tax specialists, and law-enforcement officers use such interviews. Because of the circumstances, the interviewer is sometimes dealing with an interviewee who is reluctant to respond to questions. Consequently, through the phrasing of questions and the manner in which they are verbally and nonverbally presented, the interviewer often uses psychological pressure to elicit responses.

LAW-ENFORCEMENT INTERROGATION   Law-enforcement officers are commonly trained in interrogation interviewing, a format designed to scrutinize an interviewee and, in the case of an arrest, to secure a confession to a crime. As a result, the interviewer often works to create a climate of stress during the interview to pressure the interviewee into admitting wrongdoing.

Investigators who must use this interview format keep their emotions under control throughout the interrogation. Whatever your personal feelings toward the person being questioned, or the conclusion that you have reached, keep those feelings and thoughts to yourself. In spite of this recommendation, realistically, there are situations in which strong emotions may be required to extract the necessary information.

Because the interviewee in a police investigation is likely to be quite hostile, the questioning strategy is very important. A good interrogator works to break through the hostility and get the information needed to complete the case. The interrogator should begin this process by informing the suspect of his or her rights. The U.S. Supreme Court's far-reaching *Miranda* decision requires that police officers inform suspects that they have the right to remain silent, that anything they say may be used as evidence against them, and that they have a right to have an attorney present at the interrogation.

An interrogator should establish credibility and take control of the situation. By using different types of questions, the officer constructs a picture of the incident depicted by the suspect. Lies are difficult to maintain. By noticing contradictions or improbable statements, an interrogator may be able to undermine the suspect's story, which weakens resistance and self-confidence and makes compliance with the investigator's demands easier.

Interrogation became an issue during the presidency of George W. Bush due to the controversial treatment of prisoners at Guantanamo Detention Center. It was alleged that the tactics being used were illegal and against international law.[24] Forms of interrogation intended to get prisoners to speak and reveal information included waterboarding, a controversial interrogation technique that simulates drowning.[25]

It should be noted that interrogation techniques displayed by television and movie detectives and police officers can be misleading. Remember that the scripted interaction is based on various theatrical techniques and restrictions: the length of the show, the need for dramatic tension, and the general philosophy that the "good guy wins and the bad guy loses." License is often taken with the legalities that is not allowed in real-life situations.

SECURITY INTERROGATION   Interrogation interviews extend to a variety of security interviews. Post-9/11 security needs in the United States increasingly demand that officials put in place security screenings and barriers to ensure the safety of citizens. As a result, you may find yourself to be an "instant interviewee" if stopped by a Transportation Security Association (TSA) employee at an airport screening station. Respond honestly to the questions and try not to "over talk," which is a common pattern of people under stress.

If you are applying for a sensitive position, you might be asked to take a polygraph test. Contrary to what you may be told, it is your option as to whether you desire to subject yourself to the test. In most states, polygraph results are not admissible in court, but if you refuse you may be thought guilty because you would not subject yourself to the evaluation.

LEGAL INTERROGATION   Interrogation in court is a firmly established practice. Some trial lawyers attempt to trap a witness by asking questions that elicit information outside his or her factual knowledge. For this reason, witnesses should be on guard so they do not place themselves in the position of answering questions on the basis of opinion rather than proof.

For example, one of the authors appeared as a character witness for a former student who was on trial for possession of illegal drugs. The prosecutor asked, "Do you think that the defendant has ever used drugs?" and "Would you say that there is a drug problem at the school the defendant attended?" In both questions the prosecutor was asking for information beyond the factual knowledge of the witness. The answers given were, respectively, "I have no way of knowing whether the defendant has used illegal drugs," and "I don't know what you mean by 'drug problem,' and if I did, I would have no way of knowing whether the school has such a problem." The witness was not trying to be evasive or hostile, but the questions were posed for the purpose of leading the witness to conclusions that the prosecutor could then use to influence the jury.

The courtroom interviewee always must be on guard to answer only those questions for which he or she has accurate, factual information. Saying, "I think . . ." or "I believe . . ." or "It could be that . . ." may get you in trouble.

Media Interview

The **media interview** takes place when an interviewer asks questions of a guest. The most popular format is the talk show, which can be on radio or television and can be an entire program or a segment of it. Formats vary greatly: one guest and one host, one host and open lines for listeners to phone in, or multiple guests with a single or several hosts. Such shows may cover a wide range of topics.

The host's responsibility is to set the format and tone for the program. Some choose the attack-dog approach, others the nice-person role; some are looking for facts, others to incite reaction; some hold strong biases, while others try to be more centrist. There is no one way to format such shows; therefore, the techniques vary greatly. Some hosts ask questions and politely wait for the guest to answer. Others interrupt, badger, and incite. Some hosts insist that all calls be screened; others let any call come through.

If you appear on such a show as a guest, be sure you know and approve of the format. Know if you will be asked to submit questions in advance and whether the host or the listening audience will do the asking. Agree in advance on the topic, and set any guidelines of what subjects you are and are not willing to discuss. Some guests have been amazed by both the type of the questions asked and the manners of those who ask them.

In Conclusion

The interview is a communication form used extensively to accomplish many goals. Effective participation requires that interviewers and interviewees recognize that an effective interview involves an opening that enables both parties to establish rapport and clarify their objectives, a body of questions and responses that accomplishes the communication objectives, and a closing that ties up the conversation and identifies any further steps to be taken.

Interview communicators participate in many different types of interviews, including the employment, the information-gathering, the oral history, the problem-solving, the counseling, the persuasive, the appraisal, the reprimanding, the interrogation, and the media interviews.

Learn by Doing

1. Make an appointment with a person who is or was employed in your current career or career choice. Interview the person to determine what academic courses she or he took to qualify for the job, what specific skills are required for success in the career, what the specific job responsibilities are, and what helpful hints he or she can give you about being successful in the field. Report to the class on both the results of the interview and what you learned about the interviewing process.

2. You are paired with another student according to your academic major. Each student independently researches job descriptions within the field of employment opportunities: communication skills, special talents, and abilities that are needed; types of organizations employing people trained in the field; working conditions; and salary. You are given several weeks to complete your research. You and your partner then conduct a seven- to ten-minute information-gathering interview concerning the selected career during one of your class periods. One of you acts as the interviewee and the other as the interviewer. Before the interview, develop an interview agenda and questions. If your professor prefers, the interviews can be done on audiotape or videotape and submitted for evaluation.

3. Write down five items you want an interviewer to know about you; then write a sentence about how you plan to convey each of these items. The class is then divided into groups of three, each group having an interviewee, an interviewer, and an observer. After a ten-minute interview, the observer states what he or she believes the applicant has communicated. The interviewee shares the list of five items, and then the entire group discusses how the interviewee might have communicated any items he or she failed to get across. Then change roles and repeat the process until all three members of the group have had a chance to be interviewed.

4. You are paired with another student. You are to select a subject of mutual interest and ask each other a series of questions about the topic. You should first ask each other a direct question, then an open question, then a closed question. Repeat the procedure three times to practice the types of questions. Continue the interview by asking a leading question, a loaded question, and a yes-response question. Follow up with a mirror question and a probe.

5. Select an ad from a newspaper for a job you would be interested in applying for. It should be one for which you are qualified now. Use the advice given in this chapter on how to prepare to be interviewed, and write a paper with specific examples describing what you would do to get ready for the interview.

6. Your instructor will assign groups of two people in your class various segments of Richard Bolles's *What Color Is Your Parachute?*[26] to read. Each pair conducts an information-gathering interview about the segment read. These interviews may be done in front of the entire class, outside the classroom, or in dyads while the class is in session. If either of the latter is done, each team is asked to share observations in a class discussion after the interviews have been completed.

7. Your instructor will appoint one person to be the interviewer and another to be the interviewee. The interview is to be tape-recorded. The interviewer is to ask the interviewee each of the most-asked interview questions for entry-level positions as presented in the chapter. The tape-recordings can then be used for a class discussion or can be evaluated by your instructor.

8. There are numerous family history software programs such as *Reunion, The Family Tree Software* by Leister Productions. Online sites are also of value. For example, search "Oral History Internet Resources" in Yahoo! or Google. The Indiana University Oral History Research Center offers a pamphlet on how to organize and conduct oral history interviews. Using these sources, prepare a list of statements that expand beyond the text's discussion on how to conduct a family history interview. Be prepared to share your list with your classmates.

9. Go to www.western.edu/career/Interview_virtual/Virtual_interview.html, the website of Virtual Job Interviews, and practice your job interviewing skills. Be prepared to participate in a group discussion or to give a short speech about your experience.

Key Terms

chapter 9

The Concepts of Groups

▶ **After reading this chapter, you should be able to**

- Define what a group is and compare and contrast large and small groups
- Explain the advantages and disadvantages of group decision making
- List and define the kinds of groups
- Explain and illustrate the norming, storming, conforming, performing, and adjourning group phases
- Enumerate the Six-Step Standard for Decision Making and the Berko 1-3-6 Decision-Making Technique
- Define voting and explain the four common voting methods: consensus, majority, plurality, and part of the whole
- Clarify the role of the setting in group actions

Think back over the last several weeks. How often have you been involved in group activities or heard others speaking about attending a meeting of some type? If you are typical, you probably came up with a considerable list. Businesspeople hold conferences, scientists work in teams, educators serve on committees, families meet and discuss mutual joys and problems, students attend classes and hold meetings, citizens serve on juries, and athletes play on teams. All of these are examples of groups in action.

In the United States, people join groups for various reasons. You may join because you are required to do so, such as in a work environment or classroom when there is a group project. You may affiliate because you like the members of the group. This is a common reason that individuals join fraternities or sororities. You may join because you believe in the causes that the assemblage espouses, such as their political beliefs. Organizations such as Save the Whales and the Human Rights Campaign gain membership because of their stances. Some people join because of the meaning or identity a group gives their lives. For example, you might join a church, synagogue, or the Nation of Islam because of your philosophical or religious leanings. Some people affiliate because they think they can gain contacts or socialization from the other members. Joining the American Society for Training and Development, for instance, is a way of making business contacts. Social groups may allow you to meet new friends.

In the United States, why a person joins a group can have an effect on the productivity and cohesiveness of the group. People who do not willingly become members tend to shun responsibilities and do not actively participate in collective efforts. Think of activities you were required to join. Did you actively participate? Probably not, or, at best, you did so reluctantly.

Not all cultures have the same attitudes toward groups as those practiced in the United States. The United States is generally an *individualistic society*. People are encouraged to act as individuals. In contrast, in collective societies, such as most of the Asian countries and many of the South and Central American nations, people are perceived as part of a group—a nation, a family, a work team.[1] Loyalty toward the group is strong and leaving the group is often perceived as a negative act or forbidden.

Groups Defined

A **group** traditionally has been defined as "a system which is characterized by interconnectedness of its constituent parts [the individuals who make up the group]."[2] A group is more than a collection of individuals. A group has a goal and a purpose, and the members interact with each other.[3] An aggregate of people standing in line at the bus stop is not a group. They do not have a collective goal. On the other hand, the Tibetans who, in 2008, collectively marched against what they thought was the Chinese government's oppression of Tibet, was a group. It had purpose and the participants influenced each other.

Groups often are classified by their size. **Small groups** usually consist of three to twelve persons; **large groups** normally have more than a dozen. Research shows that participation rates are affected significantly by differences in group size. For example, six-person juries offer greater vocal participation than do twelve-person juries.[4]

Group versus Individual Actions

Groups, by the very nature of their collective identity, offer participants both advantages and disadvantages over working alone.

Advantages of Groups

The group process provides an opportunity for input from many people with different points of view. Groups also offer the advantage of challenging ideas before they are put into action. Since a group may be composed of people with varying backgrounds and interests, an idea probably will receive the scrutiny of many evaluators before it receives group acceptance. Because any one person's experiences are limited, the aggregate viewpoints should result in a better thought-out decision.

In addition, taking part in group action can lead to greater commitment among participants to the decisions reached. Workers who discuss new procedures, for instance, may approach their tasks of producing or selling products or services with more enthusiasm because they helped to develop the procedures.

The *risky shift phenomenon* maintains that decisions reached after discussion by a group display more experimentation, are less conservative, and contain more risk than decisions reached by people working alone before any discussion is held. A group of managers who come together to solve a problem of worker morale, for instance, are more likely to adopt a radical strategy than any single one of the managers acting alone. A manager by himself or herself is likely to be more careful and assume less risk because he or she is acting alone rather than together with others. It has been shown that as the successes associated with this concept increase, the riskiness of the decision made will also increase.[5]

Disadvantages of Groups

Although the group process offers important advantages, it also has some disadvantages. For example, group decision making takes much longer than individual decision making because there are discussions among many people with diverse points of view. The group process also requires participants to give up some individuality for the purpose of compromising with other group members.

Yet another disadvantage of the group process may surface when people blindly commit themselves to group cohesion at the expense of careful analysis. This phenomenon, **groupthink**, is "the mode of thinking that persons engage in when concurrence-seeking becomes so dominant in a cohesive in-group that it tends to override realistic appraisal of alternative courses of action."[6] In other words, all the member of the group make decisions without concern that the conclusions are not in the best interest of anyone other than the group members' loyalty to each other or to the leader.

Although it happened almost half a century ago, the disastrous Bay of Pigs invasion in Cuba in 1961 is cited as a classic example of groupthink. President Kennedy's group of advisers blended so well as a group that they felt that any negative comments about the proposed action would be perceived as being so disloyal to the group that even those who disagreed didn't speak up.

On January 28, 1986, almost twenty-five years after the Bay of Pigs incident, the same problem presented itself. The space shuttle *Challenger* was launched from Kennedy Space

Culturally Communicating

Groupthink

The "group think" problem is particularly apropos in examining the decision-making process in international affairs, for each national group involved has to be able to consider in some detail the lens through which its own culture views the world. . . . Decision makers are not easily prepared to do so.

Source: Glen Fisher, "The Psychological Process: Perception and Reasoning," in Pamela Cooper, Carolyn Calloway-Thomas, and Cheri Simonds (Eds.), *Intercultural Communication: A Text with Readings* (Boston: Pearson Education, 2008), p. 62.

REFLECT ON THIS: Assume you are an observer in negotiations between Israeli and Arab participants who are discussing a peace agreement for the Middle East. What attitudes would be present in the negotiations that might lead to groupthink on one side?

Figure 9.1
Groupthink Framework

Source: Reprinted by permission of Sage Publications Ltd. from J. B. Shaw and E. Barrett-Power, "Group Decision Fiascoes Continue: Space Shuttle Challenger and a Revised Groupthink Framework," *Human Relations*, Vol. 44, Issue 6, 1991, pp. 539–550. Copyright © 1991 by Sage Publications, Ltd.

Center. Seventy-three seconds after the launch, the *Challenger* exploded, killing all seven aboard. The Presidential Commission that investigated that accident pointed to a flawed decision-making process as a primary contributory cause. It determined, as illustrated in Figure 9.1, that the decision makers *failed to form a group that had different perspectives,* thus falling into the same pattern as those who proposed the Bay of Pigs action. The commission further found that the decision-making team had been operating under a *time pressure* that was unrealistic. Further, the *leadership* of the group *failed to heed the known consequences of groupthink* and did not carefully monitor the proceedings. In addition, the commission found that the group had *made the decision without considering alternatives, without seeking out expert opinions beyond those of the group, and rejecting negative information* that might have cast a negative light on their preferred procedure. The *outcome was disastrous.*

The decision of the George W. Bush administration in 2003 to attack Iraq may be another example of groupthink.[7] The president had surrounded himself with his vice president and cabinet members who were hawkish and pro-war. Condoleezza Rice, who was appointed as Secretary of State during George W. Bush's second term as president, in testimony before the 9/11 commission in 2004, stated, "What emerged [at that time] was a picture of an organization with great discipline and a strong belief in orderly structures and clearly articulated concepts and policies. But it is also a top-down bureaucracy, with little capacity for hearing variant viewpoints or testing its theories against the practical wisdom of front-line operatives."[8]

To prevent groupthink:[9]

- Recognize the problem of groupthink and that it stems from pressure to conform to group norms.
- Seek information that challenges an emerging concurrence.
- Develop a norm in the group that legitimizes disagreement.
- Be aware that although cohesion is normally a positive aspect of group maintenance, the more cohesive a group is, the greater is the danger of groupthink.

Members of any group must be aware that although participation in the decision-making process can lead a person to greater commitment to his or her work or to the decision made, in some cases social loafing may take place. *Social loafing* occurs when group membership leads people to work less than they would individually. An individual who thinks that his or her own contribution to the group cannot be measured may tend to slack off.[10] A problem sometimes confronted by students is their participation in a group project in which one or more members do all the work, with social loafing being practiced by the rest of the membership. The question arises concerning who should and should not get credit for the final outcome of the project.

Types of Groups

We communicate in various types of groups, including work teams, study groups, support groups, committees, focus groups, families, public meetings, and town meetings.

Work Teams

In the professional setting, people may be involved in a number of different kinds of groups. One of the most prevalent groups in U.S. industry is the **work team:** small groups of workers who function as teams to make and implement decisions about their own work. As organizations work to accomplish their goals, they have found, based on the success of the Japanese and the Swedes, that it is important to set up work teams. For a work team to achieve its goals, management must commit to empowering the team: training the members to work in a group and allowing the group the time to carry out its functions and the decisions it makes.[11] Organizations have found that the use of work teams leads to improved employee morale, greater responsiveness to and flexibility in meeting customer needs, and better quality of services and production of goods. The Toyota Motor Sales, USA prides itself on its work teams, which it feels are responsible for the high quality of its products.

Communicating in Careers

Work Groups: How to Get Hot

When most of us hear the words "hot group," we think of Casey Kasem and America's Top 40. Not Jean Lipman-Blumen, Ph.D. She thinks of intensely focused work groups whose enthusiasm gives new meaning to the expression "I love my job."

Unlike most work teams, hot groups become so emotionally involved with their task that they actually behave like people in love. "The excitement of the task and the interaction that comes with it can be an enormous turn-on," says Lipman-Blumen, professor of organizational behavior at Claremont Graduate School. As a result, hot groups often set performance records and even volunteer for extra work.

Sounds like every manager's dream—but there's a catch. Such groups are hard to create, and when they do arise they are often short-lived. Their unorthodox work habits and tendency to isolate themselves from the parent organization can incense management, hastening their demise.

But other times they hit the jackpot. Consider Apple Computers, started by a hot group of free-spirited twentysomethings striving to build a computer for the masses rather than large businesses. Taking on corporate goliath IBM spurred them to create the revolutionary Macintosh.

Alas, there's no simple formula for spawning hot groups. Like hothouse flowers, they're exquisitely sensitive to their environment and wilt for no apparent reason. But you can optimize conditions for their growth:

- **Offer workers a thrill.** Crises and intense competition are the most powerful external motivators of hot groups. Any provocative project, however, can excite passion and intensity.

- **Feed their soul.** Hot groups are inspired by the search for truth and the feeling that they're making a difference. "Their task has to have meaning to people, society and the organization," says Lipman-Blumen. That's why hot groups are particularly common in research institutions.

- **Provide a connective leader**—an individualist with a team player mentality (and the subject of Lipman-Bluman's book, *The Connective Edge*). Such leaders are willing to share both the work and the glory.

- **Banish bureaucracy.** Freedom is essential for hot groups. Workers quickly lose enthusiasm when entangled in red tape.

Source: Roy Berko, Andrew Wolvin, and Rebecca Ray, *Business Communication in a Changing World* (New York: St. Martin's Press, 1997), p. 244.

Study Groups

Study groups are established to enable individuals to work together to study and learn with the assistance of others. Students planning to take the Graduate Record Examination, for example, often join together, with or without a tutor, to work toward learning the materials on the test.

To be productive, a study group should follow some basic principles. These include:

1. Limit the group to participants who will help in the learning process.
2. Meet on a regular basis in a location that lends itself to studying, not to socializing or interruptions, and insist that cell phones be turned off.
3. Insist that all members of the group attend all meetings and participate.
4. Require that each member be prepared for sessions.
5. Allow each member to take a turn in leading and providing explanations.

Support Groups

A **support group** is a system that allows people to interact with others who share similar goals or problems. The purpose of a support group is to increase people's knowledge of themselves and others, assist people in clarifying the changes they most want to make in their lives, and give people some of the tools necessary to make these changes.[12] Support groups may be face-to-face or online.[13]

People sometimes come together to cope with the normal processes in life. These growth groups have a vast number of purposes, including dealing with preventive and remedial aims (e.g., Alcoholics Anonymous), treating eating disorders (Weight Watchers), learning coping skills (Adult Children of Alcoholics), managing relationships (Marriage Encounter), offering support for grieving (Mended Hearts), making family adjustments (Parents Without Partners), and being the parent or friend of a gay man, lesbian, or transgendered person (P-Flag).

Study groups enable individuals to work together and to learn with the assistance of others.

In the counseling setting, support groups may be more effective than individual counseling because groups can provide the empathy and knowledge of other people who have had similar experiences and can share their thoughts and feelings.[14] Support groups are considered an effective means for working through trauma caused by rape, incest, physical abuse, battering, physical illness, and phobias. In a landmark study, a Stanford University doctor found that "women with advanced breast cancer who attended weekly support group meetings lived twice as long as 18 women with the same diagnosis who did not participate in support groups."[15]

A classic affirmation of support groups was issued by a newspaper advice columnist when she told a troubled correspondent: "I can't say enough about the groups that operate on the theory that people who share the same problem can get strength from one another. If you are having a problem with children, parents, family, friends, or with yourself, there is probably a self-help group for you."[16]

Committees

Most organizations rely heavily on committees. Because it is often difficult for a large group of people to accomplish much more than voting on policy matters, it may become necessary to send certain tasks to a **committee:** a small group responsible for study, research, and recommendations about an issue. The committee's actions usually are brought back to a larger group for action. Unfortunately, some individuals use the "refer to committee" technique as a ploy to make sure the issue is never discussed again. They know that referring a subject to committee often means no one will actually deal with it or that it will be forgotten.

To ensure that committees work effectively, a series of guidelines have been proposed:

- Have clear objectives.
- Include diverse members from throughout the organization.
- Be flexible in allowing members to move in and out of the committee.
- Be sure that everyone is allowed a voice in the deliberations.

Committees work best when they have clear objectives.

One of the most prevalent groups in industry is the work team.

- Balance the needs of the committee with the needs of the rest of the organization.
- Cooperate.
- Work as a team.
- Enjoy the experience.
- Share the results throughout the organization.
- Assume the responsibility for study, review, guidance, direction, and evaluation, but allow the implementation to be handled by management.

Focus Groups

Organizations often have to discover information to help lead them to make decisions. One of the ways, for example, that advertising agencies discern market trends, logo favorites, or attitudes of particular potential groups of consumers is to use **focus groups,** which are designed to test reactions to a particular product, process, or service offered by an organization. A randomly selected group of participants who are representative of the user or consumer group are brought together with a professional facilitator to discuss, for example, a new product. The reactions are carefully recorded and quantified in a report to the organization as input for decision making. Before advertisements are released for viewing they are often evaluated by a focus group, composed of individuals who represent the demographic description of the desired audience.

The Family as a Group

Although you may not have ever thought of it as such, the family is a group.[17] In fact, it is one of the primary groups in which most of us participate. Families are groups operating as a system by the very nature of their purposes and functions: decision making, interpersonal relationships, and mutual dependency.

A *family* is an assemblage of people who have legally been declared a group or who have defined themselves as such. Typical kinds of families are natural families (a married couple with or without children), blended families (families created by divorce and remarriage or death and remarriage), single-parent families (one parent with a child or children), extended families (a cluster of relatives who may also include friends), and self-declared families (e.g., heterosexuals living together, homosexuals living together, communal groups, religious cults).

There is no one best way for a family to operate. Some families learn to operate under stress and chaos. Some have open channels of communication and operate in cooperative harmony. Most family communication follows a structure that resembles a sculptural mobile. The parts (family members) are segments of the same unit, and any reverberation of a problem goes through the system and throws off the mobile's balance. How well the family functions depends on the members' abilities to communicate with one another and balance the various parts of the system. (See Figure 9.2.)

Family discussions center on answers to some basic communication questions. What are members allowed to talk about (e.g., death, alcohol use, sex, money)? What words can be used to talk about certain subjects (e.g., death is "passed on"; alcoholism is "Daddy is sick")? Where can members talk (e.g., in the kitchen, at the table while eating, in the bedroom, in the car, "only in our own house—this is nobody else's business")? Who can talk about it (e.g., mother and father only; father talks, others listen)?

Most families typically enforce rules randomly and lack consistency in their methods of operation. In some families, however, rules of communication are

Communicating in Careers

A Business Professional Shares Her View on Work and Groups

As a qualitative research consultant, I work for companies all over the country in their development of product lines and/or their advertising campaigns. In addition to in-depth interviewing, I make extensive use of focus groups to get reactions of typical consumers to proposed products or ads. The focus groups are an important part of my work, because the dynamics of the group enables me to get to a deeper level of response from the representative participants. I find that the synergy of the group helps the individual participants respond to products or ads both in the thinking and the feeling levels.

Source: Roy Berko, Andrew Wolvin, and Rebecca Ray, *Business Communication in a Changing World* (New York: St. Martin's Press, 1997), p. 273.

REFLECT ON THIS:

1. What do you think is a "deeper level of response"?

2. How do you think synergy helps in generating feedback?

3. Do you think that focus groups are of any real help to advertising and product development companies?

Families are groups operating as a system.

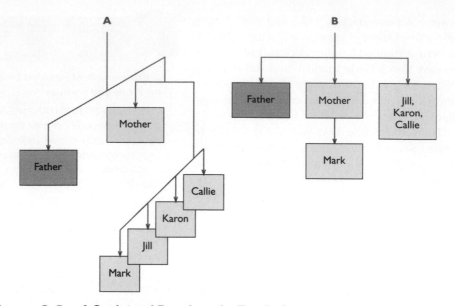

Figure 9.2   A Sculptural Drawing of a Family System

Each member of a family is important in developing the group's system. In an unbalanced system (A), for instance, as illustrated in this mobile, John (the father) has a total power. He controls the finances and is an alcoholic whose actions dominate the group's actions. Members of the family are in constant turmoil trying to live in a system where chaos reigns due to John's erratic behaior.

In example (B), Maria, John's wife, and Mark, his son, have formed an alliance to keep peace and harmony in the family, making sure that John's actions have less influence. They have worked with a counselor to get John to join Alcoholics Anonymous. Jill, Karon, and Callie, the three youngest daughters, have little real power, but their presence is important, for John has been made to feel guilty concerning his former physical abuse of the young girls. This system functions because the family members have worked out a pattern for how the rules, customs, and traditions of the group will work, thus the mobile is in balance.

Some families learn to operate under stress and chaos.

established and upheld at all costs, resulting in praise, cooperation, abuse, punishment, and/or banning.

Public Meetings

In addition to the use of internal group interactions, some organizations find it necessary to conduct **public meetings,** in which members or interested individuals may attend the sessions. Corporations must hold stockholders' meetings. Government organizations, such as school boards and city councils, may need to conduct their meetings in public to ensure that the decisions they reach are in the best interests of the public they serve and to fulfill the legal requirements of many states to hold open meetings.

Public meetings can follow a number of formats. The members may discuss the issue among themselves and then let the audience ask questions. Or there may be a series of experts or witnesses in a **symposium** format, in which participants give prepared speeches with no interaction among themselves or with the audience. These presentations are often followed by a **forum,** a question-and-answer session during which the participants field questions from each other as well as from any audience that is present.

Public meetings require skillful moderating. It is important not to let just the most outspoken people dominate a discussion so that only one point of view is expressed. "It is imperative that a diversity of participation take place in order to lend credibility to the final decisions or actions."[18] This can be done by having clear rules that indicate who can speak, how long he or she can speak, and how the process of keeping the meeting in order will be implemented. Most public meetings operate under parliamentary procedure, most commonly those practices set forth in *Robert's Rules of Order.* It is wise to have a parliamentarian present, a person well versed in the rules of order and meeting management, to assist the group in following the rules.

If the issue being discussed is highly contentious, such as what happens when school boards fire coaches or teachers or put tax levies on the ballot, the moderator must be careful to keep people from verbally (or even physically) attacking each other as emotions escalate.

Town Meetings

In a **town meeting,** a presenter opens with a short prepared statement that establishes the framework for the meeting. Individuals in the audience then engage in a forum with the speaker. In the ensuing dialogue, both speaker and audience members explain their positions and share viewpoints on issues. The town meeting has a long history in some areas of the United States, such as New England, where some communities still use it for town decision making.

The format came into contemporary prominence when President Bill Clinton conducted town meetings in various parts of the country in his 1992 and 1996 campaigns. The 2008 presidential contenders used many town meetings in their campaigns. Since town meetings are generally open for all to speak, and is considered the hallmark of democracy, President George H. W. Bush received much criticism when some Denver residents charged that they were forcibly removed from a town meeting because they opposed Bush's policies.[19]

Group Operations

As groups operate, they are continually evolving. Normally they go through six phases: forming, norming, storming, conforming, performing, and adjourning. (See Figure 9.3.)[20]

Figure 9.3
Six Phases of Group
Operations

Group Forming

Groups start by going through a process known as *group forming*. The membership can come together because they are appointed to accomplish a task. A supervisor, for instance, may want a selected number of her employees to develop a set of guidelines for conducting a survey. They can assemble because some individuals have a common mission they wish to accomplish and bring together a number of people to carry out the task. For example, residents in a community may decide that they want to work toward the election of a particular candidate for mayor. Sometimes a group forms spontaneously, such as when they are incensed over an action or lack of action. This was exemplified by "the people of London did us Brits proud today by showing their disgust at Chinese actions in Tibet and Darfur, and disrupting the running of the Olympic torch through London."[21]

Group Norming

Group norming consists of people coming together for the purpose of getting to know each other. Depending on the nature of the assemblage, an exchange of names and other demographic information usually occurs. In new organizations, discussion is often cautious and doesn't deal immediately with the purpose or goals of the group. The norming process usually proceeds more rapidly when new people enter an existing group.

During this stage, *group norms*—the rules by which the group will operate—are developed. The obligations of the members, what they can and can't do, and the mode of operation are decided. These norms can be explicit (written and agreed on, as in a constitution) or implicit (understood but not formalized).[22]

The source of the group's norms may be influenced from outside the group. They may be rules preset by others, such as when a judge charges a jury; handed down, such as when a local chapter of an organization is given rules by the national organization; developed by group members based on their past experiences or through trial and error; or influenced by a member or leader who has either experience in the group process or strong enough persuasive skills to influence others. Whatever the means, setting boundaries is a critical group function.

Group procedures that should be determined include:[23]

- *Planning an agenda.* Group meetings normally follow an *agenda:* a list of the topics to be discussed or the problems that must be dealt with in the order in which they will be acted on.

- *Handling routine housekeeping details.* Such details include taking attendance and agreeing on the rules for decision making.

- *Preparing for the next meeting.* An ongoing group must decide when it will reconvene. It is sometimes necessary to designate who will be responsible for certain details for the next session.

Group Storming

Although it might be ideal, and make group decision making much easier, groups seldom work toward their goal without some disagreements. Most groups, during either the process of setting rules or working toward their goal, enter into a period called **group storming,** when conflicts erupt. The disagreements may be caused by a power struggle among those interested in being the leader, conflict over the rules of operation, or personality conflicts among group members. Storming can be a positive aspect of group operation since it often alerts the group to underlying problems. It brings the conflicts into the open, allows the members to deal with them, and permits the establishment of an open communication environment. Although storming is common, don't assume that something is wrong if a group you are in doesn't go through storming. Just be sure that the lack of storming is not caused by groupthink (see pages 251–252).

TYPES OF GROUP TENSION   Two types of social tensions are at the base of storming. *Primary group tension* refers to the normal jitters and feelings of uneasiness that group members experience when they first congregate. Think of an experience you've had when entering a group for the first time—for example, entering a class on the first day or going to work on a new job. Group interaction at this point is usually of very low intensity. Often there are long periods of silence, discussion of frivolous topics, tentative statements, and members being overly polite. Interruptions tend to evoke apologies. There is a tendency, especially among European Americans, to want to get through this "meaningless stuff" quickly and get down to business. However, people in other cultures are interested in this relationship stage and are willing to put time into it. It is fairly common in Japan and in Arabic countries, for example, for social interactions to take initial precedence over getting down to work.

Your strategy as a competent communicator is not to avoid primary tension but to let it take its natural course. Primary tension tends to be short-lived and cause for little concern unless it escalates to an unmanageable level. With time, it normally disappears.

The other type of social tension is referred to as *secondary group tension;* it is the stress and strain that occur within a group later in its development. Frequent causes of this problem are having to make a decision, shortage of time to accomplish the task, differences of opinion, and difficult members.

Signs of secondary tension include abrupt departure from the group's routine, a sharp outburst by a member, a sarcastic comment, or hostile and antagonistic exchanges between members. Extreme secondary tension can be unpleasant. If it is left uncontrolled, the group's existence may be threatened. The goal is not to eliminate the tension, but to use it in a positive way. Tension can be energizing—a source of creative thinking—and, if effectively dealt with, can bring a group together.

Role of Power   One of the major triggers of storming is the role of power. Competition appears to be unavoidable in human transactions, and one of the major centers of competition is who holds the power. *Power role* is the ability to influence another's attainment of goals. Power can center on controlling another person or persons, influencing the efforts of others, and/or accomplishing a goal.

All groups have a power structure. It is usually held by one person, but it may be shared, such as the co-captains of a football team. The person may exert power because he or she has information or expertise that will allow the group to reach its goal. For example, a group dealing with a financial crisis may turn for advice to the person most knowledgeable about economics or accounting. In some cases, power centers on legitimate authority. The person who is appointed chairperson of the committee by the company president holds the position legitimately and therefore can act as the leader no matter what the feelings of the group may be. Sometimes the power figure has the ability to give rewards or punishments. A parent, for instance, often has the ability to decide on allowances and curfew times, thus putting her or him in a control position over children.

Another type of power centers on personal qualities. Some people have the charisma or likeability to become a power source. It is believed that our most effective leaders, whether presidents or athletic coaches, are those who get others to follow them willingly, to do so because of their charisma.[24]

The person(s) who hold power may exert it in a positive way by helping the group come to good decisions. On the other hand, some leaders are tyrants (e.g., Adolph Hitler, Sadam Hussein), whose main interest is in controlling others. Or they may be incompetent and/or have psychological problems that interfere with their exerting positive leadership.

Unresolved Storming   Do not assume that all groups make it through the storming stage. Some find that because of poor leadership, the personalities of the members, the inability to decide on norms, or the lack of clarity of purpose, they simply cannot work their way through storming. In this case, the group may disband, continue to operate in a storming fashion, or members gradually fade away and the group folds when members stop coming to meetings because nothing is being accomplished.

Storming Strategies   In order to deal with storming so that it does not remain an unresolved issue, consider following these guidelines:

- Provide a get-acquainted period before the first meeting so that group members meet each other informally.

- Schedule an informal chat period before each meeting so that there is no pressured interaction among participants.

- Remind the group that disagreement can help to achieve a superior outcome and that the purpose of the assemblage is to achieve the group goal, not individual goals.

- Tolerate, even encourage, disagreement and deviance. The trick is to keep disagreement within tolerable limits. Be aware, however, that some people can't tolerate any disagreement. They may have a history of physical or verbal abuse and panic when bickering starts, fearing it will escalate into a full-fledged war. Others have been brought up to avoid fighting at all costs. Whatever the situation, even though allowing some disagreement can be a positive force in a group, be aware of the possible deep-seated sensitivity of some members.

- If appropriate, use humor, joking, and shared laughter to lighten the mood.

- Stick to attacking the issues, not the person who disagrees with your stand. Don't keep repeating the same argument over and over.

- Be an active listener. Even though you have a clearly defined viewpoint, be aware that the other person believes his or her viewpoint is as valid as yours. If you really listen, you might find that the other's view has some validity.

- Look for possible places to compromise. Be careful, however, in reaching a compromise, that you don't water down the solution so much that it will not achieve its goal of relieving the problem.

- Monitor the leadership. If it is efficient, good. If not, either work for a change of power or work for a change in attitude by the leader. In other words, replace the leader, develop new rules of operation, or try to negotiate with the leader for a change in the way he or she is operating.

Group Conforming

Groups that work their way through the storming stage are those that can go on to work together. This coming together is called *group conforming*. The group will know that it is in the conforming stage when such issues as norms, the group's purpose, and how to handle the role of power have been settled. At that point, members feel commitment to the group. The group is ready to work toward the agreed-on mission, recognizing that it may revert back to storming and will then have to work again toward conforming.

Group Performing

Group performing is the action stage of group process. During this phase, the members clearly start to work toward goals. They have developed a history and know each other, have worked out their mode of operation, and have agreed to move forward to accomplish their task and maintenance roles.

All decision making in a group is influenced by both task and maintenance dimensions. These are not independent entities that stand in opposition to each other; they are interrelated.

The *task dimension of groups* includes decision making, informing, appraising and examining, problem solving, and creating interest in staying on track. Some consider accomplishing the goal the entire purpose of the group and concentrate solely on making sure that the group stays "on task." (Much of this and the next chapter center on how to get the group to perform effectively.) However, most groups also need to attend to the *maintenance dimension of groups:* meeting the interpersonal needs of the members. The main purpose of maintenance is developing *group cohesion:* the interconnectedness of the members.

As social beings, most people like to be with others, interact with them, and express opinions and feelings. Ignoring these aspects of group process by concentrating only on task functions can lead to an empty experience for some of the participants.

Group Adjourning

Groups may also find it necessary to go through *adjourning:* going out of existence. In business settings, certain groups are constituted to accomplish a particular task. At the completion of the task, the group disperses. Study groups are formed to prepare the participants for a test or complete a project. Once the task is completed, the group's purpose is completed. Such adjourning requires no specific action other than awareness that the task is done.

On the other hand, some groups have no specific end goal but are ongoing as they keep in existence by continuing to perform their duties (e.g., groups such as fraternities, sororities, and service clubs have the objective of continuing to work forever). But even these groups may come to an end. Members may lose interest; people may leave the organization, therefore depleting the membership; or group members determine that the group no longer has a purpose. In these cases, the members vote the group out of existence or simply stop holding meetings. It is advisable that group members take formal action to bring the group to an end. Otherwise, they may feel that they have not reached a true ending and feel incomplete, similar to not completing the process of saying good-bye to someone who dies suddenly.

Making Group Decisions

One of the most prominent functions of the group communication process is decision making. Traditionally in the European American culture, effective decision making tends to follow a step-by-step procedure that allows group members to explore the dimensions of a problem, seek out solutions, and select a solution the members think is most appropriate.

Developing a process leads a group to consider the rules of operation to be followed to reach decisions. Formal organizations, such as city councils and sororities and fraternities, develop a constitution and bylaws clearly spelling out procedures. A set of parliamentary guidelines, such as *Robert's Rules of Order,* usually is adopted as a framework for handling procedural agreements and disagreements.[25] Individuals who chair formal meetings should learn these rules of order. Less formal organizations may allow the leader of a group to determine the operational procedures. Whatever method is used, however, it should be agreed on before any formal work is undertaken by a group in order to clarify how action will occur.

Formulating an Agenda

For the members of a group to be aware of the order in which items will be handled, an **agenda**—the order of business for a meeting or discussion—is prepared. It allows the group to cover topics systematically and accomplish the task in the most efficient way possible. An agenda should be used like a road map. It should contain just enough detail to allow the group to travel the path to the task but should not be so rigid that it does not allow for any detours.

Most meetings, such as those of fraternal or civic organizations, follow an agenda to complete the group's business. A common format is:

  I. Calling the meeting to order

 II. Reading the minutes of the previous meeting

III. Presenting committee reports

IV. Discussing unfinished business

 V. Proposing new business

VI. Adjourning the meeting

Sometimes the agenda specifies not how the meeting should be run but rather how to go about solving a specific problem. The participants start their work by wording a *discussion question*—the issue or problem that will be dealt with. For example, if the group's purpose is to decide what type of grading system should be used on campus, the question could be "What should be done to solve the problem of inconsistent grading policies on campus?"

Some guidelines are useful for wording a discussion question:

- *Propose the issue in a question form.* Since the major issue of a problem-solving discussion is what the group should do to solve a specific problem, the discussion should center on answering the question.

- *Keep the question short and simple.* Clarity is important.

- *Word the question so that it does not show bias.* You cannot honestly discuss a question that states the expected conclusion.

- *Word the question as an open question so that it cannot be answered with a yes or no.* You need to allow for other alternatives.

In some instances, the group is formed because the dilemma is clear and the group's task is to solve the preworded problem. On the other hand, some groups may be given a general idea of what is wrong and need to begin by formulating the specific discussion question. One way to plan a discussion question is for each member to prepare one in advance. Then the group can meet to share individual questions and blend them into a question on which the group can agree. No discussion of the issues should take place while the question is being determined.

When the question is agreed on, a format for a discussion may be in order. This step in the process involves developing a discussion agenda. Assume that you are in a group that is going to discuss the question "What can be done at XYZ Corporation to solve the problem of computer hardware and software incompatibility?" Your problem-solving agenda might look like this:

I. What is the problem?
   A. What terms do we need to know to deal with the problem?
      1. What is computer hardware and software?
      2. What is meant by computer hardware and software incompatibility?
   B. How does this problem concern us?
      1. As professionals?
      2. As consumers?
II. What are the causes of the problem?
   A. Is the desire for profits the cause of computer hardware and software incompatibility?
      1. Is competition among leading companies a cause of incompatibility?
      2. Is the purposeful creation of more profitable products a cause of incompatibility?
   B. Does the swiftly growing and changing nature of computer design cause incompatibility?
   C. Does a lack of standards contribute to incompatibility?
III. What are possible solutions?
   A. Would government guidelines bring about greater compatibility?
   B. Would public encouragement of hardware and software compatibility solve the problem?
   C. Would forming a group of manufacturers bring about greater compatibility?
   D. Could groups dedicated to enforcing standards solve the problem?
IV. What is (are) the best solution(s)?
   A. Which of the solutions proposed is workable?
   B. Which of the solutions proposed is desirable?
   C. Which of the solutions proposed is practical?
   V. How can the best solution(s) be put into effect?

Following such an agenda allows for complete discussion and contributes to a well-thought-out solution.

Voting

In addition to developing a system for conducting business and arriving at results, a group has responsibilities for determining how decisions will be made by members.

Voting takes place when members are given an opportunity to indicate agreement, disagreement, or no opinion on an idea or candidate.

Voting takes place when members are given an opportunity to indicate agreement, disagreement, or no opinion on an idea or candidate. The purpose of voting is to ensure that members know the outcome of the discussion and the decision made. It is imperative that the method of voting be agreed on before the group starts working toward the solution to avoid conflict when it comes time to vote.

There are four common voting methods:

1. *Consensus.* The word *consensus* means "all."[26] Thus, in a consensus decision, every member of the group must agree on a proposal before it can be put into action. This is often the method used for decisions in which dire consequences can result from the outcome of the action. For example, most juries operate by consensus. In consensus, a member not voting is considered the same as a negative vote, as it stops an "all in favor" outcome.

2. *Majority vote.* Majority vote is often misunderstood. It does not solely mean more than half. In *majority voting,* the winner must receive more than half of the votes, excluding those who do not vote or who abstain (i.e., do not want to vote).[27] For example, if there are ten people in a group and all vote, it will take six votes for a majority to rule. If, however, one of the people abstains, then it will take five votes for passage according to the majority method.

3. *Plurality.* The word *plurality* means "most."[28] Often when more than two options are available, a group may turn to plurality voting. If, for example, three candidates are running for an office, in plurality voting the one getting the most votes is declared the winner. In the same way, if five ideas have been proposed as solutions to a problem, the solution selected will be the one receiving the greatest number of votes.

4. *Part-of-the-whole voting.* This method occurs when a specific number or percentage of those who are eligible to vote is required to bring about some action. For cxample, some of the rules of operation of an organization can be changed only if 75 percent of those eligible to vote agree to the change. A group has the right to set any number or percentage it wishes to allow action to take place. These numbers need to be set before starting the decision-making process.

The method selected for voting can have a profound effect on the outcome of a proposed action. In a historic case, the proposed federal Equal Rights Amendment was not enacted as a U.S. constitutional change, even though more than a majority of the states approved its inclusion. This happened because the part-of-the-whole method was used, and a two-thirds vote was needed but was not obtained. If a majority voting system had been used, the amendment would have passed. Juries, which use consensus, require all twelve jurors to agree on the vote. If the vote is eleven to one, which is clearly a majority, there is no decision. This lack of ability to reach a consensus results in a "hung" jury, one unable to reach a decision.

Decision-Making Techniques

In European American culture, there are a number of approaches to structuring a decision-making discussion. All of these center on two concepts. First, "effective group decision-making requires an analysis and understanding of a problem before members search for solutions,"[29] and, second, "effective decision-making groups normally engage in creative exploration of unusual, even deviant, ideas during initial discussions."[30] These two steps ensure that the group works toward solving an agreed-on problem and that all the resources and creativity of the members are used. Two methods of decision making are the Six-Step Standard Agenda and 1-3-6.

Six-Step Standard Agenda

The *Six-Step Standard Agenda for Decision Making*[31] is a direct outgrowth of the traditional reflective-thinking process, which stresses that a problem be identified and analyzed, solutions sought, and a solution selected and implemented.[32] The procedure for this method is comprised of six steps:

Step 1: Problem identification. A question is worded that states the problem. The query may be a *question of fact* (whether something is true, and to what extent); a *question of value* (whether something is good or bad, right or wrong, and to what extent); or a *question of policy* (whether a specific course of action should be undertaken in order to solve a problem).

Step 2: Problem analysis. Collect the information needed to identify the problem. Gather the facts, determine how serious the problem is, determine what harm is associated with the problem, decide whether the harm is serious and widespread, and identify what causes the problem.

Step 3: Solution criteria. Before the solutions are addressed, determine what criteria will be used to evaluate possible solutions. One of the most common sets of criteria centers on workability, practicality, and desirability. *Workability* is whether the solution will solve the problem. *Practicality* is whether the solution can be put into effect. *Desirability* is whether harm will be caused by implementing the solution.

Step 4: Solution suggestions. Brainstorm for possible solutions to the problem. **Brainstorming** consists of generating possible solutions without evaluation of them at the time of their proposal. Guidelines for brainstorming include:[33]

- Don't evaluate ideas while brainstorming.

- Don't clarify or seek clarification of an idea during the collection.

- Encourage zany ideas. Some of the best solutions are those that haven't been tried before or are out of the normal stream of action.

- Record all ideas without reference to who contributed the idea.

- Encourage participation by all group members.

Step 5: Select a solution. Explore the positives and negatives of all the ideas collected during brainstorming, and apply the agreed-on criteria. Another method of selecting the solution is to apply an evaluation technique known as *RISK*, which has these basic steps:[34]

- Think of any risks, fears, or problems associated with the solution.

- Brainstorm potential negative consequences either individually or as a group.

- Post all potential consequences on a chart or blackboard for all members to see.

- Give time for additions to the list.

- Discuss each negative point again.

- Weigh the risks and consequences against the perceived benefits.

- Make a decision to implement, delay for further study, modify, or kill the proposal and search for (a) better alternative(s).

Step 6: Solution implementation. Put the solution into effect and monitor it by follow-up testing and observation to make sure it is working. If it is not working, repeat steps 4 through 6.

1-3-6 Decision-Making Technique

The *Nominal Group Technique of Decision Making* centers on brainstorming without direct group interaction in the initial stage. This technique encourages idea generation from all individuals but avoids criticism, destructive conflict, and long-winded speeches.[35]

The *Berko 1-3-6 Decision-Making Technique* is a format for using the nominal group technique.[36] It takes place after the specific decision to be made or problem to be solved is agreed on by the group, and members are ready to work toward solution. The technique gets its name from how the participants work: alone (1), then in a group of (3), and then in a group of (6). The steps, illustrated in Figure 9.4, are

Step A: Each individual in the group lists what he or she thinks should be done to solve the problem or the best possible decisions regarding the issue. This process is a brainstorming session.

Step B: Participants are divided into groups of three. Each group combines its members' lists. No items are deleted, but possibilities are combined and solutions or decisions reworded. There should be no discussion of the value of the ideas during this step.

Step C: Each subgroup meets with another one, and they combine their lists. Again, duplicate ideas are eliminated and solutions or decisions reworded. No evaluations are made.

Step D: The whole group reassembles. A spokesperson for each subgroup reads its list aloud. All items are written on a long sheet of paper or on a whiteboard. (It is important that everyone in the room be able to read the lists, so large writing is imperative.)

Step E: The items are numbered.

Step F: Each person prioritizes the entire list, ranking in order all items with no ties. The most important or best solution or decision should be numbered 1, the next 2, and so forth. Each person's rankings are recorded on a sheet of paper.

Step G: The rankings are collected and tallied. The top items are identified, the final number of which should be a proportion of the number of items generated in

Figure 9.4
Berko 1-3-6 Decision-Making Technique

step D. If thirty or more items were generated, the top ten would be a reasonable final list. For fewer items, about one-half to one-third of the total is appropriate. (Determine this in advance to avoid conflict over how many should be included in the final list.)

Step H: Individuals select their top choices and then are randomly divided into subgroups of no more than six persons. If possible, a representative of each of the subgroups in step C should be in each of the newly formed units. (This is not imperative, but in cases where there is lack of clarity in a statement, the individual from the subgroup that generated the idea may be able to clarify its meaning.)

Step I: Each subgroup selects what it considers the best solution using the individual selections from step H. At this step, evaluations are made. Statements may be reworded, but no new solutions may be introduced.

Step J: Spokespersons for each subgroup report on the decision of the subgroup. If all subgroups have selected the same solution, the process is completed. If not, solutions that received the support of at least one subgroup are retained and the others eliminated.

Step K: Subgroups reassemble and select what they consider the best solution from those remaining on the list.

Step L: A spokesperson for each subgroup reports on the selection of his or her subgroup.

Steps K and L are repeated until a single solution is chosen.

Some smaller groups adopt an alternative approach, using only steps A through F, and then have all members meet together to reach a final solution. Smaller groups also can adapt the procedure to be a 1-2-4 process.

Recognize that communication factors (i.e., members are willing to listen to one another, members are comfortable expressing ideas, and members analyze information and ideas) have a major impact on the outcome of the decision making in a group. Research suggests that people believe that decisions are of high quality "when group members participate fully in the process and the group climate is characterized by the presence of respectful behaviors and the absence of negative socio-emotional behaviors."[37]

Group Setting

Although you might not have given it much consideration, where a group meets—the size, shape, color, temperature, and decor of the room—and where participants sit can affect the success of a group. Group meeting spaces represent a particularly important type of microenvironment that can influence the quality and quantity of communicative interaction, the participants' perceptions of each other, and the task performance of a given group.[38]

Two specific variables of importance in group settings that can affect group action are seating choices and the configuration of the tables.

Seating Choice

Where you sit at a meeting may determine whether you are selected as the leader, how much you will participate, and how others perceive you. This is an important concept for you to consider if you aspire to be the group's leader. For example, the person who sits at the head of a rectangular table significantly increases his or her chances of being perceived as the leader.[39]

Studies about seating have arrived at these findings:

- The person who is seated in the dominant position at a table, such as at the center of the table, is in the power position. For example, if you saw the television show *The Apprentice,* you probably noticed that Donald Trump, who had the power to hire or fire, was seated in the boss position illustrated in Figure 9.5. He placed the apprentices opposite him so that he could test their ability to communicate their expertise, defend their decisions, and counter arguments presented by others.

If one person in a group is standing and everyone else is seated, the one who is standing will command the others' attention.

Figure 9.5
Meeting Seating

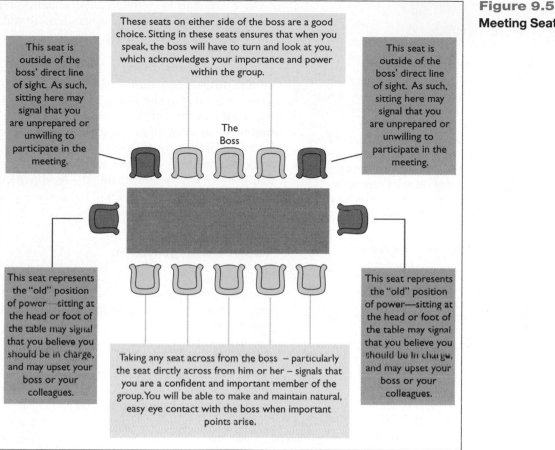

These seats on either side of the boss are a good choice. Sitting in these seats ensures that when you speak, the boss will have to turn and look at you, which acknowledges your importance and power within the group.

This seat is outside of the boss' direct line of sight. As such, sitting here may signal that you are unprepared or unwilling to participate in the meeting.

This seat is outside of the boss' direct line of sight. As such, sitting here may signal that you are unprepared or unwilling to participate in the meeting.

The Boss

This seat represents the "old" position of power—sitting at the head or foot of the table may signal that you believe you should be in charge, and may upset your boss or your colleagues.

This seat represents the "old" position of power—sitting at the head or foot of the table may signal that you believe you should be in charge, and may upset your boss or your colleagues.

Taking any seat across from the boss – particularly the seat dirctly across from him or her – signals that you are a confident and important member of the group. You will be able to make and maintain natural, easy eye contact with the boss when important points arise.

- "It seems to be a norm, in the United States at least, that leaders are expected to be found at the head or end of the table."[40] At family dinners, for example, the head of the household is usually seated at the head of the table. Elected group leaders generally put themselves in the head positions at rectangular tables, and the members place themselves so they can see the leader.

- At a round conference table, whoever sits at the twelve o'clock position is the most powerful, with power diminishing as it moves around past positions at three o'clock, six o'clock, and nine o'clock. The least powerful person sits at the eleven o'clock position.[41]

- Individuals who choose to be seated along the sides of a table not only decrease their chances of being perceived as leaders but also are likely to be perceived as individuals with lower status and less self-confidence.[42]

- People seated in a circle will feel more comfortable and interact more than they would if they were in straight rows or seated around a rectangular table.

- In a group consisting of all women, the person at the head of the table is perceived as the leader. However, in a mixed-gender group, a woman at the head position is less likely to be perceived as the leader than a man who occupies the end position.[43]

- At round tables, if several people sit at one arc of the table and the others spread themselves around the rest, the two seated together tend to be perceived as the

Culturally Communicating

Culture's Effect on Classroom Discussions

One of the significant challenges facing teachers in an increasingly multicultural educational environment is how to increase the participation level in class of some ethnic minority students. Japanese students, for example, initiate and maintain fewer conversations and are less apt to talk in class discussions than are other students. This reticence to participate verbally in class carries over to small group situations. Contributions to group decision making by ethnic minorities are consistently lower than nonminorities. In 76% of the small groups in one study, the member who contributed the least was Asian.

Source: J. Dan Rothwell, In Mixed Company, 5th ed. (Belmont, CA: Wadsworth/Thomson Learning, 2004), p. 225.

REFLECT ON THIS: Have you ever been in class with first-generation (i.e., recent immigrants, exchange students, visiting scholars) Japanese students? If so, did they follow the description in this discussion? Is the same true of other first-generation classmates from other cultures?

leaders. This is considered the visual center of the table because the others tend to turn to face the two seated together.[44]

In classrooms arranged in rows, students who participate the most tend to form a triangle from the center of the room. For example, in a room with six rows of chairs, most class participation tends to come from those seated in the first four seats of the row closest to the front, the three seats behind them, the two seats behind them, and the one seat behind them. The least participation comes from the very back corners and those seated in the end rows.[45]

Table Configuration

Table configuration or shape is an important variable in group interaction. Rectangular arrangements foster more and better communicative interaction than do T-shaped or L-shaped seating arrangements, and a round configuration is better in this regard than a rectangular table. The round configuration is the most neutral.[46] At rectangular tables, communication usually flows across the table rather than around it.[47]

People seem to be aware of the different perceptions related to different seating positions. Interestingly, when asked in one study to select seats to convey different impressions, respondents chose end positions to convey leadership and dominance, the closest seats to convey interpersonal attraction, and seats that afforded the greatest interpersonal distance to indicate they did not wish to participate.[48]

Effect of the Physical Environment

The physical environment should fit the purpose of the meeting. An informal meeting may take place around the water cooler or copy machine. For more formal meetings it should be remembered that a meeting can unravel if the room is too large or small, if it is too warm or cold, and if the lighting or the acoustics are not conducive to seeing and hearing one another. Groups often function more effectively if snacks are provided. Attention to these kinds of details will pay off in member satisfaction with the group and contribute better to the group process and product.

On the other hand, the *meet-while-standing theory* requires a meeting place without any furniture. The concept is that people forced to stand will make decisions more rapidly because the participants get tired and want to finish their business and find someplace to sit.

Mediated Meetings

Mediated meetings are electronically held teleconferences, video conferences, or computer or virtual conferences that allow for meetings to be held anyplace where someone who needs to participate in a meeting is located. Groups no longer have to meet in a conference room; they can meet in cyberspace.[49] People have both positive and negative reactions to mediated meetings. On the one hand, not only are they cost effective, but electronically supported meetings have also been found to be "more satisfying to the group members, because they can participate more equitably. The result is as much or more consensus as occurs in traditional face-to-face meetings."[50]

Types of Mediated Meetings

There are four basic types of mediated meetings:

1. *Teleconferencing* consists of telephone conference calls and speakerphone meetings.
2. *Video conferencing* includes meetings conducted with one-way video and two-way audio as well as fully interactive two-way video and two-way audio.
3. *Web conferencing* consists of meetings in which participants log on to a central conference database through their personal computer. It is similar to their sending or receiving e-mail. Computer meetings can take place as a *real-time conference*, in which all participants are at their computers at the same time, or as an *asynchronous conference*, in which participants contribute to an online conference database at different times. These meetings may go on for weeks, depending on their purpose.[51]
4. *Virtual conferencing* takes place when participants are connected to a platform such as *Second Life*, an Internet-based virtual world that enables its users, called "Residents," to interact with each other through avatars, which are a computer user's representation of himself or herself, which takes the form of a three-dimensional model or a two-dimensional icon or picture. Residents can explore, meet other "residents," socialize, and participate in individual and group activities. Avatars and objects can chat, send and receive e-mails as well as instant messages. This modality is popular for meetings among younger organizational members, as they perceive it to be much like playing computer games.[52]

Positive and Negative Aspects of Mediated Meetings

As with any other method of operation, there are advantages and disadvantages with each type of mediated meeting. Understanding these differences can help potential users or participants.

TELECONFERENCING   Most organizations have the equipment and procedures in place for multiway calls. Speakers can be on land lines at their job site, but could also be at home, in an auto, or on their cell phones. Therefore, one of the major advantages of **teleconferencing** is the ease of use. On the other hand, participants typically are sitting alone in their offices, and they may feel isolated. If there are several people in a single room with a speakerphone, regulating who will speak can be difficult. Participants cannot observe their co-participants' nonverbal feedback, so it often is hard to read feedback cues. Other drawbacks are that member participation may be inconsistent, members can do other things while participating, such as work at their desks or on computers, and not pay strict attention. It is also difficult to share visual elements such as charts or diagrams unless they have been distributed in advance or can be faxed to others while the discussion is ongoing.

VIDEO CONFERENCING   Because many organizations have on-site video equipment, such as voice-sensitive cameras and audio systems, a large-screen television set, and a set of speakers, the equipment for **video conferencing** is often readily available.

Video conferences are meetings conducted with one-way video and two-way audio as well as fully interactive two-way video and two-way audio.

Most hotels and conferencing centers have video facilities, so even holding video conferences away from the home office can be convenient.[53]

"Group videoconferencing's three most distinguishing features are its interactive capabilities, the ability to originate from any number of locations, and the capacity to reach multiple worldwide locations simultaneously."[54]

Video conferencing is effective for introducing new products to a team of salespeople or potential users, having collaborative meetings among project members in distant places, holding corporate town meetings when employees are at various worldwide sites, conducting training sessions, and participating in trade shows without leaving the office.[55]

It should be recognized that video conferencing technology is expensive and, thus, not accessible to every group. Also, as sometimes happens with electronic equipment, technical difficulties and poor usage can cause communication problems.

WEB CONFERENCING   **Web conferencing** is fairly inexpensive. Most employees have computer workstations, and the only other costs are special computer programs, if they are desired. The conferences can take place wherever a computer can be activated. General training is minimal because most people are computer literate. Participants report that dynamic interactions often take place as people get involved in each other's messages.[56]

The fact that the conference can take place over an extended period of time can be an advantage. "Members of asynchronous conferences often report being able to mull over their comments before entering them, resulting in deeper and more thoughtful discussions."[57]

Web conferencing has weaknesses as well as strengths. Some view computer meetings as impersonal, more time consuming because it takes longer to type a thought than to speak it, and unsatisfactory for those who are uncomfortable with computer technology.[58]

Additional weaknesses include that even with interactive messaging, there is a delay in message sending and retrieval and a tendency to use short and incomplete messages. Moreover, there is no nonverbal presence; the interactions are dependent on the keyboarding speed of the participants; overlapping messages can cause confusion; and with numerous participants, direct interactions become very difficult.[59]

Attempts to overcome the negative aspects of Web conferencing have led to the development of *groupware:* specially designed software that meeting participants use to perform tasks such as brainstorming and decision making.[60]

In a typical meeting in which groupware is used, each participant sits at a computer terminal. The leader begins the meeting by inputting to participants what problem must to be solved or what decision must be made. Participants input ideas and cast votes on their individual screens, which are integrated by the groupware and shown on a public screen at the front of the room. The content of the meeting is saved for later reference.[61]

"Most research suggests that groupware does improve the quality of meetings." It is reported to save time, help build consensus, and guide the uninitiated through meeting procedures.[62] On the other hand, it doesn't automatically make meetings more productive. Slow typists complain that they can't participate or that decisions are made before they can respond. It limits the amount of discussion that can take place. Extroverts complain that they can't participate enough. And because of the ease of operation, so many ideas may be presented that the volume becomes unmanageable.

GoToMeeting is one of the most commonly used groupware. It is a Web conferencing tool that allows you to meet online rather than in a conference room. It is easy to use and cost effective. Patented technology enables co-workers, customers, and prospects to view any application running on your PC in real time. With the flexibility to meet in person or online, the distributors contend, "you'll be able to do more and travel less."[63]

VIRTUAL CONFERENCING   Participating in **virtual conferencing** requires the same level of preparation as other mediated means but adds the challenge of getting attuned to the technology. Especially important is assuring that the avatar does not simulate actions that you don't want, such as sitting on a table instead of seating itself in a chair. Those who are used to playing video games usually have little difficulty in getting used to this format.

How to Make Mediated Meetings Work

Mediated meetings seem to be at least part of the answer as to how meetings should be conducted. Some techniques that are useful for planning and implementing electronic meetings include:[64]

- Speakers should be close enough to the microphones so they can be easily heard.
- Participants should control the noise of papers, tapping on the table, and other distracting habits that microphones will pick up.
- High-quality graphics must be prepared to fit the television format.
- Audio or materials that are too complex to be seen on video should be mailed or faxed to participants in time to be used for reference during the session.
- Participants should identify themselves continuously during the process.
- Participants should announce when they leave or enter the discussion.
- Wait until the camera is on you if you are participating in a video conference.
- Limit the agenda to no more than one hour. If it is longer, a break should be scheduled.

- Select the appropriate participants: people who are willing to work with media and are not being forced to do so.
- Make sure the technology is operating properly and the participants know how to work the equipment.
- Have an orientation with the participants before the actual presentation in order to answer questions about the procedure and the media.
- Prepare and distribute a written agenda in advance of the session.

In Conclusion

A meeting should be a purposeful interaction; therefore, no matter the setting or the technique, the basic questions always to be asked are (1) why the meeting is being held, (2) who should attend, (3) when the meeting should take place, and (4) what materials need to be prepared and present for accomplishing the purpose.

Groups are an assemblage of persons who communicate in order to fulfill a common purpose and achieve a goal. Group members influence one another, derive some satisfaction from maintaining membership in the group, interact for some purpose, assume specialized roles, and depend on one another. Groups often are classified by size, with small groups containing three to twelve persons and large groups more than a dozen. One of the most prominent functions of the group communication process is that of decision making. There are advantages and disadvantages to both participating in a group and having groups make decisions, versus working alone. Groups normally go through six phases: forming, norming, storming, conforming, performing, and adjourning. Where a group meets and where participants sit can affect the success of a group. Besides face-to-face meetings, organizations are using mediated meetings, which include teleconferencing, video conferencing, Web conferencing, and video conferencing.

Learn by Doing

1. Be prepared to defend or counter this statement: "The advantages of working in a group outweigh the disadvantages." Go beyond the arguments given in the chapter and use personal examples to develop your answer.

2. Consider a group in which you have worked that was *not* successful in reaching its goal or that had difficulty in reaching its goal. What specifically was the problem? How could the problem have been solved?

3. For your next examination in this class, students will be divided into study groups to prepare for the test. After the exam, a class discussion will be held on the value or lack of value of study groups.

4. Mentally revisit a group in which you have participated. Write a short paper (which may be given as an oral presentation) analyzing its norming, storming, conforming, and performing stages and adjourning.

5. Your class will be divided into groups. Each group is to contact at least two representatives of an organization that is conducting mediated meetings. Interview them in person, by telephone, or online about the pros and cons of conducting mediated meetings. Write a short report on your findings. You will present a group report to your classmates on your findings.

6. Be prepared to discuss this issue: You are a member of a classroom group that is to investigate the concept of groupthink, write a collective paper, and give an oral group report. The class has been told that everyone in the group will get the same grade for the project. There are six people in the group. One person fails to show up for any group meetings, nor does he research his segment of the paper, so others do that research. When it comes time to hand in the paper and give the oral report, what should the group do regarding the errant member?

Key Terms

chapter 10

Participating in Groups

▶ **After reading this chapter, you should be able to**

- Explain that people from different cultures possess varying attitudes about being group participants, applying procedures for working in groups, making decisions, following procedural structure, and using information

- Discuss the role of gender as a factor in group activities

- Define and explain the role of the participants, the leaders, and the leadership in groups

- Compare and contrast the role of disagreement in the group process

- Acknowledge the role of the hidden agenda in the group process

- List the types and explain the communicative role of group networks

- Define the authoritarian, democratic, and laissez-faire leader types

- Explain why a person would want to be a group leader and demonstrate how he or she would proceed to acquire the leader or leadership role

Groups are made up of people. Those who comprise a group play the roles of leaders, leadership, and participants. **Participants** are those members of a group who interact to bring about the actions of the group. **Leaders** are those who guide the group. **Leadership** refers to those who influence the group to accomplish its goal.

Members of groups, whether they are assuming a participant or leader role, come to the group with cultural influences. These influences affect the way in which group members function.

Cultural Differences in Groups

Each of us is a product of the culture in which we were brought up. We learn the customs and patterns of our culture, and these carry over into all phases of our lives. Research shows that people from different cultures possess varying attitudes about making independent decisions and being group participants, applying procedures for working in groups, making decisions, following procedural structure, and using information.

Cultures and Groups[1]

"A dominant perception in American culture assumes that the world is material [something to be used] rather than spiritual [an idea or essence to be appreciated and saved], and should be exploited for the material benefit of humanity"[2] This Euro-American point of view strongly affects how we work in groups and the purpose for which we form groups. Euro-Americans tend to use groups to get things done (e.g., commerce, getting products produced) rather than for strengthening the bonds of the

Culturally Communicating

Cross-Cultural Considerations

These guidelines can help you speak the right business language when you deal with those from other cultures:

- **Find out** if the culture you'll do business in is high-contact—expects lots of details—or low-contact—prefers a broad overview.

- **Realize that** you may have to ask permission to take meeting notes. *Reason:* Some in other cultures object because they feel it may "pin them down."

- **Assume that** in most cultures it's safer to let your counterparts bring up business issues first. That allows them to set the pace and provides signals you can use to adjust your behavior.

- **Be more** formal. Use titles and last names—and be sure to pronounce them correctly.

- **Talk clearly,** avoid slang and sports terms, and learn and use a few key phrases in the others' language. *Examples:* "Good morning," "Yes," "No," "Please," and "Thank you."

- **Adjust your** tempo to your counterparts' concept of time. Some cultures have little concern for punctuality.

- **Learn to** read cultural differences in nonverbal signals. *Example:* A smile can signal embarrassment in some cultures.

Source: Speaking the Language of Business Overseas. Prudential Relocation Global Services. Flatiron Park West, 2555 55th Street, Boulder, CO 80301. © Communication Briefings. www.briefings.com, 1101 King St., Alexandria, VA 22314. Used with permission

▶ *Note:* Throughout this text generalizations are presented regarding trends of various cultural groups. These are based, whenever possible, on research findings and expert observations. They are in no way intended to lead to the conclusion that all members of the cultural group noted conform to the generalized patterns.

The Confucian principle of i requires that a person be affiliated and identify with a small and tightly knit group of people over long periods of time.

members of the group (e.g., creating good will, supporting the emotional needs of the members, and so on).

People in the United States are highly individualistic.[3] This individualism, which stresses personal loyalty before group loyalty, has a strong historical base. The United States was founded by adventurers and dissidents. In this culture, membership in groups (except those that are mandatory because of a person's work or academic environment) tends to be voluntary. While recognizing that there may be traditions, such as membership in a particular religion, European Americans tend to decide for themselves whether they want to belong to a group. You, for example, choose whether to participate in a social group or a fraternal organization. After you become part of the group, if you don't like being a member, you can resign. Because of this ability to join and leave a group, allegiance tends not to be a lifelong commitment. This, however, is not the case in other parts of the world. For example, in many East Asian countries, Confucianism is the basic philosophy of much of the population. The *Confucian principle of i* requires that a person be affiliated and identify with a small and tightly knit group of people over long periods of time. These long-term relationships work because group members aid and assist each other when there is a need; sooner or later those who assisted others will have to depend on those they aided. This mutually implied assistance pact makes for group interdependence.[4]

Not only does the attitude toward being in groups vary by culture but there also is a difference in the training required in certain cultures for group participation. Because they participate in groups to a limited degree, many European Americans need to learn about group operational methods when they enter into organizations. The same is true of people from other countries having a high degree of individualism, such as Australia, Great Britain, Canada, New Zealand, and Denmark. In contrast, people from societies in which group adherence is stressed have a clearer sensitivity about how groups operate, since they are encased in groups all their lives. Those areas and countries that are the least individualistic are found in Asia (Japan, China, Vietnam) and South America.

Cultural differences also are reflected in the way a person works in a group. In many East Asian countries, there is a strong distaste for purely business transactions.

This is carried over into meetings, where the tendency is to mix personal with public relationships. Business meetings, for example, may take place over a long period of time in order for people to establish personal relationships, engage in activities like sports and drinking, foster an understanding of the personalities of the participants, and develop a certain level of trust and a favorable attitude.

A good example of where business is mixed with the personal is in Japan, known as a nation that stresses group culture, where individualism is submerged and expression occurs in hidden ways. This, of course, is almost the opposite of how European Americans operate. In the United States, individuals work in groups to get *tasks* accomplished. In Japan, the individual's sense of identity *is* the group. This is based on a long history of ruling families who created a social structure that bound families, villagers, and strong leaders together. In the United States, the stress has been on rugged individualism, with the group coming second to the individual. In Japan, the word for describing a group is *we*. In the United States, groups often are divided between "us" and "them." For instance, administrators and faculty members are part of the same group—the university—but too often find themselves on opposite sides when making institutional decisions.

Contrasts in Cultural Group Decision Making

If the assumption is made that one of the important tasks of a group is decision making, another cultural variation comes into play. It is important to realize, when working in decision-making groups, that there are vast cultural differences in how people think, apply forms of reasoning, and make decisions.

In the Western view, it is generally believed that people can discover "truth" if they apply the scientific method to the decision-making process. The traditional Western problem-solving sequence has four segments: identify the problem, search for solutions, test those solutions, and put a solution into practice. The final decision is often based on a majority vote of the membership, with those who will have to implement or live with the decision often not part of the decision-making team. For example, few students are included in university discussions on curriculum requirements. In Japan, on the other hand, those affected by the decision are often included in the process.

Other societies use different decision-making approaches.[5] For example, for the Chinese, though this has relaxed some during the present opening of the country to the free enterprise system, decision making is more authoritative than consensual; decisions are made by higher authorities without the inclusion of subordinates. Although subordinates are consulted informally, the leader makes the final decision.

Work groups in Mexico tend to use a *centralized decision-making process*. Mexicans often view authority as being inherent within the individual, not his or her position. Making trade-offs is common for Mexican negotiators, including adding issues that are not part of the original business at hand.[6]

Cultural Contrasts in the Role of Information for Groups

Even information or ideas that are used for making decisions may differ among cultures. European American negotiators tend to compartmentalize issues, focusing on one issue at a time instead of negotiating many issues together. In the United States, negotiating toward the final decision usually takes on a form of *proposal–counterproposal negotiating*,[7] in which a plan or solution is presented and then a counteroffer is made. For example, in a group meeting concerning salary negotiations, the employees propose a particular salary and explain why they think this is the appropriate amount. Management then typically makes an offer of a lesser amount and offers counterarguments. This process continues until an amount is agreed on. The negotiations may be accompanied by a threat of the workers going out on strike, an action unheard of in some other cultures.

The French, on the other hand, seem to have no problem with open disagreement. They debate more than they bargain and are less apt than Euro-Americans to be flexible for the sake of agreement. They start with a long-range view of their purpose, as opposed to Euro-Americans, who work with more short-range objectives. This format was evident in the French stand against the war in Iraq, where the question of the long-range purpose of the war was a point of contention between the countries.

"Japanese negotiators tend to make decisions on the basis of detailed information rather than persuasive arguments."[8] "The Japanese and most Asian cultures view [the] Euro-American version of powerful speech as immature because it indicates insensitivity to others and is likely to make agreement more difficult."[9]

Because this book is directed primarily at individuals who will find themselves most often participating in groups in the U.S. culture, the material in this chapter deals mainly with participant and leader conventions and patterns typical in the United States. However, because of the multiculturalism of this country, you likely will be working with people and in social situations with individuals from a variety of cultural backgrounds. Also, with the internationalization of business, it is becoming more and more common for businesspeople from the United States to be working in international settings, so knowledge of other cultures' group procedures can be helpful.

Male and Female Roles in Groups

Besides cultural differences based on nationality, the roles of males and females in European American culture can play an important role in leader and participant operational modes.

Is gender a factor in group tasks or maintenance? Generally, studies on leader, leadership, and the group process indicate that differences do occur in the way men and women operate in a group. For example, "women are more likely than men to

Emergent leaders exhibit a significantly higher rate of participation than do nonleaders.

engage in caring, personal communication."[10] In addition, "women tend to exceed men in collaborative, participative communication that enables others."[11] As in any instance when using research about any group, keep in mind that the results represent a norm and there are exceptions to the rule. You, for instance, may not follow the patterns, or perhaps you know people who don't.

Other studies about males and females in groups indicate that "subordinates judge male and female leaders to be equally effective, and judge both masculine and feminine styles of communication to be important in leaders."[12] In fact, one study concludes that "men and women are 99% similar and only 1% different in their communication."[13] However, "when judging a group member's expertise, men and woman are not viewed through the same lens. Men more than women are encouraged by groups to contribute their expertise, partly because group members, both males and females, don't initially think of women as experts."[14] Although men are considered to be more competitive than women,[15] "women are becoming more competitive as they enter the workforce in larger numbers."[16] As for presenting and defending ideas, "men are more argumentative than women, meaning men are more likely to advocate controversial positions during group discussion or to challenge the positions on issues taken by other group members. Women are inclined to view verbal aggressiveness and argumentativeness as strategies of dominance and control."[17]

There apparently has been a shattering of the glass ceiling (an invisible barrier of discrimination that has traditionally excluded women from top jobs in corporate and professional America), as there has been a significant change in the leader role of women in the United States. Almost half (49 percent of all managerial and professional positions in the United States are held by women.)[18]

Research in educational groups[19] indicates that students believe classes led by women are more discussion oriented, and classes taught by men are more structured and emphasize content mastery. In addition, male college professors are perceived to be less supportive and less innovative than are female instructors. It also has been shown that "male students initiate more interactions with teachers than female students initiate, and that males tend to dominate classroom talk."[20]

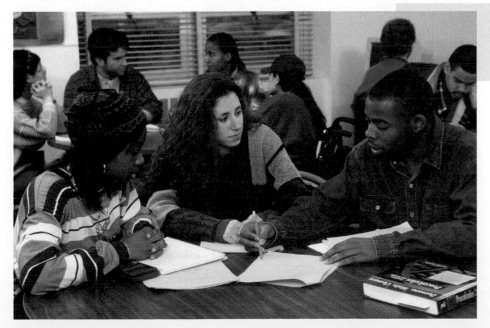

Group actions are based on proposing actions, putting forth ideas, and proposing solutions to problems.

The Group Participant

Participants in groups have various responsibilities to themselves and to the group. They normally perform communicative maintenance and task roles, form networks by which they relay messages, and must deal with other members. Researchers who study the role of the follower in a group remind us that, although there is considerable focus on understanding the dynamics of good leadership in a group, we need to remember that effective group dynamics has to start with good followership. For example, what distinguishes an effective follower from an ineffective follower is enthusiastic, intelligent, and self-reliant participation without star billing in the pursuit of an organizational goal. Further, exemplary followers are those who communicate as team members, actively engaging in the work of the group, critically assessing group decisions, and contributing creative ideas that enhance the group's goals.

Socially Communicating

Quantitative Complexity

As the size of a group increases, the possible number of interactions between group members increases exponentially.

These are the calculations:

Number In Group	Interactions Possible
2	2
3	9
4	28
5	75
6	186
7	441
8	1056

Source: J. Dan Rothwell, *In Mixed Company*, 5th ed. (Belmont, CA: Wadsworth/ Thomson Learning, 2004), p. 142.

REFLECT ON THIS: Come to several conclusions you can reach about group size based on the quantitative complexity theory.

Responsibilities of Group Members

Participants should remember that an entire group is responsible and accountable for final decisions. Thus, being a member of the **silent majority** (those who say nothing during the decision-making process) does not release you from accountability for that decision. For example, if the group decides that each member should pay fifteen dollars more in dues, you must pay the extra fee, even though you may not have said anything during the discussion and may not have even voted on the issue. Despite your lack of participation, if you expect to remain a member of the group, you cannot announce after the decision is made, "I didn't say anything and I didn't vote, so I don't have to pay!"

Being a member of the silent majority does not release you from accountability for a decision.

All group members should be knowledgeable. In the Western logic system, although personal beliefs are important, expert opinions and facts reveal what authorities believe and what testing has proved, and this is the basis for sound decision making. In other words, the use of supporting evidence can help ensure that your conclusions have substance and will probably be perceived as having credibility. Consider how you can apply evidence such as statistics, testimony, and illustrations to your discussions. Your participation is enhanced if you use this research to support your comments clearly and concisely.

Some groups are plagued by people who insist on dominating the discussion and the decision-making process. These people may, at worst, destroy the group and, at best, irritate members and make decision making difficult. Although it is sometimes very difficult when you have strong opinions and believe you are right and others wrong, each participant should try to respect as much as possible the rights of the others. This does not mean you should not participate if your views differ from those of others. It does mean, however, that a point can be reached where continued bickering can be destructive to the group's mission. Suppose that after presenting your point of view, it appears that your ideas are not going to be accepted. Your task, then, is either to try to work toward reaching a compromise into which you can enfold your ideas or to accept the fact that you have done everything you could to get your viewpoint presented and accepted but have failed to achieve your goal.

It is important not to assume that rejection of your idea is a rejection of you personally. Unfortunately, many people have difficulty making this distinction. They assume that if one of their ideas is rejected, they have been deemed unworthy. Not understanding this concept causes people to "fight to the death" for acceptance of their beliefs. In reality, what they are fighting for is to establish or retain their own legitimacy. This may lead the rejected person to start attacking others rather than sticking to the issues. Personal attacks often do little to get your stand accepted; rather, they cause alienation within the group. Personal issues lead other people to take stands not on what solution is right or wrong but on who is right or wrong. This choosing up of sides often divides the group, causing internal rifts and destroying the chances for group cohesion and goal accomplishment.

Normally, group members should take an active role in communicating with each other so that the entire group can benefit. Of course, there are times when, for whatever reason, you may feel that you do not want to participate. You may think that you do not have the necessary information, or that you might not have strong enough feelings to interject, or that your beliefs have already been presented by someone else. Whatever the reason, if you knowingly and willingly don't participate, this is your privilege. However, choosing not to participate is an act of abdicating responsibility as a group member.

Participants in a group discussion, much like therapeutic listeners, also must try to set aside their own prejudices and beliefs so as to listen and respond to what others have to say. This ability to suspend judgment is difficult. Deal with conflicts by adopting an openness to compromise and conciliation—that is, if you feel this is in the best interests of the group process and you can live with the compromise. Remember that compromises can result in giving up beliefs and moving to watered-down solutions, unsatisfying to all concerned. Do not allow a verbal bully to force you into a compromise or to adopt a solution you feel is not in the best interest of the group. Note that the focus is on the best interest of the *group,* which may not necessarily be in *your* best interest!

Communicating as a Group Member

As a group member, you perform varied communication activities. Foremost are speaking and listening. In the process of participation, you probably evaluate information, propose concepts, and agree and disagree with the ideas of others. Group interactions seem most effective when participants are aware of their maintenance and task roles.

PERFORMING GROUP MAINTENANCE TASKS   Group participants have a responsibility to attend to the maintenance functions (the interpersonal needs) of the group, because a productive group is one in which members feel positive about participating in deliberations. "*Group maintenance* focuses on the social dimension of the group. The central communicative function of maintenance roles is to gain and maintain the cohesiveness of the group."[21]

In order to effectively perform your group maintenance, you would be wise to:

■ *Treat others with respect.* For most people, treating others with respect is not a great problem. No doubt you and others realize that you will not always agree. There should be an understanding that disagreement can be helpful because it opens the decision-making process to a variety of viewpoints and allows differences of opinion to be aired.

■ *Maintain a positive attitude.* It is generally understood that having positive attitudes about what you are doing makes for a more committed and active group member. Think back to times when you have been proud of how your group acted and its achievements; perhaps you have been on a winning athletic team or planned an event and been pleased with the results. Accomplishments help build group pride.

   If group members have pride in their group and show commitment to it, the odds go up for group success. If this is not the case, maybe one of the tasks of the group should be to investigate why there are negative attitudes. Dealing with this issue may make working in the group more pleasant and increase the productivity of the membership.

■ *Encourage others.* Being encouraging rather than discouraging can keep communication channels open. Communication stoppers such as "That won't work,"

The effective group communicator should attend to nonverbal messages.

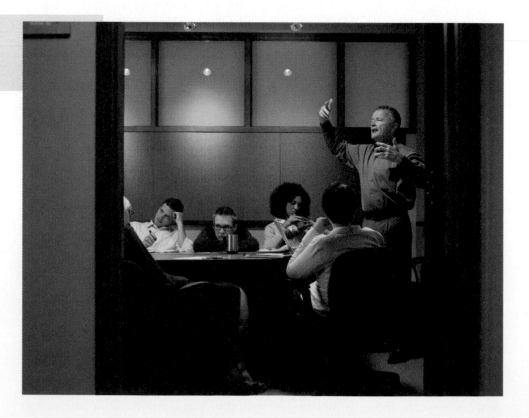

"We've tried that before," or "That's ridiculous" will have the effect of shutting down communication.

■ *Pay attention to nonverbal messages.* The effective group communicator attends to group members' nonverbal messages. Be aware of when your body is relaxed and when it tenses due to your discomfort because of the length of the discussion or your own reactions to what's transpiring in the group. Is it time to speak up? Is it time for you to stop talking? Be aware that your gestures, pace, and fluency can affect others. For example, a rapid speech rate, fluid gestures, relaxed posture, and verbal fluency are positive nonverbal communicators.[22] Be aware that people who are connecting with each other tend to face one another, looking directly in each other's eyes. When someone is turning away from an idea or a person who is presenting the idea, he or she will often literally turn away. Also, be aware that not all cultures use the same nonverbal signs. Just because someone is shaking his head and smiling does not mean the person is agreeing with you. It is common in Asian cultures, due to the politeness factor, to show agreeable signs, even when disagreeing. Also because someone is slouched in a chair does not mean that person is not paying attention. It may be his normal seating position or a cultural pattern, not discourtesy.

■ *Assume an active role.* Taking an active role in a group through volunteering ideas, showing willingness to work on subgroups and committees, and making supportive comments is important for helping a group to work cohesively.

Individuals who are communicatively supportive of maintenance functions will reinforce others' ideas, participate in constructive ways, separate people from ideas, try to remain flexible, express their feelings, and describe their reactions.

PERFORMING TASK ROLES Besides maintenance roles, participants need to perform *group task roles,* which include initiating ideas, encouraging diverse ideas, using reasoned thought, staying open-minded, being aware of hidden agendas, being cognizant of time constraints, encouraging other participants, and attending to nonverbal messages; in other words, making sure the group accomplishes its goal.

In order to effectively perform your group task role, you would be wise to:

■ *Initiate ideas.* Group actions are based on someone proposing actions, putting forth ideas, and proposing solutions to problems. Initially, people in most groups tend to be a little shy about presenting ideas. But as the group moves from norming to participating, this reluctance to put forth ideas is overcome. If others in your group aren't proposing ideas, make a suggestion. This may encourage them to participate. If you know that suggestions will be sought, and you know the topic of the discussion or the nature of the problem, come to the meeting prepared to propose ideas.

■ *Encourage diverse ideas.* Another important aspect of task roles is to encourage diverse ideas. Conservative thinkers hold to the tried and true. They tend to recreate past solutions to problems, sticking mainly to the status quo. Creative idea generators go beyond the norm and search for different solutions. Their ideas may seem crazy at first, but many seemingly outrageous ideas have satisfied major needs. Historically, space travel, the invention of the computer, and even the light bulb were all "far-out" ideas. Don't be stifled by the tried and true; think creatively, even if you risk being called a dreamer or an idealist. Join Alexander Graham Bell, Michelangelo, George Washington Carver, Madame Marie Curie, and other inventors, scientists, and explorers who have made a difference.

- *Use reasoned thought.* One of the important roles of task communication is to operate on the basis of reasoned thought. Being able to support sound ideas, develop well-thought-out concepts, separate fact from opinion, criticize weak or unsubstantiated ideas, use critical thinking, offer evidence, and integrate ideas are important obligations of a constructive task communicator.

- *Stay open-minded.* In general, most of us come to a conclusion, believe it is correct, and defend it no matter what. But ideally we should be open to the possibility that someone else's ideas may be as valid as, if not more valid than, ours. There are often ideas we haven't thought of, approaches we haven't been exposed to, ideas that challenge our beliefs. Don't overlook the possibility of joining ideas together to make for a blended solution.

- *Be aware of hidden agendas.* Be aware that not all members of a group will be as open, caring, and responsible as you are. Some individuals attempt to accomplish their goals at the expense of others. Some members of a group enter the task process with a **hidden agenda**: an objective or purpose that goes beyond the constructive interests of the group as a whole. When individuals work for their own unstated ends rather than for the group's objectives, the result is usually counterproductive. A hidden agenda is apparent, for example, when a department manager, discussing budget allocations, promises to support any plan that divides the resources equitably among departments but then opposes every plan presented. In this case, the manager has a hidden agenda: Perhaps the manager wants most of the funds for his or her department and thinks a delay will tire the participants and lead to a decision that favors that department. Thus, the manager is trying to manipulate the group toward a personal goal.

  In your role as an effective task communicator, listen carefully to the proposals and arguments of other members and be alert to the possibility of hidden agendas.

- *Be cognizant of time constraints.* A group participant should be sensitive to time factors, both to ensure that time is used wisely and that the group is not manipulated by a clever user of time. If you use a great deal of time and dominate a discussion with too many statements or lengthy comments, you run the risk that you will be tuned out or that your contributions will be so overpowering that the group process will be lost in your dominance. Use time effectively, and make sure that you allow others the time they need.

  Be wary of the participant who knows the meeting is coming to a close and that time is short, yet suggests a new, untested solution that has not been discussed. This is a device commonly used by individuals who know that when time pressures become a dominant factor, group members may act impulsively. If someone suggests a solution late in the discussion, make sure it is not acted on immediately, before the group has time to think about the advisability of taking the proposed action.

Roles of Group Members

Participants in small groups function in a variety of roles. It is helpful to recognize these roles and monitor not only your own behavior but also that of others. Monitoring enables you to understand why you and others are doing what you all are doing. And this awareness opens the possibility of altering behavior or alerting others to the role they are playing if actions being taken are detrimental to the group's progress. It also allows for self-praise and for praising others if you discover that the roles being played are productive.

Communication Networks

Groups operate by different formal and informal patterns that link members together. As participants speak, they develop patterns that result in their talking to, through, or at others. By understanding these patterns you may be able to assist the group in both its maintenance and task goals by pointing out if the use of a particular pattern is thwarting the flow of communication and stopping the group from moving forward. These patterns are called **group communication networks**.[23]

Early research on communication networks identified five basic network patterns. These are illustrated in Figure 10.1. Each of the dots represents an individual communicator; the arrows indicate the way the information flows. The leader, or the person of influence, is at the center of each flow of information. For example, in the wheel, the chain, and the Y, there is a clear leader or power figure. All information flows toward and through that person. These patterns are referred to as *centralized group communication networks, since all communication is controlled by the leader*. In general, centralized networks are most effective for groups dealing with simple problems, such as deciding who should be responsible for carrying a specific task for the group, or who will serve as secretary and record the proceedings of the group. They often depend on a strong leader to guide the proceedings. They can work more rapidly than other patterns because the leader normally has a great deal of influence and can direct participation toward accomplishing the task.

In the circle and the all-channel patterns, there is no central focal person; information does not flow from or through a single person. These are *decentralized group communication networks*. In decentralized networks, ideas flow freely. They are more effective for solving complex problems, as they often result in greater member interaction. Satisfaction with being a member of a group and backing the solution is usually high because there is much interplay among participants and less influence by a power figure. The leader in a decentralized network plays less the role of director and more that of a participant.

Specifically, in the wheel flow of information (a), each person in the group speaks to the leader, the leader speaks to each of the participants, but the participants do not

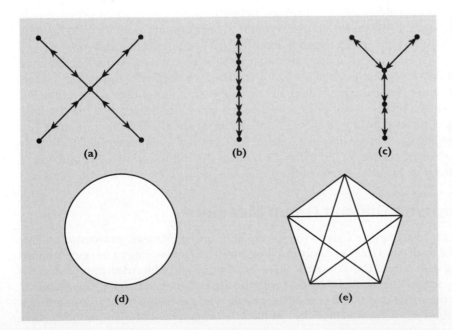

Figure 10.1

Group Communication Networks:

(a) wheel
(b) chain
(c) Y
(d) circle
(e) all-channel

Source: From Roy M. Berko, Andrew D. Wolvin, and Ray Curtis, *This Business of Communicating,* 5th ed., p. 273. Copyright © 1993 Wm. C. Brown Communications, Inc., Dubuque, Iowa. All rights reserved. Reprinted by permission.

speak directly to each other. The leader is in total control of the discussion. An example of this may be a family in which the mother is the power figure and everyone asks her for advice, and when they speak regarding making any type of family decision, she is the recipient of all the input.

The chain communication network (b) follows a format in which specific members of the group speak to each other, but they all do not communicate directly. The linchpin is the leader, who is in the center of the message chain. Again, using the family as the group being discussed, each of the children speaks to each other individually, they make a plan, and then go to the mother for approval of the action.

In the Y (c), two of the group members speak directly to the leader—but not to each other—while other members speak to each other and send messages to the other members through the leader. In this case, the oldest son and daughter speak to the mother individually, the other children speak to each other, and one of them speaks to the mother. There is no general meeting of all of the participants.

In the circle (d), each person speaks to two other people but doesn't speak directly to the others. The flow of messages is not controlled by the leader. In the all-channel communication network (e), each person in the group talks directly to all of the other members. This is the most interactive format. The family sits down and shares ideas, each speaking to the others.

How do these group formats get established? Early in the life of a group, the patterns are established. The network usually reflects the leader pattern philosophy of the person(s) in charge of the group. In the centralized networks, the leader maintains control of the flow of information. A leader less interested in controlling the flow of information will favor the decentralized networks. The members also can aid in determining the flow pattern. In groups with communication-apprehensive members, there may be a tendency for members not to want to interact with each other. Or, in some instances, the leader may encourage the members to use a more decentralized network, but the members do not assert themselves, forcing the leader to become the group's guide.

Research concerning communication networks indicates that group members have higher morale in a decentralized than in a centralized communication network; that decentralized communication networks are more efficient when groups must solve complex problems, but centralized networks are more efficient when groups must solve simple problems; and that centralized networks are more likely to result in work overload for the leader than are decentralized communication networks.

Participants in groups must realize that if the network is not working, there is a responsibility for one or more of the group members or the leader to suggest changes in the network. For example, if you are a member of a group that is operating as a chain, and information is not getting from participant to the leader, and the decisions are being controlled by one or a few of the members, and the solutions are not effective, changing the pattern may be in order. Sometimes a group outgrows the pattern being used. For example, a family may find that as the children grow older and want a more active role in the task roles of the group, the network may need to be changed.

Dealing with Difficult Group Members

Most people in groups are a joy to work with. They are cooperative, participate, assume leader and leadership roles in noncontrolling ways, and are willing to be open-minded in dealing with others. Unfortunately, there are some people who create dissent, are self-centered, attack others rather than deal with the issues, and won't stick to the agenda.

It is theorized that 90 percent of the people who are members of groups are reasonable most of the time. There are conflicts and differences of opinion, but people contribute to the good of the group and work things out. About 9 percent of the members are somewhat difficult to work with. These people have hidden agendas and disagreeable personalities, and seem to be marching to the tune of a different drummer much of the time. Then there is the remaining 1 percent. Their consistent obstructive nature gets in the way of any attempt to deal cooperatively with them.[24]

Using this concept as a basis, you can understand an aspect of conflict in a group and how to deal with different group members. To deal with the 90 percent, applying the concepts presented in this chapter on effective group communication should be sufficient to work things out and work toward tasks.

As for the 1 percent—the impossible people—there is very little you can do to work constructively with them. Reasoning with them or giving in to their demands accomplishes little. These individuals are out to make life miserable for themselves and everyone around them. They often are incapable of listening, processing, and working toward group cohesiveness. They tend to be so self-absorbed that there is no way to work things out, short of giving in. But giving in seems only to encourage their behavior, which escalates their negative actions because they know that eventually the group will give in to their tantrums and negativism again.

One coping method is to expel the impossible ones from the group. Another is to ignore them. A third is to recognize that they must have their say, but it is no one's obligation to listen. Unfortunately, if one of these is the group leader—the supervisor, the professor, the parent—the problem is compounded. Even group experts and psychologists have no recommendations for what participants should do if this is the case. Quitting a job, withdrawing from the class, or leaving a group may be your only salvation if things get too bad.

That leaves the 9 percent who are considered difficult group members. Difficult people are those who cause problems regarding the task or maintenance functions of a group—actions such as frequent disruptions, long speeches, irrational requests, insulting behavior toward others, and interruption of participants.

Before taking any action, be sure that the scenario is actually taking place and that the person is in fact difficult. Sometimes we perceive a person to be difficult because his or her ideas are different from ours. Is the person really difficult, or is the problem yours?

Experts seem to agree that to deal with difficult people, five general axioms should be followed:[25]

1. *Don't placate the troublemaker.* Allowing the disrupter to manipulate the group in order to keep the peace rewards the troublemaker for objectionable behavior and only encourages similar future actions. For example, the person might interrupt a vote by saying, "I don't want us to vote at this point. It's not fair to cut off discussion until we have all had our say." You could respond by saying, "The motion to call for the vote was made and seconded. The result was almost unanimous—except for your vote. Therefore, we have followed parliamentary procedure, and we will go ahead with the vote." To give in to the person would encourage him or her to continue to be an obstructionist in the future.

2. *Refuse to be goaded into a reciprocal pattern.* Resist the temptation to fight fire with fire. Someone might say to the chairperson, "You and your people are always making decisions that cause problems for this group. You need to be more honest in dealing with the rest of us." The person's intent is to get the chairperson upset and have her or him apologize or back down. The chair should not be pulled into such goading.

3. *Try to convert disruption into a constructive contribution.* There is a difference between being disruptive and being constructive. Use the person's idea to ask for other

ideas. Doing this takes the discussion away from the person and allows others to speak. If, for example, a member of a committee indicates that the decision-making process of the group was tainted by a lack of input, the chair might state, "That's an interesting point of view. Let's review the minutes of the meeting and reexamine the arguments for and against the selected decision." Doing this not only stops the disagreement but it may also aid in alerting the group to whether or not groupthink has been precipitated.

4. *Confront the difficult person directly.* If her or his tirades or other actions are disruptive, tell the person so. Continual disruptions and other negative actions that stop task and maintenance progress are not in the best interest of the group and need to be dealt with. Ideally, the confrontation should be assertive, factual, and focused on the issue—in other words, state exactly what the person has done. For example, instead of saying, "You are always making stupid and irrelevant remarks," state, "The last two times we have discussed the issue of selecting a new membership campaign, you changed the subject to why you believe the club should have more social events and why you believe you should be serving on the finance committee. Neither of these statements had anything to do with the topic being discussed, and they didn't help us solve the issue at hand."

5. *Separate yourself from the difficult person if all else fails.* Some individuals leave no other option but ostracism by the group. Quitting the job or leaving the group may be your only recourse. Before quitting, make an assertive statement that clearly indicates why you find the person's actions disruptive to the group and why you find yourself unable to continue working with the person. Make sure that your statements contain only facts that led you to your conclusion.

You can control only your own communication behaviors and your own responses to others' communication. Unless you are in a total power control position, you cannot change or control the actions of another person, so concentrate on dealing with yourself, and avoid getting frustrated.

The Group Leader and Group Leadership

The strength of a group is found not only in effective participation but also in meaningful guidance and decision making. The leader of a group is the person who is recognized as being responsible for guiding it through its tasks. (See Figure 10.2.) The leader

Figure 10.2

Berko-Wolvin-Wolvin Model of the Leader/Leadership Relationship

Note: The leader is the group's guide. Leadership is the ability to influence, which can be used positively or coercively. Both leader and leadership functions can be carried out by (a) the same person(s) or (b) separate persons.

The leader of a group is the person who is recognized as being responsible for guiding the group through its tasks.

may be *elected* (e.g., president of the speech honor society), may be *appointed* by an outside source (e.g., the board of trustees appoints the university president), may *volunteer* (e.g., a person volunteers to chair the social committee), or may *emerge* by taking control (e.g., a parent in a family). A group also may have more than one leader; for instance, a group may have several chairpersons. Furthermore, in some groups, the recognized leader may not be the only one guiding the group; other members may share this function by being appointed or assuming such responsibility.

The ability to influence others' opinions and actions is known as *leadership*. (See Figure 10.2.) It can be demonstrated by one or more people in a group, and the use of the power that derives from leadership can be viewed as enforcing obedience and/or the ability to influence others to perform.

Leadership power stems from various sources in the dynamics of a group. A classic study on leadership power[26] identified five sources by which leaders gain power: (1) legitimate power, inspiring a sense of responsibility in followers; (2) reward power, providing followers with things they desire; (3) coercive power, taking away rewards or administering sanctions and punishments; (4) expert power, providing others with information and advice; and (5) referent power, providing others with self efficacy, worth, or approval. In one sense, then, leadership power can be described as enforcing obedience through the ability to withhold benefits or inflict punishment. In this sense, power is coercive. **Coercion** centers on offering a selection of choices, all of them undesirable. For example, in a meeting of nurses to discuss whether shifts should be rotated, many of the participants may not want this action to be taken. But if the head nurse is in favor of rotating shifts, then the power of the position may come into play. He may say that it's his responsibility to determine staff assignments and that anyone who cannot accept his proposal can request a transfer to another department. Thus, the decision has been made through coercive power because neither of the options offered may be desirable to the nursing staff. Similarly, in a family, a mother can control the members by stating, "As long as you are living in my house, you will do as you are told or get out."

Communicating
in Careers

Advice for Meeting Leaders

To encourage creative thinking and idea generation when you're in charge of a meeting:

- **Ask open-ended** questions. *Reason:* Participants will have to answer with more than just a "yes" or "no."

- **Encourage people** to continue—even if they start to back off because they're repeating points made earlier.

- **Paraphrase ideas** when someone makes an unclear point.

- **Don't force** your views on others. Always remain neutral. *Reason:* A dominant tone will repress discussion.

- **Make sure** everyone contributes to the discussion. *How:* Direct questions to people who have not spoken. *And:* Ask for examples and elaboration.

- **Have opposing** sides state one another's opinions when conflict occurs.

- **Direct questions** to other people—or ask to hear another view—when one person tries to dominate the discussion.

- **Say to** the last person who spoke, "Tell me more."

Source: Adapted from *How to Facilitate a Productive Group Session*, by Floyd Hurt, 1004 East Jefferson St., Charlottsville. VA 29902. © Communication Briefings, www.briefings.com. 1101 King St., Alexandria, VA 22314. Used with permission.

REFLECT ON THIS:

1. Write an open-ended question your can ask regarding the group's discussion of whether your university should develop a recycling program.

2. Someone in the group says, "You know, I kind of think we should be, you know, doing something to try to get the university to become kinda greener and do recycling and stuff like that." Paraphrase this to make the point clearer.

3. Write a statement that you can make to Darnel who has not made a single contribution during the group's half-hour of discussing recycling on campus.

4. There has been a two-sided debate on whether to maybe fine those fraternities and sororities that do not develop and put into action a recycling program or put them on the honor system (whatever that means) to recycle. Neither side has been able to develop a clear statement that encompasses the wording of their stance. Write a statement that requires each side to clearly develop a specific stance.

5. Jodi jumps in and interrupts anyone who doesn't agree with her stance on recycling and keeps talking. The meeting is getting bogged down. Write a direct question that could be used to stop Jodi's dominance of the discussion.

6. Brad states, "I think that we need to really make the campus community aware of the need for recycling by doing something." Write a statement that you could direct at Brad that says, "Tell me more. Be specific."

But leadership power can also be identified as the ability to influence others to perform or produce results. This kind of power does not use force or coercion. With this type of power, the influence of the person, rather than the authority of the position, is paramount. For example, in the meeting of nurses, the head nurse may suggest a solution whereby those nurses who want to work on a rotating shift may do so, while those who do not may select a permanent shift. The head nurse presents reasons for his two options and asks the others for suggestions. Eventually the group accepts the head nurse's suggestion, with or without changes, because it was explained well and because he was willing to accept alterations and perhaps has a record of being flexible in such situations. This influence through positive leadership is a productive way to use power for the benefit of the entire group.

The tendency of certain people in leadership positions to act coercively has given rise to an examination of alternative leadership styles. One of these styles is *transformational leadership,* in which the person takes on the role of transforming agent. A transforming agent can change both the behavior and the outlook of his or her followers. This person keeps the interest of the group and its goals in mind rather than forcing her or his will on the group. Therefore, she or he gives up the command-and-control model of leadership.[27]

This approach closely resembles the way most managers operate, getting others to perform or produce by offering rewards or punishments in the process. Transactional leadership may be well suited to short-term goals of a group, but the group, to be successful, may require a more visionary approach in the long run.

Another style is *super leadership,* in which people lead themselves and thereby release the self-leadership energy within each person.[28] Such an approach is especially appropriate in today's scaled-down organizations, in which not all qualified employees have the opportunity to move up the corporate ladder into management or executive positions. This leadership format allows everyone to develop his or her leadership skills and to stay productive in changing an organization.

Types of Leaders

Regardless of leadership style, leaders use their power to influence the process of group effort. As such, leaders exhibit characteristics by which their style can be categorized. Three basic types of leaders have been identified:[29]

1. An **authoritarian leader** dominates and directs a group according to personal goals and objectives, regardless of how consistent or inconsistent these goals are with group members' goals.

2. A **democratic leader** facilitates a group according to the goals of its members and allows them to form their own conclusions.

3. A **laissez-faire leader** is nondirective and empowers group members to do their own thing.

Evidence suggests that neither the directive nor nondirective approach is consistently more effective. Each approach works under certain conditions. The key to leader effectiveness is matching the appropriate style to the group environment. Thus, if group members are very task oriented and are empowered to make decisions, they may be productive working with a laissez-faire leader. The laissez-faire style may be disastrous, however, if group members are unable to function productively on their own. A democratic leader works well with a group that requires minimal supervision. If group members cannot accomplish their tasks because they lack self-discipline, an authoritarian leader may be needed to direct activities and assign specific responsibilities.

Patterns of Leader/Leadership Emergence

If a leader is not appointed for a group, one of the questions that arises is how a person interested in becoming a leader should proceed. As illustrated in Figure 10.3, there are patterns of leader emergence. Research shows that when an official leader is not assigned within a group, the individual members accept the responsibility of carrying out the roles of the leader, and perhaps even assume the unofficial title of leader.[30]

"The general tendency is for groups to accept as a leader the person who provides the optimum

---

Culturally Communicating

Becoming a Dynamic Global Leader

After surveying 75 CEOs in 28 countries in a landmark four-year study, Rosen and colleagues (2000) contend that the following four global literacies are critical in the making of an effective global leader:

1. *Personal literacy:* Understanding and valuing yourself

2. *Social literacy:* Engaging and challenging others

3. *Business literacy:* Focusing and mobilizing your organization

4. *Cultural literacy:* Valuing and leveraging cultural differences

Source: Stella Ting-Toomey and Leeva C. Chung, *Understanding Intercultural Communication* (New York: Oxford University Press, 2005), p. 352.

Figure 10.3
Pattern of Leader Emergence

Source: From ROTHWELL. *In Mixed Company, 5/e.* © 2004 Wadsworth, a part of Cengage Learning, Inc. Reproduced by permission. *www.cengage .com/permissions.*

GENERAL PATTERN
(Process of Elimination)

Phase One
Quiet members eliminated
Members who express strong, unqualified assertions eliminated
Uninformed, unintelligent, and/or unskilled eliminated

Phase Two, Part One
Bossy, dictatorial members eliminated
Members with irritating or disturbing communication style eliminated

Phase Two, Part Two
Member who provides solution in time of crisis considered
Member who exhibits effective listening skills considered
Member who acquires a lieutenant considered
If more than one member acquires lieutenant—possible stalemate

HOW TO BECOME LEADER
Manifest conformity to group norms, values, and goals
Display proper motivation to lead
Avoid the "thou shalt nots"

MODIFYING FACTORS OF LEADER EMERGENCE
Gender bias
Ethnic bias

blend of task efficiency and sensitivity to social considerations"[31]—in other words, someone who has talent and popularity. Proving your leadership ability centers on demonstrating your competence, being accountable for your actions, and satisfying the group members' expectations.[32]

Leaders tend to conform to the group's norms, values, and goals while displaying the motivation to lead. They know the rules of order, have charisma, are positive about themselves, encourage others to communicate, and are supportive listeners.

Why People Desire to Be Leaders

Recognizing that a great deal of responsibility is laid at the feet of leaders, that leaders often find themselves the target of attacks, and that they are blamed if things don't go right, why would anyone want to be a leader? Why would people who already have wealth and power want to, for example, take on the job of President of the United States, in which they open themselves to ridicule and stress? Why would someone want to become the president of your college's Student Government? People seem to want to be leaders for various reasons:

- *Information.* The leader is privy to special information. Many leaders like to be "in the know."

- *Rewards.* Leaders receive praise, attention, payment, power, and special privileges for being in their positions. Being a corporate executive who makes several million dollars a year can be highly satisfying in spite of the responsibilities and time constraints. Some people also like to be in the public eye. A number of corporate and business leaders do advertisements for their companies.

■ *Expectations.* Certain people have enough faith in themselves to believe that they can accomplish a task or that they have better solutions than someone else. Listen to politicians campaigning for office. They have platforms that attempt to explain why they are more capable of making things better than are their opponents.

■ *Acceptance.* Some people equate the title of president, chairperson, or boss with being accepted, liked, and admired.

■ *Status.* Acquiring status in one group can bring status in other groups. That is, a record of having been a leader often is the basis for selecting someone for another leader position. Members of boards of directors of hospitals and banks are often the same people who hold the leader role in other organizations. The President of the United States almost always has been in public office as a senator, member of the House of Representatives, or state governor.

Leader/Leadership: Communicative Perspective

There is a fundamental link between human communication and leadership. Influential leaders such as Winston Churchill, Golda Meir, Martin Luther King Jr., Sitting Bull, Gandhi, Mao Tse Tung, John F. Kennedy, Ronald Reagan, and César Chavez were all compelling communicators. "Historically speaking, there seems to be a correlation between those presidents we think of as great communicators and those who are considered successful presidents."[33]

A communicative perspective emphasizes the leader as a catalyst for communication.[34] Leaders not only must use words well but also must be aware of their own nonverbal communication as well as the verbal and nonverbal communication of the group members. In addition, the leader has to listen and explain clearly while moving the group toward their task. A leader's goal is not to win a popularity contest but rather to get the task of the group completed.

Effective Leader Questioning

One of the most important responsibilities of a leader is to monitor the proceedings and interject appropriate questions to stimulate discussion, clarify ideas, and resolve conflict. Here are some ways to deal with common problems.[35]

■ *Issue: Drawing out a silent member*
Question to ask: "Does anyone who hasn't spoken care to comment?" Or "Amad, what is your opinion of . . . ?"

■ *Issue: Calling attention to points that have not been considered*
Question to ask: "Does anyone have any information about this matter?" Or "Lamont, would you care to explore this angle of the topic in more detail?"

■ *Issue: Keeping the discussion focused on the subject*
Question to ask: "That's interesting, but just how does this point fit in with the issue being considered?"

■ *Issue: Using conflict constructively*
Question to ask: "Since we do not seem to be able to resolve this difference now, could we move on to the next point?"

■ *Issue: Suggesting the need for more information*
Question to ask: "Is it agreeable to the group if we ask a subcommittee to investigate and bring back the needed information to our next session?"

- *Issue: Calling attention to the source of information*
  Question to ask: "Where did this information come from?"

- *Issue: Preventing a few from monopolizing the discussion*
  Question to ask: "May we hear from someone who hasn't expressed an opinion?"

- *Issue: Suggesting the need for closing the discussion*
  Question to ask: "We're scheduled to finish discussion in about five minutes. Is there a final comment?"

Responsibilities of Leaders

Regardless of style, a leader has the responsibility for guiding the group toward accomplishing its task and maintaining the group as a functioning unit. An effective leader needs to know when to sit back and let the group work on its own, when to step in and make suggestions, when to warn about such potential problems as groupthink, how to motivate the building of cohesion, and how to instruct on the need to evaluate ideas critically and express doubts. In other words, an effective group leader needs to know her or his responsibilities and how to carry them out.

A leader has responsibilities before, during, and following a meeting:[36]

In Preparation for a Meeting

- Define the purpose of the meeting.

- List specific outcomes that should or must be produced from this meeting.

- Establish the starting and ending times of the meeting.

- Notify members of the purpose and the agenda, their necessary preparations, and the time and place of the meeting.

- If specific resource persons are needed, advise them and prepare them for the meeting.

- Make necessary physical arrangements.

- Get necessary work items (e.g., pencils, paper, charts, data sheets, reports).

Communicating in Careers

A Business Professional Shares Her Views

What does it take to be a good group facilitator?

Most of my work as a group moderator is to be a good listener so that I can be sure that all of the group members do participate actively and so that I can provide a thorough report of the group's responses to the client. Since a focus group meets for a rather short, prescribed time frame, I have to establish trust with the members, build rapport, and develop cohesion within the first three minutes. It is important to communicate an unconditional positive regard for each member in the group. I have to "work" the group in order to engage all of the members early on in the process so that they will feel committed to the group and its goal. A focus group can't just be a serial interview of each participant; I have to understand how groups function and work to accomplish my group objectives.

Source: Barbara G. Rosenthal, Qualitative Research Consultant, as printed in Roy Berko, Andrew Wolvin, and Rebecca Ray, *Business Communication in a Changing World* (New York: St. Martin's Press, 1997).

REFLECT ON THIS: How does a leader "establish trust," "build rapport," and "develop cohesion"?

During the Meeting

- Describe the importance and purpose of the meeting.
- Make an effort to establish a climate of trust and informality (if appropriate).
- Stimulate creative thinking (if appropriate).
- Stimulate critical thinking.
- Promote teamwork and cooperation.
- Equalize opportunities to participate and influence.

Follow-Up to the Meeting

- Remind members who agreed to do after-meeting work.
- If minutes are kept, see that they are written and distributed.
- If the group decision should be forwarded to another person, see that this is done immediately.
- If work is necessary before a future meeting, be sure it is done.

In Conclusion

Groups are made up of people. People from different cultures possess varying attitudes about making decisions or being group participants. Participants are those members of a group who interact to bring about the actions of the group. Leaders are those who guide the group. Leadership refers to those who influence the group to accomplish its goal. Group members, their leaders, and their leadership perform task and maintenance roles.

Learn by Doing

1. Your class will be divided into groups. Each group is to take twenty minutes in which to agree on what a time traveler should take into the future, using this information for the decision:[37]

   > A time machine travels to the year 5847. By then, the world has been destroyed in a nuclear holocaust, and all that remains are a few men and women living a primitive existence and having no record or memory of the past. The traveler in the time machine decides to rebuild the world but can make only one trip back and forth in time. On the trip, which can encompass any years between the dawn of humanity and this year, the traveler may collect such useful items as living things, printed materials, food, toilet paper, and so forth. The only limitation is one of weight: excluding the weight of the time traveler, no more than 200 pounds of material may be carried through time. What should the time traveler take into the future?

   After the small-group discussion, the class meets to discuss these questions:

   a. What effect did differences in members' backgrounds have on the group's decision?

   b. What was the role of the leader in the group?

   c. What was the greatest problem the group encountered in reaching its decision? Could this have been resolved? How?

   d. What inferences about how groups operate can be drawn from this experience?

2. The purpose of this exercise is to illustrate how groups operate and the roles of members of a group.

   a. Before coming to class, indicate whether you thoroughly agree (TA), agree (A), disagree (D), or thoroughly disagree (TD) with each of the following statements. You must illustrate your attitude for all statements.

      (1) Prayer should be allowed in public schools.

      (2) Corporations have an obligation to their stockholders to make profits; this obligation supersedes all other obligations.

      (3) We have little control over what we communicate about ourselves to others.

      (4) Every member of an organization should be permitted to present views at a meeting, regardless of how long this process may take.

      (5) The changing ethical structure of current society has led to confusion and a breakdown of traditional morality.

      (6) Television is a major factor in desensitization of people to violence.

      (7) Advertising is necessary for continuation of the free-enterprise system.

      (8) War is an inevitable result of international conflict.

      (9) Same-sex persons should be allowed to legally marry.

   b. Your instructor will assign each member of the class to a group. Each group is to elect a leader who will be responsible for leading the discussion. Each group will be assigned one of the topics to discuss. If you finish your discussion of your topic, proceed to the next numeric topic (e.g., if you are assigned 5, and complete your discussion, discuss 6, etc.). The group must reach consensus—total agreement—on one of the four responses (thoroughly agree through thoroughly disagree). Group members may rewrite a statement if it will help them come to consensus.

   c. At the end of the discussion, each person will write answers to these questions:

      (1) What one thing did the leader do that helped the group in reaching its goals?

      (2) What one thing could the leader have done that would have helped the group in reaching its goals?

      (3) One thing I did as a participant that pleased me was . . .

      (4) One thing I did as a participant that I should not have done was . . .

      (5) This group did/did not work well because . . .

   d. After each student has completed step c, each group will meet and discuss each member's answers. Be prepared to report back to the class of your group's overall strengths and weaknesses and the process of group decision making.

3. Using the discussions that were held for either activity 1 or activity 2, each person in your group is to analyze all of the group members, including himself or herself, by identifying the specific roles each played as leader, leadership, or participant. Share your lists with the members of the group, and discuss the observations.

4. Identify a specific culture (e.g., ethnic, racial, or gender group), and prepare a short paper (which may be given as an oral presentation in class) indicating what the research shows about characteristic patterns of the specific culture as group members.

Key Terms

participants   279

leaders   279

leadership   279

silent majority   284

hidden agenda   288

group communication networks   289

leadership power   293

coercion   293

authoritarian leader   295

democratic leader   295

laissez-faire leader   295

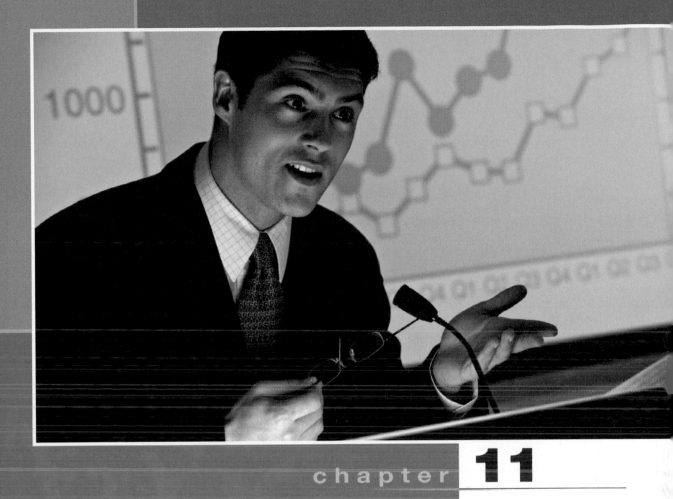

Public Speaking
Planning the Message

▶ **After reading this chapter, you should be able to**

- Define public communication/public speaking

- Be able to formulate a listenable speech

- Develop talking points for a speech

- Explain the ethical responsibility of a public speaker, including the implications of plagiarism and fabrication

- Explain the role of the participants, setting, and purpose/topic in public communication

- Define and explain the roles of prior, process, and postspeech analyses

- Clarify the role of the statement of the central idea of a public speech

- Discuss how to develop impromptu (or ad lib), extemporaneous, manuscript, and memorized presentations

- List pointers on preparing an oral-style manuscript

- Explain the advantages and disadvantages of the impromptu, extemporaneous, manuscript, and memorized modes of presentation

For many, the thought of giving a speech is exciting. For others, standing before an audience conjures up feelings of terror. No matter what your attitude is, you can learn to be a competent public speaker. Really!

The act of **public communication** involves a transaction between a speaker and an audience. You may think that public speaking is something you do not need to be concerned about, but this is not the case. In fact, "a surprising number of persons . . . do speak to audiences of ten or more people fairly frequently."[1] No matter what your college major or current position, odds are that you will be doing some type of public speaking.

The Listenable Speech

The **listenable speech**[2] is one that is formatted in a way that when it is received it is understood by listeners. Just as writers should be concerned about the readability of their text, speakers should strive to prepare and present speeches that are listenable. A listenable speech is based on words that are meant to be heard, rather than those that are meant to be read.[3] Those who prepare speeches should be careful to use words and ideas that the audience can quickly grasp and understand. For example, a speaker might use language such as "Pulchritude possesses a solely cutaneous profundity," when saying, "Beauty is only skin deep," or "All articles that coruscate with resplendence are not truly auriferous," when, in plain English, the speaker could state, "All

Listening to a speech can be an exciting, interesting, or uplifting experience.

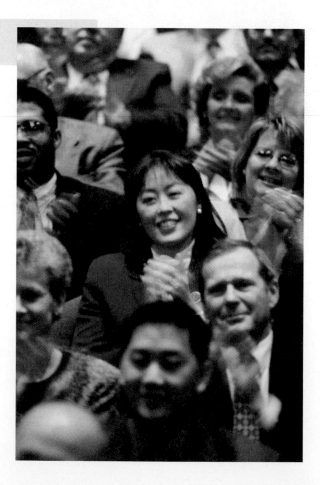

that glitters is not gold."[4] Impressing the audience with your broad or technical vocabulary does not lead to a listenable speech.

A major study of what makes a speech listenable determined that an effective presentation requires an oral-based language style (i.e., language that fits the intellectual level and experiences of the listeners); a structure that lays out clear signposts for listeners (i.e., a structure that follows a clear pattern such as chronological, problem solution, or cause to effect); phrases that tell a listener what is coming next (i.e., "First, I would like to discuss . . . "); and information that flows with cohesiveness and consistency (i.e., the statements made are backed up with facts or examples in such a way that the audience can understand and basically accept what is being presented).[5]

Further, a listenable presentation needs to be well prepared. You, as a good speaker, will have to work to develop and present a presentation that keeps the listener involved throughout the time you are speaking. Key elements of such a presentation are speaker confidence (i.e., you

Culturally Communicating

The Listenable Presentation

Listeners around the world hold different cultural perceptions as to what is a listenable presentation. A study of public speaking in Kenya revealed that the American style of speech preparation and presentation is not universally practiced throughout the world. "While Americans mainly focus on professional speaking formats, the typical Kenyan will present many ceremonial speeches (greetings, tributes, thank yous, etc.) during his/her lifetime." This difference is because Kenyans are more focused on relationships. The study also revealed that they rely on narratives and proverbs as the primary types of supporting materials, rather than facts. These supporting materials are woven together, structurally, as the speaker tells a story and then goes back to the central idea. "Often there is only one main point in such a speech, but it is developed by an abundance of supporting material."

Source: Ann Neville Miller, "Public Speaking Patterns in Kenya," in Larry A. Samovar, Richard E. Porter, and Edwin R. McDaniel (Eds.), *Intercultural Communication A Reader* (Belmont, CA: Thomson/Wadsworth, 2006), p. 243.

give the impression that you know what you are talking about and speak conversationally and with conviction rather than reading the material with little vocal emphasis); engaging nonverbal behavior (i.e., vocal animation, gesturing, direct presentation to the audience through direct eye contact); logical structure (i.e., it follows a clear pattern of speech structure that includes an introduction, a statement of a central idea, a body that consistently follows a pattern of development, and a conclusion that summarizes the presentation); conciseness of style (i.e., the speech is an appropriate length); and encouragement of listener involvement (i.e., the examples are appropriate for that particular audience, and the presentation allows for a question-and-answer session if one is appropriate).[6]

To prepare a listenable speech, you need to know yourself as a communicator. What is your style? What is your comfort level? What format will you be using (i.e., stand-up speech, table-top briefing, video cast) and how can you maximize your use of that format? What is your communication goal? And you will also need to know your listeners. Who are they? What do they know about you and your topic? What do they know or should they care about you and your topic?[7]

Let's now investigate the specific details of how to prepare a speech so that you will be able to make a listenable presentation.

Preparing a Speech: An Overview

Preparation is an important key to effective public speaking. The quality of a speech performance normally correlates positively with the total preparation time, the amount of research done, the time and effort spent in preparation of speaking notes, the time spent preparing visual aids, the number of rehearsals, and the time spent rehearsing out loud.[8]

Although there is no universally agreed-on one best way to prepare a speech, here is a process that works well for many people:

Step 1: Decide on a topic or accept the topic assigned to you.

Step 2: Formulate a statement of the central idea.

Step 3: Collect research that develops the statement of the central idea.

Step 4: Finalize the statement of the central idea, the specific purpose, and the goal that adapts to the listeners and setting of the presentation.

Step 5: Formulate and organize the body of the presentation so that the goal can be achieved.

Step 6: Prepare the necessary aids, such as audio, visuals, and computer-generated graphics.

Step 7: Develop an introduction that previews and a conclusion that summarizes the main points of the presentation.

Step 8: Polish the introduction and conclusion. The introduction should grab the attention of listeners and orient them with any necessary background. The conclusion should wrap up the presentation and clinch the purpose expressed in the central idea.

Parameters of Public Speaking

Any act of communication is based on three parameters: the participants, the setting, and the purpose of the communication. In a speech these three parameters may affect the topic selected, the language used, the types of examples and illustrations chosen, and the aids needed to support and/or clarify ideas.

The **speech participants** are the speaker and the members of the audience. The **speaking setting** encompasses where the speech is given, what the time limit is, when the presentation is made, and the attitude of the audience. The **purpose of the speech** centers on the speaker's expected outcomes for the presentation.

Ethics of Public Speaking

A major concern of any communicator should be the matter of ethics. An ethical public speaker

- Speaks with sincerity
- Does not knowingly expose an audience to falsehoods or half-truths that may cause significant harm
- Does not premeditatedly alter the truth
- Presents the truth as he or she understands it
- Raises the listeners' level of expertise by supplying necessary facts, definitions, descriptions, and substantiating information
- Employs a message that is free from mental as well as physical coercion by not compelling someone to take an action against his or her will
- Does not invent or fabricate statistics or other information intended to serve as a basis for proof of a contention or belief

■ Gives credit to the source of information and does not pretend that the information is original when it is not

An ethical speaker takes his or her audience into consideration. If the speaker does not do so, the results could be very embarrassing. For example, on August 11, 2006, Republican U.S. Senator George Allen of Virginia generated much controversy after he twice used the word *macaca* in reference to an Indian American. Depending on how it is spelled, the word *macaca* could mean either a monkey or a racial slur against African immigrants. Even though Allen claimed that he made up the word and said that he did not understand its derogatory meaning, it led to an immediate outcry. Allen later apologized, but many believe that the use of this epithet was directly related to the eventual loss of a Senate seat Allen was widely expected to retain and the subsequent Democratic Party takeover of the U.S. Senate.[9]

Another instance of negative ethical use in speaking was revealed when Scott McClellan, in a tell-all book about the supposed lies by the Bush administration that led up to the Iraq war, stated,

> The most powerful leader in the world had called upon me to speak on his behalf and help restore credibility he lost amid the failure to find weapons of mass destruction in Iraq. So I stood at the White House briefing room podium in front of the glare of the klieg lights for the better part of two weeks and publicly exonerated two of the senior-most aides in the White House: Karl Rove and Scooter Libby. There was one problem. It was not true. I had knowingly passed along false information. And five of the highest ranking officials in the administration were involved in my doing so: Rove, Libby, the Vice President [Dick Cheney], the President's chief of staff, and the President himself.[10]

The fallout from the ethical breach by the Bush administration further damaged the president's reputation.

Two specific areas of ethical concern in public speaking are plagiarism and fabrication.

Plagiarism

Plagiarism occurs when a speaker uses the ideas and words of others as his or her own without giving credit to the originator of the material. It can be as seemingly innocent as overhearing someone's idea of a solution to a problem, presenting that idea in your speech, and not giving credit to the originator of the idea. Or the speaker can copy an entire essay someone else prepared and present it as a speech with no reference to the source.

The extent of plagiarism may extend from using an idea to replicating an entire speech. There are unscrupulous people who encourage plagiarism by supplying opportunities to participate in the act. For example, theme and speech sales organizations sell prepackaged presentations. Be aware that using one of these in a classroom can result in your failing a course or even being expelled from school, plus the personal embarrassment of being identified as a cheat.

Also be aware that there are federal laws regarding the illegal use of someone else's materials, especially if the ideas are copyrighted. Materials published in a book or magazine are almost always copyrighted.

One of your authors was at a national convention and attended a session at which a graduate student presented a teaching activity that she credited as being her own. She supplemented her speech with a drawing. During the question-and-answer session, the author asked if this was the speaker's own material. She assured him that it was original and developed specifically for this presentation. He knew better. Following this session, the author was to present a workshop on creative teaching and had a copy of an instructor's manual, published several years previously, that he had written and that contained the *exact* exercise, complete with the *exact* drawing, which he pointed out to the presenter. You can imagine how difficult and embarrassing it was for the plagiarist to make a public apology.

Every idea you present in a speech does not have to be original; however, if the concept comes from another source, you are obligated as an ethical speaker to give credit. During the 2008 presidential primary campaign, Barack Obama came under fire for using some of Massachusetts Governor Deval Patrick's lines about the impact of words. Although he had Patrick's permission to use the material, the fact that he did not credit Patrick during the presentation brought forth the question of ethical responsibility.[11]

The consequences for plagiarism can be severe. "At some colleges, students who plagiarize are expelled."[12] At one prestigious southern university, thirty-three students were expelled after a professor employed software that he had designed to detect plagiarism.[13] Communication instructors at many institutions are scanning manuscripts and speaker outlines through turnitin.com, an online "proprietary system that instantly identifies papers containing unoriginal material and acts as a powerful deterrent to stop student plagiarism before it starts."[14] Besides stopping the total copying of someone else's materials, it also discourages students from just stringing one online cutting of materials to another without interjecting any of their own ideas.

All plagiarism, intentional or unintentional, is stealing! Someone else has done the work; you are taking credit for it. That is not ethical.

Fabrication

Fabrication is making up information or guessing at information and making it appear true. If research doesn't reveal the desired statistics you need for proving a point of a speech, you shouldn't just make them up. Don't assume that listeners are stupid. They read, and they watch television; they can be experts on the particular topic about which you are speaking. How would you feel if you had fabricated statistics and, during the question-and-answer session following your presentation, an audience member indicated that the information was not accurate and had proof to back up the inaccuracy? How would you feel if during a business briefing your employer was made aware by an audience member that the material you were using was made up, not accurate, and had no substantiation?

President George W. Bush found out how the public can react to fabrication when his approval rating as president dropped from a high of 66 percent in 2004[15] to 30 percent in 2007[16] after a series of misleading statements were made by Bush and members of his administration leading up to and during the Iraq war. Statements included, "Simply stated, there is no doubt that Saddam Hussein now has weapons of mass destruction" (Vice President Dick Cheney, August 26, 2002); "He has at this moment stockpiles of chemical and biological weapons" (Secretary of Defense Donald Rumsfeld, September 18, 2002). When these statements were proven to be false, a free-fall of Bush's credibility and popularity took place.

Telling half-truths because you haven't completed your work or you didn't have enough time for proper research is no excuse for making up information. Fabrication is lying, and lying is unethical.

As an ethical public speaker, you must understand that you are a moral agent. When you communicate with others and make decisions that affect yourself and others, you have a moral responsibility.

Analyzing the Parameters of Speeches

To give effective speeches, analyze the parameters in three stages: prior analysis, process analysis, and postspeech analysis. The majority of the work takes place **prior to the speech analysis,** before the speech is given. But observing the audience for feedback (the **process of the speech analysis**) and paying attention to reactions following a speech (the **postspeech analysis**) are also very important.

Prior to the Speech Analysis

In determining what you are going to say, you need to consider several factors. This information will aid in dealing with selecting or refining a topic, developing the speech, selecting appropriate language, and deciding what information to include in the presentation. This **audience analysis** consists of assessing the demographic, psychographic, and rhetorographic characteristics of your prospective listeners.

DEMOGRAPHICS **Demographics**—your listeners' characteristics based on their descriptions and backgrounds—include such factors as age, gender, religion, ethnicity, education, occupation, and race.[17]

- *Age.* The general age level of your audience should be considered. Make sure that the examples and language you use are appropriate for the age level of the group you are addressing.

- *Gender.* Knowing whether the audience will be made up primarily of males or of females may help you in deciding how to approach the topic or what types of examples to use. It is important not to stereotype all men or women as being universally the same; however, using examples that are appropriate to the gender makeup of the group can draw in the listeners. Further, be aware that sexist statements can turn listeners against the speaker.

Culturally Communicating

Cultural Listening Styles to Public Speaking

- *An Asian listening tradition:* In an Asian culture that emphasizes unity, listeners may expect speakers to develop oneness with them rather than present divisive ideas. Both speakers and audiences share the responsibility for making communication successful.

- *Another Asian tradition:* An audience may listen in silence, feeling that noise breaks the concentration required to attend to a speech. Applause can signal suspicion, similar to booing by an audience in the United States; some listeners do not even applaud at the end of the speech in order to help the speaker remain modest.

- *An African-American schema:* Within some contexts, the entire audience responds to the speaker's words.

This schema, which reflects traditional African patterns, is termed "call and response." The speaker's statements (calls) are punctuated by the listeners' reactions to them (response), with the result that the audience is, in a real sense, talking back to the speaker. Because no sharp line distinguishes speakers and listeners, both cooperate to create the message.

Source: Clella Jaffe, *Public Speaking: Concepts and Skills for a Diverse Society* (Belmont, CA: Wadsworth/Thomson Learning, 2001), p. 68.

REFLECT ON THIS: Pick one of these traditions/schemas. Indicate the implication for you as a public speaker if your audience was predominantly made up of the cultural group being discussed.

Culturally Communicating

Speaking to Diverse Groups

Today's business audiences include an increasing percentage of foreign-born people—both employees and foreigners on temporary assignments.

Speaking to these culturally diverse groups requires special preparation and understanding. Some tips from a new book on how to speak to these groups are:

- Start by finding out how many foreign-born folks will be in the audience. Ask where they are from and how well they handle the English language. Keep in mind that English taught in foreign classrooms won't qualify them to handle "words" such as, "Waddayathink?"

- When speaking, slow down and use natural pauses. "Speaking slower . . . with natural pauses . . . will allow everyone . . . a chance to absorb . . . your message."

- Avoid causing them the shame of losing face. *How?*

  —Don't call on them unless you're sure they'll understand what you'll be asking.

  —Be sure to give the instructions for an activity twice.

- Use as many visuals as possible.

- Be careful about using culturally specific examples, such as "touchdown" or "the Cosby show." Use universal themes, such as the desire for success or the importance of good friendship.

Source: Power Speaking: How Ordinary People Can Make Extraordinary Presentations, by Dr. Frederick Gilbert, Frederick Gilbert Associates, 1233 Harrison Ave,. Redwood City, CA 94062.

REFLECT ON THIS: Make a list of at least ten words or phrases that should not be used when speaking to an audience whose first language is not English, but understand basic English.

- *Religion.* A speaker can establish or destroy a common bond with specific religious groups through language and examples. If the group is all of the same religious belief, using examples of people or principles of that group could lead to the acceptance of your views, just as an inappropriate reference might turn listeners against you.

- *Ethnic background.* The ethnic background of an audience often is as important as its religious affiliation. Appropriate ethnic references, if they fit the topic, can enhance

Audience analysis, consists of assessing the demographic, psychographic, and rhetorographic characteristics of your prospective listeners.

a speaker's credibility. Select references that put the ethnic group in a positive light.

- *Educational background.* Understanding the educational background and training of your listeners is important so you can choose material appropriate to their level. For example, a highly expert audience at an informative briefing will expect a more detailed analysis of Internet capabilities than would a group of listeners who have just purchased home computers.

- *Occupation.* Occupational interests and experiences often serve as the communication bond for speakers and listeners. Using examples that are specifically aimed at members of a particular work group can result in clarity, pride, and a feeling of togetherness.

- *Racial background.* Like ethnic background, the racial composition of your audience may be a critical consideration. Just as it is important not to make stereotyped statements when addressing all men or all women, so too is it important not to make assumptions about any particular racial group, especially if you, the speaker, are not of the same race as your listeners.

PSYCHOGRAPHICS   The audience's **psychographics**—its attitudes and beliefs—are an important consideration. This profile can be determined by analyzing the listeners.

Attitudes   Attitudes are the predispositions that your listeners bring to the communication event. They will have attitudes toward you as the speaker based on their perceptions of your trustworthiness, competence, and presentational style.

Your listeners will also have attitudes toward the occasion. Usually they are part of a voluntary audience, participating in the speech event because they want to be there; but if they are a captive audience (e.g., a collegiate assembly, a required training seminar, a military briefing), it is important for you to know that. Audiences that are required to listen to a speech are less receptive, and you may need to add humor or drama to get and hold their attention. You may want to recognize that you realize that they are not there voluntarily, empathize with them, and make sure that you do an effective job of using devices to make them want to listen.

Additionally, your listeners will have attitudes toward your subject. They may agree or disagree with your stand on the subject. If they agree with you—for example, they are pro-choice when you are speaking on that subject—then they will probably need less persuading. On the other hand, if the majority of the audience is pro-life, your task is going to be more difficult, and you are going to have to use devices to attempt to change their attitude. In this case, you may want to anticipate that the pro-life audience may verbally attack you in the question-and-answer session, so you might prepare for that eventuality when assembling your materials.

Conservative/Liberal   In dealing with issues such as abortion, the death penalty, genetic engineering, homosexuality, and school prayer, you are taking on topics about which the listeners may well have an emotional investment that comes out of their conservative or liberal disposition. It is helpful to know the predispositions of your listeners as you select arguments and appeals to get them to respond.

Political Affiliation   The listeners' political affiliations usually correspond to their conservative/liberal dispositions, and may have religious roots as well. You may want to know if your listeners were primarily independent voters or registered members of a particular political party before putting together your message in order to trigger the responses you desire by appealing to their loyalties.

RHETOROGRAPHICS   Just as you analyze your audience, so must you analyze the **rhetorographics:** the place, time limit, time of day, and emotional climate for the speech.

Place   The place can affect the tone and topic of a speech. Such factors as the size of the room, temperature, lighting, furniture arrangement, and physical comfort or discomfort of the audience all affect your communication. Do the acoustics of the room enable the listeners to hear you clearly? Is there a microphone? When using slides or PowerPoint-generated graphics, can you dim the lights, or do you have to turn them off completely? How is the seating arranged?

Time   Both the time limit and the time of day affect a speaker's performance. Whatever the reason for the time limit, a speaker has an obligation to stay within the prescribed boundaries, so it is important to prepare carefully so that you don't ramble on.

Speakers also should be aware that time of day can affect an audience. Early morning and late night hours, for instance, often are difficult times to hold the attention of an audience. You might want to plan a shorter speech if you know you are speaking near the end of the day or at the finish of a conference.

Emotional Climate   The setting for public communication may be affected by its emotional climate—the overriding psychological state of the participants. A community recently devastated by a tornado, for example, certainly would have a special emotional climate. Thus, a speaker called on to present a speech in such a setting would have to adapt his or her message to the tragedy and deal with the fears, bitterness, and trauma that the audience has been experiencing.

From the information obtained in the prior analysis, you should be able to reach a reasonable conclusion about a topic that will fit you and the audience concerning the language and the supporting materials needed to develop the speech.

APPLYING THE PRIOR ANALYSIS   Assuming you have completed your prior analysis, how do you use the information?

Communicating
in Careers

Focus on Why

When preparing a presentation, conduct a "so why?" test. Pretend you're a member of the audience and ask, "So why do I need to know this?" If you don't have a clear answer, your audience won't either.

Source: Communication Briefings, as adapted from Simple Steps to a Powerful Presentation, Quill, 100 Schelter Road, Lincolnshire, IL 60069.

Topic Selection   Typically, speakers are asked to make presentations because of their knowledge, experiences, or expertise. For example, a businessperson is told to present a new plan for reorganizing her department. Or a speaker decides that he has something to say and finds an audience who should and will listen to the message.

On the other hand, sometimes a speaker is given limited leeway in selecting a topic. In the academic setting, for example, to help students learn how to plan and prepare speeches, instructors may restrict students on what topic to use for a class assignment.

The setting for public communication may be affected by its emotional climate—the overriding psychological state of the participants.

If you are given latitude in selecting your topic, know that you are your own best resource. An examination of your life experiences and interests can be useful for selecting topics. For example, consider your hobbies and special interests, places you have lived or traveled, or the skills you have. Some people like to develop a speaking inventory to help them in the topic identification process. To develop such a list, do the Your Speaker Inventory activity on the next page.

In order to assist you in preparing speeches, a list of topics is presented in the Appendix. After selecting a general topic, many speakers new to public communication have difficulty narrowing the topic to fit the audience and the time limit. One of the best ways to do this is to probe into the various aspects of the subject by asking yourself questions about the selected theme:

- What is it?
- Where does it come from?
- How has it changed?
- What are some subtopics of the subject?
- How does it operate/work?
- Why is it significant?
- What are major events of its past?
- How is it changing?
- What are its uses?
- What is its cause?
- What does it impact?
- What/how does it cause or eliminate problems?

Your Speaker Inventory

One of the keys to giving an effective oral presentation is to choose a subject you are interested in and about which you have some knowledge. To learn your interest and knowledge base, fill out this speaker inventory:

1. Hobbies and special interests _____
2. Places I have traveled _____
3. Things I know how to do (sports I can play, skills I have) _____
4. Jobs I have had _____
5. Experiences (accidents, special events) _____
6. Funny things that have happened to me _____
7. Books I have read and liked _____
8. Movies and plays I have seen and liked _____
9. Interesting people I have known _____
10. People I admire _____
11. Religious and nationality customs of my family _____
12. Talents I have (musical instruments played, athletic abilities) _____

Obviously, not all of these questions can be applied to every topic, but by asking these questions you should be able to narrow the general topic to subtopics so you can have a specific focus for your presentation. (See Figure 11.1.)

Another way to narrow a topic is to go to Google.com and google the subject. For example, in one Google attempt of the term *baseball,* a single page listed, "Negro baseball leagues," "Little League baseball," "heroes of baseball," "the science of baseball," "minor league baseball," and "baseball cards." A Google on one of these topics, "baseball cards," further narrowed the topic to "vintage baseball cards," "the best in baseball cards," "trading baseball cards online," and "Topps baseball cards."

Using the information presented so far, let's examine the process leading up to the presentation of the speech:

- Picking a General Topic: An Example

Chan is a twenty-year-old college sophomore. In filling out his speaker inventory, he discovered that his interests and knowledge all center on his having worked at McDonald's restaurants for the past four years. He is now in the management training program and is in college to fulfill requirements for becoming a district manager. He would like to talk about McDonald's! He now has a general topic. The next question is, What specifically will he speak about? The answer takes further analysis.

- Using Demographic Information: An Example

Chan remembers that during the first day of his speech communication course, everyone was introduced. Almost all of the students are health care, pre-medicine, social work, preschool, education, and psychology majors. He is one of two business majors. A number of the older students have young children. The topics he considers include how a McDonald's restaurant is managed, what his job consists of, his possible future employment with the restaurant chain, and the Ronald McDonald House program. He would feel comfortable talking about all of these, but which would be best for this audience? Based on the major academic fields of the audience, he eliminates managing the restaurant and possible employment; these would be more appropriate for

Figure 11.1
**Narrowing the
Topic of a Speech**

Source: Concept conceived
by Tony Zupancic. Notre Dame
College, South Euclid. OH.

A student athlete and sports management major used questions to select the general topic of *baseball* for a five-minute informative speech for his class. He knew he needed to narrow the topic and take into consideration the demographic, psychographic, and rhetorographic information about his audience. He began with these questions:

What is it?	Baseball is a sport that is played on the professional and amateur levels.
Where does it come from?	Baseball was invented in the United States and has a long history.
How has it changed?	Rule changes of baseball include adding of the designated hitter; differences in types of balls, glove and bats used; the banning of performance-enhancing drugs.
What are some subtopics of the subject?	Strategies including giving of signals to the batter and the pitcher; the differences between major and minor leagues; how a player gets to be a major league player.
What are major events of its past?	Black Sox scandal; excessive payment to players; major stars being suspended for use of strength-enhancing drugs

Based on the questions, his audience analysis, and his own knowledge and interests, he narrowed his specific topic choices to:

1. The controversy regarding the use of performance-enhancing drugs.
2. How signals are given to the batter and the pitcher.

Since the topic of performance-enhancing drugs was currently an issue in the press, that many student athletes were in the class, that several parents in the class had teenagers who were playing sports, and he had heard briefings on the performance-enhancing drugs, he selected the topic, performance-enhancing drugs. He will discuss what the drugs are, why athletes take the drugs, and the two major reasons why student athletes should not use these drugs.

business majors. He eliminates speaking about what his job consists of because it is of interest to him but probably not to anyone else. He selects the Ronald McDonald House program because it deals with health care and social service issues and is aimed at working with children and parents, which fits the audience demographics.

■ Using Psychographic Information: An Example

Chan reconsiders his choice based on psychographics. It doesn't appear, from what he can tell of the class, that any political or conservative/liberal disposition would be negatively stirred by his topic selection, so he decides to stick with his Ronald McDonald House choice.

■ Using Rhetorographic Information: An Example

Chan now needs to test his topic regarding place, time limit, time of day, and emotional climate. The classroom doesn't seem to have any negative effect on the topic selection, although he is aware that his idea of showing snapshots isn't going to work in the large room, with a class of thirty students, so he decides to use PowerPoint graphics instead. There doesn't seem to be any existing emotional climate he has to deal with. The time limit of the speech, however, is going to be a factor. He has a maximum of five minutes to speak. There is no way he can inform the class about all the activities of Ronald McDonald House in that time, so he is going to have to limit the breadth of the topic. He decides to tell the purpose of Ronald McDonald House and give two personal examples of children he has assisted as an active volunteer with the local project.

Language Selection   Like the topic, the language selected for use during a speech must be adapted to the audience. The average thirteen-year-old's vocabulary is not the same as an adult's, for example. By the same token, certain terms that are common to a specific occupational or cultural group may be baffling to individuals who are not members of that group. And a person who is well versed on a specific subject can easily forget that the audience may not have the same knowledge or know the same terms.

It is important to adapt your vocabulary to the level of the audience. Be careful not to talk down to your listeners and not to use language that is so technical or abstract that they do not understand.

■ Selecting Appropriate Language: An Example

Chan, in thinking about the subject, the audience, and language, realizes that he has to make sure not to use terms that are unfamiliar to those not working at McDonald's or unfamiliar with the facility. For example, he must avoid calling the site "Willard's Place," the volunteers' nickname for it. (The first person to portray Ronald McDonald was the now nationally known TV weatherman Willard Scott, who has been strongly identified with the agency.)

Statement of Central Idea   In developing a message, a speaker should know specifically what she or he wants to communicate. Thus, before even starting to put together the actual presentation, public speakers find it useful to compose a **statement of central idea,** which defines the subject and develops the criteria by which to evaluate the material to be included in the speech. A statement of central idea centers on what you want the audience to know, to be able to do, to believe. The statement of central idea typically consists of three parts: the goal of the speech, the statement of the topic, and the method or process used to develop the speech.

The **goal of the speech** is expressed in terms of its expected outcome. To *inform* (impart new information and secure understanding or reinforce information and understandings acquired in the past) or to *persuade* (attempt to get the listener to take some action, to accept a belief, or to change a point of view) are the speech goals.

The **topic of the speech**—the subject—should be stated as specifically as possible.

The **method of speech development** encompasses how you plan to approach the presentation. A topic that requires an in-depth study of one fact—for example, how cast members are chosen for a theatrical production—presents a detailed development of a single issue. If the topic requires a complete survey of ideas, a multiple number of topics may need to be covered—for example, how a play is cast, rehearsed, and performed. Just as in language selection, the method of development depends a great deal on your determination of how much your listeners know about or, indeed, need to know about the topic you have selected.

Key words can assist in developing a statement of central idea for an informative speech—for example, *by explaining, by summarizing, by contrasting, by describing, by demonstrating,* and *by analyzing.*

In a persuasive speech, key phrases for the method of development section of the statement of central idea can include *to accept that, to support, to agree with, to contribute to, to serve, to share,* and *to vote for.*

The statement of central idea thus consists of the goal of the speech, the statement of the topic, and the method or process to be used to develop the speech. Here are two examples of the statement of central idea prepared by an informative speaker:

■ To inform the audience why competency testing is being used as a determination for high school graduation by discussing the three major reasons for its use.

■ I want the audience to know of the important effect that Latino music has had on changing the self-image of Hispanic Americans. To do this, I will list and explain the effects on Hispanic Americans brought about through the cross-cultural popularity of Ricky Martin, Chayanne, Graciella Beltran, and Selena.

Here are two examples of persuasive statements of central idea:

- I want the audience to fill out and sign living wills. To do this, I will list five reasons for them to take the action.

- To persuade the audience to accept the concept that getting help from a mental health professional can be a positive act by examining the five most common reasons people seek mental health help and the statistics showing the success rate of treatment for those problems.

By keeping these factors in mind, you can avoid some of the major pitfalls of neophyte speakers: not finishing the speech in the time limit, not accomplishing the speech's purpose, and not allowing the audience to gain the information.

- Writing the Statement of Central Idea: An Example

  Chan is now ready to prepare his statement of central idea: "To inform the audience about the Ronald McDonald House project, by explaining the purpose of the project and presenting two examples of children who have been aided by Ronald McDonald House." He checks to make sure his statement contains a goal (to inform), a topic (the Ronald McDonald House project), and a method of development (explaining and presenting). Chan is now ready to develop his speech.

  The speaker's preparation also extends to doing a careful prior analysis of the audience and the setting, and drawing up a statement of central idea that will be appropriate to his or her level of expertise and knowledge and to the intended listeners.

Process of Speech Analysis

As the speech is being presented, actively analyze the feedback you are receiving. This process of speech analysis is important to the accomplishment of your speaking goal. Speakers frequently need to adjust the materials as they present. For example, President Clinton adapted good process analysis to defuse a hostile situation during his first term when he was presenting a speech about his proposed health-care plan. A man in the audience suddenly jumped up and started to verbally attack the president's efforts regarding AIDS research. Clinton paused, dissuaded the Secret Service from removing the heckler, and invited the man to present his point. The president then responded to the arguments, went back to his prepared remarks, and built references to this unplanned interaction into the remainder of the presentation.[18]

Verbal interruptions are not typical. More typical are nonverbal cues of attentiveness and agreement, or of boredom or hostility, conveyed through posture and facial expression. Some speakers are sensitive to the *cough meter*. If you have lost your audience's attention, you may hear an increasing number of people clear their throats, cough, and become physically restless.

Effective process analysis requires that you interpret cues accurately and then adapt to them. Be careful not to assume, for instance, that one person nodding off represents boredom on the part of all of your listeners. However, if most of the audience looks bored, you should be concerned.

You can adapt to the feedback you receive in various ways. For example, if you feel the audience does not understand a point, add an illustration, clarify your terms, or restate the idea. If you sense that the audience is not attentive, change the volume of your voice, use a pause, move forward, or insert an interesting or humorous story.

Another technique used in the classroom or training session is to ask questions of audience members to involve them in the presentation.

Most people don't feel totally comfortable in departing from their preplanned notes during a speech. The more confidence you have in your speaking abilities and the more comfortable you are with the topic, the more willing you will be to adjust to the feedback. Some people make mental notes about what is happening and then try to figure out afterward what went wrong so they can adjust their material or presentational style for the next speech. Besides noting what is going on during the speech, postspeech analysis can be of help in perfecting your speaking skills.

Postspeech Analysis

Postspeech analysis enables you to determine how your speech affected the audience, which offers you useful information for preparing and presenting future speeches. A direct way to conduct a postspeech analysis is to have a question-and-answer session. The questions your audience asks may reveal how clear your presentation was. The verbal and language tone of the questions may reflect the general mood of the listeners, telling you how positively or negatively they received you and your message. Informal conversations with members of the audience after the speech also can reveal a great deal.

Other postspeech techniques include opinion polls, tests, questionnaires, and follow-up interviews. Even conversations with listeners after your presentation can provide you with insight as to what works and what doesn't work. These techniques are often used by professional speakers, such as politicians, to evaluate their presentations.

Part of your preparation for a speech is to decide on the mode of presentation you will use when presenting the speech.

Modes of Presentation

Four basic **modes of speech presentation**—the preparation method and reference aids to be used during the speech—are impromptu, extemporaneous, manuscript, and memorized.

Sometimes a speaker uses information acquired from past experiences, speaks with little or no preparation, and organizes ideas while he or she is communicating.

Impromptu or Ad Lib Mode

Sometimes a speaker uses information acquired from experience, speaks with little or no preparation, and organizes ideas while he or she is communicating. This approach is referred to as **impromptu speaking.** Some speech theorists distinguish this from **ad lib speaking,** in which a speaker has no time to organize ideas and responds immediately when answering a question, volunteering an opinion, or interacting during a question-and-answer session. The impromptu mode gives a speaker a short period of time to decide what to say; therefore, the speaker does not communicate quite as spontaneously as when ad libbing. For example, when a teacher asks a question in class and gives students a minute or so to think of the answer, students use the impromptu mode when responding. Getting called on and being required to give an immediate answer is an ad lib.

These forms of speaking offer the advantage of being natural and spontaneous and tend to represent a speaker's true feelings because so little time is available to develop defenses and strategies.

Both of these modes are weakened, however, by the lack of time a speaker has to develop organized and well-analyzed statements. Another drawback, which derives from the impossibility of doing research, is the speaker's lack of opportunity to use statistics, examples, or illustrations to explain ideas clearly unless he or she is an expert on the topic. Still another liability is the speaker's tendency to ramble or use unnecessary phrases such as "you know" and "stuff like that" to gain thinking time or gloss over nonspecific information. Finally, lack of preparation also can result in oral uncertainty—a speaker's inability to present a coherent speech.

Putting together an impromptu speech requires quick work and immediate decisions. The process is the same as preparing for any other type of speech, except that there is less time to get ready. As you try to organize your thoughts, keep these ideas in mind:

Step 1: Determine what topic you wish to present.

Step 2: Word a statement of central idea that represents the topic.

Step 3: List the major headings that develop the statement of central idea. If paper is available, jot down the ideas. Write these in the vertical middle of the sheet of paper so you have time to add the introduction about them later, if time is available. Leave space between the major headings so that if you have time for developing subpoints, you will be able to write them in.

Step 4: Arrange the major headings according to one of the methods of organization—time or space order, problem solution, or a topical approach. Use the list you developed in step 3 and number the order of each heading.

Step 5: Decide on an introduction. Most ad lib/ impromptu speakers tend to use a question

Communicating in Careers

Facing a Last-Minute Speech

If you have to present with little notice, follow these tips:

- Write down a single phrase describing what you need to communicate to your audience. Then, write three actions, reasons, or qualities supporting that phrase. *Example:* If you want to communicate how to increase sales, three actions to do so could be: make more cold calls, ask for referrals, and survey customers. Mention the points during your speech. *Tip:* Write them on the back of a business card for easy reference.

- Answer the questions who, what, when, where, why, and how. *Example:* If you're talking about change that will occur in your organization, tell the audience who will be in charge of the change effort, what the change is, why it's necessary, when it will occur, where it will take place, and how it will be achieved.

- Refer to a current event or personal story and link either to your main point. Audiences will remember these more easily than facts or figures.

- Use an analogy to help get your message across. *Example:* If speaking about a new product, say, "Our new widget is like a stealth fighter because it gets the job done, and you don't even know it's there."

- Memorize four or five quotations about motivation, communication, or teamwork and include them in your talk.

Source: Adapted from *Smart Moves for People in Charge,* by Sam Deep and Lyle Sussman, Addison-Wesley Publishing Co., 1 Jacob Way, Reading, MA 01867. © Communication Briefings, www.briefings.com, 1101 King St., Alexandria, VA 22314. Used with permission.

or a reference to the topic, but often you can think of a story that relates to the topic. Because you probably will not have time to write out the whole introduction, jot down several key words so you will remember what you want to say.

Step 6: Restate the major points you made as the conclusion.

Step 7: If you have time, go back to see if you can think of any illustrations, examples, or statistics that develop the major ideas you want to present. Write them in at the appropriate place in the outline. If there is no time, try to think of some as you speak. Make sure that you clarify or define any words that may be unfamiliar to your listeners.

Extemporaneous Mode

People who have more time to prepare for their presentations often use the **extemporaneous speaking mode,** developing a set of "talking points," in notes or an outline, to assist them in presenting their ideas. The speaker knows in advance that she or he will be giving a speech and can prepare by doing research and planning the speech.

The extemporaneous mode offers significant advantages: time to find the information needed to help accomplish the statement of central idea; the security of having notes or an outline to refer to throughout the speech; the use of quotations, illustrations, and statistics in written form for backing up ideas; and a more spontaneous and natural oral presentation and physical presentation than are likely in the manuscript or memorized mode.

As with any other presentational mode, the extemporaneous mode of delivery has some disadvantages as well. For example, a speaker who does not allow sufficient time for preparation and rehearsal may get mentally lost during the presentation. Furthermore, if a speaker refers to the notes or outline too frequently during the speech or has too many notes, she or he may fail to interact with the audience. And because extemporaneous material is never written out word for word, there will be no permanent record of the speech.

PREPARING THE EXTEMPORANEOUS SPEECH   Most speakers use either notes or an outline when they present an extemporaneous speech. Notes can consist of a list of words that guide the speaker through the presentation or a series of phrases or sentences to act as clues.

Many speakers start out with a **speech planning outline,** a brief framework used to think through the process of the speech. This outline contains the major ideas of the speech, without elaboration. It is a means of thinking through the things you wish to say and putting them in a structured order. Some speakers use this for practice and while speaking. Others prepare a **speech presentation outline** in which they flesh out the outline with examples and illustrations and write in internal summaries and forecasts. (An outlining tool for formatting a speech can be found on this textbook's website.)

Outlining   The basic concept in outlining is that the speaker has a clear step-by-step structure of what will be said and in what order. Some speakers simply list the headings and subordinate points in a sequential order. Others use a formal outlining method.

Numerous rules have been developed for how to structure an outline.[19] Some speech instructors are very specific as to what the outline is to look like, indicating that the discipline of developing the outline aids the speaker in making sure that all parts of the speech are well developed and ordered. Others believe that the outline is for the speaker's benefit. They advise preparing it so that you are comfortable with the material and can remember what you need to say.

An outline generally has a balanced structure based on four major principles: parallelism, coordination, subordination, and division:[20]

- *Parallelism.* Whenever possible, when preparing an outline, you should express coordinate heads in parallel form. That is, nouns should be made parallel with nouns, verb forms with verb forms, adjectives with adjectives, and so on (*Example:* Nouns: *computers, programs, users;* Verbs: *to compute, to program, to use;* Adjectives: *home* computers, *new* programs, *experienced* users). Although parallel structure is desired, logical and clear language should not be sacrificed simply to maintain parallelism. (For example, there are times when nouns and gerunds at the same level of an outline are acceptable.) Reasonableness and flexibility of form are preferred to rigidity.

- *Coordination.* In outlining, those items that are of equal significance should have comparable numeral or letter designations: An *A* is equal to a *B,* a *1* to a *2,* an *a* to a *b,* and so on. Coordinates should have the same value. Coordination is a principle that enables a writer to maintain a coherent and consistent document. Here is a sample of good coordination:

A. Types of alternative electric energy sources
  1. Nuclear power plants
  2. Wind turbines
  3. Solar energy
B. Evaluation of programs
  1. Safety
    a. Nuclear power plants
    b. Wind turbines
    c. Solar energy
  2. Cost of building and maintenance
    a. Nuclear power plants
    b. Wind turbines
    c. Solar energy
  3. Effect on the community
    a. Nuclear power plants
    b. Wind turbines
    c. Solar energy

- *Subordination.* To indicate levels of significance, an outline uses major and minor headings. Thus, in ordering ideas, you should organize the outline from general to specific or from abstract to concrete—the more general or abstract the term, the higher its level or rank in the outline. This principle allows your material to be ordered in terms of logic and requires a clear articulation of the relationships among the component parts used in the outline. Subdivisions of each higher division should always have the same relationship to the whole. Here is a sample of good subordination form of major headings:

A. Nuclear power plants
  1. Positive features
  2. Negative features

B. Wind turbines

   1. Positive features

   2. Negative features

C. Solar energy

   1. Positive features

   2. Negative features

- *Division.* The purpose of the divisions is to flesh out the major ideas by adding clarifiers, examples, and illustrations. Some outlining purists contend that "for every *A* there should be a *B* and for every *1* there must be a *2*."[21] In general, this makes sense. If you are subdividing an idea—that is, breaking it into parts—then by definition, you must have at least two subideas. This does not mean, however, that if you are supporting an idea with an example, you must have two examples. Here is a sample of good division form:

A. Computer storage

   1. Mainframe

   2. Micro

      a. Zip drive

      b. External hard drive

      c. Flash drive

      d. Portable hard drive

B. Computer uses

   1. Institutional

      a. Individual

      b. Shared

   2. Personal

- *Form.* The most important rule for outlining form is to be consistent! Most speech outlines use either a topic structure or a sentence structure.

A **topic outline** has words or phrases for all entries and usually has little or no punctuation after entries. One advantage of this format is that it presents a brief overview of the ideas. In addition, speakers often find that they will speak more and read less with the abbreviated material on the page.

A **sentence outline** has complete sentences for all entries and usually has correct punctuation. One advantage of this format is that there is a more detailed overview of the ideas to be presented. Therefore, it may give the speaker more security since whole ideas rather than word clues are presented.

An outline can use a combination of Roman numerals and letters or a decimal form. An outline composed of Roman numerals and letters follows this format:

I.

  A.

  B.

    1.

    2.

      a.

      b.

II.

An outline composed of decimals would follow this format:

1.0
    1.1
    1.2
        1.2.1
        1.2.2
            1.2.2.1
            1.2.2.2

Here are some additional guidelines specific to speech outline format:

- *Include internal summaries and forecasts.* Internal summaries restate each major point before proceeding to the next major point. Forecasts tell the listener what is coming next. To ensure that they remember to include these in the oral presentation, many speakers write the statements into the outline.

- *Write notes in the margins to remind yourself of necessary information.* If you need a reminder to slow down in certain sections or to use a visual aid to emphasize a point, write yourself a note in the margin of the outline. Use a color of ink that stands out. Although the marginal notes are not an official part of the outline, they are yet another device to help make the speech effective and to help you feel comfortable and gain confidence.

- *Avoid over outlining.* To avoid having an excessive number of notes, limit the quantity to those you absolutely need to trigger your thoughts. In determining what is essential, you are wise to consider this analogy. The first time you drive to a particular site, you may need a detailed set of directions complete with route numbers, road markers, and indications of exact mileage. On your second trip, you need less information, and by the third trip, you need almost none. So it is with your use of notes and outlines. You should have enough information to feel comfortable and free to navigate through the presentation with no fear of getting lost. The only way to discover the extent of your readiness is to take several test drives through your speech to ascertain how much prepared information you really need to have with you in the form of written prompts.

Mind Mapping   An alternative to using an outline for the extemporaneous mode of presentation is mind mapping. **Mind mapping** is a method of arranging materials

Mind mapping is a method of arranging materials in a speech visually rather than in list form.

**Figure 11.2
Mind Maps**

"If I'm concerned about having too much to say or what to cover in a speech, I organize it by mind mapping the material. I put the topic or theme in the middle of the page. Then I brainstorm everything I can think of about that topic. I write just a word or so that represents each of those thoughts. I put little squiggles around each word, just for fun. I then look at the thoughts and number each one in the way I might use them. I don't draw pictures or get elaborate in terms of colors."—*Dr. Ken Blanchard*

Yellow elephant.

As you read that phrase, did you think of letters Y-e-l-l-o-w-e-l-e-p-h-a-n-t. Or did you see an image? Of course, you saw the image. The mind thinks in images and pictures. Mind mapping was developed by Tony Buzan, author and brain researcher, as an alternative to outlining. He suggests you organize your material by drawing pictures.

For example, you might draw a simple picture of a yellow elephant (assuming you were doing a talk that involved a yellow elephant), then a line with an arrow to the next thought you want to talk about.

When you try to force your mind to think in a traditional outline form—with words and sentences—you may wait around forever, staring at a blank paper, waiting for Roman numeral I to bounce into your head. But in mind mapping you draw each idea as it pops up, then connect the pictures later into a speech.

As you draw your mind map, you can more easily see when you've got too much stuff in one place and not enough in another. If you can't easily connect one line to another, then you can see it may not belong in the presentation at all.

Source: Reprinted by permission from Lilly Walters, *Secrets of Successful Speakers.* Copyright © 1993 by the McGraw-Hill Companies.

visually rather than in list form. This is a mode often favored by global thinkers/listeners who are stimulated by pictures rather than words. Mind mappers can use the procedure to develop the speech or to develop and then use the visual images for the presentation stage of speaking, as explained in Figure 11.2.

To mind-map, the potential speaker makes a list of all the ideas to be included in the speech. Then major headings are selected, each major idea is placed in a circle, and the subpoints are grouped around the major heading circles and connected to the circles with spokes. The speaker indicates the major heading, then orally flows from one spoke to another. When one circle and its spokes are finished, the speaker proceeds to the next circle and discusses its topical spokes. Let's say you are planning on speaking about a visit to Washington, DC, the nation's capital. You make a list of the things you did and the sights you saw (Figure 11.3). You then set the major theme ideas in circles and group the subhead ideas around those major themes (Figure 11.4). This drawing forms the basis for the extemporaneous speech.

TALKING POINTS   Some speakers like to work from talking points. **Talking points** are bullet points in an abbreviated outline format that serve as a framework for the speech and are used in a rehearsal session and as the notes for the actual presentation.

In developing talking points, you may create a detailed outline or a manuscript and then narrow those to the minimum number of statements that you will need to stay on track while presenting the material. Those points are then entered on an appropriately sized index card and used when you are rehearsing and presenting the speech. For example, a speaker talking about the need to reform the Social Security system might use these talking points:

A. Background on Social Security

- August 14, 1935: Social Security Act signed by President Franklin D. Roosevelt
- 1956: Broadened to Disability Insurance

- 1972: Provided for cost-of-living increases in benefits tied to the Consumer Price Index
- 1983: Increased age of eligibility for full retirement benefits from 65 to 67

B. Social Security Today
- Sound for today's seniors
- Only 3.3 workers are supporting every Social Security beneficiary

Figure 11.3
Mind-Mapping Procedure

A. Listing of Topics	B. Mapping Visual Outline
Subject: Visiting Washington, DC	*Outdoor Things to Do*
Smithsonian Museums	Arlington Cemetery
Georgetown	National Zoo
Kennedy Center for Performing Arts	Korean Memorial
Tyson's Corner Center	Vietnam Memorial
Korean Memorial	Lincoln Monument
Metro	Jefferson Memorial
*Outdoor things to do	Roosevelt Memorial
Vietnam Memorial	Washington Monument
Ford's Theater	Tidal Basin
Jefferson Memorial	The Mall
Beltway	*Shopping*
Bureau of Engraving and Printing	Old Town Alexandria
The White House	Mazza Gallery
Capitol Building	Smithsonian Gift Shops
Mazza Gallery	Fashion Mall
*Indoor things to do	Georgetown
Holocaust Museum	Tyson's Corner Center
Washington Monument	*Indoor Things to Do*
Arlington Cemetery	Smithsonian Museums
National Zoo	Kennedy Center for Performing Arts
FBI Building	Bureau of Engraving and Printing
Parking lots	The White House
*Transportation	FBI Building
Roosevelt Memorial	Corcoran Art Gallery
Corcoran Art Gallery	Pentagon
Lincoln Monument	Capitol Building
The Mall	Holocaust Museum
*Shopping	Ford's Theatre
Tidal Basin	*Transportation*
Pentagon	Beltway
Old Town Alexandria	Parking Lots
Smithsonian Gift Shops	Metro
Fashion Mall at Pentagon City	

*Main topics

**Figure 11.4
Mind Map Diagram**

C. Future of Social Security

- By the time today's youngest workers turn 65, only 2 workers will be supporting each beneficiary

- In 2018, the government will begin to pay out more Social Security benefits than it collects in payroll taxes

- By 2042, when today's 20-somethings begin to retire, the system will be bankrupt

Some speakers also find it helpful to create talking points to help them address potential inquiries in the question-and-answer section. The speaker talking about Social Security reform may want to have prepared responses to the arguments about how to fix the problems with the system, such as instituting privatization of accounts, increasing taxes, raising the retirement eligibility age, and reducing payments.

Some organizations have prepared talking points for their staff to use as well as for the general public to speak about educational and controversial issues. For example, the Dr. Spock Company offered parents a set of points to use when talking with their children about their fears following the attacks on the World Trade Center.[22] Families USA, a consumer health-care organization, has provided talking points for consumers to stay "on message" when interviewing medical experts about health issues.[23]

Manuscript Mode

In the **manuscript speech mode,** the material is written out and delivered word for word. This method offers the advantages of providing accurate language and solid organization. In addition, it gives the speaker a permanent written record of the speech.

But the manuscript mode also has some disadvantages. Because the manuscript provides a word-for-word record of the speech, the speaker cannot easily adapt it to suit the audience during the presentation. The speaker is stuck with the message as written. As a result, the speaker must depend on prior audience analysis to ensure that the message is tailored to the listeners.

The manuscript mode of delivery also requires the ability to read effectively from the written page. An effective speaker should use extensive eye contact, vocal inflections, and physical actions to maintain rapport with the listeners. Unfortunately, many people are not very good oral readers. They read monotonously, make reading errors, get lost in the script, and fail to establish good eye contact. Many novice speakers turn to the manuscript mode because they feel more secure with it. However, manuscript speeches, in the hands of many people, are dull and boring presentations.

As a result, accomplished speakers use the extemporaneous mode rather than the manuscript mode because it allows them to interact more freely with their audience and to adapt better to feedback. At times, however, preparing an exact word-for-word presentation is necessary. For example, the manuscript mode must be used when speakers are going to be quoted, when they must meet specific time requirements, when they need precise word selection, or when it is important to have a written record of the presentation for future reference.

PREPARING THE MANUSCRIPT   Unlike a reader, who has the opportunity to reread a passage, the listener has only one opportunity to receive, understand, and interpret the oral message (unless he or she uses an audiotape or videotape recorder and can replay passages).

When composing something that will be heard rather than read, you must write as though you are speaking, not reading. To do this, write as you would talk, say the material aloud as you are writing, and practice reading the material aloud. These pointers may help you prepare a manuscript:

- Use the active, not passive, voice.
- Keep sentences short.
- Use short, simple words.
- Use repetition to reinforce major ideas.
- Express ideas that create emotional or sensory allusions for the listener.
- Avoid using technical terms that the audience may not understand.
- Be careful in your use of pronouns so that listeners will not be confused about which "he" or "they" you are referring to.
- If a member of the audience is expected to apply the material to himself or herself, then the word *you* is appropriate. If the reference is to an experience that you, the speaker, had or something you are going to do, then use *I*.
- The word *we* is more involving than the word *you*.
- Unless it is absolutely necessary not to do so, round off any numbers you use.
- Use language with which you are comfortable. The purpose of language is to convey a message, not impress the audience.

■ Remember the rule for wording a bumper sticker: Express specific ideas by employing clear ideas in a few well-chosen words.

Memorized Mode

In the **memorized speech mode,** a speech is written out word for word and then committed to memory. Public speakers seldom use this mode of communication because it is potentially disastrous. Whereas speakers who use the extemporaneous or manuscript mode can refer to written information, those who use the memorized mode have nothing available for reference as they speak. Forgetting one idea can lead to forgetting everything. Also, the memorizer may be so concerned about getting the exact word in exactly the right place that the meaning of the words becomes secondary. The few advantages of the memorized mode include the ability to select exact wording and examples, the opportunity to look at the audience during the entire speaking process, and the ability to time the presentation precisely. The disadvantages of memorized speaking usually so overshadow its advantages that few people choose to use this mode.

In Conclusion

The act of public communication involves a transaction between a speaker and an audience. As in any other act of communication, the participants, the setting, and the purpose of the communication affect a public speech. These three parameters may affect the topic selected, the language used, the types of examples and illustrations chosen, and the aids needed to support and clarify ideas. To investigate the parameters, an audience analysis is done through prior speech analysis, process of speech analysis, and postspeech analysis. The public speaker can use one of four basic modes of presentation: impromptu or ad lib, extemporaneous, manuscript, and memorized.

Learn by Doing

1. You have two minutes to introduce yourself to your classmates. Make two outlines for the presentation. The first should follow the traditional format, the second the mind-mapping format.

2. What questions would you ask a person who has invited you to give a speech on the topic of your choice to a club or organization? Why did you pick these questions?

3. Use a topic related to your academic major to develop a statement of central idea for an informative speech to be presented to a group of classmates. Then prepare another informative statement of central idea for the same topic but for a nonclassroom audience. Based on the

different statements of central idea, how will the speeches vary?

4. Prepare a statement of central idea informing a group of high school students about your college for a speech of fifteen minutes. Now write a statement of central idea for the same speech in which you will have only five minutes to speak. Why did your statement of central idea change according to the time frame?

5. On a 3" × 5" card, list three topics you think you could speak about for a minimum of two minutes. Your instructor selects one of these for you to give an impromptu speech about. You have two minutes to get ready. You may use any notes you can prepare within that time.

Key Terms

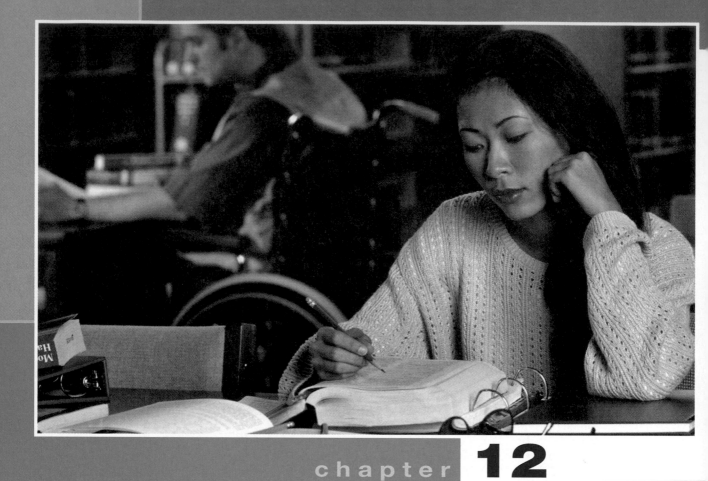

Public Speaking
Developing the Message

▶ **After reading this chapter, you should be able to**

- Identify the sources used to develop public speaking messages
- List basic reference sources used for the development of public speeches
- Illustrate the value of using and the method for finding books, magazines, newspapers, journals, indexes, government publications, special-interest group publications, and nonprint media

- Record research information
- Explain the role of support material in the development of a speech
- Identify and illustrate means of presenting and focusing supporting material

Listening to a speech can be an exciting, interesting, or uplifting experience. It also can be a frustrating, boring, or confusing one. The differences between positive and negative listening experiences often are based on whether the speaker has defined terms, offered clarifying examples, explained abstract concepts, presented proving statistics, restated ideas, and illustrated thoughts with supplementary aids.

Sources of Information

Most of the information we use to develop messages is based on personal experiences, personal observations, or learning acquired through school, the media, and reading. As we are exposed to information, we retain a certain amount of it, and this knowledge forms the core of our communication. We select words and examples from this storehouse that we use to organize messages. Sometimes, however, we need information that is not in this core to develop a message. In such cases, you need outside sources to aid you.

Since the advent of the World Wide Web, some speech researchers have relied entirely on doing a quick Web search for materials and using only what is revealed in that search. Be aware that search engines find only so much. Also be aware of the limited number of sources that a Web search can reveal.

As you search for sources of information to support your points, you should make every effort to locate **primary sources of information:** sources that represent the original reports of the observations or research. When the original work is not available, you may find it necessary to go to **secondary sources of information:** sources that report, but did not originally generate, the observations or research.

Research from major sources has been made easier with access to computerized databases. The expansion in digital networks in the U.S. research and educational community has opened up essential tools for millions of researchers and educators.[1]

Make sure the topic, examples, and language are appropriate for the age level of the group you are addressing.

Because of computers and the web research data are available, not only at the library but also at coffee shops, dorm rooms, and while sitting in the park.

In addition to locating information, a speaker must assess its validity. All sources of information reflect certain perceptions and biases. Consequently, it is wise to attempt to determine the bias of a source and interpret its information accordingly.[2] Thus, when doing research for a presentation, it is a good idea to find several agreeing authoritative sources so that your supporting details will be credible to your listeners.

Sources of information that speakers seek out include books, magazines, newspapers, special journals, indexes, government publications, and the publications of special-interest groups. Additional sources include nonprint materials such as tape recordings, records, films, CDs, DVDs, videotapes, charts, and models, as well as interviews with knowledgeable people in a particular field and computer searches.

Books

Personal, academic, and public libraries can be the sources of much information; nevertheless, you must know how to find the materials you need. In academic and public libraries, books are shelved according to a numerical system and can be located by looking in the electronic card catalog under the title, the author's name, or the general subject.

Unfortunately, not all subjects are easy to locate. For example, an average library's electronic card catalog would reveal no information if you looked under the word *Arapesh*. Thus, to learn which books contain material about this subject, you would need some additional information. By looking in an encyclopedia, you would discover that the Arapesh are a primitive, mountain-dwelling people of New Guinea, whose society was investigated by anthropologist Margaret Mead and discussed in her book *Sex and Temperament in Three Primitive Societies*. Based on this information, you

Besides using computer searches, sources of information that speakers seek out include books, magazines, and newspapers.

could look in the electronic card catalog under such subjects as *anthropology, Margaret Mead, New Guinea,* and *Sex and Temperament in Three Primitive Societies.*

Books are of great value in supplying information, but they can quickly become out of date. It generally takes at least a year for an average book to move from the author's draft through the printing process and onto the shelves of a library. Some subjects change little, and in these areas books are a good research source. But for quickly changing subjects, more up-to-date sources are needed for a thorough investigation.

Magazines

Most magazines are designed to provide recent information quickly. Many magazines are published weekly, so their information is current.

At one point the only way to access a magazine was to locate a copy of the publication. Now, however, magazines have piled up on the information highway. Many, if not most, magazines can be electronically accessed.

Researchers must be aware, however, that because these sources gather their data so quickly, some inaccuracies may occur. In addition, the editorial staffs of magazines—like the authors of books—sometimes have political and ideological biases that may temper what they write or influence what subjects they include.

To find information in magazines, you can search electronically by accessing the *Readers' Guide to Periodical Literature,*[3] a publication that indexes magazine articles by subject, title, and author, or the *International Index.* Key word or topic searches of the World Wide Web and other accessing devices will often reveal useful materials.

Newspapers

Newspapers, like magazines, contain current information that is published daily, weekly, or monthly. As is the case with magazines, because of the speed with which newspapers are written and printed, you must be aware of the possibility of error. Many libraries do not keep past issues of newspapers, but some store the information on both microfilm and microfiche, or make them available through electronic sources. Most newspapers can be directly accessed on the Web.

Journals

Professional organizations often publish journals reporting research and theories in their specific fields. The National Communication Association, for example, publishes *Communication Education, Quarterly Journal of Speech, Communication Monographs, Journal of Applied Communication Research, The Communication Teacher,* and *Critical Studies in Mass Communication.* Thus, students who are interested in finding out about some area of speech communication can refer to these journals that are published in hard copy as well as available online. The organization also has a CD-ROM for doing word, topic, and article searches.

Indexes

Encyclopedias, atlases, and bibliographical guides are indexes that provide descriptive information in certain categories. An index usually contains a minimal amount of information on many topics. Indexes may be a good starting point, but if you want in-depth material, they may not be the best sources.

In using indexes, be aware that some publish material that is factually questionable. For example, the online encyclopedia, *Wikipedia,* which is used by "36% of online

American adults,"[4] allows "anyone with an internet connection to create or alter any entry."[5] Based on this knowledge, a college student, when asked if he would recommend the use of *Wikipeida*, said, "Are you going to put the fate of your grades in the hands of total strangers who are able to make up things about a topic they might know nothing of? I think not!"[6]

Government Publications

The U.S. government publishes materials, available at minimal cost, on a variety of subjects. These can be found at bookstores in federal buildings in many major cities of the country and also can be accessed through the U.S. Government Printing Office's homepage. In addition, many major universities are designated as government depositories; all government documents are housed in those campus library systems.

Special-Interest Group Publications

Special-interest groups such as the American Cancer Society and the American Society for Training and Development publish information regarding their research and programs. A telephone call, e-mail, or letter to such an organization often brings a prompt response, or materials can be accessed through an organization's homepage on the Web. To find the name of an organization, its e-mail address, and/or its website, look in *Gale's Encyclopedia of Associations*.

Nonprint Media

Much information is available from nonprint media. Libraries and audiovisual departments of colleges and universities have collections of tape recordings, records, films, filmstrips, videotapes, DVDs and CDs from commercially and locally prepared sources covering a variety of topics. These sources usually are cataloged in a manner similar to that used for books and periodicals. Some nonprint materials are available for general circulation, but others must be used on the premises. Local and national radio and television stations and networks often sell audio or visual copies of their programs. For example, ABC News, National Public Radio, and "Dr. Phil" have catalogs of programming audiotapes and videos available for sale.[7]

Interviews

Interviews can be used to find information that is not available from written or audiovisual sources. After all, what better way is there to find out, for example, how the budget of your college is developed than by talking to the institution's treasurer or the budget director? Such interviews can be conducted in a variety of ways. If someone is not available for a face-to-face, instant messaging, or telephone session, you can submit a series of questions to be answered either through writing or tape-recording. In addition, contacting a person via e-mail often brings an immediate response.

Computer Searches

Historically, a researcher would obtain information by going to a library and looking in the electronic card catalog or the *Readers' Guide to Periodical Literature* or by asking the reference librarian what sources were available. Now you can access most of the same library materials online. Although most students go directly to Google or Yahoo! and enter the name of the topic they are searching for, this doesn't always give access to the best source. Just because something pops up first does not mean it is the best. It simply means that that item has been accessed the most. Don't just grab the initial offering. You often need to search further. Online research requires knowledge of what search engine to use as well as how to access information.

COMPUTER-BASED RETRIEVAL SYSTEMS A *computer-based retrieval system* allows the researcher to compile a bibliography or a set of facts relevant to a specific topic. Searches may be used for a variety of purposes, including gathering research or references, compiling a reading list, acquiring statistical information, or simply keeping abreast of developments in a field. Naturally, a major advantage to this method is the time saved, as a computer retrieves information in minutes that would otherwise take much longer to compile. The search can be quite comprehensive and can locate references that the most careful conventional searches may not. Another feature is the timeliness of the material since these databases are updated frequently.[8]

CONDUCTING A COMPUTER SEARCH Once you have the database you plan to search, you need a method to find what you need. There are several steps in conducting an effective computer search. The principles apply no matter what search engine or index you use.[9]

1. *Select a database* that is relevant to the kind of information you seek (e.g., education sources: Education Full Text [www.hwwilson.com]; general information: Academic Search Premier [EBSCOhost]).
2. *Narrow the hits.* Depending on the database and what you seek, you may want to select options to narrow the hits to a manageable number (e.g., 20 to 100).
3. *Examine the hits* you have for clues to what is working and what isn't working. If you have trouble finding the right sources, check to be sure you're using the right words by consulting the database's thesaurus. On the other hand, what do you do

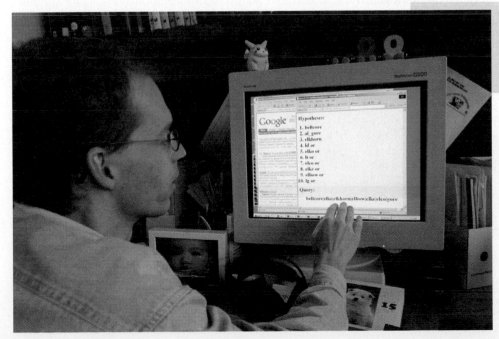

Online research requires knowledge of what search engine to use as well as how to access information.

if your search is too successful? What do you do when you get 10,000 hits and need to narrow your search?

(a) Select a database with focused content.

(b) Use a search engine that is more focused.

(c) Select only English-language articles (or articles written in whatever languages you read).

(d) Narrow to recent dates.

(e) Select only abstracts or full-text articles.

(f) Search by author, title, or subject.

(g) Conduct a *Boolean search*, a search that combines multiple words connected by *and* or *or*.

4. *Mark the sources.* When you find sources you like, check the boxes or mark them.

5. *Save your sources* by printing, e-mailing them to yourself, or saving to a disk. If they are abstracts, then go to the library and look up the full articles. If they are full text, you have all the information you need.

6. *Cite your sources.* Be sure to cite the source of the information in your speech and have the full bibliographic reference available for anyone who wants that information.

From the screen you can cut and paste information for your presentation by opening your word-processor program. Highlight the material you want, use the "Edit" function to "cut," and then move it to your word-processing program and "paste" it there.

Remember, cite the source of your ideas and information unless the ideas are ones that you already know (common knowledge) or that are truly your own. You want your speech to flow, so integrate the citation into your message. You might say, "According to the November 2009 issue of *Time* magazine . . ." or "In looking at the womenandlanguage.org website, I discovered . . . ."

Speakers are seldom criticized for citing too many sources, but just don't tag a series of quotes together. Be sure to have additional information available for audience members who might request clarifications, more ideas, or the source of the material you used. These requests might come during the question-and-answer session or following the speech.

USE OF THE INTERNET　Researchers should realize that the Internet is not always a perfect search source. As one Internet expert states, "The Internet makes readily available so much information that students think research is far easier than it really is. Students are producing superficial research papers [and speeches], full of data—some of it suspect—and with little thought."[10]

An investigation concerning the use of the Internet as a means of finding material reveals these potential problems for speech researchers:

1. *It is difficult for the uninitiated to find their way around the Internet.* Unfortunately, most students simply tinker around until they think they have found the information. If you need a primer course on the use of the Web, you might want to refer to *Internet for Dummies* or, if you are more advanced, *More Internet for Dummies*.

Socially Communicating

Internet Info

Do you need permission to copy and use copyrighted material that you get off the Internet? *Answer:* Generally, you should not copy—and certainly not use—copyrighted material without permission from the copyright holder.

Source: J. Dianne Brinson, coauthor of *The Multimedia Law and Business Handbook,* writing in *PhotoStockNotes,* Pine Lake Farm, 1910 35th Road, Osceola, WI 54020. © Communication Briefings, www.briefings.com, 1101 King Street, Alexandria, VA 22314. Used with permission.

2. *"Because information is so accessible, students stop far too quickly."*[11] Researchers often assume that everything about a particular topic will be revealed through a quick Internet exploration. Consequently, they find one or two sources and stop looking. The best advice that can be followed is to use the Internet as a part of, not as the whole, process of researching a topic.

3. *"Many sites neglect to stay up-to-date."*[12] Don't assume that because something appears on the Internet, it is current and accurate. For example, a computer software company that was supplying information regarding a specialized program went out of business and left its homepage active. Individuals who took information after the site was no longer being maintained used useless concepts.

4. *Some information is fabricated by the source.* People with biases and prejudices who manipulate information for their own means enter material on the Web. For example, anyone can access the entries on Wikipedia and alter the material. In addition, anyone can start a blog or a webpage and post anything. There is no requirement that this information be correct, as there is no one to monitor it. Just because information has been posted on the Internet doesn't mean that it is true, well researched, or up to date. Some websites are refereed journals, but for most there are no editors, evaluators, or research scholars who screen much of what appears.

SELECTING INTERNET SOURCES   It is imperative, as an ethical and competent public speaker, that you make wise choices when using evidence. Here are some suggestions for selecting and using Internet sources:

Find Valid Sources   Remember, some Internet sources are completely inaccurate. You'll want to check carefully for accuracy. The online source www.snopes.com is valuable in checking out truth versus *urban legends* (hoaxes). For example, students in a public speaking class were assigned to give a speech on a topic that may or may not have involved urban legends. Some of the topics included the notions that the fashion of wearing sagging pants was originally a prison mode for signaling sexual availability; that when Barack Obama was sworn into office as a senator from Illinois he did not use *The Bible,* but used *The Koran;* and that the game of basketball was invented in the United States.

Following each speech, the students voted to tell whether they believed that the material was true, false, or undetermined. How many of the statements did you think were true?[13]

Claim: The fashion of wearing sagging pants was originally a prison mode for signaling sexual availability.

Status: False. Although sagging pants were first worn in the U.S. prison system, this was not a style originating with imprisoned homosexuals intent on advertising their interest in casual flings. Sagging pants became the behind-the-bars fashion thanks to ill-fitting prison-issue garb: Some of those incarcerated were provided with clothing a few sizes too large. That oversizing, coupled with the lack of belts available in prisons, led to a great number of prisoners whose pants were falling off their waists. Belts are not permitted in most correctional facilities because all too often the lifeless bodies of inmates had been found hanging from them.

Claim: When Barack Obama was sworn into office as a senator from Illinois he did not use *The Bible,* but used *The Koran.*

Status: False. During his run for the Democratic presidential nomination, lots of rumors circulated about Obama. *The Koran* rumor was one of them. In fact, as a

Christian, Obama did use *The Bible*. The circulators mixed up Obama with Keith Ellison, a Muslim congressman from Minnesota, who did use *The Koran* at his swearing-in ceremony.

Claim: The game of basketball was invented in the United States.

Status: False. James Naismith, a Canadian physical education instructor, invented basketball in 1891. It all started with a soccer ball and two peach baskets affixed to a ten-foot-high railing.

The moral? What seems to be true may, in fact, not be.

With this in mind, be especially careful when using blogs as a research source. "In size and scope, blogs are low-budget, one-person operations that could not be more different from the country's newsrooms. There is no editorial layer—no reporters, editors, copy editors, or producers constantly verifying and tweaking what is reported before it is seen by the public. There is no call to be objective and strike a balance in the stories."[14] In other words, you have no way of knowing whether the information on a blog is truthful, has been well researched, or is total fantasy.

Look for sources noted for generally doing accurate investigation, such as universities, scholarly organizations, and the government. If you are looking for statistics for a speech about rape, for example, you may be able to find information from your local police department, the FBI, or a local rape crisis center. In addition, associations such as the American Psychological Association and the American Counseling Association have homepages that can lead you to information that has been published after being reviewed by experts in the field. "Search engines, such as Google and Ask.com, are not bad places to start, but the results aren't always reliable or relevant, because popularity or paid placement can determine which sites turn up first."[15] Some sites to consider are Library Spot (www.libraryspot.com), Bigchalk (www.bigchalk.com), and the Library of Congress (www.loc.gov).[16]

Use the Databases Available through College Libraries   Your university or college is probably part of a library consortium. Each consortium member pays a fee for a site license so that you and other students can have full access to the sources available in all of the libraries that are part of the consortium. These databases give citation information, abstracts, and often full-text articles, so you can find the articles you need. Because these databases are academically based, you are likely to get more accurate material than you would from a generic database.

Set a Stopping Point   How much time will you spend on your research? Theoretically, you could research your topic for minutes or years. Realistically, you have only so much time to prepare a speech. Set a logical stopping point. This is usually when you think you have enough information to flesh out the speech and have the aids you need to assist in the speech's development. If necessary, as you prepare the speech itself, you can go back and find some additional support to plug some holes in your message. Of course, this theory is based on the supposition that you have left yourself enough time to research, prepare, practice, and adjust the speech. If you are a procrastinator, you may be rushed to find material and not find enough or the right kind.

For a recap of how to evaluate Internet sources, see Figure 12.1.

ANALYZING SOURCES   It is important, as you identify and collect information, to do a careful analysis of the validity of the information that you plan to use in your speech. Unfortunately, some people are so happy just to find information that they use it without any thought that they have an ethical responsibility to present accurate, truthful support to the claims that they make.

Figure 12.1
The Ten Cs for Evaluating Internet Sources

Source: Adapted from "The Ten C's for Evaluating Internet Sources," McIntyre Library, University of Wisconsin-Eau Claire, and "Evaluating Internet Research Sources" at www.VirtualSalt.com/evalu8it.htm.

The "Ten Cs" provide criteria to consider in evaluating Internet resources.

1. **Content.** What is the intent of the content? Are the titles and author identified? What is the date of the document or article? Do you have the latest version?
2. **Credibility.** Is the author identifiable and reliable? Is the content credible?
3. **Critical Thinking.** Can you identify the author, publisher, edition, and so on, as you would with "traditionally" published resources?
4. **Copyright.** If the material falls under the copyright laws, is the credit given?
5. **Citation.** Is credit given to the author? Does the format of the citation follow a standard style?
6. **Continuity.** Will the Internet site be maintained and updated? Can you rely on this source over time to provide up-to-date information?
7. **Censorship.** Does your search engine or index look for all words, or are some words excluded?
8. **Connectivity.** Does access to the resource require a graphical user interface? Are you familiar with the tools and the applications required to access the material?
9. **Comparability.** Does the Internet resource have an identified comparable print or CD-ROM data set or source? Does the Internet site contain comparable and complete information (e.g., full text versus partial information)?
10. **Context.** How does the Internet information fit in the overall information context of your subject?

In general, information from government agencies and educational institutions is perceived to be credible since they tend to have less of a vested interest in persuading people to a particular point of view. For instance, the Central Intelligence Agency's *World Factbook* offers an exhaustive collection on the population, geography, government, and economy of other countries (www.odci.gov/cia/publications/factbook). Subscription-based sites that provide reliable, advertising-free information also can be dependable sources. Publications with long-standing reputations such as the *New York Times* and the *Economist* are generally considered credible sources. Like panning for gold, the quality of information that you use is central to the quality of your communication. "Use credible information providers. Identify sources. Authenticate what they say. Then ask yourself: Is this gold or garbage?"[17]

RECORDING AND USING YOUR RESEARCH   When you do research, keep a record of where your information came from so you can refer to the source to find additional information, answer questions about a source, or give oral footnotes during a speech. When you write a term paper, *you must footnote quotations*—material written or spoken by a person in the exact words in which it was originally presented—and *paraphrases*—someone else's ideas put into your own words. You do the same in public speaking, except orally. For example, in a speech concerning male–female communication, this **oral footnote** would be appropriate:

Dr. Julia Wood, in discussing nonverbal behaviors of women and men in her book, *Communication, Gender, and Culture,* states, "Nonverbal behaviors expected of women emphasize communality—building and sustaining relationships and community. Nonverbal behaviors considered appropriate for men emphasize agency—displaying power and initiative, achieving."[18]

In some instances, it might be necessary to establish a quoted author as an authority. You do this because you think the audience doesn't know the author's credentials or the person, or because you want to reinforce the author's credibility. In this case, for an oral footnote, you could say:

> Julia Wood is one of our nation's eminent communication scholars and professors. Recently the Council for Advancement and Support of Education (CASE) in Washington, DC, and the Carnegie Foundation for the Advancement of Teaching in Princeton, New Jersey, named Julia Wood Professor of the Year for North Carolina. Her interest in gender led her to teach graduate-level courses in Feminist Research in Communication and a seminar in Communication in Personal Relationships. In her book, *Gendered Lives, Communication, Gender, and Culture,* Dr. Wood states, "Nonverbal behaviors expected of women emphasize communality—building and sustaining relationships and community. Nonverbal behaviors considered appropriate for men emphasize agency—displaying power and initiative, achieving."

In recording your research, you may select from a variety of formats. The most commonly used patterns are those of the Modern Language Association (MLA) and the American Psychological Association (APA).[19]

When actually inscribing your bibliographical information and notes from your research, you need to be careful to keep track of where you got the material. Notes can be taken on 3 × 5 or 4 × 6 cards or on sheets of paper. They can also be keyboarded into a computer. Whichever method you use, be sure to transcribe the source of the material, including the writer, where the material was obtained (newspaper, book, the Internet), the date of the publication, the publisher and city, and the page number.

One method of recording the research is to use a running bibliography. The list is numbered so that it can be used while you are taking notes. For those who are unfamiliar with formats for coding bibliographical entries, patterns for (1) a book, (2) a newspaper story, (3) a magazine or journal article, and (4) an online article are presented.

Bibliography

1. Julia T. Wood, *Gendered Lives: Communication, Gender, and Culture,* 7th ed. (Belmont, CA: Thomson Higher Education, 2007), p. 152.
2. John Campanelli, "A Show of Affection Can Be Good for a Guy. Really," *Cleveland Plain Dealer* (June 19, 2005), p. L1.
3. Peg Tyre and Julie Scelfo, "Why Girls Will Be Girls," *Newsweek* (July 31, 2006): 46–47.
4. Jeanna Bryner, "Clueless Guys Can't Read Women," March 20, 2008, www.msnbc.msn.com/id/23726891/.

As you do your research and record information, you can refer to the source by number, thus eliminating the necessity for continually writing out the same bibliographical material. You can refer to Wood's male–female quotation, for example, as 1-152 (source 1 in the bibliography, page 152). Because the material is directly quoted, put quotation marks around it. If it is paraphrased, the use of quotation marks is not necessary, but make sure you remember that the material is not your original ideas but from another source. If cards are used, a footnote reference would look like Figure 12.2.

If a computer is used, keyboard a running bibliography and enter the reference material by keyboarding or scanning it. Double-space between entries. After assembling all of your research, you can print out the material. Then cut the reference material into strips, separate them by topic, write or outline directly from these slips of paper or arrange the slips on sheets of blank paper and attach the slips to the pages

Figure 12.2
Source Card

Topic: Gender Communication

Reference: 1–152

Information: "Nonverbal behaviors expected of women emphasize communality—building and sustaining relationships and community. Nonverbal behaviors considered appropriate for men emphasize agency—displaying power and initiative, achieving."

with transparent tape, and use these as an outline for the speech. An alternative is to connect the strips and then duplicate them on a copy machine, thus creating a working outline. The advantages of using or copying the actual slips of paper center not only on saving time but also having all your footnote sources available if you are asked about them during the question-and-answer session.

If you used notecards, arrange them in a sequential order and follow the procedure described in the previous paragraph to complete the speech.

Supporting Material

Supporting speech material should clarify a point you are making in the speech or offer evidence of the validity of the argument presented. The challenge for the speaker is to find material that supports the main point being discussed so that the listener pays attention because she or he is interested. Characteristics that constitute the most memorable material are those that are (1) simple, (2) unexpected, (3) concrete, (4) credible, (5) emotional, and (6) story based so that the listener will be engaged as the point is developed.[20]

The forms of support you select depend on your purposes, but the most common are stories, specific instances, exposition, statistics, analogies, and testimony.

Stories

Stories are the most interesting form of supporting material. "The delivery of the message is enhanced with stories because stories help us reach our deepest level of understanding."[21]

Humans connect with each other through the stories they tell, whether they are in interpersonal situations or in public speaking. Speakers who use stories tend to be perceived as being more engaging. For this reason, many politicians attempt to enhance their credibility and listenability by telling stories to illustrate that the plan they are presenting has worked in specific cases or that the "pain" they are feeling comes from their examining the plight of a particular person or family. For example,

Socially Communicating

Putting Humor in Its Place

Humor has a place in your presentations and your work with others. Even if you feel you can't tell a joke, you can still make humor work for you.

Humor should be relevant to the message you are giving. Link it to a point you are making, and make it the type of humor that is in good taste.

- Analogies are one way to use humor. Linking your present situation or problem to something else often provides an opportunity for humor. The link can be either logical or illogical and could even be a personal anecdote.

- Another way to use humor—and an easy one for the person who falls into the "cannot-tell-jokes"

category—is to use funny quotes. Get a book of humorous quotes.

Also: Have you seen an amusing cartoon in the paper or in a magazine? Describe it. Show it on a screen. Some specifics on using humor:

- When you are telling jokes or quips, don't pre-announce them. Just insert them here and there.

- Avoid anything offensive or sarcastic. If in doubt, leave it out.

- Remember that sometimes things occur—such as power failures, dead mikes, etc.—during presentations. Have a joke or comment ready for emergencies.

Source: Dr. Stephenie Slahor, P.O. Box 2615, Palm Springs, CA 92263.

Barack Obama, in his "A Perfect Union" speech, in which he explained his relationship with the controversial Reverend Wright, told this story:

> There is a young, twenty-three-year-old white woman named Ashley Baia who organized for our campaign in Florence, South Carolina. Ashley said that when she was nine years old, her mother got cancer. And because she had to miss days of work, she was let go and lost her health care. They had to file for bankruptcy, and that's when Ashley decided that she had to do something to help her mom. She knew that food was one of their most expensive costs, so Ashley convinced her mother that what she really liked and really wanted to eat more than anything else was mustard and relish sandwiches, because that was the cheapest way to eat. She did this for a year until her mom got better, and she told everyone that the reason she joined our campaign was so that she could help the millions of other children in the country who want and need to help their parents too. Now Ashley might have made a different choice. Perhaps somebody told her along the way that the source of her mother's problems were blacks who were on welfare and too lazy to work, or Hispanics who were coming into the country illegally. But she didn't. She sought our allies in her fight against injustice.[22]

The stories may be hypothetical or factual. If the illustrations are hypothetical, the speaker should make this clear by saying something like "Suppose you were . . ." or "Let us all imagine that . . . ." A medical technician can use a hypothetical illustration, for instance, by taking a listener on an imaginary trip through the circulatory system. In contrast, a factual illustration is a real or actual story. A speaker developed a speech on safety codes with this illustration:

> Where Memorial School stands today, Jefferson School once stood. One day a devastating fire struck Jefferson School. Eighty students and four teachers lost their lives in that tragic fire, and hundreds of others were seriously injured. The new Memorial School can never eradicate the memories of those who died during the tragic fire.

Stories can be powerful tools of persuasion. "Narratives—from novels to sitcoms— pervade our lives and can affect what we believe about topics as sweeping as historical events or as personal as safe sex."[23] A speaker, for example, who is giving a speech

Democratic candidate Barack Obama presents "Perfect Union" speech addressing race and politics.

about why the classroom audience should sponsor her in an upcoming Multiple Sclerosis Walk told the story of her daughter's brave ongoing battle with the crippling disease.

Be careful when using stories. Don't assume that your telling of a story is factual proof of your contention. Stories are *illustrations*, devices for explanation, clarification, and attracting attention. They are not generally intended to offer proof.

Specific Instances

Condensed examples that are used to clarify or prove a point are *specific instances*. Because they are not developed in depth, you can say a great deal quickly by using them and provide listeners with evidence they can relate to your point.

If you want to develop the idea that speech communication is an interesting major for college students, for example, you can support your point with specific instances of careers that employ communication majors: speech writing, teaching, research and training in business and industrial communication, political campaigning, health communication, and public relations.

Exposition

An *exposition* gives the necessary background information to listeners so that they can understand the material being presented. Sometimes, for example, a speaker needs to define specific terms, give historical information, explain the relationship between herself or himself and the topic, or explain the process that will be used during the presentation. In using exposition, the speaker must also anticipate or alter a message to provide listeners with the background information they need for understanding the transaction.

The speaker, realizing an obligation to aid the audience in understanding the message, may feel a need to define terms and ideas that will be used in the presentation. For instance, a speaker who wants to explain the advertising campaign to be used in marketing a product may find it necessary to clarify such terms and phrases as *bandwagoning* and *plus-and-minus factor of surveying*.

An audience may need historical information as well. In order for listeners to understand the rationale for the American intervention in Iraq from the standpoint of the George W. Bush administration, they would need to have quotations from President Bush himself as well as from members of his administration.

Listeners may need a bridge between the speaker and the topic to understand why the speaker is discussing the subject or to establish the speaker's expertise. For example, a student nurse who is explaining the nursing program he recently completed should share his educational background with the audience.

In addition, indicating the process to be followed during a presentation or the results the speaker wants to achieve may be helpful to listeners. An outline of the major points to be made can be distributed or displayed, or the speaker can explain what she or he will do and will want the audience to do as the speech proceeds.

Statistics

Any collection of numerical information arranged as representations, trends, or theories makes up *statistics*. For example, in discussing the changing world, a speaker might state, "The planet's population continues to explode: from 1 billion in 1820, to 2 billion in 1930, 3 billion in 1960, 4 billion in 1974, 5 billion in 1988, and 6 billion in 2000. For the 21st century, the continued exponential growth in science and technology raises both hopes (e.g., advances in medicine) and fears (e.g., development of even more lethal weapons of war),"[24] or "70.8% of the world's surface is water, 29.2% is land."[25]

Caption TK

Before accepting statistics as proof, the wise speaker asks:

- Who says so?
- How does he or she know?
- What is missing?
- Did somebody change the subject?
- Does it make sense?[26]

When statistics have been accurately collected, are properly interpreted, and are not out of date, their use is a valid aid in reaching conclusions. Unfortunately, not all statistical studies are accurately conducted, properly interpreted, or current.

STATISTICAL SURVEYING Statisticians have developed methods for collecting data—statistical surveying—that can be used with some degree of assurance that the resulting information will be correct.[27] Ideally, to discover everyone's opinion on a particular issue, everyone should be asked, but of course this is usually impossible for large groups of people. Thus, to make educated guesses, statisticians have devised methods of random sampling that allow less than the entire population to be surveyed. These methods recognize the probability of error, and a speaker should indicate this fact when giving the statistical results of a survey.

Proper Interpretation of Data If a particular group or person is trying to get a specific result, that tester may keep testing until she or he gets the desired conclusion or ignore results that do not agree with the goal. For this reason, be wary of statistics that are taken out of context, are incomplete, or do not specify the method used to collect the data.

Currency of Data Studies and surveys conducted in the past may have been perfectly accurate at the time they were done. This does not mean that they are accurate now. It is important that you use or receive the latest data and not allow yourself to be influenced by information that is out of date.

Reporting the Data Remember that a person can retain only a limited amount of information. Thus, extensive lists, complicated numerical combinations, and long numbers may well be lost if you do not help listeners by simplification or visualization. For example, a long list—such as the figures representing the cost of each material used to produce a piece of machinery—can be written on a chalkboard or poster or projected on a screen. In this way, listeners view as well as hear, and they can refer to the numbers as needed.

Simplify numbers. A statistic such as $1,243,724,863 is difficult to comprehend, but the phrase "approximately $1.25 billion" is within the grasp of an audience. If a statistic is important enough to include in a speech, you must be sure that the listener can grasp the information.

Analogies

A speaker may use an *analogy* to clarify a concept for listeners; that is, the speaker compares an unfamiliar concept to a familiar one. For example, in the section of this text dealing with the processing capacity of the human cortex, an analogy was drawn between a cybernetic process and a computer process. This comparison was not intended to indicate that the cortex and the computer are one and the same, but to demonstrate that if a reader understands the functioning of a computer, he or she may also understand the basic operation of the cortex.

Remember that an analogy is effective only if listeners are familiar with the object, idea, or theory being used as its basis. Contrasting a patient on an operating table to stars in the sky may confuse listeners who are unfamiliar with either astronomy or surgical techniques.

A speaker also should be careful not to overextend the comparison or contrast. A college president once developed an inaugural speech by comparing the school to a football team. The analogy compared faculty members to team players, students to spectators, the president to the coach, and on and on and on! After a while, the listeners became confused and stopped paying attention; the intended effect was lost.

Testimony

Testimony may be a direct quotation (actual statement) or a paraphrase (reworded idea) from an authority. Speakers provide testimony to clarify ideas, back up contentions, and reinforce concepts. Thus, a speaker may turn to this type of supporting material when it is believed that an authority is more knowledgeable than the speaker about the topic being discussed or that the opinion of an authority will make listeners more receptive to a particular idea.

An *expert* is a person who, through knowledge or skill in a specific field, gains respect for his or her opinions or expertise. We trust experts' opinions because their knowledge has been acquired through personal experience, education, training, research, and/or observation. We also respect people who have academic degrees, who are licensed or accredited, or who are recognized by peers as leaders in their fields. Many useful quotations are available to speakers on The Quotes Home Page at www.lexmark.com/data/quote.html.

Selected quotations should be true to the intention of the source. Before you accept testimony as support, assess its validity by asking some basic questions:

- Is the material quoted accurately?
- Is the source biased because of position, employment, or affiliation? A quotation by the chairperson of the board of directors of a major tobacco company that cigarette smoking may not lead to cancer should be suspect because of the speaker's biased position.
- Is the information relevant to the issue being discussed?
- Is the source competent in the field being discussed? For example, what qualifies an actor to recommend changes in U.S. foreign policy?
- Is the information current, if currency is important?

Techniques for Presenting Supporting Material

Four means of presenting and focusing supporting material are internal summaries, forecasting, signposting, and use of supplementary aids.

Internal Summaries

As a listener, have you ever been on the receiving end of a message and found yourself totally confused because of the amount of material involved? To avoid listener confusion, summarize each segment of a presentation by providing an **internal summary,** a short restatement of what has just been said in the section that you are about to leave, before proceeding to the next segment. For example, after spending several minutes proposing that the United States should adopt a more aggressive foreign policy, the speaker could bridge out of that unit with the internal summary, "Our nation, then, needs to pursue a more vigorous, definitive approach to its international relations."

Forecasting

A **forecast** is a statement that alerts the audience to ideas that are coming. An example of a forecast is, "Let's now examine the three examples of how bulimics purge food." This forecast alerts the audience to get ready to listen for the three points.

Signposting

An additional vehicle for presenting supporting material is signposting. In **signposting**, a speaker reviews where the listeners have been, states where they are presently, and forecasts where they are going. This aids the listener by recapping what has been presented and telling where the speech is going. An example of a signpost is, "We've seen how the effects of cholesterol could result in clogged arteries. I've just reinforced this idea by presenting information from the American Medical Association proving the theory to be correct. Now, let's examine what you can do to lower your cholesterol and, therefore, lessen your chances of having a heart attack."

Supplementary Aids

Many speakers find **supplementary speech aids**—visual, audio, audiovisual, and computerized graphics—valuable in augmenting the oral segments of their presentations. Aids are intended to facilitate listener understanding, not to function as decorative touches; therefore, a speaker should ask two questions before using aids: Is the aid relevant to the presentation? And will listeners better understand the material through the use of an aid?

In a speech, statistical differences can be greatly enhanced by the use of charts. In a classroom, supplementary aids can be used to teach particular techniques. For example, student nurses sometimes inject needles into grapefruits so they can learn how to give shots, and a videotape of an interrogation can supplement a discussion on how to question suspects for law enforcement students. These aids are intended to supplement the speaker's voice.

VISUAL AIDS **Visual aids** appeal to our sense of sight. And since so many listeners are visual in orientation, visual support of a speaker's message can be a key to enhancing comprehension. As in using any supplementary aid, speakers must be sure that the visual aid truly *aids* the presentation; that is, be sure that it doesn't just replace you and your message. Some speakers use the basic rule that if something can be said orally, without any assistance, then an aid should not be used. Others contend that right-brained listeners often depend on visual stimulation both in order to comprehend and to pay attention. Too many speakers bring in a huge number of pictures or PowerPoint slides and proceed to overwhelm listeners with no real supporting purpose.

A speaker can choose from a variety of visual aids:

1. *Real objects.* To demonstrate the process of swinging a hammer, why not use a real hammer? Or use an actual form to show how a traffic ticket is filled out. These are examples of using real objects as visual aids.

2. *Models.* At times, it is impossible to use real objects. In such cases, a scale model (in exact proportion to the dimensions of the real object) or a synthetic model (not in proportion but nevertheless representative) may be used. For example, although a Boeing 757 jet cannot be brought into an aviation classroom, a scale model certainly can be.

3. *Photographs, pictures, and diagrams.* A photograph of a death scene and the victim can be shown to a jury in a murder trial in order to reconstruct the scene or the violence.

4. *Charts.* A chart is a visual representation of statistical data that gives information in tabular or diagrammatic form. For example, a series of columns representing the number of doctors available to a hospital compared with the number needed presents a striking visual image of the problem.

5. *Cutaways.* It is often difficult to look inside certain objects. A cutaway allows us to see what we normally would have to imagine, thus enabling us to visualize and understand better. To show the layers of materials used to construct a house, a wall is cut in half so that we see the siding, the insulation, the studding, the wallboard, and the wallpaper.

6. *Mockups.* A mockup shows the building up or tearing down of an article. For example, a biology textbook may include an outline drawing of the human body on a page with a series of clear plastic sheets attached. Each of these plastic overlays shows a specific drawing that, as it is flipped onto the original sketch, adds an aspect of the human anatomy.

7. *Flip charts and chalk/whiteboards.* You may be presenting in a classroom or training room with little or no technological support. In such a setting, make use of the chalkboard or whiteboard or bring a flip chart with newsprint paper so that you can list your major points or illustrate numbers as you speak. A good rule is to start at the far left and let your material "flow" across the board in the sequence in which you present it. Write legibly and large enough for your writing to be seen from the farthest point of the room. A traditional chalk mark or wide-tipped felt marker line can be seen clearly up to a distance of about twenty feet. If you know in advance that you will be using a flip chart, you can prepare the pages before your presentation and flip through them as you speak.

8. *Presentation graphics.* Presentation graphics are a series of visuals that are projected using an overhead projector while the speaker is discussing each point. The slides enable the speaker to illustrate visually with statistics, cartoons, short quotations, maps, and other materials.

In order to supplement computer-generated materials in lengthy presentations, it often is helpful to provide listeners with a copy of the slides and space for taking notes.

AUDIO AIDS   *Audio aids* appeal to our sense of hearing. Such devices as records, tape recordings, or duplications of sounds may be the only way to demonstrate particular sensations accurately for listeners. For example, playing a segment of Martin Luther King's "I Have a Dream" speech is an excellent way to demonstrate his dynamic oral style.

AUDIOVISUAL AIDS *Audiovisual aids* such as films, videotapes, and tape–slide presentations combine the dimensions of sight and sound. A video clip of a seeing eye dog assisting his or her person can illustrate the support that such animals can provide. In the same way, a videotape of an executive's speech is an excellent way to illustrate his or her vocal and physical mannerisms.

Computerized Graphics

Computerized graphics programs such as Power-Point provide speakers with the opportunity to outline a speech, create slides with animated bullets that follow the outline, and import visual graphics, photos, video or audio clips, and Internet connections. Many courtrooms, classrooms, and organizations are equipped with projectors so that speakers can display computerized graphics. A speaker who uses the program effectively can provide listeners with multimedia messages, stimulating their visual and auditory senses.

Computer graphics allow people who are not artists to prepare attractive visuals. In addition, apprehensive speakers may be less fearful because they perceive that audience members are looking at the visuals, not at them.

A computerized presentation allows for varying the visuals through a variety of media and media techniques. The inclusion of visuals will tend to hold an audience member's attention better than just words. It will also give a visual impression that the listener can retain.

Socially Communicating

The Controversy over PowerPoint

In 2007, one of the most elegant, most influential and most groaned about pieces of software in the history of computers was 20 years old.

While PowerPoint has served as the metronome for countless crisp presentations, it has also allowed an endless expanse of dimwit ideas to be dressed up with graphical respectability.

"Graphics guru Edward Tufte says the software "elevates format over content, betraying an attitude of commercialism that turns everything into a sales pitch."

Robert Gaskins, one of the inventors, states that "a PowerPoint presentation was never supposed to be the entire proposal, just a quick summary of something longer and better thought out." He cites as an example his original business plan for the program: 53 densely argued pages long. The dozen or so slides that accompanied it were but the highlights.

Source: Lee Gomes, "PowerPoint Turns 20, as Its Creators Ponder a Dark Side to Success," *The Wall Street Journal* (June 20, 2007): B1.

Besides the advantages, recognize that there are also drawbacks to using computer programs:

- If the projection equipment is substandard, it may be necessary to turn out the lights so the audience can see the slides, a move that creates a sleep-inducing environment and makes it difficult for people to take notes.

- There is a risk of putting so much on the screen that the material becomes overwhelming.

- A speaker can get so carried away with the program's technological abilities to dissolve, fade, or fly transitions that the medium becomes more important than the message.

Since many speakers want to and may even be required to use electronic techniques and equipment, this text presents a discussion of their preparation and use. It is understood, however, that some instructors may request that their students not use computer-assisted presentational programs, just as some organizations are requesting that their employees avoid using this type of equipment. Be aware that this attitude is not universal; many organizations expect their employees to be proficient in the use of presentation graphics.

In planning the use of PowerPoint, remember that presentation graphics, like any visual aids, are designed to assist your oral presentation, not replace it. As a result, you will want to plan carefully how best to incorporate the graphics so that they reinforce or clarify your verbal points. Recognize that some speakers rely far too extensively on visuals, putting their entire presentation on the screen. Remember that audiences are expected to comprehend word slides at a glance, without breaking their concentration on the speaker. When bombarded with word slides, audiences can only pretend that they're taking in both the visuals and the voice. Also be aware that, depending on your projector system, the audience may have to sit in the dark during the use of the equipment. Darkness can be depressing, lead to sleepiness, and make it difficult for people to take notes.

Keep in mind the purpose of supplementary aids. If you can say something without any visual assistance, do so. Do not use visuals as decoration or to show off your computer skills. Make sure that the materials aid your speech, not detract from it. After a while the novelty of graphics wears off, and audience members find themselves bored, or they pay attention to the process rather than to what you are saying.

Developing PowerPoint Presentations

The materials should be easy to read, visible to all, and simple to understand. (See Figure 12.3.) Each slide or visual should focus on a single idea and convey that information clearly. Punctuation and capitalization should be consistent throughout. Spelling and punctuation should be correct. Select a neutral color for your ending slide. This way you avoid having a glaring white screen after your last visual.

Make sure that when preparing the graphics, you parallel your speech materials with the visuals. Listeners shouldn't have to struggle to comprehend the connection between the visual and verbal message.

If you are going to utilize electronic presentational programs to their full advantage, you also need to understand not only how to input the information but also how to use the process during a presentation. Many colleges and organizations offer classes on how to prepare and use the programs, and some packages have video or computer tutorials. The PowerPoint package, for example, comes with PowerPoint Wizard, a program that

Figure 12.3
Design Elements and PowerPoint Slides

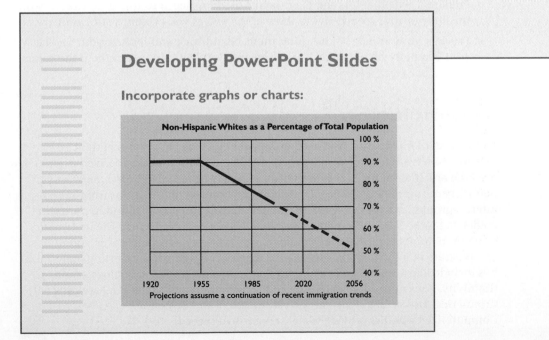

directs you through each step of creating the visuals. For those who prefer to read instructions, books specifically written for the presentational packages are available. In addition, there are some good online sources such as speechmaster.com (www.speechmastery.com/power-point.html). You'll want to give careful consideration to the design elements of your PowerPoint presentation. For clarity, keep these suggestions in mind:

- Use a clean-looking font, such as **Arial**.
- Use the rule of 5 × 5, which indicates that no slide should use more than five words per line and no more than five lines per slide.
- Phrases are easier to grasp than full sentences, but full sentences may be useful to express complete thoughts.
- Bulleted and/or numbered lists and topic outlines are useful.
- Be aware that different computers may project colors differently, so standard colors may work best.
- Use the same font and format on all slides so that your words don't seem to jump all over the screen with each new slide.
- Keep the lights on during the speech (in most rooms).
- Use a very light background with black or dark lettering.
- Plan the presentation so that you deliver one page in thirty seconds (or more).
- Use one visual per minute.
- Present only one major idea per slide or viewgraph.
- Use no more than four subordinate ideas per minute.
- Each bulleted point should be horizontal on the slide.
- Use colors that can be seen (avoid putting black print on a dark-blue background).
- Pay attention to the print and background colors in the preformatted designs.
- Incorporate video and film clips, maps, graphs, and charts, if appropriate.
- Use the same graphics, colors, and fonts on all of your slides.
- Prepare a slide that lists the main points of your speech to use as an overview of the body of your speech and to show at the end as you present your summary.
- Preview your visuals before using them. Stand back and look at your visuals as your listeners will see them. This is the only way you can determine if the colors, layout, and format work.

In Conclusion

The sources of information available to a speaker include personal experiences, personal observations, and accumulated learning, plus information derived from research and interviews. Research information may be found in books, magazines, newspapers, journals, indexes, government publications, publications from special-interest groups, and the Internet. Additional information can be found in nonprint media and interviews. When doing research, keep a record of where the information came from. Supporting material is used in a speech to clarify the speaker's point or to demonstrate that the point has some probability of being true. Supporting material can include illustrations, specific instances, expositions, statistics, analogies, and testimony. Four means for presenting and focusing supporting material are internal summaries, forecasting, signposting, and the use of supplementary aids. Computerized graphics provide visual support to a speech.

Learn by Doing

1. Select a controversial subject area (e.g., abortion, euthanasia, legalization of drugs, confiscation of handguns), and identify an authority on the subject. Interview that person (in person or via the phone or Internet), and give an oral presentation to the class about your interview. You should clearly state the interviewee's stand concerning the issue and the reasons for the stand. After all of the presentations have been made, participate in a class discussion on the value of the interview as a means for collecting data for a speech.

2. Use the information collected from the interview in activity 1 to research the same topic. Look for the views of other authorities on the subject. Prepare a presentation in which you compare and/or contrast the results of your interview with the results of your research.

3. Make a presentation to the class in which a supplementary aid is absolutely necessary for the listeners' comprehension of the message (e.g., a description of Van Gogh's style of brush stroke, the music of Michael Buble in comparison with that of Josh Grogan, the architectural styles of the Maya of the Yucatan).

4. Research each of these items and compile a set of notecards or notes and a running bibliography as explained in the chapter:

   a. The name of one book about the teachings of Aristotle

   b. A magazine article about nuclear-waste disposal

   c. The longitude and latitude of Omaha, Nebraska

   d. Three encyclopedia entries about the White House

   e. The name of a journal exclusively about nonverbal communication

   f. The definition of the word *cacophony*

   g. The 1950 population of the United States

   h. The name of the university that sponsors the Semester at Sea academic program

   i. The title of a government pamphlet dealing with AIDS

   j. The gross national product of the United States in 2006

   k. The name of the lyricist for the musical *Rent*

5. Use the format explained in the chapter to make three notecards or notes for a speech with the purpose statement "to inform the class of the effects of the Salk polio vaccine." Two are to be quotations and one should be a paraphrase. Use a different source for each entry.

6. Find a factual or hypothetical illustration that could be used for the speech described in activity 5.

7. What background information do you think would be needed by members of your class if you were to present the speech in activity 5?

8. Locate and footnote three sources of testimony concerning the effects of secondary smoke on nonsmokers.

9. Find a humorous story that you could use as an introduction for a speech about the U.S. educational system, gender similarities or differences, or sports.

10. Prepare a three- to five-minute speech that depends on the listeners' viewing a PowerPoint presentation.

11. Select one feature of preparing a PowerPoint presentation that you can demonstrate to the class in a speech of three minutes or fewer. Since everyone in the class will be doing this assignment, try to select an aspect of the program that is unusual. Then present the speech to the class.

Key Terms

primary sources of information   329

secondary sources of information   329

oral footnote   337

supporting speech material   339

internal summary   344

forecast   345

signposting   345

supplementary speech aids   345

visual aids   345

chapter 13

Public Speaking
Structuring the Message

▶ **After reading this chapter, you should be able to**

- Explain why it is important to structure speeches carefully

- Structure a speech to meet the needs of the listeners

- Explain what makes an effective introduction, central idea, body, and conclusion for a speech

- List and give examples of introduction attention getters for a speech

- Identify the purpose and types of orienting materials

- Explain the purpose of and develop a central idea for a speech

- List and give examples of the methods of issue arrangement for the body of a speech

- List and give examples of the methods for concluding a speech

- Identify and illustrate the methods for the overall organization of a speech

- Have the ability to make transitions into a question-and-answer session

- Explain how culture has a role in speech organization

Have you ever sat through a class lecture and found yourself thoroughly confused because the instructor kept jumping from idea to idea and then back to a previous one while discussing still another thought? If so, you were experiencing organizational confusion.

Listeners have limited and fluctuating attention spans, constantly tuning in to and out of a speaker's message. Consequently, it is important to present a carefully structured message that enables listeners to get back on track when they tune back in to the speech. In addition, if the major points in the speech are well supported with statistics and examples, listener understanding will be enhanced.

Basic Elements of a Speech

What is the basis for the need to effectively organize a speech? "Languages differ in the very assumption of how information should be organized, of what is to be or not to be described and expressed."[1] In other words, as we develop our language skills, we hear ideas presented in certain patterns. If concepts are presented in an alternative pattern, it can cause listener problems. It is important, therefore, to understand that not all cultures organize ideas in the same way. For example, historically, speakers of Western cultures, based on the concepts developed by the Greek rhetorician Aristotle, make use of a process that calls for stating a contention, supporting that contention, and drawing a conclusion for the listeners. This is accomplished in a step-by-step manner. As you will discover later in the chapter, other cultures are exposed to, and therefore tend to listen best in, different structures.

Because this book is written primarily for public speakers for whom the Western mode of reasoning and organization is the general format, the discussion of how to structure a speech will follow Western guidelines. This is not to say that other formats or approaches should not be learned or used when appropriate. In fact, a European American whose analysis shows that the audience is composed primarily of individuals who are not European Americans should adapt the message and its presentation to that audience.

The Western system requires a careful plan for preparing and developing effective presentations.[2] The plan should foster listening comprehension, aid in eliminating confusion, produce a well-supported presentation, and maintain attention. (An outlining tool for formatting a speech can be found on this text's website.)

To make the most effective use of this plan, it is helpful to look first at the basic elements (introduction, central idea, body, and conclusion) of a speech and how each of these four elements are put together.

A public communication message should be arranged in four parts:

1. *Introduction*—attention-gaining and orienting material.
2. *Central idea*—the purpose of the presentation and a specific statement of its main idea.
3. *Body*—the major points to be expressed in the presentation. The body of the speech may be organized into as many divisions as necessary to develop the intent of the message.
4. *Conclusion*—a summarizing and possibly a motivating statement.

The Introduction

The purposes of the **introduction to a speech** are to gain the listeners' attention and orient them to the material that will be presented.

Culturally Communicating

A Navajo (Diné) Speech Introduction

Not all cultural groups begin their speeches by first gaining attention, next relating to audience interests, then establishing their credibility. Speakers at Diné Community College (formerly Navajo Community College) first answer the listeners' question, "Who are you and what's your clan affiliation?" Students thus begin their classroom speeches by telling their names (who they are) and identifying their clan affiliation (knowing this helps listeners understand the roots of their life). Until this personal, identifying information is shared, neither the speakers nor their listeners can feel at home.

Source: Clella Jaffe, *Public Speaking: Concepts and Skills for a Diverse Society* (Belmont, CA: Wadsworth/Thomson Learning, 2001), p. 194.

Attention Material

It is imperative to gain your listeners' attention at the start of the speech. If a speaker fails to convince the audience to listen immediately, getting them to tune in later is almost impossible. Attention-getting techniques include presenting personal references, humorous stories, illustrations, rhetorical questions, action questions, unusual or dramatic devices, quotations related to the theme, and a statement of the theme.

PERSONAL REFERENCES   Introductions containing personal references give a speaker's reasons for undertaking a presentation on a specific topic. For example, to introduce a presentation that appeals for funds, a speaker may relate the personal experience of receiving aid from the Muscular Dystrophy Association.

HUMOROUS STORIES   People like to laugh and enjoy themselves; therefore, humorous stories can be an effective way to start a presentation. The humor should fit the audience and the occasion, be relevant to the material being presented, and set the desired tone.

The humor should parallel the intent of the speech. A speaker, for example, could begin a presentation with a humorous anecdote: "A railroad agent in Africa had been

Communicating in Careers

Try These Speech Starters

Successful presenters use these techniques to quickly establish a connection with their audiences:

- Quiet a talkable group with the silent treatment. Just stand there and look at them until all the eyes—and the ears—in the room focus on you. At the precise moment that occurs, hit them with a statement that gives them a good reason to keep listening.

- Imply that you need their help. *Example:* "I have something on my mind, and I'd like to share it with you to see what you think."

- Dramatize what you're planning to tell them. *Example:* "I'm deeply troubled by something, and I'm wondering if the same thing is also troubling you."

- Ask them how they feel about the topic of your presentation. *Example:* "I'm fed up with the tax system. Are you?"

- Say something that will involve them. *Examples:* "I'm going to ask you to think about an important topic." "I'd like you to do something for me."

Source: Steve Adubato, PhD, Emmy Award-winning author and communication trainer, Bloomfield, NJ, writing in *Business News New Jersey,* Snowden Publications, Inc., 104 Church St., New Brunswick, NJ 08901. © Communication Briefings, www.briefings.com, 1101 King Street, Alexandria, VA 22314. Used with permission.

bawled out for doing things without orders from headquarters. One day headquarters received a telegram from the agent which read, 'Tiger on platform eating conductor. Wire instructions.'"[3] From this story, listeners would expect a speech about worker empowerment or creative decision making.

It is important to consider, too, whether humor is appropriate to your own communication style. Some people are not very comfortable telling funny stories or jokes, and that discomfort will be revealed to the audience. Other speakers have a good ear (and memory) for relaying humorous anecdotes and find the form successful for them.

Likewise, a humorous introduction may not always be appropriate for the audience or the topic at hand. A briefing on the current state of affairs in war-torn Afghanistan, for instance, certainly does not call for a light, humorous opener.

ILLUSTRATIONS Illustrations such as stories, pictures, and slides help make ideas more vivid for listeners because they create a visualization or image of the topic to be discussed. For example, showing pictures of the results of a new skin-grafting process for burn victims clearly illustrates the topic to be discussed. Similarly, a speaker who is going to talk about the need for well-equipped police cars can begin a speech by saying, "Picture yourself on a dark road some night with car trouble or maybe even an injury that prevents you from driving. Suddenly you see the headlights of a car. It could belong to almost anyone. But wouldn't you feel better if it turned out to be a police officer with all the equipment you needed?"

One form of illustration is a historical reference in which the speaker tells a story or uses instances of historical happenings that draw the listeners' interest into the topic of the speech. For example, a speaker at the dedication of the newly renovated Stamp Student Union on the University of Maryland campus began with a series of historical events that had occurred in the old student center during the past fifty years, including that in 1963, Bill Cosby met the woman who was to be his wife; in 1979, Kermit the Frog delivered a homecoming speech; in 1992, author Alex Haley presented his last lecture, and in 2008, a presidential nomination debate took place in the venue.

Introductions containing personal references give a speaker's reasons for undertaking a presentation on a specific topic.

Humorous stories often are an effective way to start a presentation.

RHETORICAL QUESTIONS Questions for which no outward response is expected are *rhetorical questions*. For example, a speaker may say to an audience, "Have you ever asked yourself what you would do if someone tried to rob you?" In this case, the speaker does not intend to count how many people in the audience have or have not asked themselves the question. Instead, the purpose is to have audience members ask themselves the question so as to build their curiosity or interest.

Although they are sometimes overused, rhetorical questions can be an effective method of getting the audience to ponder a topic and to engage them right from the start.

ACTION QUESTIONS *Action questions* are a means of getting the audience involved in a speech and making listeners think and respond. For example, a speaker started a presentation by asking, "How many of you have been involved in an auto accident?" After the hands went up, the speaker said, "For those of you with your hands up, do you remember that instant when you knew the accident was going to happen and you couldn't do anything about it? What flashed through your mind?" After getting some answers from the audience, the speaker said, "Yes, a common response is helplessness and fear." Thus, the speaker involved the audience and was able to move their attention to the next segment of the speech, which centered on how to overcome the feelings of helplessness caused by fear and despair.

UNUSUAL OR DRAMATIC DEVICES Unusual or dramatic devices get the audience's attention because of their curiosity or shock value. In one dramatic opening, a medical lab technician set up equipment and drew blood from a student volunteer to show how blood is analyzed.

QUOTATIONS RELATED TO THE THEME Speakers sometimes begin by quoting a famous person or expert, reading an account of a specific event, reciting a section of a poem or play, or reading a newspaper editorial. The quotations should be relevant to the topic and be read meaningfully. The greatest mistake many speakers make in presenting a quotation is to select an appropriate piece and then speed through the reading or fail to stress the meaning.

STATING THE THEME Theme statements indicate to the audience exactly what the speaker is going to talk about. Unfortunately, many untrained speakers start out their presentations by saying, "Today I am going to tell you about . . . ." This is not a creative or attention-getting opener.

A more creative theme statement is likely to hold the audience's attention. For example, a police officer started her presentation by saying, "There is a right way and a wrong way to respond to a police officer who has stopped you for speeding. Even

Unusual or dramatic devices get attention because of their curiosity or shock value.

though this is a stressful situation, you need to make the right choices when communicating with the officer. Let's look at those choices."

Orienting Material

Orienting material gives an audience the background necessary to understand the basic material of the speech. It is designed to tie the material to the central idea, provide necessary information, establish personal credibility for the speaker, and make the subject important to the listener. Orienting material can include such clarifiers as providing a historical background, defining terms that will be used in the presentation, tying the speaker's personal history to the subject, using statistics to identify how many people are affected, and illuminating the importance of the ideas to the listener.

HISTORICAL BACKGROUND   Often a speaker has to explain what led up to the present time so an audience can gain the necessary historical background. For example, a speech intended to persuade the audience to vote for a renewal of a school levy ought to include the facts that illustrate the history of the levy.

DEFINING TERMS   Although terms usually are defined at the place they are used in a speech, sometimes the very nature of a speech depends on the audience's having an understanding near the start of the presentation. For example, in a speech about agoraphobia, its definition as an emotional illness that manifests itself in a person's not wanting to appear in public should appear near the beginning of the presentation. Only terms that are universal to the speech should be included in the orientation.

PERSONAL HISTORY AND/OR TIE TO THE TOPIC   A speaker can gain credibility if she or he has some personal tie or experience related to the topic. A speaker intending to demonstrate the steps in mouth-to-mouth resuscitation could refer to his Red Cross training and his background as a lifeguard. This documentation establishes the speaker's authority to speak about the subject.

IMPORTANCE TO THE LISTENERS   One of the most critical parts of the orienting material is relating the subject to the listeners in some way. Listeners pay attention to ideas and issues that are relevant to them, so it is helpful if the speaker makes that link at the outset. One good strategy is to show the importance of the topic based on the interests of the audience. For example, "The Internal Revenue Service reports that an average of 107 million income tax forms are filed yearly. Many of these are incorrect and result in millions of lost refunds. Hopefully, your tax form was not one of these."

The Central Idea

The **statement of the speech's central idea** is intended to keep the speaker on course for developing a purposeful and well-organized speech. It also indicates the response the speaker wants from listeners. If, for example, the central idea of a speech is stated as "There are two reasons why we should all vote for the school bond issue on November 2," both the speaker and the audience are clear about the topic, the method of developing that topic, and what is desired from the audience.

The importance of stating the central idea in a speech cannot be overemphasized. Speakers who skip this important part of the speech deprive the listeners of the clue they may need to determine the exact point of the speech. The central idea should be presented as a statement, because a speaker who uses a question (e.g., "Should the federal government provide financial aid to private educational institutions?") is not indicating to listeners what the main point really is. But a speaker who presents the point as a statement ("There are three reasons that I believe the federal government should not provide financial aid to private educational institutions") is clarifying the stand that will be advocated and how the body of the speech will be organized.

In some persuasive speeches, when listeners initially may disagree with some aspect of the speaker's purpose, an effective speaker might choose to delay an indication of listeners' response by starting with common ground and unfolding ideas that move listeners from initial disagreement to some acceptance of the speaker's proposal.

The Body

The **body of a speech** develops through major points as well as any subpoints needed to develop the speaker's central idea. The major points are placed in a structured format. In this way, the listeners should have little trouble understanding the message.

One of the questions often asked by those learning the techniques of structuring and organizing a speech centers on how many points to use in the body of the speech. "Cognitive psychologists tell us we learn better when we portion blocks of information into 3 to 7 major units."[4] Most communication instructors "recommend 3 to 5 major points."[5]

Traditional Methods of Arrangement for the Body of a Speech

The **method of issue arrangement for the body of a speech** in the Euro-American culture traditionally takes one of six forms: spatial arrangement, time arrangement, topical arrangement, causal arrangement, comparison–contrast arrangement, or problem-solution arrangement. The method selected acts as a guide for sequencing information for listener clarity. *Note:* These examples do not list the sources of the material by indicating the oral footnotes that would be included in the speeches. In a speech, these sources would be included.

SPATIAL ARRANGEMENT   Many people organize information automatically even though they are not aware of it. Suppose some friends are visiting you at your college. They have never been on your campus before, so they ask you to tell them about the institution. You start by describing the buildings located on the south end of the campus and then proceed to talk about all the other buildings, noting their locations from south to north. You have organized your presentation according to the **spatial method of issue arrangement.** You have set a *point of reference* at a specific location and followed a *geographic pattern.* The pattern can be left to right, north to south, or from the center to the outside. This is a common method for giving directions or describing something by its location.

We can see how spatial arrangement can be used for the body of a speech whose central idea is "to inform the audience of the financial tax base of Maryland by examining the state's patterns from west to east." Here is a possible outline of the body of the speech with major headings spatially arranged according to geographical location:

III. Financial Tax Base of the State of Maryland

    A. Western Maryland

        1. Cumberland

        2. Hagerstown

    B. Central Maryland

        1. Baltimore

        2. Rockville

        3. Potomac

    C. Eastern Maryland

        1. Annapolis

        2. Ocean City

The body of a speech develops through major points as well as any subpoints needed to develop the speaker's central idea.

TIME ARRANGEMENT   The **time method of issue arrangement** orders information from a beginning point to an ending one, with all the steps developed in numerical or time sequence. Research shows that using a time method of issue arrangement increases a listener's retention of a speaker's information.[6]

For example, chronological arrangement can be used to develop the body of the speech whose central idea is "to inform the audience of the accomplishments of the last four Chinese dynasties." The outline of the body for the speech would read:

III. Four dynasties mark the end of China's experience with monarchy and foreshadowed modern times.

   A. AD 960–1280: Song (Sung)

      1. Paper money invented

      2. Primitive printing press developed

      3. Scholars active

         a. Books printed

         b. Painting reached zenith

   B. AD 1280–1368: Yuan

      1. Became part of an empire that stretched to Europe

      2. Silk Road reopened

      3. New religions introduced

   C. AD 1368–1644: Ming

      1. Agricultural methods of production developed

      2. Great sea expeditions undertaken

   D. AD 1644–1911: Qing (Ching)

      1. Tobacco and corn industries developed

      2. Lost Korea, Taiwan, and the Pescadores Islands

TOPICAL ARRANGEMENT   Ideas can be organized on the basis of their similarities or other relationships. Thus, in using a **topical method of issue arrangement,** a speaker explains an idea in terms of its component parts. For example, in speaking about dogs, a speaker may discuss cocker spaniels, poodles, and then collies, developing ideas about each breed (the component part) completely before going on to the next one. The speaker also can organize the presentation of ideas by talking about the temperament of each breed, and then about the sizes of each breed, and finally about the coloring of each breed. In this way, the speaker is organizing ideas by classifying the animals according to specific identifiable characteristics (the component parts) and then developing each subsection into identifiable patterns of information.

Although there is no set sequence in which topics must be presented in the topical arrangement, main points might be made in their order of relevance, importance, or priority, or even given alphabetical order. The key to an effective topic arrangement is for the speaker to create and communicate a rationale for the main points.

As illustrated in the following example, with a central idea of exposing the audience to the topics and the order in which they will be discussed, you might say, "There is a misconception among Americans that since there has been a decrease in AIDS, the epidemic is over. Some of this reasoning is based on a lack of knowledge about the disease. I think a refresher course in AIDS is necessary, so today I'm going to define *AIDS/HIV,* reveal the origin of HIV, and give a brief history of HIV in the United States.

III. HIV/AIDS

  A. What is HIV/AIDS?

    1. Viral infection

      a. Gradually destroys the immune system

      b. Results in infections that are hard for the body to fight

    2. Occurs by the transfer of fluids

      a. Blood

      b. Semen

      c. Vaginal fluid

      d. Pre-ejaculate

      e. Breast milk

    3. Routes of transmission

      a. Unprotected sex

      b. Contaminated needles

      c. Breast milk

      d. Transmission from an infected mother to her baby at birth

  B. Origin of HIV

    1. Scientists identified a type of chimpanzee in West Africa as the source of HIV infection in humans

    2. Virus most likely jumped to humans when chimpanzee meat was eaten

    3. Virus spread across Africa to other parts of the world

  C. History of HIV in the United States

    1. First identified in 1981

    2. Test for virus developed

    3. During early 1980s, 150,000 people a year were infected with HIV

    4. AIDS cases began to fall dramatically in 1996

      a. New drugs

      b. Awareness of how disease is spread

    5. About one-quarter of people with HIV or AIDS do not know they are infected

      a. Put themselves at risk

      b. Put others at risk

CAUSAL ARRANGEMENT   The **causal method of issue arrangement** shows how two or more events are connected in such a way that if one occurs, the other will necessarily follow. In other words, if one incident happened, it caused the second incident to happen. This is a good method to use when a specific observable result can be understood by determining what happened.

    This outline was developed for the body of a speech whose central idea was "to list and discuss the theory that a series of identifiable events can result in the development of agoraphobia":

III. Series of Events Resulting in the Development of Agoraphobia

  A. Sequence of events

    1. First event

    a. Physical symptoms such as heart palpitations, trembling, sweating, breathlessness, dizziness

    b. No apparent cause for the physical symptoms

  2. Second event

    a. Duplication of physical symptoms in a place similar to the site of the first event

    b. Increasing awareness of fear of going to certain places

  3. Third event

    a. Symptoms occurring when there is a thought of going to a place similar to the site of the first event's occurrence

    b. Feeling of being out of control when thinking of leaving the safety site (usually the home)

B. Result: agoraphobia

  1. Personality changes

    a. Frequent anxiety

    b. Depression

    c. Loss of individual character

  2. Emotional changes

    a. Impassiveness

    b. High degree of dependence on others

    c. Constant alertness

Note that the events leading up to the final result are listed, with the final result discussed last. An alternative form would have been to give the final result first and then list the events leading up to it. The former method is called *cause(s) to effect;* the latter is *effect from cause(s).*

COMPARISON–CONTRAST ARRANGEMENT   Suppose you are asked to explain the similarities between a community college and a four-year institution. Your explanation could follow the **comparison method of issue organization,** in which you would tell how the two types of institutions are alike. In the case of the colleges, you could talk about the similarities in curriculum, staff, facilities, activity programs, and costs. If, however, you are asked to tell the differences between the two, you would use the **contrast method of issue arrangement,** developing the ideas by giving specific examples of differences between the two types of institutions. A speech based on the **comparison–contrast method of issue arrangement** shows both similarities and differences.

Here is the body of a speech with a central idea of "informing the audience of some similarities and differences between high-context and low-context society's communication patterns":

III. Similarities and differences regarding high- and low-context society's communication patterns

  A. Similarities

    1. Both high- and low-context communication societies express ideas in verbal messages

    2. Both high- and low-context communication societies express ideas in languages

  3. General consistency within each society as to the context of the system used

B. Differences

  1. Expression of intentions

    a. High-context emphasis is on how intention or meaning can be conveyed through the social roles or positions of the participants by both verbal and nonverbal means

    b. Low-context emphasis is on how meaning is best expressed through explicit verbal messages

  2. Value base of expression

    a. High-context emphasis is on collectivistic values

    b. Low-context emphasis is on individualistic values

  3. Verbal style

    a. High context—indirect verbal style

    b. Low context—direct verbal style

An alternative way of presenting the material would be to explain by examining how the communication of high- and low-context societies are different. The outline for that speech would be:

III. There are differences between the way high- and low-context communication takes place

A. High-context societies

  1. Collectivistic values

  2. Spiral logic

  3. Indirect verbal style

  4. Verbal reticence or silence

B. Low-context societies

  1. Individualistic values

  2. Linear logic

  3. Direct verbal style

  4. Verbal assertiveness or talkativeness

PROBLEM-SOLUTION ARRANGEMENT The **problem-solution method of issue arrangement** is used when a speaker attempts to identify what is wrong and to determine how to cure it or make a recommendation for its cure. This method can be used to think through a problem and then structure a speech. A person dealing with the problem of child abuse, for instance, may wish to begin by analyzing the problem: the influence of family history, the lack of parental control or knowledge, and the different types of child abuse. Such an analysis could then lead to a consideration of various solutions, such as stricter legislation mandating penalties for child abuse, stronger enforcement of child abuse laws, improved reporting procedures, and greater availability of social services to parents and children alike.

When you develop a problem-solution message, your sequence should state the problem, its cause, its possible solutions, and the selected solution. This organization allows your listeners to share a complete picture of your reasoning process.

Here is an example of a speech outline using problem-solution for the body of a speech with the central idea "to inform the audience what anger is and some methods of coping with anger":

III. What is anger and how can it be dealt with?

   A. Anger defined

      1. Anger is an emotional state that may range in intensity from mild irritation to intense fury and rage

      2. Anger can have such physical effects as an increase in heart rate and blood pressure

      3. Biological influences

         a. Temporal lobe epilepsy

         b. Temperament

         c. Substance abuse

         d. Chemical imbalance

      4. Psychological influence

         a. Cognitive/Perceptual style

         b. Interactional/Interpersonal style

         c. Coping style

   B. Treatment for anger

      1. Venting

         a. Free expression to the anger

         b. Volcanic reactions

      2. Ventilation

         a. Talking out of feelings rather than acting them out

         b. Talking them out in a positive way

Speakers who don't have a clear purpose risk not getting their point across to the audience.

3. The lifesaver technique

    a. Suck on a lifesaver until it's all gone before your respond to your anger

    b. Delays action and gives the mind a chance to change from the emotional to the logical state

4. The Keep My Cool Technique

    a. Label the anger

    b. Respond, don't react; emotions come and go

    c. Reconnoiter—identify the who, where, why, and what

    d. Review your options

    e. Respond by ventilating

    f. Reward yourself

A more detailed presentation of the speech can include discussions of testing each of the solutions. This can be accomplished by including subdivisions under each of the statements of the solution to explore whether it is *workable* (developing why the suggestion will solve or help solve the problem), *desirable* (explaining why the suggestion will not cause greater problems), and *practical* (indicating if and how the suggestion can be put into practice).

An alternative form of the problem-solution method is the *see-blame-cure-cost method*. In this approach, the evil or problem that exists is examined (see); what has caused the problem is determined (blame); solutions are investigated, and the most practical solution is selected (cure); and what finances, time, or emotions will have to be expended (cost) are examined.

MAJOR AND INTERNAL METHODS OF ARRANGEMENT   For each speech, the speaker usually selects one major method of development, always keeping in mind that other methods may be used as necessary to present subdivisions of the complete idea. For instance, in developing a presentation on the causes of World War II, a speaker may decide to use a chronological arrangement as the major method of development and a spatial method for some of the subtopical segments of the presentation. Thus, the speaker may talk about the political and social changes in the 1920s in England, France, Germany, Russia, and Japan; then proceed to tell about events in the early 1930s in these countries; and then discuss happenings in these countries in the mid-1930s. In this way, the audience can develop a listening pattern that allows for clarity of comprehension through the decade span and then the location.

No matter which pattern you use to develop a message, maintain that pattern consistently throughout your presentation. Otherwise, your audience will be confused by sudden shifts or failure to follow a sequence to its logical conclusion.

The Conclusion

Depending on the purpose of a speech, the **conclusion of a speech** can be used to summarize and/or motivate listeners to take a prescribed action.

Summary

Whatever the purpose, a presentation should end with a *summary of a speech* that restates the major points to recap what has been covered. The guide for developing the

Socially Communicating

Openers and Closers: Using Stories and Jokes

The Roman Gladiator, Androcles, developed quite a reputation for staying alive. He was frequently thrown to the lions, and, just as frequently, he returned alive. He always used the same approach. Just as the lion was about to eat him, Androcles would whisper in his ear, and the animal would appear to lose his appetite and slink away with a defeated look.

Finally, the Roman emperor called him to his court. "Androcles," he said, "I can take it no longer. I need to know your secret." "It's this way, your highness,"

Androcles said. "I merely remind the lion that when he has finished dinner, he'll be asked to say a few words. I'm living proof that lions don't like to give after-dinner talks!"

The key is to make sure the story fits your topic and can lead right into it. After this story, I say, "I know a lot of people, too, who don't like to make after-dinner talks, or after-lunch talks, or before-lunch talks, . . ."

Source: Lillian D. Bjorseth, "Improving Your Public Speaking: Openers and Closers," *The Sideroad,* www.sideroad.com/Public_Speaking/ improve-public-speaking.html, 2007.

summary is to refer to the major headings in the body of the speech and indicate how they develop the statement of central idea.

Clincher

Many speakers, speechwriters, and speech coaches agree that all speeches should end with a summary of the major points, followed by a *clincher to the speech,* which gives the speaker one more chance to reinforce the major ideas presented and then wraps up the presentation with a final message to clinch the selling of the central idea. The outline of the conclusion section of a speech that includes a clincher would be:

IV. Conclusion

    A. Summary

    B. Clincher

Clincher techniques are similar to attention-getting introduction methods—for example:

- *Personal reference.* A speaker who established expertise at the start of a speech can reestablish his or her authority in the conclusion.

- *Humorous story.* A humorous story summarizes the speaker's ideas. For example, a presentation about public speaking anxiety could end with "The mind is an amazing thing; it starts working the moment you are born and never stops until you get up to give a speech."

- *Illustration.* A drug counselor can end a speech on substance abuse with a story about a client's success in turning away from the drug scene.

- *Rhetorical question.* A speaker who posed a rhetorical question at the beginning of a presentation can conclude by answering it.

- *Unusual or dramatic devices.* A speaker concluded a speech about the necessity of proper dental hygiene by passing out a small cup of disclosing solution and small mirror to each member of the audience. She then asked each of them to rinse out their mouths with the solution, which turned plaque and other substances on or between the teeth bright red. This activity effectively illustrated the importance of proper brushing—and the value of unusual or dramatic devices.

- *Quotations.* A quotation that restates the major theme of a presentation can be used in ending it. A speaker could summarize a speech against the death penalty, for example, by reading the vivid description of an execution presented in Truman Capote's classic book *In Cold Blood.*

- *Repetition.* Closing a speech with repetition ties it back to the introduction. It makes for a circular presentation, which many speakers find to be the most effective concluding device because it clearly wraps up the speech by coming back to the statement of central idea which laid out the topic and format for the speech.

Transition into the Question-and-Answer Session

If a question-and-answer session is to follow the prepared address, the speaker should incorporate a transition into the conclusion section. The speaker might say, for example, "And so we've seen what I consider to be the effects of our current policy on the national security database. I'd be happy to respond to any questions you may have." If there are going to be restrictions on the question-and-answer session, this would also be the appropriate place to mention them. For instance, you might also say, "I would appreciate it if you would restrict your comments to a specific question rather than express your stand on the issue."

If the question-and-answer transition is used, the outline of the conclusion section of a speech would be:

IV. Conclusion

    A. Summary

    B. Clincher

    C. Transition to question-and-answer session

Alternative Methods for Organizing the Speech

"In addition to the traditional patterns usually taught in U.S. public speaking classes, communication theorists are constantly looking at other organizational patterns."[7] These methods include those used by women, ethnic, religious, and racial speakers, as well as some concepts developed by those who perceive that there may be some alternative ways to structure the bodies of speeches to allow for ease in both preparation and receipt of the message. The search for alternatives centers on the idea "that many speakers are uncomfortable with the standard organizational patterns due to cultural backgrounds or personal inclinations."[8] As a speaker, you should choose that organizational pattern that will best meet your communication goals and your listeners' needs.

In organizing a speech, you, the speaker, must make careful decisions about the type of introduction, statement of central idea, methods of arranging the material in the body of your speech, and various techniques you can use to conclude. Alternative methods include the partitioning, unfolding and case methods.[9]

Partitioning Method

The **partitioning organizational speech structure** is a deductive format in which, as the speech proceeds, the speech is partitioned into a number of points. In developing the speech, you state your point and then develop each point with supporting details. This format lends itself to informative speaking (see Chapter 15).

When using this type of organization, you start with the introduction (I), state the central idea (IIA), then preview the points you will be making in the speech (IIB), and then specifically tell the audience the main issues you will be covering in the body of the speech (IIC). The main issues should be organized by one of the traditional methods of organization discussed on pages 359–365.

Part IIC, the listing of how the main issues will be presented in the speech, is the **partitioning step,** as it divides (partitions) the topic. Part IIC may be viewed as the "road map" of the speech because it specifically tells the audience where the "main stops" will take place on the road through the body of the speech. A speaker, for example, whose central idea is that "there are several problems with the use of radiation therapy" might say, "To understand these radiological difficulties, we will look at the harmful effects of radiation therapy, the after-effects of receiving radiation, and the poor quality of radiation facilities in hospitals." The "stops," as the speech progresses, will be at "harmful effects," "after-effects," and "poor quality of the radiation facilities." These segments are arranged by the topic method of arrangement.

As you proceed from segment to segment, you should use transitions, which are statements of what the next segment will be. The *transition* forecasts the coming issue. For example, you could say, "Turning, then, to our first point, let's consider the current state of facilities and equipment that exists today for radiation therapy." You would continue to use transitions for each connection between major segments of the body to help listeners understand and remember.

Except for the first transition, which forecasts only what is going to be presented in the upcoming section, the other transition consists of two parts: a restatement of the previous issue and a forecast of the next one. When moving from the second segment of the body of the speech to the third, you, the speaker, would state, "Yes, there are harmful effects of radiation therapy. Let's now examine the after-effects of receiving radiation."

Once the last issue in a partitioned speech has been discussed, the presentation ends with a conclusion that restates the central idea and the main issues. As in any good conclusion, this summary gives listeners a chance to review the points that have been discussed.

A general outline for the partitioning sequence looks like this:

I. Introduction

   A. Attention material

   B. Orienting material

II. Central Idea

   A. Statement of central idea

   B. Preview of how the central idea will be developed

   C. Listing of issues arranged by the method of issue arrangement

      1. First main issue

      2. Second main issue

      3. Third main issue

      (and so on)

III. Body (Transition: forecast of the first issue)

   A. First main issue

      1. Discussion of first main issue through examples, illustrations, and explanations

    2. Additional discussion of first main issue through examples, illustrations, and explanations (and so on)

      (Transition: restatement of first main issue and forecast of second issue)

  B. Second main issue

    1. Discussion of second main issue

    2. Additional discussion of second main issue (and so on)

      (Transition: restatement of second main issue and forecast of third issue)

  C. Third main issue

    1. Discussion of third main issue

    2. Additional discussion of third main issue (and so on)

IV. Conclusion

  A. Summary (restatement of issues and central idea)

  B. Clincher

Here is an example of a speech following the partitioning method of organization. Its central idea is "to inform the audience of the alternatives an intake counselor has by listing and discussing the alternatives available":

I. Introduction

  A. Attention material: Each of us probably makes hundreds of decisions every day. We decide what to eat, what to wear, what television program to watch, what time to go to bed.

  B. Orienting material: In my work as an intake counselor with the Department of Juvenile Services, I must make decisions that can seriously affect a child's life. An intake counselor gets the police report when a juvenile commits a crime, calls in the parents and the child to decide what actions should be taken, and counsels them. An investigation of such work can help you understand some of the procedures that local governments use to combat the problems of juvenile delinquency.

II. Central Idea

  A. Let us consider the alternatives an intake counselor has.

  B. The counselor can select from three major decisions.

  C. These decisions are to

    1. Send the case to court.

    2. Close the case at intake.

    3. Place the child on informal supervision for forty-five days.

III. Body

  (One decision a counselor may make is to send the case to court.)

  A. The law states that you must send the case to court if

    1. The charge is denied.

    2. The juvenile has a prior record.

    3. You notice signs of trouble in the family.

    4. The case is like Felicia's. Felicia . . .

      (Thus a case may be sent to court. A counselor also may decide to close a case at intake.)

B. There are several reasons for closing the case at intake.

1. The child admits guilt.

2. The incident was a first offense.

3. The parents are supportive, and the home life is stable.

4. An example of a case closed at intake was Henrietta's. Henrietta . . .

(As a result, a case may be closed at intake. A counselor also may decide to put a juvenile under informal supervision.)

C. Supervision for forty-five days is warranted if

1. The child or the family is in need of short-term counseling.

2. The procedure is not used often.

3. The court has never ordered this in the past.

4. The case is like Lamont's. Lamont . . .

(Through informal supervision, some children can be helped.)

IV. Conclusion

A. Summary: The basic decision is whether to arrange court appearances, stop the action at the beginning, or supervise the client.

B. Clincher: The goal of the whole intake process is to provide whatever is best for the child so that he or she will have proper care, treatment, and supervision.

Although partitioning organization can be used for a speech of any purpose, it is especially well suited to informative speaking and informative briefing. Because the aim of such a speech is to increase the listener's comprehension of a particular body of information, a clear structure and repetition of the major points are warranted.

Unfolding Method

Another alternative pattern that can be used is the **unfolding organizational speech structure.** This is an inductive style in which the speaker lays out supporting evidence and then draws a conclusion, leading the listeners to be drawn into the argument.

The *inductive reasoning process* begins with specific instances or examples, then formulates a reasonable generalization or conclusion from them.[10] One test of whether the instances effectively develop the concepts presented is "Is the conclusion reached *expected*" and "*accepted*."[11] If, for example, you said to someone, "One plus one is two." The person would accept what you said since the expected answer to "one plus one is ___" is "two." On the other hand, if you said, "One plus one is nine," the person should reject your solution. The expected outcome is "two," not "nine." Since the expected answer is not presented, the answer will not be accepted. Moral: In developing the arguments to prove your various contentions, be sure to use statistics, examples, and other information that will lead audience members to accept your answer because the conclusion you reach is the expected conclusion.

Three major tests can be used to evaluate the examples that are used to reach the conclusions:[12]

1. Are enough cases represented to justify the conclusion? Or are you forming a conclusion based on only a few examples?

2. Are the examples typical? That is, do they represent the average members of the population to which the generalizations are applied? Or are they extreme cases that may show what could happen, but not what usually happens?

3. Are the examples from the time under discussion, or are they out of date?

The unfolding format lends itself to persuasive speaking (as will be discussed in Chapter 16). The basic format for the unfolding method, as the title indicates, is to get the audience's attention and provide the necessary orienting material in the introduction, state the central idea, and then present the body of the speech in an order that unfolds the arguments in favor of the proposal one at a time, one building on the other, so the speaker's arguments for the speech build one on the other. For example, a speaker who believes that a particular candidate for office is the best candidate would give a basic reason for his belief (the candidate has shown good character), another factor (she has used that good character to do good deeds), then (her good deeds have resulted in progressive legislature being passed which has helped the community), then (this help for the community is the basis for her seeking higher office which she has proven she is capable of holding.)

Here is a sequence for an unfolding format:

I. Introduction

    A. Attention material

    B. Orienting material

II. Statement of Central Idea

III. Body (organized by some method of issue arrangement)

    (Transition)

    A. First issue

        1. Discussion of first issue through examples, illustrations, and explanations

        2. Additional discussion of first issue through examples, illustrations, and explanations (and so on)

        (Transition)

    B. Second issue

        1. Discussion of second issue through examples, illustrations, and explanations

        2. Additional discussion of second issue through examples, illustrations, and explanations (and so on)

        (Transition)

    C. Third issue

        1. Discussion of third issue through examples, illustrations, and explanations

        2. Additional discussion of third issue through examples, illustrations, and explanations (and so on)

IV. Conclusion

    A. Restatement

    B. Clincher

This next outline develops a speech according to the unfolding method of organization. The central idea is "to persuade each member of the audience, by listing and discussing the reasons, that he or she should donate his or her body to science":

I. Introduction

    A. Attention material: Picture a three-year-old girl attached to a kidney dialysis machine once a week for the rest of her life. Picture a little boy whose world is blackness, or a father who is confined to his bed because he has a weak heart.

B. Orienting material: Such pictures are not very pleasant. But you can do something about them.

II. Statement of Central Idea: You should donate your body to science.

III. Body

A. Organ banks need organs so that people who need them may function normally.

1. List of organs that can be donated

2. The need for speed in transplanting organs (thus specific organs can be used)

B. Organ donations have been used both to save lives and to improve the quality of life of the recipients.

1. Statistics on the number of donors

2. Statistics on the number of lives saved

3. Examples of the improved quality of life of recipients

C. Your body can also be used as an instrument for medical education.

1. Who can donate and how

2. The need to eliminate shortages

(As a result, your entire body can continue to serve a useful purpose.)

IV. Conclusion

A. Summary

1. Organs are needed so that others can function normally.

2. Your body can be used for medical education.

B. Clincher

1. I am a benevolent person who believes that everyone is born with a benevolent nature. I know that you and I will help those less fortunate than we are. I am a potential organ and cadaver donor through my will. A donor's card can be obtained through any medical foundation. I cannot overemphasize the need for body and organ donations.

2. Don't, as the proverb states, wait for George to do it. You do it! Take immediate action to become an organ and cadaver donor.

There are alternative formats that can be used for the unfolding method, but the general idea is the same. For example, if your prior analysis reveals that members of the audience oppose your stand, you should not state the central idea early in the presentation. If this is the case, you actually present the body of the speech before stating the central idea, thus not "tipping your hand" too early and giving yourself a chance to build your case before you come to your stand. For example, if you are trying to persuade an audience composed of Republicans to vote for the Democratic candidate you favor, it would be wise to lay the foundation of the stands your candidate has taken that agree with the views of the audience and can benefit the listeners. Then propose they vote for her. Some members may be swayed to your side.

In this variation, you present the main points, moving from areas of shared agreement. If you arrange and develop the main issues carefully, establishing your purpose statement just before you reach the conclusion, you may be able to get your desired effect. This outline illustrates this alternative method for using the unfolding format:

I. Introduction

A. Attention material

B. Orienting material

(Transition)

II. Body (organized by some method of issue arrangement)

A. Discussion of first issue

1. Examples and illustrations

2. Examples and illustrations (and so on)

B. Statement of first issue

(Transition)

C. Discussion of second issue

1. Examples and illustrations

2. Examples and illustrations (and so on)

(Transition)

III. Statement of Central Idea

(Transition)

IV. Conclusion

A. Restatement

B. Clincher

Case Method

Another alternative method is the **case method of organizational speech structure** in which the speaker discusses the central idea without breaking it into subpoints. As a result, this format is especially suitable for a single-issue speech. If, for example, your central idea is that "left-handed people are discriminated against," then the body of the speech includes a series of examples of how left-handed people are discriminated against.

Here is the general format for a speech developed by case organization:

I. Introduction

A. Attention material

B. Orienting material

(Transition)

II. Central Idea

(Transition)

III. Body (organized in a sequence)

A. Example (a case)

(Transition)

B. Example (a case)

(Transition)

C. Example (a case, and so on)

(Transition)

IV. Conclusion

A. Summary

B. Clincher

The following outline develops a speech according to the case method of organization. As with the partitioning method, cases or examples may be arranged chronologically, spatially, or by a speaker's own creativity. The central idea is "to inform the audience of some ways in which left-handers are discriminated against from their fingers to their souls (spatial method of development)":

I. Introduction

    A. Attention material: Have you ever pondered the design of a butter knife or the structure of a gravy ladle?

    B. Orienting material: These structural problems are important to all of us who are afflicted with a key social problem: left-handedness.

    (Those of us who are left-handed believe that . . .)

II. Statement of Central Idea

    A. Left-handers are discriminated against.

    B. Let's look at some examples.

III. Body

    A. Example: Tell a story of the difficulties encountered when using scissors.

    (Transition: Another experience I've had . . .)

    B. Example: Tell a story of the problems with school desks designed for right-handed people.

    (Transition: This experience points out another one . . .)

    C. Example: Tell a story of the problems with words such as *gauche* and *south-paw*.

    (Transition: So you see . . .)

IV. Conclusion

    A. Summary: Left-handers are discriminated against all the way from the design of scissors to the names they are called.

    B. Clincher: If you are left-handed, however, no matter the discrimination, you are in good company: Eleven presidents of the United States have been left-handed!

 ## Role of Culture on Speech Structure

It should be recognized that the American way of structuring speeches is not the way listeners from other cultures are accustomed to attending to presentations. Here are some examples of how culture affects the organization of ideas:

- In some cultures, a *spiral form of explanation* is used. In this mode, a statement is made and then a story or analogy that deals with the statement is presented. It is left to the listener to apply the parallels and draw outcomes related to the original statement. (In other words, the traditional conclusion step is not included in the speech.) This is a method often used in Arabic, Native American, and some Asian cultures.

- Arabic speakers value telling a story or a series of parables and letting the listeners figure out the moral of the narrative. This indirect presentational style, with little structure, often confuses those who are used to a direct format in which a statement is made and evidence is presented to clarify the proposition.

Culturally Communicating

Foreign Audience? Differences in Cultural Patterns

■ You might think you are putting your audience to sleep in Japan, but don't worry. In Japan it is common to show concentration and attentiveness in public by closing the eyes and nodding the head up and down slightly.—Then again, maybe you really are boring.

■ Applause is accepted as a form of approval in most areas of the world. In the United States, applause is sometimes accompanied by whistling. If you hear whistles in many parts of Europe, you better run because it is a signal of disapproval.

■ If you were finishing a speaking engagement in Argentina and you waved goodbye, U.S. style, the members of the audience might all turn around and come back to sit down. To them the wave means, "Hey! Come back." In other parts of Latin America and in Europe the same wave means "no."

■ Do not expect standing ovations when speaking in public in Australia. It doesn't seem to be part of their culture.

■ South of the border people don't like us to refer to ourselves as Americans. We must remember that we are not the only ones. There are North Americans, Central Americans and South Americans.

Source: "Public Speaking: International Perspective on Humor," Advance Public Speaking Institute, www.public-speaking.org/public-speaking-international-article.htm, 2007.

■ Arabs use "a completely different persuasive style than that set in Western logic. The Arabic argumentative style depends greatly on parables from the *Koran*, which are based on the concept 'because Islam says so.'"[13] This organizational style often causes Western listeners to disregard the information because it is not based on logic proofs, such as statistics and research findings.

■ Because discourse for Navajos is designed to secure order, harmony, and balance, they are interested in dialogue, not a speaker who is expounding a point of view to silent listeners. Public speaking, Navajo style, is interactive, with no prescribed structure.[14] Most Native Americans, representing the communication style of high-context cultures, resort to hints and implicit analogies, rather than direct statements.[15]

■ The overall Russian persuasion style centers on a structure pattern that starts with "an agreement in principle (i.e., the big picture) and then fills in the details. Russian negotiators, consider compromise as a sign of weakness, a retreat from a correct and morally justified position, therefore, they are prepared to wait out their opposition."[16]

■ The Chinese tend to present ideas through a variety of indirectly related views. Their pattern is the opening, amplification, preliminary exposition, first argument, second argument, third argument, final argument, and conclusion. The most important part is the amplification, which consists of two or

Communicating in Careers

Considering Organizational Culture

Whenever you speak within an organization, learn as much as you can about its culture before you create your speech—even expectations for introductions can differ in specific settings. Today, for example, was graduation day at my university, and a business leader from the community gave the commencement address. She did not start with a statistic, a visual aid, or any other attention strategy mentioned in this chapter; instead, she first referred to the occasion, congratulated the graduates, and expressed respect for the university—acknowledging both the organization and the cultural event (graduation) before introducing the topic of her speech. It would have seemed abrupt and strange to the graduates and their families on this special occasion if she had launched into her speech immediately.

Source: Clella Jaffe, *Public Speaking: Concepts and Skills for a Diverse Society* (Belmont, CA: Wadsworth/Thomson Learning, 2001), p. 193.

REFLECT ON THIS:

1. Where can you find out about a corporation's culture?

2. Why would it have seemed abrupt and strange to the audience if the speaker had launched into her speech immediately?

African American rhetoric depends on a unique style of language for its effectiveness.

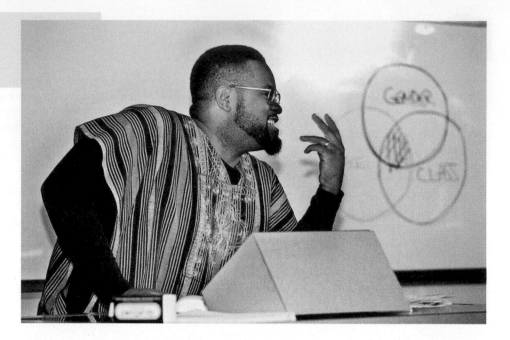

three sentences that express the topic. This is in contrast to the European American tradition of the body being the most important part of the presentation because it amplifies the reason for taking specific actions.

- Japanese speakers can be indirect in what they want the listener to know. The Japanese language forces the listener to construct meaning based on shared knowledge between the listener and the speaker.[17]

- African Americans are a high-context culture in which the group is more important than the individual. Often there is no specific theme or organizational pattern but a stringing together of stories, anecdotes, and biblical quotations in a random order.[18]

- Athabaskans, an oral-based society of native Alaskan speakers, "think it rude to explicitly state the conclusions they want listeners to draw. It is enough for them to simply present a set of facts and let audience members draw their own conclusions."[19]

- "Members of Italian, Slavic, Jewish, and many African cultures have a tendency to use effusive metaphors, parables or stories to dramatize the emotional impact of their message."[20]

In Conclusion

A public communication message is usually divided into four parts: introduction, central idea, body, and conclusion. Attention material can be personal references, humorous illustrations, references to the occasion or setting, rhetorical questions, action questions, unusual or dramatic devices, quotations related to the theme, or statements of the theme.

Orienting material, which includes historical background, definition of terms, personal history and/or the speaker's tie to the topic, and the topic's importance to the listeners, gives an audience the background necessary to understand the basic material of the speech.

The body of a speech in the Western world normally takes one of six forms: spatial arrangement, time arrangement, topical arrangement, causal arrangement, comparison–contrast arrangement, or problem-solution arrangement. A summary restates the major points of the speech. Clinchers can include personal references, humorous stories, illustrations, rhetorical questions, unusual or dramatic devices, or quotations.

Alternate modes of speech organization are the partitioning, unfolding, or case methods.

It must be remembered, however, that not all audiences will be European American and that cultures and languages differ in the very assumption of how information should be organized, of what is to be or not to be described and expressed. A speaker is wise to take into consideration the general culture of the audience and adapt the speech materials accordingly.

Learn by Doing

1. Your instructor asks for a volunteer and gives him or her a card with a drawing on it. Each member of the class has a sheet of paper and a pencil. The volunteer explains to the class how to draw the diagram exactly as it appears on the card. No one is allowed to ask any questions. When the volunteer has finished giving directions, the members of the class compare their drawings with the original. After the activity, the class discusses these questions:

   a. If the volunteer did not do so, would it have helped if he or she had given a general overview of what to draw before beginning to give directions? Discuss this question in relation to your reading about the purpose of an introduction.

   b. Did the instructions have a conclusion? How could a conclusion restating the major points have helped you?

   c. Did any words used in the directions confuse you, causing you to make an error or not be able to follow the instruction? What were they? How did they cause problems?

   d. Was the structure of the directions clear?

   e. Do you think a question-and-answer session following the instructions would have been valuable? Why or why not?

2. Do activity 1 again using a different diagram. This time, a different volunteer builds on the positive things the first volunteer did and makes improvements based on the class discussion. This time, the activity is followed by a question-and-answer session. Note how many people altered their drawings during the question-and-answer session. Reach some conclusions about the value of question-and-answer sessions.

3. A speaker informs the class about an unusual topic—something about which the audience probably has no knowledge. Sample topics are the language of bees, the Kaballah, the country of Malawi, or organic architecture. Be sure the speech has a clear structure and lasts no more than five minutes.

4. Select a subject about which you are an expert, and present a speech to your classmates in such a way that when you finish, they too have an understanding of the topic. Clearly structure the speech, and take no more than six minutes to deliver it.

5. Prepare a speech of no more than five minutes informing the class about a controversial theory. Sample topics: The Loch Ness monster exists, Rational Emotive Therapy can alter behavior, Alcoholism is an inherited disease. Explain the theory and the various arguments concerning the theory. Do not include your own views in the presentation. Be sure the speech is clearly structured.

6. You are assigned to give a speech about your education (elementary, high school, college). Prepare an introduction for the presentation representing each of these introductory devices:

   a. Personal reference

   b. Humorous story

   c. Rhetorical question

   d. Unusual or dramatic device

Key Terms

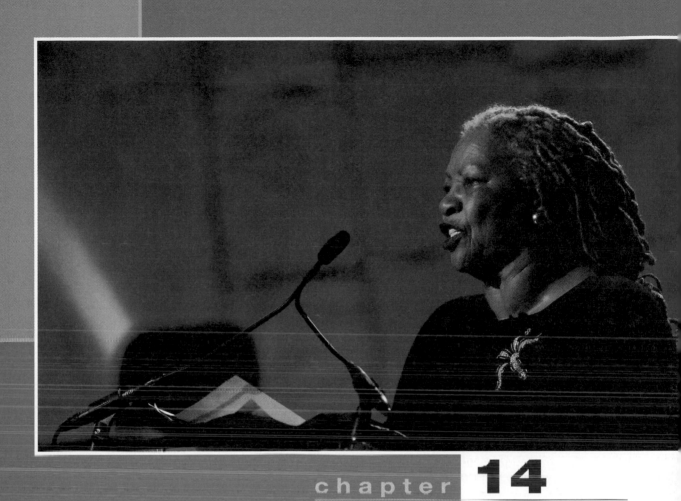

chapter 14

Public Speaking
Presenting the Message

▶ **After reading this chapter, you should be able to**

- Identify the oral and physical factors that lead to an effective presentation

- Clarify how to use visuals in a presentation

- Know how to use an outline or manuscript while speaking

- Appreciate the necessity of rehearsal as a requirement for successful public speaking

- Acknowledge the role of culture in public speaking presentations

- Put into practice the concept of speaking with confidence

- Explain public speaking anxiety and some ways of dealing with it

- Understand the role of culture in speech apprehension

After the speech is prepared, it must be presented to the audience. The delivery has two components: the oral and the physical aspects.

Aspects of Oral and Physical Speech Presentation

Speakers who capture their listeners' attention are likely to share certain qualities: confidence, ease, authority, conviction, credibility, sincerity, warmth, animation, enthusiasm, vitality, intensity, concern, and empathy. They also make effective use of eye contact, conversational tone, and a variety of pitch, pacing, projection, and phrasing.

Vocal Delivery

A speech can be enlivened by effective vocal and physical delivery. Audience members tend to listen with more attention when a speaker is dynamic and enthusiastic.

VOCAL VARIETY   A question often asked by novice public speakers is: How fast or slow should I speak? There is no accurate rate, but speaking with vocal variety, speaking in a number of different speeds to match the mood of the ideas you are presenting, is desirable.

"The average speech rate in the mid-Atlantic states is about 120 to 140 words per minute. It is faster in some places such as New York City, and slower in other locales."[1] In general, in preparing a manuscript the normal rate would be the equivalent of one-half to two-thirds of a double-spaced keyboarded page. Speaking slower than that can lead to listener boredom.

Someone who speaks in a *monotone*—a flat, boring sound resulting from a constant pitch, volume, and rate—will often cause the audience to tune out. On the other hand, speaking so rapidly that the listener can't understand will result in confusion.

Therefore, the goal should be to speak in a manner that will allow you to be understood, hold the audience's attention, and allow for clarity of ideas. A factor that can affect how rapidly you speak is your pronunciation. If you can't be understood, no matter how fast or slowly you speak, you will not achieve your speaking goal.

PRONUNCIATION   "There are many different and acceptable ways of pronouncing American English, because our language is spoken differently in various parts of the United States."[2] Standard American English—the language generally recognized by linguists as representative of the general population of the United States—spoken in most of the Midwest and West Coast—tends to be the most acceptable of the regional dialects. Speech becomes substandard if pronunciations cause misunderstandings and set a negative tone for the presentation.[3]

Because you will be evaluated on the basis not only of what you say but also on how you say it, you should be aware of some common pronunciation problems, their causes, and how to correct the sounds:[4]

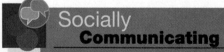

Start and Finish Your Talk without Notes

Few people can actually memorize an entire speech. Most of us have to rely on some sort of notes or outline. But you should make every attempt to anchor your opening and closing statements firmly in your mind so that you can look directly at your audience while delivering those lines.

Source: American Speaker, Briefings Publishing Groups, 2008.

REFLECT ON THIS: Give three reasons why it is a good idea to memorize the opening and closing remarks of a speech.

- *Sloppy or incorrect articulation.* If you say "air" for *error* and "dint" for *didn't,* you are mispronouncing because of lazy use of the articulators (tongue, jaw, teeth). Be conscious of dropping the *g* sound at the end of words ending in *-ing,* such as *going, doing,* and *watching.* Also be aware of slurring words together. "Alls-ya-godado" is not an understandable substitute for *all you have to do.*

■ *Unaware of correct pronunciation.* Listening and reading vocabularies are far greater than speaking vocabularies. In preparing a speech, look up in a dictionary or a pronunciation guide any word for which pronunciation is unfamiliar.

■ *Vowel distortion.* Some of us have grown up in environments in which words are mispronounced because of vowel substitutions. *Milk* may have been pronounced as "melk," *secretary* may have been "sekatury," and *many* may have been "minny." Being aware of the distortions allows some people to begin monitoring their own pronunciations and correcting themselves.

■ *Pronunciation outside the normal pattern.* Assuming that Standard American English is the norm, certain pronunciations usually are not considered acceptable in the marketplace of business, education, and the professions. *Asked* is not "ax" and *picture* and *pitcher* are not the same word.

■ *Those who speak American English as a second language.* Individuals who speak American English as a second language will often carry with them pronunciations from their native language. All languages do not have the same sounds. For example, Japanese does not have an *l* sound (e.g., the *l* in *look*). To the Japanese ear, the word *plastic* sounds like "prastic," so that's the way it will be pronounced. This type of "mispronunciation" is not intentional; rather, it is simply a reaction to the difference in sounds.

Physical Elements

The physical elements of public communication include gestures and eye contact. The way you use visual aids is another physical element.

GESTURES   Gestures incorporate the use of hands, body movements, and facial expressions. Hand gestures can add the extra emphasis to a point in a speech. A good speaker keeps his speech flowing smoothly with both his voice and his hands. When you're passionate about a subject, hand gestures can non-verbally convey the purpose and intent behind the words.[5] "Your gestures and movement should grow out of your response to your message. They should always appear natural and spontaneous, prompted by your ideas and feelings."[6] The more emotional you are, the more dynamic will be your gestures.

Knowing the importance of movement, students in speech classes sometimes ask their instructors to teach them how to gesture. Unfortunately, it is impossible to do so, because gesturing is the result of the speaker's degree of involvement, excitement, dynamism, and personality. Each person uses his or her own characteristic gesture pattern while communicating. Some people use a great number of gestures, whereas others use just a few.

Gestures should be natural. That is why you should not worry about what to do with your hands. Forget them, and they will take care of themselves. Your hands will be active when your body calls for movement. Avoid gripping the lectern so tightly that you cannot let go, and do not have your hands jammed inside your pockets and be unable to get them out. If you are orally dynamic, your body will be too. If you are orally boring, so will be your body. Your gestures, while speaking before an audience, should parallel the gestures you use when speaking in a conversation. You don't ask yourself when speaking to a friend, "What should I do with my hands?" Your hands just do their own thing, move naturally. The more excited you get, probably the more

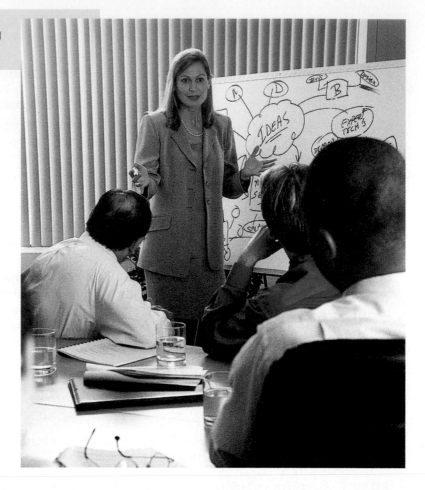

People who use hand movements when they talk appear to be freer, more open, and more honest to an audience.

you use your hands. The less dynamic, the less you will exhibit physical, facial, and body movements.

EYE CONTACT   Establishing **eye contact**—looking into the eyes of your audience as you speak—is another key to effective speaking. Members of an audience will tend to feel involved in the presentation if you look at them. Maintaining eye contact also helps you receive feedback so you can adjust your presentation accordingly. To use eye contact effectively, look directly at listeners, not over their heads. Shift your focus so that you are not maintaining contact with just one section of the audience, and be especially careful not to overlook those in the front or back rows.

Sometimes you may speak to a larger audience. It is difficult to maintain eye contact with everyone in an auditorium or large classroom. So, as illustrated in the Socially Communicating box, you can use *zoned eye contact* to look at segments of the audience to ensure that each segment receives attention. In doing this, try to directly contact the eyes of at least several people in that zone.

Using a Script or Outline

Using a script (manuscript or outline) can be difficult because you must look at the audience at the same time that you are trying to present your material with animation and naturalness. You will have to work out some system for following the script in an unobtrusive way so that you also can look at the audience without losing your place.

Socially
Communicating

The Magic V

Let's say there are 500 people in your audience. It's very difficult to make actual eye contact with 500 people. However, there's a trick to help called the Magic V (see the figure). When you look at someone, all of the people in a V behind that person think you are looking at them.

Divide the room up into a tic-tac-toe board. Look at one of the "squares" and use the V and the mind touch to lift that section. Once you have them, move to another square.

When the crowd is large, use the Magic V. Draw a "tic-tac-toe" in your mind over the crowd. As you look at each square, you are actually looking at all the people in a "V" behind the person you are really looking at.

After you have made contact with that group emotionally, switch to another square. Make sure you work the squares at random.

Source: Reprinted by permission from Lilly Walters, Secrets of Successful Speakers. Copyright © 1993 by the McGraw-Hill Companies.

REFLECT ON THIS: The Magic V is a controversial device because some people think it is too automatic and the audience will know you are not looking directly at some people. On the other hand, it does give a person a way of "looking" at the entire audience in a formatted way. Which stand do you believe is correct?

Be careful not to move or flip manuscript pages unnecessarily; this draws attention away from you and toward the manuscript.

Some speakers run the index finger of their hand down the side of the script so that they are continuously pointing to the start of the next printed line or major point they will be presenting. Then when they look up, they can find their place when they return to the script.

One method for establishing eye contact with an audience while following a manuscript in an unobtrusive way is *eye span*. You can train your eyes to glance down, pick out a meaningful phrase or a sentence, and deliver it to the audience. As you reach the end of the phrase, but before you have finished saying it, glance down and grasp the next idea to be spoken.

Avoid a flat-sounding reading style. Instead, read and speak according to the meaning by stressing important words and ideas, and vary your tone of voice so that you are speaking naturally. It is helpful to underline key words and to mark off phrases. Slash marks (*virgules*) can be used to indicate a pause or a stop. Usually, a / is used for a short pause, / / for a longer pause, and / / / for a full stop.

Underscores can be placed beneath a word or a phrase to indicate that it should be <u>stressed</u>. Usually a single underscore indicates a minor stress, and a double signifies a stronger stress; a triple underscore represents the point at which you should increase the volume and the power of your vocal delivery. For example, the word <u>*now*</u> is to be stressed in the sentence: Do it <u>now</u>. Notice that the entire meaning of the sentence changes if the underscoring becomes: Do <u>it</u> now. How about: Do it. <u>Now!</u> If you think underscoring will help you to present the material in a meaningful way, use it.

It also helps to arrange the script in a manner that keeps you from getting lost. Double- or triple-space the information, number the pages, do not divide sentences by starting them on one page and finishing them on another. Do not write on the backs of the pages. Use a large font size (e.g., 14) so you can easily read the notes.

If you are using standardized sheets of paper, place them on a lectern or place them on a table so that your hands are free. If you plan to move away from the lectern, put that segment of material on a note card so you can take it with you.

If you are going to use notecards, write on only one side so you don't get lost, and number each card. It is best to hold the notecards with one hand rather than two as it leaves the vacant hand free for gesturing.

Use of Visual Aids

Visuals can assist you in making the presentation listenable and in maintaining attention. Keeping in mind that visuals are aids for making your presentation comprehensible and engaging, you can use these guidelines to employ visuals effectively:

■ Use the visual aid as an aid, not as a replacement for your oral presentation (i.e., don't just display a projection or chart and expect the audience to read and understand the information).

■ Be sure the visual is large enough for the entire audience to see.

■ Display the visual only at the point when you are speaking about that particular information. Don't expose it before you need it or after you've referred to it.

■ Don't block the audience's view by standing between the visual and the audience.

■ Speak to your listeners, not to your visual.

■ Know the visual aid well enough that you don't have to study it while you are speaking.

■ Point to the particular place on the aid that you are discussing as you discuss it. (For example, if you are using a map, use a laser pointer to illustrate exactly what country you are discussing.)

■ Integrate the aid into your presentation at the point when it will have the greatest impact.

■ Limit the amount of text on a slide or chart. Remember the 5/5 formula (no more than five lines on a slide/chart and no more than five words on a line).

■ If you use handouts, be sure to integrate them fully into your presentation by passing them out at the point when you are going to refer to the material so that your listeners will not be distracted by reading the material rather than listening to you.

Using PowerPoint

If you are using PowerPoint or a similar presentation program, recognize that like any communication strategy, using a computer presentation program probably will not be comfortable for you at first.

Here are some suggestions on how to make your presentation work well:

1 *Practice thoroughly.* One of the questions often asked is: How much should I practice with my supplementary aids? A valuable rule here is to spend at least as much time practicing your delivery as you spend on preparing the visuals. If it takes an hour to pull together the visuals, then plan to spend an hour with those visuals in actually practicing your delivery. Because of differences in equipment, it is best to practice with the actual equipment that you will use during the presentation. Once you get your materials developed, work with the computer and/or the projector so that you can use the equipment smoothly.

2 *Learn how to use the mouse or remote control so that you can get to the right slide at the precise time in the sequence of your talk when it should appear.* While practicing, remember that listening to a speaker read word for word from a slide that is visible to all is both uncreative and boring.

3 *Be patient.* Accidentally advancing two slides instead of one takes control away from the speaker. If something goes wrong—and with the use of electronic equipment, it well may—don't panic. Adjust to the place in the presentation where you need to be and go on. Some people apologize or make a joke about the problem. Theories differ about whether to try to cover up the error. If it's a one-time occurrence, the best advice is to correct the problem and go on. Doing this does not draw attention to the error. If the cause of your error is your apparent lack of preparation or familiarity with the equipment, the audience will probably be less forgiving than if the cause is a mechanical glitch or a slip of the finger.

4 *Maintain control of the presentation.* The speaker, not the technology, must maintain control. For example, just as you should cover your chart until you want the audience to see it, have a neutral colored blank page in your PowerPoint inserted so that the audience isn't looking at the previously used image or distracted by the frame that will be used next.

5 *Be prepared for the worst.* Have a contingency plan available in case of equipment failure. Ask yourself what you will do if at the start or during the speech, the equipment malfunctions. Many speakers print copies of the necessary graphics for distribution as a hedge against negative possibilities, others present the material as if no visual had been intended. In general, avoid statements such as, "If I had the slide to show, it would illustrate . . ." or "This point would be clearer if I had the visuals." Statements such as these add nothing to the message development and diminish your credibility as a speaker.

6 *When you get to the room or auditorium where you will make your presentation, check out the facilities.*

   a. If you did not bring your own equipment, make sure any equipment that has been ordered is present and working. If you are using computer equipment, be sure the right software has been loaded.

   b. Pull down the projection screen.

   c. Check the lighting to determine the appropriate level for the audience's viewing.

   d. Check the power connections to be sure that they are operational.

e. If you are using an overhead projector, check to ensure that the machine comes with a spare light bulb, just in case the bulb burns out.

f. Check the focus. Walk around the room to make sure that the visuals are readable from all seats in the room.

7   *Don't talk to the screen.* Avoid the "death by PowerPoint" style of turning (or even occasionally glancing) back at the screen. The projection is there to support, not replace, what you're saying. Maintain your eye contact and interaction with your listeners so they focus on you and your message, not your slides.

Unfortunately, examples abound of speakers who failed to use presentation tools effectively. Consider, for example, Alex's biology instructor. She prepared a PowerPoint presentation for every class meeting in the course, an activity that took many hours of work on her part. Sound like a good idea? Not the way she did it! The slides were a dark background with white lettering, and the projector was so weak that the room had to be totally dark the entire presentation time. The students found it hard to stay awake. And the controls were located at the back of the room, so she stood behind the class. As a result, they couldn't see her, nor could she read feedback on the students' faces. Instead of using bullets, phrases, and outlines, the instructor wrote a paragraph on each slide, which she read aloud. The students felt that if she had intended to read to them, she should have just put the information on a handout, let them read the material themselves, and skipped the class session. The biology instructor's intentions were good, but her lecturing with the overused and poorly developed PowerPoint program was a boring, nonadaptive disaster. Don't be like Alex's biology teacher when you prepare and use an electronic program for your speeches.

One of the major concerns brought up in introduction to public speaking courses is: I get stage fright or speaker anxiety when I give a speech. Why? What can I do about it? In order to understand what public speaking anxiety is, the topic will be discussed and, following that discussion, some specific techniques will be used to aid you to become a more proficient public speaker, and to cope with some of the anxiety.

Public Speaking Anxiety

Very few speakers escape the "butterflies." "Speech anxiety is a serious problem for a large number of people and has been found to affect career development as well as academic performance."[7] "Millions of professionals make themselves sick at the thought of having to get up in front of people to give a speech."[8]

"Speaking in public is easily one of the most common fears facing Americans. Now, a little bit of anxiety before getting up in front of an audience is quite natural (some estimates say that as much as 75 percent of the population does not like speaking in public), but a significant portion of us (estimates say around 30 percent) have a real, sometimes debilitating, fear of public speaking."[9] Yes, research shows that "the fear of public speaking is the No. 1 rated fear in America."[10]

Interested in ascertaining your speaking anxiety level? If so, complete the Do You Have Public Speaking Anxiety? questionnaire on the next page.

Although it is often referred to by the generic name *stage fright*, public speaking anxiety is actually a phobia: **speechophobia.** It is classified as a phobia because of its psychological and physical characteristics: (1) there is persistent fear of a specific situation out of proportion to the reality of the danger, (2) there is a compelling desire to avoid and escape the situation, (3) the fear is unreasonable and excessive, and (4) it is not due to any other disorder.[11] As with most phobias, it is curable. A lack of knowledge of how to prepare and present a speech leads to anxiety.[12] As you read this book

Do You Have Public Speaking Anxiety?

This instrument is composed of six statements concerning feelings about speaking in public.[13] Indicate the degree to which each statement applies to you by marking whether you (1) strongly agree, (2) agree, (3) are undecided, (4) disagree, or (5) strongly disagree. Work quickly. Record your first impression.

____ a. I have no fear of giving a speech.

____ b. Certain parts of my body feel very tense and rigid while I am giving a speech.

____ c. I feel relaxed while giving a speech.

____ d. My thoughts become confused and jumbled when I am giving a speech.

____ e. I face the prospect of giving a speech with confidence.

____ f. While giving a speech, I get so nervous I forget facts that I really know.

Scoring: Add 18 to your scores from items a, c, and e, and then subtract your score from the total of items b, d, and f. This is your final score.

Interpretation: Scores can range from a low of 6 to a high of 30. If your score is 18 or above, you are like the overwhelming majority of Euro-Americans in that you display public speaking apprehension.

and practice developing speeches, you will gain the knowledge to overcome this roadblock to public speaking.

Conquering Public Speaking Anxiety[14]

Here are some principles that might help you both understand public speaking anxiety and work toward conquering it:

- *Speaking in public is* not *inherently stressful.* "Most of us believe parts of life are inherently stressful. In fact, most of us have been taught to believe that life as a

The number-one fear of Americans is speaking in public.

Communicating in Careers

How the Best Speakers Do It

Successful business speakers share certain practices and techniques.

Among other things, they make it a point to entertain as well as inform—just as good teachers do. They also deepen and expand the bond with their audiences through openness, sensitivity and humor.

Based on observations of successful and unsuccessful speakers, the good ones:

- **Are thoroughly** prepared and comfortable with their material. They outline their main points on a blackboard, slide or easel. They also make sure that all audiovisual equipment functions smoothly.

- **Involve** their audiences by soliciting answers and information. *Example:* One speaker, addressing "Downsizing in the '90s," had all the participants stand, then sit down in stages if they or someone they knew had been affected by firings, layoffs, takeovers, etc. Eventually the entire group was seated.

- **Enhance** their presentations by creative use of newspaper clippings, cartoons, music, appropriate quotes or relevant experiences.

- **Often use** self-deprecating humor to get a point across. This allows the audience to identify with the speaker's foibles.

- **Move around** the room rather than remain fixed behind a lectern, a technique that makes them seem accessible. Many greet people individually as they enter the room.

- **Avoid boring** business audiences with material that's common knowledge.

Source: Carol Driscoll, writing in *The Toast-master*, P.O. Box 13888, Mission Viejo, CA 92690.

REFLECT ON THIS: Think of a speech you have recently heard (e.g., a student presentation in your speech class or a professor's lecture). Analyze the speech using the six criteria for a successful speaker presented by this author.

---

whole is very stressful! To deal with any type of stress effectively, you first must understand that life itself, including public speaking, is *not* inherently stressful. Thousands of human beings have learned to speak in front of groups with little or no stress at all."[15] "If they can conquer the fear of public speaking, so can you!"[16]

- *You don't have to be brilliant or perfect to succeed.* "You don't have to be brilliant, witty, or perfect to succeed. That is not what public speaking is all about. It may look that way, but it's not. You can be average. You can be below average. You can make mistakes, get tongue-tied, or forget whole segments of your talk. You can even tell no jokes at all and still be successful."[17] "The essence of public speaking is this: give your audience something of value."[18] If you have a clear statement of central idea and have developed it effectively, you will have succeeded.

- *When you speak in public, nothing that bad can happen!* "One thing that adds to the fear of public speaking is the dread people have that something awful, terrible, or publicly humiliating will happen to them."[19] The odds of this happening are remote. In all the years your authors have been teaching public speaking, no student or client has ever passed out from nervousness, and no one has died. A few speakers have forgotten what they intended to say, or didn't say exactly what they had intended, but no one has been humiliated because of it unless a speaker imposed the humiliation on himself or herself. No one is perfect. Unless you are totally unprepared, all you can do is the best you can do, and that is not a crime.

- *You don't have to control the behavior of your audience.* "To succeed as a public speaker, you don't have to control the behavior of your audience. There are certain things you do need to control—your own thoughts, your preparation, arrangements for audiovisual aids, how the room is laid out—but one thing you don't have to control is your audience. They will do whatever they do."[20] This does not mean that you should ignore the audience. Audience analysis and adaptation are important, but thinking you need to change or control other people is a hidden cause of stress in many areas of life. This is just as true for relating to a group as it is for relating to your friends, spouse, children, and other acquaintances.

■ *Your audience truly wants you to succeed.* "Your audience truly wants you to succeed. Most of them are scared to death of public speaking, just like you. They know the risk of embarrassment, humiliation, and failure you take every time you present yourself in public. They feel for you. They will admire your courage."[21] "This means that most audiences are truly forgiving. While a slip of the tongue or a mistake of any kind might seem like a big deal to you, it's not very meaningful or important to your audience. Their judgments and appraisals will usually be much more lenient than yours. It's useful to remind yourself of this point, especially when you think you've performed poorly."[22]

These suggestions for dealing with speaking anxiety may also be helpful:

■ *Do not avoid the experience of giving a presentation.* The more you speak, the more comfortable you will get. Although your nervousness may not go away completely, it should let up as you get more practice.

■ *Accept that you will experience some anxiety.* All speakers encounter at least a moment of anxiousness as they begin because they are, essentially, facing the unknown.

■ *Do not take drugs or alcohol because you think they will relax you.* Although there has been some recent research that shows that in extreme cases such prescription drugs as Paxil can help in containing physically caused anxieties, self-prescribed drugs and alcohol tend to dull your reflexes and increase your chances of forgetting and making a fool of yourself. (Just picture how a person who is drunk tends to act.)

■ *Use relaxation techniques.* Before beginning a presentation, some speakers find it helpful to take several deep breaths and expel all the air from their lungs. Others like to shake their hands at the wrists to "get out the nervousness." Some people favor grabbing the seat of their chair with both hands, pushing down, holding the position for about five seconds, and repeating this movement about five times. This tightens and then loosens the muscles, which causes a decrease in physical tension.[23]

■ *Recognize the anxiety.* Another approach is to think of the experience of getting up before the audience and to feel the anxiety. Let it stay in your mind, imagining that you are going through the experience. Let yourself be as nervous as you can; psychologically push it as far as you can. Some people report that by imagining the upcoming experience in its worst way, the actual experience becomes much easier.[24]

■ *Prepare.* Highly anxious speakers are less likely to spend time preparing and rehearsing their speech.[25] Ironically, this avoidance of getting ready is exactly the opposite of what most research shows aids a person to overcome speechophobia. It is well documented that preparation and rehearsal develop security, one of your basic needs and a key to effective speech performance.[26]

■ *Practice visualization.* We all tend to perform the way we expect to perform, so expectancy restructuring is based on the idea that if you expect to do well, then you will do well. To overcome the fear, prepare a well-structured and well-documented speech so that you have confidence in your material. Then go through the process of visualization—seeing yourself in the actual setting in which you are going to give the speech and making a successful presentation. Picture yourself getting out of your chair, walking to the front of the room, arranging your materials on the lectern, looking at the audience, and giving the speech. As you see yourself presenting the material, look at various people. They are nodding their heads in agreement; they are interested and are listening attentively. Finally, imagine yourself ending the speech, the audience applauding, and returning to your chair, feeling good about yourself. The more you visualize this positive experience, the more your expectation level of success should increase. You will be expecting success, not failure.

The goal for the public speaking–challenged should not be to eliminate all stress and anxiety associated with the task. Some butterflies are necessary to help keep you focused. But when anxiety becomes so great that it hinders performance, it crosses the line into social phobia. Such sensitivity to criticism or social scrutiny can be passed along from one generation to the next, like hair color. The phobia often can be beaten by consciously changing our behavior and the way we think. Those who suffer such debilitating fear are filled with irrational thoughts. They think they have to be perfect, that they can't tolerate any anxiety or stress during a speech. What should be ingrained is that perfection is not possible, that discomfort can be tolerated and eventually will pass, and that tanking a speech does not make you a complete flop. One great tip is to not even think of yourself as a public speaker but as someone simply sharing information with a friend. Recognize that your audience is just fallible human beings like yourself.[27]

After following the suggestions just presented, individuals who are still traumatized by the prospect of giving a speech may need mental health support. Some hospitals and health centers have phobia clinics that could be of assistance.[28]

Speech Apprehension and Culture

Cultural differences have been found regarding anxiety as related to public speaking. Research in the United States indicates that speechophobia is highest among Asian Americans and lowest among Jewish Americans.[29]

International research showed that speaking apprehension varied from a low of 31 percent in Israel to a high of 57 percent in Japan and 55 percent in Taiwan.[30] In Mexico, Germany, India, and Newfoundland, speech anxiety was more similar to the U.S. statistic.[31] There is no gender difference reported in the United States, but men have typically learned tactics for concealing their shyness because it is considered a feminine trait in most countries.[32] In Mexico, males are less likely than females to report speaking apprehension.[33]

Research shows that "fifty percent of Japanese students would be classified as highly apprehensive about giving speeches."[34] "United States college students show less apprehension than Japanese college students."[35] This is likely the result of the cultural norms in Japan that do not value talkativeness; therefore, the Japanese tend not to be outspoken in contrast to Euro-Americans who are encouraged to speak out for their rights.[36]

Rehearsing the Speech

If possible, start to prepare far enough in advance so that you have sufficient material, the speech is well structured and well organized, and you have a chance to practice it. Some speakers try to convince themselves that they will do better if they just get up and talk, with little or no thought about what they will say. This is a fool's contention. It is usually the excuse of a procrastinator or a person who is not properly aware of his or her responsibility to the audience and self. Yes, some speakers can get up and "wing it," but the normal mortal usually cannot. Rehearsal is a key to effective speech performance.[37] So prepare and practice! Professional speakers with whom your authors work often go through as many as 20 dry runs of their presentation so that they feel totally comfortable with what they're going to say (ensuring that the introduction, main points, transitions, and conclusion are easily accessible from their long-term memory) and with their polished, natural presentation style.

There is no one best way to rehearse. For some people, sitting at a desk and going over the material by mumbling through the outline or notes is the starting point. This will alert you to ideas that do not seem to make sense, words you cannot pronounce, places where you go blank because you need more notes, and areas that need more or fewer examples. Make the changes, and continue to review your notes orally until you are satisfied with the material. You might ask someone to listen to the speech. The person can then give you feedback on your presentation. If you're on a campus or in an organization that has a communication lab or media center, take advantage of that facility and

Communicating in Careers

Prepare!!!

I was making a sales presentation to a group of potential buyers about a new product line that my company had developed. I had been to a briefing about the products, but didn't have time to read all of the specifications before the meeting. During the speech I was feeling very uncomfortable and kept verbally stumbling. In the question-and-answer session I was asked a series of questions about the products. I didn't have answers for most of the inquiries. It was obvious that I didn't know what I was talking about. I really felt like a fool. A speaker has to prepare for a speech.

Source: Roy Berko, Andrew Wolvin, and Rebecca Ray, *Business Communication in a Changing World* (New York: St. Martin's Press, 1997), p. 307.

REFLECT ON THIS: What specific lesson did you learn from the words of this sales representative?

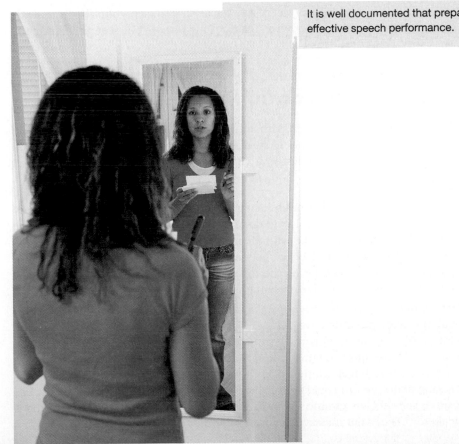

It is well documented that preparation and rehearsal are keys to effective speech performance.

schedule a run-through before the video camera. The center may even have a speech tutor/coach who can review your recorded presentation to help you polish the presentation to a professional level.

Once you are satisfied with the material, try to construct the setting in which you are going to speak. Duplicate as closely as possible what you are going to do. If you are going to use visual aids, practice using them. The more familiar you become with exactly what you are going to do, the more likely it is you will be comfortable doing it.

Stop practicing when you are comfortable with your material and have worked out the problems related to using notes and supplementary aids. You are striving to become as comfortable as you can in what is a stressful situation for almost all of us.

For many speakers the most important part of rehearsing is to run a positive movie in your head of your speaking experience.[38] "You may not know this, but the brain and body can't tell the difference between something you vividly imagine and reality. When you learn something new, a pathway is created in your brain between neurons. This pathway is your brain's way of remembering. Because the brain can't tell the difference between real and vividly imagined events, even mental practice can help establish new patterns."[39] "So, formulate an indelible stamp on your mind of a mental picture of yourself as succeeding. Hold this picture. Never let it fade."[40] Mohammad Ali, former heavyweight boxing champion, used what he called "future history" in preparing for his fights. "He said he always rehearsed the fight in his head, again and again before he even stepped foot in the ring."[41] His success rate was 17 wins out of 19 fights. He credits his future history practice for his accomplishments. You too can take on and whip the world of public speaking, by using the technique of imaging as part of your rehearsal process.

Practice just before you go to sleep. As you lie in bed, see yourself successfully going through your speaking experience, from getting out of your seat, to hearing the applause at the end of the presentation.

Speaking with Confidence

"Audiences are drawn to a speaker with confidence."[42] But what is confidence and where does it come from? "A confident speaker exudes positive energy that feeds and excites the audience."[43] She exudes positive energy because she believes in herself and what she is saying. What can you do to become a confident speaker?[44]

- *Always be prepared.* One of your basic needs is security. If you believe that you are in control of what you are going to do and what you are going to say, and have rehearsed and feel comfortable with the material, it is likely that you will feel positive about the experience. Why? You feel secure. If you are speaking about a topic you believe in, you know the topic inside and out, and you've organized your thoughts into a cohesive presentation, you will feel secure.

- *Embrace your uniqueness and imperfections.* A confident speaker doesn't worry about what the audience thinks of him. Do you perceive yourself as too tall? Too skinny? Do you speak with an accent, have a lisp, or a hearing impairment? So what? Make the most of your uniqueness. Be proud of who you are. Only you can make yourself feel inferior. And, if you allow what you perceive others are thinking about you to control your thoughts, then you victimize yourself. "Use positive self-talk to reframe the way you perceive yourself as a person and a speaker."[45] The major message to yourself should be, "I'm confident."

Socially
Communicating

McCain Bumbles the Delivery

At the start of the 2008 presidential campaign, a great deal of attention centered on Republican nominee John McCain's poor oral and physical speech presentation style. One of the questions being asked was, "Is there a way John McCain can win the presidency without giving another speech?" The reason? "Not good," a McCain adviser conceded, critiquing their nominee's presentation of a major speech. "It's never going to be his strong suit, and it will always be Obama's." "We were appalled at the candidate's performance," said a strategist. "It's

a serious problem—the contrast is so clear that it's demoralizing." One of McCain's ad-makers said, "This is not a speechmaking contest," he said. "Thank God."

Source: Jonathan Martin, "McCain Bumbles the Delivery, Capitol New Company, http://Dyn.Politico.Com/Printstory.Cfm?Uuid=5a63304b-3048-5c12-004afca417f9386f, June 6, 2008.

REFLECT ON THIS: Is the ad-maker's view correct? Is the race for the presidency a speechmaking contest?

■ *Don't apologize.* Confident speakers are often nervous. However, they don't let the audience know it by using the trite "I'm really nervous" or "I really am not very good at giving speeches." Why? Because instead of the audience feeling sorry for them, they feel pity. A confident speaker doesn't want pity; he wants respect! A confident speaker appears calm and relaxed, even when nervous. What if you make a mistake, trip over the mike chord, or drop your notecards? "Take care of the problem as quickly as possible, lighten up the situation with a little humor, and then move on."[46]

The Role of Culture on Speech Presentation

"Culture has a powerful effect on communication. Whether the culture derives from our nationality, race, ethnicity, religion, work environment, peer group, or even gender, we can't ignore its effect on communication."[47]

It is important to recognize that not all people are trained to speak and present ideas in the same way. Culture plays a major role in the way you use words and what your body does during a speech. To this point in the chapter we have placed an emphasis on Euro-American speakers, not separating out gender or cultural factors. Because of the multicultural nature of this nation, you will probably be listening to and speaking before people of various cultures. In addition, you may be placed in situations where, because of your career or interests, you will speak and listen to people from differing cultures. To illustrate the differences, let's examine a few public speaking cultural variations.*

Because Black Americans come from traditions where storytelling, preaching, gospels, spirituals, dancing, and speaking are all part of the public speaking environment, audiences often expect to be entertained, comforted, and inspired.[48] Listening

▶ *Note:* As in all other parts of this text that deal with generalizations—in this case, cultural generalizations—do not assume that the statements fit every member of the particular group being described. The conclusions reached are based on research findings. You may find, as a member of the group being described, that you do not fit the generalization. The nature of most research is to find norms that describe, recognizing that not every member of the group is being described.

Black American public speaking and preaching traditions encourage the speaker to be innovative, novel, and dynamic.

to Jesse Jackson, or some of the other Black spokespersons, is often a unique situation for those not used to the history of African American speechmaking and preaching. "The rhetorical situation demands that the rhetoric be innovative and novel, for unlike the traditional public speaking situation where the speaker talks without interruption to a usually passive audience, a formal Black speaking situation shows how the speaker, the message, and the audience are one."[49] Listeners often shout out in agreement or repeat the message of the speaker for emphasis. This is not being disrespectful; rather, it is showing support for the speaker and the involvement of the members of the audience in the proceedings.

The message for those not familiar with Black American listeners is that "the language and delivery components are necessary to capture an audience, for many Black audiences are notoriously unresponsive to small voiced, unimaginative and uncreative speakers."[50]

Do not be lulled into a false sense of security when speaking before a Chinese audience. Listeners will often shake their heads up and down as they listen, thus giving Euro-Americans the idea that the listeners are agreeing. This is not necessarily so. Chinese people are very polite, and nod their heads vertically only to indicate that they are receiving the message. Chinese seem to avoid free expression of personal views and feeling, so don't be concerned if they do not ask questions during the question-and-answer session, even when encouraged to do so.[51] The same is to be said for the Japanese, who will seldom ask questions in public forums. The concept of "saving face" is so ingrained that they will not put speakers on the spot for fear that the speaker will be embarrassed in the eyes of others for not knowing the answer.

"The traditional West African storyteller, called the *griot,* weaves a story with song and dance, and enlivens a tale with all sorts of sound effects."[52] Pops, clicks, and clapping sounds dramatize the presentation, and members of the audience respond like a chorus.

In Arab cultures, the poetic words of speakers are often accented with fiery harangues of sound.[53] This is also true of Arab American speakers.[54] Hispanic and other Latino males "favor an elegant, expressive, or intense narrative form of public communication."[55]

Native American speakers, as well as some Asian and Asian American speakers, do not use direct eye contact, as it is a form of disrespect.[56]

"Differences in feminine and masculine communication patterns also surfaced in public contexts. Historically, men have dominated politics. Thus, it's not surprising that the assertive, dominant, confident masculine style is the standard for public speaking."[57] Women who are effective in public speaking often "manage a fine balance in which they are sufficiently feminine to be perceived as acting appropriately for women and sufficiently masculine to be perceived as acting appropriately."[58] Speakers such as former Texas governor Ann Richards, Golda Meir (the first woman Prime Minister of Israel) and Margaret Thatcher all fit that mold. While a candidate for the 2008 Democratic party presidential nomination, Hillary Clinton had trouble finding the "right" style, as she sometimes was declared too masculine or at times too feminine in her presentational style.[59]

Sarah Palin, 2008 Republican vice presidential candidate, polarized audiences by her speaking style. As one pundent stated, "I've seriously had enough of the winking, the giant-chinned-smirking, the too-sibilant forks-on-a-chalkboard "s" sounds, the "nookyooler," the "you betchas," and especially her Romper Room-like penchant for naming and labeling everyone in her audiences: "Romper bomper stomper boo, tell me, tell me, tell me, do! I see Joe the Plumber, Roscoe the Racist, Zed the Gimp . . . ."[60]

Another observation of her public speaking abilities was, "Palin is also alarmingly unskilled when it comes to a more indigenous matter: speaking the English language. Or, as I wouldn't be too surprised to hear her put it, talking American. The petrified McCain team has, wisely, barely permitted Palin to speak in public. They are so worried about her oratorical ineptitude, in fact, that they successfully negotiated to limit the amount of time she could be interrogated on a single topic during [the] vice-presidential debate."[61]

These cultural differences suggest that there is more than one way to present a public speech. None of the cultural-bound styles is either correct or incorrect, just different. But knowing that there are different styles can alert you, as a speaker, to be aware that you may not get the same response from one audience as from another because of the difference in presentation and receiving styles.

Culturally Communicating

Immigrants, Don't Be in Such a Hurry to Shed Your Accents

This letter to the editor appeared in the New York Times, March 21, 1993.

To the Editor:
You report that immigrants in New York City are turning to speech classes to reduce the sting of discrimination against them based on accent. . . . I'd like to tell all my fellow immigrants taking accent-reduction classes: As long as you speak fluent and comprehensible English, don't waste your money on artificially removing your accent.

I am fortunate enough to be one of the linguistically gifted. I even acquired an American accent before I left China for the United States five years ago. From the day I set foot on this continent till now, the praise of my English has never ceased. What most people single out is that I have no, or very little accent. However, I know I do have an accent. . . . I intend to keep it because it belongs to me. I want to speak and write grammatically flawless English, but I have no desire to equip myself with a perfect American accent. . . .

America is probably the largest place for accents in English because the entire nation is composed of immigrants from different areas of the world. This country is built on accents. Accent is one of the most conspicuous symbols of what makes America the free and prosperous land its own people are proud of and other people long to live in.

I work in an urban institution where accents are an integral part of my job: students, faculty and staff come from ethnically diverse backgrounds. Hearing accents confirms for me every day that the college is fulfilling its goal to offer education to a multicultural population.

I wonder what accent my fellow immigrants should obtain after getting rid of their own: a New York accent? a Boston accent? Brooklyn? Texas? California? Or go after President Clinton's accent?

Source: Clella Jaffe, Public Speaking: Concepts and Skills for a Diverse Society (Belmont, CA: Wadsworth/Thomson Learning, 2001), p. 289.

Dealing with Difficulties During a Speech

As you proceed through your speech, you can do several things to help make this a positive experience for both you and the audience:

- *Accept that mistakes are going to happen.* If you are well prepared, you are more likely to be able to adjust to problems. For example, if the light blows out on the projector, and you know your material, you can speak rather than use the Power-Point program.

- *Try to be relaxed as you speak.* A psychological theory conceptualizes that how you stand affects your ability to avoid your body's tightening.[62] The tightening often results in shallow breathing, dry mouth, and shaking hands and legs. Using the *triangle stance* can help you stop your body from stiffening. In the triangle stance you place foot A at a slight angle and foot B at about a 45-degree angle, as if it were coming out of the arch of foot A. Keep your feet about six inches apart. Shuffle your feet slightly until you feel comfortable and balanced. Place your weight on foot A. You will feel leg and foot B relax. You may also find that it helps if you slightly extend the hip on the foot-A side of your body. As you proceed through a speech, you can alter your stance by changing the positions of feet A and B, but always remember to put your body weight on the foot that is farther back. It may sound silly and simplistic, but it does work!

- *Look at the people in the audience who are alert during the presentation.* You can find these people by watching for those who nod in agreement or smile at you as you speak. Typically, presenters feel good when they get positive reactions.

- *Remember that we all make mistakes.* Even professional speakers and media announcers fumble words. If you make a minor error, just ignore it and keep going. If it is a major error, fix it. Simply repeat the correct word or words and continue your speech, recognizing that you can't erase the mishap.

Communicating in Careers

Handling a Hostile Audience

Consider these techniques to keep cool when your listeners turn up the heat:

- A heckler or adversary interrupts you. *Solution:* Get audience support by reminding listeners of why you're speaking. *Example:* "I can discuss that shortly, but let's first finish tackling the critical issues that affect all of us."

- An angry listener stands and refuses to sit down. *Solution:* Ally yourself with the group. Say something such as: "If you'll please sit down so others can see, the audience would appreciate it."

- A coworker tries to score points with the boss by throwing you a loaded question or contradicting you. *Solution:* Say you want to stick to the agenda and cover what people came to hear. That subtly suggests that the opponent is keeping them from getting needed information.

- Someone shouts an emotion-laden question such as, "Why did the company have to fire such a loyal group of employees?" *Solution:* Respond in a soft-spoken tone and restate the question before you try to answer it. *Example:* "Why did the company, in a fight for survival, have to resort to layoffs?"

Source: Moray Stettner, writing in *Investor's Business Daily*, 12655 Beatrice St., Los Angeles, CA 90066.

REFLECT ON THIS: Have you ever been at a speech or lecture when an audience became hostile? How did the speaker or moderator handle the person or persons?

- *Take time to get yourself organized at the lectern.* Arrange your notes on the lectern so that page 1 is on the left and the rest are on the right. Halfway through page 2, slide (don't flip) the page over to cover page 1. Continue to do this so that you are not pausing at the end of each page to move it over. Sliding allows you to move pages without calling attention to the act; flipping pages can be distracting as it draws attention to the pages for no reason.

In Conclusion

In presenting the speech, the vocal elements and the physical elements are important. Competent speakers are confident. Some people have anxiety associated with giving a speech. Techniques are available for lessening the fear. Major ways of coping with speech anxiety include being prepared, rehearsing, and visualizing being successful. Some cultural differences will require that you adapt your speaking style in order to be most effective speaking to representatives of a particular culture.

Learn by Doing

1. The class sits in a circle. The instructor throws a ball to someone in the circle and passes an envelope to that person. The person selects a statement from the envelope, takes a minute to prepare, and gives a one- to two-minute presentation on the topic. Before speaking, the first person tosses the ball to someone else, who will be the second speaker. While the first person is speaking, the second person selects a topic and prepares a speech. Each speaker tosses the ball to another speaker until all members of the class have spoken.

2. Some of the most commonly mispronounced words in Standard American speech are *across, acts, actually, all, ambulance, any, asked, because, catch,* *doing, familiar, fifth, genuine, get, going, horror, hundred, introduce, just, library, next, nuclear, particular, picture, prescription, probably, pumpkin, recognized, sandwich, secretary, Washington, with.* Look up each word in a dictionary or pronunciation guide. During a class session, you will be asked to pronounce these words and use them in sentences .

3. Videotape one of your classroom presentations. Watch the video. Pay attention to your gestures, facial expression, vocal variety, and rate of speed. Did you look comfortable and confident? If you were to give the speech again, what changes would you make in your physical and vocal actions?

Key Terms

gestures   381

eye contact   382

speechophobia   386

chapter **15**

chapter **15**

Informative Public Speaking

▶ **After reading this chapter, you should be able to**

- Define informative speaking
- Discuss the need for informative speaking in the information age
- List and explain the classifications of informative speeches

- Explain how to develop an informative speech
- List and explain the steps a successful informative speaker takes in developing a speech

We live in "the information age." The name alludes to the global economy's shift in focus away from the production of physical goods (as exemplified by the industrial age) and toward the manipulation of information.[1] Technological advances have changed lifestyles around the world and spawned new industries around controlling and providing information.[2]

With the ever-expanding development of information, we must have reliable sources for obtaining the ideas. The previously used sources of television, radio, and newspapers have been supplemented by the Internet and CD-ROMs. In addition, businesses and organizations have come to depend on information resource people, such as trainers and guest speakers, to provide needed information.

Role of Informative Speaking

Oral briefings and informative presentations, given one on one, one to group, or via media such as closed circuit television broadcasts, have become major vehicles for disseminating, managing, and dealing with the dissemination of information. Thus, many employees are called on to present and listen to oral presentations, and to be trained and to instruct others.

Informative speaking is not limited to the workplace. Educators, knowing that students learn best from personal involvement, have increased the number of public communication assignments in various subject matter classes. For example, you may be asked to give an informative speech on the life of an author, a psychological theory, or the operational method of a computer system.

Informative speaking is also a function in governmental, community, and cultural venues. Clarifying a zoning change that has been enacted, sharing the design specifics for a new high school, or giving information about upcoming seasonal offerings at the local community theater are all examples of informative speaking.

Concept of Informative Speaking

Traditionally, **informative speaking** has been defined as discourse that imparts new information, secures understanding, or reinforces accumulated information. This may appear to be a straightforward concept, but there is a question about whether there really is such a thing as informative speaking, or that all speaking is persuasive.

Socially Communicating

The Ethics of Informative Speaking

1. Be sure you can ethically defend your choice of a topic.
2. Mention all major positions on a topic when there are differing perspectives.
3. Present all information on a topic that is important for audience understanding.
4. Do not distort information that is necessary for audience understanding.
5. Do sufficient research to speak responsibly on your subject.
6. Do not omit relevant information because it is inconsistent with your perspective.
7. Strive to be as objective as possible.

Source: Michael Osborn, Suzanne Osborn, and Randy Osborn, *Public Speaking*, 8th ed. (Boston: Pearson, 2009).

REFLECT ON THIS: Why do you think it is necessary for you to understand the "Ethics of Informative Speaking"?

This textbook recognizes that all communication contains elements of persuasion. After all, the audience in the traditional informative speaking format must be persuaded to accept information that the speaker presents. Indeed, even the act of using materials to gain attention is persuasive because the speaker is asking listeners to pay attention to the speaker rather than to any other competing stimuli.

It is our contention that there are distinguishing elements between an informative and a persuasive speech. They center on the structure of the message and the appeals used in the persuasive format. The importance of understanding this argument, for you, the student, is to be alert that an informative speech and a persuasive speech are not exactly the same, as they have different communication goals. Some informative presentations are designed to create awareness of the new information about a topic, whereas others are designed to enhance understanding of information that the speaker already knows.

As you study this and the next chapter, you will be introduced to what your authors think are the unique differences between informative and persuasive speeches and to your responsibilities as a preparer, presenter, and listener of each of these types of speeches.

Characteristics of Informative Speaking

As in any other type of speaking, the development of an informative presentation depends on audience analysis. Consideration must be given to the listeners' knowledge about the subject, the concepts they know that can function as a foundation to their gaining the information, and the extent to which definitions, understandable analogies, examples, and clarifiers need to be used. A speaker also must determine the appropriate language level, attention devices, and structure of the message that will best fit the recipients. An astute speaker determines the real needs of the listeners by thorough audience analysis and then uses that information to develop the speech.

In an informative presentation, a speaker must always keep the purpose of the presentation in mind. Thus, a clear statement of central idea is essential. Consider these two examples:

- To inform the audience of what the Heimlich maneuver is, how it was developed, and how this technique can prevent people from choking to death.

- At the conclusion of this speech, I want the members of the audience to know what the Heimlich maneuver is and what steps are necessary to do the maneuver.

In the examples, the subject is the same, but the goal is different. The first statement explains the maneuver and its value. The second explains the maneuver and then teaches the steps for performing it. Both, however, are stated in a manner that narrows the subject and indicates specifically what will be included in the speech. Thus, the statement of central idea serves as a fence around the territory to be covered in a presentation and indicates how to "corral" the information. If you do not set up boundaries, you may find yourself discussing many things but not achieving your desired outcome.

Classifications of Informative Speaking

Informative presentations may be classified as speeches about objects, processes, events, and concepts. In addition, there can be specific types of informative speeches, including informative briefings, team briefings, one-on-one briefings, technical reports,

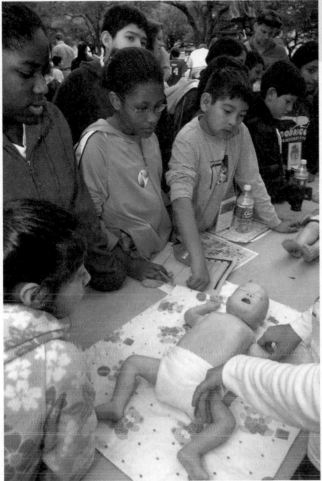

Speeches about processes instruct the audience about how something works, is made, or is done so that they can apply the skills learned.

presentations of professional papers, lectures, question-and-answer sessions, and speeches of introduction.

Speeches about Objects

Speeches about objects describe a particular thing in detail. The object may be a person, place, animal, structure, machine, or anything else that can be touched or seen. First the object is identified, and then details concerning some specific attribute of the object are discussed.

Here are some examples of statements of central ideas for informative speeches about an object and each presentation's method of arrangement: "To inform the audience about the three purposes of the Office of Global Communication" (topical arrangement); and "To inform the audience of the history of the Internet by examining the most important advances from 1995 to 2008" (chronological arrangement).

Speeches about Processes

Speeches about processes instruct the audience about how something works, is made, or is done so that they can apply the skills learned. The purpose may be to gain understanding of the process or to be able to do something. This technique, for example, can be used in training workers to operate a piece of equipment or in

Speeches about processes instruct the audience about how something works.

explaining a manufacturing process. Speeches about processes often lend themselves to development according to a chronological method of organization. In this method, the speaker describes the first step of the process, then the second, and so on.

Statements of central idea for informative speeches about processes include: "To inform listeners of the step-by-step process of creating a PowerPoint slide" (chronological arrangement); and "To demonstrate the process used to fill out the income tax short form" (chronological arrangement).

Speeches about Events

Speeches about events inform the audience about something that has already happened, is happening, or is expected to happen. This type of presentation tends to work well in a chronological, comparison–contrast, or spatial arrangement. Here are some statements of central ideas for informative speeches about events: "To inform the audience of the spread of the AIDS virus in the United States through a statistical examination of the years 1980 to 2008" (chronological arrangement); "To inform the audience of the similarities and differences in the United States and Russian revolutions based on their economic causes" (comparison–contrast arrangement); and "To inform the audience about the major battles fought in the U.S. Civil War by discussing them from the most northern to the most southern conflicts" (spatial arrangement).

Speeches about Concepts

Speeches about concepts examine theories, beliefs, ideas, philosophies, or schools of thought. Much of your academic life is spent listening to speeches about concepts. Concept topics include explanations and investigations of business theories, philosophical movements, psychological concepts, and political theories.

Because some of the ideas relating to concepts are abstract, the speaker must be sure to use precise language, define terms, give historical background, avoid undefined slang and jargon, and use clarifying support materials such as audio, visual, and audiovisual aids. Examples of statements of central ideas for informative speeches about concepts are "To inform the audience about three classical research theories that disprove the myth that abused children do grow up to be child abusers" (topical arrangement); and "To inform the audience of the similarities and differences between the I-phone and a Blackberry" (comparison–contrast).

Informative Briefings

Business, organizational, and technical communicators often gain up-to-date knowledge in their fields as a result of informative briefings. The fundamental objective of an **informative briefing** is to present information to a specialized audience, followed by the exchange of data, ideas, and questions among participants. Organizations, for example, use this technique to explain new or existing organizational policies, procedures, and issues. For instance, a sales manager of an automobile agency may inform her staff about the new models, or a Dean of Students may explain a college's academic policies to a group of entering freshmen.

As with any other speech, preparation for an informative briefing requires careful analysis of the audience to determine what background and definitions will be needed to ensure audience comprehension. If the audience has extensive knowledge, the speaker does not have to cover background material in as much depth as he or she would for uninformed listeners. The automobile agency sales manager does not have to go into detail with her experienced staff about the auto manufacturer and the history of the agency. On the other hand, she would give this background for a meeting of new salespersons. The Dean of Students does not have to explain the layout of the campus or the college's grading policy to upper-level students who will be advising the new freshmen, but must explain both of these factors to new freshmen.

Team Briefings

In a college course or at work, you may find yourself acting as part of a team asked to complete a project. The group may be asked to present a **team briefing** on its findings or recommendations. Team briefings, for example, are used in technology organizations in which design projects or project proposals must be pitched to potential clients or funding agents. In a classroom, teams often are formed to do research or perform an experiment. For example, a group in your communication class, while studying nonverbal communication, may be asked to do research on the effect of invasion of territory by one person while carrying on a conversation with another person. The group would do research on territorial invasion, write a hypothesis, design an experiment to prove the hypothesis, carry out the experiment, and then present a team briefing to the class about its findings.

Team briefings must be well planned and rehearsed. The rehearsal stage can be stressful because the group has to work with each individual's time schedule and differing speaking styles. In order to use group time efficiently, each member

Communicating in Careers

McDonalds, Hamburgers and Informative Speaking

McDonald's owner Ray Kroc once asked if anyone in a particular audience knew what business they were in. The reply came back, "Hamburgers." How would you reply? Probably the same as most do, "Hamburgers."

No, they are not in the hamburger business. They are in the real estate business. They own more prime commercial real estate than just about any body else.

So what is the real meaning of the information you are presenting? List all of the various meanings. Share or weave the most relevant meanings into the body of the talk. Help the audience to see past the hamburgers to the real estate as it were.

Source: Jonathan Steele, "The Informative Speech Body," speechmastery.com, May 31, 2008.

REFLECT ON THIS:

1. Did the title of this tidbit of information catch your attention? If so, why?

2. What are the implications for you as an informative speaker?

should first prepare and rehearse her or his individual briefing. Then, when the team meets, the entire presentation should be blended together. This will entail deciding the format for the program, the speaking order of the presentations, and whether each speaker will have a question-and-answer session or whether there will be an inquiry session for the entire group in which any panel member can answer the audience's probes.

Since a common communication format for team briefings is to have one individual serve as the facilitator, someone will have to be selected, appointed, or elected. The facilitator's role is usually to introduce the presentation and the speakers, make transitions between each of the speakers, conduct the question-and-answer session, and then provide a final summary.

One-on-One Briefings

You may find yourself giving a **one-on-one briefing** to a person or a small group of individuals. Financial analysts, for example, may be called on to brief key decision makers in an informal, conversational presentation, For example, the analyst may present a short summary of the latest projections of the financial status of the organization. Although the presentational climate is informal, it still must follow the basic rules of effective public speaking regarding audience adaptation, clear structuring, and effective oral and physical presentation. The process is sometimes referred to as a *table-top briefing* because it commonly takes place with the participants seated around a conference table.

The briefer usually makes an opening statement about the topic and then presents a short statement of the findings, followed by an extensive question-and-answer session.

Technical Reports

The **technical report** is a statement describing a process, explaining a technique, or discussing new elements to people within a business or industry or to people outside it, such as customers or researchers who may be interested in the topic.

Because the information is often scientific or dependent on knowledge of special terminology, the speaker must do careful audience analysis. If the report is to be given

A speaker should know exactly how much time has been allotted for the presentation and plan to stay within that time limit.

to nontechnical people, all specialized words must be defined, and analogies familiar to the audience should be included to clarify the ideas. This does not mean a speaker has to "water down" the material, but the presenter must give examples and present ideas in a variety of ways to make sure that the audience understands the concepts.

For a more technically oriented audience, a depth of background information would not be necessary. For example, a representative of a medical machinery corporation, in presenting information about a new fMRI (functional magnetic resonance imager) to a group of psychologists interested in the potential for using the device for brain examination who had little technical background, was careful to avoid explaining the mechanical theory behind the equipment. Instead, she demonstrated the ease of operation and the results of the brain scans that could be achieved through using the device. If she were speaking to a group of MRI salespeople, however, who already had the necessary technical knowledge, she would detail the development of the machinery, the technical aspects of the machinery, how it operated, and its various uses.

If your presentation includes technical drawings or a number of statistics, use handouts so that everyone can examine the materials.

If the group is small, consider using an interactive model of communication in which audience members are encouraged to ask questions so you can adapt your message to ensure they get immediate clarification.

When you structure a technical report that involves a recommendation, it is usually wise to start with a statement of the proposal in which you state exactly what you are suggesting or are going to discuss. After you have stated the idea, explain how you arrived at the conclusions or recommendations.

On some occasions, you may want to deviate from this organizational method. For example, you may want to hold the recommendation until the end if you know the audience will be hostile to the proposal, or if you want to lead up to the recommendation by giving total background before revealing your solution or recommendation.

Professional Papers

Another type of speaking that you may encounter or need to present is the professional paper. A **professional paper** is a speech in which the presenter briefs his or her audience on some findings that relate to the speaker or the listeners' area of interest. For example, some colleges stage graduate or undergraduate research conferences for students to present their research findings. Or some students and college professors present their research findings or theories at a professional or academic meeting such as the National Communication Association's yearly convention or an American Psychological Association regional conference.

Some presenters choose to present their papers word for word, while the listeners follow along, but that is not a very engaging presentational style. The most effective presenters will speak extemporaneously and, following the presentation, hand out copies for listeners to read at another time. This method avoids having the listeners reading your paper while you are speaking. If the listeners need some specific information as you are speaking, an outline can be distributed before you make your speech, or a PowerPoint program of the highlights may be used.

Another format for presenting research at these conferences is the poster session. In a **poster session** you prepare a poster, a series of charts, or a PowerPoint program that visually highlights your research or idea. The posters or electronic equipment are usually set up in a room with other charts, displays, and speakers. You will be asked to explain your work and answer questions posed by those who have come to look at your work. For example, if you have ever been to or participated in a high school science fair or a product sales show, you've been part of a poster session. Most of the presentations will be made one on one or to a very small group. Since the audience will be circulating, you must be aware of the time factor and the setting. In general, you will want to prepare a one- or two-minute briefing and be ready to answer questions when they are asked.

Here are some guidelines for preparing for a poster session:

- Divide the contents of the poster into appropriate sections: title, author, affiliation, project abstract, method of determining the idea or recommendation, data, results, and conclusions.
- Use a font larger than 16 point for headings or major information.
- Avoid fonts that are difficult to read (for example, avoid using letters with serifs [flags] such as *Apple Chancery*) and erratic fonts such as **Sand**.
- You don't have much space, so be concise.
- If appropriate, use graphs, pictures, and tables to display your results or conclusions.
- Generally, use a neutral-colored posterboard unless you are trying for a specific result (e.g., a student at a college science fair who was making a presentation on explosives intentionally selected a red poster board to visually highlight her work).
- If possible, have copies of your entire paper available for people to take with them.

The format for preparing PowerPoint displays can be found on pages 348–350.

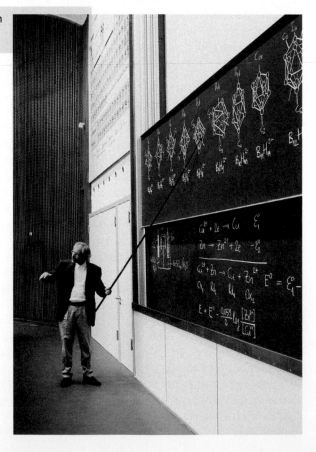

Lectures are an integral part of academic life, serving as the main vehicle for presenting information in many subject fields.

Lectures

Probably the most familiar type of informative speaking is the **lecture,** the formal presentation of material to facilitate learning. Lectures are an integral part of academic life, serving as the main vehicle for presenting information in many subject fields. Lectures also are used in other settings, including speakers for lunch or dinner seminars in corporate headquarters and public lectures by distinguished authorities in museums, arts, religious, or public settings.

A good lecture should be adapted to the intended audience so that the speaker's topic, language, and examples fit the listeners' levels of knowledge and vocabulary. An effective lecture, like any good speech, should be clearly organized, with transitions that allow listeners to stay on track and anticipate what is coming next. The speaker should use supporting details to elaborate on each of the points made. A variety of supporting materials (stories, statistics, analogies) should be used.

Humor is also a way of getting and holding attention. Even if you are not a joke teller, you can still make humor work for you. Of course, the funny story or humorous incident should be relevant to the theme and purpose of the speech. And, unless there is an overriding reason for it not to be, the humor should be in good taste. Audience analysis is important here. What might be appropriate at a roast of a retiring football coach would be inappropriate for a speech to the high school football team.

Some types for inclusion of humor in a speech include:[3]

- Analogies are a good source of humor. Linking your present situation or problem to something else often provides an opportunity for humor. The line can be either illogical and could even be a personal anecdote.

- Use a funny quote. These can be found online (e.g., amusingquotes.com or allfunnyquotes.com) or in books of quotations (e.g., Dick Enberg, Brian Morgan, and Wendy Morgan, *Dick Enberg's Humorous Quotes for All Occasions* (Riverside, NJ: Andrews McMeel Publishing, 2000) or Allen Klein, *The Wise and Witty Quote Book: More than 2000 Quotes to Enlighten, Encourage, and Enjoy* (New York: Gramercy, 2005).

- Use an amusing cartoon from the newspaper or magazine. Show it, read it, or describe it.

Culturally Communicating

Humor and Diversity

What if you are an outsider, not a member of a group? I generally recommend to a speaker presenting to nurses to avoid nursing jokes if the speaker is not a nurse. The reason? They have heard the jokes before. And you do not have the inside knowledge to judge whether the joke is truly funny or in good taste. So, if you are speaking to a group of Republicans or doctors or Mormons or blacks, it is probably risky to target jokes toward their specific group if you are not one of them.

Inside knowledge helps. Is it safe to tell a physically challenged joke, a black joke, a Jewish joke, gay joke, a joke about women? It's probably safe if you are a black Jewish Lesbian in a wheelchair. One of the safety factors is "are you part of the group"? Being blind, if you are telling a blind joke, may give you better insight on whether or not the joke is funny or in good taste. Being part of the group may also give you "permission" from the audience to tell the joke as someone who is not an outsider.

Source: John Kinde, "Humor and Diversity," http://humorpower.com/art-diversity.html, 2006.

REFLECT ON THIS:

1. Of what value is knowing this attitude toward speaking to groups of which you are not a member?

2. Have you ever been in an audience where these "rules" were not followed? What was the reaction of people in the audience.

- Don't announce when you are about to use humor (e.g., "I'm going to tell you the funniest joke," "You are going to love this one"). Both of those lines give a forecast that might not be true and it could turn out to be an embarrassment when no one laughs after your joke or quote. Instead, just unobtrusively insert humor here and there.

- If you are in doubt about the quality or the appropriateness of a joke or quote, leave it out.

Another attention technique is to use questions, probing for information, and inviting inquiries during the presentation instead of waiting until the question-and-answer session. Asking questions where the audience can vote for solutions or verbally suggest ideas gets attention. A lecturer, about half-way through his presentation on nonverbal communication, inserted a series of questions regarding masculine and feminine perceived body movement and gesture patterns. He polled the audience to determine their ideas about whether men or women used the described actions. The audience became animated and were curious as to whether they had answered the questions correctly. As the answers were given, they cheered when they were correct.

Insertion of supplemental aids (charts, handouts, PowerPoint graphics) can facilitate listeners' understanding and keep them interested.

The timing of a lecture is another key to success. The audience expects a lecturer to stay within the assigned time (such as a class period).

We have all sat through good and bad classroom lectures—lectures that held your attention and from which you learned. You probably have also sat through some that put you to sleep. If you are ever asked to present a lecture, recall what kept you engaged when you listened to the good presentations and use those techniques in your own presentation.

Question-and-Answer Sessions

The **question-and-answer session** that follows many speeches is a type of informative speech in itself. The questions asked and the speaker's responses can be useful to measure a speaker's knowledge, alert a speaker to areas in a speech that were unclear

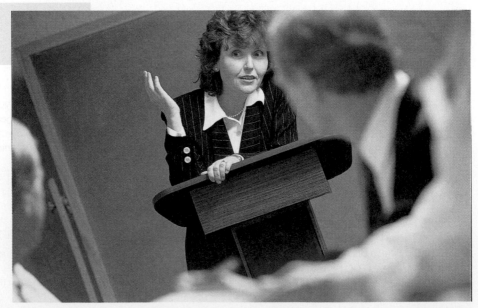

The question-and-answer session is an on-the-spot set of unrehearsed answers.

or needed more development, and give listeners a chance to probe for ideas.

In preparing for a question-and-answer session, you should anticipate the types of questions you are likely to be asked and prepare some potential responses. This will help you to compose your thoughts and might help to avoid being blind-sided by questions you had not expected.

When you enter into a question-and-answer session, set the ground rules. Ask the program chairperson about the process to be used and the time limit. Tell him or her of any restrictions you wish to place on this segment of the speech and inform the audience of the rules. Some speakers like to call on participants themselves; others prefer that the chairperson entertain the questions. Some presenters want all questions written out beforehand so they can select the questions they will answer.

The most difficult part of many question-and-answer sessions is to get the first question asked. Once this hurdle is overcome, questions usually flow readily. To overcome the first-question trauma, you may want to have someone in the audience prepared in advance to ask a question. Another technique is to ask a question yourself. This can be accomplished by stating, "I've often been asked my views concerning . . ." and then answering by indicating your views.

Communicating in Careers

The Question-and-Answer Session in an Informative Speech

Most business presentations have a question-and-answer (Q&A) period at the end of the talk. Unless your presentation is interactive, this is the time your audience may ask questions. The Q&A section of your presentation should mark the beginning of your close, not the end. How many times have you seen a speaker ask "Are there any questions?" only to look out into an audience of blank stares and what feels like an eternity of silence. For this section to be successful, you must have audience participation.

To prevent an ocean of blank stares, use one of the following techniques to get your Q&A session rolling. First, have a friend in the audience prepared to ask a question the minute you open the floor to questions. It's a good idea to know the question ahead of time so you're ready with an answer; however, it's not absolutely necessary. Another approach that works well is for you to lead with a question you're typically asked. Start by saying, "A question I'm typically asked is . . . ." Both methods will give your audience time to formulate questions and prevent an awkward silence. Afterward, thank members of your audience for their questions before moving to your invitation (call to action).

Source: "The Three-Step Close That Attracts Clients Like Crazy," www.persuasivespeaking.blogspot.com, March 31, 2008.

Here are some additional suggestions for conducting a question-and-answer session:

- Before you answer a question, restate it so that everyone hears the inquiry. If the question is complicated, simplify it in the restatement.

- Speak to and look at the entire audience rather than only at the questioner.

- Be patient. If you have to repeat material you have already covered, do so briefly.

- If a question goes on and on, prompt the questioner to summarize the question.

- Keep your answers short. Restate the question, give your response, clarify any vocabulary necessary, give an example if appropriate, and then stop. Following the response, some speakers ask the questioner whether the answer was satisfactory.

- Back up your responses with examples, statistics, and quotations.

- If a question is overly complicated or of interest only to the asker, suggest a discussion with the questioner after the speech or via correspondence.

- If a question is irrelevant, indicate that it is interesting or thought provoking but does not seem appropriate to the presentation. Do not get sidetracked from the purpose of the speech or pulled into a private debate with a questioner.

- If you do not know an answer, say so. You can offer to find out the answer and report back later.

- Limit the discussion to one question per person, and avoid getting caught in a dialogue with one person. Others who have questions will become frustrated, and those who do not will get bored.

- Be willing to be corrected or at least to recognize another's viewpoint. Thank a person for clarification or acknowledge that more than one point of view is possible (e.g., "That's an interesting idea" or "The idea can be viewed that way"). You may win a battle of words by putting down or insulting a questioner, but you will usually lose the respect of your listeners in the process. It is futile to get involved in a battle of words with a heckler or a person with a preconceived attitude or bias.

- Know when to end a session. Do not wait until interest has waned or people begin leaving. You can lose the positive effect of a speech by having an overly long question-and-answer session.

- Display the points of your presentation for the audience. It is helpful for listeners to have the points of the presentation before them so they can be reminded of what you have covered. If you use PowerPoint, have a slide to display during the question-and-answer session that has the bullet points of the speech. Leave this slide on the screen during the question-and-answer session. Or, if you are not using PowerPoint, you might prepare a handout with the major points so that the audience can follow along during the presentation and then use the points during the question-and-answer section. Alternatively, you can hand out the talking points following your speech.

- Summarize the speech, including the question-and-answer session. Wrap up the entire presentation when you have completed all aspects, perhaps with a closing such as, "Current policy on a national security database just begins to address the many issues that must be considered by security organizations, law enforcement, and policymakers alike. As our interaction together suggests, the impact of these issues is profound. Thank you for being with me today to explore these ideas."

In some instances, a question-and-answer session allows listeners to point out weaknesses in a speaker's arguments or present alternative views. These occur more frequently after persuasive speeches than after informative presentations. If confronted by a hostile questioner, the speaker has to determine whether to deal with the issue or remind the prober that the purpose of this part of the speech is to ask questions, not give a counterspeech or engage in debate. One way to avoid getting into a confrontation is to say to the questioner, "That's an interesting question. I'd be more than glad to discuss that with you following the presentation."

Speeches of Introduction

The purpose of a **speech of introduction** is to identify the person who will be speaking to the audience and give any other information that may spark listeners' interest in the speaker or the topic. Too often, speeches of introduction are ineffective because the presenter has not carefully prepared remarks appropriate to listeners' needs. When you introduce a speaker, clearly identify who the speaker is by name, title, and the identification he or she wants used. You can talk about where the speaker is from as well as his or her accomplishments and when they were achieved. Establish the credibility of a speaker by highlighting aspects of his or her credentials and background that indicate knowledge or expertise in the subject being discussed.

Remember that listeners have come to hear the speaker, not the person making the introduction, so a speech of introduction should be short and to the point. Here are some suggestions for a speech of introduction:

- Get the information you need from a speaker as far in advance as possible so that you have time to work on the presentation.

- Be sure you can pronounce a speaker's name as he or she wants it pronounced.

- If possible, ask what background information a speaker wishes to have highlighted.

- Do not overpraise a speaker. Indicating that he or she is the best speaker the audience will ever hear, for example, gives the presenter an almost impossible goal.

- Avoid using a statement such as "It is an honor and a privilege" or "This speaker needs no introduction." These are overused and often sound insincere.

- Set the proper tone for the speech. If, for example, you know that the speech is going to be humorous, try to fit humor into the introduction.

One of your authors was asked to give a speech to an audience of alumni of the communication program of the school at which he taught. He was introduced by one of his former students, who said, "We all know our speaker tonight as an author, entertainment reviewer, theater director, counselor, and a teacher, but to me, his greatest talent is that of an inspirer. My life, and those of countless many of you, has been drastically changed by having him as a professor and friend. He inspired us to 'reach for the highest star and to do the very best you can.' Our speaker, who will share the importance of setting high personal goals, is . . . ."

Development of the Informative Speech

Every informative speaker has a challenge: to get the audience to understand and retain the information presented. The basis for retention and understanding is the establishment of relationships (associations and connections) with physical or mental activities. We can learn through repetition—hearing ideas over and over again. We can learn through experiencing—doing a task to see what it is. We are more likely to remember things that have relevance to us. We remember information we are exposed to that will somehow make life easier or teach us something we did not know before or for which we will be rewarded. In other words, we remember when we see a reason to do so. We also remember when something makes sense to us—when the order in which the material is presented makes the idea(s) easy to understand or the examples and other developing materials make the idea clear.

When you plan an informative speech, consider using supplementary aids to help your listeners remember your message. Understanding how people learn can be of assistance in determining the approach to take. Such devices as slides, charts, illustrations, pictures, and models help to reinforce and clarify what you say. Keep in mind these pointers when developing an informative speech:

- *Order your ideas clearly.* Select a method of organization that helps your audience follow the step-by-step development of the speech.

Socially Communicating

What Structure Will Best Suit the Audience?

The structure of an informative speech body is usually in the form of main points.

Because of the way the human mind works, three is the best number to limit it to. If necessary, some go as high as five. Beyond that, most will not remember and the effectiveness of your public speaking will be diluted.

Sometimes it is possible to structure an informative speech in the form of a story or through an illustration. The points can be woven into an illustration to aid the audience to remember and motivate them to use the information. Real life stories have the ability to motivate as well.

Note: Caution needs to be used here as the story can overshadow the points so that everyone remembers the story and not the main points.

The goal is to try to find a fresh way of looking at the information. Look for creative ways to share and create an informative speech that touches the audience. Be able to deliver the information differently than it has been shared before.

Source: Jonathan Steele, "The Informative Speech Body," speechmastery.com, May 31, 2008.

- *Use a time sequence method of delivery if a speech lends itself to a first-second-third progression or is date oriented (years or ages). Sample subject:* Explaining an experiment that requires a specific progression.

- *Use a spatial method of organization if a speech has some geographical basis that lends itself to an east-west, top-bottom, or inside-out organization. Sample subject:* Tracing the voyage of Christopher Columbus from Spain to the New World.

- *Use a topical method of delivery if a broad subject area can be divided into specific parts. Sample subject:* Describing the life cycle, characteristics, and dangers of the killer bee.

- *Use comparison–contrast when a topic centers on illustrating similarities and differences. Sample subject:* Comparing Nebraska's unicameral (one-house) legislature with the two-house legislative system of other states.

- *Use the familiar to explain the new.* An excellent clarifying technique is to use an analogy that compares something unfamiliar to the familiar. For example, you can explain how an AM radio signal travels by comparing it to the way a bow and arrow work. The arrow goes as far as the bow projects it. If something gets in its way, the arrow stops moving. Similarly, an AM signal goes as far as its thrusting signal power allows it to move, unless something gets in its way and stops it.

- *Use vivid illustrations.* Descriptions, stories, comparisons, contrasts, and verbal pictures add to the possibility of gaining and holding the audience's attention. An audience member who can visualize something is likely to remember it.

- *Avoid being too technical.* If you have ever tried to follow directions for using a computer program when you knew nothing about computer language, you know the difficulty of understanding materials geared for an expert, not a layperson. If your subject is technical, evaluate the vocabulary level of audience members and choose terms that are unlikely to confuse or that will clarify the technical terms you do use. The purpose of a speech is not to impress an audience with your vast vocabulary; it is to accomplish an informative objective. Select words that will help, rather than hinder, your task.

- *Personalize your message.* Audiences are more attracted to real, human-element examples than to fictional or hypothetical examples. If at all possible, use illustrations that allow your audience to identify with the plight of a victim, understand the joy of what happened to someone who mastered the process you are teaching, or learn how someone's life was altered by the historical event you are sharing.

- *Do not speak down to your audience,* but do not overestimate audience knowledge. There is no clear guideline for evaluating an audience's knowledge level other than to learn as much as you can about what the audience knows, specifically and generally. It is senseless to draw an analogy to the familiar if it is not familiar. For instance, professors who grew up in the 1960s, when John Kennedy was president, often forget that most college students today were not even born during JFK's presidency. Drawing comparisons between today and that time may be beyond the conceptual level of students.

- *Use as much clarification and detail as you think necessary to ensure listener understanding.* If anything, err on the side of overexplanation. Most audience members appreciate a speaker who makes an effort to communicate clearly.

The Informative Process in Action

It is helpful to study the process of speech preparation by investigating a model. Figure 15.1 outlines a speech that follows the principles you've learned for developing informative speeches.

Statement of Central Idea: To inform the audience about the importance of the impact of nanotechnology on our future by examining what nanotechnology is and providing individuals with examples of how it can change lives.

Opening material to grasp the listeners' attention	**I. Introduction** A. Attention material: Nanotechnology is so small, if an experiment in the lab were to be hit by a single particle of dust, it would be the equivalent of your car windshield getting hit with a bowling ball at 65 mph. B. Orienting material: With the further development of nanotech, the medical opportunities are endless, which could help cure disease and allow people to live longer healthier lives.
Topic of speech	**II. Central Idea** A. Nanotechnology is currently being developed in all fields, from electronics to medicine. This powerful technology has the ability to truly change the world.
Preview of nanotechnology	B. Let us explore the world of nanotechnology by looking at facilities requirements, size, and medical applications.
First issue (keeping facilities clean)	**III. Body** A. The development of nanotechnology requires extremely clean facilities.

Discussion of nanotechnology labs and equipment	1. Any dust or dirt particles will destroy the nanotechnology experiments.
	  a. People working in the facilities must wear specialized suits that cover their bodies.
	  b. They must also wear gloves, goggles, as well as shoe covers to prevent any unwanted debris from entering the lab.
	2. Special air filtration systems (hepafiltration) have been installed in nanofabrication labs.
	  a. These systems do not allow any dust or dirt particles to enter the air.
	  b. They are extremely expensive to run, but must remain on at all times to protect the nanotechnology experiments.

Transition	Now that we have an idea about how fragile these nano particles are, let's take a deeper look at their actual size.
Second issue (size of nanotechnology)	A nanometer is one-billionth of a meter. A single strand of hair is 100,000 nanometers wide!

Discussion of the process of making nanotechnology products	B. The making of nanotechnology parts
	1. Nanotechnology parts are made with a process called photolithography, since the parts are too small to see with the human eye.
	  a. Photolithography is three-dimensional.
	  b. Photolithography uses light.

Transition	Understanding how these small parts are made is the first step to seeing how nanotechnology can be made possible in medicine.

(continued)

Figure 15.1   Informative Process in Action

Third issue (putting nanotech into medicine)	Nanotechnology has the capability in the near future to help people with various diseases, like heart disease.

Discussion of nanorobots	C. As futuristic as it may seem, there is currently talk on developing "nanorobots" to enter the human body and literally eat away the plaque and cholesterol buildup in arteries.
	   1. Heart disease is the number-one killer in America. Heart attacks occur when arteries become severely or completely blocked.
	      a. The nanorobots would be able to enter the human body through veins.
	      b. They would then be directed to the clogged arteries.
	      c. Last, they would be retrieved back out of the body.
	   2. These nanorobots have the ability to eliminate clogged arteries and save lives.

Reiteration of main points	IV. **Conclusion**
	   A. Summary
	      1. In order to make nanotechnology experiments possible, facilities must be extremely clean.
	      2. A nanometer is one-billionth of a meter.
	      3. Developments such as the nanorobot have the opportunity to reduce heart disease and save lives.

Restatement of theme to emphasize the importance of the impact of nanotechnology	B. The impossible can be made possible with further developments of nanotechnology.

Figure 15.1   (continued)

In Conclusion

Informative speaking imparts new information, secures understanding, or reinforces accumulated information. Types of informative speaking include presentations about objects, processes, events, and concepts. Informative speeches, when classified by setting or uniqueness, include informative briefings, team briefings, one-on-one briefings, technical reports, presentations of professional papers, lectures, question-and-answer sessions, and speeches of introduction. The challenge for an informative speaker is to get the audience to understand and retain the information presented. To develop an informative speech, order your ideas clearly, use the familiar to explain the new, use vivid illustrations, avoid being too technical, personalize the message, and do not speak down to the audience.

Learn by Doing

1. In class, your instructor will match you with a partner. With the assistance of your partner, select a topic for a speech based on audience analysis (your class), setting (your classroom), and purpose (an informative speech of three to five minutes). After both of you have selected your topics, meet with another duo. Each of you will present a short informative speech indicating what topic you

have selected and why this subject suits you, the audience, the setting, and the purpose. The speech should have an introduction, statement of central idea, body, and conclusion.

2. Bring to class an object or piece of machinery (e.g., a digital camera, electronic wall stud finder, microscope) that you think members of your class cannot operate or that you have a different approach to operating. Be prepared to teach someone else how to use the equipment. In class, you are placed in a group with four of your class-mates. Decide the order in which you will present the material. After this is done, the first speaker gives a two- to four-minute presentation on how the object works. Then the second speaker demonstrates how the object operates. Your success as a speaker is based on whether the person following you can operate the object.

3. Before a series of speeches is to be given by class members, your instructor assigns you the name of a person in your class whom you will later be introducing. Interview that person and collect all the information you will need to prepare a speech of introduction (topic of the speech, some background information on the speaker, why the subject was chosen, the qualifications of the speaker to present a speech on this topic, and so on). On the day of your partner's speech, introduce her or him.

4. You are going to give a "what-if" speech. On each of three 3 × 5 notecards, indicate something that could go wrong immediately before, during, or after a speech (e.g., you drop your speech outline in a puddle of water just outside your classroom building, or an audience member challenges your statistics during the question-and-answer period). The instructor collects the cards, shuffles them, and hands them out one by one. When you get your card, immediately give a presentation that includes a restatement of the occurrence and a contingency plan for dealing with the situation. (This assign-ment may take place when a short amount of time remains at the end of any class period.)

5. All students present one-minute speeches in which they state something that bothers them in everyday life. They should tell what the peeve is, why it is a peeve, and what they would like to see done about it, if anything.

6. Use your vocational preference, or an occupation you may be interested in, to investigate some phase of the career and present an informative speech about it. The presentation must include the use of a supplementary aid. Sample speech topics include a future audiologist explains the differences among several brands of hearing aids, a theater major discusses the famous actors who graduated from this college, an aspiring musician demonstrates how music is scored.

Key Terms

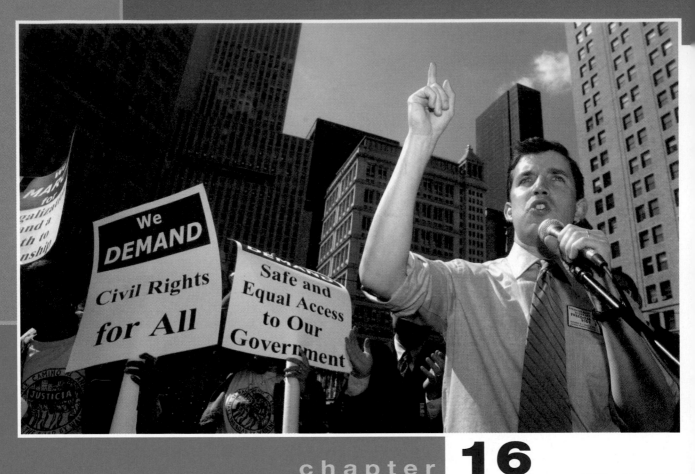

Persuasive Public Speaking

chapter 16

▶ ### After reading this chapter, you should be able to

- Explain how people are influenced by persuasive messages

- Explain how people are influenced by coercive messages

- Illustrate how speaker credibility, logical arguments, and psychological appeals can affect listeners

- List and explain how speaker credibility, logical arguments, and psychological appeals can be used in the preparation of a persuasive speech

- Analyze a persuasive speech to ascertain its potential effectiveness based on logical arguments and psychological appeals

- Prepare a persuasive speech using credibility, logical arguments, and psychological appeals

E very day, as a listener you are bombarded with messages intended to convince you to take some action, accept some belief, or change some point of view. And almost every day, as a speaker, you, knowingly or unknowingly, attempt to bring about these changes in others. These are all acts of persuasion.

Persuasion is the process of influencing attitudes and behaviors. The route to being a successful persuader is to find the means to answer the question, "What's in it for *you?*" The bottom line for the person who is the recipient of a persuasive message is, "Is what the speaker proposing in my best interests?" Most people will take actions or adopt beliefs if they can figure out how they can benefit from them—monetarily, socially, physically, philosophically, or spiritually.

Persuasive Speaking

A **persuasive speech** is intended to influence the opinion or behavior of an audience. Its materials are derived from problems about which people hold differing beliefs and opinions, such as controversial matters that call for decisions or action. The persuasive speaker tells listeners what they ought to believe or do.

A persuasive speech may have as its end goal either conviction or actuation.

In a **speech of conviction,** the speaker is attempting to convince the listener to believe as the speaker does. Topics that fall into this category could include "There is no real danger of nuclear fallout from atomic plants" or "XYZ Corporation has developed a clear set of equal opportunity guidelines."

A **speech of actuation** should move the members of the audience to take the desired action that the speaker has proposed—for example, buy the product, sign the petition, go on strike, or adopt the plan presented. Topics that fall into this category could include "Please support my candidacy for President of the University's Student Body" or "Purchase products that are bio-green."

Process of Persuasion

Much is known about what motivates people to act. Unfortunately, in spite of our knowledge, there are flaws in the system, or no candidate for office would ever lose, no charity would fail to reach its fund-raising goal, and no advertised product would go unsold. This chapter presents the theories that explain the process of persuasion and how—if you are developing a persuasive speech to individuals from the European American culture—you might use those theories to accomplish your goal.

The basic process of persuasion centers on making a claim, then backing up the claim with reasons and emotional appeals that will lead listeners to accept the claim. To do this, you must analyze the audience and develop arguments that will appeal to that particular group.

Several concepts, including the theories of field-related, group, and individual standards, help explain what to do.

The *theory of field-related standards* proposes that not all people reach conclusions in the same way and thus may react differently to the same evidence or psychological material. Therefore, in establishing your arguments, you want to include as many appeals as you can to cover the various thought processes of members of your audience. For example, in establishing arguments for why your listeners should vote for a particular candidate, you can list several of the candidate's positions rather than just one and select the positions that most align with the attitudes of the audience.

Group norm standards—the thinking of a particular group—may be used as a guide for developing your arguments. If you are speaking to a group of union members, for instance, you can assume that on labor-related issues, they will have views that favor the union rather than management. Thus, if you are going to propose a change in the plant operation, show how it will be good for the union and its members.

In any group there are those who have power. The theory of *individual norm standards* proposes that being on the side of or getting the backing of that person or persons may be a powerful tool to influence the group's members to side with your stand. For example, if the elected president of the city council agrees, the rest of the group who elected her may follow her lead.

To be persuasive, you also should develop your arguments to encourage listeners to believe that the solution, plan of action, or cure that you are presenting is the best solution. Two methods you might consider using to accomplish your persuasive goal are critical thinking and comparative-advantage reasoning.

To apply *critical thinking*, you establish criteria and then match the solutions with the criteria. For example, if you are proposing a plan of action for solving a fraternity's financial problems, you can set criteria that include not having to raise members' dues and planning an activity that can raise money quickly, without extensive planning. You may then propose that the organization stage a lottery and sell raffle tickets, establishing how the lottery fulfills the established criteria.

In contrast, when you use *comparative-advantage reasoning*, you begin by stating possible solutions. Then you demonstrate how the proposal is the most *workable* (can solve the problem), *desirable* (does not cause any greater problems), and *practical* (that it can be put into operation). Establish why your particular proposal has fewer disadvantages than any other. To achieve the goal of raising funds, for example, in using the comparative-advantage reasoning process, you could propose that a lottery be set up, explain why this is a workable plan by referring to other organizations that have used the process, and present statistics on the amount of money these groups have raised. Then indicate that a lottery is desirable because it will not cost members a great deal of money and the risk that the organization will lose money is not great. Next, show that the proposal is practical because the tickets can be ready by the next week and the finance committee has worked out a plan for distributing the tickets and handling the money. Finally, you explain why this system is better than raising dues.

An alternative persuasive process is the *Monroe's Motivated Sequence*.[1] This plan describes the psychological sequence by which a listener is taken through a five-step persuasive message:

1. *Attention*. Get the listener to focus on your message.
2. *Need*. Identify a problem and show how it relates to the listener.
3. *Satisfaction*. Propose a plan of action that will meet the need that has been identified.
4. *Visualization*. Describe the beneficial results when the plan is implemented (or the detriments if it is not undertaken).
5. *Action*. Challenge the listener to do as requested.

The motivated sequence fits the traditional speech structure (introduction, statement of central idea, body, conclusion; see pages 353–367 in this text). The attention step is the first section of the introduction. The statement of central idea establishes your purpose for speaking. The need is developed in the first section of the body of the speech, followed by how the need is satisfied by the proposed plan, which is followed by the visualization, which describes the benefits of the plan. (Traditionally, these would be III. A, B, and C in the speech outline.) And the action step starts with the summary part of the conclusion in which the need (problem), satisfaction (plan of action), and visualization (benefits of the proposed solution) are presented, followed by a clincher in your conclusion in which you challenge the listener to do as requested.

Persuasive Strategies

The aftermath of the September 11, 2001, terrorist attacks and the Iraq war have led to increasing questions of the government's persuasive powers and whether our leaders can or should be trusted. Americans have been bombarded with reports on the dangers of drugs and food products, economic downturn, West Nile virus, climate change, AIDS, bio-terrorism, and obesity warnings. Because we receive so much bad news, many listeners have become skeptical of what they hear. Consequently, persuaders are hard-pressed to know how best to get people's attention and how to target appeals that will lead to their desired response; therefore, persuasive strategies are constantly under scrutiny.

Researchers have renewed and refined their efforts to ascertain how people are influenced.[2] Their exploration centers on such factors as personal involvement, saving face, the Elaboration Likelihood Model, values clarification, and the sense of social support.

It is understood that a person who has something at stake, a *personal involvement*, will be most likely to be persuaded by a message that solves a personal problem, gives advice on how to fulfill a personal desire or need, or allows him or her to "save face," fulfill an ego need, or feel better about himself or herself. If the message has little or no relevance to the listener, certainly he or she is not going to focus much energy on processing it.

The *Elaboration Likelihood Model* has been used to explain how listeners process persuasive messages.[3] The model illustrates the theory that if the issue being discussed is one that the listener has encountered before, is interested and involved in, and enjoys thinking about, he or she is more likely to engage in centrally processing the persuader's arguments. This attention does not necessarily guarantee that the listener will be persuaded, but at least it gives the speaker the attention of the receiver and, if the arguments are emotionally and logically sound, there is a chance for persuasive results.

The listener also may be persuaded because the message resonates with his or her values or things in which he or she believes. Such factors as change/mobility, equality, individualism, free enterprise, informality, directness, practicality and materialism are important to many U.S. citizens.[4] (See Figure 16.1.) Messages that tap into these values probably have the greatest effect in eliciting change, because listeners can connect with the appeals.

To be persuaded, listeners also may rely on a strong sense of *social support*. The long-term staying power of messages depends not only on how the appeal resonates with the individual but also on the degree to which the individual perceives that he or she has the support of others, thus enabling the person to feel that "we are all in it together."

Some principles that persuaders who are keying on social support should consider when attempting to get people to respond include:[5]

- *The principle of liking.* People like those who like them, so find a common bond and offer genuine praise and support.
- *The principle of reciprocity.* People will repay in kind, so a good strategy is to give what it is you want to receive in return.
- *The principle of social proof.* People will follow the lead of those similar to them, so use the examples of peers to reinforce your effort.

Figure 16.1

The Values Americans Live By

Source: Adapted from L. Robert Kohls, "The Values Americans Live By." Published 2006 by Meridian International Center.

1. Personal Control over the Environment
Americans no longer believe in the power of Fate, and they have come to look at people who do as being backward, primitive, or hopelessly naive.

2. Change
In the American mind, change is seen as an indisputably good condition.

3. Time and Its Control
Time is, for the average American, of utmost importance.

4. Equality/Egalitarianism
Equality is, for Americans, one of their most cherished values.

5. Individualism and Privacy
Each individual is seen as completely unique, totally different from all others.

6. Self-Help Concept
In the United States, a person can take credit only for what he or she has accomplished by himself or herself.

7. Competition and Free Enterprise
Americans believe that competition brings out the best in any individual.

8. Future Orientation
Valuing the future, and the improvements Americans are sure the future will bring, means that they devalue the past and are, to a large extent, unconscious of the present.

9. Action/Work Orientation
Americans routinely plan and schedule an extremely active day. Any relaxation must be limited in time, pre-planned, and aimed at "recreating" their ability to work harder and more productively once the recreation is over. Americans believe leisure activities should assume a relatively small portion of one's total life.

10. Informality
Americans are one of the most informal and casual people in the world. American bosses often urge their employees to call them by their first names. Dress is another area where American informality will be most noticeable.

11. Directness, Openness, and Honesty
Many other countries have developed subtle, sometimes highly ritualistic, ways of informing other people of unpleasant information. Americans, however, have always preferred the direct approach.

12. Practicality and Efficiency
Americans have a reputation of being an extremely realistic, practical, and efficient people.

13. Materialism/Acquisitions
Americans value and give higher priority to obtaining, maintaining, and protecting their material objects than they do in developing and enjoying interpersonal relationships.

- *The principle of consistency.* People will make their commitments if they're based on active, voluntary choices.

- *The principle of authority.* People defer to experts, so don't assume that your expertise is self-evident. Let people know your background and experience.

- *The principle of scarcity.* People want more of what they have less of, so limiting opportunities to act so they can get more of the scarce commodity will have a mobilizing effect.

Persuasiveness is a complex matter that requires careful understanding of your listeners and adaptation of your message to them.

Role of Influence in Persuasion

One of the purposes of the persuasive process is to influence, to get the listener to take some action or believe in a concept. The persuasive process occurs, for instance, when salespersons from different data corporations present speeches in an attempt to sell their systems to the purchasing agents of clients. Based on the presentations, the purchasing agents may be influenced to buy products from a salesperson because of her arguments stressing her product's lower cost and ease of operation.

Normally, the intended audience has a choice of what actions to take. However, a particular form of influencing takes place when listeners are not given a voluntary choice. For example, a speaker at a union meeting says, "Either we accept the proposal as presented or we go on strike." You might not want to choose either of those options, yet if the vote is set up with only those two, you must choose. This attempt to change behavior relies on force and is known as *coercion*. Coercion results when the listener perceives that he or she has no choice but to accept what the speaker proposes.

Another type of attempt to use influence includes presenting *psychological appeals* aimed at emotionally stirring audience members to action. Such factors as fear, hatred, social pressure, and shock can be used to dull listeners' senses to the point where they perform acts they may not consider if they were to step outside the emotion of the situation and objectively evaluate potential consequences. German dictator Adolf Hitler before and during World War II used emotional appeals focused on building a "master race" that included killing all those he deemed inferior: Jews, gypsies, homosexuals, and his political enemies. Many people responded to these appeals and participated in the destruction of other human beings as a result.

Persuasion can be accomplished by repeated exposure to messages. Seldom does one persuasive message result in any major change of belief on the part of the receiver. As a result, massive amounts of time and money are spent waging persuasive campaigns by systematically and repeatedly exposing listeners to a message with the objective of enhancing retention of its basic persuasive thesis. This is the reason that the electorate is inundated with speeches and other publicity about candidates during political campaigns, and advertisers run ads over and over until they make their impact.

Do not assume that all persuasion is negative or immoral. Persuasive communication strategies are essentially *amoral*—neither good nor bad. It is only the ways in which the strategies are used, and to what ends, that give communication a dimension of morality. By knowing this, and being equipped to recognize manipulative and coercive methods, you may be able as a listener to protect yourself from being exploited.

Socially Communicating

Achieve Change with 2-6-2

To persuade a group to accept change, consider the "2-6-2" principle: Two out of ten will oppose it, six out of ten will wait and see, and two out of ten will embrace it.

Strategy:

- Don't try to sway the opposing 20 percent.

- Give the pro 20 percent all they need to make the change work. *Reason*: They'll quickly produce results. And when the fence-sitting 60 percent see that, they'll join the pro team.

Source: Go-Go Tools: Five Essential Activities for Leading Small Groups, by Shigehiro Nakamura, Productivity Press, P.O. Box 13390, Portland, OR 97213. © Communication Briefings, www.briefings.com, 1101 King St., Suite 110, Alexandria, VA 22314. Used with permission.

REFLECT ON THIS: You have been appointed to be the speech writer for a political candidate. What are the implications of the "2-6-2" principle for your preparation of "vote for me" persuasive speeches for the candidate?

As demonstrated by such speakers as World War II
German leader Adolf Hitler, fear, hatred, social pressure,
and shock can be used to dull listeners' senses to the
point where they perform acts they may not consider if
they were to step outside the emotion of the situation
and objectively evaluate potential consequences.

Components of Persuasive Message

The classical Greek philosopher-rhetorician Aristotle first described what has become
Western culture's system of persuasion as based on three components: speaker
credibility (**ethos**), logical arguments (**logos**), and psychological appeals (**pathos**)
(discussed later).[6] Although Aristotle developed his rhetorical model more than 2,000
years ago, his theory still characterizes what are considered to be the components of
the development of an effective persuasive message.

Speaker Credibility

The reputation, prestige, and authority of a speaker as perceived by the listeners all
contribute to *speaker credibility*. In most persuasive situations, listeners' acceptance of
the speaker as a credible person will make it easier for the speaker to get acceptance of
the message. For example, one of the major tasks of a politician is to try to establish his
or her credibility. The candidate's opponent tries to make the electorate question that
credibility. This can be illustrated in the race for the Democratic nomination for president in 2008. Barack Obama attempted to build his credibility as having experience in
foreign affairs by stating, "Both as a consequence of living in Indonesia and traveling
in Pakistan, having friends in college who were Muslim, I was very clear about the history of Shia-Sunni antagonism which is why, as an Illinois senator, I opposed the war

Culturally Communicating

Australian View of Public Speaking

Public speaking is taught in Australian universities to local students and to students from Asian countries studying in Australia. The advice given to students about public speaking follows American or Australian texts, which are generally similar in approach. However, the way of speaking advocated takes little account of a multicultural audience, and an implicit assumption appears to be that there is but one way of communicating in public—that given to us by rhetoricians in Greece and Rome who set the "rules" for public speaking centered around *logos* (or reason), *ethos* (or good character) and pathos (the evocation of feelings of pity or sympathetic sadness; a play on emotions). However, students of intercultural communication can find that scholars suggest that the rhetorical tradition of Europe and North America reflect not a universal communication style but rather the cultural patterns of logical, rational and analytic thinking favored in those countries.

Source: Mary R. Power and Camille Galvin, "The Culture of Speeches: Public Speaking across Cultures," *Culture Mandala: The Bulletin of the Centre for East-West Cultural and Economic Studies,* 2(2) (1997), Article 2.

REFLECT ON THIS:

1. Do you agree that there is no universal communication style?

2. If so, what are the implications for you as a public speaker?

in Iraq".[7] His opponent, Hillary Clinton, and later John McCain, alleged foreign-policy inexperience on Obama's part. Clinton went so far as to suggest in a TV ad that Obama "was the wrong man to answer the phone at 3 a.m. during a crisis."[8]

A person's reputation can help or hinder his or her persuasive ability. For example, if Clint Eastwood, the winner of two Academy Awards for Directing, addressed an audience about the skills needed to be an effective motion picture director, he would have initial credibility, so he would get a positive reception and his views would be accepted.

A negatively perceived speaker would have a much more difficult persuasive task. If, as a listener, you dislike, mistrust, or question the honesty of a person, she or he will have a difficult time persuading you to accept her or his beliefs. President Bush

Psychological appeals are aimed at emotionally stirring audience members.

encountered increasingly negative approval ratings as the war in Iraq dragged on during the final months of his administration. In May of 2008, for example, USA Today/Gallup reported Bush had a 28 percent approval and 67 percent disapproval rating.[9] Consequently, the White House undertook efforts to position President Bush more aggressively on other important foreign and domestic issues, including the sinking economy and the rising fuel costs so that his speeches and legislative proposals might receive more positive response from the public and legislators.

A speaker who has a reputation for being knowledgeable about the topic, or is a celebrity, or has a positive personal reputation with the audience comes to speak with preacknowledged credibility. Think of credibility as managing three Cs: competence, charisma, and character.

COMPETENCE   *Competence* refers to the wisdom, authority, and knowledge a speaker demonstrates. For an audience to feel that you are competent in the subject area being discussed, you must demonstrate that you know what you are talking about. This ordinarily means including up-to-date information and showing your familiarity with the material. A salesperson who has just made a presentation to a group of executives can ruin a potential sale, for example, if he displays a lack of knowledge about the product during the question-and-answer session.

Another way to establish credibility is to build on someone else's knowledge. For example, if you aren't an expert on a topic, you can strengthen your position by quoting recognized experts in the field. In this way, listeners draw the conclusion that if experts agree with your stand, then your contention must have merit. This is an appropriate device commonly used by students in their public speaking classes when presenting persuasive speeches. In quoting material, establish the qualifications of your sources with such phrases as, "Grady Sizemore, Cleveland Indian's All Star center fielder, explained how difficult it is to make the transition from the minor to the major league. He said . . . ."

Connect yourself with the topic. Suppose you are proposing a plan of action concerning safety regulations. If you have had experience on a construction crew and refer to this experience, your listeners will more readily accept your point that the construction industry needs more stringent safety regulations than if you did not have the personal experience. To establish the tie, use statements such as, "It has been my experience that . . ." and "I have observed that . . . ."

CHARISMA   Another characteristic of credibility is *charisma*. Words synonymous with charisma are *appealing, concerned, enthusiastic,* and *sincere.* People with charisma are compelling and have the ability to entice others. A charismatic speaker grabs and holds attention. John F. Kennedy and Martin Luther King Jr. were masters at getting masses of people to follow them because of their ability to mesmerize audiences. Oprah Winfrey has that effect on television viewers. Television psychologist Dr. Phil McGraw holds viewers' attention by successfully using humor, knowledge, and a down-home, folksy approach. Illinois Senator Barack Obama mesmerized the nation as the keynote speaker at the 2004 Democratic Convention with his youthful, dynamic, sincere, and articulate presentation and continued to impress voters during the 2008 Democratic presidential primary campaign. Indeed, the *New York Times* characterized the effect as "The Charisma Mandate."[10]

Some televangelists are capable of getting their followers to give vast amounts of money because of the power of the listeners' unwavering belief in the messenger. The late Pope John Paul II was considered to be a great communicator. "He didn't use a dignitary tone but connected to his audience by speaking from his heart, from the gut, soul-to-soul."[11] On the other hand, his successor, Pope Benedict, evokes such comments as,

People with charisma, such as President John F. Kennedy, are compelling and have the ability to entice others by grabbing and holding attention.

"He's cold."[12] "A hard-liner."[13] "The truth is that among American Roman Catholics, excitement about this pope and his trip [April 2008] is remarkably low."[14] "Benedict pales in comparison to his predecessor John Paul II in almost every respect, including looks, vitality, charisma, showmanship, tenure and popular appeal."[15]

CHARACTER Your reputation, honesty, and sensitivity all aid in developing your *character*. People who are assumed to be of high character based on the experiences they have had, the positions they hold, or the comments others have made about them engender trust.

Positively perceived speakers often find audiences receptive to their messages. Speakers who are viewed negatively need to try to alter their listeners' beliefs by emphasizing qualities about themselves that the audience may respond to positively. For example, a former convict, speaking to an audience about the need for altering prison procedures, started his presentation with these comments:

> I am a paroled convict. Knowing this, some of you may immediately say to yourself, "Why should I listen to anything that an ex-jailbird has to say?" It is because I was in prison, and because I know what prison can do to a person, and because I know what negative influences jail can have on a person, that I want to speak to you tonight.[16]

Sometimes speakers can change the attitudes of audience members who disagree with their views by directly taking on the issues of disagreement and asking listeners to give them a fair chance to be heard. For example, a Democratic candidate speaking before a predominantly Republican audience stated:

> I realize that I am a Democrat and you are Republicans. I also realize that we are both after the same thing: a city in which we can live without fear for our lives, a city in which the services such as trash and snow removal are efficient, and a city in which taxes are held in check. You, the Republicans, and I, the Democrat, do have common goals. I'd appreciate your considering how I propose to help all of us achieve our joint objectives.[17]

Not only are competence, charisma, and character important, but developing a logically constructed speech is critical to persuading listeners.

Logical Arguments

If it doesn't make sense, the audience is less likely to be swayed. To a European American audience, "making sense" generally means that statements and the supporting evidence add up to a reasonable match. Listeners, especially when they are dealing with information about which they know little or are skeptical, look for logical connections in the messages they are receiving.

Be aware that the use of logic, although important in the Western world, is not universal. If you are speaking to an audience primarily composed of Arabic or Hispanic members, for example, know that their basic method of conveying information is through the use of stories that illustrate the point being made but do not necessarily directly state the conclusion to be reached. It may be more persuasive, then, to tap into the listeners' narrative and use their stories to convince them of your point of view. A story about the devastating cyclone that hit the southwest coast of Myanmar on May 3, 2008, should lead listeners throughout the world to recognize the need for better worldwide plans for distributing aid in time of crises.

Therefore, in planning a presentation, be sure to recognize that cultural adjustments may be necessary. If you are to speak outside of your norm culture, you may need to consult an expert in the persuasive cultural patterns of the listeners.

STRUCTURE OF LOGICAL ARGUMENTS   There is no one best way to get everyone to agree with you. However, these qualities of a presentation will provide a good foundation:

- A clear statement of the purpose of the speech so that the audience knows what you are proposing

- Reasons that you believe or want the audience to believe in the proposal

What is perceived to be the most persuasive form of supporting material—evidence—includes testimony from experts, statistics, and specific instances.

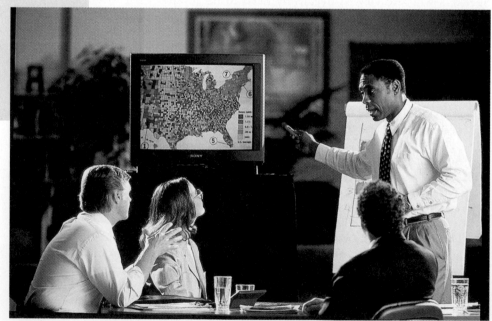

Communicating in Careers

Cultures and Acceptable Evidence

Reasoning plays an important part in business contexts. Yet, not every culture reasons in the same way. . . . Cultures differ in what is considered acceptable evidence, reasonable, and persuasive styles (the preferred way to convince others).

European Americans prefer facts as evidence. The myriad detective stories on television suggest this emphasis on facts: the physical aspects of the crime scene, the accounts of people who saw the events, the scientific data from DNA. These facts lead investigators to not only the behavior of individuals involved in the crime, but also their motivation.

For some cultures, facts are not as acceptable. For Muslims, stories or parables, particularly from the Koran, are acceptable as well as powerful forms of evidence. The story is told and the lesson from the story is assumed conclusive. In cultures influenced by Confucianism, metaphors analogies are used for evidence. In African cultures, testimony is not powerful

from of evidence as it is in the U.S. legal system. Some African cultures believe that the word of a witness should be disregarded because if the person speaks up about seeing something, she or he must have an agenda and is therefore not objective.

Source: Reprinted by permission from Rick Hoel, "How Do I Criticize? Let Me Count the Ways," in Pamela Cooper, Carolyn Calloway-Thomas, and Cheri J. Simonds, *Intercultural Communication: A Text with Readings.* Copyright © 2007 by Allyn & Bacon.

REFLECT ON THIS:

1. Assume you are going to give a speech with the central idea, "To persuade the audience that television mystery shows use facts to lead investigators to identify a perpatrator of a crime." Use a specific case from a TV mystery show to illustrate your point.

2. Using the same show, indicate how the show would have been developed if it had been developed for either a Muslim or an African audience.

- Reference to credible sources if you are not a recognized expert on the topic
- Arguments that follow some structure for ease of understanding and that develop the main point(s)
- A statement of the desired outcome, stand, or action
- Absence of false facts, partial information, and biased stands

To lead your listeners to your conclusion, it often is wise to choose an argumentative structure that fits your analysis of what approach is most likely to engage your listeners and lead them to accept your persuasive claim. These persuasive claims—your central idea—are argument propositions.

A *proposition of fact* states the existence of something in the past, present, or future by offering the reasons why the proposition should be believed (e.g., The New England Patriots will win the Super Bowl this year).

A *proposition of value* offers an evaluation of a person, place, or thing. In the proposition of value (e.g., Cleveland, Ohio, is a wonderful place to live), there is always a value term (e.g., *good, bad, right, wrong).*

A *proposition of policy* is the most commonly used persuasive method. It centers on stating that something should or should not be done (e.g., The United States should disengage from Iraq). The most familiar Western logical structures are the inductive or deductive formats.

An *inductive argument* is based on probability: what conclusion is expected or believed from the evidence. The more specific instances you can draw on in an inductive argument, the more probable your conclusion will be. Inductive argument can take one of two forms: the generalization conclusion or the hypothesis conclusion.

At a nuclear energy conference, the chairman of the U.S. Nuclear Regulatory Commission spoke of opportunities for growth and investment in the nuclear industry.

Socially Communicating

Factual Claims

Here you argue what exists or does not exist, what's led to a current situation, or what will or will not happen; you assess their validity using terms such as *true* or *false*, *correct* or *incorrect*, *yes* or *no*. The following three types of **factual claims** are common:

1. **Debatable points** (there is life on other planets; Lee Harvey Oswald acted alone in killing President Kennedy)

2. **Causal relationships** (secondhand smoke leads to lung disease; television violence influences children to commit violent acts)

3. **Predictions** (this mutual fund will gain value; Y2K will shut down global economies and cause widespread anarchy)

Source: Clella Jaffe, *Public Speaking: Concepts and Skills for a Diverse Society* (Belmont, CA: Wadsworth/Thomson Learning, 2001), p. 339.

REFLECT ON THIS: Write two debatable points, two causal relationships, and two predictions that could be used for topics of persuasive speeches.

He talked about the expanding workload of the commission and how the challenge will be to balance an increase in staff positions with the loss of key employees to retirement—all at the time of major nuclear expansion. He used these points to stress that "a major industry effort is necessary to address every level of education in this country, starting with a commitment to fostering interest in science and engineering at the elementary and middle school level."[18]

In a *generalization conclusion*, a number of specific instances are examined. From these, you attempt to predict some future occurrence or explain a whole category of instances. Underlying this is the assumption that what holds true for specific instances will hold true for all instances in a given category.

In a *hypothesis conclusion*, a hypothesis is used to explain all the evidence. For the argument to have substance, however, the hypothesis must provide the best explanation for that evidence. For example, in overriding the decision of the Texas Department of Child Protective Services (TDCPS) to remove children from a polygamist group, the Supreme Court ruled that the TDCPS overreached when it swept the children into foster care, knowing little about the religious group; used a mysterious telephone call of questionable validity; accepted as truth the word of disgruntled former members; and did not learn from a brush with another Texas-based religious sect that led to the fiery death of 21 children at the Branch Dividian compound.[19]

In addition to inductive arguments, persuasive speakers can make use of the *deductive argument*, which is based on logical necessity. If you accept the premise of the deductive argument—the proposition that is the basis of the argument—then you must also accept its conclusion.

One type of deductive argument is the *categorical syllogism*, an argument that contains premises and a conclusion. For instance, in a speech with the central idea of persuading the listeners of what the symptoms are that lead doctors to diagnose chronic fatigue syndrome, a speaker might state:

> *(Premise)* A proven sign of chronic fatigue syndrome is an off-balance immune system.

> *(Premise)* A proven sign of chronic fatigue syndrome is a positive diagnosis for human herpes virus 6.

> *(Premise)* A proven sign of chronic fatigue syndrome is a positive diagnosis for human B-cell lymphotropic virus.

> *(Conclusion)* Therefore, a person diagnosed with an off-balance immune system, human herpes virus 6, and human B-cell lymphotropic virus can be diagnosed as having chronic fatigue syndrome.

As communicated, a syllogism usually takes the form of an *enthymeme*, in which a premise usually is not directly stated. The omitted premise is shared by the communicators and therefore does not need to be verbalized. For example, while speaking to those attending a conference on writing assessment, a speaker might state, "If we can teach our children, from all backgrounds, to write with joy, originality, clarity, and control, then I don't think we have much else to worry about," a conclusion based on the premise shared by his listeners that children should be taught effective writing skills. An important step in analyzing your audience is to determine if the listeners share the unstated premise on which you base your argument. If you believe they do not, then you ought to build that assumption into the argument you spell out for your listeners.

Another type of deductive argument is the *disjunctive argument*—an either-or argument in which true alternatives must be established. For example,

In a professional baseball game between the Boston Red Sox and the Cleveland Indians,

Either the Boston Red Sox win or the Cleveland Indians win.

The Red Sox did not win.

Therefore, the Indians won.

Still another form of deductive argument is the *conditional argument,* which sets up an if-then proposition. In this form, there are two conditions, with one necessarily following from the other. The chief executive officer of a major accounting firm proposed that the federal government adopt a new accrual accounting system so that the public and Congress could monitor the federal budget. He could argue, "*If* citizens demand the financial information to which they are clearly entitled, incentives would be created for sound fiscal management—and perhaps for more enlightened political leadership—*then* we could expect to see better-informed decision making (i.e., less fiscal recklessness) and a reduction in the risks caused by the misallocation of capital."

PERSUASIVE EVIDENCE   The persuasive speaker, in Western cultures, not only must structure the persuasive argument but also must support these contentions. What is perceived to be the most persuasive form of supporting material—*evidence*—includes testimony from experts, statistics, and specific instances. If you can offer solid data to support your contentions, they will lend substance to your argument. For example, a speaker who attempts to persuade listeners that the U.S. Food and Drug Administration (FDA) needs more funds to hire inspectors can cite specific instances from the agency's files. Real cases are on record that show that potatoes contaminated with insecticide and ginger ale containing mold were sold to consumers. The speaker also can cite statistics indicating that only 500 FDA inspectors are available to monitor 60,000 food-processing plants in the United States.

When using evidence, verify that the evidence has a factual base. Make sure that your sources are valid and current. Many students look online for their information and assume that if it appears online, it is valid. That assumption is wrong! For example, a student who was speaking about the changing image of gays and lesbians stated that Marcia Cross, an actress on the television show *Desperate Housewives,* was a lesbian. One of the other students challenged the speaker about the validity of the information during the question-and-answer session that followed the speech. The speaker agreed to do further research, including determining whether the information was an *urban legend* (traditional story popularly regarded as true but usually containing a mixture of fact and fiction), and to report back to the class. At the next session she reported that the information was not true. She had searched on Snopes.com (a source for ascertaining whether urban legends are true or false) and showed classmates a clip from the television show, *The View,* which showed cohost Barbara Walters questioning Cross on rumors regarding her sexuality. "I'm not gay," said Cross.[20]

Culturally Communicating

Gender and Reasoning

Although both men and women reason inductively, a number of feminist philosophers believe inductive reasoning is a *major* way that women draw conclusions. Women typically describe specific experiences of real people—the rape victim, the family without medical insurance, the student athlete whose sport was eliminated—then generalize from these examples. In short, women's reasoning is grounded in personal experiences that arise out of their interpersonal relationships.

A common stereotype of women is that they reason with their hearts rather than their heads—an overgeneralization that may have some basis in fact. Studies of women's patterns of thinking show the importance of emotion in their reasoning process. Alison Jaggar, for example, believes that emotions are essential to knowing. Although they are obviously different from "dispassionate investigation," emotions complement logic, and they are intertwined with rational proofs. Feelings, in this view, are not inferior to reason; furthermore, they are not something that women must overcome in order to think clearly. Instead, emotions can be a source of knowledge in themselves, and "truth" or "knowledge" without them is distorted.

Source: Clella Jaffe, *Public Speaking: Concepts and Skills for a Diverse Society* (Belmont, CA: Wadsworth/Thomson Learning, 2001), p. 369.

REFLECT ON THIS: Take a stand as to whether you do or do not believe that "women's reasoning is grounded in personal experiences that arise out of their interpersonal relationships." Back up your arguments with research.

The lesson for public speakers is to be sure to confirm the validity of the information you use, don't always rely on a single entry, and surely don't assume that a blog or online source is accurate.

REASONING FALLACIES Speakers sometimes, intentionally or not, present material that contains flaws in reasoning. As a speaker, you should be aware that you might fall prey to using these fallacies. Wise listeners are aware that they must protect themselves from accepting fallacious reasoning. Types of reasoning fallacies include hasty generalizations, faulty analogical reasoning, faulty causal reasoning, ignoring the issue, *ad hominem* argument, *ad populum* argument, and *ad ignorantium* argument.

A speaker who makes a *hasty generalization* reaches an unwarranted general conclusion from an insufficient number of instances. For example, a speaker may argue that gun control legislation is necessary and demonstrate this argument with examples of college campus shootings such as Virginia Tech or Northern Illinois University, thus limiting the scope and numbers of possible cases in support of the need for gun control.

Another reasoning fallacy is *faulty analogical reasoning*. No analogy is ever totally "pure" because no two cases are ever identical. Speakers use faulty analogies when they assume that the shared elements will continue indefinitely or that all the aspects relevant to the case under consideration are similar. The speaker who argues that the AIDS crisis is analogous to the bubonic plague that ravaged medieval Europe, for example, overlooks the medical advances that make the AIDS crisis very different (although no less serious).

Faulty causal reasoning occurs when a speaker claims, without qualification, that something caused something else. If the claim overstates the case, faulty reasoning has been used. Rather than saying "a common cause" or "a probable cause," the speaker would argue, for example, that the increase in the number of illegal immigrants into the United States is the direct result of liberal welfare laws.

An entire set of reasoning fallacies can result from *ignoring the issue*. In ignoring the issue, the speaker uses irrelevant arguments to obscure the real issue. The *ad hominem argument*—attacks on the personal character of a source—is one example. For instance, some attacks on the proposal for health system reform in the mid-1990s centered on the fact that Hillary Rodham Clinton was one of its codevelopers. Since she wasn't elected by the people, it was argued, she shouldn't have been on the proposal commission, and therefore the bill should not be passed.

The *ad populum argument*—an appeal to people's prejudices and passions rather than a focus on the issue at hand—is another characteristic of ignoring the issue. For example, in 2008, when singer Britney Spears was accused of "being a bad mother," many music fans insisted she was innocent. Their devotion to her as an entertainer overshadowed any implicating evidence.[21]

Yet another example of the fallacy of ignoring the issue is the *ad ignorantium argument*—an attempt to prove that a statement is true because it cannot be disproved. For example, supporters of pit bull terriers argue that they are not dangerous pets because dog bite statistics show pit bulls to rank ninth in number of bites, after poodles and cocker spaniels. Of course, the number of pit bulls in this country is minuscule in comparison with the number of more popular breeds such as poodles and cocker spaniels.

Structure of the Persuasive Message

The structure of a persuasive speech should allow the listener to reach the behavioral or mental change the speaker desires. The most common method of developing a persuasive message is to use the problem–solution arrangement. The speaker identifies what is wrong and then presents the cure or recommendation for its cure.

A structure of the body of a speech that develops inductively would be:

III. Body

    A. Identify the situation (what is wrong).

    B. Identify the problem (what has to be changed).

    C. List the possible solutions to the problem.

    D. Evaluate the solutions for workability, desirability, practicality.

       1. Workability—Can the proposed solutions solve the problem?

       2. Desirability—Will the proposed solutions cause bigger problems?

       3. Practicality—Can the proposed solutions be put into effect?

    E. Recommendation of the solution that is most workable, desirable, and practical.

When you are listing the possible solutions (section C), two strategies are available: placing the strongest argument first so that it will have the greatest impact on listeners at the outset, or placing the strongest argument last to ensure that listeners retain it.

Another consideration is whether to develop section D—evaluation of solutions—by simply listing the reasons that the solution to be proposed is workable, desirable, and practical, or to investigate both sides of each solution, including the one to be recommended. One potential problem in developing both sides of an argument is that you may raise issues and ideas that your listeners have not previously considered.

An alternative to the illustrated pattern would be to place what is section E—identification of best solution—at the start of the body, thus beginning by revealing the solution and then explaining why this solution was selected. In general, if you feel that the audience is or may be on your side, state your arguments first and allow your listeners to believe along with you for the rest of your presentation (a deductive mode of reasoning). But if you perceive your audience to be hostile to your position, build the background and then present the arguments when you think that your listeners are ready for them (a more inductive line of reasoning).

Psychological Appeals

The third component of the persuasive message, *psychological appeals,* enlists listeners' emotions as motivation for accepting your arguments. Just as you must select your

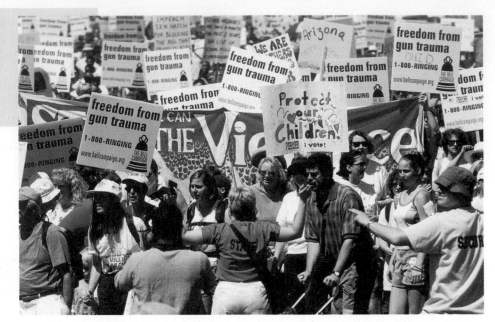

Persuasive speakers using the survival-of-the-species theory try to appeal to such factors as the physical and psychological safety of the person and his or her family.

arguments and enhance your credibility on the basis of what you know about your listeners, so must you also select psychological appeals on the basis of what you think will stir their emotions. The purpose of incorporating some emotional appeals in your speech is to keep your listeners involved as you spell out your persuasive plan, even though they may not distinguish the emotional from the rational in your presentation.

People tend to react according to whether their needs are being met. Several theories attempt to illustrate what needs people have, and persuasive speakers can use these as a guide to organizing emotional appeals to trigger need satisfaction.

One approach to understanding need satisfaction is (Abraham) *Maslow's Hierarchy of Human Needs* (Figure 16.2). Based on this view, a speaker must determine the level of need of a particular group of listeners and then select appeals aimed at that level.[22]

Figure 16.2
Maslow's Hierarchy of Needs

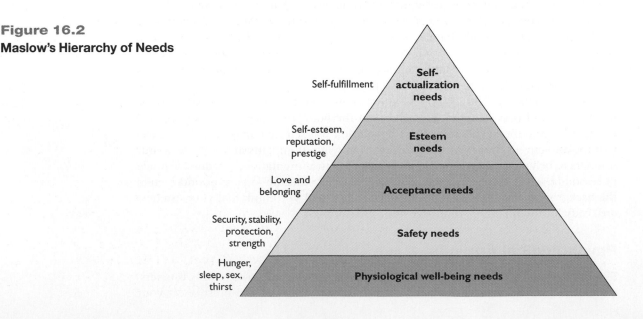

Although Maslow's theory is hierarchical, these need levels may all function at the same time. Therefore, a speaker need not deal with only one level at a time.

Maslow suggested that all human beings have five levels of needs. The first, most basic level is *physiological needs:* hunger, sleep, sex, and thirst. Normally all of these needs must be satisfied before a person can be motivated by appeals to higher levels of need. For example, the U.S. Agency for International Development offers aid to developing nations in order to persuade them, through appeals to physiological needs, that the democratic form of government offers housing and food and medical care.

The second level of human need, *safety needs,* encompasses security, stability, protection, and strength. Organizations that have had to reduce their workforces and lay off employees have found it persuasive to offer seminars on job searches, résumé preparation, and other career skills. Employees concerned about the security of their positions are quick to sign up for such offerings.

The third level consists of *acceptance needs:* the needs for love and belonging. College and university alumni representatives use this need in speeches intended to motivate alumni to contribute to endowment funds for the sake of being part of their alma mater.

Esteem needs form the fourth level that Maslow identified. Human needs at this level involve both self-esteem (desire for achievement and mastery) and esteem by others (desire for reputation and prestige). Athletic coaches use appeals to esteem in their pep talks before games to persuade team members to do their best.

Finally, Maslow identified the fifth level in the hierarchy as *self-actualization needs:* desire for self-fulfillment or achieving one's greatest potential as the ultimate level for which people reach. Recruiters attempt to influence potential military personnel with slogans such as "Be the best that you can be."

The *Ethnographic Theory of Human Drives,* another attempt to explain human needs, proposes that survival of the species, pleasure seeking, security, and territoriality must be satisfied. (See Figure 16.3.)

Persuasive speakers using the *survival-of-the-species* aspect of this theory try to appeal to such factors as the physical and psychological safety of the person and his or her family. Speakers talking to teens, for example, regarding the need for safe sex, use AIDS and sexually transmitted diseases as life-threatening illustrations.

Pleasure seeking centers on the idea that people spend a great deal of their lives seeking happiness. For example, in discussing why a city income tax is needed, a municipal spokesperson might indicate that the funds would be going toward refurbishing the city's recreation facilities.

Security means keeping things on an even keel, in balance, under control. In analyzing an audience, look for fears about change, insecurity, and uncertainty. For example, in light of the seeming increase in the number of child abductions, when speaking to audiences, police stress ways for parents to feel secure by forming neighborhood watches, being aware of sexual offenders in the neighborhood, walking their children to school, and having children play in large groups. Airline spokespersons stress that plane travel is safer than automobile travel, that cockpits can no longer be opened, that sky marshals travel on many flights, and that the security checking system is better than it was before the 9/11 terrorist attacks. All this is done in order to make potential passengers feel secure about flying.

We mark off and defend territory. This is *territoriality*. To activate this appeal, you must ascertain that audience members are concerned about what is already theirs, or you can instill the belief that something will belong to listeners.

**Figure 16.3
Ethnographic
Theory of Needs**

Territoriality　　Security

Pleasure
seeking　　Survival of
the species

Culturally Communicating

International Negotiation

Many cultures are realizing the benefits of persuasive speaking—at least in their dealings with representatives of the West. Because of trade negotiations, the existence of the United Nations, peace talks, and other international exchanges, many nations with different persuasive traditions are adopting strategies of Western rhetoric. Their leaders are often educated at American universities, and they adapt their rhetorical strategies to communicate their nation's views to international audiences. For example, Takakazu Kuriyama, the Japanese Ambassador to the United States (1992–1995), studied at Amherst College (Massachusetts) and Lawrence University (Wisconsin). He intentionally adopted some U. S. rhetorical strategies when he dealt with members of Congress and representatives of the U.S. media.

Source: Clella Jaffe, *Public Speaking: Concepts and Skills for a Diverse Society* (Belmont, CA: Wadsworth/Thomson Learning, 2001), p. 337.

REFLECT ON THIS: Do you think it is ethical to require that Western rhetorical patterns be adopted by persuasive speakers from other cultures? Is this requirement a form of ethnocentricism?

Homeowners, for example, may give speeches to a planning commission by taking on zoning issues when it appears that a jurisdiction will change laws that might alter the nature of their neighborhoods.

Human needs connect with human values and principles that are held in esteem. European American values shape the way persuaders appeal to listeners and establish themes. These values include improvement, practicality, freedom, responsibility, equality, and individuality.[23]

APPEALS TO MOTIVATE LISTENERS   Once you understand your listeners' need level(s), you can build into the speech motivational appeals to engage your audience and get them to respond to your persuasive message. Research in persuasion (including psychology, communication, marketing, advertising, and public relations) offers us a catalog of different motivational appeals. As a speaker, you should select those appeals that will be most appropriate for your particular listeners and for your persuasive goal. The appeals that you select can then be incorporated into your discussion of your arguments and evidence, especially examples. Being aware of the appeals can assist you in determining which ones will be appropriate for your listeners.[24]

As a speaker, then, you can select from among these appeals and build them into your presentation:

- *Adventure.* The speaker stresses the listeners' desires to explore new worlds, see exciting places, take part in unusual experiences, or participate in different events. A speaker in the travel industry might motivate potential travelers by describing a tour to an unusual place.

- *Anger.* Anger can be a strong motivator if listeners are worked up about a particular issue. A speaker can tap into this emotion and use it to keep listeners engaged. People who are upset about a proposed highway that will displace neighborhoods will respond to appeals to express their anger and disagreement to highway planning commissioners.

- *Companionship.* This taps the human desire to be with other people. A speaker might make this appeal in an attempt to recruit membership for a senior citizens' group.

- *Deference.* Showing respect for the wiser, more experienced, higher authority can be a successful strategy. Political candidates who are running for office often emphasize their record of civil service to remind voters that they are the most experienced candidate. Local candidates may also try to get respected community leaders and national office holders to endorse their candidacy and appear with them at rallies and in television commercials.

- *Fear.* This appeal is used to raise apprehension in a listener. A representative of the food industry speaking to individuals who have had heart attacks or bypass surgery could use this approach to discuss no-salt and low-cholesterol products. Although the fear appeal can be powerful, there can be a danger in its use. Listeners can become frightened if they perceive the situation as hopeless. Long-time smokers, for example, may assume that because of their long history of smoking, there is no sense in quitting because the damage has already been done.

- *Gender.* Appealing to women's rights, stressing the need for understanding the male point of view, or criticizing sexual harassment can all be useful in persuasion.

- *Guilt.* People may feel guilty for either doing or not doing something. Clergy turn to this appeal in some sermons. The "greening" of America movement taps into citizen guilt for polluting the environment, leaving carbon footprints, and causing global warming.

- *Happiness.* We seek happiness (pleasure) in life, and persuaders should understand the psychological appeal of this need for satisfaction and well-being.

- *Health.* A strong appeal is the need for good health. The complexity and the increasing cost of the health-care system serve as strong reminders that individuals need to do all they can to preserve their good health. We're persuaded to slim down and stay fit. A healthy you is the bottom line for motivational appeals in advertising, public service messages, and speeches stressing the need to change the nation's physical and psychological health care system.

- *Hero worship.* Audiences are often motivated by hero worship. Referring to a famous person who feels as they do about a subject may be the motivating factor

People may feel guilty for both doing and not doing something.

to convince an audience to take a desired action. Following the September 11, 2001, terrorist attacks, speakers who needed a hero image referred to the firefighters and police officers who had lost their lives while trying to save others. Presenters who want to speak about modern-day heroism may evoke the memory of military personnel who gave their lives during the Iraqi war. You might want to recruit volunteers for a "reading in the schools" program. If so, video references to Cleveland Cavaliers' basketball superstar LeBron James as an in-school reading volunteer does wonders for motivating through hero worship.

- *Humor.* People enjoy laughing and are often taken off guard when they are enjoying themselves. Humor has also been credited with relieving pain, helping aid in the cure of illnesses, and helping in the development of positive mental health.

- *Independence.* The appeal to independence ("Do your own thing"; "Be your own person") is strongly entrenched in European American values. Since the United States was built on a spirit of independence, European Americans like to be able to express their individuality and have a sense of control over their own decisions.

- *Liking.* As we have seen with the appeal to companionship, people have a strong need to affiliate with each other. This motivation can extend to the need to be liked by others—and even to be perceived as being similar to others.

- *Loyalty.* Appeals to commitment—to respect the nation, friends and family, or organizations—motivate. The "Buy American" campaign is an example of an appeal to national pride.

- *Nostalgia.* People like to look back at "the good old days" and appreciate being reminded of events and people of the past that evoke warm, pleasant memories. A speaker can refer to Fourth of July picnics, community family days, and how wonderful things were in the 1950s.

- *Revulsion.* An appeal to disgust can be effective. A speaker, for instance, can illustrate the effects of water pollution on the Chesapeake Bay by showing listeners some water samples in an attempt to motivate them to support legislation to clean up the bay. As with fear, revulsion can arouse such strong feelings that listeners may tune out the message. For example, antivivisectionists risk overwhelming their listeners with photographs of maimed laboratory animals.

- *Safety.* Concern for safety ranks high in human needs, as the Maslow hierarchy indicates. Safety—airline safety, school safety, vehicle safety, home safety—is a major issue. Advocates for gun control appeal to parents to ensure the safety of their children by disallowing the sale of firearms. Those desiring controls over the sale of natural herbs as medicine stress the issue of safety because there is no national testing of the ingredients in the products.

- *Savings.* Fluctuations of the world economy continue to convince people that they need to save money—both in terms of bargain purchasing power and for retirement. Speakers representing financial institutions appeal to individuals to save and to invest their money. Retail institutions convince us that the "price is right."

- *Sex.* Sex sells. Sex is a major motivational appeal in the global marketplace and almost inescapable in advertising messages. A controversial but effective advertising campaign for Candies, a perfume product, showed a woman in front of an open medicine cabinet filled with condoms. The attention drawn to the explicit sexual nature of the advertisement caused sales to skyrocket.

- *Sympathy.* By showing photographs or films of starving children or impoverished elderly people, a speaker can compel listeners to give time, money, or other resources. A sympathetic bond, often coupled with guilt, is created with those less fortunate.

Persuasive Process in Action

Psychological appeals, coupled with a speaker's credibility and well-reasoned and well-supported arguments, provide a sound, honest approach to influencing others to change their beliefs or actions. The sample speech outlined in Figure 16.4 illustrates the interaction of these persuasive elements.

Statement of Central Idea: To persuade the audience that stem-cell research is beneficial by explaining the ethical issues behind stem-cell research, showing how stem cells can be used to test new drugs, as well as how stem cells may be used to treat diseases that can save lives in the near future.

Attention material to involve listeners	**I. Introduction** A. Attention material: Millions of people in the world suffer every single day from devastating diseases, ones for which we have no cure. Stem-cell research creates a promise to better our lives.
Orienting materials to relate topic to listeners and to help establish the speaker's credibility **Topic of speech**	B. Orienting material: Stem cells may one day have the ability to treat diseases such as Parkinson's, Alzheimer's, diabetes, and even cancer. Stem cells can provide a great advantage to our world. However, much more research is needed in order to perfect this method that has the opportunity to treat diseases that beslege people like you and me everyday.
Central point of speech	**II. Central Idea** Although there are some ethical issues that surround stem-cell research, it is essential that we look at the numerous benefits that surround the idea of stem-cell research.

First issue: The "problem" behind stem cell research	**III. Body**
	
	A. Main ethical issue surrounding stem-cell research
	
	  1. Embryonic stem-cell studies are controversial because they involve the destruction of human embryos.
	
	    a. The embryos used are only three to five days past conception, and are known as blastocysts. In fact the cells are so small that they cannot be seen with the human eye.
	
	    b. The embryo has absolutely no consciousness, no feeling, and no self-awareness.

Second issue: Discussion of how stem cells could be useful in the treatment of Parkinson's disease	2. Those in favor of pro-life feel this is wrong.
	
	    a. However, with a surplus of created embryos due to in vitro fertilization they could be donated to help the research, since not all of them will be created into life anyway.
	
	    b. There is also a program called "Store-a-tooth."
	
	      i. Recent studies have found that there are potent stem cells in baby teeth and wisdom teeth.
	
	      ii. Instead of throwing baby teeth away, they can be donated for research.

Transition	(Although there seem to be a few ethical concerns about stem-cell research, the pros outweigh the cons, as this science has the potential to cure disease and prolong life.)

(continued)

Figure 16.4   The Persuasive Process in Action

B. Stem cells for future treatment of disease

   1. Parkinson's Disease

      a. What is it?

         i. Neurodegenerative disorder that affects over 5 million people over the age of 50 worldwide.

         ii. PD results from the loss of brain cells called dopaminergic neurons in the area of the brain called the substantia nigra.

         iii. Effects of PD are tremors, muscles becoming rigid, and shaking of the limbs uncontrollably.

      b. How can stem-cell research help?

         i. This research has the ability to take stem cells and grow them into new brain cells.

         ii. The next step would be transplanting them into the patients, which would help with the effects of PD.

Transition

(Not only can stem-cell research help patients with Parkinson's disease, but there are also an enormous amount of other benefits that stem-cell research can provide to our world.)

Third issue: Explanation of how stem cell research can be used to test drugs

C. Stem cells can be used to test new drugs and the new generation of cell tissue.

   1. New medicines can be tested for safety on differentiated cells.

   2. Cancer cell lines can be used to screen for anti-tumor drugs.

   3. Stem cells offer the possibility to be a renewable source of replacement cells. These replacement cells can be used to treat Alzheimer's, spinal cord injuries, stroke, burns, heart disease, and many other diseases.

Reiteration of main points

IV. Conclusion

A. Restate the issues

   1. The current debate surrounding stem-cell research is whether the destruction of embryos is ethical, but keep in mind there are many ways to donate stem cells.

   2. If stem-cell research were permitted, we would be able to treat diseases that we are unable to treat now.

   3. Stem cells can also be used to test new drugs as well as the generation of cell tissues.

Final appeal

B. Clincher

   1. Stop and think for a minute about someone you know who has or has had Parkinson's, cancer, Alzheimer's, or diabetes. Think about how hard it was to watch them struggle through these terrible diseases with no hope for a treatment or cure. Now imagine this would never have to happen again. We should all support stem-cell research, so both you and I never have to lose another loved one to disease again.

Figure 16.4   (continued)

In Conclusion

Persuasion is the process by which one party purposefully secures a change of behavior on the part of another party. The basic process of persuasion centers on a speaker making a claim and backing it up in such a way that listeners accept the claim. Successful persuasive strategies center on the use of speaker credibility, logical arguments, and psychological appeals. The most persuasive speaker will combine these persuasive elements to reach the listeners and accomplish their communication goal.

Learn by Doing

1. Prepare a speech on a topic about which you have strong feelings. Propose a change in a current procedure, take a stand on a view concerning the subject, or propose a plan of action. The topic should be one to which your listeners can relate and react so that you can persuade them. An example of a topic for this speech might be "This college should not raise tuition."

2. Select a controversial topic and prepare a speech in which you advocate a particular solution to the problem. Your task is to persuade your listeners to accept your solution. A topic for this speech might be "Euthanasia should be a legal option for terminally ill patients."

3. Prepare a speech analyzing the persuasive strategies used by some group in advocating a particular cause (e.g., gay rights or Native American rights). Select a number of persuasive messages by spokespersons for the group you choose, and use examples from these messages to illustrate your analysis of the persuasive strategies.

4. Find a speech or letter to the editor that illustrates one or more of the psychological appeals described in this chapter.

5. Make a list of what you perceive to be the differences in preparing persuasive speeches and informative speeches.

6. Prepare a speech in which you persuade your classmates as to which of "The Values Americans Live By," illustrated in Figure 16.1 (p. 420), is the most important.

Key Terms

persuasion   417

persuasive speech   417

speech of conviction   417

speech of actuation   417

ethos   422

logos   422

pathos   422

Informative Speech Topics

General Topics

The life and times of _____ (e.g., Abraham Lincoln, Julius Caesar, Winston Churchill, Bob Dylan)

My pop music idol

The evolution of _____ (e.g., the railway locomotive, windshield wiper, the street light)

On this day in history

The first moon landing

Top Internet searches

The value of snopes.com

Socializing health care

The contributions of Alfred Kinsey

The Darwin Awards

Origami in action (show how you can make things out of paper)

Color blindness

10 uses for a _____ (e.g., paperclip, tennis ball, bus ticket)

Who says that crime doesn't pay?

My dream holiday

How to escape the earth's gravity

Homing pigeons: The heroes of World War I

Why the *Titanic* really sank

Origin of cornbread

The history of fireworks

The history of basketball

Formula One race cars

Healthy eating

How lie detectors work

Kangaroos

The impact of flooding

Five-minute dating

How to find a good job

Easy ways to make money

Why humans use speech

Making a living will

Are cell phones overused?

The scientific reason why guys like pornography

▶ *Source:* Modified from www.presentationhelper.co.uk/more_informative_speech_topics.htm.

Ten fun things to do with your Internet connection
How the electoral college works
How cheap will PCs become?
Why people procrastinate
Selling myself in an interview
The Ken Burns effect
Evolution
Globalization
Video games
The musicals of Lerner and Loew (or Rogers and Hammerstein or Stephen
  Schwartz)
Genetic modification
Money laundering
Guide dogs for the blind
Mac versus PC
What is inside your tap water?
Easy ways to pass exams
Motivating people in boring jobs
Why businesses fail
Test marketing your idea
The problems of being left-handed
Time management for dummies
Emotional intelligence
My worst summer job
Psychological problems (autism, dual-personalities, alcoholism, anorexia, bulimia)

Famous People

Winston Churchill
Robert Falcon Scott
Lawrence of Arabia
Julius Caesar
Charles Dickens
Longfellow
Ronald Reagan
Marie Curie
Joan of Arc
General Douglas McArthur
Nelson Mandela
Henry VIII
Robert Burns
Charles Darwin
Sir Isaac Newton
The Queen
Mahatma Gandhi
Duke of Wellington
Frank Lloyd Wright
Sitting Bull
Abraham Lincoln
Stephen Hawking
Louis Pasteur
Benjamin Franklin

History

The six wives of Henry VIII
Custer's Last Stand
The Spanish Civil War
The rise of Nazism in Germany
Decline and fall of the Roman Empire
The importance of the year 1066
The Gettysburg address
Roman military hardware
The telegraph: The "Internet" of the 19th Century
Who really invented the Internet?
Woodstock

Nature

Wolves in the living room: How the wolf evolved into the domestic dog
The secret life of an eel
Is an owl really wise?
A day in the life of a Beluga Whale
Why dolphins jump out of the water
Cats and lions: How do they compare?
The cortex: Its importance to you

Famous Musicians

The Rolling Stones
Arctic Monkeys
Mika
Van Morrison
Elton John
Robbie Williams
John Lennon
Moby
Edward Elgar
Mozart
Beethoven
The Beatles
Elvis Presley

Persuasive Speech Topics

(The topic needs to be restated as a stand—for or against—or a belief.)

iPod music downloads should be free
Dogs are man's best friend
Princess Diana: Cover up or accident?
The case for organ donation
The need for recycling
Why the death penalty should be abolished
The need for gun control
The dangers of taking illegal steroids

Cloning should be federally funded

How to pay off your credit card

Avoiding drinking or drunk driving

Why we should require school uniforms in public schools

Global warming: What should we do about it?

Why we should wear seat belts in cars

Why you should become a blood donor

The dangers of gambling

Gay marriage should be federally legalized

Euthanasia: You should be responsible for your own death

Marijuana should be legalized for medicinal purposes

Prostitution should be legalized

Credit cards should not be given to anyone who is not fully employed

Junk foods should not be sold at schools

Animal rights

What you should wear for your job interview

Don't pay off your student loan

Volunteering: What can you do about it?

Golf: The best hobby in the world or a complete waste of time?

Ten tips for legal tax avoidance

Three ways to improve your time management

Drugs can reverse the aging process

A man landed on the moon: Is it really a hoax?

George H. W. Bush: Worst/best President in history

The Internet: The death of the newspaper

We can eradicate AIDS in Africa

Broadband is economical for rural areas

What good is keeping physically fit?

Sex, drugs, and rock and roll: Good fun or a major health hazard?

Road congestion, the way of the future

The five-day detox

Botox is dangerous

The Loch Ness monster does exist

The DaVinci code was fantasy, not fact

There should be a United States of Europe

The death penalty should be abolished in the United States

We should not consume genetically modified crops

The war in Iraq was not justified

Organized religion: The world's biggest problem

Glossary

accent   a nonmainstream pronunciation and intonation used by a person. It may represent a specific region of a country (e.g., southern dialect).

accenting relationship between verbal and nonverbal communication   nonverbal behavior intended to accent parts of a verbal message, much as underlining or italicizing emphasizes written language (e.g., pounding on a desk while saying, "I want it done now!").

action chain   a behavioral sequence between two or more participating organisms in which there are standard steps for reaching a goal (e.g., meeting and greeting customs).

action questions   queries intended to get the audience involved in a speech and to make listeners think and respond.

ad lib speaking   a speech in which a speaker has no time to organize ideas. The speaker responds immediately when answering a question, volunteering an opinion, or interacting during a question-and-answer session.

adaptors   movements that accompany boredom, show internal feelings, or regulate a situation (e.g., glancing continually at your watch while waiting for a friend who is late).

adjourning   the stage of group operation in which it goes out of existence.

aesthetics   the study of communication of a message or mood through color or music.

affect display   facial gestures that show emotions and feelings, such as sadness or happiness.

affirmation   saying something that inspires positive beliefs and actions (e.g., "I can give a speech without being scared").

agenda   the order of business for a meeting or discussion.

aggressive behavior   a response to conflict that centers on domination and focuses on the communicator getting his or her own way at all costs.

all-channel communication network   each person in the group talks directly to all the other members. This is the most interactive format.

analogy   a comparison of an unfamiliar concept to a familiar one.

androgyny   the possession of both masculine and feminine communication patterns.

anger   an emotional response to stimuli; serves as an emotional defense mechanism to relieve the stress of an overly stressful situation; the feeling of being upset with yourself or others (or both).

anxiety   the perception of a real or perceived threat or danger that affects your perceptions and your intrapersonal or interpersonal performance; based on negative intrapersonal messages.

apologizing   the act of a person saying he or she is sorry.

appraisal interview   sometimes referred to as a performance review, the interviewer helps the interviewee realize the strengths and weaknesses of his or her performance.

appreciative listening   takes place when a person engages in enjoyment of or sensory stimulation to a message, such as listening to humorous speakers, comedians, or music videos.

arbitration   a process for deciding disputes in which a third party, who is an expert in a particular field, decides how the conflict will be resolved.

artifactics   the study of those things that adorn the body and send messages to others about us as well as our selection of these items (e.g., clothing, makeup, eyeglasses, and jewelry)

Asian American dialect   a dialect of English spoken by Asian Americans that generally follows Standard American grammar rules with deviant pronunciation of Standard American words, as well as using vague and imaginative statements to develop arguments.

asking   seeking out information by inquiring.

assertive communication   a form of communication within conflict resolution that takes place when a person stands up for his or her right without attacking others.

assignment of meaning   the process of putting the stimulus into some predetermined category.

attention   the step in listening in which the receiver focuses on a specific stimulus selected from all the stimuli received at any given moment.

audience analysis   assessing the demographic, psychographic, and rhetorographic characteristics of your prospective listeners.

audio aids   supplementary aids that allow the listener of a speech to hear what would normally have to be imagined (e.g., records, tape recordings, or duplications of sounds).

audiovisual aid   supplementary aids that allow the listener of a speech to see and hear what would normally have to be imagined (e.g., films, videotapes, and tape-slide presentations that combine the dimensions of sight and sound).

authoritarian leader   a leader who dominates and directs a group according to his or her personal goals and objectives, regardless of how consistent or inconsistent these goals are with group members' goals.

avatars   a three-dimensional virtual conferencing model that allows users to represent themselves.

avoiding stage of relationships   the stage in Knapp's Relationship Termination Model that is highlighted by the partners physically separating, resulting in little or no discussion taking place since the relationship is probably about to end.

behavioral interview   designed to allow employers to know what skills the applicant may have and how these skills would translate into performance on the job.

Bem Sex-Role Inventory   a questionnaire developed by Sandra Bem that allows an individual to evalute how he or she perceives himself or herself on a masculine/feminine scale.

Berko 1-3-6 Decision-Making Technique   a format for using the nominal group technique that takes place after the specific decision to be made or problem to be solved is agreed on by the group and members are ready to work toward solution.

bipolar questions   a form of closed interview question, requiring a yes or no response (e.g., "Would you like to work for this company?").

Black English   an alternative name for Ebonics.

blended families   families created by divorce and remarriage or death and remarriage.

blink rate   the pattern by which individuals blink their eyes while communicating. The normal blink rate for someone speaking is 31 to 50 blinks per minute. Faster or slower blink rates can indicate nervousness.

blog   a website with dated entries, usually by a single author, often accompanied by links to other blogs; a person's electronic public diary.

body of a speech   the segment of the speech that is developed through major points as well as any subpoints needed to discuss the speaker's central idea.

body synchrony   the study of posture and the way a person walks and stands as a means of communication.

bonding stage of relationships   the fourth stage in the Knapp Relationship Escalation Model; it centers on a formal, sometimes legal, announcement of the relationship taking place, which includes the use of such terms as *marriage* and *civil union,* or the forming a business partnership.

brain dominance   the pattern by which an individual learns and listens, which reflects whether a person is linear, global, or combined linear and global.

brainstorming   consists of generating possible solutions without evaluation of them at the time of their proposal.

bullying   verbally or physically attacking someone.

Bushisms   peculiar words, phrases, pronunciations, malapropisms, and semantic or linguistic errors and gaffes that appeared in the speeches and communication of President George W. Bush.

business casual   the relaxed clothing style worn in business and corporate environments.

case method of organizational speech structure   a speech organizational mode, which is suitable for a single issue speech, in which the speaker discusses the central idea of the presentation without breaking it into subpoints.

causal method of issue arrangement   a method of arrangement for the body of a speech in which the speaker shows how two or more events are connected in such a way that if one occurs, the other will necessarily follow.

centralized decision-making process   a method of making decisions, common in Mexico and other Central and South American countries, that centers on the view of authority as being inherent within the individual, not his or her position. Making trade-offs is common for negotiators, including adding issues that are not part of the original business at hand.

centralized group communication network   all communication in this group communication network pattern is controlled by the leader.

chain communication network   follows a format in which specific members of the group speak to each other, but they all do not communicate directly. The linchpin is the leader who is in the center of the message chain.

channel   the mode by which the communication is conveyed from source to source, usually by some or all of the five senses, as it flows one on one or via electronic channels or physical contact.

chronemics   the study of time as a communication tool.

circle communication network   each person speaks to two other people but doesn't speak directly to the others. The flow of messages is not controlled by the leader.

circular time   the use of time in which precise time is not of importance; integration of past and future into a peaceful sense of the present (e.g., present in Native American and eastern societies).

circumscribing stage of relationships   the stage in Knapp's Relationship Termination Model that is highlighted by the diminishment of volume and quality of the intercouple communication.

clincher to a speech   the section of a speech that gives the speaker one more chance to reinforce the major ideas presented and then wrap up the presentation with a final message to clinch the selling of the central idea.

closed question   interview questions that provide alternatives, narrowing the possibilities for response, and probe for opinions on opposite ends of a continuum (e.g., "Do you think knowledge of a product or possessing communication skills is the most important asset of a salesperson?").

clusters   grouping of nonverbal factors such as gestures, posture, eye contact, clothing styles, and movement together in order to attempt to ascertain the meaning of the message being conveyed.

Code of Ethics for Speakers   a credo approved by the National Communication Association, the major organization of communication educators, which states specific traits that define an ethical speaker in the European American culture.

coercion   centers on a leader offering a selection of choices, all of them undesirable, to the membership, but making the group member or members select one of them for action or compliance.

coercive power   influence based on possible negative outcomes that are used as weapons. To exercise coercive power, a person needs to (1) know what weapons the other person fears most, (2) acquire them, (3) communicate that he or she has them, and (4) persuade the other person that such weapons will be used.

cognitive dissonance   the imbalance between your values, attitudes, and beliefs.

cognitive language   conveys information, generally through denotative words.

cognitive modification teaching a person how to modify his or her negative thinking.

cognitive processing how people process information in relationship to their values, attitudes, and beliefs by comprehending, organizing, and storing ideas.

comfort space bubble the personal space distance within which people feel comfortable.

committee a small group responsible for study, research, and recommendations about an issue whose actions are usually brought back to a larger group for action.

communication a conscious or unconscious, intentional or unintentional process in which feelings and ideas are expressed as verbal and/or nonverbal messages that are sent, received, and comprehended.

communication apprehension speech anxiety; the fear of participating in the communication act. Also identified as shyness, Social Anxiety Disorder, or Social Phobia.

communication ethics the principle that speakers should give the audience assistance in making wise decisions and that speakers' decisions about what to say should be based on moral principles.

communication system a pattern by which people relate to and interact with each other; if the system changes, the communication changes; the way in which the participants, the setting, and the purpose interact in the process of communication.

comparison method of issue organization a method of arrangement for the body of a speech in which the speaker describes how the two types of entities are alike.

comparison–contrast method of issue arrangement a method of arrangement for the body of a speech in which the speaker shows similarities and differences of the entities being discussed.

complementing relationship of verbal and nonverbal communication the supporting of a verbal message with nonverbal actions (e.g., shaking the head up and down while saying "yes").

compliance gaining the process of getting others to agree with or otherwise engage with you by using the skills of persuasion.

comprehension listening listening that attempts to recognize and retain the information of a message.

computer-based retrieval system an online search engine, such as Google.com or Ask.com, that allows researchers to compile a bibliography or a set of facts relevant to a specific topic.

computerized graphics programs electronic techniques, such as PowerPoint, that provide speakers with the opportunity to outline a speech, create slides with animated bullets that follow the outline, and import visual graphics, photos, video or audio clips, and Internet connections.

conclusion of a speech the ending section of a speech; its purpose is to summarize what has been said and/or motivate the listeners to take a prescribed action.

conflict any situation in which you perceive that another person with whom you're interdependent is frustrating or might frustrate the satisfaction of some concern, need, want, or desire of yours. The source of conflict could be your perception of a limited resource (such as money) or an individual difference between you and the other person (such as differences in how you and the other person define your relationship.)

conflict accommodation managing conflict by putting the needs of others ahead of your own, thereby giving in and not asserting your displeasure.

conflict avoidance not confronting a conflict by sidestepping, postponing, or ignoring a problem, no matter how unpleasant.

conflict competition a form of conflict resolution, often referred to as *aggression,* whose purpose is to get another person to comply with or accept your point of view, or to do something that person may not want to do, without concern for the other person.

conflict compromise conflict resolution that attempts to satisfy the needs of both parties, but often results in trading some of what you want for some of what the other person wants.

conflict integration a form of conflict resolution where there is concern about both persons' needs. Unlike compromise, both parties realize that they can participate in a win-win resolution and are willing to collaborate.

conflict smoothing over a form of conflict accommodation in which a person seeks to preserve the image that everything is okay.

conflicting relationship between verbal and nonverbal communication a difference of intent between the verbal and nonverbal messages (e.g., a person verbally saying that she does not have to leave while continually glancing at her watch and moving away from the speaker).

Confucian principle of l a theory, part of the Confucian philosophy, that requires that a person be affiliated and identify with a small and tightly knit group of people over long periods of time.

congruency the relationship between current and past patterns of behavior, as well as the harmony between verbal and nonverbal communication.

connotative words words with implied or suggested meanings.

consensus means "all"; thus, in a consensus decision, every member of the group must agree on a proposal before it can be put into action.

contact cultures those cultures characterized by strong tactile modes of communication (e.g., Latin Americans, Mediterraneans, French, Arabs).

context the physical and the cultural setting where the communication is taking place and the general psychological attitude of those assembled.

contrast method of issue arrangement a method of arrangement for the body of a speech in which the speaker tells the differences between two entities.

conversation an interpersonal interaction between at least two people.

counseling interview an interview format used by mental health professionals, friends, and family members, among others, that is designed to provide guidance and support to the interviewee.

credibility the listener's perception of the speaker's trustworthiness, competence, and dynamism that can lead the listener to accept or reject a message.

critical listening centers on the listener's comprehending and evaluating the message that has been received.

criticism the act of judging.

cultural noise communication problems that result from preconceived, unyielding attitudes derived from a group or society about how members of that culture should act or believe.

cultural relativism   worldview and standpoint that no culture is superior to any other one, and that any culture deserves to be described, understood, and judged on its own premises.

culture   all those individuals who have a shared system of interpretation. Cultural group identifiers are the region of a country, religious affiliation or orientation, political orientation, socioeconomic status, gender, sexual orientation, age or generation, vocation, avocation, family background, marital status, and parental status.

cutaway   a visual aid that allows the listener of a speech to see what would normally have to be imagined, enabling one to visualize and understand better (e.g., to show the layers of materials used to construct a house, a wall is cut in half so that one sees the siding, the insulation, the studding, the wallboard, and the wallpaper).

cyber addiction   a psychological compulsion in which individuals are so involved in Internet usage that they use it to the point of neglecting personal and work responsibilities, and, consequently, become socially isolated.

cyber bullying   harassment that takes place using an electronic medium.

cyber stalking   following and harassing others online.

cybernetic process   the process that describes that the human cortex functions much like a computer, receiving, storing, and processing some of these incoming signals and putting forth some of the necessary information when called on to do so.

Cybernetics   the study of the nervous system and the role it plays in the internal control of communication in humans.

decentralized group communication networks   all communication in this group communication network pattern flow with no set pattern or control by the leader or any group member.

decode   the process of translating the received messages.

democratic leader   a leader who facilitates a group according to the goals of its members and allows them to form their own conclusions.

demographics   speech listeners' characteristics based on their descriptions and backgrounds; includes such factors as age, gender, religion, ethnicity, education, occupation, and race.

denotative words   words with direct, explicit meanings of words.

DESC scripting   a way of dealing with interpersonal conflicts that centers on the process of **D**escribing, **E**xpressing, **S**pecifying, and stating **C**onsequences. This process allows you to analyze conflicts, determine your needs and rights, propose a resolution to the conflict, and, if necessary, negotiate a contract for change.

desirability   a test of a solution to a problem that centers on whether the suggested solution will cause greater problems.

devil effect   a negative evaluation of a person because of the way the person looks, regardless of his or her intelligence or job performance.

dialect   a social or regional variation of a language.

differentiating stage of relationships   the stage in Knapp's Relationship Termination Model that is highlighted by one or both of the partners being aware that he or she needs to assert independence, which results in one or both persons realizing that "we" is no longer as important as "me."

difficult group members   group members who create dissent, are self-centered, attack others rather than deal with the issues, and won't stick to the agenda.

direct aggression   an outward expression of dominating or humiliating communication.

direct questions   explicit interview questions that require specific replies (e.g., "Where did you last work?").

directions   instructions for accomplishing a task, achieving an effect, or getting somewhere.

directive intervention   an interview technique used by mental health professionals in which specific activities should be carried on outside the counseling session (e.g., writing a letter to or directly confronting a person who has abused the client).

discriminative listening   listening that attempts to distinguish auditory and visual stimuli.

discussion question   the issue or problem with which a group, interview, or discussion will deal.

doublespeak   a form of vagueness that is deceptive, evasive, or confusing with the intention of misleading, distorting reality, making the bad seem good, creating a false verbal map of the world, or creating incongruity between reality and what is said or not said.

dyad   two people.

dysfunctional relational system   a relationship that has established rules and processes of actions that are not satisfying to one or both of the participants.

Ebonics   a private language also called Vernacular Black English of many African Americans people; reflects the common national culture of the African American community; it is characterized by a systematic grammar and a vocabulary system that differs from Standard American English.

Economic Model of Relationships   a systematic way to evaluate relationships by applying the concept that people make judgments about interpersonal contacts by comparing relational rewards and costs. As long as rewards are equal to or exceed costs, the relationship will usually become more intimate; however, once costs exceed rewards, the relationship may begin to stagnate and eventually dissolves.

egospeak   the art of boosting our own ego by speaking only about what we want to talk about, and not caring at all what the other person is speaking about.

electronically mediated communication (EMC)   all forms of communication using electronic devices—including cell phones, electronic mail, instant messages, blogs, social networks (e.g., texting, Facebook, MySpace, Twitter, You Tube), and computer-conferencing—that become substitutes for faxes, voice mail, letters, and even face-to-face interactions.

e-mail   electronic messages sent via the Internet.

emblems   cultural-specific nonverbal acts that have a direct verbal translation or dictionary definition consisting of one or two words (e.g., the Euro-American A-OK sign).

emotive language   employs emotional connotative words to express the feelings, attitudes, and emotions of the speaker (e.g., riveting, gripping).

empathic assertion   a statement or statements that recognize the other person's position but that state your own needs. It may follow a simple assertion or be the first step in the assertive process.

employment interview   an interview that provides a way of entering the job market; changing positions; getting promotions; achieving salary increases; gaining admission for universities, internships, or assistantships, and graduate and professional programs.

employment stress interview designed to determine how an interviewee might function under pressure.

encode the process of creating a message.

environmental noise outside interference that prevents the receiver from getting the message.

ethical communicators those who "respect the integrity of ideas and concerns from the listeners."

ethical public speaker speaks with sincerity, does not expose the audience to falsehoods or premeditatedly alter the truth or invent or fabricate statistics, raises the listeners' level of expertise, employs a message that is free from mental or physical coercion, and gives credit to the source of information.

ethics the systematic study of what should be the grounds and principles for acceptable and unacceptable behavior. Ethics are not just something that individuals practice; instead, they are the perceived values shared by a society.

ethnocentrism the belief that the views and standards of an individual's own in-group is superior to the views and standards of the out-group.

ethnographers researchers who study cultures.

Euro-Americans people living in the United States who either emigrated or had ancestors who emigrated to the U.S. from the European continent. They are usually Caucasian, members of the Judeo or Christian faith, and speak English. Traditionally, they have been members of the in-group, the majority population, and are individualistic in their worldview.

Expectancy Violation Theory concept of communication as the exchange of information that is high in relational content and can be used to violate the expectations of another, which will be perceived either positively or negatively depending on how much the two people like each other (e.g., people allow those whom they like to stand closer to them than people they do not like).

experimenting stage of relationships the second stage in the Knapp Relationship Escalation Model; it centers on determining whether there is interest in furthering the relationship.

expert a person who, through knowledge or skill in a specific field, gains respect for his or her opinions or expertise.

expert power a person's capacity to influence another person because of the knowledge and skills the person has or is presumed to have.

exposition information included in a speech that gives the necessary background information to listeners so that they can understand the material being presented (e.g., definition of specific terms, historical information, relationship between herself or himself and the topic, the process that will be used during the presentation).

extemporaneous speaking mode the speaker knows in advance that she or he will be giving a speech, can prepare by doing research and planning the speech, and develops a set of talking points, such as notes or an outline, to assist in presenting ideas.

extended families a cluster of relatives who may also include friends.

eye-accessing cues a neurolinguistic psychological theory that eye movements aid in accessing inner speech since the eye movements stimulate different parts of the brain.

eye contact looking into the eyes of the audience as a presenter gives a speech.

eye gaze the length of time that people look into each other's eyes while communicating. Members of different social classes, generations, ethnic groups, and cultures use their eyes differently to express messages.

eye span a method for establishing eye contact with an audience while following a manuscript in an unobtrusive way, which takes the form of the speaker glancing down, picking out a meaningful phrase or a sentence, delivering it to the audience, then, as the end of the phrase is reached, but before the speaker finishes the idea, glances down and grasps the next idea to be spoken.

fabrication making up information or guessing at information and presenting it as if it were factual.

Facebook an online social network community (facebook .com).

facebooking a term meaning to connect with someone through Facebook.

FACS (Facial Action Coding System) a process used to collect data about how the face conveys messages.

facsics the study of how the face communicates.

fair fighting a pattern of conflict resolution in which the participants work toward an amicable solution to the problem and keep in mind that although the issue is important, the relationship is also important.

family an assemblage of people who have legally been declared a group or who have defined themselves as such. Kinds of families are natural families (a married couple with or without children), blended families (families created by divorce and remarriage or death and remarriage), single-parent families (one parent with a child or children), extended families (a cluster of relatives who may also include friends), and self-declared families (e.g., heterosexuals living together, homosexuals living together, communal groups, religious cults).

feedback a verbal and/or a nonverbal reaction or response to the message.

first brain/second brain theory the first brain to develop was the emotional brain (the right lobe), and therefore it triggers first causing instinctively action; it has been estimated that 90 percent of people's actions are emotional. Then the second brain, the logical brain, is triggered. The logical brain contains the information people are taught: reasoning patterns, the rules of civilized behavior, and cultural rules.

flaming e-mail aggression that occurs when individuals exchange hostile or insulting remarks.

flat world platform a convergence of the personal computer, with fiber-optic cable, with workflow software that enables individuals all over the world to collaborate regardless of the distance between them.

focus groups a group designed to test reactions to a particular product, process, or service offered by an organization.

follow-up assertion a statement or statements used when the simple or empathic assertion is not successful in getting the desired action. It takes the form of a restatement of the simple or empathic assertion and then a statement of your own position, which may include a direct statement of the action you need or want.

forecast   a statement that alerts the audience to ideas that are coming.

formal time   the division of time into specific referents, such as centuries, years, months, weeks, days, hours, and minutes.

forum   a question-and-answer session that often follows a symposium, during which the participants field questions from each other as well as from any audience member.

frame of reference   a perceptual screen used by receivers to filter message ideas based on their background and culture.

freedom of speech   the protected right to speak without restrictions—to be free to say what a person wants.

functional relational system   a system that is operating to the general satisfaction of the participants.

funnel schedule   an interview format in which the questions are sequenced to take the interview from more general to more specific information.

gender   one's psychological, social, and interactive characteristics (man/woman), in contrast to sex, which is one's biological or physical self (male/female).

gestics   the study of the movements of the body, such as gestures, that can give clues about a person's status, mood, cultural affiliations, and self-perception.

gestures   the speaker's use of hands, body movements, and facial expressions while speaking; can either substitute for, complement, conflict with, and/or accent verbal communication.

global listeners/learners   individuals who tend to have preference for a generalized rather than specific description.

go to meeting   a Web conferencing tool that allows participants to meet online in real time rather than in a conference room.

goal of the speech   the purpose of a speech (e.g., to inform or to persuade), which is expressed in terms of its expected outcome.

green-flag words   emotional trigger words that create positive stimulations that trigger emotional responses.

griot   the traditional West African storyteller who weaves a story with song and dance, and enlivens a tale with all sorts of sound effects.

group   a system characterized by interconnectedness of its constituent parts (the individuals who make up the group). It is more than a collection of individuals, as it has a goal and a purpose and the members interact with each other.

group cohesion   the interconnectedness of the members of a group.

group communication networks   visual illustrations of the way members of a group communicate.

group conforming   the stage of group operation when the members of the group have worked through the storming stage.

group forming   the first phase of group operation with the purpose of group members getting to know each other.

group maintenance   focuses on the social dimension of the group in which the central communicative function is to gain and maintain the cohesiveness of the group.

group norming   the second phase of group operation with the purpose of developing the rules by which the group will operate.

group norms   the rules by which the group will operate. These norms can be explicit (written and agreed on, as in a constitution) or implicit (understood but not formalized).

group performing   the action stage of group process in which the members start to work toward accomplishing the group's goals.

group setting   where a group meets; includes the size, shape, color, temperature, and decor of the room.

group storming   the stage of group operation when conflicts erupt.

group task roles   focuses on the group accomplishing its goals by initiating ideas, encouraging diverse ideas, using reasoned thought, staying open-minded, being aware of hidden agendas, being cognizant of time constraints, encouraging other participants, and attending to nonverbal messages.

groupthink   the mode of thinking in which people engage when concurrence seeking becomes so dominant in a cohesive in-group that it tends to override realistic appraisal of alternative courses of actions. Takes place when all the members of the group make decisions without concern that the conclusions are not in the best interest of anyone other than the group members' loyalty to each other or to the leader.

groupware   specially designed software that meeting participants use to perform tasks such as brainstorming and decision making.

gustorics   the study of how taste communicates.

halo effect   positive evaluation of a person or thing, not because of his or her talents or display of proficiency, but because of such factors as physical appearance.

Halogen eAppraisal   an electronic program intended to enhance the appraisal process by aligning employee goals and developing a high-performing workforce.

haptics   the study of the use of touch as communication.

hearing   a biological activity that involves reception of a message through sensory channels.

hedges   powerless language in the form of an inarticulate that adds meaningless words to a statement (e.g., "It's *like* difficult to concentrate").

hesitations   powerless language in the form of an inarticulate in which verbal pauses are placed within communication (e.g, "um," "you know").

hidden agenda   when individuals work for their own unstated ends rather than for the group's objectives; the result is usually counterproductive.

high-context communication societies   emphasis is on how the verbal message can best be conveyed through indirect language and the nonverbal channels of silence and subtle tone of voice. High-context nationalities are Japan, China, South Korea, Vietnam, Nigeria, Mexico, Kuwait, and Saudi Arabia.

high-context cultures   cultures in which the information is situated in the communicators themselves and in the communication setting, so fewer words are necessary. In high-context cultures, it is the responsibility of the listener to understand. Japan and Saudi Arabia are recognized as high-context cultures.

IABC Code for Ethnical Business Communicators   a code of ethics established by the International Association of Business, which indicates that business communicators must practice "honest, candid and timely communication and [foster] the free flow of essential information in accord with the public interest."

ideal self   who you would like to be or think you should be.

identifying language   centers on naming persons or things specifically, thus being able to clarify exactly what a person is speaking about.

illustrators   kinesic acts accompanying speech that are used to aid in the description of what is being said or trace the direction of speech (e.g., pointing at an object while speaking about it.)

I–Me dichotomy   the difference between your self-perceived "me" and your other-perceived "me" the difference between the way you perceive yourself and others perceive you.

impromptu speaking   a speech given with little or no preparation.

inarticulates   uttered sounds, words, or phrases that have no meaning or do not help the listener gain a clear understanding of the message, such as the phrase *stuff like that*.

inferences   interpretation beyond available information or jumping to conclusions without using all of the information available.

informal time   a flexible use of time exemplified by such terms as *soon* or *right away*.

information-gathering interview   an interview in which the interviewer sets out to obtain information from a respondent. This type of interview is important to journalists, law-enforcement authorities, health-care workers, students, businesspeople, and mental health professionals.

in-group   a collectivity with which an individual identifies, or the group in a society that has the most influence (e.g., for many years the group who had the power in the United States were white, Christian males, thus they composed the in-group).

initiation stage of relationships   the first stage in the Knapp Relationship Escalation Model; it centers on the exchanging of basic information about the participants.

innate neurological programs   automatic nonverbal reactions to stimuli with which people are born.

integrating stage of relationships   the third stage in the Knapp Relationship Escalation Model; it includes the relationship described by such terms as *best friends, couple, boyfriend–girlfriend/boyfriend–boyfriend/girlfriend–girlfriend, engaged*. Others perceive the dyad as a pair, as they have developed a shared relational identity.

intensifiers   powerless language in the form of an inarticulate that adds meaningless stress words within a sentence (e.g., "It's *so awesome* of you to come").

interactional model of communication   a schematic that illustrates how a source encodes and sends a message to a receiver (through one or more of the sensory channels). The receiver receives and decodes the message, as in linear communication, but then encodes feedback and sends it back to the source, thus making the process two-directional. The source then decodes the feedback message. Based on the original message sent and the feedback received, the source encodes a new message that adjusts to the feedback (adaptation).

intercultural communication   communication between individuals with whom there is little or no cultural bond (e.g., Japanese citizen with little knowledge of New Zealand and a New Zealander with little knowledge of Japan or its customs who are speaking with each other).

intercultural-intimate conflict   any antagonistic friction or disagreement between two partners due, in part, to cultural or ethnic group membership differences.

internal summary   a short restatement of what has just been said in the section that you are about to leave before proceeding to the next segment.

Internet   a worldwide, publicly accessible series of interconnected computer networks that transmit data by packet switching using the standard Internet Protocol (IP); a "network of networks" that consists of millions of smaller domestic, academic, business, and government networks, which together carry various information and services, such as electronic mail, online chat, file transfer.

interpersonal communication   communication that is based on communicators' recognition of each other's uniqueness and the development of messages that reflect that recognition; an interactional process in which two people send and receive messages. Communication takes place between two or more persons who establish a communicative relationship. Forms of interpersonal communication include face-to-face or mediated conversations, interviews, and small-group discussions.

interpersonal relationships   social associations, connections, or affiliations between two or more people that can vary from intimacy and sharing to establishing a common ground, and are usually centered around something shared in common.

interrogation interview   an interview used by lawyers, credit officers, tax specialists, and law-enforcement officers, designed to secure information from an interviewee through extensive use of probing techniques.

interview   a purposeful conversation between two or more persons that follows a basic question-and-answer format.

interview agenda format   outlines the procedures that will be followed to achieve the purpose of the interaction.

interviewee   the person who is the subject of the interview.

interviewer   the person responsible for arranging for and conducting the interview.

intimate space distance   in the Euro-American culture, a space varying from direct physical contact with another person to a distance of eighteen inches.

intracultural communication   interaction between those who have a common cultural bond (e.g., Spaniard to Spaniard, female to female, Catholic to Catholic).

intrapersonal communicator   a person internally communicating with himself or herself.

intrapersonal communication   communicating with yourself, encompassing such activities as thought processing, personal decision making, listening, and determining self-concept.

introduction to a speech   the segment of a speech with the purpose of gaining the listeners' attention and orient them to the material that will be presented.

Johari window   a graphically represented theory that helps you ascertain your willingness to disclose who you are and allows others to disclose to you.

kinesics   the study of communication through the body and its movements.

Knapp's Relationship Escalation Model   a communication-based explanation of how relationships develop and continue.

Knapp's Relationship Termination Model   describes how, at any stage of the Knapp's Relationship Escalation Model, participants may work toward ending the relationship.

laissez-faire leader a leader who is nondirective and empowers group members to do their own thing.

language a system of arbitrary signals—such as sounds, gestures, or symbols—that is used by a nation, people, or distinct community to communicate thoughts and feelings. The system includes rules for combining its components, referred to as *grammar.*

language distortion the intentional or unintentional distortion of information through ambiguity, vagueness, inferences, or message adjustment.

Language-Explosion Theory humans build language skills from a central core of influence, often the mother–infant dyad, and then expand the skills through the circles of influence in which a person is involved (e.g., schools, media, religious institutions).

large groups a group consisting of more than a dozen persons.

leaders those who guide the group.

leadership refers to those who influence the group to accomplish its goal.

leadership power the ability of a member or members of a group to influence others' opinions and actions.

leading questions interview questions that encourages a specific answer—for example, "You wouldn't say you favor gun control legislation, would you?" This is a leading question because it implies how the interviewee should answer the question.

left hemisphere of the brain responsible for rational, logical, sequential, linear, and abstract thinking.

legitimate power influence that stems from one person's perception that another person has the right to make requests of him or her because of the position that the other person occupies or because of the nature of the relationship.

linear one-dimensional; going in one direction.

linear learners/listeners individuals who tend to take information at face value, and who prefer knowing that the information is useful and can be applied.

linear model of communication a schematic that illustrates the process by which a source encodes a message and sends it to a receiver through one or more sensory channels without a feedback loop. The receiver then receives and decodes the message.

linear time the use of time that centers on punctuality (e.g., present in most of Western Europe, North America, and Japan).

linguist a social scientist who studies the structures of various languages—to provide concepts that describe languages.

Linguistic Relativity Hypothesis theorizes that a person's understanding of the world, and how the person behaves in it, are based on the language a person speaks. Also known as the Sapir-Whorf Hypothesis.

linguistics the study of the sounds, structure, and rules of human language.

listenable speech one that is formatted in a way that when it is received, it is understood by listeners.

listener apprehension the fear of misinterpreting, inadequately processing, and/or not being able to adjust psychologically to messages sent by others.

listening a process that involves reception, attention, perception, the assignment of meaning, and the response to the message presented.

litigation a conflict resolution in which a dispute is settled by presenting evidence to a judge or a jury.

loaded questions a type of leading interview question designed to elicit an emotional response. Asking a job applicant who was an officer of the union at a previous job to defend this company's policy of nonunion affiliation would, for example, be a loaded question.

lose-lose resolutions a style of negotiation in which neither person is satisfied with the outcome because neither gets what he or she wants.

low-context communication societies emphasis is on the expression of ideas through explicit verbal messages. The British, Germans, Danes, Swedes, Euro-Americans, Canadians, and Australians tend to be low-context communicators.

low-context cultures cultures in which communicators expect to give and receive a great deal of information. The speaker is responsible for making sure the listener comprehends all. The United States and Canada are considered to be low-context cultures.

maintenance dimension of groups the members of a group meeting their interpersonal needs.

majority voting a vote in which the winner must receive more than half of the votes, excluding those who do not vote or who abstain (i.e., do not want to vote).

manuscript speech mode a speech in which the material is written out and delivered word for word from a text.

material self your possessions and physical surroundings.

media radio, television, the Internet, magazines, newspapers, and films as types of communication.

media interview takes place when an interviewer asks questions of a guest.

mediated meetings electronically held teleconferences, video conferences, and computer or virtual conferences that allow for meetings to be held any place where someone who needs to participate in a meeting is located.

mediation a conflict resolution process in which a neutral person, who has no vested interest in the outcome, facilitates communication between parties without imposing a solution in order for the participants to understand and resolve their dispute.

Meet-While-Standing Theory a meeting procedure that requires a meeting place without any furniture, forcing people to stand while making decisions in a more expedient use of time.

memorable language word selections, which are colorful, rhythmical and compelling, selected to compel the listener to remember the presentation.

memorized speech mode a speech is written out word for word and then committed to memory.

MERMER a system of brain fingerprinting that records messages emitted by the brain before the body physically reacts in an attempt to establish whether the person is lying or telling the truth.

messages the content of communication.

method of issue arrangement for the body of a speech the way the body of a speech is organized. In the Euro-American culture, the format traditionally takes one of six forms: spatial arrangement, time arrangement, topical arrangement, causal arrangement, comparison–contrast arrangement, or problem-solution arrangement.

method of speech development encompasses how you plan to approach the presentation.

mind mapping a method of arranging materials visually rather than in list form. This is a mode often favored by global thinkers/listeners who are stimulated by pictures rather than words.

mirror questions an interview question intended to get a person to reflect on what he or she has said and expand on it. For example, the interviewer may say, "I've worked for this corporation for years, and I'm getting nowhere."

mockup a visual aid that allows the listener of a speech to see the building up or tearing down of an article (e.g., a biology textbook may include an outline drawing of the human body on a page with a series of clear plastic sheets attached).

multicultural a society consisting of varied cultural groups (e.g., the United States is a multicultural society due to its population that is composed of people of many nationalities, races, sexual orientations, and genders).

multiculturalism a political and attitudinal movement to ensure cultural freedom.

MySpace an online social network community (myspace .com).

nationality the nation in which one was born, now resides, or has lived in or studied for enough time to become familiar with the customs of the area. Some nationality identifiers are Irish and Korean. Nationality is one aspect of culture.

natural families a married couple with or without children.

noise any internal or external interference in the communication process.

negotiation the act of bargaining to reach an agreement with at least two people or groups working on a mutual problem that is intended to satisfy all parties.

Nominal Group Technique of Decision Making centers on brainstorming without direct group interaction in the initial stage with the purpose of encouraging idea generation from all individuals but avoids criticism, destructive conflict, and long-winded speeches.

nonassertive behavior a form of communication that centers on avoiding conflict.

noncontact cultures those cultures characterized by a lack of strong tactile modes of communication (Germans, Japanese, English, North Americans).

nondirective interviewing techniques a counseling interviewing technique in which the interviewer takes a passive role by leading an interviewee to a solution to a psychological problem.

nonstandard dialects low-prestige dialects (e.g., dialects other than Standard American English in the United States).

nonstandard English dialects deviations of English that do not conform to the rules of Standard American English (e.g., Spanglish, Asian American English).

nonverbal communication all messages that people exchange beyond the words themselves.

ocalics the study of the eyes as a receiver and conveyer of communication.

olfactics the study of smell as a communicator.

online interview using cyberspace for recruiters to meet with candidates; may take place on instant messaging and may be conducted with or without the use of Web cameras.

open questions interview questions that specify only the topic (e.g., "What is your educational background?").

oral footnote an oral reference used in a speech that indicates that the material being presented is a paraphrase or quotation generated by a source other than the speaker (e.g., "In her book, *Gendered Lives, Communication, Gender, and Culture,* Dr. Julia Wood, an eminent communication scholar, states, 'Nonverbal behaviors expected of women emphasize communality—building and sustaining relationships and community'").

oral history interview an informative interview as a way for families to preserve their history by questioning members of the family who have stories and customs they can share on audiotape or videotape.

organizational noise communication problems created by the lack of a clear structural order in which the information presented.

orienting material provides the background necessary to understand the basic material of the presentation. It is designed to tie the material to the central idea, provide necessary information, establish personal credibility for the speaker, and make the subject important to the listener.

other-perceived Me the person who others perceive you to be. It may be the same as or different from your self-perceived I.

out-group a collectivity with which an individual does not identify or the group or groups in a society who have little or not power (e.g., during the time of slavery in the United States, Blacks were the out-group).

paralanguage/paravocalics the study of how vocal quality (rate, volume, pitch, pause, and stress) communicate nonverbally to the listening ear.

paraphrases someone else's ideas put into your own words.

paraphrasing a concise restatement of what has been presented by the speaker.

parliamentarian a person well versed in the rules of order and meeting management, to assist the group in following the rules.

participants those members of a group who interact to bring about the actions of the group.

partitioning organizational speech structure a deductive format to a speech in which, as the speech proceeds, the presentation is partitioned into a number of points. In developing the speech, the speaker states a point and then develops the concept with supporting details.

partitioning step a device used in a speech that lists how the main issues that will be presented in the presentation.

part-of-the-whole voting voting method that occurs when a specific number or percentage of those who are eligible to vote is required to bring about some action (e.g., some of the rules of operation of an organization can be changed only if 75 percent of those eligible to vote agree to the change).

passive aggression communication that is done by pretending that there is nothing wrong but, at the same time, derailing any attempt to solve a problem that isn't to your liking in a way that doesn't appear to be aggressive.

perception a screening process that attempts to analyze what has been input.

perceptions the way a person views the world.

perceptual filter   strains the stimuli the listener receives and separates what makes sense from what doesn't.

personal ethical value system   the basis for your decision making and your understanding of why you will or will not take a particular stand or action.

Personal Report of Communication Apprehension (PRCA-24)   a questionnaire designed to ascertain whether a person has a fear of participating in the communication act.

Personal Report of Intercultural Communication Apprehension (PRICA)   a measure whose purpose is to evaluate a person's comfort or discomfort in communicating with individuals from different cultures.

personal space distance   in Euro-American culture, a space distance varying from eighteen inches to four feet, sometimes called the *comfort space bubble*.

persuasive interview   an interview with the purpose of changing or reinforcing a person's beliefs or behavior.

phatic language   the function of the words is to perform a social task (e.g., informal personal greetings).

physical characteristics   the study of what height, weight, and skin color communicate about an individual.

physical elements of public communication   the gestures and eye contact used by a speaker while presenting a speech.

physical self   our physical being.

physiological-impairment noise   a physical problem that blocks the effective sending or receiving of a message (e.g., deafness or blindness).

plagiarism   occurs when a speaker uses the ideas and words of others as his or her own without giving credit to the originator of the material.

pleasure seeking (as a basic need)   reflexive, inborn reactions that people instinctively use for communicating pleasure or lack of pleasure as they exploit their conquests, stress their influences, and reinforce their accomplishments.

pluralism   the concept that stresses that individuals can maintain their individual identities and still be part of the larger group (e.g., the salad bowl concept of some in the United States who believe that each person is uniquely different and does not have to become the same).

plurality   means "most." In voting, the option receiving the most votes wins.

polygraphs/lie detectors   devices used to read the body's reactions by measuring changes in blood pressure, respiration, and/or skin response in order to detect a conflicting relationship between the verbal and the nonverbal in order to attempt to establish whether the person is lying or telling the truth.

positive relationship   a relationship that allows freedom of expression and reflects acceptance of the feelings of both people.

postspeech analysis   evaluating the effect of the speech following the presentation through the question-and-answer session, questionnaires, and personal feedback.

power   the ability to control what happens—to create things you want to happen and to block things you don't want to happen.

power role   the ability to influence another's attainment of goals. Power can center on controlling another person or persons, influencing the efforts of others, and/or accomplishing a goal.

practicality   a test of a solution to a problem that centers on whether the suggested solution can be put into practice.

presentation graphics   a series of visuals, usually from the PowerPoint program, that are projected using an overhead projector while the speaker is discussing each point.

primary group tension   the normal jitters and feelings of uneasiness that group members experience when they first congregate.

primary signal system   the senses: seeing, hearing, tasting, smelling, and touching.

primary sources of information   sources used in a speech to develop clarification or proof that represent the original reports of the observations or research.

prior to the speech analysis   audience analysis before the speech is given.

probes   interview questions that are used to elicit a detailed response, including his or her point with more direction and depth, such as "Why do you feel that way?"

problem-solution method of issue arrangement   a method of arrangement for the body of a speech in which the speaker attempts to identify what is wrong and to determine how to cure it or make a recommendation for its cure.

problem-solving interview   the interviewer and interviewee meet to solve a dilemma. The end goal is to develop a solution that can solve the problem, won't cause bigger problems, and can be put into effect.

process of the speech analysis   observing the audience for feedback during the speech.

proposal–counterproposal negotiating   a method of negotiation, common in the United States and some other Western countries, in which a plan or solution is presented and then a counter offer is made.

proxemics   the study of how people use and perceive their social and personal space.

psychographics   speech listeners' attitudes and beliefs.

psychological noise   communication problems created by emotional issues such as stress, frustration, or irritation.

psychological vulture   a person's negative self-thoughts and beliefs. It attacks a person's perceived weaknesses and eats at the person's self-worth.

public communication   characterized by a speaker sending a message to an audience. It may be direct, such as a face-to-face message delivered by a speaker to an audience, or indirect, such as a message relayed over radio, television, or the Internet.

public meetings   a group gathering in which members or interested individuals may attend the sessions (e.g., corporation stockholders' meeting, school board meeting, city council meeting).

public self   the one you let others know; the you that you have decided to let others see.

public speaking   involves a transaction between a speaker and an audience.

public speaking anxiety   the fear of giving speeches, sometimes referred to as *speechophobia* or *stage fright*.

pupilometrics   a theory that indicates that pupils dilate when the eyes are focused on a pleasurable object and contract when focused on an unpleasurable objects.

purpose of the speech   centers on the speaker's expected outcomes for the presentation.

quotations   material written or spoken by a person in the exact words in which it was originally presented.

real self   what you think of yourself when you are being most honest about your interests, thoughts, emotions, and needs.

receiver   the recipient of the message.

reception   the initial step in the listening process.

red-flag words   emotional trigger words that create intrapersonal negative reactions.

referent power   influence based on personal loyalty, friendship, affection, and admiration.

reflective nonverbal reactions   the display of culturally learned nonverbal behavior (e.g., touching/nontouching patterns, length of eye contact while conversing).

reflexive nonverbal reactions   automatic reactions to stimuli based on inborn neurological drives (e.g., eye blinks, facial flushing, facial expressions).

regulators   nonverbal acts that maintain and control the back-and-forth nature of speaking and listening between two or more people (e.g., nods of the head, eye movements, and body shifts are all regulators used to encourage or discourage conversation).

relational conflict   disagreements in a relationship; recognizable stages are tension develops, false ignoring, resentment, and unforgiveness.

relational fusion   a process in relationships in which one partner defines, or attempts to define, reality for the other; one partner, the controller, dictates what is good, right, and acceptable for the other partner.

reprimanding interview   an interview in which the interviewer helps the interviewee analyze problems caused by the latter so that corrections can be made. It is usually scheduled after an appraisal interview so that an employee has had an opportunity to correct problematic behavior.

requesting   the process of asking, expressing a desire, or soliciting for something.

reward power   influence based on a person having the best or only source of desired rewards.

rhetorical language   used to influence thoughts and behaviors (e.g., often used in advertisements).

rhetorical questions   queries for which no outward response is expected.

rhetorographics   the place, time limit, time of day, and emotional climate of a speech.

right hemisphere of the brain   responsible for intuitive, spatial, visual, and concrete matters.

risky shift phenomenon   holds that decisions reached after discussion by a group display more experimentation, are less conservative, and contain more risk than decisions reached by people working alone before any discussion is held.

Robert's Rules of Order   a book that lists and organizes the rules of parliamentary procedures by which groups operate.

rule of 5 × 5   indicates that no PowerPoint slide or chart should use more than five words per line and no more than five lines per slide.

sales interview   a cultural-specific interview with the purpose of persuading someone to purchase a product or service.

salon conversation clubs   groups of people form for the opportunity to participate in interactions about various topics such as books, politics, religion, or the arts.

Sapir-Whorf Hypothesis   theorizes that a person's understanding of the world, and how the person behaves in it, are based on the language a person speaks. Also known as the *Linguistic Relativity Hypothesis.*

schemata   mental representations carried in the brain that are shaped by the language categories and the way brains process information.

second employment interviews   provides more detailed information about an employment position and, at the same time, further determine the candidate's fit to the organization and the job.

Second Life   a virtual conferencing Internet-based vitural world that enables meeting participants to interact with each other through use of avatars.

secondary group tension   the stress and strain that occur within a group later in its development. Frequent causes of this problem are having to make a decision, shortage of time to accomplish the task, differences of opinion, and difficult members.

secondary sources of information   sources used in a speech to develop clarification or proof that report, but did not originally generate, the observations or research.

security (as a basic need)   reflexive, inborn reactions that cause people to seek equilibrium, a balance. When security is absent, people feel a lack of control, get uneasy, and become overly cautious and uncertain.

selective communication   the ability of humans to choose the symbols that best represent the idea or concept to be expressed.

self-concept   your idea or picture of yourself; the accumulation of knowledge about the self, including such dimensions as beliefs regarding personality traits, physical characteristics, abilities, values, goals, and roles.

self-credentialing verbal mode   a communication style in which emphasis is placed on drawing attention to or boasting about one's accomplishments. A style encouraged in the United States, Switzerland, and in some Arabic and African cultures.

self-declared families   a group who has decided to live together as a declared group, usually without legal recognition (e.g., heterosexuals living together, homosexuals living together, communal groups, religious cults).

self-disclosure   intentionally letting the other person know who you are by communicating self-revealing information.

self-fulfilled person   the person who confidently chooses what to reveal and to whom; a person who is not intimidated into a negative self-concept and realizes that there will always be problems, frustrations, and failures in life.

self-humbling verbal mode   a communication style in which emphasis is placed on lowering oneself via modest talk, verbal restraints, and the use of self-deprecation. A style encouraged by Native Americans and some areas of West Africa.

self-love   accepting yourself as a worthy person because you choose to do so.

self-perceived I   the image you project; the way you perceive yourself. It is revealed through the words, ideas, actions, clothing, and lifestyle you choose.

self-talk   intrapersonally communicating within yourself; an inner dialogue.

semantic noise   communication problems created by the meaning of words.

semantics   the study of the relationship of language and meaning.

sensorium   frames the listener's perceptual filter so that all of the senses are brought to bear so the listener can logically and emotionally respond to information.

sentence outline   a speech presentation tool that has complete sentences for all entries and usually has correct punctuation.

sex   one's biological or physical self (male/female), in contrast to gender, which refers to one's psychological, social, and interactive characteristics (man/woman).

sexual harassment   generalized sexist remarks or behavior; inappropriate and offensive sexual advances; solicitation of sexual activity or other sex-linked behavior by promise of rewards; coercion of sexual activity by threat of punishment; assaults; unwanted and unwelcome sexual actions in work and educational contexts.

shyness   the fear of participating in the communication act. Also identified as *communication apprehension, Social Anxiety Disorder,* and *Social Phobia.*

Significant-Other Theory   the selection of specific people or groups whose language, ideals, and beliefs we allow to influence us.

signposting   speaker stating, during a speech, where the listeners have been, where they are presently, and where they are going.

silent majority   those who say nothing during the decision-making process.

simple assertion   a statement or statements in which a person states the facts relating to the existence of a problem.

single-parent families   a family consisting of one parent with a child or children.

Six-Step Standard Agenda for Decision Making   a six-step decision-making procedure that is a form of reflective thinking; it stresses that a problem be identified and analyzed, solutions sought, and a solution selected and implemented.

slang   words that are related to a specific activity or incident and are immediately understood by members of a particular group.

small group ecology   The physical placement of members of small groups in relation to one another; includes placement of chairs and the size and shape of the tables and desks.

small groups   a group consisting of three to twelve persons.

small talk   an exchange of information between two people that normally is on the surface level, usually centering on biographics (name, occupation, college major, hometown, college attended or attending).

smell adaptation   occurs when people gradually lose the distinctiveness of a particular smell through repeated contact with it.

smell blindness   occurs when people are unable to detect smells.

smell memory   the ability to recall previous situations when encountering a particular smell associated with them.

smell overload   takes place when an exceptionally large number of odors or one extremely strong odor overpowers the smeller.

social networking   talking online in such communities as facebook.com, MySpace.com, and twitter.com.

social orientation   a person's nationality, race, gender, sexual orientation, and religion that are the basis for her or his identity.

social self   your interactions with others.

social space distance   in Euro-American culture, a four- to twelve-foot zone that is used during business transactions and casual social exchanges.

source   the originator of the message.

Spanglish   a dialect of English in which the vocabulary is mostly Spanish, with a smattering of English words and some fractured traditional English syntax.

spatial method of issue arrangement   a method of arrangement for the body of a speech in which the speaker sets a point of reference and follows a geographic pattern. The pattern can be left to right, north to south, or the center to the outside.

speaker inventory   an examination by a prospective speaker of his or her life experiences and interests that can be useful for selecting a topic for a presentation.

speaking setting   encompasses where the speech is given, what the time limit is, when the presentation is made, and the attitude of the audience.

specific instances   condensed examples that are used to clarify or prove a point in a speech.

speech-independent gestures   bodily movements tied to speech, referred to as *emblems.*

speech to inform   a speech with the purpose of imparting new information and securing understanding, or reinforcing information and understandings acquired in the past.

speech outline   a clear step-by-step structure of a speech that indicates what will be said and in what order.

speech participants   the speaker and the members of the audience.

speech to persuade   a speech that attempts to get the listener to take some action, to accept a belief, or to change a point of view.

speech planning outline   a brief framework used to think through the process of the speech.

speech presentation outline   a framework in which the speaker fleshes out the planning outline with examples and illustrations and writes in internal summaries and forecasts.

speech-related gestures   bodily movements directly tied to or that accompany speech; referred to as *illustrators, affect displays, regulators,* and *adaptors.*

speech topic   the subject of a speech.

speechophobia   public speaking anxiety, sometimes referred to as *stage fright.*

spiral form of explanation   a method of speech structure in which a statement is made and then a story or analogy that deals with the statement is presented, with the responsibility for interpretation left to the listener.

spiritual self   what we are thinking and feeling.

stagnating stage of relationships   the stage in Knapp's Relationship Termination Model that is highlighted by the individuals starting to avoid discussing the relationship because one thinks he or she knows what the other will say and is afraid of the consequences that can result in the air of suspended animation; little or no mutual feelings or actions take place at this stage.

Standard American English   the language generally recognized by linguists as representative of the general population of the United States (e.g., words and grammatical forms are those of nationally published magazines, such as *Time* and *Newsweek,* and newspapers such as *USA Today* and the *New York Times*. These words tend to represent the vocabulary of the West, the Midwest, the Midland, and the southern section of New England.

standard dialects   high-prestige dialects.

statement of central idea defines the subject and develops the criteria by which to evaluate the material to be included in the speech; it centers on what you want the audience to know, to be able to do, to believe; consists of three parts: the goal of the speech, the statement of the topic, and the method or process used to develop the speech.

statement of the speech's central idea the segment of a speech intended to keep the speaker on course for developing a purposeful and well-organized speech, while indicating the response the speaker wants from listeners.

statistical surveying methods developed by statisticians for collecting data.

statistics a collection of numerical information arranged as representations, trends, or theories.

study group established to enable individuals to work together to study and learn with the assistance of others.

study of language examining meaning based on the words used, the way the words are placed together, and the backgrounds and experiences of the communicators.

substituting relationship of verbal with nonverbal the replacement of verbal communication with nonverbal communication (e.g., shaking the head up and down to indicate "yes").

super leadership guidance in which people are led to lead themselves and thereby release the self-leadership energy within each person.

supplementary speech aids visual, audio, audiovisual, and computerized graphics used during a speech with the intention of facilitating the listeners' understanding.

support group a system that allows people to interact with others who share similar goals or problems whose purpose is to increase people's knowledge of themselves and others, to assist people to clarify the changes they most want to make in their life, and to give people some of the tools necessary to make these changes.

supporting speech material information used by a public speaker that clarifies a point being made in the speech or offers evidence of the validity of presented argument.

survival (as a basic need) reflexive, inborn reactions that we instinctively use to communicate our fear of a possible ending of our existence.

symbol a word or sound that is designated in a language system to represent an image or idea (e.g., *pencil, beautiful*).

symposium a group format in which participants give prepared speeches with no interaction among themselves or with the audience.

syntactical noise communication problems created by grammatical usage.

systematic desensitization people are taught first to recognize tension in their bodies and then how to relax through a step-by-step process.

tag questions inquiries added onto the end of statements, such as "That movie was terrific, don't you think?" The intent is to get the communicative partner to enter the conversation; powerless language in the form of an inarticulate that asks a question that is not a meaningful part of the statement (e.g., "Put away your toys, *okay?*").

talking points bullet points in an abbreviated outline format that serve as a framework for the speech and are used in a rehearsal session and as the notes for the actual presentation.

task dimension of group the members of a group meeting the goal of the group, which may include decision making, informing, appraising and examining, problem solving, and creating interest in staying on track.

technical time precise time, as in the way some scientists look at how things happen in milliseconds.

techno-babble computer language used for personal communications. Technobabblers interface with each other and debug their relationships.

teleconferencing consists of telephone conference calls and speakerphone meetings.

telephone job interview an employment interview which, in some cases, has replaced the first personal interview that an applicant used to have with a company.

terminating stage of relationships the final stage of Knapp's Relationship Termination Model; it is highlighted by a breakup of the relationship.

territory (as a basic need) physical or perceptual areas that you mark off or possess and within which you feel secure.

testimony a direct quotation (actual statement) or a paraphrase (reworded idea) from an authority that is provided by a speaker to clarify ideas, back up contentions, and reinforce concepts.

text messaging sending of short messages (160 characters or fewer), using the Short Message Service from mobile phones.

Theory of Listening Fidelity postulates that how much listeners understand a speaker's message is consistent with the speaker's understanding of the message received.

therapeutic listening the type of listening used in mental health, social work, and counseling that requires a listener to learn when to ask questions, when to stimulate further discussion, and when, if ever, to give advice.

time method of issue arrangement a method of arrangement for the body of a speech that orders information from a beginning point to an ending one, with all the steps developed in numerical or time sequence.

topic outline a speech presentation tool that has words or phrases for all entries and usually has little or no punctuation after entries.

topic selection the subject about which the speaker selects to speak.

topic of the speech the specific subject of a speech.

topical method of issue arrangement a method of arrangement for the body of a speech in which a speaker explains an idea in terms of its component parts. For example, in speaking about dogs, a speaker could discuss cocker spaniels, poodles, and then collies.

touch avoidance the degree to which an individual dislikes being touched.

town meeting a meeting in which a presenter opens the session with a short prepared statement that establishes the framework for the meeting, followed by individuals in the audience engaging in a forum with the speaker.

transactional model of communication a schematic that illustrates how communicators simultaneously process messages. Communicator A encodes a message and sends it. Communicator B then encodes feedback and sends it to A, who decodes it. But these steps are not mutually exclusive; encoding and decoding may occur simultaneously. Speakers may send a verbal message and at the same time receive and decode a nonverbal feedback message from listeners. Because messages can be sent and received at the same time, this model is multidirectional and the message overlaps.

transformational leadership   the role of a leader who takes on the role of changing both the behavior and the outlook of his or her followers.

triangle stance   a posture/stance technique used by speakers to aid in relaxing their bodies as they speak.

turnitin.com   an online proprietary system that instantly identifies papers containing unoriginal material and acts as a powerful deterrent to stop student plagiarism before it starts.

two-valued reasoning   dividing all decisions into a right or wrong/good or bad structure so that there is no flexibility in reaching conclusions.

unfolding organizational speech structure   an inductive style of organizing a speech in which the speaker lays out supporting evidence and then draws a conclusion, leading the listeners to be drawn into the argument.

urban legends   myths, often spread on the Internet, which consists of stories thought to be factual by those circulating them. They are not necessarily untrue, but they are often distorted, exaggerated, or sensationalized.

victim   a person who is denied the right to decide how to live his or her own life.

victimizer   a person or establishment that interferes with another person's right to decide how to live his or her own life.

video conferencing   meetings conducted with one-way video and two-way audio as well as fully interactive two-way video and two-way audio.

virgules   slash marks inserted into a manuscript that can be used to indicate a pause or a stop.

virtual conferencing   takes place when meeting participants are connected to an Internet-based virtual world that enables its users, called "Residents," to interact with each other through avatars, a computer user's virtual representation of himself or herself.

visual aids   supplementary aids, which appeal to the sense of sight, that are used during a speech to facilitate the listeners' understanding.

visualization   a technique in which a public speaker sees himself or herself in the actual setting in which he or she is going to give the speech and making a successful presentation.

voting   a procedure that takes place when members are given an opportunity to indicate agreement, disagreement, or no opinion on an idea or candidate.

Web conferencing   meetings in which participants log on to a central conference database through their personal computer.

western problem-solving sequence   a method of solving problems that has four segments: identify the problem, search for solutions, test those solutions, and put a solution into practice. The final decision is often based on a majority vote of the membership, with those who will have to implement or live with the decision often not part of the decision-making team.

wheel flow of information communication network   each person in the group speaks to the leader, the leader speaks to each of the participants, but the participants do not speak directly to each other.

Wikipedia   a widely used online encyclopedia of questionable facts because it allows anyone with an Internet connection to create or alter any entry; a source generally not recommended for use as a primary or secondary source of information.

willingness to communicate   a person's willingness to take risks, analyze his or her communication, and make adjustments in order to participate in the communicative act.

win-lose negotiations   a style of negotiation that centers on one person getting what he or she wants while the other comes up short.

win-win negotiation   a style of negotiation in which the goal is to find a solution that is satisfying to everyone.

work team   a small group of workers who function as teams to make and implement decisions about their own work.

workability   a test of the solution to a problem that centers on whether the suggestion solution will solve or help solve the problem.

working memory capacity   the dual-task process made up of both the memory and the attention functions as listeners attempt to process the speaker's message.

World Wide Web   a collection of interconnected documents linked by hyperlinks and URLs accessible via the Internet.

Y communication network   two of the group members speak directly to the leader—but not to each other—while other members speak to each other and send messages to the other members through the leader.

yes-response questions   a form of leading interview question that is stated in such a way that the respondent is encouraged to agree with the interviewer (e.g., "You would agree with me, wouldn't you, that this company's policies are fair?").

Notes

PREFACE

1. Doug Hunter, dhunter@lamcastermorgan.com. (printed with permission).
2. Dr. Sandy Nesbit Tracy, University of Arkansas at Pine Bluff.
3. S. P. Morreale & J. C. Pearson, J.C. (2008). "Why Communication Education Is Important: The Centrality Of The Discipline In The 21st Century," *Communication Education*, 57(2) (2008): 224–240.
4. Ibid.
5. Ibid.

CHAPTER 1

1. Sherwyn Morreale and Judy C. Pearson, "Why Communication Education is Important: The Centrality of the Discipline in the 21st Century," *Communication Education*, 57(2) (2008): 11 (original manuscript).
2. Ibid.
3. See Andrea Koncz and Mimi Collins, "'Perfect' Job Candidate Pairs Communication Skills with Strong Work Ethic," National Association of Colleges and Employers website, NACEWeb, www.naceweb.org/press/display.asp?year=&prid=270, December 5, 2007.
4. "Class of 2008 Steps into Good Job Market," National Association of Colleges and Employers, www.jobweb.com/Jobs/market.aspx?id=1219.
5. Morreale and Pearson, pp. 224–240.
6. B. R. Brunner, "Listening, Communication & Trust: Practitioners' Perspectives of Business/Organizational Relationships," *International Journal of Listening*, 22(1) (2008): 73–82.
7. Stella Ting-Toomey and Leeva C. Chung, *Understanding Intercultural Communication* (Los Angeles: Roxbury Publishing Company, 2005), p. 2.
8. Thomas L. Friedman, *The World Is Flat: A Brief History of the Twenty-First Century* (New York: Picador/Farrar, Straus and Giroux, 2007), pp. 10–11.
9. Richard Emanuel, "A Rationale for the Basic Course: Fundamentals of Oral Communication vs. Public Speaker," National Communication Association website, 2005, referring to the work of G. Crawley and K. Klomparens, *The 1997–98 MSU Ph.D. Alumni Survey*. Michigan State University, East Lansing, M1.
10. Ibid.
11. Ibid.

12. For an extended discussion of public-speaking apprehension, see Virginia P. Richmond and James C. McCroskey, *Communication: Apprehension, Avoidance, and Effectiveness*, 5th ed. (Boston: Pearson, 2000), Chapter 3.
13. "National Workplace Survey Reveals American Professionals Overwhelmed, Headed for 'Breaking Point,'" www.lexisnexis.com/media/press-release.aspx?id=1041.asp, February 26, 2008.
14. Based on David K. Berlo, *The Process of Communication* (New York: Holt, Rinehart and Winston, 1960).
15. Advertisement, "WordPerfect-Macintosh," WordPerfect Corporation, Ogden, UT.
16. Factors that cause communication difficulties are sometimes called *interference*. In this text, these factors are referred to as *noise*.
17. James Neuliep, *Intercultural Communication: A Contextual Approach*, 2nd ed. (Boston: Houghton Mifflin, 2003), p. 219.
18. Berlo.
19. Michael Bloom, Notre Dame College, South Euclid, OH, in correspondence of February 2, 19, 2008, regarding the need to acknowledge the sociological theories of media.
20. "American Time Use Survey Summary," United States Department of Labor news release, www.bls.gov/news.release/atus.nr0.htm, June 28, 2007.
21. "Internet World Stats, Usage and Population Statistics," Miniwatts Marketing Group, www.internetworldstats.com, December 31, 2007, p. 1.
22. Dirk Johnson, "A Bloody Day on the Rez," *Newsweek* (April 4, 2005): 3.
23. Neal Justin, "Political Moments in Radio, TV That Defined People and Times," *The Cleveland Plain Dealer* (April 12, 2007): E5, as reprinted from *Minneapolis-St. Paul Star Tribune*.
24. Ibid.
25. Ibid.
26. Dita Smith, "How Wide a Web?" *Washington Post* (July 28, 2001): A13.
27. Michael Liedtke, "Facebook Revamps New Advertising System," Associated Press, November 30, 2007.
28. "Sophos Facebook ID Shows 41% of Users Happy to Reveal All to Potential Identity Thieves," www.sophos.com, August 14, 2007.
29. See Vinton Cerf, "How the Internet Got Started," *Online Success* at www.webmastercourse.com/articles/internet/history.

30. Neil Postman, "The Antidote to Trivialization," *NPQ* (Fall 1990): 55.

31. For a discussion on pluralism, see Larry Samovar, Richard Porter, and Edwin McDaniel, *Intercultural Communication: A Reader* (Belmont, CA: Thomson Higher Education, 2006), pp. 156–158.

32. A treatise on the concept of multcultualism: William A. Henry III, "The Politics of Separation," *Time* (Fall 1993, special edition): 75. For a contemporary view, see "Culture and Multiculturalism," The Ayn Rand Institute, www.aynrand.org/site/PageServer?pagename=media_topic _multiculturalism&JServSessionIdr007=8j6x3uvd32.app5a, 2008.

33. Robert Pear, "U.S. Minorities Are Becoming the Majority," *International Herald Tribune* (August 23, 2005), www.iht. com.

34. Ibid.

35. J. W. Neuliep and J. C. McCroskey, "The Development of Intercultural and Interethnic Communication Apprehension Scales," *Communication Research Reports,* 14 (1997): 385–398.

36. Stella Ting-Toomey and Leeva Chung, *Understanding Intercultural Communication* (New York: Oxford University Press, 2005), p. 234.

37. Americans for Legal Immigration, www.alipac.us, 2007.

38. Brian Williams quoting exit poll statistics collected by selected NBC reporters on NBC News, February 5, 2008. For additional information, see "Early Feb. 5 Exit Poll Highlights," Associated Press, February 5, 2008, quoting from exit polling by Edison Media Research and Mitofsky International for the Associated Press and television networks.

39. Samovar et al., p. 433.

40. A comment included on a student evaluation of the Intercultural Communication course for the Fall/Winter 1999–2000 school year.

41. David L. Hudson, Jr., "Free Speech on Public College Campuses," Overview, First Amendment Center, www .firstamendmentcenter.org, September 13, 2005.

42. Ibid.

43. May Beth Marklein, "On Campus: Free Speech for You but Not for Me?" *USA Today* (March 11, 2003), www.usatoday .com.

44. Franklyn S. Haiman has written extensively on the First Amendment to the Constitution of the United States and the Speech Arts. This quote appeared in Franklyn Haiman, *Speech Arts and The First Amendment* (Carbondale: Southern Illinois University Press, 1993), p. 3. He expanded on this and other first amendment concepts in Franklyn Haiman, "Articles by Franklyn Haiman," *The American Prospect,* www .prospect.org, 2008.

45. Ibid.

46. Alan Dershowitz, "Finding Jefferson: A Lost Letter, a Remarkable Discovery, and the First Amendment in an Age of Terrorism," www.alandershowitz.com, 2008.

47. Ibid.

48. Scott Jaschite, "Nominee Reflects on 'Hate Speech,' Sees Supreme Court Taking Up the Issue," *Chronicle of Higher Education* (August 4, 1993): A-23.

49. Gina Holland, "Free Speech Cases Pile Up on Docket at Supreme Court," *Cleveland Plain Dealer* (August, 20, 2002): A7.

50. Nancy Chang, "The USA Patriot Act," Center for Constitutional Rights, November 2001.

51. Susan Herman, "The USA Patriot Act and the U.S. Department of Justice: Losing Our Balances?" Jurist Legal Intelligence News, jurist.law.pitt.edu, 2003.

52. Richard L. Johannesen, *Ethics in Human Communication,* 5th ed. (Prospect Heights, IL: Waveland Press, 2001), p. 2.

53. Ibid.

54. Stewart M. Powell, "Kerry Strikes Back at GOP Attacks on His War Record," *Cleveland Plain Dealer* (August 25, 2004): A7.

55. Michael Osborn and Suzanne Osborn, *Public Speaking,* 7th ed. (Boston: Houghton Mifflin, 2006), p. 19. For a discussion on ethical communication and ethical speakers, see pp. 19–24.

56. Douglass K. Daniel, "Study: False Statements Preceded War," The Associated Press, January 23, 2008, reporting the results of a study done by the Center for Public Integrity, www.publicintegrity.org/defaule.aspx.

57. www.hist.umn.edu/~ruggles/Approval.htm, a compilation of the ratings of Gallup, Zogby, Ap/Ipsos, Quinnipiac, ARG, Harris, Newsweek, CBS/NYT, CNN, Fox, NBC/WSJ, ABC/WP, and Pew.

58. Bill Barger, "Ethics in Business Communication," http:// ezinearticles.com/Ethics-in-Business-Communication&id=603856, June 12, 2008.

59 "IABC Code of Ethics for Professional Communicators," www.iabc.com/about/code.htm, 2008.

60. Ibid.

CHAPTER 2

1. "Obama Rips Rev. Wright," CBS Corporation, April 30, 2008, http://wbztv.com/national/obama.rips.wright.2 .711401.html.

2. Ibid.

3. Ibid.

4. Definition is based on "Language," *American Heritage Dictionary of the English Language,* 4th ed., www.ask.com/ reference/dictionary/ahdict/46762/language, 2005.

5. Michael C. Corballis, *From Hand to Mouth: The Origins of Language* (Princeton, NJ: Princeton University Press, 2002). Also see Justin Gillis, "Gene Mutations Linked to Language Development," *Washington Post* (August 15, 2002): A13.

6. The social construction of reality concept has its roots in Peter L. Berger and Tomas Luckman, *The Social Construction of Reality: A Treatise in the Sociology of Knowledge* (New York: Doubleday, 1966). For a contemporary discussion, see Stephen W. Littlejohn, "Theories of Social and Cultural Reality," *Theories of Human Communication* (Belmont, CA: Wadsworth, 2005).

7. Emily Eakin, "Before the Word, Perhaps the Wink: Some Language Experts Think Humans Spoke First With Gestures," *New York Times* (May 18, 2002): B7, Column 5, based on Michael C. Corballis, *From Hand to Mouth: The Origins of Language* (Princeton, NJ: Princeton University Press, 2002).

8. Ibid.

9. Ibid.

10. Ibid.

11. Adam Gorlick, "Merriam-Webster Picks Words to Go by the Book," *Cleveland Plain Dealer* (July 7, 2006): 2.

12. Ibid.
13. "What's the Good Word? 'Crackberry,'" *USA Today* (January 2, 2006): 1D.
14. Ashley M. Heher, "McDonald's Seeks to Refine 'McJobs,'" Associated Press, March 21, 2007, www.oed.com, www.mcdonalds.com.
15. Ibid.
16. Ibid.
17. Ibid.
18. Randolph E. Schmid, "Regions of Dying Languages Named," Associated Press, September 18, 2007, based on research funded by the Australian government, U.S. National Science Foundation, and National Geographic Society. Further information can be found at www.languagehotspots.org and www.livingtongues.org.
19. Terry Leonard, "Knowledge Fades as African Languages Die," *Science-AP* (March 7, 2005).
20. Ibid.
21. Schmid.
22. The theory was proposed by Norbert Wiener, *The Human Use of Human Beings* (New York: Da Capo Press, 1950), republished in 1988.
23. George Herbert Mead, *Mind, Self, and Society* (Chicago: University of Chicago Press, 1934).
24. A theory developed by American linguists Edward Sapir and Benjamin Whorf. For an updated discussion of the theory, see "Current Interpretations of the Sapir-Whorf Hypothesis," www.geocities.com/CollegePark/4110/whorf.html.
25. Peter Farb, *Word Play* (New York: Alfred A. Knopf, 1993), p. 197.
26. For a discussion of the function of language, see Barbara Warnick and Edward S. Inch, *Critical Thinking and Communication* (Upper Saddle River, NJ: Prentice-Hall, 2005).
27. For a discussion of phatic language, see Richard Nordquist, "Phatic Communication," about.com, and "What Is Phatic Communication?," www.wisegeek.com/what-is-phatic-communication.htm, 2008.
28. Diane Catellano Mader, "The Politically Correct Textbook: Trends in Publishers' Guidelines for the Representation of Marginalized Groups," paper presented at the Eastern Communication Association Convention, Portland, ME, May 3, 1992.
29. Ibid.
30. Ibid.
31. For a discussion of language distortion, see Harrison Koehl, "Psycho-Babel: A Ponerological Approach to Modern Doublespeak and the Distortion of Language," *Signs of The Times* (November 24, 2006), www.sott.net/signs/editorials/signs.php and Kimball Atwood, "Misleading Language: The Common Currency of 'CAM' Characterizations," *Science Based Medicine* (March 7, 2008), www.sciencebasedmedicine.org.
32. For a complete discussion of doublespeak, see William Lutz, *Doublespeak* (New York: Harper and Row, 1989). To see examples of doublespeak, go to www.doublespeakshow.com/.
33. Boston Globe, quoting from a speech by Governor Romney, October 24, 2005, as found in "Did Romney Up Taxes or Close Loopholes?", www.msnbc.msn.com/id/2193946, November 2, 2007.
34. Ibid.
35. Ibid.
36. Jacob Weisberg, "The Complete Bushisms," *Bushisms: President George Herbert Walker Bush in His Own Words* (New York: Workman Publishing Company, 2002).
37. about.com: Political Humor.
38. Ibid.
39. Lutz, pp. xii, xiii.
40. Roger Brown, *Words and Things* (New York: Free Press, 1959), p. 22.
41. Based on the classic work of Howard Mims. See Howard A. Mims, "On Black English: A Language with Rules," *Cleveland Plain Dealer* (August 31, 1979): A21.
42. Ibid.
43. Definition is based on Joseph DeVito's comprehensive dictionary dedicated to the exclusive study of communication terms. Joseph A. DeVito, *The Communication Handbook: A Dictionary* (New York: Harper and Row, 1986), p. 94.
44. Mims.
45. Jeffrey Collins and Kristen Wyatt, "Whither the Southern Accent?," Associated Press, www.antimoon.com, November 23, 2005.
46. "Nashville Mayor Vetoes English-Only Measure," *USA Today* (February 13, 2007): 4A.
47. Material in this section is based on the work of W. Zelinsky, as discussed in Peter A. Andersen, Myron W. Lustig, and Janis F. Andersen, "Regional Patterns of Communication in the United States: A Theoretical Perspective," *Communication Monographs* 54 (June 1987): 128–144.
48. Jessica Weintraub, "From AOK to Oz, The Historical Dictionary of American Slang," *Humanities*, 25(2) (March/April 2004), www.neh.gov/news/humanities/2004-03/slang.html and "People, Etc.," *Elyria (Ohio) Chronicle-Telegram Scene* (April 10, 1977): 2.
49. Larry Neumeister, "'Cool' Still as Cool as Ever in Slang," *Cleveland Plain Dealer* (February 12, 2006).
50. For a discussion of techno-babble, see "Technobabble," http://en.wikipedia.org/wiki/Technobabble.
51. Michael Lawrence, "Slanguages," Ellis, IL., 1996–2007, as found on www.slanguage.com.
52. "What's in a Word? A Job, Hood Senior's Study Says," *Washington Post* (June 6, 1991): Md8.
53. David Walton, "Um, Pardon Me While I Figure Out What I'm Saying," *Cleveland Plain Dealer* (August 26, 2007): M5.
54. Ibid.
55. Ibid.
56. A concept proposed by Orlando Taylor, Howard University.
57. Robin Henry, "'Black English' Causes Confusion in the Classroom: An Interview with Dr. Howard Mims, Associate Professor of Speech and Hearing, Cleveland State University," *Elyria (Ohio) Chronicle-Telegram* (July 26, 1987): G2. Mims was one of the forerunners in the examination of Ebonics/Black English.
58. "Teaching Standard English: A Sociological Approach," unpublished handout based on the syllabus for the Basic Communication Strategies course at LaGuardia Community College, New York, n.d.

59. "Teaching Standard English," with reference to Randall Miller, *Dictionary of African American Slang* (Working Title Publishing, 2006), workingtitlepublishing .com@earthlink.net.

60. Ibid.

61. Ibid.

62. Ibid.

63. The theory of Sheila Mayers.

64. Ibid.

65. Janice Castro, "Spanglish Spoken Here," *Time* (July 11, 1988): 53.

66. Ibid., as stated by Carmen Silva-Corvalan, University of Southern California.

67. Ibid.

68. For a discussion of Asian language styles, see Stella Ting-Toomey and Leeva Chung, *Understanding Intercultural Communication* (New York: Oxford University Press, 2005).

69. Steven B. Pratt, "Razzing: Ritualized Uses of Humor as a Form of Identification among American Indians," paper presented at Central States Speech Association, Oklahoma City, April 1994; see also H. B. Mokros (Ed.), *Interaction and Identity: Information and Behavior*, vol. 5 (New Brunswick, NJ: Transactions, 1994), p. 4.

70. Ibid.

71. Gerry Philipsen, "Navaho World View and Culture Patterns of Speech: A Case Study in Ethnorhetoric," *Speech Monographs* (June 1972): 134.

72. Ibid., p. 135.

73. Pratt, p. 2.

74. Ibid.

75. Rene Sanchez, "After Ebonics Controversy, Oakland Seeks Viable Lesson Plan," *Washington Post* (April 19, 1998): A10.

76. Howard A. Mims, Cleveland State University, symposium lecture, 2000.

77. "Hispanic and Black High School Graduation Rates Very Low," *ParaPundit* (February 26, 2004), reported by the Civil Society Institute's Results for America (RTFA) Project and Advocates for Children of New York, www.parapundit.com.

78. Based on research by Sandra Terrell and Francis Terrell.

79. Adapted from the concepts of Thomas R. Nilsen.

80. Sarah Smith, "Words That Sting," *Psychology Today* (September/October, 2000): 24.

81. Ibid.

82. Ibid.

83. Name of student withheld to protect his identity.

CHAPTER 3

1. For an in-depth discussion of nonverbal communication, see Mark Knapp and Judith Hall, *Nonverbal Communication in Human Interaction*, 5th ed. (Belmont, CA: Thomson Wadsworth, 2007). For a business orientation to nonverbal communication, see Tonya Reiman, *The Power of Body Language: How to Succeed in Every Business and Social Encounter* (New York: Pocket Books/Simon & Schuster, 2007).

2. For an extended discussion of universal nonverbal clues, read "Darwin's Universal Faces," in Peter Anderson (Ed.), *The Complete Idiot's Guide to Body Language* (New York: Penguin Group, 2004), pp. 53–56. Anderson is also the author of the scholarly text, *Nonverbal Communication: Forms and Functions*, 2nd ed. (Longwave, IL: Waveland Press, 2007).

3. Judee K. Burgoon, David B. Buller, and W. Gill Woodall, *Nonverbal Communication: The Unspoken Dialogue*, 2nd ed. (New York: McGraw-Hill, 1996), p. 1. (The book is no longer in print, but is considered as a precedent-setting text in the field of nonverbal communication and is still used as a classic reference by communication instructors.)

4. Ibid., p. 136.

5. Ibid., p. 1.

6. Ibid., p. 136.

7. Anderson, pp. Foreword 1 & 2.

8. Mark L. Hickson III, Don W. Stacks, and Nina-Jo Moore, *NVC: Nonverbal Communication Studies and Applications*, 4th ed. (Los Angeles: Roxbury Publishing, 2004).

9. Anderson, p. 55, based on the research of Eible-Eibesfeldt.

10. Ibid.

11. Anderson, p. 39.

12. Clifford Wright, *NLP Workbook, Introductory Level*, Books 1 and 2 (Portland, OR: Metamorphous Press, 1989). For a description and discussion of neurolinguistic programming, see www.nlpinfo.com/ and http://www .neurolinguisticprogramming.com/.

13. Ibid., p. 4.

14. Ibid.

15. Ibid.

16. For a further discussion of thinking and eye movement, see Eric Adler, "Speak to Me with Thine Eyes (and Head and Arms)," *Washington Post* (November 26, 1998): C5.

17. G. Doheryt-Sneddon, "Non-Verbal Communication," *SPECTRA*, National Communication Association (March, 2006). For the complete report, go to http://insidehighered .com/workplace/2006/01/13tips.

18. Edward Hall and Mildred Hall, "The Sounds of Silence," *Playboy* 18 (June 1971), p. 148. The concept was later included in Edward Hall, *Beyond Culture* (New York: Longitude, 1977).

19. "World Citizens Guide," Southern Methodist University and Business for Diplomatic Action, traveler@worldcitizensguide.org, 2005.

20. For an extensive discussion of international gestures, see Roger E. Axtell, *The Complete Guide to International Business and Leisure Travel* (Hoboken, NJ: John Wiley and Sons, 2007). Also see Anderson, pp. 317–328 and Roger Axtell, *Gestures: The Do's and Taboos of Body Language Around the World* (New York: John Wiley and Sons, 1991).

21. Sigmund Freud, *The Columbia Word of Quotations*, entry 23110, www.bartleby.com/66/10/23110.html.

22. The primary article that defined and explained expectancy violation theory: J. K. Burgoon, "A Communication Model of Personal Space Violation: Explication and an Initial Test," *Human Communication Research*, 4 (1978): 129–142. For a further explanation, see Daniel Canary, Michael Cody, and Valerie Manusov, *Interpersonal Communication: A Goals-Based Approach* (Boston: Bedford/St. Martins, 2008), p. 130.

23. "Honors: Communication Capstone, Interpersonal Context," www.uky.edu/~drlane/capstone/interpersonal/ evt.html.

24. www.psychologymatters.org/polygraphs.html (website of the American Psychological Association), 2008.

25. Randolph Schmid, "Lie Detectors Called Too Inaccurate for National Security," *Cleveland Plain Dealer* (October 9, 2002): A10.

26. Ibid.

27. Kaja Perina, "Truth Serum, Brain Scans May Be Foolproof Lie Detectors," *Psychology Today* (January–February 2002), p. 15.

28. Ibid.

29. Neil Parmar, "Deception Detection: Brain Fingerprinting Spots Crime and Innocence," *Innovation* (PBS documentary series, Episode 8, 2004).

30. Ibid.

31. No specific identifying channels of nonverbal communication have been universally defined. The names used here are a compilation of those that have appeared in various textbooks on communication.

32. Hickson et al., p. 222.

33. A research study conducted by Joe Teece, Boston College neuropsychologist.

34. "What to Keep an Eye On," *Cleveland Plain Dealer* (January 31, 2006): A3, originally printed in the *Baltimore Sun*.

35. Hickson et al., p. 155.

36. Adler, p. C5.

37. Ibid.

38. Anderson, pp. 81–82.

39. Axtell, p. 87.

40. Anderson, p. 81.

41. Burgoon, p. 41.

42. Anderson, p. 68

43. Ibid.

44. Larry Samovar, Richard Porter, and Edwin McDaniel, *Intercultural Communication: A Reader* (Belmont, CA: Thompson Higher Education, 2006), p. 253.

45. For a discussion on gender and touch, see Hickson et al., p. 78.

46. Jessie Graham, "A Hands-On Approach," *Psychology Today* (November/December 2007), p. 24.

47. Ibid.

48. Anderson, p. 75.

49. Anderson and Leibowitz, *Environmental Psychology and Nonverbal Behavior. 3* (2): 89–106. Reprinted with kind permission from Springer Science and Business Media.

50. Knapp, pp. 273–284.

51. Martha Irvine, "Employers, Schools Issue New Dress Codes," U.S. National–AP, as found in www.wjla.com/headlines/0904/171582.html, September 8, 2004.

52. Christina Binkley, "Business Casual: All Business, Never Casual," *The Wall Street Journal* (April 17, 2008): D1.

53. Judith Gumbiner, "What's Business Casual Attire?" http://career-advice.monster.com/business-etiquette/Whats-Business-Casual-Attire/home.aspx, retrieved May 12, 2008.

54. Kathy Gurchiek, "Workers: Comfort Is Main Criterion for Attire," Society for Human Resource Management, www.shrm.org/hrnews_published/archives/CMS_019057.asp.

55. "Dressing Down: Most Readers Back Office Dress Codes," *Boston Business Journal* (July 14, 2006). http://boston.bizjournals.com/boston/stories/2006/07/17/story15.html.

56. Paul Burnham Finney, "Redefining Business Casual," *The New York Times* (October 23, 2007). www.nytimes.com/2007/10/23/business/23attire.html.

57. Marina Krakovsky, "Haven't We Met?" *Psychology Today* (September–October 2003): 17.

58. "Black Bodies," 20/20 ABC-TV, April 19, 1999, available from ABC News Home Videos, #T990419.

59. Roberto Olivardia, Harrison G. Pope Jr., John J. Borowiecki III, and Geoffrey H. Cohane, "Biceps and Body Image: The Relationship Between Muscularity and Self-Esteem, Depression, and Eating Disorder Symptoms," *Psychology of Men and Masculinity* (July 2004): 112–120. Abstract available at www.sciencedirect.com/science.

60. Dale Leathers and Michael H. Eaves, *Successful Nonverbal Communication, Principles and Applications* (Boston: Pearson Education, 2008), p. 154. The statistics are from a classic study reported in "The Eyes Have It," *Newsweek* (December 3, 1973): 85. For an extensive discussion on personal appearance, see Leathers, Chapter 7.

61. Hickson et al., p. 162.

62. Ibid.

63. John Mangels, "Society Doesn't Let Short Boys Stand Tall," *Cleveland Plain Dealer* (December 20, 2006): M4. Based on the writings of Stephen S. Hall, *Size Matters* (Boston: Houghton Mifflin, 2006).

64. Hickson et al., p. 161.

65. Burgoon, p. 224, referring to research by Edward Hall.

66. Ibid.

67. Burgoon, p. 224, based on the work of S. M. Jourjrard and N. M. Genley.

68. Anderson, pp. 117–120, based on the research of Edward and Mildred Hall.

69. For an extensive discussion of paralanguage, see Reiman, pp. 187–207.

70. William Harms, "Verbal Gestures Unconsciously Used During Speech," *Advice for Speech-Language Pathologists & Audiologists* (December 4, 2006): 16.

71. Ibid.

72. Ibid.

73. Knapp, pp. 204–205.

74. Young Yun Kim, "Intercultural Personhood: An Integration of Eastern and Western Perspectives," in Larry Samovar, Richard Porter, and Edwin McDaniel (Eds.), *Intercultural Communication: A Reader* (Belmont, CA: Thomson Higher Education, 2006), p. 411.

75. Ibid.

76. For a discussion on culture and chronemics, see Hickson et al., pp. 315–320.

77. The incident reported was at George Washington University. The student's name was omitted by request.

78. Hickson et al., p. 319.

79. The classic observations regarding procrastination can be found in Albert Ellis and William Knaus, *Overcoming Procrastination* (New York: AEI Publications, 1979). For help in overcoming procrastination, see "Overcoming Procrastination/Eliminating Procrastination," Wikibooks, http://en.wikibooks.org/wiki/Overcoming_Procrastination/Eliminating_Procrastination, March, 2008.

80. Maral Szalavitz, "Stand and Deliver," in Karen Duffy (Ed.), *Personal Growth and Behavior* 35th ed. (Dubuque, IA: McGraw Hill, 2007), pp. 62–63.

81. Linda Andrews, "The Hidden Force of Fragrance," *Psychology Today* (November/December, 2007): 57.

82. Hickson et al., p. 300.

83. For a discussion of these and other influence of smell as a communicator, see Hickson et al., 299–306.

84. Andrews, p. 8.

85. Ibid.

86. Ibid.

87. Results from tests run by Muzak Limited Partnership, n.d.

88. "Music's Affects on the Human Body," http://hs.riverdale.k12.or.us/~dthompso/exhib_03/jasonc/Music's_Affects_on_the_Human_Body.html. Also see H. Sakamoto, "Psycho-Circulatory Responses Caused by Listening to Music, and Exposure to Fluctuation Noise or Steady Noise," *The Journal of Sound and Vibration,* 250(1) (September 2002): 23–29.

89. Patricia McCormick, "Rock Music Can Weaken Muscles," *Elyria (Ohio) Chronicle-Telegram,* (January 12, 1979): "Encore," p. 15. Stephanie C. Change & Jacquline S. How, "La La La: The Effects of Music on Muscle Strength," California State Science Fair, 2005, http://search.yahoo.com/search?p=rock+music+can+effect+muscles&fr=yfp-t-501&toggle=1&cop=mss&ei=UTF-8.

90. Lindsey Tanner, "Physicians Take Note of Music's Power to Heal," *Cleveland Plain Dealer* (December 26, 2005): A-2, based on research done by Dr. Ary Goldberger of the Harvard Medical School and Abraham Kocheril of the Carle Heart Center in Urbana, IL.

91. Ibid.

92. Robert Britt, "Red Outfits Give Athletes Advantage," *Live Science, Health SciTech* (May 18, 2005), based on the research of Russell Hill and Robert Barton, University of Durham, as reported in the May 19, 2005 issue of *Nature.*

93. Ibid.

94. Sara Goudarzi, "Study: Seeing Red Lowers Test Scores," *Live Science, Health SciTech,* (March 5, 2007), based on research by Andrew Elliot, University of Rochester.

95. Ibid.

96. For a discussion of taste/gustoric communication, see Hickson et al., pp. 294–295.

97. Leslie Miller, "Airport Security Watching Behavior Patterns," *Cleveland Plain Dealer* (April 17, 2004): A10.

CHAPTER 4

1. Kelly J. Watkins, "How Much Time Do You Spend Listening?, www.alumbo.com/article/39652-How-Much-Time-Do-You-Spend-Listening.html, December 3, 2007.

2. Ibid.

3. Concept proposed by Marilyn F. Buckley.

4. Laura Ann Janusik and Andrew D. Wolvin, "24 Hours in a Day. A Listening Update to the Time Studies." Paper presented at the meeting of the International Listening Association, Salem, OR, April 2006.

5. See Larry Barker and Kittie Watson, *Listen Up* (New York: St. Martin's Press, 2001), Chapter 4.

6. National Institute on Deafness and Other Communication Disorders. (n.d.). "Quick Statistics." Retrieved May 30, 2008, from www.nidcd.nih.gov/health/statistics/quick.htm.

7. Ibid.

8. Ibid.

9. Interview with Marcia Warren, CCC-A, licensed audiologist, July 10, 2008.

10. "Why Use Active Learning?" Active Learning Online (The Abilene Christian University Adams Center for Teaching Excellence), e-mail: activelearning@acu.edu.

11. Paul Mobley, "Listening," ez@articles, http://ezinearticles.com/?Listening&id=397732, December 28, 2006.

12. Jeff Davidson, *The Complete Guide to Public Speaking* (Hoboken, NJ: Wiley, 2002).

13. Brad Vander Zanden, "Preparing an Effective Presentation," www.cs.utk.edu/~bvz/presentation.html.

14. Ibid.

15. Ibid.

16. See Laura Ann Janusik, "Building Listening Theory: The Validation of the Conversational Listening Span," *Communication Studies,* 58 (June 2007): 139–156, for a discussion of the applications of working memory to understanding listening cognition.

17. "Are People Speaking Faster (and Are They Being Heard)?," http://answers.google.com/answers/threadview?id=112576, November 30, 2002.

18. Ibid.

19. Academic Skills Center, Dartmouth College, 2001, based on the research of Ralph Nichols, www.google.com/search?hl=en&q=average+rate+of+listening&btnG=Google+Search.

20. Concept developed by Andrew Wolvin and Carolyn G. Coakley.

21. A concept developed by Renee Edwards and Janet L. McDonald.

22. For a discussion of global and linear brain theory, see Dr. Carolyn Hopper, *Practicing College Study Skills: Strategies for Success,* 3rd ed. (Boston: Houghton Mifflin, 2003) and Kendra Van Wagner, "Right Brain vs. Left Brain," About.com, August 22, 2007.

23. Based on instruments developed by Paul Torrance, Bernice McCarthy, and Rebecca Cutter.

24. Ibid.

25. Edward T. Hall and Mildred R. Hall, *Understanding Cultural Differences* (Yarmouth, ME: Intercultural Press, 1989).

26. Parthenia Franks, "Native Americans and the Value of Silence/Listening." Paper presented at the International Listening Association convention, Chicago, IL, 2001.

27. Carl R. Rogers and F. J. Roethlisberger, "Barriers and Gateways to Communication," *Harvard Business Review,* 30 (July–August 1952): 46–52.

28. Taxonomy developed by Andrew Wolvin and Carolyn Coakley.

29. William G. Powers and Graham D. Bodie. "Listening Fidelity: Seeking Congruence Between Cognitions of the Listener and the Sender," *International Journal of Listening,* 17 (2003): 19–31.

30. B. Scott Titsworth, "Students' Notetaking: The Effects of Teachers' Immediacy and Clarity," *Communication Education* 53(4) (October 2004): 3–5.

31. Ibid.

32. Ibid.

33. Ibid.

34. Alton Barber and Alvin A. Goldberg, "Principles of Confirmation," in Kathleen M. Galvin and Pamela J. Cooper (Eds.), *Making Connections* (Los Angeles: Roxbury, 2000), pp. 139–141.

35. In 1975, Lawrence Wheeless differentiated *received apprehension* from *communication apprehension.* It was reported in Lawrence R. Wheeless, "An Investigation of Receiver Apprehension and Social Context Dimensions of Communication Apprehension," *Speech Teacher,* 24 (September 1975): p. 263. For a current discussion of listener/receiver apprehension, see A. Kathleen Wilcox, "Receiver Apprehension and College Students: An Examination of Remediation via Interactive Skills Training," Lewis-Clark State College, Lewiston, Idaho,

November 2002, www.lcsc.edu/humanities/Wilcox-paper
.htm.

36. The concept of egospeak was developed by Edward Addeo
and Robert Burger and presented in their classic book,
Egospeak (New York: Bantam Books, 1974), p. xiv.

37. Based on W. James Potter, *Media Literacy* (Thousand Oaks,
CA: Sage, 2007).

CHAPTER 5

1. A concept presented by Roy Berko on the role of self-talk as
the basis for all human communication as part of the course
"The Psychology of You," Cuyahoga County Community
College, Fall 2006.

2. A concept developed by Robert McGarvey, www.mcgarvey
.net.

3. Ibid.

4 Donna R. Vocate, *Interpersonal Communication: Different
Voices, Different Minds* (Hillsdale, NJ: Erlbaum, 1994), p. 176.
For a discussion of the work of L. S. Vygotsky, see Vocate.

5. Ibid.

6. A concept stated in Ronald B. Adler, Lawrence B.
Rosenfeld, and Russell F. Proctor II, *Interplay: The Process of
Interpersonal Communication*, 10th ed. (New York: Oxford
University Press, 2006).

7. For an in-depth discussion of language development, see
Rita C. Naremore and Robert Hopper, *Children Learning
Language: A Practical Introduction to Communication
Development* (Clifton Park, NY: Thomson/Delmar Learning,
1997).

8. Norman Geschwind, "Language and the Brain," *Scientific
American*, 226 (April 1972): 76–83. Also see Naremore and
Hopper.

9. Mary Duenwald, "Baby Talk Linked to Origin of Language."
Cleveland Plain Dealer (October 15, 2002): E3.

10. Ibid.

11. Jeannette M. Alvarez, "Self Concept and Self Esteem,"
more-selfesteem.com, 2007.

12. Adapted from items presented in *Tennessee Self-Concept Scale*
(Nashville, TN: Counselor Recordings and Tests, 1964).

13. Ibid.

14. Louis Janda, *The Psychologist's Book of Self-Tests* (New York:
Berkley Publishing Group, 1996), p. 72.

15. Ibid.

16. Ibid.

17. Gail Dusa, as noted in Robert McGarvey, "Talk Yourself
Up," *USAir Magazine* (March 1990): 90.

18. Gail Dusa, as noted in McGarvey, p. 90.

19. A theory developed by Joan Aitken based on the concepts
of Sidney Simon.

20. Dave Grant, as noted in McGarvey, p. 93.

21. Bernie Zilbergeld, as noted in McGarvey, p. 94.

22. Leon Festinger, A *Theory of Cognitive Dissonance* (Evanston,
IL: Row, Peterson, 1957).

23. Sveri Wahlross, *Family Communication* (New York:
Macmillan, 1974), p. xi.

24. Long Beach City College of Theatre Arts and Speech,
Communicate, 3rd ed. (Dubuque, IA: Kendall/Hunt, 1976).

25. William James, *The Principles of Psychology* (New York: Holt,
Rinehart and Winston, 1990).

26. Barbara M. Byrne, *Measuring Self-Concept Across the Lifespan:
Methodology and Instrumentation for Research and Practice*

(Washington, DC: American Psychological Association,
1996).

27. The verb *to be* provides us with our basic label of ourselves.
Native Americans and those from some other cultures, such
as West Africans, may have difficulty understanding and
applying this concept because of linguistic and cultural
differences. Most U.S. Americans, however, should find it
an understandable concept.

28. Joseph A. Luft, *Group Process: An Introduction to Group
Dynamics* (Palo Alto, CA: National Press, 1963), Chapter 3.

29. Based on Lawrence Rosenfeld, "Relational Disclosure and
Feedback," unpublished paper developed by Lawrence
Rosenfeld, Department of Communication, University of
North Carolina, Chapel Hill, NC. Final format developed by
Lawrence Rosenfeld and Roy Berko.

30. For a discussion of communication and ethnography, see
Stuart Sigman, "A Matter of Time: The Case for
Ethnographics of Communication," unpublished paper
presented at the Speech Communication Association
Convention, November 23, 1996. See also H. L. Goodall,
"Transforming Communication Studies Through
Ethnographic Practices," unpublished paper presented at
the SCA Convention, November 23, 1996.

31. The description presented is based on a synthesis of theories
about ethnography.

32. Paul Foxman, "Fear, Anxiety, Worry and Panic," lecture
presented at the Free Clinic of Cleveland, June 21, 2004.

33. Ibid.

34. Ibid.

35. Ibid.

36. Ibid.

37. Ibid.

38. Ibid.

39. Ibid.

40. A concept presented by Dr. Joy Browne on her national
syndicated radio program. For more information about
Dr. Joy Browne, go to www.drjoy.com/contact.

41. Foxman.

42. Joannie M. Schrof and Stacey Schultz, "Social Anxiety,"
U.S. News and World Report (July 21, 1999): 50.

43. See, for example, Joe Ayres, A. Kathleen Wilcox, and
Debbie M. Ayres, "Receiver Apprehension: An Explanatory
Model and Accompanying Research," *Communication
Education* 44 (July 1995): 223–235; Joan E. Aitken and
Michael R. Neer, "College Student Question Asking: The
Relationship of Classroom Communication Apprehension
and Motivation," *Southern Communication Journal* 59
(Fall 1993): 73–81; and Virginia P. Richmond and James C.
McCroskey, *Communication: Apprehension, Avoidance, and
Effectiveness*, 5th ed. (Englewood Cliffs, NJ: Prentice-Hall,
1997).

44. Beth Azar, "Shy People Have Inaccurate Self-Concepts,"
American Psychological Association Monitor (November 1995):
24.

45. Ibid.

46. Joe Ayres and Tim Hopf, *Coping with Speech Anxiety*
(Norwood, NJ: Ablex, 1993), p. 4.

47. John A. Daly, James C. McCroskey, Joe Ayres, Tim Hopf,
and Debbie M. Ayres (Eds.), *Avoiding Communication:
Shyness, Reticence and Communication Apprehension*, 2nd ed.
(Cresskill, NJ: Hampton Press, 1997). In addition, see
www.jamescmccroskey.com/.

48. James McCroskey and Virginia Richmond, *The Quiet Ones: Communication Apprehension and Shyness* (Dubuque, IA: CommComp, Gorsuch Scarisbrick, 1980), p. 21.

49. Schrof and Schultz, p. 50.

50. Ibid.

51. Bill Hendrick, "Biology Might Be at Root of Some People's Shyness," *Cleveland Plain Dealer* (July 27, 2003): L5.

52. Schrof and Schultz, p. 50.

53. Ibid., p. 53.

54. Daly et al. In addition, see www.jamescmccroskey.com/.

55. James W. Chesebro et al., "Communication Apprehension and Self-Perceived Communication Competence of At-Risk Students," *Communication Education*, 41 (1992): 345–360.

56. For a discussion of the effects of communication apprehension on math, English, reading, and intelligence scores, as well as on grades in general, see John Bourhis and Mike Allen, "Meta-Analysis of the Relationship Between Communication Apprehension and Cognitive Performance," *Communication Education*, 41 (1992): 68–76.

57. Based on an unpublished investigation of speech reticence conducted by Doug Pederson, Pennsylvania State University, 1971.

58. See Daly et al.

59. Richmond and McCroskey.

60. Ibid.

61. Ibid.

62. From Virginia P. Richmond and James C. McCroskey, *Communication: Apprehension, Avoidance, and Effectiveness,* 4th ed. Published by Allyn and Bacon, Boston, MA. Copyright © 1985 by Pearson Education. Reprinted by permission of the publisher.

63. Hendrick.

64. Ibid.

65. Ibid.

66. "Is Shyness Inherited?" *Healthy Decisions* (Georgetown University Medical Center) (Winter 1997): 2.

67. Azar, "Shy People."

68. For an extended discussion of the causes of communication apprehension, see Virginia Richmond and James McCroskey, *Communication: Apprehension, Avoidance, and Effectiveness,* 4th ed. (Scottsdale, AZ: Gorsuch Scarisbrick, 1995).

69. Lawrence R. Wheeless, "An Investigation of Receiver Apprehension and Social Context Dimensions of Communication Apprehension," *Speech Teacher*, 24 (September 1975): 261–268.

70. Azur, "Shy People."

71. Results have been documented by Dr. Roy Berko, crisis counselor, while working with communicative apprehensive clients in "Overcoming Shyness and Communication Anxiety" workshops.

72. Erika Casriel, "My Friend Joe Raffeto, A Desert Guide," *Psychology Today* (March/April, 2007): 70, based on the work of Bernardo Carducci, Director of Indiana University Southeast's Shyness Research Institute.

73. Ibid.

74. Richmond and McCroskey, pp. 97–101.

75. Ibid., p. 36.

76. Ibid., p. 49.

77. Virginia P. Richmond and K. David Roach, "Willingness to Communicate and Employee Success in U.S. Organizations," *Journal of Applied Communication Research,* 20 (February 1992): 104.

78. Schrof and Schultz, p. 54.

79. Ibid. See also Anduradha Raghunathan, "Drug Firms Work on Treatment for Extreme Forms of Shyness," *Cleveland Plain Dealer* (May 18, 1999): 8A. (Paxil was the first selective serotonin reuptake inhibitor to win approval by the Food and Drug Administration for treatment of debilitating shyness. In addition, the drugs Zoloft and Prozac may be of some value.)

80. Pamela Cooper, Carolyn Calloway-Thomas, and Cheri Simonds, *Intercultural Communication: A Text With Readings* (Boston: Pearson Education, 2007), p. 86.

81. Stella Ting-Toomey and Leeva C. Chung, *Understanding Intercultural* Communication (Los Angeles: Roxbury Publishing Company, 2005), p. 192.

82. Ibid.

83. Ibid.

84. A concept described in Myron Lustig and Jolene Koester, *Intercultural Competence: Interpersonal Communication Across Cultures,* 5th ed. (New York: HarperCollins, 2006).

85. Ibid.

86. Ibid.

87. Ting-Toomey and Chung, p. 70.

88. Ibid.

89. Cooper, Calloway-Thomas, and Simonds, p. 98.

90. Ting-Toomey and Chung, p. 169.

91. Ibid., p. 170

92. Ibid.

93. Guo-Ming Chen and William J. Starosta, *Foundations of Intercultural Communication* (Boston: Allyn and Bacon, 1998), p. 131.

CHAPTER 6

1. Rebecca Cline, "Seminar in Interpersonal Communication," unpublished syllabus, Temple University, Philadelphia, n.d.

2. Roy Berko, Lawrence Rosenfeld, and Larry Samavor, *Connecting: A Culture-Sensitive Approach to Interpersonal Communication Competency* (Ft. Worth: Harcourt Brace, 1997), p. 16. For additional information on interpersonal communication, see Ronald B. Adler, Lawrence B. Rosenfeld, and Russell F. Proctor II, *Interplay: The Process of Interpersonal Communication,* 10th ed. (New York: Oxford University Press, 2007).

3. Valerie Marchant, "What Bosses Really Want," *Time* (June 28, 1999).

4. Ibid., p. 303.

5. For further discussion of the "I," see Calvin S. Hall and Gardner Lindzey, *Theories of Personality* (New York: Wiley, 1957), p. 483.

6. Gerald Marwell and David R. Schmitt, "An Introduction," in James Price Dillard (Ed.), *Seeking Compliance: The Production of Interpersonal Influence Messages* (Scottsdale, AZ: Gorsuch Scarisbrick, 1990), pp. 3–5.

7. For a discussion of left brain/right brain theory, see Betty Edwards, *Drawing on the Right Side of the Brain* (Los Angeles: Jeremy Tracher, 1989); Constance Pechura and Joseph Martin (Eds.), *Mapping the Brain and Its Function* (Washington, DC: Institute of Medicine National Academy Press, 1991); and Rebecca Cutter, *When Opposites Attract: Right*

Brain/Left Brain Relationships and How to Make Them Work (New York: Dutton, 1994).

8. A theory of Murray Banks, a professional speaker, who speaks extensively on leadership, change, performance, and lifestyle.

9. For an extensive investigation of emotional expression, see Berko et al., pp. 84–95.

10. Berko et al., p. 428. Also see Robert A. Barraclough and Robert A. Steward, "Power and Control: Social Science Perspectives," in Virginia P. Richmond and James C. McCroskey (Eds.), *Power in the Classroom* (Hillsdale, NJ: Erlbaum, 1992), pp. 1–4.

11. Adapted from Pamela Cumming, "Empowerment Profile," *The Power Handbook* (Boston: CBI, 1981), pp. 2–5.

12. George A. Bordon, *Cultural Orientation: An Approach to Understanding Intercultural Communication* (Englewood Cliffs, NJ: Prentice-Hall, 1991), p. 116.

13. Jan Servaes, "Cultural Identity in East and West," *The Howard Journal of Communication,* 1 (Summer 1998): 64.

14. Thomas Carlyle. See www.landofwisdom.com/category/heart/.

15. Deborah Tannen, *You Just Don't Understand* (New York: Morrow, 1990), p. 14.

16. Matt Crenson, "Summers' Remarks Supported by Some Exports," Yahoo! Reprinted from Associated Press News, February 28, 2005.

17. Peg Tyre and Julie Scelfo, "What Girls Will Be Girls," *Newsweek,* (July 31, 2006): 46, quoting neuropsychiatrist Louann Brizendine, author of *The Female Brain.*

18. Ibid., p. 7

19. Ibid, quoting from the works of Janet Hyde.

20. Ibid.

21. Ibid., quoting Dr. Nancy C. Andreasen, a psychiatrist and neroimaging expert.

22. Deana J. Goldsmith and Patricia A. Fulfs, as quoted in "Hot Type," *Chronicle of High Education* (June 18, 1999): A22, from their article in the *1999 Communications Yearbook.*

23. Ibid.

24. For a preliminary discussion on early writings concerning the differences between male and female communication, see Lauri P. Arliss and Deborah J. Borisoff, *Women and Men Communicating: Challenge and Changes* (Ft. Worth: Harcourt Brace, 1993); Deborah Tannen, *You Just Don't Understand* (New York: Morrow, 1990); John Gray, *Men Are from Mars, Women Are from Venus: A Practical Guide for Improving Communication and Getting What You Want in Your Relationships* (New York: HarperCollins, 1992); Julia T. Wood, *Gendered Lives: Communication, Gender, and Culture* (Belmont, CA: Wadsworth 1994); and Lea Stewart, Pamela Cooper, Alan Stewart, and Sheryl Friedley, *Communication and Gender,* 4th ed. (Boston: Pearson, 2003).

25. Lauri P. Arliss and Deborah J. Borisoff, *Women and Men Communicating: Challenge and Changes* (Ft. Worth: Harcourt Brace, 1993), p. 3.

26. Anne Moir and David Jessel, "Sex and Cerebellum: Thinking about the Real Difference Between Men and Woman," *Washington Post* (May 5, 1991): K3.

27. Ibid.

28. Arliss and Borisoff, p. 9.

29. Barbara Mathias, "Male Identity Crisis," *Washington Post* (May 3, 1993): C5.

30. Gray, p. 16.

31. Mathias, p. C5.

32. Brant Burleson, Kathryn Dindia, and Celeste Condit, "Gender Communication: Different Cultural Perspectives," a panel discussion at the National Communication Association Conference, Chicago, 1997.

33. Adapted from Sandra L. Bem, "The Measurement of Psychological Androgyny," *Journal of Consulting and Clinical Psychology,* 42 (1974): 155–162. The original inventory developed by Bem contains sixty items—twenty masculine, twenty feminine, and twenty neutral (neither masculine nor feminine exclusively).

34. "What's in a Word? A Job, Hood Senior's Study Says," *Washington Post* (June 6, 1991): MD8.

35. Tannen, pp. 43–44.

36. Matthias Mehl, Simine Vazire, Nairan Ramirez-Esparza, Richard Slatcher, and James Pennebaker, "Are Women Really More Talkative Than Men?" *Science,* 6 (July 2006). Details on methods and analysis are available on *Science* online.

37. For a discussion on interruptions, see Stewart, Cooper, Stewart, and Friedley, p. 54; and Wood, pp. 31, 144.

38. Based on the research of H. G. Whittington, James P. Smith, Leonard Kriegel, Lillian Glass, and Hilary Lips.

39. Ibid.

40. Ibid.

41. Gray, p. 26.

42. Ibid., p. 25.

43. Ibid., p. 15.

44. Patrick Fanning and Mathew McKay, *Being a Man: A Guide to the New Masculinity* (Oakland, CA: New Harbinger, 1993), p. 13.

45. David Zinczenko, "Why Men Don't Talk," *Men's Health,* as posted on http://health.yahoo.com/experts/menlovesex/73762/why-men-dont-talk, December 17, 2007. Additional material on this subject is discussed in David Zinczenko, *Men, Love and Sex: The Complete User's Guide for Women* (Tantor Media), November 2006.

46. Ibid.

47. Gray, pp. 11–13.

48. Janet Cho, "The Great Divide: Learning to Talk So the Other Sex Hears You Is More Complicated Than You Think," *Cleveland Plain Dealer* (June 28, 2004): E1.

49. Ibid.

50. Ibid., p. E2.

51. Ibid.

52. Ibid.

53. Ibid.

54. Ibid.

55. Gary Kreps, *Sexual Harassment: Communication Implications* (Cresskill, NJ: Hampton Press, 1993), p. 11. For more information, see Mark Walsh, "Court Asked to Define Sex Harassment in the Workplace," *Education Week* (October 20, 1993): 37.

56. Kreps, p. 186.

57. Adapted from Andrea P. Baridon and David R. Eyler, *Working Together* (New York: McGraw-Hill, 1994).

58. "Sexual Harassment in the Workplace," sexualharassmentsupport.org, 2006.

59. Ibid.

60. Ibid.

61. Ibid.

62. Ibid.
63. Ibid., p. 133.
64. Ibid., p. 13.
65. Ibid., p. 134.
66. Richard Morin, "Harassment Consensus Grows," *Washington Post* (1992): A22.
67. Based on the writings of Rebecca Ray, senior vice president, director of training, American Skandia Corporation.
68. Marilyn Elias, "Bullying Crosses the Line Into Workplace," *USA Today* (July 28, 2004).
69. Ibid.
70. Ibid.
71. Ibid.
72. Ibid.
73. Based on a theory of Jon Nussbaum.
74. Ibid.
75. Stella Ting-Toomey and Leeva Chung, *Understanding Intercultural Communication* (Los Angeles: Roxbury Publishing, 2005).
76. The information in this section is based on Mark Knapp, *Interpersonal Communication and Human Relationships* (Boston: Allyn and Bacon, 1984), as appearing on the Allyn and Bacon Home Website, Communication Studies, Allyn and Bacon, 1998.
77. For a discussion of the economic model of relationships, see Berko, p. 289.
78. Based on the research of Anthony Brandt.
79. The discussion in this section is based on the writings of Vince Lindgren, "Recognizing Relationship Warning Signs," www.lindgrenmt.com/warning.htm.
80. Knapp, as appearing on the Allyn Bacon Home Website, Communication Studies, Allyn and Bacon, 1998.
81. The section "The Internet as a Means of Interpersonal Communication" was written with the advice and editorial assistance of Joan Aitken, Park University, Parkville, MO.
82. "Wiredville, U.S.A." *Newsweek* (September 20, 1999): 62.
83. Michael J. Miller, "Do-It-All Cell Phones," *PC Magazine, 23* (February 17, 2004): 6.
84. "Fatal Wreck Spurs Cell Phone Fight," *Pittsburgh Tribune-Review* (January 10, 2003), www.pittsburghlive.com, based on research by the Center for Cognitive Brain Imagery at Carnegie Mellon University.
85. Suggestions synthesized from Nokia, "Cell Phone Courtesy Month: Five Basic Cell Phone Rules," July 1, 2003, www.classbrain.com; "Proper Cell Phone Etiquette," n.d., cellphonecarriers.com; Mark Toft, "Cell Phone Etiquette," 2004, www.staples.com.
86. "Broadband Adoption, 2007," *The Pew Charitable Trust* (July 6, 2007), www.pewtrusts.org/our_work_report _detail.aspx?id=25474&category=54&WT.srch&source =google
87. N. J. Slabbeert, "The Technologies of Peace," *Harvard International Review* (June 2006).
88. Ibid.
89. gotomeeting.com.
90. K. Sherer, "College Life On-Line: Healthy and Unhealthy Internet Use," *Journal of College Student Development,* 38(6) (November–December 1997): 655–665.
91. Patrick Carnes, "The Criteria of Problematic Online Sexual Behavior," stated in a workshop presented at the Free Clinic of Cleveland, February 27, 2004.
92. Ibid.
93. W. Payne, "More People Say Heavy Internet Use Is Disrupting Their Lives, and Medical Experts Are Paying Attention," *The Washington Post* (November 14, 2006): F01.
94. Results reported by Jonathan Kandell, Assistant Director of the Counseling Center University of Maryland, College Park, May 2008.
95. Based on psychiatrist Nathan Andrew Shapira's study on obsessive Internet use, referred to in Nathan A. Shapira, Mary C. Lessig, Toby D. Goldsmith, Steven T. Szabo, Martin Lazoritz, Mark S. Gold, and Dan J. Stein, "Problematic Internet Use: Proposed Classification and Diagnostic Criteria," *Depress Anxiety,* 17(4) (2003), pp. 207–216.
96. Adapted from materials presented at a workshop by Patrick Carnes, "The Criteria of Problematic Online Sexual Behavior," Cleveland (OH) Free Clinic, February 27, 2004.
97. Ibid.
98. Ibid.
99. Martin Corbett and Mike Thatcher, "People Management," *Personal Publications* (June 6, 1997), p. 26.
100. The concepts of sociologist Sherry Trukle, author of *Life on the Screen,* and psychiatrist Esther Gwinnell, author of *Online Seductions,* as referred to in Wray Herbert, "Getting Close, But Not Too Close," *U.S. News and World Report* (March 22, 1999): 56–57.
101. Alanna Mitchell, "Bullied by the Click of a Mouse," www .globeandmail.com/servlet/story/RTGAM.20040124 .wbully0124/BNStory/, January 24, 2004.
102. Ibid.
103. P. J. Huffstutter, "Fatal Cyber-Bullying Hits Home," *Los Angles Times,* as reproduced in *Cleveland Plain Dealer* (November 23, 2007): A12.
104. Ibid.
105. Ibid.
106. Ibid.
107. *1999 Report on Cyberstalking,* www.usdoj.gov/criminal /cybercrime/cyberstalking.htm.
108. Ibid.
109. George Siemens, "The Art of Blogging—Part 1: Overview, Definitions, Uses and Implications," www.elearnspace. org/Articles/blogging_part_1.htm, December 1, 2002, p. 2.
110. Ibid.
111. Chad Dickerson, "Blogging to Ourselves," *InfoWorld,* 26(21) (May 24, 2004): 34.
112. Scott Sherman, "Lies, Libel and Ethics," www. TheHowlerMonkey.com, March 11, 1005.
113. Ibid.
114. Ibid.
115. For a detailed discussion about blogging skills, see Cory Doctorow, Rael Dornfest, J. Scott Johnson, Shelley Powers, Benjamin Trott, and Mena G. Trott, *Essential Blogging* (Sebastopol, CA: O'Reilly, 2002).
116. For further information on blogger sites, see "How to Find Your Kind of Blog," *Time* (June 21, 2004): 70.
117. Sara Sklaroff "E-mail," *U.S. News and World Report* (March 22, 1999): 54.
118. Soraya Nadina McDonald, "Facebook Frenzy," The Associated Press, July 5, 2005.
119. "St Xavier Get Pokes in, But Fails to Rattle Tanski," *Cleveland Plain Dealer,* December 1, 2007, D1.

120. Bill Tancer, "My Space v. Facebook: Competing Addictions," *Time* (October 24, 2007), www.time .com/time/printout/0,8816,1675244,00.html.

121. "Facebook," Wikipedia.com.

122. Ibid.

123. Ibid.

124. Steven Levy, "Facebook Grows Up," *Newsweek* (August 20/27, 2007): 41.

125. "Facebook, the Privacy and Productivity Challenge," sophos.com.

126. Joan Swartz, "Soon Million of Facebookers Won't Be Incognito," *USA Today* (September 12, 2007): 3B.

127. "What You Need to Know about Facebook," Office of Career Services, University of Central Missouri, adapted from materials developed by Kathleen Mcabe, Director of Peer Education at Creighton, University.

128. www.ucalgary.ca/nlsewar/text/culture.htm.

129. "The Online Rocket," September 07, 2007, comment section, http://media.www.theonlinerocket .com/media/storage/paper601/news/2007/09/07 .Opinion/Ourview.Textmessaging.Service.Should.Be .Used.Properly-2954612.shtml.

130. www.smh.com.au/articles/2004/07/11/1089484242565 .html.

131. Jeff Stanton, Associate Professor of Information Sciences, as quoted in Thomas L. Friedman, *The World Is Flat* (New York: Picador/Farrrar, Straus and Giroux, 2007), p. 522.

132. Todd Ogasawarea, "Please Practice Safe Text(-Messaging)," O'Reillymacdevcener.com, November 7, 2005.

133. "Arizona May Ban Vehicular Text-Messaging," United Press International, December 15, 2007. www.upi .com/NewsTrack/Top_News/2007/08/15/ arizona_may_ban_vehicular_textmessaging/2863.

134. "The Techdirt Blog," Techdirt, The Insight Company for the Information Age, www.techdirt.com/articles /20031027/0024253F.shtml.

135. "Pitfalls of Child Text Messaging," October 5, 2007, Info on Text Messaging MSN.com.

136. www.smh.com.au/articles/2004/07/11/1089484242565 .html.

CHAPTER 7

1. Pam Kruger, "How to Talk to Anyone about Anything," *Redbook* (April 1994), p. 132.

2. Larry Samovar, Richard Porter, and Edwin McDaniel, *Intercultural Communication: A Reader* (Boston, MA: Wadsworth Cengage Learning, 2009), p. 436.

3. For a discussion of cultural personal space, refer to Samovar, pp. 281–286.

4. For an in-depth discussion of salon clubs, see Jaida Nha Sandra and John Spayde, *Salons: The Joy of Conversation* (Minneapolis, MN: Utne Reader Books, 2002).

5. Ibid.

6. "Request Definition," Request, www.yourdictionary.com/ request, referring to *Webster's New World Telecom Dictionary* (Indianapolis, IN: Wiley Publishing, 2008).

7. LaVerne L. Ludden and Tom Capozzoli, *Supervisor Savvy: How to Retain and Develop Entry-Level Workers* (Indianapolis, IN: JIST, 2000).

8. Roy Berko, Lawrence Rosenfeld, and Larry Samovar, *Connecting: A Culture-Sensitive Approach to Interpersonal Communication Competency,* 2nd ed. (Fort Worth: Harcourt Brace, 1997), p. 372.

9. Ibid.

10. William A. Donohue with Robert Kolt, *Managing Interpersonal Conflict* (Newbury Park, CA: Sage, 1992), p. 2.

11. Ibid., p. 3.

12. Ibid.

13. For a further discussion, see Joseph A. DeVito, *The Interpersonal Communication Book,* 12th ed. (Boston: Allyn & Bacon, 2010), Chapter 12.

14. Donohue and Kolt, pp. 12–17.

15. Harriet Goldhor Lerner, *The Dance of Anger* (New York: Perennial Library, 1985), p. 1.

16. Based on the concepts of Marlene Arthur Penkstaff.

17. A theory of Dr. Susan Forward, media psychologist and author.

18. Ibid.

19. The principles are based on the theories of Sonya Friedman.

20. A crisis counseling concept presented by Roy Berko, May 17, 2008, the Society for the Scientific Study of Sexuality, May 17, 2008, Cleveland, OH.

21. This is a principle of Gestalt therapy, as explained by Les Wyman, Gestalt Institute, Cleveland, OH.

22. "Activity 1," a handout developed by Mary Adams Trujillo and Laurie Miller and distributed at the workshop, "Responding to Conflict around Issues of Difference," National Conference for Community and Justice, Northern Ohio Region, February 19, 1999, Cleveland, OH.

23. Ibid.

24. Ibid.

25. Ibid.

26. Dr. Andrew Slater introduced the concept of assertiveness in the 1940s. It is commented on in Robert Epstein, "Ask Dr. E.," *Psychology Today* (March/April 2002).

27. Discussion based on shyness-workshop materials prepared by Phyllis DeMark, Lorain County Community College, Elyria, OH, n.d.

28. Sharon Bower and Gordon Bower, *Asserting Yourself* (Reading, MA: Addison-Wesley, 1976), p. 87.

29. For a discussion on business negotiation, see Deborah A. Cai and Laura E. Drake, "The Business of Business Negotiation: Intercultural Perspectives," *Communication Yearbook,* 21, (1998): 153–189.

30. Concepts in this section are based in part on "12 Skills [Negotiation Skills]," Conflict Resolution Network, www. crnhq.org.

31. Martha Lagace, "Becoming an Ethical Negotiator," Harvard Business School, www.hbswk.hbs.edu.

32. "12 Skills [Negotiation Skills]."

33. Armond Budish, "What's Arbitration? What Options Do Consumers Have?" *Cleveland Plain Dealer* (April 12, 2005): C5.

34. Ibid.

35. *Code of Virginia,* Chapter 20.2, Section 8:01-576.4 (July 1993).

36. For information on mediation, see Jonathan G. Shailor, *Empowerment in Dispute Mediation: A Critical Analysis of Communication* (Westport, CT: London, 1994); and Dorothy J. Della Noce, *Mediation Fundamentals: A Training Manual* (Richmond, VA: Better Business Bureau Foundation of Virginia, 1993).

37. For a discussion of culture and conflict, see Samovar, Porter, and McDanile, pp. 141–143 and Stella Ting-Toomey

and John Oetzel, "Intercultural Conflict: A Culture-Based Situational Model," in Pamela Cooper, Carolyn Calloway-Thomas, and Cheri Simonds, (Eds.), *Intercultural Communication: A Text with Readings* (Boston: Pearson Education, 2007), pp. 121–129.

38. Diana Rowland, Japanese Business Etiquette (New York: Warner Books, 1985), p. 5.

39. Lennie Copeland and Lewis Griggs, Going International (New York: Random House, 1985), p. 109.

40. Mia Doucet, "Costly Western Assumptions," Control Engineering, 54(10) (October 2007), p. 32.

41. Berko, Rosenfeld, and Samavor, p. 374.

42. Stella Ting-Toomey and Leeva C. Chung, *Understanding Intercultural Communication* (New York: Oxford University Press, 2005), p. 268.

43. Ibid.

44. For a discussion of cross-cultural conflict styles, see Ibid, pp. 274–275.

45. Ibid.

46. Ibid.

47. Ibid.

48. Ibid.

49. "When and How to Apologize," a pamphlet produced by the University of Nebraska Cooperative Extension and the Nebraska Health and Human Services System, n.d.

50. Dennis R. Tesdell, "The Top 10 Ways to Apologize to Someone You Have Hurt or Offended," lifecoach@coachdt.com, February 10, 1997.

51. Ibid.

52. Rosamund Stone Zander, "The Power of An Apology," *Parade* (July 29, 2001), p. 8.

53. "Japanese Language, Expressing Apologies," http://search .about.com/fullsearch.htm?terms=Japanese%20Language.

54. Ibid.

55. Ibid.

56. Ibid.

57. This concept was described in Stella Ting-Toomey, *The Challenge of Facework* (Albany: State University of New York Press, 1994), p. 185. A search of the current literature in the field of apologies shows no contradictions of these findings.

58. Ibid.

59. Ibid.

CHAPTER 8

1. www.quintcareers.com/interview_questions.html.

2. For an resource on questions and job searches, see Katharine Hansen and Randall Hansen, *The Quintessential Guide to Job Interview Preparation* (DeLand, FL: Quintessential Careers Press, 2007).

3. Frank S. Endicott, *Making the Most of Your Job Interview* (New York: New York Life Insurance Company, n.d.).

4. John Decker, "Interviewing," www.RetirementJobs.com.

5. Ibid.

6. Robert McGarvey, "Tailoring an Image," *USAir Magazine* (May 1990): 76.

7. Ibid., p. 78.

8. Alison Doyle, "How to Dress for a Job Interview," About.com: Job Searching. http://jobsearch.about.com/od/ interviewattire/a/interviewdress.htm.

9. Ibid.

10. Ibid.

11. Ibid.

12. "What Not to Wear to an Interview: Top 20 Wardrobe Malfunctions," www.careerbuilder.com.

13. U.S. Department of Labor, Employment and Training Administration, *Merchandising Your Job Talents* (Washington, DC: Government Printing Office, n.d.), pp. 7–8.

14. *EEO Interview Guidelines*, 29 C.F.R. § 1602 *et seq.*; DC Code § 1-2501 *et seq.*; and DCMR, Title 4, Ch. 5, Employment Guidelines. Updated link 10/15/04. Information can be found at http://counsel.cua.edu/employment/questions.

15. Ron Grant, president of Meridian Resources, Greenville, SC.

16. Kathleen Schlach, "Virtual Recruiting for Real-World Jobs," www.npr.org/templates/story/story.php?storyId=13851345 &sc=emaf.

17. Ibid.

18. Ibid., quoting Polly Pearson, an EMC vice president.

19. Ibid.

20. A psychological theory developed by Roy Berko, certified crisis counselor, in teaching clients how to be nondirective in their communication.

21. Judi Brownell, "Applied Research in Managerial Communication: The Critical Link between Knowledge and Practice; Applying the Lessons of Managerial Communication Studies Can Help Managers Become More Influential and Effective in Their Daily Activities," *Cornell Hotel & Restaurant Administration Quarterly*, 44 (April 1, 2003).

22. www.performance-appraisal.com/methods.htm.

23. www.halogensoftware.com.

24. For a discussion of this issue, see the websites of Amnesty International, www.amnesty.org/en/campaigns/Counter +Terror+with+Justice/issues, and American Civil Liberties Union, www.aclu.org/safefree/detention/closeguantanamo .html.

25. "Waterboarding: Interrogation or Torture?," www.cbsnews .com/stories/2007/11/01/national/main3441363.shtml, May 23, 2008.

26. Richard N. Bolles, *What Color Is Your Parachute?* (Berkeley, CA: Ten Speed Press, 2008).

CHAPTER 9

1. For a discussion of individualism versus collectivism as it relates to groups, see J. Daniel Rothwell, *In Mixed Company, Communicating in Small Groups and Teams*, 5th ed. (Belmont, CA: Wadsworth/Thomson Learning, 2004), pp. 13–14.

2. Ibid., p. 48

3. Ibid., p. 48.

4. Ibid., p. 42.

5. Robert W. Armstrong, Robert J. Williams, and J. Douglas Barrett, "The Impact of Banality, Risky Shift and Escalating Commitment on Ethical Decision Making," *Journal of Business Ethics*, Part 2, 53(4) (September 2004): 365–370.

6. The term *groupthink* was conceived by Irving Janus, as explained in Irving Janis, *Victims of Groupthink* (Boston: Houghton Mifflin, 1972) and further discussed in Irving Janis, *Groupthink: Psychological Studies of Policy Decisions and Fiascoes* (Boston: Houghton Mifflin, 1983). For another discussion of the concept, see Rothwell, pp. 199–206.

7. David S. Broder, "Rice Reveals Missing Steps at White House," *Cleveland Plain Dealer*, (April 11, 2004): A3.

8. Ibid.

9. Gregory Moorhead, Richard Ference, and Chris P. Neck, "Group Decision Fiascoes Continue: Space Shuttle *Challenger* and a Revised Groupthink Framework," in Mark H. Davis (Ed.), *Social Psychology 2001–2002*, (Guilford, CT: McGraw-Hill/Dushkin, 2001), p. 201.

10. The theory of Bibb Latane, Kipling Williams, and Stephen Harkins.

11. For an examination of work teams, see "Work Teams— Building Effective Teamwork," www.strategosinc.com/team_series.htm.

12. For a discussion about and a list of support groups, see http://dailystrength.org/.

13. For an example of an online support group, go to www.supportpath.com/.

14. A concept confirmed by Roy Berko, certified crisis counselor.

15. Study was done by Dr. David Spiegel as reported on www.cancerandcareers.org/women/strength/cancer_support_groups, 2008.

16. "Ann Landers," *Washington Post* (March 15, 1990): B12.

17. For a discussion on the various definitions of a *family*, see Lynn H. Turner and Richard West, *Perspectives on Family Communication*, 3rd ed. (Columbus, OH: McGraw-Hill, 2006).

18. "Planning and Conducting Effective Public Meetings," *Ohio State University Extension Fact Sheet*, www.ohioline.osu.edu/cd/fact/1555html, April 2, 2005.

19. Jim VandeHei, "Three Were Told to Leave Bush Town Meeting," *The Washington Post* (March 30, 2005): A04. Washingtonpost.com.

20. Rothwell, pp. 55–80.

21. http://boards.historychannel.com. Further information available at http://news.bbc.co.uk/1/hi/uk/7332942.stm, April 6, 2008.

22. Ibid., pp. 65–66.

23. Rothwell, p. 142.

24. Wynton C. Hall, "Do Effective Speakers Make Effective Presidents? USAtoday.com, February 28, 2008.

25. Henry M. Robert III and William J. Evans, *Robert's Rules of Order, Newly Revised* 10th ed. (Glenview, IL: Scott, Foresman, 2000). The source is also available on CD and in an online searchable version: www.robertsrules.com.

26. In parliamentary procedure, the term *consensus* means "unanimous." In nonparliamentary use, the term is often assumed to mean "generally." For voting purposes, it is synonymous with "all." See Robert and Evans, pp. 52–55.

27. Robert and Evans, pp. 399–400.

28. *Part-of-the-whole voting* is sometimes referred to as *2/3 voting*. For a discussion, see Robert and Evans, pp. 396–397.

29. Rothwell, p. 195.

30. Ibid.

31. Janis, p. 197.

32. The classic Dewey inductive process was first discussed in John Dewey, *How to Think* (Boston: D. C. Heath, 1910), pp. 68–78.

33. Janis, p. 219.

34. Ibid., p. 203.

35. A process refined by Roy Berko from a concept of Eileen Breckenridge.

36. Rothwell, p. 221.

37. Michael Mayer, "Behaviors Leading to More Effective Decisions in Small Groups Embedded in Organizations," *Communication Reports* 11 (Summer 1998): 123–132.

38. For a discussion on group meeting spaces, see Dale Leathers, *Successful Nonverbal Communication*, 2nd ed. (New York: Macmillan, 1997), pp. 407–411.

39. Ibid.

40. Mark Knapp and Judith Hall, *Nonverbal Communication in Human Interaction*, 4th ed. (Ft. Worth: Harcourt Brace, 1997) p. 175.

41. Leathers.

42. Ibid.

43. Mark Knapp and Judith Hall, *Nonverbal Communication in Human Interaction*, 3rd ed. (Ft. Worth: Harcourt Brace, 1992), p. 168.

44. For a discussion of round and rectangular tables, see Knapp and Hall, pp. 177–179.

45. From the research of R. Sommer, as found in Knapp and Hall, pp. 116–118.

46. Leathers.

47. Knapp and Hall, p. 168.

48. Ibid.

49. Isa Engleberg and Dianna Wynn, *Working in Groups*, 3rd ed. (Boston: Houghton Mifflin, 2003), pp. 338–340.

50. Research reported by Janet Fulk, University of Southern California, Annenberg School for Communication, in Barbara Langham, "Mediated Meetings," *Successful Meetings* (January 1995), p. 75.

51. The 3M Meeting Management Team with Jeannine Drew, *Mastering Meetings: Discovering the Hidden Potential of Effective Business Meetings* (New York: McGraw-Hill, 1994), pp. 114 115.

52. For information regarding Second Life, go to secondlife.com.

53. Lee Fehl, "The World at Your Fingertips," *Successful Meetings* (March 1999), p. 91.

54. Ibid.

55. Ibid.

56. Engleberg and Wynn.

57. 3M, p. 115.

58. Ibid.

59. Engleberg and Wynn.

60. Fulk, p. 75.

61. 3M, p. 116.

62. Ibid., p. 123.

63. GotoMeeting.com.

64. *Group Problem-Solving and Meeting Dynamics*, blind review manuscript, n.a. (Cincinnati, OH: Southwestern, 1993), pp. 30–31.

CHAPTER 10

1. For an extended discussion on culture and its effect on groups, see J. Dan Rothwell, *In Mixed Company*, 5th ed. (Belmont, CA: Wadsworth/Thomson Learning, 2004) and Stella Ting-Toomey and Leeva Chung, *Understanding Intercultural Communication* (New York: Oxford Press, 2005).

2. Edward C. Stewart, Jack Danielian, and Robert Foster, "Cultural Assumptions and Values," in Pamela Cooper, Carolyn Calloway-Thomas, and Cheri Simonds (Eds.), *Intercultural Communication A Text with Readings* (Boston: Pearson Education, 2007).

3. Rothwell, pp. 13-15.

4. Larry Samovar and Richard Porter, *Intercultural Communication: A Reader,* 11th ed. (Belmont, CA: Thompson High Education, 2006), pp. 24–25.

5. For a discussion on cultural decision making, see Ting Toomey and Chung, pp. 340–341, 344–347.

6. Ibid.

7. For a discussion on Euro-American decision making, see Rothwell, chapter 7.

8. For explanations of Japanese communication styles, see Judith Martin and Thomas Nakayama, *Intercultural Communication in Contexts* (New York: McGraw-Hill, 2007), p. 54, and Ting-Toomey and Chung, pp. 274–275.

9. Rothwell, citing the work of P. Wetzel.

10. Julia Wood, *Gendered Lives: Communication, Gender, and Culture* (Belmont, CA: Thompson High Education, 2007), p. 236.

11. Ibid.

12. Ibid., p. 237.

13. Rothwell, p. 21, citing the work of D. J. Canary and K. S. House.

14. Rothwell, p. 258, referred to research by K. Propp.

15. Rothwell, p. 91, based on the research of A. Kohn.

16. Ibid.

17. Rothwell, p. 254, based on research by L. Stewart and by A. Nicotera and A. Rancer.

18. Rothwell, p. 132, citing the research of M. M. White.

19. Ideas were originally explained by Lea Stewart, Alan Stewart, Sheryl Friedley, and Pam Cooper, *Communication between the Sexes* (Scottsdale, AZ: Gorsuch Scarisbrick, 1990), p. 162, and further expanded on in Lea Stewart, Pamela Cooper, Alan Stewart, with Sheryl Friedley, *Communication between the Sexes* (Boston: Pearson Education, 2003), pp. 155.

20. Ibid.

21. Rothwell, p. 123.

22. Based on the work of James E. Eikell, Florida Maxima Corporation.

23. For a discussion on communication networks, see Dale Leathers and Michael Eaves, *Successful Nonverbal Communication: Principles and Applications* (Boston: Pearson Education, 2008), pp. 357–358.

24. A concept developed at the Gestalt Institute of Cleveland during a workshop regarding dealing with difficult people, as reported by Roy Berko, one of the workshop participants.

25. Rothwell, pp. 31–33.

26. John R. P. French & Bertram J. Raven, "The Bases of Social Power," in D. Cartwright (Ed.), *Studies of Social Power* (Ann Arbor, MI: University of Michigan Press, 1959). For an update, see Value Based Management.net, www.valuebasedmanagement.net/methods_french_raven_bases_social_power.html, March 25, 2008.

27. "What Is Transformational Leadership?," www.leadingtoday.org/Onmag/feb03/transform22003.html, February 2003.

28. For a discussion of superleadership, see Vadim Kotelnikov, Ten Business e-Coach, "What Is SuperLeadership?," www.1000ventures.com/business_guide/crosscuttings/leadership_super.html, 2008, and Chris Neck and Charles Manz, *Mastering Self-Leadership: Empowering Yourself for Personal Excellence,* 4th ed. (Upper Saddle River, NJ: Prentice-Hall, 2006).

29. For a discussion on perspectives of leadership, see Rothwell, pp. 135–140.

30. Traci A. Carte, Laku Chidambaram, and Aaron Becker, "Emergent Leadership in Self-Managed Virtual Teams: A Longitudinal Study of Concentrated and Shared Leadership Behaviors," *Group Decision and Negotiation,* 15(4) (July 2006): 323–343.

31. Rothwell, p. 131.

32. Ibid.

33. Martin J. Medhurst, in Wynton C. Hall, "Do Effective Speakers Make Effective Presidents?", USAToday.com, February 28, 2008.

34. Michael Hackman and Craig Johnson, "Teaching Leadership from a Communication Perspective," unpublished paper, Department of Communication, University of Colorado, Colorado Springs, CO, n.d., p. 6.

35. Based on a concept developed by Patricia Hayes, Indiana University–Bradley.

36. A concept developed by Julie Ann Wambach.

37. Contributed by Isa Engleberg. Used with permission.

CHAPTER 11

1. The study that revealed this is Kathleen Kendall, "Do Real People Ever Give Speeches?" *Central States Speech Journal,* 25 (Fall 1974): 235. Other follow-up studies have affirmed the conclusion.

2. The concept of the listenable speech as discussed by Donald Rubin, "Listenability = Oral-Based Discourse + Considerations," in Andrew D. Wolvin and Carolyn Gwynn Coakley (Eds.), *Perspectives on Listening* (Norwood, NJ: Ablex, 1993), pp. 261–281. The explanation and recommendations presented in this text are those adapted by Andrew Wovlin and Roy Berko .

3. Cindy L. Griffin, *Invitation to Public-Speaking,* 3rd ed. (Boston: Wadsworth, Cegage Learning, 2009), p. 52.

4. Ibid,, pp. 52 and 55.

5. Rubin.

6. Ethel C. Glenn, Philip Emmert, and Victoria Emmert, "A Scale for Measuring Listenability: The Factors That Determine Listening Ease and Difficulty," *International Journal of Listening,* 9 (1995): 44–61.

7. The Wolvin Listenability Paradigm, in Andrew D. Wolvin, Roy M. Berko, and Darlyn R. Wolvin (Eds.), *The Public Speaker/The Public Listener* (Los Angeles: Roxbury, 1999), pp. 68–78.

8. Kent Menzel and Lori Carrell, "The Relationship Between Preparation and Performance in Public Speaking," *Communication Education,* 43 (January 1994): 17.

9. Tim Craig and Michael D. Shear, "Allen Quip Provokes Outrage, Apology, "*Washington Post* (August 15, 2006): A01.

10. Dan Eggen, "White House Strikes Back at Tell-All-Book," *Washington Post,* as reprinted in *Cleveland Plain Dealer* (May 29, 2008): A4. Quotation is from Scott McClellan, *What Happened: Inside the Bush White House and Washington's Culture of Deception (*New York: Public Affairs Books, 2008).

11. Jack Shafer, "Don't Call It Plagiarism," *Slate,* February 19, 2008, www.slate.com/id/2184070.

12. Brigid Schulte, "Web of Cheating," *Cleveland Plain Dealer* (October 8, 2002): E1.

13. Ibid.

14. www.Turnitin.com.

15. Richard Morin and Dan Balz, "Bush's Popularity Reaches New Low," washingtonpost.com, November 4, 2005.
16. PollingReport.com.
17. For an extended discussion of demographics, see Griffin, pp. 101–103.
18. For details of the interaction between Bill Clinton and Bob Rafsky, see, "Heckling" (Transcript 1992) in Clella Jaffe, *Public Speaking: Concepts and Skills for a Diverse Society,* 3rd ed. (Belmont, CA: Wadsworth/Thomson Learning, 2001).
19. For an extended discussion of speech outlining, see Griffin, pp. 218–224.
20. Based on http://owl.english.purdue.edu/handouts/esl/index.html. If your server will not access this website, go to http://dept.kent.edu/english/eslowl/resources.htm and access the Purdue site through this portal.
21. Ibid.
22. www.drspock.com.
23. www.familiesusa.org.

CHAPTER 12

1. *Frequently Asked Questions Regarding: Information and Intelligent* Design (Arlington, VA: National Science Foundation, 2005), NSF 05-551, www.nsf.gov/funding/pgm_summ.jsp?pims_id=13503&org=IIS and AEC Koehler, *Some Thoughts on the Meaning of Open Access for University Library Technical Services,* 32(1) (2006), p. 17.
2. The classic book on the use of evidence and the role of bias is Robert Newman and Dale Newman, *Evidence* (Boston: Houghton Mifflin, 1969). For additional information, see "Evidence," *Handouts and Links,* www.unc.edu/depts/wcweb/handouts/evidence_use.html, 2008.
3. To access *Readers' Guide to Periodical Literature,* go to www.hwwilson.com/Databases/Readersg.htm#Literature.
4. "Popularity of Wikipedia," techxplolrer.com, May 1, 2007.
5. Brian Sack, "More Accurate Wikipedia Warnings," www.cracked.com
6. Thomas Smith, "Wikipedia—A Reliable Source for Students-Nay," www.nuimsu.com/spoke/november-2007/wikipedia-reliable-source-students-nay, November 2007.
7. The catalog can be obtained from ABC News by calling 800-505-6139.
8. For a discussion of library research, see "Basic Library Research," www.dushkin.com/online/study/dgen1.mhtml. For computer searches, see Maura Shaw, *Mastering Online Research* (Cincinnati, OH: F & W Publishing, 2007) and Terrence Doyle and Linda R. Barr, *Research Navigator Guide* (Boston: Allyn and Bacon, 2004).
9. Process described by Joan Aitken, Park University, Parkville, MO.
10. Steven R. Knowlton, "How Students Get Lost in Cyberspace," *Washington Post* (November 2, 1997): 18.
11. Ibid.
12. Ibid.
13. www.snoopes.com.
14. Jen Christensen, "Jeff vs. the Bloggers," *The Advocate* (May 10, 2005), 48.
15. Christina Pino-Marina, "Online Resources for Legitimate Research," *Cleveland Plain Dealer* (October 8, 2002): E3.
16. Ibid.
17. Jim Cope, "Data Overload: Separating Gold from Garbage," *Hemisphere* (April 1998): 33.

18. Julia Wood, *Gendered Lives: Communication, Gender, and Culture* (Belmont, CA: Thomson Higher Education, 2007), p. 153.
19. For an in-depth discussion of styles, see John Bourhis, Carey Adams, Scott Titsworth, and Lynn Harter, *Style Manual for Communication Studies* (New York: McGraw-Hill, 2002).
20. Chip Heath and Dan Heath, *Made to Stick* (New York: Random House, 2007).
21. Joanna Slan, *Using Stories and Humor* (Boston: Allyn and Bacon, 1998), p. 26. This book is strongly recommended by The National Speakers Association and Toastmasters International. For a discussion of humor in speeches, see Michael Osborn and Suzanne Osborn, *Public Speaking* 7th ed. (Boston: Houghton Mifflin, 2006), pp. 490–491.
22. Barack Obama, "A More Perfect Union," a speech given in Philadelphia on March 18, 2008.
23. Melanie C. Green and Timothy C. Brock, "Persuasiveness of Narratives," in Timothy C. Brock and Melanie E. Green (Eds.), *Persuasion* (Thousand Oaks, CA: Sage, 2005), pp. 117–142.
24. "World Factbook," http://kids.yahoo.com/reference/world-factbook/country/xx—World, 2008.
25. Ibid.
26. Darrell Huff, *How to Lie with Statistics* (New York: Norton, 1993), pp. 123–142. Although dated, this book still appears to be one of the definitive discussions of how statistics are manipulated. Also see Joel Best, *More Damned Lies and Statistics: How Numbers Confuse Public Issues* (Berkeley, CA: University of California Press, 2004).
27. For extended discussions of communication research, see Rebecca Rubin and Alan Rubin *Communication Research: Strategies and Sources,* 5th ed. (Belmont, CA: Wadsworth/Thompson Learning), 2005.

CHAPTER 13

1. Senko K. Maynard, "Contrastive Rhetoric: A Case of Nominalization in Japanese and English Discourse," *Language Sciences* 18 (1996): 944.
2. Richard A. Lindeborg, "A Quick and Easy Strategy for Organizing a Speech," *IEEE Transactions on Professional Communication,* 33 (September 1990): 133–134.
3. Morris Mandel, *Stories for Speakers* (New York: Jonathan David, 1996).
4. Clella Jaffe, *Public Speaking: Concepts and Skills for a Diverse Society,* 3rd ed. (Belmont, CA: Wadsworth/Thomson Learning, 2001), p. 166.
5. Jaffe, p. 174.
6. Annie Lang, "Effects of Chronological Presentation of Information on Processing and Memory for Broadcast News," *Journal of Broadcasting and Electronic Media,* 33 (Fall 1989): 441–452.
7. Jaffe, p. 174.
8. C. Jorgensen-Earp, "Making Other Arrangements: Alternative Patterns of Disposition." Unpublished course handout, Lynchburg, VA: Lynchburg College, n.d., as found in C. Jaffe, p. 174.
9. Based on theories of organization proposed and developed by Donald Olson, University of Nebraska.
10. Jaffe, p. 365.

11. A concept proposed by Fran Bostwick, speech professor, Lorain County Community College, Elyria, Ohio.
12. Jaffe, p. 366.
13. Ibid., p. 36.
14. One of the experts in the field of Native American languages is Gerry Philipsen. For an investigation of his works, see Part IV of Judith Martin, Thomas Nakayama, and Lisa Flores, *Readings in Intercultural Communication: Experiences and Contexts* (New York: McGraw-Hill, 2001).
15. Stella Ting-Toomey and Leeva Chung, *Understanding Intercultural Communication* (New York: Oxford University Press, 2005), p. 190.
16. Ibid.
17. Myron W. Lustig and Jolene Koester, *Intercultural Competence,* 5th ed. (Boston: Pearson Allyn and Bacon, 2006).
18. For extended discussions on African American communication, see Ronald L. Jackson, II, *African American Communication & Identities: Essential Readings* (Thousand Oaks, CA: Sage, 2004), and Michael Hecht, Ronald L. Jackson, and Sidney Ribeau, *African American Communication: Exploring Identity and Culture,* 2nd ed. (Mahwah, NJ: Lawrence Erlbaum Associates, 2002).
19. Jaffe, p. 337.
20. Ting-Toomey and Chung, p. 190.

CHAPTER 14

1. Katie Schwartz, "Speech Rate Too Fast? Tips to Slow Down," Ezine Articles, http://ezinearticles.com/?expert=Katie_Schwartz, April 9, 2008.
2. Stuart W. Hyde, *Television and Radio Announcing,* 4th ed. (Boston: Allyn & Bacon, 2003), p. 81.
3. For an extended discussion of pronunciation and articulation, see Jeffrey Hahner, Martin Sokoloff, and Sandra Salisch, *Speaking Clearly: Improving Voice and Diction,* 6th ed. (Columbus, OH: McGraw-Hill, 2001).
4. Hyde, pp. 83–85.
5. "How to Use Hand Gestures in Public Speaking," eHow Careers and Work Editor, www.ehow.com/how_2274513_use-hand-gestures-public-speaking.html, 2008.
6. Michael Osborn and Suzanne Osborn, *Public Speaking,* 8th ed. (Boston: Allyn & Bacon, 2007), p. 361.
7. Joe Ayres and Tim Hopf, *Coping with Speech Anxiety* (Norwood, NJ: Ablex, 1993), p. xi.
8. Debbye Turner, *The Early Show,* CBS-TV, July 31, 2002.
9. "Fear of Public Speaking: Where This Popular Fear Stems From and Seven Tips to Overcome It," The Sedona Training Association, Sedona, AZ, www.Sedona.com, 2007.
10. Psychologist Shirley Impelizari, appearing on *The Early Show,* CBS-TV, July 31, 2002. The original source for identifying public speaking anxiety as the number-one fear was Bruskin/Goldring Research Report, February 1993. This finding was duplicated by a February 2001 Gallup Poll (http://answers.google.com/answers/threadview?id=47686).
11. Ayres and Hopf, p. 1.
12. Ibid., p. 5.
13. This is a section of the Personal Report on Communication Apprehension (PRCA-24), developed by James McCroskey. For a more comprehensive public speaking apprehension test, students should take the PRPSA (Personal Report on Public Speaking Anxiety), which is reprinted in the Instructor's Resource Manual accompanying this text and can be found online.
14. These principles are based on the concepts of Morton C. Orman, MD, as presented in "How to Conquer Public Speaking Fear," www.stresscure.com/jobstress/speak.html. For additional information on Dr. Orman's theories, see M. C. Orman, *The 14-Day Stress Cure* (Sparks, MD: TRO Productions, n.d.).
15. Ibid., p. 1.
16. Ibid., p. 2.
17. Ibid.
18. Ibid.
19. Ibid., p. 6.
20. Ibid.
21. Ibid., p. 7.
22. Ibid.
23. Only anecdotal evidence is available to demonstrate that these activities are effective.
24. Discussion based on information given by Les Wyman, Gestalt Institute, Cleveland, OH.
25. John A. Daly, Anita L. Vangelisti, and David Weber, "Speech Anxiety Affects How People Prepare Speeches: A Protocol Analysis of the Preparation Processes of Speakers," *Communication Monographs,* 62 (1995): 383–397.
26. Kent E. Menzel and Lori J. Carrell, "The Relationship between Preparation and Performance in Public Speaking," *Communication Education,* 43 (2001): 17–26.
27. Peter Krouse, "Preparation Is Key to Conquering Your Communication Fears," *Cleveland Plain Dealer* (November 1, 2004): E1, E5.
28. There are mental health centers that specifically deal with public performance apprehension such as the Public Speaking–Social Anxiety Center of New York (www.speakeeezi.com).
29. Lynn Henderson and Phillip Zimbardo, "Shyness," *Encyclopedia of Mental Health,* (San Diego, CA: Academic Press, in press), p. 9, www.shyness.com/encyclopedia.html.
30. Ibid.
31. Ibid.
32. Ibid.
33. Ibid.
34. Earl E. McDowell and Noriko Yotsuyanagi, "An Exploratory Study of Communication Apprehension, Willingness to Communicate, and Sense of Humor between College Students from the United States and Japan," an unpublished paper, Educational Resources Information Center, n.d., p. 12.
35. Ibid.
36. Ibid.
37. Menzel and Carrell, pp. 17–26.
38. Jo Jameson, "The Number One Tip for Overcoming Fear of Public Speaking—Part Two—The Science Bit," Ezine Articles, http://ezinearticles.com, January 24, 2008.
39. Ibid.
40. Ibid.
41. Ibid.
42. Lisa Braithwaite, "Public Speaking—What's Confidence and How Do I Get It?," EzineArticles, http://ezinearticles.com, April 7, 2008.
43. Ibid.

44. Based on the concepts of Braithwaite.

45. Ibid.

46. Ibid.

47. Cindy L. Griffin, *Invitation to Public Speaking,* 3rd ed. (Boston: Wadsworth Cengage Learning, 2008), p. 7.

48. For an extensive discussion of African American/Black communication, see S. Ribeau, M. Hecht, and R. Jackson, *African American Communication,* 2nd ed. (Mahwah, NJ: Lawrence Erlbaum, 2002).

49. Melbourne S. Cummings, "Teaching the Black Rhetoric Course," an unpublished paper, Educational Resources Information Center, n.d., p. 5.

50. Ibid.

51. For a discussion of Chinese gestures and physical expression see James Neuliep, *Intercultural Communication: A Contextual Approach,* 2nd ed. (Boston: Houghton Mifflin, 2003), pp. 240, 243, 249.

52. Griffin, p. 7.

53. Ibid.

54. Griffin, p. 8.

55. Griffin, pp. 7–8.

56. Ibid.

57. Julia Wood, *Gendered Lives, Communication, Gender and Culture,* 7th ed. (Belmont, CA: Thomson Wadsworth, 2007), p. 133.

58. Ibid.

59. Robert Schlesinger, "Hillary's Speaking Style," Huffingtonpost.com, www.huffingtonpost.com/robert-schlesinger/hillarys-speaking-style, April 3, 2008; and, Bruce Newman, "Comparing Style Apples and Oranges," Faith Writers, Faithwriters.com, March 7, 2008.

60. Bob Cesca, "The Mandatory Rejection of Sarah Palin," www.huffingtonpost.com/bob-cesca/the-mandatory-rejection-o-b-139062.html, November 8, 2008.

61. Maura Kelly, "Sarah Palin's Political Gibberish," www.guardian.co.uk/profile/maurakelly, October 2, 2008.

62. A concept proposed by Dr. Les Wyman, Gestalt Institute, Cleveland.

CHAPTER 15

1. "Information Age," answers.com, Chapter 15, www.answers.com/topic/informationage?cat=technology.

2. Ray Strackbein, "How to Succeed in the Information Age, Survive the Transition:Industrial Age to Information Age," www.strackbein.com/.

3. Concept developed by Stephenie Slahor, P.O. Box 2615, Palm Springs, CA.

CHAPTER 16

1. Bruce E. Gronbeck, Douglas Ehninger, and Alan H. Monroe, *Principles and Types of Speech Communication,* 16th ed. (Boston: Pearson, 2007).

2. The concepts presented are classical theories of persuasion that were proposed in Sarah Trenholm, *Persuasion and Social Influence* (Englewood Cliffs, NJ: Prentice-Hall, 1989), Chapters 3 and 10. For additional discussion of these concepts, see Kendra VanWagner, "Persuasion Techniques: The Psychology of Persuasion," about.com,

2008, and "Theories about Persuasion," changingminds.org, 2008.

3. The theory was proposed by Richard E. Petty and John T. Cacioppo and explained in, "The Elaboration Likelihood Model of Persuasion," in Leonard Berkowitz (Ed.), *Advances in Experimental Social Psychology* (New York: Academic Press, 1986), pp. 123–181.

4. Adapted from L. Robert Kohls, "The Values Americans Live By," www.uri.edu/mind/VALUES2.pdf, last revised January 2006.

5. Robert B. Cialdini, "Harnessing the Science of Persuasion," *Harvard Business Review,* 79 (October 2001): 72–79.

6. Aristotle, *The Rhetoric of Aristotle,* trans. Lane Cooper (New York: Appleton-Century-Crofts, 1932).

7. Richard Wolffe and Michael Hirsh, "A Man at Home in the World, *Newsweek* (April 21, 2008): 22.

8. Ibid.

9. PollingReport.com, May 6, 2008.

10. Kate Zernike, "Follow Me: The Charisma Mandate," *New York Times* (February 17, 2008): WK1.

11. Del Jones, "Business Leaders Can Learn From Pope," *USA Today* (April 5, 2005): 3B.

12. "A Papal Pilgrimage," *Newsweek* (April 21, 2008): 14.

13. Ibid.

14. Lisa Miller, "Why This Pope Doesn't Connect," *Newsweek* (April 21, 2008): 41.

15. Ibid.

16. Based on a speech given by an inmate of the Grafton Prison Farm, Grafton, OH. Name and setting withheld by request.

17. Congressman Donald Pease, 13th Ohio Congressional District, speaking to the Elyria (OH) Republican Women's Club.

18. Dale E. Klein, U.S. Nuclear Regulatory Commission, "Opportunities for Growth and Investment in North America," speech delivered at the Third Annual Platts Nuclear Energy Conference, February 8, 2007. www.nrc.gov/reading-rm/doc-collections/commission/speeches.

19. Michelle Roberts, "Polygamist Raid Now a Fiasco," Cleveland *Plain Dealer* (June 1, 2008): A12.

20. "Marcia Cross Denies 'Coming Out,'" Associated Press, February 9, 2005, as found on www.msnbc.msn.com/id/6942214, explaining that the *Desperate Housewives* star said she wasn't a lesbian after *The View* cohost Barbara Walters questioned her on rumors regarding her sexuality. "I'm not," said Cross.

21. "Britney Spears Bad Mother Backlash Begins," http://defamer.com/hollywood/britney_spears/britney-spears-bad-mother-backlash-begins-176117.php and www.idontlikeyouinthatway.com/2007/02/britney-spears-is-wonderful-mother.html.

22. Abraham Maslow, *Motivation and Personality* (New York: Harper & Row, 1970), pp. 35–58. How Maslow's hierarchy is reflected in societal needs is demonstrated in M. Joseph Sirgy, "A Quality-of-Life Theory Derived from Maslow's Developmental Perspective," *American Journal of Economics and Sociology* 45 (July 1986), pp. 329–342.

23. John Harmon McElroy, *American Beliefs* (Chicago: Ivan R. Dee, 1999), p. 220.

24. Discussion adapted from the theories of Gronbeck.

Index

INDEX OF ACTIVITIES/QUESTIONNAIRES

The online website to this text contains activities that will help you become a more aware communicator. Included are chapter quizzes, speech outlines, questionnaires, and inventories. These include:

Note: Definitions of all key terms used in the text, as well as important other terms, may be found in the Glossary of this book.

Photo Credits

Chapter 1: Page 1: Alan Abraham/Corbis; page 2: José Luis Pelaez/Corbis; page 5: Louise Grubb/The Image Works; page 10: Bob Handelman/Getty Images; page 15: Peter Turnley/Corbis; page 23: Bob Daemmrich/The Image Works; page 27: Digital Vision/Getty Images **Chapter 2:** Page 35: Jeff Maloney/Photodisc/Getty Images; page 39: Geri Engberg/The Image Works; page 50: Javier Pierini/Corbis; page 53: Molly Riley/Reuters/Corbis; page 55: AP/Wide World Photos; page 58: Jim Cummings/Corbis; **Chapter 3:** Page 60: Jock Fostick/The Image Works; page 66: Bob Daemmrich/The Image Works; page 69: *(left)* Jim Watson/Getty Images; page 69: *(center)* Charles Dharapak/AP Images; page 69: *(right)* Jim Watson/Getty Images; page 71: Spencer Grant/PhotoEdit; page 75: Gerard Pile/Tony Stone Images; page 77: Digital Vision/Getty Images; page 80: Dion Ogust/The Image Works; **Chapter 4:** Page 86: Ed Bock/Corbis; page 92: Frank Herholdt/Stone/Getty Images; page 97: Paula Bronstein/Stone/Getty Images; page 99: Moodboard/Corbis; page 107: Getty Images; **Chapter 5:** Page 114: Ted Levine/Zefa/Corbis; page 118: Steven S. Miric/Superstock; page 125: Sonda Dawes/The Image Works; page 130: Sonda Dawes/The Image Works; page 131: David Young-Wolff/PhotoEdit; **Chapter 6:** Page 142: Blend Images/Getty Images; page 147: Don Smetzer/PhotoEdit; page 155: David Young-Wolff/PhotoEdit; page 164: Bob Daemmrich Photography; page 168: Ronnie Kaufman/Corbis; page 174: Colin Young-Wolff/PhotoEdit; **Chapter 7:** Page 183: Iconica/Jetta Productions/Getty Images; page 188: Redlink Productions/Corbis; page 189: Jeff Greenberg/The Image Works; page 198: David Young-Wolff/PhotoEdit; page 208: Raveendran/AFP/Getty Images; page 211: Jeff Greenberg/PhotoEdit; **Chapter 8:** Page 219: Jeff Greenberg/PhotoEdit; page 221: *(top)* Michael Newman/PhotoEdit; page 221: *(bottom)* Chet Gordon/The Image Works; page 225: Bob Daemmrich/PhotoEdit; page 235: Meg Takamura/IZA Stock/Getty Images; page 236: David Kelly Crow/PhotoEdit;

page 241: Artiga Photo/Corbis; page 245: Bob Daemmrich/The Image Works; **Chapter 9:** Page 249: Tony Hopewell/Stone/Getty Images; page 254: Jacobs Stock Photography/PhotoDisc; page 256: Walter Hodges/Stone/Getty Images; page 257: Elizabeth Crews/The Image Works; page 266: David Young-Wolff/Stone/Getty Images; page 270: Fancy/Veer/Corbis; page 274: Syracuse Newspapers/Gloria Wright/The Image Works; **Chapter 10:** Page 278: Bernd Thissen/DPA/epa/Corbis; page 280: John Burbank/The Image Works; page 283: Bob Mahoney/The Image Works; page 286: Karen Moskowitz/Taxi/Getty Images; page 293: Yellow Dog Productions/Image Bank/Getty Images; **Chapter 11:** Page 301: Flying Colours Ltd./DigitalVision/Getty Images; page 302: Ed Boc/Corbis; page 308: Jeff Greenberg/The Image Works; page 311: Marc Serota/Getty Images; page 316: Jeff Greenberg/The Image Works; **Chapter 12:** Page 328: Bill Lai/The Image Works; page 330: Yellow Dog Productions/Digital Vision/Getty Images; page 333: Catherine Karnow/Corbis; page 341: William Thomas Cain/Getty Images; page 347: Mitch Wojnarowicz/Amsterdam Recorder/The Image Works; **Chapter 13:** Page 352: Asia Images Group/Getty Images; page 355: Bob Daemmrich/The Image Works; page 356: Bob Daemmrich/The Image Works; page 357: David J. Sams/Stone/Getty Images; page 376: Syracuse Newspapers/Dick Blume/The Image Works; **Chapter 14:** Page 379: Brad Barket/Getty Images; page 382: José Luis Pelaez/Corbis; page 391: David Young-Wolff/PhotoEdit; page 394: Tim Boyle/Getty Images; **Chapter 15:** Page 398: John G. Mabanglo/epa/Corbis; page 401: Bob Daemmrich/The Image Works; page 406: A. Huber/U. Starke/Zeta/Corbis; page 408: Bruce Ayers/Stone/Getty Images; **Chapter 16:** Page 416: Ramin Talaie/Corbis; page 422: Popperfoto/Getty Images; page 425: Bettmann/Corbis; page 426: Don Bosler/Stone/Getty Images; page 432: Cleve Bryant/PhotoEdit; page 435: BillAron/PhotoEdit